POTTERY ANAL

PRUDENCE M. RICE

POTTERY ANALYSIS

A SOURCEBOOK

The University of Chicago Press/Chicago and London

The University of Chicago Press, Chicago 60637
The University of Chicago Press, Ltd., London
© 1987 by The University of Chicago
All rights reserved. Published 1987
Paperback edition 2005
Printed in the United States of America

19 18 17 16 15 14 13 12 11 10   7 8 9 10 11 12

Library of Congress Cataloging-in-Publication Data

Rice, Prudence M.
  Pottery analysis.

  Bibliography: p. 487.
  Includes index.
  1. Pottery—History.   2. Pottery—Expertising.
3. Pottery—Analysis.   4. Ceramics.   1. Title.
NK3780.R53   1987   738   86-24958

ISBN-13: 978-0-226-71118-8 (cloth)
ISBN-13: 978-0-226-71116-4 (paper)
ISBN-10: 0-226-71118-8 (cloth)
ISBN-10: 0-226-71116-1 (paper)

♾ The paper used in this publication meets the minimum
requirements of the American National Standard for Information Sciences—Permanence of Paper for Printed Library
Materials, ANSI Z39.48–1992.

In memory of Ralph,
who was always
on top of everything

Contents

Figures

Tables

Preface

This book is about concepts and issues in the study of pottery. It addresses many aspects of the topic—the nature and properties of the resources of pottery making; the history of pottery; its modern manufacture, use, trade, and discard; and the different perspectives from which it is analyzed. Above all, the book deals with pottery as a source of insights into people and cultures, and it is directed toward those with such interests: primarily to social scientists such as anthropologists, archaeologists, and ethnoarchaeologists, but also to the physical and materials scientists—ceramic engineers, chemists, physicists, and geologists—whose expertise is increasingly being engaged in technical analyses of pottery.

The title was chosen to emphasize the properties and methods of study of *pottery*—that is, relatively low-fired containers made of clay, which have constituted the *batterie de cuisine* of millions of households worldwide throughout the past eight thousand years. The much wider ranges of high-fired, glazed *ceramic* products—including art objects, tableware, structural clay products, plumbing fixtures, and so forth—is intentionally though regretfully slighted. Illustrative material has been selected in light of this emphasis, and examples drawn from historical or modern glazed, high-fired ceramic traditions are relatively infrequent.

This book addresses several objectives. First, it was prepared as a "source-book"—it is intended as a relatively broad reference work, but on some levels it must also act as an introduction to the subject. I have thus endeavored to identify and define concepts and terms used in different scientific approaches to pottery analysis, since I believe communication among their practitioners will be promoted by a shared understanding of what such terms mean and how they have come to be used in particular ways.

Second, pottery analysis is undeniably a growing concern. Many national and international symposia are being convened to address various aspects of the topic, and an increasing number of collections of research papers or review articles on pottery analysis are being published. It is more and more difficult to keep up with this expanding literature, and as the field is changing new questions and methods are continually coming to the fore. In consequence, some synthesis—however preliminary—is needed. Much of the current research into past and present pottery traditions addresses complex relations between technical and cultural phenomena—for example, between paste chemical composition and clay resource selection, between vessel shape and functions, and between decorative style and social organization, not to mention investigation of the factors governing assemblage size, determination of original firing temperature, and so forth. Hence this book also attempts to weave the many approaches to pottery—field and laboratory, archaeological and ethnographic, technical and cultural, empirical and theoretical—into a single fabric.

Third, and related to the need for synthesis, the study of archaeological pottery has undergone many recent developments in technical eleboration and precision (in excavation, quantification, coding, compositional analysis, physical and mechanical characterization, etc.). These advances are certainly laudable, but there has not been a commensurate development of theory, or integrated approaches to analyzing and interpreting ceramic data, so that this technical expertise can be optimally utilized. Lacking such theory and integration, researchers may waste time reinventing the wheel, repeating mistakes, and dismissing much of the variability in pottery as insignificant "noise." Because it is such a complex subject, it is easy in pottery analysis (as in other complex areas of research) to oversimplify, reducing complex factors of multivariate correlation and causality to a single attractive or easily comprehended dimension. I hope that efforts to synthesize a variety of approaches to ceramic problems and call attention to the complexity of the issues will not be discouraging but instead will prove challenging and thereby encourage further study.

With these as the objectives of *Pottery Analysis,* I have tried to maintain a balance between depth, spread, and synthesis in identifying focal concepts and issues. I selected some important behavioral questions and research methods in the study of pottery, and for each one—to a greater or lesser extent—I discuss the history of its development, provide an overview of alternative approaches, summarize their advantages and disadvantages, summarize the most recent findings, and confront the problems yet to be satisfactorily resolved. In all these discussions I have endeavored to provide enough basic information to cover the issue adequately, and also to include enough references to pertinent literature so that the interested reader can delve more deeply. Throughout, I have tried to avoid pronouncements on how one should conduct pottery studies, developing instead a broader picture of the ramifications of various procedures or viewpoints. I have also eschewed detailed treatments of archaeological field processing and recording of data, since this is an extremely individualized matter, varying from one field project to another.

Pottery Analysis is organized into three primary divisions treating raw materials, ethnographic and ethnoarchaeological studies, and analytical approaches to pottery, plus a short introduction and concluding section. Each primary division is broadly related to the preceding section(s): for example, the discussion of the properties of raw materials in part 2 helps lay the foundation for understanding aspects of pottery manufacturing and use (part 3), and these perspectives in turn establish a basis for identifying research problems and issues for technical analysis (part 4).

Part 1 (chap. 1) introduces the topic of pottery and ceramics within a historical and geographical framework, summarizing what is known about the origins and history of pottery (and related materials) in different parts of the world. Part 2 treats the raw materials of pottery making, establishing both how their properties affect the construction of pottery vessels and their use and how they shape scientific analysis of the pottery and its interpretation. Within part 2, chapter 2 discusses clay as a geological material, the origins of clays, and different kinds of clays; chapter 3 describes the properties of clays when water is added or removed, that is, plasticity and shrinkage; and chapter 4 explains changes in clays fired under different conditions and the composition of glazes.

Part 3 highlights ethnographic and ethnoarchaeological perspectives on various aspects of pottery production and use, with particular attention to the concerns and data base of archaeology. Chapter 5 surveys the technology of manufacture, including clay preparation, shaping, decorating, and firing, and chapter 6 examines the organization of pottery production and distribution. In chapter 7 various approaches to the many functions of pottery are addressed, including clues from vessel form, composition, and direct investigation of the contents. Chapter 8 focuses on decorative style and on the many ways decoration (particularly painting) on pottery has been analyzed and interpreted by archaeologists and ethnoarchaeologists. In chapter 9 some special topics in pottery analysis are investigated: classification, quantification, and use life and assemblage formation.

Part 4 treats characterization of pottery by its physical, mechanical, thermal, mineralogical, and chemical properties. Chapter 10 introduces the background and goals of characterization studies, together with some general questions concerning their design (especially sampling) and interpretation. Chapter 11 is directed toward color characterization—the source and interpretation of differences in pottery colors—and chapter 12 reviews physical, mechanical, and thermal properties, including porosity, hardness, strength and thermal stress resistance. Physiocochemical analysis methods are outlined in chapter 13, which summarizes the general principles, sampling requirements, and information about pottery that are yielded by petrographic analysis, X-ray diffraction, thermal analysis, optical emission spectroscopy, X-ray fluorescence, atomic absorption, neutron activation, electron microscopy, and other methods. Chapter 14 addresses some special research questions to which pottery characterization studies are often directed, such as temper identifications, provenience studies, estimates of firing temperature, and dating and authentication of pottery.

Part 5 (chap. 15) identifies the effects of modern technological developments, colonialism, and tourism on patterns of change and continuity and explores the implications of these findings for archaeological studies of pottery change in prehistory. As cheap utilitarian containers of plastic and metal become widely available, the number of potters making traditional cooking pots and water jars is rapidly dwindling, and with them is disappearing an invaluable source of insights into prehistoric cultures and their artifacts.

A number of people helped me in preparing this book. Among them I would like to thank Wendell Williams and Warren DeBoer, who read various sections of the manuscript, and especially Alan Franklin, who bravely tackled chapters 12–14. Chuck Nelson helped with table 7.1 and Bruce Edwards with Figure 7.9. Don Rice took pictures, switched files, and assisted with matters of design. Parts of this manuscript were drafted while I held a National Science Foundation Visiting Professorship for Women, and I am grateful for that support.

When you hold a pot in your hands, when you go over its walls with your fingers, you feel the hands of the potter, his fingermarks, his touch. You may not know who he was or what he looked like, but, handling the pot, be it hundreds or thousands of years old, you can still feel the imprint of his hands. It is this fact about a pot that makes it so endearing, so very personal. It makes the physical handing of a pot such an important part of its appreciation, as important as its visual impact, and at times even more so.

O. Natzler, *Ceramics*

Pottery and Its History

1

Pottery was the first synthetic material humans created—artificial stone—and it combines the four basic elements identified by the Greeks: earth, water, fire, and air. As one of many materials within the large sphere of technology known as ceramics, pottery has transformed a broad range of human endeavors, from prehistoric cuisine to the twentieth-century aerospace industry.

Besides prehistoric vessels and fragments, common ceramics include terra cottas, earthenwares, and stonewares such as craft items and flowerpots, and also china and porcelain tableware. Less obviously, perhaps, ceramics also encompass bricks, roof and floor tiles, sewer pipe, glass, and vitreous plumbing fixtures, as well as cements and plasters, abrasives, refractories, enameled metals, electrical insulation and conduction parts, space-shuttle tiles, spark plugs, and dentures (see Norton 1970, 408–74), and recently ceramic materials have been invented that can bond to living human tissue, opening up new medical applications (Hench and Etheridge 1982, 126–48). The connection between ancient pottery fragments, outer space, and modern medicine may seem tenuous, but it is present in the realm of ceramics.

1.1 Pottery and Ceramics: Definitions and Products

The term "ceramic" derives from the Greek *keramos,* variously translated as "burned stuff" or "earthenware"; it describes a fired product rather than a clay raw material (Oldfather 1920; see also Washburn, Ries, and Day 1920). Although in popular usage ceramics denotes materials made of clay, modern science applies the term far more broadly to chemical compounds combining metallic elements (which give up electrons) with nonmetallic elements (which add or share electrons). Thus one definition calls ceramics "the art and science of making and using solid articles which have as their essential component, and are composed in large part of, inorganic nonmetallic materials"

3

(Kingery, Bowen, and Uhlmann 1976, 3). Although some ceramics are compositionally complex, they may also exist as simple oxides of aluminum (Al_2O_3), magnesium (MgO), or barium ($BaTiO_3$).

The word ceramics has two sets of overlapping meanings, one set common to materials science and another employed in art and archaeology, which complicates its precise definition and usage. In materials science ceramics is a broad generic term, referring either to the entire range of compounds of metals and nonmetals or, sometimes slightly more restrictively, to materials manufactured from silicates (usually clays) and hardened by applying heat. The term also encompasses the research and applied fields developed around these products, that is, ceramic science, ceramic engineering, and ceramic industries. Pottery is one of several specific industries within the overall ceramic field (table 1.1) and includes low- and high-fired tableware, utensils, and tiles; the other ceramic industries manufacture structural, electrical, refractory, or glass products (Grimshaw 1971, 35).

In art and archaeology the term ceramics usually excludes construction or industrial products (cements, bricks, abrasives, etc.) and conforms more closely to dictionary definitions, which emphasize the plastic arts and clay working. Within these fields, ceramics refers to cooking and serving utensils and objets d'art manufactured of clay. Even here the term is sometimes employed more specifically to distinguish ceramics—high-fired, usually glazed, and vitrified—from pottery, which consists of low-fired, unvitrified objects and/or cooking and storage vessels. In Oriental studies an even finer distinction may be made, whereby ceramics denotes glazed and vitrified material intermediate technologically between low-fired pottery and high-fired translucent porcelain.

In terms of these several criteria of function, firing, and composition, prehistoric archaeologists and anthropologists investigating traditional crafts commonly treat only a subset of the diverse field of ceramics, that is, low-fired, unglazed, relatively coarse pottery vessels or art objects. (It is clear, however, that in the historical period as well as in much of Asia, high-fired glazed and vitrified ceramics provide a major component of the data base.) The fine distinction between ceramics and pottery is difficult to uphold in many situations, for example, in time periods or regions where domestic vessels were of vitrified clay. Nevertheless, given both the extremely broad tech-

Table 1.1   Principal Ceramic Industries

Industry	Product
Structural ceramics	Bricks, tiles, drainpipes, concrete, flowerpots
Pottery	Artware, tableware
	Terra-cotta
	Earthenware, glazed and unglazed
	Stoneware
	China
	Porcelain
Refractories	Fireclay bricks, crucibles, insulation
Electrical	Spark plugs
Abrasives	Abrasives
Glass	Glasses, glaze

Source: After Grimshaw 1971, 35.

nical meaning and the narrow art-historical meaning of the term ceramics, the bulk of low-fired, unvitrified material treated by anthropologists and prehistoric archaeologists is more properly referred to as pottery.

Prehistoric, historical, and modern pottery and ceramics are grouped into a number of categories called wares or bodies (table 1.2) on the basis of their composition, firing, and surface treatment (see Norton 1970, 1–7). The broadest division is into unvitrified versus vitrified wares, a distinction based on whether the composition and firing are such that the clay melts and fuses into a glassy (i.e., vitreous or vitrified) substance. Low-fired, porous, unvitrified pottery includes terra-cottas and earthenwares, while high-fired, vitrified ceramics include stonewares and porcelains.

Terra-cottas are relatively coarse, porous wares fired at low temperatures, usually 900°C or less. The earliest fired pottery in all areas of the world falls into this category. Terra-cotta vessels, sculptures, and tiles are generally not covered with a glaze, but they may exhibit several surface treatments that enhance their function. Roughening surfaces by beating with a carved or a cord- or fabric-wrapped paddle can increase the ability of vessels to absorb heat and prevent them from slipping out of the hands when wet. Alternatively, surfaces may be covered with slip or engobe, a liquid solution of fine clays and water that, in addition to cosmetic effects of coloring and smoothing, lowers the vessel's porosity and retards seepage of liquid contents. Terra-cottas are often subsumed within the broader category of earthenwares.

Earthenwares also include porous, unvitrified clay bodies, but they are fired at a wide range of temperatures from 800/900°C or so up to 1100/1200°C. In the lower part of the range they are roughly equivalent to terra-cottas. Earthenwares may be glazed or unglazed; although the body itself is not vitrified, the firing temperature may be high enough to allow a glaze to form properly. These wares are made from "earthenware clays," usually relatively coarse, plastic red-firing primary clays. This category of ceramic material includes a wide range of products, ranging from coarse earthenwares (sometimes called "heavy clay products") such as bricks and tiles to fine earthenwares such as tin-enameled majolicas, made with more refined white-burning

Table 1.2   Ceramic Bodies and Their Characteristics

Body Type	Porosity	Firing Range	Typical Applications	Comment
Terra-cotta	High: 30% or more	Well below 1000°C	Flowerpots, roof tiles, bricks, artware; most prehistoric pottery	Unglazed, coarse, and porous; often red-firing
Earthenware	Usually 10%–25%	Wide: 900–1200°C	Coarse: drainpipes, filters, tiles, bricks Fine: wall and floor tiles, majolicas	Glazed or unglazed; body nonvitrified
Stoneware	0.5%–2.0%	Ca. 1200–1350°C	Glazed drainpipes, roof tiles, tableware, artware	Glazed or unglazed; vitrified body
China	Low: usually less than 1%	1100–1200°C	Tableware	White, vitrified
Porcelain	Less than 1%; often nearly 0%	1300–1450°C	Fine tableware; artware; dental, electrical, and chemical equipment	Hard body; fine, white, translucent; "rings" when tapped

clay bodies. Earthenwares have served an enormous variety of household and construction purposes throughout the world for many millennia.

Stonewares are fired at temperatures of roughly 1200 to 1350°C, high enough to achieve at least partial fusion or vitrification of the clay body, depending on its composition. The body is medium coarse and opaque rather than translucent and often is gray or light brown. It is usually composed of "stoneware clays," which are typically sedimentary deposits such as ball clays (see Rhodes 1973, 22), highly plastic and low in iron. Stonewares may be unglazed or may have a lead glaze or, more frequently in modern times, a salt glaze. A distinctive fine, hard, porcelainlike European stoneware is Wedgwood jasper ware, containing high quantities of barium sulfate, which began to be made in England in the mid-eighteenth century.

The pinnacle of the potter's art, at least in terms of technical accomplishments, was reached with the Chinese production of porcelain, a thin, white, translucent vitrified ceramic that is customarily fired at temperatures of 1280–1400°C or higher. Porcelains are made of a white-firing, highly refractory kaolin clay (sometimes called "china clay"), relatively free of impurities, mixed with quartz and with ground, partially decomposed feldspathic rock that acts as a flux. When fired to high temperatures the feldspar melts, giving the product its characteristic translucency, hardness, and melodious ring when tapped. High-fired (but nontranslucent) porcelains in China are well known from the T'ang dynasty in the ninth and tenth centuries A.D. (Hobson 1976, 148), although "protoporcelains" or "porcellanous" stonewares are sometimes claimed to have been manufactured a millennium earlier in the Han dynasty (Laufer 1917; Li Jiazhi 1985, 159).

When Chinese porcelains of the Song, Ming, and later dynasties reached Europe, potters there tried a variety of experiments to achieve the same hardness and translucency, including adding ground glass to the clay, but they met with little success. The translucency of porcelain could be achieved but not the hardness, and the European product up through the eighteenth century was a "soft porcelain" or *pâte tendre* (Kingery and Smith 1985). Porcelains today are composed of 40% to 50% kaolin (sometimes with the addition of a more plastic ball clay), 25% to 30% feldspar, and 20% to 25% quartz or flint (Norton 1970, 336; Rhodes 1973, 53–54). "Bone china" is a late eighteenth-century English innovation in which calcined ox bones provide the desired translucency. Bone china, consisting of 40% to 50% bone ash, today is made almost exclusively in England (Norton 1970, 346–60).

1.2 History of Pottery and Ceramics

It is impossible to trace precisely the beginnings of human exploitation of the world's resources of earthy and clay substances. Although early stone tools from Africa are more than a million years old, the oldest objects of clay that archaeologists have found date only in the tens of thousands of years. Humans may have experimented with soft, plastic earthy materials considerably before this, perhaps hundreds of thousands of years ago, in uses as ephemeral as painting their bodies with colored clays. But the essential features in the history of use of this resource is the application of heat to transform the soft clay into something hard and durable. A relatively recent achievement by the yardstick of prehistory, it is this transformation that allowed broken bits of pottery to survive millennia and come into archaeologists' hands for study.

Any discussion of the history of pottery and ceramics must begin with the recognition of clay itself as a useful raw material (see table 1.3). Clay is certainly one of the most abundant, cheap, and adaptable resources available for human exploitation. Earliest archaeological evidence for its use ties it to the diverse artistic expressions of the Upper Paleolithic period of central and western Europe. Many Paleolithic caves have designs traced into wet clay on walls and floors, in addition to the more familiar animal paintings. At the Tuc

Table 1.3 Chronological Sequence of Developments in Pottery and Ceramic Technology

Development	Europe	Near East	Far East	Western Hemisphere
Fired clay figurines	Dolní Věstonice, Czechoslovakia, 30,000 B.C.			
Pottery		Anatolia, 8500–8000 B.C.	Japan, 10,000 B.C.	Various, 3000–2500 B.C.
Kiln	[England, late 1st millennium B.C.]	Iran, 7th millennium B.C.	China, 4800–4200 B.C.	Mexico, A.D. 500
Wheel		3500 B.C.	China, 2600–1700 B.C.	[16th century A.D.]
Brick—adobe		Zagros, 7500–6300 B.C.		Coastal Peru, 1900 B.C. Mexico, 900–800 B.C.
Brick—fired		Sumer, 1500 B.C.		Mexico, A.D. 600–900
Stoneware	Germany, 14th century		China, 1400–1200 B.C.	
Glazes				
Hard		16th century B.C.	China, 1028–927 B.C.	
Lead		100 B.C.	China, 206 B.C.–A.D. 221	
Celadon			China, 4th century	
Fritted			China, 8th century	
Tin	Southern Italy, 13th century England, 17th century	Assyria, 900 B.C.		
Salt	Germany, 16th century			
Porcelain	Germany 1709 France 1768		China, 9–10th century Japan, 1616	
Bone china	England, late 18th century			
Gypsum plaster mold	Italy, 1500			
Jiggering	1700			
Slip casting	1740			
Pyrometric cones	1886			

d'Audoubert cave in France two modeled bison were found, formed of unfired clay. Among the famous "Venuses"—female figurines with exaggerated sexual characteristics—are specimens formed of fired and unfired clay from Dolní Věstonice in Czechoslovakia; dating to about 30,000 B.C. (Zimmerman and Huxtable 1971), some of the figurines were made of clay mixed with crushed mammoth bone.

These examples suggest that by the late Paleolithic period three significant principles of clay use were already known. One is that moist clay is plastic: it can be shaped and formed and will retain that form when dried. Another principle is that fire hardens clay. A third is that adding various substances to clay can improve its properties and usefulness.

The use of clay to make pottery containers does not seem to have originated in any single time and place in human history; rather, the idea seems to have been independently invented in an unknown number of centers. Several scenarios have been proposed to explain the origins of pottery; all are intuitively appealing and may have some basis in fact. Unfortunately, though, simple answers to "Why?" questions in archaeology are not easy to come by, and the whys and hows of pottery origins are no exception. Multiple causes are more probable explanations for almost all prehistoric cultural developments; thus the beginnings of pottery may be a consequence of numerous lines of experimentation and accumulation of practical experience.

One unusual suggestion is that pottery vessels may have developed out of "soil crusts," the surfaces of fine clay deposits that, during sun drying, shrank and warped into shallow bowllike forms (Goffer 1980, 108).

A more typical reconstruction of pottery origins calls attention to the fact that in many parts of the world the earliest pottery known archaeologically occurs in forms or with decorations that resemble earlier containers made of other materials. These pottery skeuomorphs often mimic containers of birchbark (Speck 1931), metal (Trachsler 1965), gourds (Joesink-Mandeville 1973), wood (Mellaart 1965, 220), or soapstone (Griffin 1965, 105–6), or leather bags or baskets. The similarities have led to suggestions that pottery utensils may have developed out of the use of clay to line, mend, or reinforce containers such as baskets (see, e.g., Wormington and Neal 1951, 9). This was once a popular explanation for the origins of Southwestern United States pottery, but the theory was based on the basketlike "corrugated" ceramic wares from this area, which actually occur relatively late in the technological sequence rather than early (Morris 1917; Gifford and Smith 1978).

Alternatively, clay could have been used alone, perhaps to form containers that were only dried and hardened in the sun; these would have served well for holding dry goods such as grains, seeds, nuts, or herbs. In prepottery Neolithic settlements at both Jarmo and Jericho in the Near East, clay-lined storage pits, "baked in place" basins set into house floors, fire pits, and ovens have been found (see Amiran 1965, 242). It is not difficult to imagine that once people recognized the durability and impermeability of the hardened clay that lined these pits they would have experimented with firing clay to create portable containers.

For archaeologists, the problem in all these reconstructions is that unfired clay objects are ephemeral and leave only rare traces in the archaeological record. They are easily broken, crushed, or dissolved by liquid and quickly return to their original state. Thus the early use of clay for making or modifying containers is still poorly documented.

The use of unfired clay for artistic or utilitarian objects is not restricted to the earliest stages of cultural development, however. Unfired clay vessels were found in tombs in Nubia from A.D. 300–550 (Williams, Williams, and McMillan 1985, 46); in the Near East unfired clay objects come from excavations into structures dating to the early Sumerian civilization, and a variety of unfired "mud" dishes and other utensils are made by Bedouins in the same area today (Ochsenschlager 1974); and some Eskimo pottery from A.D. 1000 to 1600 was unfired (Stimmell and Stromberg 1986, 247). Unfired, sun-dried clay objects are made and used today in Papua New Guinea (May and Tuckson 1982, 7). Nonetheless, in most cases it is only when clay items were subjected to fire—intentionally or accidentally, through burning of dried clay parching trays or setting a clay-lined basket too close to the fire—that they survived and allow us to piece together a technological history of pottery.

The appearance of pottery vessels in the archaeological record was at one time interpreted within evolutionary theories as marking the development of human societies out of "Upper Savagery" into "Lower Barbarism" (Morgan 1877), but in more recent thinking pottery is seen as part of the so-called Neolithic technocomplex. This is an assemblage of tools and containers for food preparation and storage, together with the associated technology of their manufacture and use, that correlates in a very general way with worldwide changes in human lifeways at the end of the Paleolithic period or soon thereafter. These changes are dramatic, involving the adoption of food production rather than collecting, and settlement in villages rather than temporary encampments. Although there is no necessary causal relationship between agricultural life and pottery making, it is true that even today pottery is primarily made in sedentary as opposed to nomadic societies (table 1.4). When scrutinized on a smaller scale, however, the Neolithic changes appear as the culmination of a long series of connected adjustments and alterations in social and ecological relationships. The changes took place over several millennia and occurred in different ways at different times in different areas.

Pottery, rather than being a spectacular new achievement at this time, is better considered as a transformed exploitation of an already familiar raw material. The appearance and widespread adoption of fired pottery reflects both continuing and new needs for tools and resources—principally storing and

Table 1.4   Relation between Pottery Making and Sedentism among Fifty-nine Ethnographic Societies

	Settlement Type			
	Nonsedentary	Partially Sedentary	Fully Sedentary	Total
Pottery-making societies	2	12	32	46
Non-pottery-making societies	6	4	3	13
Total	8	16	35	59

Source: Arnold 1985, table 5.3. From the Human Relations Area Files Probability Sample Files.

preparing newly important foods such as domesticated grains—and new ways of meeting these needs. In fact one theory of the origins of pottery relates it to the need to detoxify plant foods by heating (Arnold 1985, 129–35). All of this is not to minimize its significance from the viewpoint of the history of technology, however, The technological achievements that underlie pottery making established the foundations for many other ancient and modern technologies such as metallurgy, brick architecture, and engineering.

1.2.1 Pottery and Ceramics in the Old World

1.2.1.1 THE NEAR EAST

In the Near East, although Paleolithic use of clay has not been documented archaeologically, after about 10,000 B.C. clays were used for a variety of purposes including architecture, pottery, and small modeled clay objects. Their order of appearance varies from region to region within the area.

Architectural use of clay is widespread very early (by 7500 B.C.) in all areas of the Near East and calls attention to the integration of clay exploitation with sedentary agricultural settlements. Clay was used by itself or mixed with chaff or straw from the fields as poured or "puddled" adobe for constructing walls of permanent houses, as plaster or mortar over rock or pole walls, and for floors and roofs. Indeed, wheat and barley kernels are often found embedded in the clay of these buildings (Amiran 1965, fig. 1). Adobe bricks began to be used as early as 7500–6300 B.C. in the Zagros area (Schmandt-Besserat 1974). Planoconvex bricks, formed in a mold and dried in the sun, continued to serve in the construction of residences, temples, and burial chambers for millennia; fired bricks were probably regularly in use by 1500 B.C.

Pottery containers appear perhaps as early as 8500–8000 B.C. at Beldibi (Bostanci 1959, 146–47, cited in Schmandt-Besserat 1977a, 133) and Çatal Hüyük (Mellaart 1964, 1965) in southern Turkey, whereas in Syria pottery did not occur until about 6000–5500 B.C. (Schmandt-Besserat 1977b, 40). In the Zagros area, figurines and geometric cones, spheres, and disks were made of clay as early as 8500–7500 B.C., and in the succeeding millennium pottery containers—which may or may not have been fired—began to be made (Schmandt-Besserat 1974). The earliest vessels in the Near East were hand built by coiled or segmental building (Mellaart 1965, 220) and then scraped, paddled, or rubbed to produce an even finish; they were fired without kilns in open bonfires, using wood or dung cakes for fuel. These and later vessels come in a range of shapes, including bowls, cups, and trays, and later are decorated with paint and incised lines. Their decoration depicts a variety of plant and animal forms (fig. 1.1), human activities, and costuming; and the context of recovery—burials, household activity areas, refuse deposits—provides many clues to their diverse functions.

Despite the common use of fired clay, objects formed of unfired clay continued to be important. At Cayönü, in Anatolia, in the period about 6500 to 6000 B.C., before the manufacture and use of fired pottery, various unfired clay objects have been found, including models of houses, a bowl formed by lining a basket with clay, animal and human figurines, and a clay-lined bin (Redman 1978b, 160).

Figure 1.1 Painted Samarran-ware bowl from the site of Hassuna, a sixth-millennium B.C. village in Iraq. After Redman 1978b, fig. 6-9.

At a number of sites in the Near East, unfired or low-fired clay tokens, inscribed with various notations, may constitute early records of economic transactions that can be linked to the later development of writing (Schmandt-Besserat 1978; cf. Lieberman 1980). The variety of sizes and shapes of the objects (cones, disks, etc.) may correspond to kinds and quantities of goods. These shapes are echoed in the earliest examples of writing, which appear in cuneiform on clay tablets by the late fourth millennium. When fired, as at Ebla (Tell Mardikh), whether intentionally or accidentally, these clay tablets formed a permanent "library" of knowledge and activities of the time (Matthiae 1977).

Female figurines, "mother goddesses," were widely produced in early agricultural towns and villages in the Near East and may have connections with fertility or household religious practices. Numerous other items of clay were also manufactured, including toys, models of houses, and tools. Among the tools are "administrative artifacts" such as stamp and cylinder seals used for recording and identification in economic transactions, loom weights and spindle whorls used in weaving and spinning, and clay sickles, with inset stone blades, for harvesting grain.

By 1500 B.C. three major characteristics of ceramic manufacture—ancient and modern, craft and industrial—had developed in the Near East. These include the use of kilns (open topped) for firing, the potter's wheel, and glazes. These developments had far-reaching significance in pyrotechnology and in the organization of craft production beyond simply providing household cooking pots and drinking cups.

Kilns, or firing chambers, are significant innovations because the enclosed space concentrates available heat, permitting higher temperatures, better control of the firing process, and more efficient use of fuel. The earliest kilns were probably open topped—either pit kilns or built aboveground—and fulfilled these functions only minimally. Later changes in kiln design, involving enclosed chambers to provide maximum firing control, permitted successful manufacture of high-fired vitrified ceramics. Such high-temperature firing control also contributed to the beginnings of bronze metallurgy (smelting of metal ores) and glassmaking. Several kilns are known from the fifth millennium B.C. in the Near East, and one near Susa in Iran is dated to the seventh millennium B.C. (Majidzadeh 1975–77, 217).

The potter's wheel allowed rapid mass production of standardized forms and development of a ceramic industry serving a large market. The true potter's wheel, on which vessels are "thrown," combines the principle of the pivot, also used in wheeled vehicles, with the principles of rotary and centrifugal motion. It was probably preceded by a "slow wheel," "hand wheel," or tournette on which vessels could be turned during shaping but where the actual rotary force was not a fundamental part of vessel forming as it is in the true wheel. One line of evidence—not entirely reliable—for the use of potter's wheels is the characteristic "rilling" or spiraling ridges on vessel surfaces formed by pressure of the potter's hands during throwing. Archaeological discovery of actual potter's wheels is of course the best evidence of this technique, but those made of wood may not have survived. Wheels or pairs of socketed hand wheels of stone or clay seem to have been common in the Near East after about 3500 B.C. (Amiran and Shenhav 1984; Lobert 1984).

Glazes are vitreous (glassy) coatings melted on the surfaces of vessels to make them watertight. Their manufacture is dependent both on knowledge of how to prepare a substance that will melt to form a glass and on the ability to sustain a high enough temperature in firing so this melting can take place. Glazed faience beads were made in Egypt during the Predynastic period, about 4000–3100 B.C. (see Vandiver 1982), and there is some evidence that alkaline glazed pottery manufacture may have begun about the sixteenth century B.C. in the Near East (Hedges and Moorey 1975).

One of the major kinds of glazes on earthenwares, ancient and modern, is the lead glaze. Lead acts as a flux in glaze composition; that is, it lowers the melting or fusion point of the glaze mixture, allowing it to form a glass at lower temperatures. Lead glazes are generally clear and often green though yellows and reds are also common; copper was a typical colorant. They apparently developed in China during the Han dynasty, 206 B.C. to A.D. 200 (Shangraw 1978, 44), and in the Near East about 100 B.C.

A second kind of earthenware glaze is the tin glaze, a thick white coating made opaque by adding stannic (tin) oxide to a lead glaze. These opaque glazes mask defects in finish or color of the vessel body and provide a clean background for painted decoration, often executed in blue or in polychrome colors. Tin glazes (or enamels) were first used in decorating brick panels by the Assyrians after 900 B.C., then the knowledge of their manufacture was lost until it was rediscovered by Islamic potters in the ninth century A.D. Never popular in China, tin-glazed pottery and tiles were produced in the Islamic Near East and North Africa; knowledge of their manufacture traveled with the Moors to Spain and Italy and later to the New World in the sixteenth century.

1.2.1.2 THE FAR EAST

It is in the Far East—primarily China, Korea, and Japan—that the earliest innovations in virtually all stages of the potter's art can be found. Because of these outstanding technical and aesthetic advancements throughout the history of the craft, little attention has been paid to the earliest "primitive" stages, and as a result many questions remain concerning the beginnings of clay use in this area.

The oldest pottery known in Japan is a very well made type called Jōmon, or "cord pattern," because of its distinctive cord-marked or string-impressed decoration (fig. 1.2). The dates of Jōmon pottery are highly controversial, because radiocarbon measurements suggest some pieces may be over twelve thousand years old (Ikawa-Smith 1980, 138). A thermoluminescent dating program on some Jōmon material, while not yielding evidence of such antiquity, generally supported the radiocarbon ages of the various periods and gave mid-sixth millennium B.C. dates for the earliest Jōmon period pottery (Ichikawa, Nagatomo, and Hagahara 1978). Jōmon pottery is hand built and consists primarily of beakers or deep jars with small bases, which often seem unstable and poorly suited for practical use. Although the entire range of early through late Jōmon pottery is characterized by impressed and modeled (rather than painted) decoration, the most elaborate of these products were produced in the Middle Jōmon period (second millennium B.C.), with heavy appliquéd fillets and buttons, castellated rims, and deeply incised grooves (see Kidder 1968; Rathbun 1979).

In China little is known of the very earliest stages of the potter's art, though the late prehistoric and historical periods are very well studied. The earliest pottery in the area comes from coastal southeast China and adjacent regions and consists of a variety of cord- and shell-marked and incised types (Chang 1977, 85–90). Dating is somewhat uncertain; although dates in the fifth millennium range seem most acceptable, a new radiocarbon determination from the interior of Jiangxi Province gives a date of 6875 ± 240 B.C. (Chang 1977, 511). Nine thermoluminescence dates on pottery from Zenpiyan, in Guangxi

Figure 1.2 A late Jōmon jar from Japan, showing characteristic cord marking; height 47 cm. Courtesy Royal Ontario Museum, Toronto, Canada.

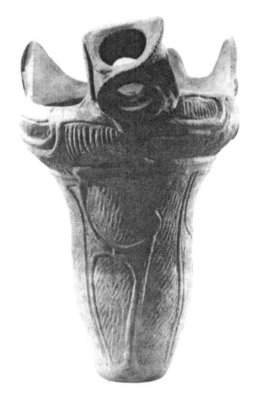

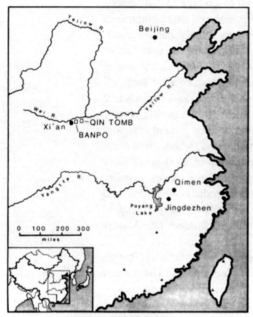

Figure 1.3   Map of east-central China, showing locations of interest in ceramic history. Small triangles show locations of sites with early cord-marked pottery.

Figure 1.4   A late Yangshao funerary urn of Banshan type, from northwest China. After Blandino 1984, 15.

Province, range from 6990 to 10,340 B.P. (Wang and Zhou 1983, tables 1 and 3).

The best-known early Chinese pottery (see Shangraw 1978) comes from the Yangshao culture in the Yellow River valley (fig. 1.3), between 4800 and 4200 B.C. Potters at Banpo and other Yangshao villages produced beautiful hand-formed jars and dishes painted with red-and-black geometric decoration (fig. 1.4), so skillfully made that they could not represent the beginnings of the craft. Furthermore, these wares were fired in small, subterranean horizontal and vertical updraft kilns (fig. 1.5) on the outskirts of the villages (Shangraw 1977); these Neolithic kilns could achieve firing temperatures of 950°C (Li Jiazhi 1985, 143). The date of production of these wares is comparable to the fifth-millennium dates of the early kilns in the Near East. Incised marks on some of the Banpo vessels have been interpreted as maker's marks associated with particular family lines (Chang 1983, 84–86) and may show

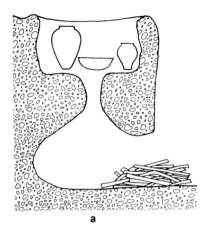
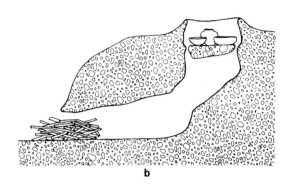

Figure 1.5 Reconstruction of early bank   b, horizontal kiln. After Shangraw 1977, 389.
kilns found at Banpo, China: a, vertical kiln;

some relation to later characters, particularly numerals, in Chinese writing (Cheung 1983).

There is little evidence for the beginning of use of the potter's wheel in China. It has recently been suggested that a low, thick-walled dishlike vessel commonly found at Yangshao sites between 4800 and 3600 B.C. may actually have been used as a slow or low-speed wheel (Zhou Zhen-xi 1985). The fast or true wheel was apparently used during the Zhou (Chou) period, roughly the first millennium B.C. (Hobson 1976, 2).

One of the most spectacular finds of archaeological pottery is the army of 7,500 life-size soldiers and horses found in 1974 near Xian, China. Guarding the tomb of Emperor Qin Shi Huang, the first unifier of China in 221 B.C., the terra-cotta army was formed in separate pieces but without molds. Solid or hollow legs support hollow torsos made of coils of clay; heads, arms, and legs were shaped separately, then attached to the bodies with strips of clay; individualized facial features and costume details were sculpted or appliquéd to finish the pieces before firing, then after firing the pieces were painted with red, green, black, and other colors (Hearn 1979, 46–48; Museum of Qin Shi Huang 1981, 11–14).

Chinese ceramic history is marked by numerous technical achievements of lasting impact, particularly in the field of high-fired bodies and in glazes (Li Jiazhi 1985; Zhang Fukang 1985). By the Middle Shang period, between the fifteenth and thirteenth centuries B.C., stonewares were being produced in kilns capable of reaching 1200°C (Li Jiazhi 1985, 144). At about the same time, glazes were produced using a combination of CaO (lime) and wood ash as fluxes (Zhang Fukang 1985, 164, 170), so vessels may have been given a "natural kiln glost" from wood ash during the firing. True hard (feldspathic) glazes began to be used a few centuries later in the Early Western Zhou period (Shangraw 1977, 383; 1978, 43–46).

One of the most beautiful of Chinese wares is celadon, identified by its distinctive sea green, apple green, or olive green glaze. The delicate color, described as "the blue-green color of distant hills," is so similar to jade that the ware was sometimes called "false jade." The origin of the term celadon is uncertain: one theory is that it was named after Saladin, a twelfth-century Islamic potentate, while another calls up the gray-green costume of Celadon, the shepherd hero in a seventeenth-century French pastoral comedy (Wykes-Joyce 1958, 54). Although celadon glaze manufacture has been dated as early as the fourth century A.D. (Mikami 1979, 12), the most famous of the celadons were those produced in the Longquan (Lung Ch'uan) District of the Southern Song dynasty (A.D. 1127–79) and later (Hobson 1976, 16; Li Hu Hou 1985; Vandiver and Kingery 1984). Celadons were widely popular throughout Asia, which can be attributed not only to their beauty but also to their supposed magical or curative powers. It was believed in India and Persia, for example, that a celadon bowl would crack or change color if its contents were poisoned, and a famous Song celadon censer, shaped like a bird, was said to make birds burst into song and to cry out to its owner if danger was near (Spinks 1965, 98–99). Medications were also thought to be more powerful if prepared in a celadon vessel or if such a vessel or its glaze was ground and mixed into the potion (Spinks 1965, 99–100).

The most enduring legacy of Chinese potters is porcelain, originally called *porcellana* (shell) by Marco Polo becaue of its delicate translucency. The origins of porcelain are uncertain. Historical texts are not conclusive: there is no single Chinese word for porcelain as distinct from other kinds of pottery, although the beginning of a new written character, *tz'u* (or *ts'e*) during the Han dynasty (206 B.C. to A.D. 220) has sometimes been interpreted as signaling the creation of a distinctive new ceramic product (see Hobson 1976, 140–42). Compositionally, some of the hard-fired stoneware ceramics manufactured in this period or earlier (Shang-Zhou) have been called "porcellanous" stoneware (Laufer 1917) or protoporcelain (Li Jiazhi 1985, 135), but they lack the characteristic white color and translucency of true porcelain. Excavations of tombs in the region of Anyang and Xian in northern China yielded white porcelains, revealing that its manufacture dates as early as the Northern and Sui dynasties (late sixth century A.D.), though no kiln sites of this early date have been found (Li Guozhen and Zhang Xiqiu 1986, 217). Until recently, it was the recovery of Chinese porcelains from outside China that provided the basis for inferring a somewhat later date of production, that of the T'ang dynasty, A.D. 618–906 (Hobson 1976, 148). A set of thirty polychrome porcelain headrests was excavated at an ancient Nara period (A.D. 649–794) temple in Japan (Mikami 1979, 110), and porcelains were also found in the ninth-century Moslem center of Samarra, on the Euphrates River in modern Iraq, which flourished from A.D. 836 to 883 (Wykes-Joyce 1958, 51). White, hard, translucent, and resonant, porcelain reached its finest development in the Song dynasty (A.D. 960–1279) and thereafter and was compared by lyrical Chinese poets to jade, snow, and lotus leaves.

Chinese porcelains are most closely identified with the "imperial kilns" at Jingdezhen (formerly Ching-tê-chên, or Ch'ang-nan). This city (see Tichane 1983) rose from humble origins as an old market town (*chên*) on the east bank of the Chang River in northern Jiangxi (Kiangsi) Province, to become "the metropolis of the ceramic world, whose venerable and glorious traditions outshine Meissen and Sèvres and all the little lights of Europe, and leave them eclipsed and obscure" (Hobson 1976, 152). Although skilled potters were to be found in the area centuries earlier, the meteoric rise of Jingdezhen as one of the world's great potting centers began when Emperor Ching Te (A.D. 1004–7) of the Song dynasty decreed that its kilns should produce wares for the imperial capital (Hobson 1976, 45, 156). Most of the later Chinese export porcelains (see Gordon 1977; Weiss 1971, 44–46) were manufactured at Jingdezhen for shipment to Europe and the New World.

Chinese pottery and porcelains exerted incalculable influence on the ceramic industries of other nations for more than a millennium. The earliest evidence for long-distance export of Chinese products is in the time of the T'ang dynasty, when porcelains came to be popular among the Asian aristocracy (Mikami 1979, 35). Celadons reached Korea by the eleventh century (Mikami 1979, 13), and porcelains arrived there in the fourteenth century. The arrival of Korean potters in Japan, allegedly by force during the "Ceramic Wars" (1592–98) involving trade with Europeans, led to the beginnings of porcelain manufacture there, and the discovery of kaolin clay stimulated the founding of the famous kilns at Arita in 1616 (see Weiss 1971, 48–49). Archaeomagnetic dating has been used to confirm some of the legends surrounding the beginning of porcelain at the time (Fleming 1976, 173).

Contacts with the Near East flourished especially during and after the Mongol Yuan dynasty (A.D. 1280–1367), when there was considerable interchange between the Chinese and Islamic ceramic arts. One significant import from the Near East during this period was pure cobalt pigment—called "Mohammedan blue" or "sacrificial blue" (Zhang Fukang 1985, 173)—for underglaze decoration; the local cobalt in China was contaminated with small amounts of manganese and did not fire well (Wykes-Joyce 1958, 57). The result of this trade was the foundation of the Chinese blue-on-white decorative tradition that has continued to the present (see Weiss 1971, 26–29).

1.2.1.3 EUROPE AND THE MEDITERRANEAN

Europe was not an independent center of pottery development; the appearance and development of the craft were tied to the broader range of technology associated with agriculture and sedentary life pioneered in the Near East.

Two kinds of pottery in Europe and the classical world, Greek figured pottery and Roman Arretine ware, represent outstanding technical achievements. Both these wares, judged by their firing and other characteristics, probably should be classed as high-fired terra-cottas or low-fired earthenwares. Neither is glazed, though their fine glossy slips have sometimes been erroneously referred to as glazes.

Greek black- and red-figure pottery (Noble 1966; Richter 1976) was manufactured during the sixth through fourth centuries B.C. in Athens. The distinctive painted decoration (fig. 1.6) was applied by potters or by a separate group of vase painters who sometimes signed their work, and the painted scenes depict a variety of activities of Greek life, both ceremonial and prosaic (Beazley 1945; Thompson 1984; Von Bothmer 1985). The occurrence together of both red and black iron paints and slips on these vessels entranced and perplexed scholars for generations, but experiments to reproduce them did not succeed until the early twentieth century (Schumann 1942; Stross and Asaro 1984,

Figure 1.6   A Greek red-figure vase, showing painters at work. Courtesy of Joseph V. Noble.

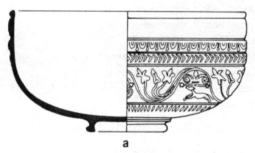

a

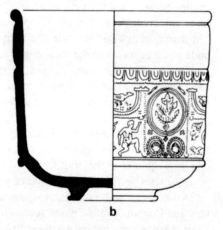

b

Figure 1.7   Gaulish Samian-ware bowls, moldmade with raised decoration and covered with a red slip: *a*, hemispherical bowl (known as form Drag 37), used in the third century B.C.; *b*, slightly less common deep bowl (Drag 30) made in the first and second centuries B.C. After Anderson 1984, fig. 27.

181–83). It was found that the colors and gloss of the paint derived from a particular clay mineral (illite) and from careful control of kiln atmosphere in firing.

Roman Arretine ware dates from the first century B.C. to the fourth century A.D.; the name comes from ancient Arretium (modern Arezzo), a center of production in northern Italy. These beautiful lustrous red bowls and jars were copied at multiple centers of manufacture (Johns 1977a; Peacock 1982, 114–28) and were widely traded throughout Roman Europe. Wares made in what is now France and Germany, for example, are referred to as samian or Gaulish Samian (from Samos) ware (fig. 1.7) or as *terra sigillata* (meaning "clay impressed with designs"). Like the Greek gloss paints, the distinctive red slips of Arretine and Samian wares are fine illite clays fired in a carefully controlled atmosphere at temperatures between 980 and 1260°C (Lawrence and West 1982, 212; Bimson 1956; Tite, Bimson, and Freestone 1982). Vessels were formed in wheel-thrown molds and often feature the name or mark of either the vessel maker or the mold maker on their surface (see Hoffman 1983).

During the Renaissance, the technique of tin glazing moved from the Mahgreb (North Africa) to southern Italy by the fourteenth century (Whitehouse 1980) and then to Spain, France, Germany, and the Netherlands, finally reaching England in the seventeenth century. The type of pottery on which this glaze appears is a fine earthenware known variously as majolica or maiolica, faience, or delft after the hypothesized (and often confused) locations of manufacture or distribution throughout Europe (Wykes-Joyce 1958, 74). Maiorca (or Majorca) is an island from which tin-glazed wares were shipped to Italy, so Italians named the pottery after the island, maiolica; Faenza is a city in Italy from which Italian tin-glazed wares were exported to France, so the French called the pottery faience (not to be confused with a much earlier Egyptian silica-rich glazed material also called faience). Delft wares (Fourest 1980) are later products from the town of Delft in the Netherlands, made in imitation of Chinese blue-and-white porcelains.

European potters continued making tin-glazed earthenwares, and by the fourteenth century Germany had taken the lead in producing a well-developed stoneware. Potters also experimented with reproducing the highly desirable "hard" Oriental porcelains (Weiss 1971, 60–83), but they were hindered in that endeavor by a lack of suitably plastic and white-firing kaolins. Although an experimental porcelain had been made by Grand Duke Francesco Maria de' Medici in Italy in the late sixteenth century (Wykes-Joyce 1958, 78–79; Weiss 1971, 69; Kingery and Smith 1985), it was not until the early eighteenth century that a viable product was achieved. Two Germans, "alchemist" Böttger and physicist von Tschirnhausen, found a local source of kaolin clay that permitted them success in creating a hard, white, translucent porcelain body—a success achieved, according to Böttger's notes, at 5:00 P.M. on January 1708, after a twelve-hour firing (Weiss 1971, 60). With that discovery in 1710 a royal porcelain factory was later established at Meissen, near Dresden (Wykes-Joyce 1958, 136–39). The French continued to produce soft porcelains at Vincennes (d'Albis 1985) and Sèvres until kaolin was discovered at Limoges in 1768, at which point true hard porcelain soon began to be manufactured in that country. In the late 1700s in England, Josiah Spode added calcined ox bones to a porcelainlike fine stoneware body formula, producing "bone china," which is white, translucent, and very hard.

1.2.2 Pottery in the New World

In the Western Hemisphere the development of pottery proceeded independent of that in the Old World, and from several apparently unrelated areas of origin. As in the Old World, its beginnings in the New World archaeological record are broadly correlated with the transition to horticulture and sedentary settlement in several regions after the end of the Pleistocene. But because these developments themselves varied considerably in time and mode of occurrence, the association of pottery with them is general, not specific.

Two facts are striking about the development of pottery in the New World as compared with the Old. One is that its earliest appearance is considerably later in the New World, by five thousand years or so. Second, two of the hallmarks of Old World ceramic production, glazes and the potter's wheel, never appeared in the pre-Columbian New World, nor were kilns ever widely used.

Surfaces of aboriginal vessels were covered by clay-rich slips rather than glazes, although vitreous glaze paints were manufactured and used in the Southwestern United States after A.D. 1000 (Shepard 1942a, 1965; DeAtley 1986). A shiny, lead-colored surface appeared on a widespread trade pottery called "Plumbate" in Mesoamerica about A.D. 1000 and is sometimes mistakenly referred to by archaeologists as a glaze. The coating was actually a clay-rich slip, however, its distinctive color and shine resulting from peculiarities in composition and firing (Shepard 1948a), and although it is vitrified in places it is not a true high-fired vitreous glaze. Similarly, potter's wheels were unknown in the New World. Although several devices (e.g., the *kabal* in Yucatán [Thompson 1958] and the *molde* in Oaxaca [Foster 1959] were used by potters to help turn the vessel during forming, the continuous, high-speed rotation of the true wheel was not attained.

Probable pottery kilns have been identified in highland Mexico (Abascal 1975; Payne 1982) as well as a few other areas, and these were primarily used after A.D. 500. In general, however, most New World pottery was fired in open bonfires rather than enclosed chambers. Firing temperatures were most commonly in the range of 700 to 900°C (see Shepard 1976, 84, 87). Stonewares and porcelains were never manufactured in the New World because in the general absence of kilns the consistently high temperatures necessary for vitrification could not be attained, and thus all New World aboriginal pottery falls into the category of terra-cottas or earthenwares. Glazes, wheels, and kilns were introduced to the Americas in the sixteenth century by European explorers and settlers.

Identification of the earliest pottery in the New World is a matter of some disagreement. A very early complex of vessel forms and decorative styles from Valdivia, on the coast of Ecuador, dates to approximately 2500 B.C. (Meggers and Evans 1966). The pottery is similar in some general characteristics (chiefly decoration) to Jōmon pottery from Japan. This has prompted some speculation that a group of Japanese fishermen blown off course and shipwrecked in this area may have managed to persuade or coerce local inhabitants to make what was to be the first New World pottery. But subsequent excavations at the site revealed an earlier pottery style stratigraphically below the Jōmon-like material (Bischoff and Viteri Gamboa 1972), so the Japanese-origins hypotheses is at present given little credence.

The early development of pottery in other areas of the New World at approximately the same time, 2500 to 2000 B.C. or earlier, also supports hypotheses of indigenous development rather than diffusion. These areas of early pottery assemblages include the coast of Colombia (Reichel-Dolmatoff 1961), Pacific coastal Mexico (Brush 1965), and the southeastern United States (Sears and Griffin 1950). Relatively simple forms, often echoing the shapes of gourds or stone bowls, were hand modeled and decorated with incising or, in Mexico, with a red wash or slip. Both the Colombian and the southeastern United States examples were made of clay mixed with plant fibers, stimulating hypotheses that they may represent interrelated technologies resulting from population movements through the Caribbean islands (Bullen and Stoltman 1972).

From these beginnings, the next four thousand years of New World pottery development reveal great elaboration of forms and decoration, particularly in polychrome painting. Architectural uses of clay varied from area to area. Adobe bricks were commonly used in ceremonial buildings on the Peruvian coast, beginning by the Initial Period (1900–1800 B.C.) at the northern site of Las Haldas, whereas in the Andes highlands stone was more typically used. In Mesoamerica stone was employed far more often than adobe; adobe bricks were used in Late Formative period (ca. 900–800 B.C.) ceremonial architecture at Oaxaca (Flannery 1976, 24), and fired bricks are rare, being particularly associated with a Late Classic (ca. A.D. 600–900) lowland site of Comalcalco, in Tabasco, Mexico.

Lacking the wheel and kiln, New World potters were rarely able to attain the same levels of technical achievement and standardized production as did their stoneware- and porcelain-producing Old World contemporaries. In consequence, the artistic and utilitarian excellence of their products, while entirely the equal of Greek figured or Arretine pottery, is often denigrated as "primitive" or simply ignored by Old World scholars. Yet outstanding examples of the potter's craft are to be found all over the ancient New World.

In South America, from 200 B.C. to A.D. 700, Nazca (Proulx 1968) and Moche (Donnan 1965) potters on the coast of Peru produced stirrup-spouted vessels decorated with modeled and painted houses, animals, plants, and human faces so individualized as to suggest actual portraits (fig. 1.8). These polychrome designs included red, black, brown, yellow, blue, green, pink, and white colors. Other elaborate polychrome vessels, decorated with geometric and stylized natural motifs, were made throughout the Andes up to the coming of the Spaniards.

In Guatemala and Mexico, Maya potters of the Late Classic period civilization, A.D. 600 to 900, produced a variety of bowls and vases with modeled and painted decoration of exceptional technical skill (see Rice 1985). Cylindrical vessels and plates portrayed human and animal figures in a graceful natural style, featuring mythical (fig. 1.9) and ritual scenes such as dances, processions, or royal audiences and often had brief glyphic texts that apparently identified the persons, locations, or events represented (Coe 1973, 1978; Robicsek and Hales 1981; Quirarte 1979). They were painted with subtly toned pigments, often resist applied and underlying a sheer, glossy pale orange slip. After about A.D. 1000, much of the pottery decoration from Mexico through northern South America changed from multicolored designs to combinations of red, black, and white painting. The Aztecs in central Mexico made and used an orange-paste pottery with painted decoration of fine black lines.

Pueblo pottery in the Southwestern United States from A.D. 700 to 1300 (Dittert and Plog 1980) featured geometric and stylized life-form representations, with polychrome or black-and-white painted decoration (fig. 1.10). At the same time, in the southeastern and south-central United States, sophisticated plastic decorative techniques, especially incising and modeling, rather than painting were the outstanding modes of embellishment. Modeled heads of dogs or birds were often added to rims of simple globular vessels, or the vessels themselves might be in human or animal form, the features accented by paint or incising (Rice and Cordell 1986).

The prehistoric pottery vessels made in the New World included the standard repertoire of cooking, serving, and storage vessels—plates, bowls, jars, vases, cups—with local variations on shape and elaboration. In addition, braziers, griddles for toasting tortillas or manioc cakes, and "chile grinders" (bowls with incised interiors for grinding chile peppers) were common. Among the more distinctive of the manufactures are pottery incense burners from Mesoamerica (fig. 1.11), plain vases or bowls with elaborate modeled, ornamented faces and figures of humans and gods (Caso and Bernal 1952). Often two feet or more in height, these censers were painted in bright colors, and openings were placed so that the smoke from the incense would emerge from the figure's nose and mouth. Huge urns were made in South America and used for burials, the deceased being placed inside in a flexed or "fetal" position; elsewhere, smaller vessels were often used to hold cremated remains. Modeled and moldmade figurines of humans and animals and elaborately formed and

Figure 1.8 (left) Moche portrait vessel, Peru. Peabody Museum, Harvard University, photographed by Hillel Burger. Copyright by the President and Fellows of Harvard College, 1985, all rights reserved.

Figure 1.9 (below) Interior of an Early Classic (A.D. 300–600) Maya polychrome bowl from Belize, illustrating a myth in which the sun god, dressed in a deerskin (*right*), appears with a hummingbird and two vultures while waiting to recover his wife, the moon goddess, who has eloped with a vulture. The vessel is painted red, orange, and black. After Hammond 1982, fig. 10.4.

Figure 1.10 Zuñi jar, from New Mexico, painted in black and red on white; height 26 cm. Florida State Museum, catalog number P-1861.

Figure 1.11 A Zapotec effigy urn from Oaxaca, Mexico, depicting the god of rain and lightning. These urns, which usually have a cylindrical vase behind the effigy figure, are approximately 18–24 inches in height and were placed in tombs during the Classic period (ca. A.D. 200–700). After Willey 1966, fig. 3-96.

painted model houses, villages, groups of dancers, and so forth were often found in burials in western Mexico. More utilitarian ceramic manufactures included spindle whorls for spinning cotton fibers, net and line sinkers used in fishing, pipes for smoking, and musical instruments such as whistles, drums, and flutes.

In the early years of the sixteenth century, Europeans arrived in the New World and began exploring and colonizing the land and trading with its native peoples. Their presence is marked by the distribution of European ceramics such as olive jars (Goggin 1970), majolicas (Lister and Lister 1982), stonewares, and porcelains as well as many nonceramic artifacts at missions, forts, trading posts, and settlement locations throughout the Americas. The centuries of European conquest of the native states and chiefdoms had variable effects on the craft of pottery making. Despite the drastic social, demographic, and economic events associated with the conquest—famines, disease, settlement relocation, and depopulation—utilitarian pottery making among the Incas, Mayas, and Aztecs continued virtually unchanged from its pre-European pattern in terms of resources used, form, and decoration. Gradually, however, by introducing the wheel, kilns, and glazes and by stimulating the local manufacture of glazed pottery and tiles for construction and trade, the Spaniards and English transformed and Europeanized the organization and products of the native ceramic craft in the Western Hemisphere.

1.3   Overview of Pottery Studies

Pottery has had a long and varied history of manufacture and use. This range of ceramic products traditionally has been studied from a wide variety of points of view, including artistic, aesthetic, archaeological, historical, classificatory, mechanical, mineralogical, and chemical. Appreciation of the aesthetic qualities of early Chinese porcelains stimulated Islamic potters to try to reproduce them in the ninth century. The antiquarianism of the Renaissance and post-Renaissance centuries fostered interest in collecting Greek and Roman wares and an awareness of early civilizations and their achievements. Finally, mineralogical and chemical experiments by western European potters and scientists trying to imitate Far Eastern porcelains led to improvements in their own manufactures, such as bone china.

Modern archaeological studies have generally devoted a great deal of attention—in fact, disproportionate attention—to pottery in their reports, and this is true for myriad reasons. First, pottery has a long history and is found in virtually all parts of the world; its presence is rarely controlled by a particular geological or environmental situation or conditions of preservation. Second, as a function of its physical properties, pottery is essentially nonperishable: although a pot may break, the fragments (called sherds) are virtually indestructible. Third, unlike stone projectile points, which are attractive to collectors and easily gathered for display in decorative "point board" arrangements, sherds are not particularly appealing to pothunters (though unfortunately the same cannot be said of intact vessels). Hence the potsherds are less likely to be selectively removed from sites.

Figure 1.12 A *tanga*, or pottery pubic cover from Brazil, painted in tones of dark brown on tan. After Palmatary 1950, plate 104d.

Fourth, in general pottery is not an exotic or highly valued good, like gold or jade, restricted to the residences and tombs of the upper stratum of society. Although certain kinds of pottery may be confined to elite, ceremonial, or mortuary usage—porcelain headrests, figurines, tea jars, life-size statues—pottery as a general artifact class is not so restricted. Pottery served very ordinary, day-to-day functions in cooking, storage, and hygiene for all members of society. Thus archaeologists and anthropologists have encountered a variety of goods made of fired clay, everything from ordinary bowls and jars to baby bottles in Greece (Noble 1972), footscrapers in Pakistan (Rye and Evans 1976, plate 49b–3), and *tangas* (fig. 1.12) or female pubic coverings in Brazil (Palmatary 1950, 327–328).

A final and perhaps most significant reason pottery has been useful to archaeologists is its manufacturing method. Pottery is formed and *in*formed: pottery making is an additive process in which the successive steps are recorded in the final product. The shape, decoration, composition, and manufacturing methods of pottery thus reveal insights—lowly and lofty, sacred and profane—into human behavior and the history of civilizations. Potters' choices of raw materials, shapes to be constructed, kinds of decoration, and location of ornamentation all stand revealed, as do cooking methods, refuse disposal patterns, and occasional evidence of clumsiness and errors in judgment. The sensitivity, spatial as well as temporal, of pottery to changes in such culturally conditioned decisions has fed archaeologists' traditional dependency on this material for defining prehistoric cultures and their interrelations.

Most modern archaeological studies of pottery are based on three approaches: classification, decorative analyses, and compositional studies. Classificatory studies of pottery form and compare groupings of vessels or sherds representative of a particular culture at a particular time. These groupings are the basis for archaeological dating and go back to the late nineteenth-century work of Sir Flinders Petrie in Egypt. Study of the decorative motifs and styles of pottery, whether expressed in painting or in plastic decoration (incising, molding, appliqué), has always yielded insights into the lifeways of a people as well as their aesthetic perceptions and ideological systems. The third and growing focus of pottery study is technological analysis, which focuses on the paste or composition of a ceramic rather than on the way it is decorated or shaped and on the properties conferred by that composition.

Archaeologists' and anthropologists' attention has increasingly turned to pottery manufacture and use among Third and Fourth World groups being rapidly acculturated during the twentieth century. In both hemispheres the traditional craft of the potter, often a household livelihood passed down from generation to generation within a family, is suffering at the hands of modernization. Plastic and metal utensils are relentlessly usurping the utilitarian functions of jars and bowls formerly made of clay, because these new materials permit cheaper, more durable products. Although traditional people everywhere are likely to believe that water is more refreshing when cooled in a porous terra-cotta jar or beans are more flavorful when cooked in an earthenware pot, indulging these preferences is more and more difficult as potters abandon their craft to "progress."

Modern ceramic industries, sensitive to the needs of a technologically oriented society, now produce ovenware, flameware, and freezer-to-stovetop cooking utensils, plumbing fixtures, refractory brick for steel furnaces, dentures, and containers for radioactive waste. Meanwhile, the dwindling numbers of traditional potters turn to producing flowerpots, ashtrays, and figurines for a tourist market that too often has little appreciation for the dignity and history of their craft. Fortunately, the value of studing contemporary potters and their products has not gone unrecognized, both as an aid to archaeological interpretation of the distant past and also in helping many peoples recover part of their heritage before it is irretrievably lost.

1.4   References

Abascal 1975
Amiran 1965
Amiran and Shenhav 1984
Anderson 1984
Arnold 1985
Beazley 1945
Bimson 1956
Bischoff and Viteri Gamboa 1972
Blandino 1984
Bostanci 1959
Brush 1965
Bullen and Stoltman 1972
Caso and Bernal 1952
Chang 1977, 1983
Cheung 1983
Coe 1973, 1978
d'Albis 1985
DeAtley 1986
Dittert and Plog 1980
Donnan 1965
Flannery 1976
Fleming 1976
Foster 1959
Fourest 1980

Gifford and Smith 1978
Goffer 1980
Goggin 1970
Gordon 1977
Griffin 1965
Grimshaw 1971
Hammond 1982
Hearn 1979
Hedges and Moorey 1975
Hench and Etheridge 1982
Hobson 1976
Hoffman 1983
Ichikawa, Nagatomo, and Hagahara 1978
Ikawa-Smith 1980
Joesink-Mandeville 1973
Johns 1977a
Kidder 1968
Kingery, Bowen, and Uhlmann 1976
Kingery and Smith 1985
Laufer 1917
Lawrence and West 1982
Li Guozhen and Zhang Xiqiu 1986
Li Hu Hou 1985

Li Jiazhi 1985
Lieberman 1980
Lister and Lister 1982
Lobert 1984
Majidzadeh 1975–77
Matthiae 1977
May and Tuckson 1982
Meggers and Evans 1966
Mellaart 1964, 1965
Mikami 1979
Morgan 1877
Morris 1917
Museum of Qin Shi Huang 1981
Noble 1966, 1972
Norton 1970
Ochsenschlager 1974
Oldfather 1920
Palmatary 1950
Payne 1982
Peacock 1982
Proulx 1968
Quirarte 1979
Rathbun 1979
Redman 1978b
Reichel-Dolmatoff 1961
Rhodes 1973
Rice 1985
Rice and Cordell 1986
Richter 1976
Robicsek and Hales 1981
Rye and Evans 1976

Schmandt-Besserat 1974, 1977a,b,
  1978
Schumann 1942
Sears and Griffin 1950
Shangraw 1977, 1978
Shepard 1942a, 1948a, 1965, 1976
Speck 1931
Spinks 1965
Stimmell and Stromberg 1986
Stross and Asaro 1984
Thompson 1984
Thompson 1958
Tichane 1983
Tite, Bimson, and Freestone 1982
Trachsler 1965
Vandiver 1982
Vandiver and Kingery 1984
Von Bothmer 1985
Wang and Zhou 1983
Washburn, Ries, and Day 1920
Weiss 1971
Whitehouse 1980
Willey 1966
Williams, Williams, and McMillan
  1985
Wormington and Neal 1951
Wykes-Joyce 1958
Zhang Fukang 1985
Zhou Zhen-xi 1985
Zimmerman and Huxtable 1971

The Raw Materials of Pottery Making

In an age that glorifies celestial mechanics, matters "of the earth, earthy" have to be etherealized before they appeal to earthlings. . . . Water, air, and fire—the admired constituents—can all be conceived as pure. But "pure earth" seems to be a contradiction in terms, earth being the one unpurifiable element that sullies everything else. My subject being a turbid mixture of earth and pure water . . . I find the public preoccupation with unearthly problems a little unrealistic; but it warns me not to try to make mud glamorous.

E. S. Deevey, Jr., "In Defense of Mud"

Clays: Their Origin and Definitions

2

Of all the materials and processes involved in making a pottery bowl or jar or dish, the most important are clay and its manipulation. Hence a discussion of pottery making must begin with the raw materials: with clays and their origin, composition, and properties.

Clays are complex substances. It is of little use to minimize this complexity, for it is clays' very diversity that enhances their desirability as raw material and leads to the variety of objects manufactured from them. Although anthropologists and archaeologists have always had an interest in pottery, they have not consistently involved themselves in studying potters' raw materials. Clays are primarily studied by mineralogists, soil chemists, agronomists, ceramic engineers, and geologists. Consequently the material has been defined and described with respect to a variety of standards or properties that depend on the context and purpose of a given study. These definitions may focus on the origin of clays, on their chemical or mineral composition, or on their contemporary (commercial or industrial) usage. Each of these definitions involves a constellation of properties and characteristics relating to that particular view of the material. An understanding of clays as defined in all these ways will be enhanced by a brief review of some principles of geology and geochemistry that underlie the origins and properties of clays.

2.1 Earth Materials

The planet Earth may be envisioned as a series of concentric zones—the core, the surface, and the surrounding air. The core comprises three subzones, composed of mixtures of iron, nickel, silicon, and magnesium; it is over 6,000 km thick, and its center is presumed to be molten and fluid. Overlying this core is a thin (average 24–32 km) "crust" known as the lithospere (from Greek *lithos,* "stone"), composed of rocks and sediments. Above the crust is the atmosphere, consisting of various gases, including oxygen. In studying clays, the most important of these zones is the lithosphere, in terms of its composition and formation.

The lithosphere or crust is composed of elements such as silicon (Si), aluminum (A1), and iron (Fe) (fig. 2.1). These elements do not exist as free silicon or aluminum but instead are typically combined with other elements to form compounds (see sec. 2.3.3). The most common of these compounds are chemical combinations of elements with oxygen, the most abundant element in exposed rocks, to form oxides. Table 2.1 shows the composition of the earth's crust in oxides of the most common elements. Oxygen also combines with other elements such as carbon (C), sulfur (S), and hydrogen (H) to form additional oxides that may be gases or liquids rather than solids: for example, CO_2, SO_2, and H_2O (water).

Elements, oxides, and other compounds combine in various ways to form minerals. A mineral is a homogeneous solid with a characteristic chemical composition and a regular ordered structure of its constituent atoms. This systematic structural arrangement is referred to as the crystal structure, and all

Table 2.1   Composition of the Earth's Crust (Percentage by Weight)

SiO_2	60.1
Al_2O_3	15.6
Fe_2O_3	3.4
FeO	3.9
MgO	3.5
CaO	5.1
Na_2O_3	3.9
K_2O	3.2
TiO_2	1.0
P_2O_5	0.3

Source: After Mason 1966, chap. 3.

Figure 2.1   The periodic table of the elements, showing element symbol and atomic number (upper left corner).

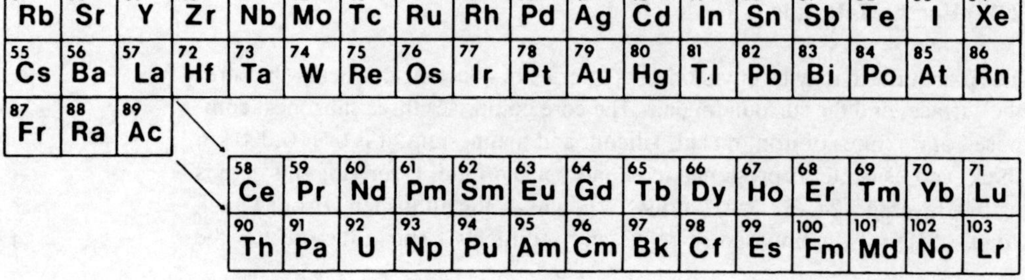

minerals, because they exhibit one of several kinds of atomic ordering, are said to be crystalline. Substances without these regular or periodic atomic arrangements are called amorphous.

Minerals may be described or classified in many ways. In addition to their distinctive crystalline forms, characteristic properties of specific gravity, hardness, fracture, luster, and color distinguish one mineral from another. Some of these properties are visible to the unaided eye, while others can be measured only with elaborate equipment. One can also distinguish rock-forming minerals from ore minerals—those that can be processed to yield iron ore, copper ore, gold ore, phosphate, and so forth.

In studying clays it is appropriate to focus on rock-forming minerals, because all clays are derived from rocks. The most common rock-forming minerals are silicates, that is, minerals with SiO_2 as a major part of their composition. Referring back to table 2.1, which shows the abundance of various oxides in the earth's crust, it is easy to see why the most abundant rocks are silicates of aluminum, magnesium, iron, calcium, sodium, and potassium. Silicate minerals having these elements in their composition include feldspars (see sec. 2.2), which compose 39% of the surface rock-forming minerals: quartz (28%); clay minerals and micas (18%); and ferromagnesian silicates (2%). Besides these silicates, another 9% of surface rock-forming minerals are carbonates, which have CO_3 as a major part of their composition.

Rocks are composed of minerals. Although some rocks comprise only one kind, typically several minerals combine in a single rock. The constituent minerals of rocks may be described as either essential, that is, the major components of the rock, or "accessory" minerals, minor components that occur in small but distinctive amounts.

The most usual classification of rocks is by their origin: the familiar igneous, metamorphic, and sedimentary classes. Almost all rocks are ultimately derived from igneous sources, however. Metamorphic rocks, for example, are igneous rocks transformed by heat or intense pressure or both. Sedimentary rocks are primarily the result of transport and redeposition of the products of weathering of older igneous or metamorphic rock, though some kinds of sedimentary rock are organic deposits formed by compaction of shells or diatoms. Sedimentary rocks account for approximately 66% of the rocks in the continental surfaces of the earth (the lithosphere); of these, approximately 65% are classed as mudrocks, which primarily comprise clay minerals and clay in silt-sized particles (Blatt 1982, 5, 6).

Although potter's clays are sediments, their origin is igneous rock, so it is useful to understand something about the formation and compostion of igneous materials. Igneous rocks (from Latin *ignis*, "fire") are formed from magma, or molten silicate material under the earth's crust. They are differentiated into two principal categories, volcanic and plutonic, based on where the molten material cooled. Volcanic rocks erupted or were extruded to the surface as lava or ash, then cooled rapidly, forming typically fine-grained rocks. Examples of volcanic rocks are basalts, obsidian, and pumice. Plutonic or intrusive rocks formed deep in the earth, cooled slowly, and are coarse-grained; examples are granites and diorites.

Both volcanic and plutonic rocks may be further described by their chemical composition, on a continuum from acid to basic. Acid rocks (such as granites) are high in SiO_2 and have a light color and a low specific gravity, whereas basic rocks (such as basalts) have less SiO_2, are dark in color and heavy, and have a high specific gravity. The color and weight of basic rocks come from large quantities of iron and magnesium in the ferromagnesian or "mafic" (containing Mg and Fe) minerals.

Within this continuum of acid through basic igneous rocks, the rock-forming minerals—primarily with silicates as essential constituents—may be divided into several families. The most common of these are the feldspars (also spelled felspars), followed by micas, amphiboles (e.g., hornblende), pyroxenes (e.g., augite), and olivines. The distribution of these families among acid versus basic rocks may be seen in table 2.2.

Because clays are formed by weathering, the relative resistance of rocks to disintegration and alteration by physical or chemical means is important to the origins of clays. The most common rock-forming minerals, whether they occur in volcanic rocks or have been altered by heat or pressure to form metamorphic rocks, will undergo some changes through abrasion or chemical action. Their stability or susceptibility to such alteration varies with their composition and texture. Table 2.3 lists eighteen common rock-forming minerals in order of most resistant to least resistant to alteration.

Clays are products of the breakdown and decomposition of particular kinds of silicate rocks: those containing a significant proportion of alumina (Al_2O_3). In the list of minerals in table 2.3, olivine, augite, and hornblende are the least resistant to decomposition and contain little Al_2O_3; olivine lacks alumina and therefore cannot alter into clay minerals. It is the high-alumina minerals, principally micas and feldspars, that alter most quickly to clay. But

Table 2.2   Mineral Composition of Acid through Basic Rocks

Acid	Intermediate	Basic
Quartz	—	—
K-feldspar (orthoclase)	K-feldspar (orthoclase)	—
[Na/Ca feldspar] (plagioclase)	Na/Ca feldspar (plagioclase)	Na/Ca feldspar (feldspar)
Mica	[Mica]	—
—	Hornblende	[Hornblende]
—	[Augite]	Augite
—	—	Olivine

Source: Cardew 1969, 10. Brackets indicate that the mineral may or may not be present. Minerals in parentheses are common names for feldspars of varying composition.

Table 2.3   Rock-Forming Minerals in Order of Resistance to Alteration

1. Quartz (most resistant)	10. Albite feldspar (Na/Ca)
2. Zircon	11. Oligoclase feldspar (Na/Ca)
3. Tourmaline	12. Andesine feldspar (Ca/Na)
4. Magnetite	13. Anorthite feldspar (Ca)
5. Ilmenite	14. Apatite
6. Rutile	15. Biotite mica
7. Muscovite mica	16. Hornblende (amphibole)
8. Orthoclase feldspar (K)	17. Augite (pyroxene)
9. Garnet	18. Olivine (least resistant)

even within these mineral families differences in stability are evident, as indicated by the relative positions of muscovite versus biotite mica and orthoclase (K-feldspar) versus anorthite (Ca-feldspar) in the series.

2.2 Feldspars, Weathering, and Clay Origins

Feldspar is the most abundant mineral in the earth's crust, constituting 39% of the rock-forming minerals of the surface. Feldspar is an alumina silicate; that is, it consists of SiO_2 and Al_2O_3, with the relative proportion of SiO_2 varying from roughly 43% to 65%. Three additional elements—potassium (K), sodium (Na), and calcium (Ca)—are also present in feldspars in differing proportions. These elements are responsible for the division of the mineral family into potash or alkali feldspars (containing potassium; e.g., orthoclase and microcline), soda-lime feldspars (containing different relative quantities of sodium and calcium; e.g., albite, oligoclase, andesine, labradorite, bytownite, and anorthite), and lime feldspars (containing calcium; e.g., anorthite). These last, the soda-lime feldspars, are collectively called plagioclases.

Alkali felspars (orthoclase and albite) have relatively high percentages of silica and are characteristic of more acid rocks, occurring with quartz in granites, for example, whereas the calcic or plagioclase feldspars are characteristic of the more basic rocks (diorites and basalts). The presence of potassium, sodium, and calcium in feldspars and in the clays that develop from them helps determine the firing characteristics of the clays (see sec. 4.2.3). These elements are also important in determining the weathering characteristics of the feldspars and the products—clays and other minerals—that result from such disintegration. During chemical weathering, in the presence of water and free hydrogen ions, all the abundant minerals in igneous rocks except quartz (and perhaps olivine) form clays. The products of such weathering are clay minerals, alkali and alkaline earth cations, and silica in solution. Different kinds of rocks and different kinds of decomposition produce different kinds of clays, however.

Decomposition or weathering of the rocks and minerals composing the earth's crust involves mechanical, chemical, and biochemical agents. In general the surface weathering (or epigenic changes; see Grimshaw 1971, 39–43) can be described in terms of two processes: fragmentation, the mechanical disintegration of the rock; and hydrolysis, the chemical reactions of the minerals with liquid solutions, forming new minerals. These two processes vary according to climatic conditions and are especially responsive to temperature and rainfall.

Physical mechanisms of fragmentation include abrasive forces such as wind, water (rainfall, flooding, percolating groundwater, wave or stream action), or glacial ice as agents of rock decomposition and transport of fine particles. Both the mean temperature and the range of seasonal temperature changes can also be important in the breakdown of rocks. For example, in zones with extreme seasonality, the alternate freezing and melting of water that penetrates cracks in a rock is a major cause of disintegration. The change of water from a liquid to a solid at 0°C causes a 9 percent expansion in volume at an equivalent force of up to 2,000 pounds per square inch.

Chemical or hydrolytic weathering involves solution, hydration, and oxidation processes in which chemical and biochemical agents such as organic or humic acids and gases as well as algae, bacteria, and rootlet penetration all play a part. All these actions take place in liquid solutions, which may be dilute acids (carbonic or sulfuric), and result in mineral decomposition.

Depending upon the climate, one or another process may dominate. In cold or dry climates fragmentation is predominant, chemical weathering and decomposition being minimal. Mineral composition is altered relatively little, the principal weathering products being micas. In warm, humid environments hydrolysis is the dominant weathering process: decomposition is largely a function of temperature, rainfall, drainage, and leaching. Leaching and dissolution are accelerated by high rainfall and high temperatures, and these influence the plant cover, which in turn governs the acidity of the groundwater. Plants release organic acids and CO_2 gas, which combines with moisture to form carbonic acid, an important leaching agent. Thus leaching and chemical weathering remove elements from the rocks in accordance with their relative solubility (first sodium, then potassium, calcium, and magnesium), leaving weathered products that are rich in relatively insoluble iron, silicon, and aluminum. The red, clayey, leached laterite soils of humid, tropical regions, as well as the high-alumina minerals gibbsite and bauxite, are products of such extreme hydrolysis.

2.3   Definitions of Clays

As noted above, clays are complex materials that are of practical use and academic interest in a variety of sciences and applied fields. For this reason clays may be defined from several points of view, each highlighting a different, but equally important, aspect of the material. The term clay usually denotes a fine-grained earthy material that becomes plastic or malleable when moistened. More specifically—and confusingly—clay refers to a particular group of minerals, a category of rocks and soils in which these minerals predominate, and a specific particle-size grade that constitutes the major fraction of those minerals, rocks, and soils. The significance of these distinctions will become clearer as we examine five definitions or descriptions of clays, based on the following characteristics: depositional situation, granulometry, chemical composition, mineralogy, and commercial usage.

2.3.1   Depositional Situation of Clays

Clays are sedimentary deposits that, in their geological age, are comparatively recent accumulations of the products of weathering and disintegration of much older rocks (table 2.4). The depositional situation of clays—that is, the location of the decomposed material relative to the parent rock—is one basis for classifying clays. By this criterion clays are either primary (also called residual) or secondary (transported or sedimentary). In a sense, all clays are of secondary origin, because they are products of rock decomposition rather than of original rock formation processes. This is largely a seman-

Table 2.4 Processes of Origin of Clay Minerals

1. Weathering of silicate minerals and rocks
2. Weathering of clay minerals
3. Diagenesis, reconstitution, and ion exchange
4. Crystallization from solution
5. Replacement by clay minerals
6. Hydrothermal alteration of minerals and rocks

Source: After Keller, 1964, table 1.

tic technicality, however, and understanding the origin of the clay deposit provides one basis for understanding many clay properties.

Primary or residual clays are those deposits remaining in more or less the same location as the parent rock from which they developed. They are formed by a series of hydrolytic reactions involving percolation of groundwater and chemical action, plus other weathering factors (such as freezing). These clays develop from many different kinds of rock, such as feldspathic rock, granite, basalt, diorite, and volcanic ash or tuff; and even if the parent rock is sedimentary (e.g., limestone or shale), the clay is still a primary clay if it occurs near that parent. In the case of limestones, clays are usually present as detritus in the initial sediment during or before consolidation of the rock. They remain after weathering processes, and especially acidic solutions, have leached away the calcareous and carbonaceous material.

Because the alteration and decomposition of the parent rock, whatever its composition, is not always complete, residual clays frequently contain coarse, unaltered, angular fragments of the parent material. These minerals, which may constitute as much as 90% of the deposit, most commonly include quartz, feldspar, mica, and pyrite. Primary clays usually have a low organic content (less than 1%) and are often coarse and of low plasticity.

Secondary, transported, or sedimentary clays are found in deposits or beds some distance from a probable parent source, having been moved by waves, tides, streams, wind, glaciation, erosion, or other forces. Transported clays are more abundant than residual clays and may be more homogeneous, as well as finer in texture, as a result of sorting and redeposition. They often have a relatively high—5% to 10%—organic content, which varies with depositional context. Sedimentary clays may be further categorized by the conditions or methods of deposition and transport, such as marine clays, fluviatile clays, lacustrine clays, aeolian clays, and glacial clays.

Marine clays are probably the largest sedimentary clay deposits, formed when extremely fine clay particles in rivers were carried to their ultimate destination and settled out after contact with and adsorption of the ions in brackish seawater. Marine clays may be subdivided into pelagic (deepwater deposits, usually extremely fine), littoral (coarse, organic-rich clays deposited between the high- and low-water marks), and estuarine (also coarse, organic-rich materials, principally useful for structural products). Glacial clays are generally coarse and unsorted, high in impurities, and useful for structural products or earthenwares. Lacustrine or swamp clays often occur in lenticular deposits, decreasing in fineness near the edges; they are often high in organic matter. Flint clays are stiff, organic-rich, low-plasticity clays deposited in swamps.

2.3.2   Granulometry of Clays

Differences in formation and deposition provide another means of defining
and understanding clays: granulometric—or particle-size grade—definitions.
One of the most important characteristics of clays is their small particle size,
which is the source of their most salient property, plasticity (see sec. 3.2).
Generally, the smaller particles in the clay or the greater the quantity of the
smallest particles, the more plastic the clay.

As defined in the fields of geology, soil science, and agriculture, as well as
the branches of engineering and the construction industry, "clay" refers to a
specific particle-size range; that is, particles smaller than about 2 micrometers
(μm), or two-thousandths of a millimeter (0.002 mm) in diameter. This limit
is by no means absolute: the widely used Wentworth scale (Wentworth 1922,
1933) for classifying sediment particle sizes allows slightly larger particles
within the clay range, setting the upper limit at 4 μm (or 0.004 mm) (see
fig. 2.2). The upper limit of 2 μm seems to be almost a natural boundary,
however, because numerous analyses of argillaceous (clayey) sediments have
shown that clay minerals tend to be concentrated in a size fraction smaller
than 2 μm, while nonclay minerals rarely occur in particles this small (Grim
1968, 2).

The extremely small particle size of clays gives them the properties and
behavior of colloids (see also sec. 3.4.2). The term colloid refers to a state in
which very fine particles (of a solid, liquid, or gas) are dispersed or suspended
in another material (solid, liquid, or gas). Examples of the colloidal state include fog (liquid dispersed in a gas), blood (solid in a liquid), and foam (gas
in a liquid). Colloidal particles are extremely tiny, 1 μm (0.001 mm) or less in

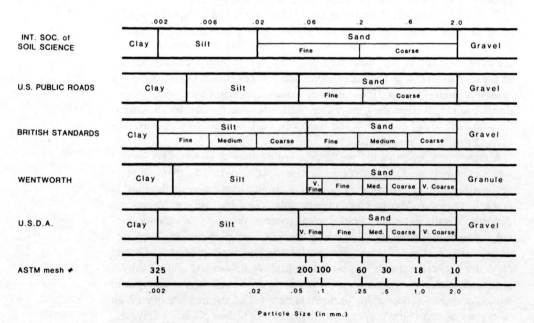

Figure 2.2   Six common standards for classification of particle sizes.

diameter; this is merely the lower range of the clay particle size, however, and not all clay-size particles are also colloid-size.

The proportion of clay-grade particles in a sediment varies depending upon how the deposit was formed. Most argillaceous sediments contain a considerable quantity of much coarser particles, either fragments of the original parent rock from which a primary or residual clay deposit weathered or particles picked up during transport of a secondary or sedimentary clay. The term "clay" is reserved in mechanical analyses of consolidated (rock) and unconsolidated (soil) sediments for materials in which the clay particle size grade predominates. Rocks or consolidated sediments dominated by clay-sized particles are called mudrocks; these include claystone and shale.

Frequently in soil analyses the relative mixture of clay-grade particles with larger particle sizes forms the basis of descriptive categories such as "clay loam," "silty clay," and so forth (fig. 2.3). To be designated a clay by soil scientists, the soil must carry at least 35% of the fine particles less than 0.002 mm according to some classifications; by other schemes this fraction must be not less than 40%. Silty clay sediments contain 80% to 100% of their composition as silt-sized (0.05–0.002 mm) and clay-sized particles in approximately equal proportions.

The distribution of clays, silty clays, and clay loams in a region typically may be found on soil maps, which have been plotted by soil scientists and agronomists. In most cases the scale of these maps is not sufficiently fine to pinpoint the precise location of clays suitable for pottery, however, and in many areas modern construction prohibits access to particular deposits. Nonetheless, the maps give a general picture of the kinds of soils in an area and the locales with some potential for yielding clayey resources.

Fine-textured plastic clays are apt to be found as deposits in shallow, quiet lakes, slow-flowing streams, or estuaries rather than as primary clays, although some glacial clays may contain a variety of nonclay minerals in extremely small particle sizes. Hydrothermal clays, which are formed by alteration through contact with hot—100–300°C—often acid, mineralized solutions, may have as little as 5% coarse particles (Grim 1968, 2). But for a soil material to exhibit plasticity, that essential characteristic of clays, it may contain as little as 15% of the fine particle size range.

Figure 2.3   Ternary diagram of soils classification by particle size.

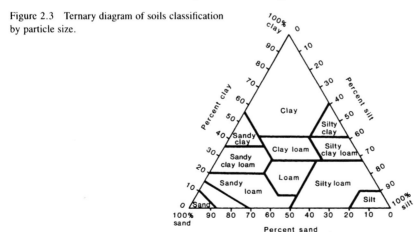

2.3.3 Chemical Definitions of Clays

Another useful way to define and describe clays is by their chemical composition. Because clays are the end products of weathering of silicate rocks, most are primarily composed of silica and alumina, the two chemical elements most resistant to weathering. Most clays may be described as hydrous aluminum silicates and are variants of the general (or theoretical) formula $Al_2O_3 \cdot 2SiO_2 \cdot 2H_2O$ (table 2.5). The relative percentages of these three components—alumina, silica, and water—vary considerably in different kinds of clays. The average composition of silicate clays is 39.4% alumina, 46.6% silica, and 13.91% water, but because different kinds of clays (or clay minerals) vary in atomic structure, the ratio of silica to alumina may range from $1:1$ to $4:1$ or higher, and water may constitute as much as 30% to 35% of the clay body.

In addition to the silicate clays, another chemical group consists of the iron and aluminum hydrous oxide clays. These clays are particularly associated with acid weathering in tropical and semitropical regions, and they represent the most advanced stage of alteration (laterization) of soil/rock material. Generally red or yellow, the hydrous oxide clays may be intermixed with silicate clays and are represented by the formulas $Fe_2O_3 \cdot xH_2O$ and $Al_2O_3 \cdot xH_2O$ (the amount of water of hydration in these clays is variable).

The distinctive properties of clays that are important for pottery manufacture and use result in large part from their chemical composition and structure, and it is useful to think of clays as composed of two kinds of "building blocks." Each of the blocks is an arrangement of two of the three chemical components of clays—atoms of silicon combined with oxygen and atoms of aluminum with several oxygens or hydroxyls (OH)—and the arrangement of these units is indicated by the terms of the chemical formulas given above. These components of the clay structure exist as ions, which have electrical charges that can be understood on the basis of the structure of individual atoms.

Atoms of all elements consist of two major parts—a nucleus and an electron distribution—and each of these parts is electrically charged. The nucleus comprises positively charged protons ($+$) and uncharged neutrons that together give it a net positive electrical charge. Electrons have a negative charge ($-$) and revolve around the nucleus in a series of nested orbits (also called shells or energy levels). Atoms are electrically neutral, because they have an equal number of protons ($+$) and electrons ($-$).

Atoms having either two or eight electrons in their outermost orbit are electrically stable and unreactive. If, however, there is any other number of elec-

Table 2.5 Ideal Chemical Formulas of the Clay Minerals

Kaolinite	$Al_2(Si_2O_5)(OH)_4$
Halloysite	$Al_2(Si_2O_5)(OH)_4 \cdot 2H_2O$
Montmorillonite	$\left(Al_{1.67} \begin{smallmatrix} Na_{0.33} \\ Mg_{0.33} \end{smallmatrix}\right)(Si_2O_5)_2(OH)_2$
Illite	$Al_{2-x}Mg_xK_{1-x-y}(Si_{1.5-y}Al_{0.5+y}O_5)_2(OH)_2$
Mica	$Al_2K(Si_{1.5}Al_{0.5}O_5)_2(OH)_2$

Source: After Kingery, Bowen, and Uhlmann 1976, 7.

trons in the outer shell, the atom will tend to lose or gain one or more electrons in order to bring the total number to either two or eight and thereby attain electrical stability. This loss or gain of electrons transforms the atom from an electrically neutral or balanced state into a charged ion. A loss of one or more electrons causes the atom to become a positive ion (called a cation), while the gain of one or more electrons changes the neutral atom into a negatively charged ion (or anion). An ion that needs to gain or lose one electron to stabilize its outer shell is called a monovalent ion (e.g., Na^{1+} and K^{1+} are monovalent cations, while Cl^{1-} is a monovalent anion); an ion with two to gain or lose is divalent (e.g., Mg^{2+}), and one with three is tervalent (e.g., Al^{3+}).

Because the transition from a neutral atom to a positive ion (cation) commonly involves losing electrons to eliminate an incomplete outermost energy level, the effective size (ionic radius; see table 3.1) of a cation is reduced (compared with that of a neutral atom of the same element) whenever a positive ion is formed. Conversely, the formation of a negative ion (anion) involves filling this outermost shell, and thus negative ions increase in size compared with neutral atoms. In general, cations are smaller than anions.

The creation of positively and negatively charged ions by the sharing of electrons between atoms produces stable chemical compounds—combinations of one or more elements in definite proportions. This process of combination often occurs when large anions are arranged in a close-packed structure, with the smaller cations fitting into the spaces between.

With respect to the structure of clay particles specifically, aluminum and silicon are both cations (i.e., small and positively charged). Aluminum must lose three electrons to attain chemical and electrical stability (as Al^{3+}), and silicon must lose four to become Si^{4+}. In clays, both these cations lose their electrons to oxygen atoms, each of which needs two electrons to complete its outer shell and become O^{2-}.

The form and arrangement of the silicon and aluminum cations with the oxygen (or hydroxyl) anions is distinctive. Silicon combines with oxygen to form tetrahedrons consisting of the small central silicon cation surrounded by four larger oxygen atoms equally spaced around it (fig. 2.4a). This silicon-oxygen tetrahedron is the basic building block of all silicate rocks. In clays the tetrahedrons typically join together in sheets by sharing oxygen atoms at their "corners." This occurs because in the transfer of four silicon electrons to four oxygen atoms, the oxygen atoms' electrical charge requirements are not satisfied, since four oxygens require eight electrons to become O^{2-} ions. To achieve electrical completion, the oxygens in one tetrahedron bind with four oxygens at the bases of five additional tetrahedrons, forming hexagonal rings of tetrahedrons (fig. 2.4b,c). This process repeats indefinitely, forming a sheetlike structure composed of hexagons.

Similarly, aluminum cations form octahedrons with two oxygens and four hydroxyls equidistantly spaced around the aluminum (fig. 2.5). Because aluminum is tervalent, giving only half a charge to each of the six other particles, it is still electrically unsatisfied. As a result, alumina octahedrons join to each other by sharing the corner oxygens and hydroxyls to form sheetlike layers as do the silica tetrahedrons. Many of the silicate clay minerals are composed of "sandwiches" of stacked layers of alternate sheets of alumina octahedrons and silica tetrahedrons, which are weakly bound to each other by sharing oxygens between the two layers (see sec. 2.3.4). This flat, sheetlike crystalline structure, with weak bonding between the layers, results in the lamellar, platelet shape of the particles of many clays and their easy cleavage.

This configuration is the theoretical or compositional ideal structure of a pure silicate clay. It may be confounded, however, because silicon and aluminum, the basic cations of these tetra- and octahedral arrangements, can be replaced by other elements to varying degrees. For example, Mg^{2+}, Fe^{2+}, or Fe^{3+} may replace Al^{3+}, or Al^{3+} may replace Si^{4+}, owing to satisfaction of electrical charge requirements or similarities of sizes of the ions (ionic radii). These cations can then "fit" between the oxygens and hydroxyls. It is this compositional complexity that gives rise to the many different kinds of clays—approximately fifty clay mineral "species."

In addition, because the edges of the clay particles are unsatisfied electrically, they tend to bond readily with other elements. This tendency, along with the attached elements themselves, plays a significant role in the behavior and properties of individual clays. Elements such as iron, titanium, calcium, sodium, and magnesium may substitute within the atomic structure of different clays, or they may be bonded to the particles as impurities in the form of oxides of soluble salts to satisfy electrical charge requirements. These ele-

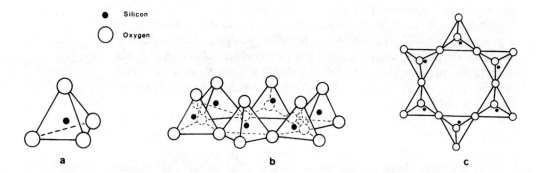

● Silicon

○ Oxygen

a   b   c

Figure 2.4 The configuration of silica: *a*, *b, c*, the hexagonal arrangement of silica tetrahedral arrangement of silicon and oxygen; tetrahedrons.

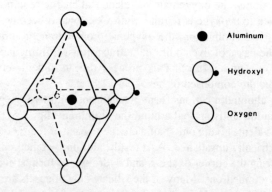

● Aluminum

○ Hydroxyl

○ Oxygen

Figure 2.5 The octahedral arrangement of aluminum, oxygen, and hydroxyls.

ments and compounds, plus carbon compounds, are common as trace or minor constituents in clays and can significantly affect their properties (see chaps. 3 and 4).

2.3.4 Mineralogical Definitions of Clays

Despite the long history of clay use, the knowledge that clays are minerals was achieved rather recently. For a long time it was thought that all clays were a single substance very similar to what is now known as kaolinite. This material was thought to exist in particles invisible to the naked eye, and clays were considered to be amorphous (noncrystalline) colloid-sized particles. Variations in the properties of clays and soils were believed to be a consequence of impurities in this kaolinite-like product (Ashley 1909; Grim 1968, 13–18).

Then, beginning in the 1920s, a series of studies used improved techniques to examine the structure and properties of the microscopic particles (Rinne 1924). Optical petrography and especially X-ray diffraction (see secs. 13.2.1 and 13.2.2) revealed that clays are extremely fine crystalline solids rather than amorphous materials, and that they have a definite internal structure and arrangement of atoms (Hendricks 1942; Brindley, ed. 1951, 1961). This internal structure in most clays comes primarily from the layered arrangement of sheets of silica tetrahedrons and alumina octahedrons described above (though not all clays have this structure). By the early 1930s the clay-mineral concept was firmly established, following publication of works on clay mineralogy and efforts at classification of the minerals (see Ries 1927; Ross 1928; Ross and Kerr 1931a; Grim 1939, 1950, 1965; Keller 1964; Rich and Kunze 1964; Keeling 1965).

It is now known that there are many kinds of clay minerals, and imposing an orderly classification has proved extraordinarily difficult. No consensus has been achieved among clay mineralogists on a satisfactory taxonomy, or even on the most appropriate criteria for creating one, although crystalline structure and properties (shape, expandability) have been most commonly used. The classification problem is complicated because there seem to be "transitional" clays with properties intermediate between one clay mineral category and another. This suggests that clays vary on a continuum and cannot easily be divided into discrete categories. What follows here is an effort to simplify this complexity and discuss some of the major or most commonly accepted categories of clay minerals (see Brindley et al. 1951; Grim 1965; Millot 1979).

Most of the major clay minerals or mineral groups fall into the category of layered silicates or phyllosilicates (from Greek *phyllon*, "leaf"), although a number of important minerals have a chain or lath type of structure (table 2.6). Additionally, a small group of clay minerals (the allophane minerals) are noncrystalline and amorphous to X-ray diffraction, making them very difficult to analyze. Because they are not common or well known, they will not be further treated here, and attention is given principally to the phyllosilicates and chain-structure clay minerals. Table 2.7 summarizes some of their important properties.

Table 2.6   Classification of the Major Clay Minerals

        I. Phyllosilicates (layered structure) clays
            A. Two-layer clays
                1. Kaolin group
                    a. Kaolinite
                    b. Nacrite
                    c. Dickite
                2. Halloysite group
            B. Three-layer clays
                1. Expanding lattice clays
                    a. Smectite group
                        i. Montmorillonite
                        ii. Bentonite
                        iii. Beidellite
                        iv. Saponite, stevensite
                        v. Nontronite
                        vi. Sauconite
                    b. Vermiculite group
                2. Nonexpanding lattice clays
                    a. Illite group
                        i. Illite
                        ii. Glauconite
            C. Mixed-layer clays (mica structure)
                1. Chlorite group
        II. Hydrous-magnesian clays (lath or chain structure)
            A. Attapulgite, palygorskite
            B. Sepiolite

Table 2.7   Properties of Some Clay Minerals

Property	Kaolinite	Smectites (Montmorillonite)	Illite	Chlorites, Hydrous Micas
Occurrence	Highly weathered, especially by acid leaching; widespread; occurs as primary and secondary clays	Not heavily weathered; especially characteristic of arid and alkaline environments	Especially in marine and calcareous sediments	Commonly mixed with other clays
Type	Two-layer	Three-layer expanding	Three-layer nonexpanding	Mixed layer
Particle size and shape	Relatively large hexagonal plates, $0.3\ \mu m$–$0.01\ \mu m$ diameter	Very small and poorly defined; much less than $1\ \mu m$ diameter	Small, thick, poorly defined	Variable and poorly defined
Plasticity	Sedimentary—good; residual—low	Very good	Good	Poor
Shrinkage	Low	High	—	—
Fired color	Sedimentary—sometimes white; residual—variable	Variable—cream, red, light brown	Variable	Brown, red, black
Refractoriness	High, 1710°C	Moderate, 1350–1450°C	Low, 1000–1300°C	Low to moderate, 1200–1500°C
Other	Sometimes has natural luster	High base exchange, high absorption, low luster	Natural luster, good for slips	—

2.3.4.1 PHYLLOSILICATES

The phyllosilicates or layered silicates consist of a regular ordering of layers of the silica and alumina structural components as described above. Differences in the arrangement of these layers, plus substitutions of various cations for the aluminum, provide the basis for three major subdivisions within this larger group. One division is the two-layer clays, which have one layer of silica tetrahedrons and one layer of alumina octahedrons; these include kaolinites and halloysites. A second group consists of the three-layer clays, which have one layer of alumina octahedrons sandwiched between two sheets of silica tetrahedrons. These may be further divided into expanding-lattice clays (smectites and vermiculites) and nonexpanding-lattice clays (illites). The third subdivision is the mixed-layer clays, the chlorite group, which have alternating layers of different types stacked on top of each other.

2.3.4.1.1 Kaolin Group. Clays of the kaolin group are composed principally of the clay mineral kaolinite (Ross and Kerr 1931b; Gruner 1932; Brindley and Robinson 1946). The name kaolin is believed to come from Chinese *kao lin* or *kau ling,* "high hill," designating a locale near Jau Chou in Jiangxi (Kiangsi) Province, where white clay for porcelains was obtained. The use of the term kaolinite began in 1867.

Kaolinite represents an advanced stage of weathering of the parent material, usually an acid rock such as a pegmatite (granitic rocks high in feldspar and quartz) or micaceous schist. The mineral is most often formed in warm tropical or subtropical regions with high rainfall and good soil drainage, resulting in acid leaching, which removes most elements—especially bases such as calcium, magnesium, iron, sodium, and potassium—except silicon and aluminum from the parent. Kaolinite is generally high in alumina, which often exists in a ratio of two to one with silica. The mineral is described by the idealized formula $Al_2O_3 \cdot 2SiO_2 \cdot 2H_2O$ and has an average chemical composition of 39.4% alumina, 46.6% silica, and 13.9% water. When weathering and leaching are extreme, especially in tropical equatorial regions, even more silica is removed, forming the hydrous oxide clays and deposits of the high-alumina minerals bauxite and gibbsite.

Kaolinite particles usually occur as flat hexagonal plates (fig. 2.6) of moderate to large size, ranging in diameter from 0.3 μm to 0.01 mm and approximately 0.05 μm thick. Their two-layer silica-alumina structure (fig. 2.7) involves a relatively strong bond, providing little opportunity for cation substitutions in the structure (low base exchange capacity), and therefore the composition and properties of kaolinites are relatively constant.

Kaolin clays may exist as residual or sedimentary deposits, and they are widespread in temperate and tropical zones. Residual kaolin clays are usually low in plasticity, coarse, and full of impurities, chiefly remnants of the parent rock, including partially decomposed feldspar and unaltered rock minerals. Sedimentary kaolins usually benefit from sorting during transport and deposition, which eliminates impurities and makes them finer grained. Depending upon the location of the deposit, however, the sediment may be highly organic (e.g., lacustrine deposits).

In ancient sediments, kaolinite is abundant in clays of fluviatile origin and nearshore deposition. In modern soils, kaolinite minerals are common in red

Figure 2.6 Platelets of kaolin clay, as seen in a scanning electron microscope under 3,700x magnification. Although individual particles may be less than half a micron thick, they frequently occur as stacks of platelets that require mixing to break apart and bring about good plasticity. Reproduced with permission from W. D. Kingery and P. Vandiver, *Ceramic Masterpieces: Art, Structure and Technology* (New York: Free Press, 1986), fig. 1.8.

and gray, usually acidic, podsols and laterites. Alkaline or calcareous (e.g., limestone-derived) sediments tend not to include kaolinite, and calcium may inhibit the formation of the mineral (Millot 1942, cited in Grim 1968, 548).

Certain kinds of kaolin clays, primarily sedimentary deposits, are relatively free of impurities such as iron and other colorants, and they fire to a white color. These deposits are industrially important for paper sizing (nearly one-third the weight of slick-paper magazines is kaolinite; Mason and Berry 1968, 443), vitreous plumbing fixtures, and china tableware. Indeed, kaolin clays are often called "china clays" (though this term usually refers more specifically to primary kaolin deposits). China clays are typically refractory, very low in impurities, low in plasticity, and have comparatively large particle sizes, averaging 0.6 to 1.0 μm (Cardew 1969, 20). Among the white-firing kaolin deposits that are commercially significant today are the deep residual kaolins formed from hydrothermal alteration of granites in Cornwall, England, and the plastic, sedimentary kaolins of South Carolina, Georgia, and

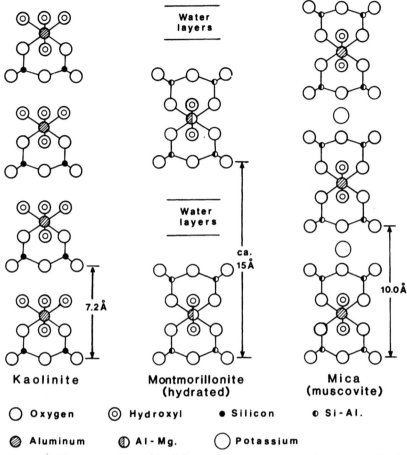

Figure 2.7 The layer structure of kaolinite, montmorillonite, and mica, showing the position of common cation substitutions, water layers, and average lattice constants (the distance between repeated layers). After Kingery, Bowen, and Uhlmann 1976, fig. 2.35.

Florida, formed by erosion of kaolinized granite and subsequent transport and redeposition of the kaolin.

From the viewpoint of ceramics, kaolin clays are extremely important because kaolinite is a common clay mineral and thus very widespread, and because some of the material fires to a white color. Because of their high alumina content and resistance to absorbing impurities, they are relatively refractory (that is, they do not melt at low temperatures). Their large particle size makes them rather low in plasticity, and they also have a low drying shrinkage. Products formed of kaolinite clays may attain a high natural luster without polishing.

Halloysite, the second major mineral category in the two-layer group, has some irregularity in the stacking of its silica and alumina layers, leading to more water in the mineral structure and a tendency for the thin platelets of halloysite to be curved or rolled into tubelike forms. Halloysite has been found to develop fairly rapidly from volcanic ash as recent as four thousand years old in tropical environments (Hay 1960). Like the other two kaolin

group minerals, nacrite and dickite, halloysite tends to be formed by hydrothermal action.

2.3.4.1.2 Smectite Group. The smectite clay group, previously referred to
as montmorillonite (the most common member, named in 1948 after Mont-
morillon, France), is one of two categories of clay minerals having a three-
layer structure (Ross and Hendricks 1945). Many interesting properties result
from this three-layer structure and make these clays valuable in a variety of
commercial applications.

Smectites comprise units of two sheets of silica tetrahedrons separated by
an intermediate layer of alumina octahedrons, all joined by loose bonds. The
silica tetrahedrons are oriented in both sides of the "sandwich" with three corners outward and a single point directed inward toward the alumina layer.
Thus, in joining with the alumina octahedrons, bonding occurs only between
the oxygen tips of the silica tetrahedrons and the oxygen tips of the alumina
octahedrons; the hydroxyls remain unbonded and electrically unsatisfied. Additionally, only a weak bond exists between one three-layer silica-alumina-
silica unit and the next one stacked on top of it. As a result, water molecules
and atoms of a variety of elements can easily penetrate the spaces between
these unit layers (fig. 2.7). This makes the layers expand, cleave apart, or
simply adsorb additional ions with ease, a property known as high "base exchange" (Foster 1953; Brown and Stephen 1959). In most of the smectites this
expandability is present only in the structure of the mineral, whereas in
bentonite clays the actual clay volume swells to a degree visible to the naked
eye. Bentonites are highly absorbent and are often used commercially as de-
colorizers, and as clarifiers and stabilizers in wine production.

Smectites are formed chiefly by alteration of basic rocks and minerals high
in calcium, magnesium, and iron, such as basalts and calcic plagioclases, or
by decomposition of volcanic ash. They are formed under conditions of relatively poor drainage, reduction, low rainfall, and leaching, and when bases
such as magnesium, iron, calcium, sodium, and potassium are relatively
abundant in the zone of weathering. Smectites tend to be common in recent
sediments and are major components of soils in arid regions. They are largely
absent from many ancient (pre-Mesozoic) sediments. They are not as highly
weathered as kaolinites; in fact alteration—especially the leaching that occurs
under conditions of high rainfall, high temperature, and good drainage—will
remove bases and so transform smectites into kaolinites. Chemically, smectites
have a higher ratio of silica to alumina (on the order of four to one) and more
of the alkali metal elements (lithium, sodium, potassium, rubidium, and
cesium). The lower proportion of alumina makes them less refractory (i.e.,
they will melt at lower temperatures) and more fusible than the kaolin clays.

The theoretical composition of smectites is 66.7% silica, 28.3% alumina,
and 5% water. Because of the water adsorption and substitutions within the
lattice structure, however, the theoretical formula virtually always differs from
the actual chemical composition. The most common substitutions for the
major cations in montmorillonite are Al^{3+} and P^{5+} for Si^{4+}, and Mg^{2+},
$Fe^{2+, 3+}$, Zn^{2+}, Ni^{2+}, or Li^{1+} for Al^{3+} (Grim 1968, 83). If these substitutions
are extensive, the result is a completely different clay mineral. Replacement

of Al^{3+} by Mg^{2+} yields saponite, and replacement by Fe^{3+} yields nontronite, both of which have a lathlike structure. Substitution of Zn^{2+} for Al^{3+} yields sauconite, while replacement of Si^{4+} by Al^{3+} yields beidellite.

As with kaolinites, smectite particles are thin and platy, but they do not exhibit the regular hexagonal shape of kaolinite crystals. In addition, the particles of smectites are considerably smaller than kaolinite particles, ranging from 0.05 μm to 1 μm in diameter. Because of this small particle size, smectite clays are usually very plastic and "sticky." In terms of their behavior in pottery making, these fine particles plus their tendency to adsorb water between the layers means that the clays usually have high shrinkage, often cracking as they dry. Also, the fineness may give them the characteristics of colloids, and this plus their open lattice structure—which confers a considerable capacity for adsorbing other ions (e.g., colorants)—makes them useful for paints or slips. Smectites generally do not attain high luster.

A clay mineral related to the smectites is vermiculite (Walker 1961), named in 1824 from the Latin *vermiculus*, "worm," because vermiculite particles, when heated, look like small worms. Vermiculites are similar to smectites in having an expanding lattice, but their expansion is not as great as that of smectites. This may be partly because vermiculites occur in larger particle sizes, and there is less randomness in the ordering of the layers of the particles (Grim 1968, 111). Because they expand to become light and porous, vermiculite clays are useful in industry as insulation material and as fillers in concrete.

2.3.4.1.3 Illite Group. The second major group of three-layer clays (besides smectites and related vermiculites) is the illite group (Gaudette, Eades, and Grim 1966), named in 1937 for the state of Illinois. Illite clay minerals have structures similar to those of well-crystallized micas (fig. 2.7; Bradley and Grim 1961), and these in turn are very similar to those of smectites. In the illite clays, however, about one-sixth of the silicon is replaced by aluminum, leading to a charge deficiency that is balanced chiefly by potassium (K^{1+}), but also by Ca^{2+}, Mg^{2+}, and H^{1+}. This charge deficiency is primarily in the outer silica layers of the unit structure and therefore close to the surface, rather than in the interior alumina layer as it is in smectites. It is largely for this reason that the illite clays are nonexpanding. Like smectites, illite mineral particles occur in poorly defined flakes of very small sizes, but they are thicker and larger than smectites, with diameters ranging between 0.1 μm and 0.3 μm. The fineness of these illite clays, and their tendency to have a natural luster, makes them useful for pottery slips. Slips on two famous categories of archaeological pottery, Greek black-figure ware and Arretine/Samian ware, were manufactured from illite clays (see sec. 1.2.1.3).

Illite clays are particularly characteristic of marine deposits, especially offshore or in deep water. There is some evidence that these minerals are formed there by diagenesis, an in-place physical and chemical alteration that converts sedimentary deposits to rock. Alternatively, their existence may relate more directly to the weathering and deposition of these sediments. In the alkaline marine environment, illite may form from the alteration of kaolinites and smectites, owing to the absence of leaching and the presence of ions of calcium, potassium, and magnesium. In other situations illites may alter to smectites over thousands of years. Illites seem to be the most common clay minerals in calcareous sediments.

Glauconite is an unusual mineral that may be classed as part of the illite group or the chlorite group (see below). Formed during nearshore or shallow-water marine diagenesis, its formation is enhanced by organic and calcareous material as well as potassium, and it may be a product of alteration of biotite as well as other minerals.

2.3.4.1.4 Chlorite Group. The chlorite clay minerals (Brindley 1961) are mixed-layer minerals colored light green by ferrous iron (Fe^{2+}). The name chlorite was first used about 1800 and comes from the Greek *chloros,* "green." Chlorites comprise alternating micalike biotite layers (see Illite Group, above) and "brucite" layers of magnesium-aluminum hydroxide. There are a number of variants within this group that arise from partial substitution of Fe^{2+} and Mn^{2+} for Mg^{2+} and from Fe^{2+} or Cr^{3+} partially replacing Al^{3+}, all in the brucite layer. Chlorites are highly susceptible to destruction, are commonly mixed in small amounts with other clay minerals, and are often difficult to identify.

2.3.4.2 LATH-STRUCTURE CLAYS

The lath-structure hydrous-magnesian clays have a chainlike rather than sheetlike arrangement of silica tetrahedrons, and the octahedrons contain magnesium atoms surrounded by oxygens and hydroxyls. These lathlike or fibrous minerals fall into two groups, the attapulgite-palygorskite group and the sepiolite group. They frequently occur mixed with other clay minerals as well as in calcareous material, and they are easily destroyed by acid solutions, making them difficult to isolate and study. The lath-structure clay minerals are typically associated with soils of arid and desert regions, and they are also weathering products of basalts.

2.3.4.2.1 Attapulgite-Palygorskite Group. Attapulgite was identified in 1935 in fuller's earth from Attapulgus, southern Georgia. Magnesium ions in the octahedral units in this mineral are replaced to a considerable degree by aluminum. Attapulgite occurs as laths and bundles of laths, usually several microns long, often bent and tangled. These clays are highly absorbent and are used commercially as decolorants as well as ingredients in antidiarrheal preparations.

Palygorskite is intermediate in composition between attapulgite and sepiolite, with some replacement of magnesium by aluminum, but this substitution is not as extreme as in attapulgite.

2.3.4.2.2 Sepiolite Group. Sepiolite is a light mineral named in 1847 from the Greek *sepion,* meaning cuttlebone or cuttlefish. It has often been equated with meerschaum, the light-colored and lightweight material used to make tobacco pipe bowls. Sepiolite occurs in laths that are thicker, shorter, and more densely packed than those of attapulgite.

2.3.5 Commercial Uses of Clays

Clays may also be categorized by their modern industrial or commercial uses, a system of classification that cuts across the former clay classes based on mineralogy and depositional context. Clays are used for a staggering variety of products and purposes beyond their well-known functions as tableware, tiles, bricks, pipes, and plumbing fixtures. Some of the other uses have been mentioned above in connection with specific minerals: clays may be used in insulation, medication, decolorants, concrete filler, and paper sizing. In addition, clays or ceramic materials are employed as furnace linings, filters, agents in dry cleaning, drilling lubricants, and a wide variety of goods from spark plugs to dentures to porcelain hand grenades.

The major commercial categories of clays are ball clays, refractory clays, and heavy clay products (also known as building or structural) clays, although other uses and descriptive terms, including stoneware clays, fire clays, china clays, and flint clays, are common in the literature (see Grimshaw 1971, 290–311).

Ball clays are important in the manufacture of whitewares, which include china tableware, tiles, and sanitary ware. These clays are composed principally of the clay mineral kaolinite, although some may contain smectites and illites. Ball clays usually have 40% to 60% silica and 30% alumina. In addition, they include significant amounts (5% or more) of organic material and soluble salts, the organic material making them gray or black in the unfired state. Ball clays are very fine textured, highly plastic, secondary clays that are usually water transported and deposited in lakes or swamps, and they fire to a white or cream color. They usually have a fairly high drying shrinkage yet are strong when dried but unfired (Holdridge 1956), a property called green strength. Ball clays typically are not used alone but are added to a mixture to improve its working properties.

Refractory clays have a melting point above 1,600°C. They are usually residual kaolinites that are high in alumina—over 30% of their composition in most cases—and low in alkali impurities, which act as fluxes, lowering the melting and vitrification point. Some refractory clays are also called fire clays. Refractory clays are used for furnace linings, high-temperature brick, and other industrial products that must withstand high temperatures.

A third important use category is "building clay" or "heavy clay products clay," used for structural products such as bricks, roof tiles, and sewer pipes. These clays are generally red firing, as a consequence of an iron content of 3% to 8%, and they may be high in impurities such as calcium and magnesium, which act as fluxes. Usually coarse textured and variable in plasticity, structural clays are associated with a variety of poorly sorted primary and secondary deposits, including fluviatile and glacial clays and surface clay soils.

2.4 Functional Definitions of Clays

For anthropologists or archaeologists studying pottery, these issues of depositional context, particle size, chemical structure, and mineralogical composition are essential in a way, but in another sense they are of little importance. The significance of these different viewpoints depends on the questions being asked. Chemical or mineralogical data on clays are not informative unless research questions are framed so that chemistry and mineralogy can provide answers.

To answer the crucial question, What is a clay? it is helpful to look at contemporary, nonindustrialized peasant or traditional potters who produce their wares under relatively simple conditions, frequently without a wheel or kiln (see chap. 5). Although these potters often demonstrate considerable expertise in selecting their materials and modifying them for use, their requirements for a usable clay are also much less rigorous than those of modern industry. For the most part, traditional potters must choose and use what is available. They may be very selective when a wide spectrum of resources is available, recognizing special and desirable properties, but their criteria and limitations are not those of twentieth-century Western science and industry. Most noncraft or nonindustrial potter's clays are not "pure" in either a mineralogical or a granulometric sense: they may be surface clay soils; they may consist of a mixture of interlayered clay minerals; and they do not have all the coarse, nonclay material separated out from them. Traditional potters have a number of ways to purify and increase the fineness of their clays, such as crushing, sifting, or levigation, but in general their materials are highly impure and contain a variety of substances besides clay minerals or clay-sized particles.

It is entirely likely that the conditions current among modern village potters also obtained in prehistory. Furthermore, in studying ancient pottery, we must remember that firing clays usually destroys their mineral structure, rendering them unidentifiable. Thus archaeologists studying ancient potsherds may find ceramic technological research futile if questions are based solely on clay mineral (or chemical) identifications.

Presenting the varied definitions of clays illustrates why archaeologists and anthropologists seeking assistance from geologists, mineralogists, or ceramic engineers in understanding the properties of potters' resources should be aware of different approaches to the same topic. Chemists, mineralogists, geologists, and engineers may define what is or is not a clay based on strict definitions of particle size, mineral composition, or potential for commercial use. They may be skeptical when asked to analyze a clay sample collected from an archaeological survey area.

Functionally, however, in terms of selection and use by potters in the ethnographic present, clays may be defined solely by their most important property, plasticity. Plasticity (see sec. 3.2), the property that allows wet clay to be shaped by pressure, is the fundamental, pragmatic, and operational criterion in identifying a clay for the purposes of traditional potters and anthropologists, regardless of chemical, mineralogical, or particulate character. Because prehistoric potters could not select or reject resources strictly on the basis of their being smectite rather than kaolinite minerals, or being 5 μm in diameter rather than 1 μm, these technical distinctions are generally not of primary interest. The ultimate concern in making clay vessels is a material's plasticity or workability. (An important exception to this generalization, of course, is the use of particular substances for paints or slips, in which plasticity per se is not the primary consideration.) Thus most of the discussion in this book, unless otherwise specified, focuses on what might be called "natural" clays: clay materials that can be worked and shaped into a desired form.

On the other hand, for some analytical purposes technical properties may be of the highest significance to anthropologists and archaeologists. Mineral composition, chemical composition, particle size, and such, determine the characteristics that *did* influence prehistoric potters' selection—workability, shrinkage, strength, thermal shock resistance, and color development. Thus these properties of clays provide the basic limits of variability within which one must seek answers to questions that interest anthropologists—questions concerning resource selection, production, and function. So while ancient and contemporary village potters may not knowingly select smectite clays, they may select for some of the *properties* of smectite clays, such as absorption and plasticity. Similarly, it may be of little use to obtain an ultimate chemical analysis of a given clay, because most clay deposits differ chemically from each other as well as varying internally within a single deposit. Yet knowing the role of high alumina content (as a refractory) or high alkaline content (as a flux) will be significant in understanding the behavior of particular clay sediments in pottery manufacture.

The point is that chemical, mineralogical, or granulometric analyses should not be undertaken as pro forma descriptive techniques; rather, they should be conducted with a very clear idea of what kind of information they can and cannot provide about the pottery or resources of interest (chaps. 12–14). It is not the composition itself, then, but the properties it confers that are of interest in the study of pottery, whether ancient or contemporary. In looking for answers, in ceramic study as in other areas of research, it is important not to lose sight of the questions.

2.5 References

Ashley 1909
Blatt 1982
Bradley and Grim 1961
Brindley 1961
Brindley, ed., 1951, 1961
Brindley and Robinson 1946
Brindley et al. 1951
Brown and Stephen 1959
Cardew 1969
Foster 1953
Gaudette, Eades, and Grim 1966
Grim 1939, 1950, 1965, 1968
Grimshaw 1971
Gruner 1932
Hay 1960
Hendricks 1942
Holdridge 1956

Keeling 1965
Keller 1964
Kingery 1960
Kingery, Bowen, and Uhlmann 1976
Kingery and Vandiver 1986
Mason 1966
Mason and Berry 1968
Millot 1942, 1979
Rich and Kunze 1964
Ries 1927
Rinne 1924
Ross 1928
Ross and Hendricks 1945
Ross and Kerr 1931a, b
Walker 1961
Wentworth 1922, 1933

3 Properties of Clays I: The Clay/Water System

A number of characteristics of clays are significant to potters because they determine whether the clays can be easily and safely formed, dried, and fired into durable containers or other objects. These qualities vary among the clay mineral groups and are in part the bases for some of the industrial or commercial use classifications of clays. The most fundamental property of a clay is its plasticity, which is in turn founded on the idea of the "clay/water system." A clay becomes plastic only when mixed with some amount of water; hence this primary property is based on the relationship between the two most basic ingredients of a ceramic, clay and water.

This chapter looks at the nature of the clay/water relationship, at plasticity, and at shrinkage—the consequence of removing water from the clay. The discussions of clay and the clay/water system here refer almost exclusively (and except where noted) to the layered silicate clays.

3.1 The Clay/Water System

Clay is defined in most general, functional terms as a material that becomes plastic when mixed with a limited amount of water. One must understand the nature of this added water to comprehend the property of plasticity as well as other important characteristics of ceramic materials. The water of interest here is not the interlayer lattice water between the silica and alumina sheets of the smectite minerals; nor is it the chemically combined water—the hydroxyls—or water of hydration that is part of the chemical structure of clays. Instead, the water involved in the clay/water system is that which is *adsorbed* by the clay particles, or weakly bound to their surfaces and edges. This consists primarily of the water that makes dry clay malleable when "mechanically combined" with the clay (or "physisorbed") rather than being bound as part of the chemical structure ("chemisorbed") of the clay particles (Phelps and Maguire 1956; Dal and Berden 1965; Norton and Johnson 1944; Williamson 1947). This weakly bound water is easily removed from the clay at low temperatures (see sec. 3.3).

The atomic structure of water molecules is similar in some ways to that of silica. As discussed in section 2.3.3, atoms of silicon join with oxygen to form tetrahedrons, and these in turn combine into hexagonal rings of tetrahedrons, a structural arrangement common in many clays. Water molecules, like silica, tend to join with each other into tetrahedrons, and these tetrahedrons will join into hexagonal rings.

Water molecules are made up of one oxygen anion (O^{2-}) and two cations of hydrogen (H^{1+}) (fig. 3.1a). Because of a noncentrosymmetric charge distribution, the water molecule acts as if it had two charges, positive and negative, even though the net charge of the molecule is zero. One end of the molecule, the end with the two hydrogen ions, has a partial positive charge, while the other end associated with the oxygen ion has a partial negative charge. A molecule with this structure is called a dipole because it has two electrical charges, or poles, separated by some distance.

Dipolar molecules may interact with other molecules and ions in two important ways. One results because their dipolar character (dipole moment) leads them to interact electrostatically with other dipolar molecules. Water molecules commonly associate with four other water molecules, the positive "ends" forming four ionic bonds with the negative "ends" of other molecules (fig. 3.1b), leading to a hexagonal ring structure (fig. 3.1c). Unlike the layered clays, however, in water this hexagonal structure develops in three dimensions, not just in a two-dimensional sheet structure. The bonds holding the molecules together are weak because the dipolar charges are only partial, and hence the electrostatic attraction is reduced. Further, the weak dipole/dipole interaction is a strong function of distance and falls off rapidly with increasing separation.

Figure 3.1 The structure of water: a, a single molecule, showing the dipolar structure resulting from the arrangement of two hydrogen nuclei. After Lawrence and West 1982, fig. 3-1. b, the tetrahedral arrangement of molecules and, c, the hexagonal ring structure of water, formed by arrangements of tetrahedrons. After Lawrence and West 1982, fig. 3-2a, b.

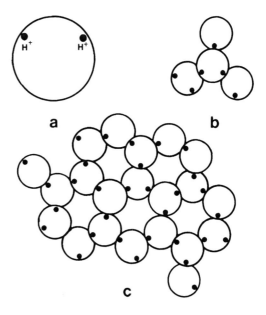

The second important result of this dipolar charge distribution concerns interaction with single ions. Ions with a positive charge (cations) will be attracted to the negative side of water molecules, while ions with negative charges (anions) will be attracted to the positive side. In addition to the effect of the charge of the ion, the size of the ion is also important. Small ions, such as Ca^{2+} or Al^{3+}, that fit into the center of the hexagonal water structure will enhance its stability. Conversely, ions with radii larger than the size of the central area (greater than approximately one Ångstrom [Å], or 1.0×10^{-8} cm, or 0.0000001 mm), such as K^{1+}, will disrupt the hexagonal arrangement (fig. 3.2). Table 3.1 gives the ionic radii of some common ions.

One more aspect of the ion/dipole relationship of water deserves mention—the effect of adding ions to the water structure. An electric field is cre-

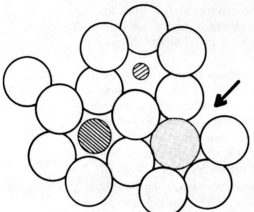

Figure 3.2   Accommodation of ions of different sizes in the hexagonal water structure; arrow indicates disruption of the water structure caused by the large K^{1+} ion. After Lawrence and West 1982, fig. 3-6b.

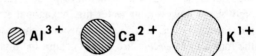

Table 3.1   Ionic Radii of Some Common Elements (Coordination Number = 6)

Element	Ion	Atomic Number	Ionic Radius (Å)
Lithium	Li^{1+}	3	0.74
Oxygen	O^{2-}	8	1.40
Sodium	Na^{1+}	11	1.02
Magnesium	Mg^{2+}	12	0.72
Aluminum	Al^{3+}	13	0.53
Silicon	Si^{4+}	14	0.40
Chlorine	Cl^{1-}	17	1.81
Potassium	K^{1+}	19	1.38
Calcium	Ca^{2+}	20	1.00
Manganese	Mn^{2+}	25	0.67
Iron	Fe^{2+}	26	0.77
	Fe^{3+}	26	0.65
Copper	Cu^{1+}	29	0.96
	Cu^{2+}	29	0.73
Zinc	Zn^{2+}	30	0.75
Arsenic	As^{3+}	33	0.53
	As^{5+}	33	0.50
Tin	Sn^{2+}	50	0.93
	Sn^{4+}	50	0.69
Barium	Ba^{2+}	56	1.36
Lead	Pb^{2+}	82	1.18

Source: After Kingery, Bowen, and Uhlmann 1976, table 2.3.

ated in the water surrounding the ion. The water molecules that are adsorbed immediately onto the ion are in a different physical state than ordinary water; they become organized and "immobilized" into a state sometimes referred to as "nonliquid" or "quasi-crystalline" (fig. 3.3). The molecules are fixed or restructured by the ion/dipole attraction: with a cation, their negative regions are directed inward; with an anion, the positive ends are directed inward. As a result, the water in the immediate region of the ion is in some senses like a thin layer of a solid, analogous to ice. There may be a sort of disordered "buffer" between the immobilized region and the normal liquid water structure of dipole/dipole attraction. The thickness or size of the area of nonliquid water around the ion is in turn a function of the ion's size and charge. This area is enlarged by small, highly charged ions, which fit into the water structure without disrupting it, whereas large, monovalent ions decrease its immobilization and stability.

These considerations are important to the clay/water system because wet, plastic clays consist of individual particles surrounded by a film of water. Clay platelets have active, electrically charged sites on their surfaces and edges that, depending on imperfections and the location of the broken bonds, result from the exposure of unsatisfied Al^{3+}, Si^{4+}, O^{2-}, and OH^{1-} ions. Most generally, in kaolinites at least, the break is such that the surfaces of the platelets consist of O^{2-} or OH^{1-} ions, while the edges are Al^{+3} or Si^{4+} ions. In other words, the edges of the particles have a positive charge and the surfaces a negative charge; clay particles thus have a dipole moment, but with an overall negative charge (monopole) as well.

To satisfy the charge deficiency of these ions, the surface sites of the clay particles attract the dipole water molecule (and other ions), the OH^{1-} and O^{2-} bonding with H^{1+} in water and the Al^{3+} and Si^{4+} bonding with the O^{2-} in water. This forms a layer or hull of adsorbed water around the platelet, which then acts as a large ion or series of ions surrounded by a water layer. This water can be either structured (immobilized) or unstructured in the way described above.

The degree of structuring (i.e., the size of this immobilized region) is partly a function of the size and charge of the charge-deficient ions on the clay platelet as well as their positioning. It also varies among the clay minerals

Figure 3.3 Model for the modification of the structure of water produced by the presence of a small ion (+). Heavy stipple indicates region of immobilization; light stipple indicates region of high disorder between immobilized water and normal water structure outside stippling. After Lawrence and West 1982, fig. 3-4.

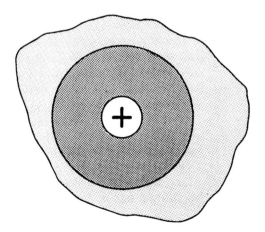

(Grim and Cuthbert 1945). Kaolinite platelets, for example, have a pattern of charges on the edges that matches the hexagonal structure of water, making an interlocking and stable structure. The water structuring is also in part a consequence of the ions in the water solution. For example, both sodium and calcium cations have the same ionic radius, 0.98 Å, but sodium is monovalent (Na^{1+}) while calcium is divalent (Ca^{2+}). In clays with adsorbed sodium cations, the nonliquid water zone is smaller than in clays with calcium cations, and there is a considerably greater transition region to liquid water (Grim 1962, 251–52). This is doubtless also related to the fact that sodium-rich clays require less water to develop plasticity than do calcium-rich clays.

3.2 Plasticity

Plasticity allows a clay, upon addition of a limited amount of water, to be shaped by pressure, and to retain that form when the pressure is relaxed. The property of plasticity is lost when this adsorbed water is removed from the clay in drying (see sec. 3.3), but the form will be retained. Plasticity can be restored by wetting the clay again, but the shaped form will disappear. Upon heating or burning (see chap. 4), clays become hard and extremely resistant to weathering, and above certain temperatures the capacity for plasticity is permanently eliminated.

3.2.1 Factors Influencing Plasticity

Plasticity has its origins in the clay/water system and arises from a number of factors (Bloor 1957; Norton 1948; Marshall 1955; Grimshaw 1971, 496–504). Among the major concerns are the following: (1) clay particle size, (2) clay particle shape, (3) surface tension of the water, (4) rigidity of the water, (5) adsorbed ions, (6) clay mineral component, (7) clay deposit location, (8) organic content, (9) nonclay mineral component of the material, and (10) temperature (important primarily in commercial applications of clay working).

Of the many factors influencing plasticity, among the most important are the size and shape of the clay particles. As discussed in section 2.3.2, clay particles are extremely small, generally less than 2 μm in diameter, and a considerable proportion of the smallest clay particles behave like colloids (see sec. 3.4.2). In addition, they have a flat lamellar or platelet shape, with a ratio of thickness to diameter on the order of 1:12. These shape and size considerations mean the clay particles in a clay mass have a very large total surface area. Most of the properties of clay/water systems (especially plasticity) in large part result from the interaction of clay and water at the surfaces of the clay particles.

Some idea of the surface area involved with clay-sized particles, compared with sand or other particle-size grades, may be given by calculating the surface area produced by successively subdividing a cube of some material (Lawrence and West 1982, 21). A cube of one cubic centimeter (1 cm³) has a total surface area of 0.93 square inches. Dividing that cube into particles on the order of 0.1 mm in diameter would produce 93.0 square inches of surface area. If the original cube were divided into fine clay-sized particles 0.1 μm (or 0.0001 mm) in diameter, the total surface area would be just under 650 square feet. Another way to express this is to say that 1 cm^3 of clay-sized particles has 1,000 times the surface area of an equal volume of coarse sand-sized particles.

When water is mixed with a clay, a thin film of adsorbed water surrounds the clay particles, acting as a lubricant that allows the platelets to slide over one another. The finer the particle size of a given volume of clay, the greater its plasticity, in part because a larger number of platelets, and hence a larger surface area, is present. Clay owes much of its plasticity to the characteristics of this adsorbed water. Specifically of interest are surface tension and the "rigidity" of the water film.

Surface tension refers to the intermolecular interactions of the thin film of water coating the clay particles, which acts weakly to hold the clay particles together (Schwartz 1952). Although in a plastic clay mass the water serves as a lubricant, so the particles slide easily over each other, at the same time the surface tension forces are sufficiently strong to make it difficult to pull the platelets apart or to shear the entire mass. The greater the total surface tension resulting from finer particles and thus more surrounding water, the greater the plasticity in the clay/water system. If, however, excess water is added, the surface tension is reduced and there is less resistance to shear: plasticity, yield point, and extensibility (see sec. 3.2.2) are all diminished. A final point concerns the channels or capillaries through which the water flows. Because surface tension increases with greater surface area and capillary volume per unit volume of clay, finer clays are more plastic than coarse ones, which have less surface area and a smaller total pore structure.

The rigidity of the adsorbed water film refers to the characteristics of the nonliquid or semicrystalline water that is initially adsorbed around the clay particles (Grim and Cuthbert 1945). There seems to be an optimal—and very small—amount of water necessary for a clay to reach a plastic state. There must be enough water to satisfy the charge requirements on all available particle surfaces and to form the nonliquid configuration, plus a very little more to act as normal liquid water in achieving lubrication, surface tension, and flow. If too much water is added, the surface tension is lowered and the body moves beyond a plastic state to become soft and weak. If insufficient water is added, the quasi-crystalline structure may not develop, or the particles may not be close enough to each other.

Adsorbed ions on the clay platelets or in the surrounding water film affect plasticity by influencing the dispersion of the platelets and their orientation to one another (see sec. 3.4.2). The effects of the ions depend primarily on their size and valence, but also on their shape and tendency to hydrate. Other things being equal, the plasticity of a clay increases as the charge of the ions in the adsorbed waters increases, and their size decreases. This is because the large monovalent ions tend to disrupt the nonliquid water structure and promote disorder, whereas the smaller, more highly charged ions fit more securely into the holes in the lattice and have little disordering effect. More simply put, large monovalent cations such as Na^{1+}, K^{1+}, or NH_4^{1+} tend to suppress plasticity, whereas smaller and highly charged divalent and trivalent ions such as Mg^{2+}

or Ca^{2+} will increase plasticity. It was mentioned earlier that clays with Ca^{2+} cations have a larger nonliquid zone around the particles than do sodium-rich clays and a more abrupt transition to liquid water. This is a factor not only in the variable amounts of water required to develop initial plasticity in these clays, but in the effects these ions have on plasticity when they are added in excess.

Clay surfaces may adsorb ions from the surrounding water film, and the rigid water structure itself may contain ions that will affect plasticity. The enormous surface area afforded by the colloid-sized particles in clay mixtures is important here, since they present a significant region for adsorption of ions, and their behavior alters in response to the resultant charge. As noted above, the clay platelets themselves may have a net negative charge, which makes them act like ions and repel each other. Because of this repulsion, they remain stable and separated, dispersed in an "edge-to-face" structure with the negatively charged surfaces associated with the positively charged ends of the particles. This arrangement of particles with respect to their electrical charges, and the role of ions in this arrangement, is important in determining whether clays are in a flocculated or deflocculated state (see sec. 3.4.2) and affects their appropriateness for a variety of uses.

Clay minerals vary in plasticity. In general, other things being equal, clay minerals with smaller particles, such as smectites, tend to be more plastic than those with larger particles, such as kaolinites. A further consideration is individual clay mineral categories' propensity to adsorb ions. The clay minerals, because of their different crystal structures and particle sizes, vary in their ability to adsorb and hold ions—their base exchange capacity. Kaolins, for example, because of their two-layer structure and the arrangement of charges on the edges of the particles, have little tendency to adsorb ions (low base exchange), whereas smectites, with their expanding lattices, have a high adsorptive capability.

The origins of clays and their depositional locations affect their plasticity. Because of sorting and additional weathering in transport and redeposition, sedimentary clays such as ball clays are usually finer in particle size and more plastic than are primary clays such as china clay. Primary clays may also include relatively large amounts of coarse and angular parent material, which means that particles in the clay size-grade range make up only a small fraction of the total, so they are very low in plasticity.

Sedimentary clays may also be finer than primary clays because in the process of deposition they are often mixed with organic matter such as bacteria and acids, increasing plasticity. Ball clays, for example, in addition to being fine in texture, are typically high in organic matter. The same is true of estuarine or lacustrine clays, which are often gray to black from organic matter; if not too sandy, these may be plastic to the point of stickiness.

3.2.2 Measuring Plasticity

No satisfactory means of measuring plasticity has been developed, in part because the property is influenced by so many factors, and in part because its applications require that it be measured in different ways (Grout 1906; Whittemore 1935; Norton 1938; Greger and Berg 1956; Bronitsky 1982). The definition of plasticity focuses on deformation of the clay by force, and for this reason it is useful to address the kinds of forces and deformations concerned, because each enters into some component of plasticity.

Three major forces are involved (see also sec. 12.3.2). One is compressive force—pressing on a wet clay, which will eventually cause it to crack. Another is tensile force—stretching or extension of the clay mass, which will also cause cracking beyond a certain limit. A third force is shear—simultaneous application of opposing forces on the clay, which will cause it to crack or rupture.

For ceramic engineers, plasticity may be described as the product of two specific characteristics of a clay, yield point and extensibility. At the yield point compressive stresses start changing the shape of the plastic mass, as the clay begins to become soft and malleable rather than remaining stiff and unyielding. The yield point may be measured by the force per unit area applied to the test material in pounds per square inch (psi) or kilograms per square meter. Extensibility refers to the amount of deformation a clay can withstand (in inches or meters) beyond the yield point before cracks appear.

Yield point and extensibility are inversely proportional: a clay with a high yield point will have low extensibility and is often described a "stiff," tending to crack when pressure is applied. A good clay balances the two opposed characteristics, so that it has both a moderate yield point and a moderate extensibility.

Potters assess a clay's plasticity according to its "working range," "workability," or "plastic limits," characteristics that can be determined adequately, though nonquantitatively, by a skilled potter through "feel" and experience. Potters will squeeze a clay, bite it, rub a small pinch between thumb and forefinger, or make a loop of it to judge its plastic characteristics. Even someone inexperienced can make some determination of a clay's working properties based on intuitive concepts of plasticity.

The terms working range and plastic limits have specific meanings, however. Both refer to the variable amount of water that must be added to a dry clay to make a mass that can be satisfactorily formed. The limits of plasticity and the working range thus refer to the interval between yield point and the upper boundary of extensibility. These limits vary with the kind of clay mineral, the intended use, and the pressure individual potters exert as they form their pots. A good clay for throwing on a wheel should have a relatively wide plastic region, because it must flow easily with the centrifugal forces of the wheel, but it should not dry out excessively or lose plasticity from the evaporation caused by rapid spinning. For hand modeling a stiffer clay (with a higher yield point and lower extensibility) might be serviceable. Some clays have a wide working range and can be worked into the desired forms without cracking when both relatively wet and relatively dry. Other clays have a narrow range: they are stiff until a certain amount of water has been added, but with just a little more they slump and lose their firmness.

Clays that have a relatively broad working range and are useful at a range of consistencies (wetter versus drier) for hand building or throwing are sometimes described as "fat" or "rich." They are typically sticky, fine, and very plastic. Montmorillonite clays are often fat clays, as are ball clays. By contrast, "short" or "lean" clays are those that are usually coarse, mealy, and stiff, with a relatively narrow working range. In general, the coarser the texture, the narrower the range.

One of the most commonly used quantitative assessments is a clay's percentage water of plasticity, or %WP, defined as the percentage (by weight) of water required to develop optimum plasticity in a dry clay. "Optimum plasticity" is a subjective judgment, dependent upon intended use and the individual potter's sense of what feels right. Thus for any given clay, %WP calculations are given as a range rather than a single number.

Water of plasticity is calculated by slowly adding water from a graduated cylinder to a standard weight of dry clay (for example, 100 g) and noting first the amount of water required to develop initial plasticity and then the additional amount giving full plasticity and stickiness after continued mixing. Because 1 cc (or 1 ml) of water equals 1 g of weight, the volume is equivalent to the weight of water; the amount added to 100 g of clay is equal to the clay's %WP. The two quantities give the range of workability, from initial plasticity to stickiness.

Generally, finer clays require more water to develop plasticity, because they have more particles per unit volume and also a more extensive pore or capillary system for carrying water. Coarser clays have larger capillaries (but a smaller total pore structure), and usually need less water to make them plastic. Table 3.2 gives ranges of %WP for some common clays.

Another way to measure water of plasticity is by comparing the weight of a wet clay object with its dry weight. This figure is multiplied by 100 to express it as a percentage:

$$\%WP = \frac{weight_{wet} - weight_{dry}}{weight_{dry}} \times 100.$$

In effect, this calculation bases the measure of plasticity on the amount of water lost from the clay in drying (see sec. 3.3), the weight loss corresponding to the water added to the dry clay to achieve plasticity. A similar concept of plasticity is expressed by the "coefficient of plasticity," which is the ratio of the shrinkage water to the total water content required for forming and provides a relative degree of plasticity (Barna 1967, 1092).

Plasticity is a desirable characteristic of clays up to the point of excessive stickiness. Because plastic clays are preferred by studio or craft potters, ceramic engineers, and village potters making traditional pottery for household

Table 3.2   Water of Plasticity Ranges of Several Clays

Clay Type	%WP
Washed kaolin	44.48–47.50
White sedimentary kaolin	28.60–56.25
Ball clays	25.00–53.50
Plastic fireclays	12.90–37.40
Flint fireclays	8.89–19.04
Saggar clays	18.40–28.56
Stoneware clays	19.16–34.80
Brick clays	13.20–40.70

Source: After Nelson 1984, 322.

use, a variety of techniques may be used to increase plasticity in a relatively stiff clay. Adding organic material, particularly acids (vinegar, for example), will increase plasticity by lowering the pH to a neutral level (of 6 or 8), if the clay mass was originally alkaline, and thereby bringing about flocculation of the clay particles (Grimshaw 1971, 505; Fina 1985). Some craft potters add yogurt, beer, or starch to alkaline commercial clays, thereby increasing acidity as well as adding bacteria, both of which enhance plasticity. Aging a clay—over weeks or even generations—also increases plasticity; the process apparently works by allowing the water to reach all clay particles and by promoting the action of bacteria and acids, perhaps increasing the fineness of the clay, altering the pH, and causing flocculation (see Glick 1936). The growth of molds during aging, particularly if organics have been added to the clay, can cause other problems in forming and firing, however (Fina 1985).

Other ways to increase plasticity include mixing a stiff clay with another clay that is finer and more plastic and mixing a fresh clay with part of an older batch that has been mixed and aged, even for a short while. Ceramic engineers may add cations of a high charge or decrease the amount of monovalent ions in the system, both of which will disrupt the rigidity of the adsorbed water, cause deflocculation, and thereby increase plasticity.

3.3 Drying and Shrinkage

After a clay/water mass is formed into a desired shape, it is allowed to dry. Drying is a dangerous step in the forming process, because stresses within the formed body can cause cracking and deformation. The unfortunate consequences may be immediately noted in pieces that crack or warp during drying, or the flaws may not be apparent until the piece is fired. Most of the stresses occur because, during drying, the water films surrounding the clay platelets evaporate and the platelets draw closer together, causing the clay body to shrink and decreasing plasticity (Kingery and Francl 1954; Moore 1961).

Understanding shrinkage begins—as did understanding plasticity—with the clay/water system. There are two kinds of water loss and two kinds of shrinkage in the ceramic manufacturing process: the water lost is both mechanically combined and chemically combined water, and shrinkage may be measured both in linear and volume dimensions. Chemically combined water is almost never lost in normal low-temperature air-drying of clays. Its loss begins with the application of heat and firing, the ultimate dehydration of clays. The water loss and shrinkage that occur in firing are taken up in chapter 4; for the present, the concern is with air-drying.

3.3.1 Water in the System

In considering dehydration and shrinkage, it is useful to discuss the location of water in a clay/water system and the means by which it is held. There are four kinds of water in a wetted clay throughout the transition from a plastic to an air-dried state, whether or not the mass has been shaped: shrinkage water, pore water, surface-adsorbed water, and interlayer and crystal lattice water (Norton 1970, 157–60; see also Grimshaw 1971, 443–49).

Shrinkage water separates the particles in the clay/water mass by a substantial distance so that the mass has a low density (fig. 3.4a). It constitutes most of the water that was mechanically combined with a dry clay to develop plasticity. Shrinkage water could also be called film water, for it primarily constitutes the films that surround and separate the clay platelets and act as a lubricant. When this shrinkage or film water is removed, the mass shrinks as the surface tension of the remaining water draws the particles together. The clay platelets become more densely packed, until finally they are no longer separated (fig. 3.4b). During the earliest stages of drying, volume change and moisture content are linearly related, and this stage is known as the "constant rate period of drying" (Grimshaw 1971, 544–45).

Once this water is eliminated, air-temperature shrinkage of the clay bulk effectively ceases, though water is still present in the system. The shrinkage ends because the particles have come into contact with each other, creating a rigid framework or skeleton. This framework cannot be significantly reduced in size, even when the remainder of the water in the pores between the platelets is removed by room-temperature or low-heat (105–10°C) drying. Further appreciable shrinkage takes place only in firing. After the shrinkage water is

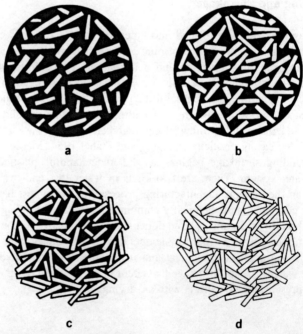

a   b

c   d

Figure 3.4 Types of water and particle arrangement in a clay during drying. Letters correspond to points on the drying curve in fig. 3.5: a, excess free water (shrinkage or film water and pore water) in a plastic clay; b, the critical point or leather-hard stage, when particles come into contact and water exists as pore water; c, water (as pore water and adsorbed water surrounding clay platelets) evaporates from the center throughout the ends of capillaries; d, dry clay. After Grimshaw 1971, fig. IX.7; Norton 1970, fig. 11.1; Lawrence and West 1982, fig. 6-1.

gone a formed clay piece can be safely handled, because the clay is rigid and is no longer plastic. This state is also known as leather-hard, and the amount of water remaining in the body is termed the critical moisture content.

The "pore water" remaining in the system after shrinkage water is lost fills the pores and capillaries of the clay-particle framework (fig. 3.4c). As part of the mechanically combined water that was added to make the clay plastic, it is loosely held in the clay and therefore easily given up to the air. After shrinkage, however, the pores it moves through are very small, so it takes longer to move outward from the interior. Drying beyond the leather-hard state is thus slower than evaporation of shrinkage water, but there is less pore water to be lost.

Pore water may compose 10% to 26% of the true volume of the clay body, depending on particle size; fine clays have more pores and hence more pore water. Because pore water does not surround and separate the clay platelets, which are now touching, its loss will not affect the bulk volume of the clay or cause further shrinkage. The weight of the piece will continue to decrease, but because pore water is replaced by air, only the true volume of the clay will be reduced, not the bulk volume.

Surface-adsorbed water is adsorbed from the atmosphere by the surface of a dried or drying clay mass. It is not the same as water adsorbed onto the surfaces of individual clay platelets, which allows plasticity. A dry clay, or even a drying clay that appears to have a dry exterior, actually holds a microscopic film of water on its surface. This surface-adsorbed water represents an equilibrium between the water vapor pressure of the clay and that of the atmosphere. This water layer is only one molecule thick, though it may penetrate capillaries from the surface, and therefore is not included in volume loss, weight loss, or shrinkage calculations.

Interlayer water exists between the unit layers of the three-layer clay minerals (such as montmorillonite; see fig. 2.7). Because it occurs only in these minerals, its contribution to shrinkage is usually negligible. This water is strongly held, because it is part of the internal structure of the clay platelets, and it is the last water lost in drying. Crystal lattice water is the chemically combined water held as hydroxyls (or OH^{1-}) within the layer structure of the clay minerals, referred to in describing clays as "hydrated" alumina silicates. Normally this lattice water is lost only by heating beyond 110°C, usually in the range of 450–600°C.

3.3.2 Processes of Drying and Shrinkage

One can envision the relation between water loss and volume shrinkage by an idealized diagram of a clay/water mass (fig. 3.5). Point A represents a clay/water mass at optimum plasticity, consisting of 55% clay and 45% water by volume (or 75% clay and 25% water by weight), that is beginning to air-dry. Two stages of drying and shrinkage are indicated by roman numerals along the top of the figure.

I: Drying proceeds by constant-rate loss of shrinkage or film water, as described above. After 69 hours (point B), the volume has been reduced to 78% of the original. The clay fraction has not changed (it is still 55% of the origi-

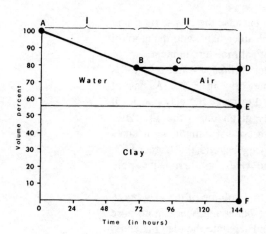

Figure 3.5 Relative changes in volume of water and pores as a clay/water mass is air-dried. After Salmang 1961, 33, and Norton 1970, fig. 11.2.

nal volume), but the amount of water has been severely reduced. Water now constitutes only 12% of the original bulk (compared with 45% water in the starting mix). Thus at point B, sometimes referred to as the critical point, the clay has attained the leather-hard stage; the particles are in contact, and pore water has not yet been replaced by air (see also fig. 3.4*b*). At this point all the shrinkage has been accomplished with loss of the shrinkage water, reducing the original bulk by 22%. The water that remains in the system is pore water (plus lattice and perhaps interlayer water, depending on the clay mineral[s] involved), and its loss will not bring about any appreciable further shrinkage.

II: At point D, after 144 hours of drying, all water except chemically combined (lattice) water is lost. Line DF on the figure represents the bulk volume of the dry clay, or the clay particles plus air in the pore spaces. Line EF represents the true volume of the clay itself, which has remained unchanged from the original mass. Line DE represents the volume of pores in the clay; these are occupied by air and do not contribute to the true volume, only the bulk volume. As water moves through the clay and is eventually lost from the system by evaporation, it causes the many defects, such as cracking, associated with the drying of ceramics (sec. 3.3.3).

Water is lost by capillary action, or movement through the clay pores from the interior to the exterior of the body, because evaporation begins at the surfaces and edges of the clay piece. As surface evaporation proceeds, water is continuously drawn outward to the surface and also evaporates. Two mechanisms seem to be at work. A moisture gradient within the clay tends to force a flow of water from the moist interior to the drier surfaces. And the pressure gradient within the capillaries between the outer vapor pressure and the interior liquid forces the liquid from the filled interior capillaries into the exterior ones, which are only partially filled.

The role of capillary flow becomes clearer when the drying process in a coarse clay is compared with that in a fine clay. Sandy or coarse clays have a more open structure; though there are fewer pores per unit volume than in fine clays, they are larger. Furthermore, the nonclay particles have no water films, and therefore there is less water in the system. The flow of water from the interior to the surface, where it evaporates, is easier; drying is rapid, shrinkage is low, and the danger of warping is relatively slight.

In extremely fine clays, however, drying is hindered by the very characteristic that makes them desirably plastic: the fine particle size means that to develop plasticity more water is needed to cover the extensive surface area of the platelets, and it exists in a more extensive network of finer capillaries than in a coarse clay.

3.3.3 Drying Defects and Green Strength

Drying of fine clays is a slow process; shrinkage is high, and there are many opportunities for defects to occur. Clay minerals show different susceptibilities to cracking during drying, and one test suggests most cracking occurs in illites and least in well-ordered kaolinite (West and Ford 1967).

One important determinant of drying defects is particle size. In fine clays, water may evaporate from the surface faster than it can be resupplied from the interior. The surface will then shrink more rapidly than the entire mass can accommodate, a strong moisture gradient will be present within the piece, and the stresses of the surfaces compressing over the interior may cause warping or cracking. Though visible warping and cracks are a clear indication of structural defects in the dried and unfired product, frequently the cracks may be invisible and the damage may become apparent only after firing accentuates the defects. Because of this problem, it is extremely important that products formed from fine clays be dried very slowly.

An additional problem is that when very fine clays are sedimentary and highly organic—as they often are—the water in the pores may contain dissolved or dispersed matter such as salts or organic colloids. As water is drawn from the interior, these salts and minute organic particles also flow to the surface, where they may form a residue or scum and also change the density, color, or hardness of the piece (see Brownell 1949). Colloidal clay particles may also migrate in this fashion, affecting the density and hardness of the surface and causing fine surface cracks owing to compressive tensions during drying.

The method of shaping a clay body can lead to anisotropic shrinkage, which occurs at different rates along two directions of measurement. This anisotropy may be caused by forming and casting operations that result in different proportions of water and clay particles, or different alignments of clay particles, in various parts of the finished object. The most severe differential shrinkage occurs where the orientation of the clay platelets changes sharply—at corners, seams, and angles.

The method of shaping a clay body may contribute to uneven shrinkage, and hence warping or cracking, through differential water—uneven water content in different portions of the body. Areas that are repeatedly stroked and smoothed during forming generally are wetter than other parts; on a pot thrown on a wheel, for example, the exterior will be wetter than the interior and the base wetter than the upper portion. The portion of the body containing

Figure 3.6   An S-shaped crack on the base of   defect (exaggerated in firing) caused by differ-
a small wheel-thrown ashtray, a typical drying   ential water and resultant uneven shrinkage.

more water will shrink more than the drier portion, causing stresses that lead to warping or cracking (fig. 3.6).

Another factor involved in such shrinkage is the preferred orientation of the clay particles—nonrandom or directional positioning in which the clay platelets become oriented parallel to each other like courses of brickwork rather than occurring randomly or in the "face-to-edge" arrangement. Preferred orientation is more easily observed in clay minerals with relatively larger particle sizes, and it also can be noted in platy nonclay inclusions in the clay body, such as micas or shell particles (see Mehran, Muller, and Fitzpatrick 1981). It may be caused to varying degrees by virtually all operations of forming a clay body (extruding, coiling, throwing), because all involve stroking the clay repeatedly. The absorptive properties of the mold used in casting and the pressure of the hands are sufficient to realign the clay particles "floating" in their water films with their long dimension perpendicular to the forming pressure. Preferred orientation may also be caused by the natural settling behavior of the particles in slip casting or slipping. Also, the light pressure used in burnishing a clay surface is enough to reposition particles, and the low luster of the burnished surface is a consequence of preferred orientation as well as compaction of the very finest particles brought to the surfaces.

Shrinkage occurs differentially according to the direction of particle orientation because of the varying volumes occupied by water films versus clay particles in each linear dimension and the variable densities of particle pack-

Figure 3.7 Particle-orientation effects: *a*, effects in a rolled cylinder of clay (after Norton 1970, fig. 10.11); *b*, effects in a slip-cast piece. (after Lawrence and West 1982, fig. 64*a*); *c*, warpage of slip-cast piece during drying. (after Lawrence and West, 1982, fig. 64*b*).

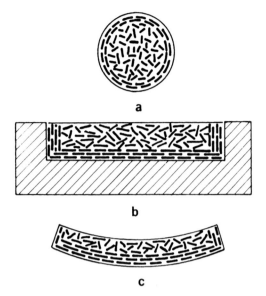

a

b

c

ing after shrinkage water is lost (fig. 3.7). Shrinkage will be greatest perpendicular to the orientation of the platelets, because more water films occur per unit area in that direction. Shrinkage will be least in the direction parallel to the particles. Where the platelets are in a random, unordered arrangement (and where more pore water is retained), shrinkage is intermediate. Because of this uneven shrinkage in all directions of the clay mass, again the final product may warp or crack if the tensions exceed the strength of the dry clay body (e.g., fig. 3.6).

Preferred orientation may be caused by forming an object from a wet clay or by dispersion of the particles within the clay/water system owing to their electrical charges and the presence of ions. Certain kinds of ions will alter the pH of the system as well as modify the arrangement of the particles within the system, leading to flocculation or deflocculation. A deflocculated system has a loose packing of particles in a face-to-edge arrangement (the positive ends of particles joined to the negative surfaces); there are many pores in the system, and drying takes place with relatively low shrinkage. A flocculated system settles with particles arranged in preferred orientation and densely packed; shrinkage is high.

Resistance to cracking and warping as a clay body dries is a function of its strength in the dried but unfired state—dry strength or green strength (Ryan 1965; Holdridge 1952; McDowell and Vose 1952; Pask 1953). A dried body with considerable green strength has a significant integrity resulting from the forces bonding the clay platelets together; it is resistant to cracking and warping in the dry state. The attributes that enhance green strength include fine rather than coarse particle size, the presence of Na^{1+} ions, and a deflocculated state. In addition, common organic materials may be added to a clay to increase its green strength, such as flour, cornstarch, milk solids (casein), and gums of various trees and bushes (Norton 1970, 99). Green strength increases as moisture is lost and is greatest in completely dry bodies; ware that is only leather-hard, for example, is more susceptible to deformation. The cause of this is not fully known; it has been attributed to variations in the weak elec-trostatic attraction between molecules known as van der Waals forces, which in this case holds the clay mineral layers and particles together.

Clearly, drying does not take place uniformly, and this can lead to defects and a loss of strength. The principal difficulty is that evaporation and shrink-age are more rapid on external surfaces exposed to the air. This is particularly a problem if pieces are set to dry in an area subject to fluctuating tempera-tures, air currents, or humidity levels. Sudden changes in temperature or rate of evaporation may disturb the temperature and moisture gradients within the clay or on various surfaces, affecting the rate of drying and causing warping.

Shrinkage of a clay/water mass during drying is unavoidable, but defects are not inevitable. It is useful to summarize some of the circumstances that permit deformation-free dehydration. Two approaches may be taken: one is that reducing overall shrinkage reduces the chance of defects; the other is that controlled drying permits relatively great shrinkage without damage to the product.

Among the many variables of drying are size of the clay particles, floccu-lated versus deflocculated state (or presence/absence of preferred orienta-tion), amount of water present, temperature, humidity, and air currents. It has already been mentioned that fine clays—which require a lot of water for plas-ticity—shrink more than coarser clays. Thus one way to lessen the risk of warping and cracking is to raise the proportion of coarser particle sizes to in-crease the pore space and promote water movement from the interior to the exterior. But this procedure decreases green strength (table 3.3). Defloccu-lated clays have lower shrinkage than flocculated clays, at least along one di-mension, as well as greater green strength, and therefore adding deflocculants such as basic salts or Calgon will reduce shrinkage.

Despite the dangers of deformation, a major problem in drying is econom-ics. There must be a balance between the delays caused by drying slowly for the sake of safety and the risk of damage if drying is accelerated by heat and air circulation. Defects are more likely during the first part of the drying time, when shrinkage water is lost and the vessel is shrinking in response. During this period drying is best carried out slowly. After shrinkage has stopped, dry-ing can be more rapid.

Clearly atmospheric conditions are important: temperature and humidity and presence of air currents. Heating both the ceramic body and the air, either

Table 3.3 Comparative Green Strength (psi) of Clays with and without Sand

Clay Type	Dried Clay			Dried Clay Plus 50% Sand		
	Compressive Strength	Tensile Strength	Transverse Strength	Compressive Strength	Tensile Strength	Transverse Strength
Ball clays	565–1,148	135–210	375–558	464–777	124–80	242–330
Plastic clays	631–954	155–72	484–520	476–553	113–50	216–80
Plastic kaolins	455–539	104–47	239–325	286–559	54–110	122–210
Primary kaolins	205–349	34–69	74–166	164–72	29–35	56–82

Source: After Ries 1927, 221.

artificially or by placing the clay pieces in sunlight, permits rapid dehydration because heat enables water to migrate to the surfaces of the piece more easily. In addition, heated air can absorb more moisture from the ceramic than cooler air. But the heat can cause more rapid surface evaporation than can be accommodated by internal water movement and the strength of the vessel, and this may give rise to defects. Modern commercial operations may use humidity driers; the ceramic pieces are heated in a very humid atmosphere, then drying proceeds by controlled reduction of humidity. Nonindustrial village potters similarly adjust drying procedures to the characteristics of their clays and environment (sec. 5.4).

3.3.4 Measuring Shrinkage

Loss of mechanically combined water (film water) during the air-drying or low heat drying of a plastic clay causes shrinkage of the body. This may be measured as linear drying shrinkage or volume drying shrinkage, also referred to as linear air shrinkage and volume air shrinkage. Linear drying shrinkage (%LDS) is computed by marking the wet clay with lines a specified distance apart; after complete drying at 105°C, the distance is remeasured and subtracted from the original measurement. The result is divided by the wet length measurement and converted to a percentage:

$$\%LDS = \frac{length_{wet} - length_{dry}}{length_{wet}} \times 100.$$

Volume air or drying shrinkage (%VDS) is computed by measuring the volume of the thoroughly dried clay piece in a volumeter filled with kerosene. The piece is then removed, dried, and soaked for twelve hours in kerosene of the same specific gravity as that used in the volumeter, after which its volume is again measured in the volumeter. The formula is as follows:

$$\%VDS = \frac{volume_{wet} - volume_{dry}}{volume_{wet}} \times 100.$$

Table 3.4 compares some linear and volume drying shrinkage measurements for several clays. For a uniform, isotropic body, %VDS = 3%LDS if the shrinkage is small; inhomogeneous shrinkage or large shrinkage values will cause deviations from this general relationship.

Table 3.4   Ranges in Air-Drying Shrinkage for Several Clays

Clay	%LDS	%VDS
Crude kaolin	5.00–7.60	14.11–20.92
Ball clay	5.25–12.00	21.90–31.92
Refractory clay	4.25–11.00	30.48–45.00
Stoneware clay	4.80–9.30	15.11–41.20
Flint fireclay	0.78–6.59	2.36–21.12
White sedimentary kaolin	4.50–12.50	7.53–36.46
Saggar clays	2.80–10.80	9.10–25.00

Source: After Ries 1927, 227.

3.4 Inclusions and Impurities

Naturally occurring clays rarely exist as pure, monomineral deposits (for the reasons outlined in chap. 2). Minerals from the parent material and from rocks and sediments encountered during transport typically are present as well. Primary or residual clays usually include fragments of their parent rock material and may consist of several clay minerals in combination, depending on the degree of weathering. Sedimentary or secondary clays, as a result of the processes of deposition, may contain a mixture of minerals from several sources as well as organics and salts.

The inclusions and impurities of interest here are present in all size ranges, but for the present they can be divided into two categories: extremely fine colloid-sized material (excluding the clay mineral fraction itself), and the nonplastic, relatively large particles in the clay body. Particles in either size range may occur naturally in the sediment or may be added by potters to modify a particular characteristic.

3.4.1 Coarse Inclusions

The coarser particles or clastics in a natural clay are largely responsible for the property known as texture—the proportion, size, and shape characteristics of the particles in a clay material, whatever their origin or their chemical or mineral identity. The texture of an unfired clay/water mass can be judged imprecisely—but often very effectively—by "feel" when a small amount of the clay is rolled between the fingers or nibbled. A very plastic clay that feels smooth and "fat" or slimy is usually a fine clay material, while one that is stiff and "lean" usually feels coarse and gritty.

The texture of a clay is not measured directly, but by comparing the particle-size fractions of the clay material against some standard scale established by geologists or pedologists (see figs. 2.2 and 2.3). Most clays contain a range of particle sizes, sometimes as large as pebbles (very coarse, greater than 4 mm in diameter), granules, or gravel (between 2 and 4 mm), but more frequently in the sand, silt, and clay-sized range. One should remember that sand refers to a particle-size category, not to a specific mineral, although the predominant mineral of the sand and silt size in clays is quartz. "Sand" may be quartz sand, calcium carbonate sand, volcanic sand, or a mixture of many materials such as micas, feldspars, hornblende, and ferric minerals (the last often occurring as finely particulate coatings on the sand grains).

Because some soils with as little as 15% of the finest clay-sized particles may exhibit plasticity, two related substances are of interest in the study of natural clays: mud and muck. Mud is a term sedimentary geologists use to refer to sediments with particle sizes less than 0.06 mm, that is, in the range of silts and clays. Muck is a fine sediment usually associated with wet environments and peat deposits and consists of 50% or more fine organic matter.

Two methods are commonly used to separate particle-size fractions of sediments: the suspension (or sedimentation) method and the sieving method. The suspension method is based on Stokes' law, which permits calculation of the settling time of particles of different size (diameter) and density in a given

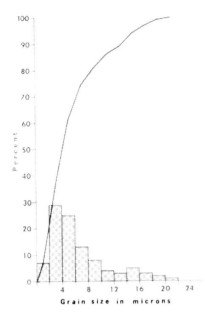

Figure 3.8 The particle-size distribution of a hypothetical clay determined by the suspension method, showing by histogram and cumulative percentage graph the percentage weight of the sample finer than a particular size (in micrometers). After Grimshaw 1971, fig. VII.7.

fluid of known density and viscosity (Shackley 1975, 116). Various techniques employ pipettes, hydrometers, and settling tubes, and they are usually applied to fine, subsieve-sized sediments such as silts (Shackley 1975, 116–33). Figure 3.8 shows the particle-size distribution of a clay achieved by the suspension method.

Sieving may be done either dry or wet (Shackley 1975, 109–15), but because clay usually consists of aggregated particles it is usually necessary to use wet sieving. A weighed amount of clay, dried at 110°C, is soaked in water, then washed through a series of graded sieves, such as the American Society of Testing Materials (ASTM) series. The sieves should represent the approximate size divisions of sand (coarse, medium, fine), silt (coarse, medium, fine), and so forth. By comparing the relative percentages left on the sieves with a scale such as the Wentworth scale (fig. 2.2) or with a triangular diagram (fig. 2.3), the clay may be described as sandy or silty.

Wet sieving is not very accurate, especially for the finest particle sizes, which are usually lost (for the fine fraction, sedimentation methods should be used). Furthermore, it is necessary to dry the sieved fractions before reweighing. Nonetheless, sieving provides a relatively easy laboratory method for studying the particle-size distributions of sandy or silty natural clays (fig. 3.9), and the extracted fractions can be used for additional microscopic analyses (see sec. 13.2.1.3.2).

Not only is microscopic analysis useful for identifying the minerals represented by the clastics, but the shape of the grains can give clues to their origin and hence to the depositional origin of the clays. The rounding or sphericity of grains is often interpreted in terms of the abrasion they have received from wind, stream, or wave action. Their shape is also important in terms of shrinkage, drying, and strength of an unfired or fired clay body. In principle, clay will shrink less and dry more easily if all grains are spherical, uniform in size, and closely packed. Such a state rarely exists, however, except perhaps

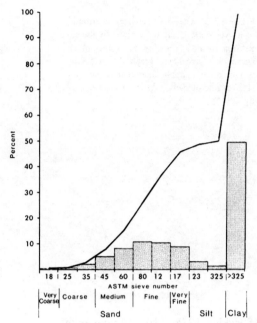

Figure 3.9 The particle-size distribution of clay C-16 from Suwanee County, Florida, determined by sieving, showing the percentage weight of particle-size fractions left on ASTM sieves of different sizes (see fig. 2.2 for mm equivalents). Data from Cordell 1984, appendix L. Figure 4.3 below shows coring in fired coarse and fine fractions of this clay.

in very well-sorted, highly abraded wind- or waterborne sediments. Indeed, this set of characteristics is not totally desirable, because the rounded surfaces do not develop strong interlocking frameworks of clay particles and therefore may lead to a weak body. An abundance of platy flat inclusions, such as micas and chlorites, may make the clay body laminated or fissile through preferred orientation. Although it may be strong and well bonded across the laminae, the body will be weak along the orientation of the plates and may crumble in layers. Clay materials with little range in particle size—for example, silty clays lacking a considerable clay-sized fraction as well as coarser material—may be extremely weak and lack green strength.

To be a good pottery clay, then, a natural deposit needs inclusions that are angular and occur in a wide range of sizes. In such a deposit the smaller particles and the clay itself bond and interlock with the angles and edges of the inclusions, conferring strength in both dry and fired states.

These nonclay clastic materials are so important in modifying clay bodies that ancient and modern potters alike have added them to their clay mixtures. These additions, commonly called "temper" by archaeologists (see sec. 14.1), correct stickiness, increase porosity, reduce shrinkage, decrease drying time, reduce deformation in drying, and improve firing characteristics. Available raw materials such as sand, plant fiber, volcanic ash, crushed shell, rock, or pottery itself (called grog) were added by prehistoric and contemporary village potters the world over to solve these problems of workability. Distinctive combinations of inclusions and clays form the basis for many archaeological reconstructions of events in ancient times, from dating sites to tracing patterns of trade, subjects taken up at length in parts 3 and 4.

In the modern world, studio potters and commercial ceramic industries use triaxial bodies in ceramic manufacture—various mixtures of three basic components, the proportions varying with the product desired (see fig. 3.10). One

Figure 3.10   Raw ceramic materials and tri-axial bodies: *a*, American electrical porcelain; *b*, Chinese and Japanese porcelain; *c*, stoneware; *d*, European cookware; *e*, European electrical bodies; *f*, raw kaolin; *g*, washed kaolin; *h*, quartz sands; *i*, feldspar sand; *j*, American dental porcelain; *k*, feldspars. After Norton 1970, figs. 12.2, 12.3, 12.4.

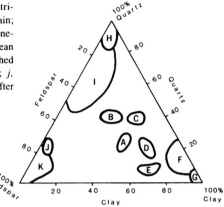

component is a clay (or more than one clay), which provides plasticity and dry strength. To this is added a filler or aggregate, typically flint, quartz sand (Johnson 1976), or a chemically inert material such as grog, which limits shrinkage, reduces drying time, and eliminates cracking. The third constituent is a cementing component (a flux), which promotes melting, helps develop fired strength, and reduces porosity. This is typically a feldspar or other alkali mineral, such as nepheline syenite. Triaxial bodies are attempts to create, though with a much finer mean particle size and range of variation, the mix of particle sizes described above for an ideal natural clay deposit, in which a range of particle sizes interlocks for strength and porosity and which will have the desired strength or purity (as at high temperatures, or for cooking, etc.). A typical triaxial body might have 50% clay, 25% quartz, and 25% feldspar; the clay might be a mix of kaolin with particle sizes of 2 μm and ball clay at 0.5 μm, while the quartz and feldspar particles might average 40 μm in diameter (Norton 1970, 259).

The irony of having to add these materials to the commercially available overrefined clays that once contained them naturally has not gone unnoticed. Bernard Leach, a famous potter and philosopher of art pottery, has commented on the paradox (1976, 43–44):

> Western potters from the early days of industry and especially in making porcelain, have travelled further and further away from a natural conception of clay towards an ideal of over-refined mixtures which are aptly called pastes. Up to a point this has been a necessary tendency in the stages of standardization, but . . . the sooner we return to a healthier understanding of clay and melted stone the better. To dig a single clean clay in the vicinity of the kilns was the habit of the old country potters and it is one which can be recommended to the studio potter of today. . . . He should not want to standardize, or to depend entirely on those reliable but uninteresting substances which the potter's merchant offers to the trade. What usually happens is that the studio potter in search of quality is forced by ignorance or convenience to buy standardized raw materials and then to introduce impurities artificially in order to obtain, not nearly so successfully, what he might have had direct from nature.

3.4.2   Colloids, Ions, and Organics

The colloidal fraction of a clay comprises particles 0.001 mm (or 1 μm) or less in diameter. Colloid also refers to very fine particles suspended or dispersed in another material, such as clay particles in water (see van Olphen 1963). Particles in colloidal suspensions repel each other, being kept apart by their like charges as well as by Brownian movement, the continuous agitation of colloidal particles caused by collisions with molecules in the surrounding solution. Two kinds of colloidal matter are important in understanding clay sediments: inorganic colloids (represented almost entirely by very fine clay mineral particles) and organic colloids.

Colloid-sized particles in a ceramic system primarily affect plasticity and shrinkage, mainly through their enormous surface area (see also sec. 3.2.1), which increases the volume of water in a clay mass and also expands the opportunities for adsorption and exchange of ions, which can change the dispersion of the clay platelets (Grimshaw 1971, 465–73). A clay's base exchange, ion exchange, or cation exchange capacity refers to the ability of fine clay particles, surrounded by water films, to adsorb loosely ions that are dissolved in the water. Some surfaces can preferentially adsorb certain ions from solution, and one ion may be exchanged for another because the bonding is loose, but not all ions are replaceable or exchangeable. The property of cation exchange is traditionally expressed in milliequivalents (meq, or equivalent atomic weight) per 100 g of dry clay at a neutral pH of 7.

Clay minerals differ in their ability to adsorb ions. In general, the finer the clay (and hence the greater the surface area), the greater the exchange capacity (see Johnson 1949; Johnson and Lawrence 1942). Several explanations of adsorption in clays have been advanced, and all may be accurate in part. One is that ion exchange satisfies broken bonds on the edges of clay particles, which themselves act as anions (negatively charged ions), adsorbing positive ions onto the cleavage planes of their surfaces and negative ions onto their edges. A second type of ion exchange is lattice substitution, that is, the substitution of certain ions for others in the lattice structure or on the cleavage surfaces. This appears to be particularly common in smectites and vermiculites and largely accounts for their high exchange capacity. Most of these substitutions occur in the octahedral layer, with magnesium and iron particularly substituting for aluminum. A third mechanism involved in cation exchange is the adherence of small quantities of three-layer minerals to the surfaces of other clay particles (e.g., kaolins), thus increasing the base exchange capacity.

Table 3.5 gives the exchange values of some common clays: clays with extremely fine particle size and expanding lattices (smectites, montmorillonites), as well as vermiculite clays, have high exchange capacities, and substitutions within the lattice (rather than on the surfaces) account for about 80% of their total exchange capacity (Grim 1968, 194). Kaolinites, on the other hand, because of their two-layer structure and the arrangement of charges on the ends of particles (an arrangement very close to the hexagonal structure of the water film), have low exchange capacity, and exchange takes place only on the basal oxygen surface of the layer of silica tetrahedrons.

Table 3.5 Range of Cation Exchange Capacity (meq) of Some Clay Minerals

Clay	Norton	Grim
Kaolinite	2–5	3–15
Dickite	1–10	
Halloysite	3–15	5–10
Hydrated halloysite	20–35	40–50
Vermiculites	100–150	100–150
Illites	10–40	10–40
Sepiolites, attapulgite	20–30	3–15
Montmorillonite	75–150	
Ball clays	7–30	
Smectite		80–150
Chlorite		10–40
Allophane		25–50

Source: Norton 1970, table 9.1; Grim 1968, table 7-1.

Clays also selectively adsorb ions. In general, trivalent ions are adsorbed more strongly than bivalent ions, and bivalent more strongly than univalent. The most common exchangeable cations in clays are Ca^{2+}, Mg^{2+}, H^{1+}, K^{1+}, NH_4^{1+}, and Na^{1+}; common anions are SO_4^{1-}, Cl^{1-}, PO_4^{3-}, and NO_3^{1-}. The order of their replacement power is highly variable, depending on concentration, size, temperature, and the presence of other ions. In addition to being less adsorbed, the monovalent ions are usually larger; they have lower bonding energy, are more mobile, and diminish plasticity by disrupting the nonliquid structure of the water films surrounding the clay particles. The trivalent and divalent ions, more highly charged and smaller, increase plasticity because they fit more securely into the holes in the nonliquid water lattice. Clays with Ca^{2+} ions have a larger nonliquid zone surrounding the particles than do clays with Na^{1+} ions and a more abrupt transition to liquid water; this is also a factor in developing plasticity.

Ions are important in a clay/water mix because by filling the electrically unsatisfied sites on the particle surfaces, they affect the arrangement of the clay particles, giving rise to a flocculated or deflocculated state (see Scripture and Schramm 1926; Johnson and Norton 1941), which is also partly a function of the pH (hydrogen ion concentration, or acidity versus alkalinity) of the clay.

In a deflocculated clay particles repel each other and are ordered face-to-face or in a preferred orientation. Deflocculation usually occurs under neutral to alkaline conditions when the clay particles all have the same charge on edges and surfaces (because ions satisfy the unsatisfied charges). These clays exist as stable dispersed suspensions that resist settling; when they do settle or dry, they exhibit low shrinkage and high green strength. Deflocculated clays are the usual basis for slips, which may be used as surface coatings of a clay body or for casting in molds (slip casting). Such slips are stable suspensions with minimum viscosity or resistance to flow as well as a high solids content—many clay particles per unit volume. This state can be achieved by adding ions that will change the charge on the clay particles. Adding (1+) cations such as sodium, basic salts such as Na_2CO_3 or Na_2SiO_3, or alkalies such as ammonia or Calgon will deflocculate a flocculated clay system or make a soft, plastic clay stiffer (though too much can reflocculate it; see Brody 1979, 28–29). Adding (2+) cations such as calcium or magnesium (e.g., Epsom salts) will flocculate a system, increasing its stiffness.

There is some evidence that there are two types of flocculated clays: one existing in acid conditions, in which the particles are dispersed in a "house of cards" arrangement, and the other more closely resembling the face-to-face orientation of deflocculated clays and occurring under conditions of high pH (alkalinity). Flocculated systems settle rapidly and dry in a loosely packed arrangement with large amounts of water trapped between the particles. Drying shrinkage is usually high.

Flocculation/deflocculation and plasticity may also be affected by organic colloids, collectively referred to as "humus" in soils studies, which comprise three classes of materials: fulvic acid, humic acid, and humin. These materials contribute to the acidity of soils or clays, particularly in moist, humid areas, and thus to a flocculated state. Colloidal humus particles are very small (at least as small as the smectite clays), are thought to be noncrystalline, and have an extremely high exchange capacity. Although the charge of the particles is pH dependent, it is generally negative so that, like clay particles, humus may be thought to consist of negatively charged particles surrounded by positively charged cations.

Organic material in a clay (see Worrall 1956) generally increases plasticity (sec. 3.2.1) and may be suspected when raw clay is sticky. Organic matter may also add to the dry strength of extremely sandy clays by increasing the total amount of finely particulate binding matrix in the mix.

When organic clays are being dried in the laboratory, the colloidal humus particles frequently migrate to the surface of the clay as pore water moves outward by capillary action. This leaves a dark brownish film on the upper surface of the clay. Virtually all clays contain some organic material, if only a very small percentage. Primary or residual clays typically contain less organic matter than secondary or sedimentary clays, and surface clay soils may have 5% to 10% or more. Ball clays are commonly high in organics (as well as salts). Besides affecting plasticity, organic matter also influences the color of a fired clay piece, as discussed in chapter 4.

3.5 References

Barna 1967

Bloor 1957

Brody 1979

Bronitsky 1982

Brownell 1949

Cordell 1984

Dal and Berden 1965

Fina 1985

Glick 1936

Greger and Berg 1956

Grim 1962, 1968

Grim and Cuthbert 1945

Grimshaw 1971

Grout 1906

Holdridge 1952

Johnson 1949

Johnson and Lawrence 1942

Johnson and Norton 1941

Johnson 1976

Kingery, Bowen, and Uhlmann 1976

Kingery and Francl 1954
Lawrence and West 1982
Leach 1976
McDowell and Vose 1952
Marshall 1955
Mehran, Muller, and Fitzpatrick
  1981
Moore 1961
Nelson 1984
Norton 1938, 1948, 1970
Norton and Johnson 1944
Pask 1953

Phelps and Maguire 1956
Ries 1927
Ryan 1965
Salmang 1961
Schwartz 1952
Scripture and Schramm 1926
Shackley 1975
Van Olphen 1963
West and Ford 1967
Whittemore 1935
Williamson 1947
Worrall 1956

4 Properties of Clays II: Firing Behavior

After plasticity, the second most salient property of clay is its hardening when subjected to heat. Plastic clay begins to lose water on air-drying, and water loss continues under elevated temperatures so that ultimately the original mineral structure changes and the clay becomes permanently hardened. A fired clay object is in some senses an artificial stone.

This chapter outlines the changes that occur in a clay material as it is heated or fired. Increasing temperatures cause progressive and usually irreversible physical modifications of the clay/water system, which occur at different temperatures and take varying times in particular clay minerals or mixtures of clay minerals. The preceding discussion of clay properties such as shrinkage has touched on some of these transformations, but here they are examined in terms of increasing temperature of firing and the contribution of individual components of the clay body.

4.1 Variables of Firing

Applying heat to a clay alters its physical and chemical characteristics, beginning at relatively low temperatures and continuing through very high temperatures. These changes are all functions of three primary variables of firing: duration, temperature, and the atmosphere in which the heat is applied and later allowed to dissipate.

Anthropologists and archaeologists studying the products of nonindustrialized potters, ancient or modern, also are interested in how these three variables are affected by the technology of firing. The same physical and chemical changes will occur whether the firing takes place in an electric kiln or an open bonfire, and the three primary variables of firing will be operative in either situation. The difference is in their uncontrolled variation and the effects on the final product (see sec. 5.4).

In dealing with the firing of any ceramic body, time, temperature, and atmosphere must always be considered together. It is not appropriate to discuss (or infer) the firing technology of any ancient piece by estimating temperature alone. The duration of firing at that temperature and the atmosphere in which it took place are also important and should not be ignored.

The atmosphere of firing refers to the presence of gases, particularly oxygen, while the clay is heated and cooled. Where there is free air circulation and ample free oxygen to bind with elements on or in the clays, the atmosphere is said to be oxidizing. An atmosphere lacking free oxygen is said to be reducing and is frequently smoky, though not always.

Some gases in the firing atmosphere are simply those present in the earth's atmosphere, such as oxygen and nitrogen. Others result from combustion, for example, water vapor and carbon dioxide. Carbon monoxide results from an atmosphere lacking enough oxygen for complete combustion. Sulfurous gases (SO_2) may also escape from burning fuel. A third source of gases is the clay material itself, which on heating may emit water vapor, carbon dioxide, or sulfur dioxide, depending upon its inclusions and impurities.

In kilns the atmosphere may be controlled by the selection of fuel and by regulating air circulation within the kiln. In open-air or bonfire firings, used before the development of kilns and throughout most of the pre-Columbian New World, the atmosphere was more difficult to control because of wind and irregularities in fuel combustion.

The atmosphere of firing affects several properties of the finished product, especially color and hardness, but also porosity and shrinkage. Discussions of the firing atmosphere should specify—if there is variability—the atmosphere in which the maximum temperature was attained, the atmosphere in which the maximum temperature was held, and the atmosphere during cooling. These atmospheres frequently fluctuate as fuel is added to attain a desired temperature (wood, for example). In addition, cooling may take place in a different atmosphere than the heating if the air is allowed to circulate or if the pieces are covered with a layer of ash.

Where kilns were not used, or where kiln technology was relatively simple, the atmosphere is likely to have been highly variable, neither completely oxidizing nor completely reducing at any stage of firing, and may best be described as incompletely oxidizing. A completely reducing atmosphere during firing is difficult to attain except under well-controlled or extreme conditions (such as complete smothering of the firing load).

Determining the temperature of firing seems to be the goal of most studies of ancient technology: at what temperature was the vessel fired? Yet this is relatively insignificant unless one knows the duration of the maximum temperature and the atmosphere at that temperature. In modern electric or gas kilns the rate of heating can be carefully controlled and monitored up to the maximum desired temperature. The same is not true of ancient and modern kilns burning wood or other fuel, though skilled potters carefully judge temperature by the color of the hot ware in the kiln or the smoke emanating from it.

The maximum temperature of firing can be approximated by a number of analytical techniques (see sec. 14.3) based on certain mineralogical and structural changes within the ceramic components. These changes usually occur over a range of temperatures, however, and they are also affected by the atmosphere of firing. For example, some reactions may be essentially completed, and certain properties may develop at lower temperatures if the firing atmosphere is reducing rather than oxidizing.

The temperature at which a ware is fired is one important variable distinguishing classes of pottery such as earthenware, stoneware, and porcelain (see sec. 1.1). Equally important, of course, are the composition of the body and the ingredients that allow certain reactions to take place at that temperature (sec. 4.2.3). Terra-cottas are low fired at temperatures below 1000°C; virtually all non-kiln-fired, unglazed pottery of interest to prehistoric archaeologists consists of terra-cottas. Earthenwares are fired at from 900°C to approximately 1200°C; stonewares at 1200–1350°C; and porcelains at approximately 1400°C. Glazed ware frequently needs two firings, which may be at different temperatures (see sec. 4.2.4).

Pottery firing temperatures are usually given in degrees Celsius (or centigrade); a conversion chart from Celsius to Fahrenheit is given in table 4.1. Art-pottery firing temperatures are usually achieved with reference to pyrometric cones—small pyramids compounded of materials similar to glazes, whose precise composition varies so that the cones will melt and bend at specific temperatures given a standard rate of temperature increase. Several kinds and sizes of cones are used, all of which are numbered from 020 through 01 to 15 (table 4.2), measuring temperatures from roughly 635°C to 1430°C.

Typically, several cones will be selected to bracket the desired kiln temperature: one that melts at a higher temperature, one at a lower temperature, and one at the desired maturing point. The three cones are set upright in a pad of clay and placed in the kiln so as to be visible to the potter. When the lowest cone melts and bends into a semicircle, the proper temperature is approaching and adjustments should be made to hold the temperature constant; when the highest cone bends, it indicates overfiring (fig. 4.1).

Of greatest interest is how long the ceramic materials were subjected to maximum temperature. The entire heating time must be considered, however, and this can be broken down into three stages: the period when the temperature is raised; the period when the maximum temperature is sustained (the soaking period); and the period when no fuel is added, temperatures decline, and the vessels cool to ambient temperature.

Because time and temperature are so closely related, what is really of interest is the "work heat" in the kiln, or the effect of a given amount of heat in a

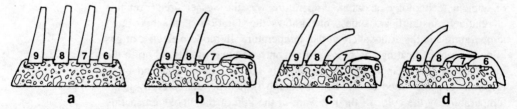

Figure 4.1 Pyrometric cones used in gauging a hypothetical firing: *a*, unfired cones; *b*, overfiring for cone 7, underfiring for cone 8; *c*, proper firing for cone 8; *d*, overfiring for cone 8, but not quite proper firing for cone 9.

Table 4.1   Temperature Conversion Chart, Celsius (°C) and Fahrenheit (°F)

°C	*	°F	°C	*	°F
−17.8	0	32	399	750	1382
−15.0	5	41.0	404	760	1400
−12.2	10	50.0	416	780	1436
−9.4	15	59.0	427	800	1472
−6.7	20	68.0	438	820	1508
−3.9	25	77.0	449	840	1544
−1.1	30	86.0	454	850	1562
1.7	35	95.0	460	860	1580
4.4	40	104.0	471	880	1616
7.2	45	113.0	482	900	1652
10.0	50	122.0	493	920	1688
15.6	60	140.0	504	940	1724
21.1	70	158.0	510	950	1742
26.7	80	176.0	516	960	1760
32.2	90	194.0	527	980	1796
37.8	100	212.0	538	1000	1832
49	120	248	549	1020	1868
60	140	284	560	1040	1904
71	160	320	566	1050	1922
82	180	356	571	1060	1940
93	200	392	582	1080	1976
100	212	413	593	1100	2012
104	220	428	604	1120	2048
116	240	464	616	1140	2084
121	250	482	621	1150	2102
127	260	500	627	1160	2120
138	280	536	638	1180	2156
149	300	572	649	1200	2192
160	320	608	660	1220	2228
171	340	644	671	1240	2264
177	350	662	677	1250	2282
182	360	680	682	1260	2300
193	380	716	693	1280	2336
204	400	752	704	1300	2372
216	420	788	716	1320	2408
227	440	824	727	1340	2444
232	450	842	732	1350	2462
238	460	860	738	1360	2480
249	480	896	749	1380	2516
260	500	932	760	1400	2552
271	520	968	771	1420	2588
282	540	1004	782	1440	2624
288	550	1022	788	1450	2642
293	560	1040	793	1460	2660
304	580	1076	804	1480	2696
316	600	1112	816	1500	2732
327	620	1148	827	1520	2768
338	640	1184	838	1540	2804
343	650	1202	843	1550	2822
349	660	1220	849	1560	2840
360	680	1256	860	1580	2876
371	700	1292	871	1600	2912
382	720	1328	882	1620	2948
393	740	1364	893	1640	2984

(*continued*)

Table 4.1   *(cont.)*

°C	*	°F	°C	*	°F
899	1650	3002	1282	2340	4244
904	1660	3020	1288	2350	4262
916	1680	3056	1293	2360	4280
927	1700	3092	1304	2380	4316
938	1720	3128	1316	2400	4352
949	1740	3164	1327	2420	4388
954	1750	3182	1338	2440	4424
960	1760	3200	1343	2450	4442
971	1780	3236	1349	2460	4460
982	1800	3272	1360	2480	4496
993	1820	3308	1371	2500	4532
1004	1840	3344	1382	2520	4568
1010	1850	3362	1393	2540	4604
1016	1860	3380	1399	2550	4622
1027	1880	3416	1404	2560	4640
1038	1900	3452	1416	2580	4676
1049	1920	3488	1427	2600	4712
1060	1940	3524	1438	2620	4748
1066	1950	3542	1449	2640	4784
1071	1960	3560	1454	2650	4802
1082	1980	3596	1460	2660	4820
1093	2000	3632	1471	2680	4856
1104	2020	3668	1482	2700	4892
1116	2040	3704	1493	2720	4928
1121	2050	3722	1504	2740	4964
1127	2060	3740	1510	2750	4982
1138	2080	3776	1516	2760	5000
1149	2100	3812	1527	2780	5036
1160	2120	3848	1538	2800	5072
1171	2140	3884	1549	2820	5108
1177	2150	3902	1560	2840	5144
1182	2160	3920	1566	2850	5162
1193	2180	3956	1571	2860	5180
1204	2200	3992	1582	2880	5216
1216	2220	4028	1593	2900	5252
1227	2240	4064	1604	2920	5288
1232	2250	4082	1616	2940	5324
1238	2260	4100	1621	2950	5342
1249	2280	4136	1627	2960	5360
1260	2300	4172	1638	2980	5396
1271	2320	4208	1649	3000	5432

Source: After Lawrence and West 1982, app. A-9.

Note: This chart can be used in two ways: (1) Any Celsius temperature in the left column can be converted into Fahrenheit by reading across on the same line to its equivalent in the center column. Similarly, any Fahrenheit temperature in the right column can be expressed in Celsius by reading across on the same line to its equivalent in the center column. (2) The temperature of interest can be found in the center column, and its Fahrenheit equivalent may be found to the right, or its Celsius equivalent to the left.

Temperature conversion formulas: $°F = (°C \times \frac{9}{5}) + 32$; $°C = (°F - 32) \times \frac{5}{9}$.

given amount of time. The "work-heat ratio" is registered by pyrometric cones, but not by measurement of temperature alone.

As mentioned above, the changes that occur as a ceramic is heated usually

Table 4.2 Pyrometric Cone Equivalent (PCE) Temperatures, Orton and Seger Cones (°C)

Cone Number	Orton Cones		Seger Cones
	Large Cones[a]	Small Cones[b]	
020	635	666	670
019	683	723	690
018	717	752	710
017	747	784	730
016	792	825	750
015	804	843	790
014	838		815
013	852		835
012	884		855
011	894		880
010	894	919	900
09	923	955	920
08	955	983	940
07	984	1008	960
06	999	1023	980
05	1046	1062	1000
04	1060	1098	1020
03	1101	1131	1040
02	1120	1148	1060
01	1137	1178	1080
1	1154–1160	1179	1100
2	1162–1165	1179	1120
3	1168–1170	1196	1140
4	1186–1190	1209	1160
5	1196–1205	1221	1180
6	1222–1230	1255	1200
7	1240–1250	1264	1230
8	1263–1260	1300	1250
9	1280–1285	1317	1280
10	1305	1330	1300
11	1315–1325	1336	1320
12	1326–1337	1335	1350
13	1346–1349		1380
14	1366–1398		1410
15	1431–1430		1430–1435
16	1491		1460
17	1512		1480
18	1522		1500
19	1541		1520
20	1564		1530

Source: After Nelson 1984, 325; Grimshaw 1971, tables XIIa,b.

Note: Orton cones are used in America, Seger cones are used in Europe.

[a]Bending temperatures for large Orton cones are based on a heating rate of 150°C (temperature rise per hour). Nelson and Grimshaw give different temperatures for the cones; where two temperatures are given, the first temperature is from Nelson, the second from Grimshaw.

[b]Bending temperatures for small Orton cones are based on a heating rate of 300°C (temperature rise per hour).

take place within a range of temperatures, and whether they are completed may depend on how long a given temperature is held. Nonkiln bonfire firings are generally short, a matter of minutes (Shepard 1976, 87, 89; see also sec.

5.4.1.1); the rate of heating is usually uncontrolled but very fast, and the highest temperature is held only briefly before cooling begins. Kiln firings are considerably longer, and higher temperatures are achieved more gradually. Cardew (1969, 176) suggests that for a terra-cotta firing with wood as the fuel, a safe rate of temperature rise is twelve hours to 900° C. This slow rate of heating to high temperatures is in part a response to the temperature differential, or thermal gradient, between the surfaces and interior of the walls of a ceramic piece; different physical and chemical changes are taking place at different times within the body of the clay, which can set up damaging stresses (see sec. 4.2).

The changes that occur in a fired ceramic have been studied under the controlled conditions of scientific laboratories with clays of known chemical, mineral, and particle-size composition. Yet it is dangerous to apply such conclusions too stringently to the materials and products of nonindustrial potters in interpreting their choices and procedures. Neither clay composition nor firing conditions in the past were subject to modern industrial quality control and testing. For example, the clays used in much ancient pottery were probably not pure kaolins or smectites; nor was the firing process identical to heating experiments lasting one-hundred hours or more in the lab, which allow the clay body ingredients to change completely and reach equilibrium. Furthermore, it is certain that in the rapid bonfire firings common in many parts of the world, the clay body does not even approach maturity—the maximum hardness and minimum porosity of a particular composition or ware. There are many exceptions to these generalizations, the most outstanding being the production of Chinese porcelains, in which the quality control from clay preparation to firing seems to have been extraordinary, to judge from eighteenth-century accounts (e.g., Staehelin 1965; Burton 1906, 84–122).

Engineering tests do, however, provide a framework for understanding the development of the distinctive characteristics that for millennia have made ceramic materials so useful as utensils. If due caution is employed in their interpretation, these investigations let us appreciate the sophistication of ancient potters in successfully manipulating raw materials—clay and heat—to achieve their desired ends.

4.2 Physical and Chemical Changes in Firing

The changes that begin at the lowest temperatures and last longest are continuations of the drying process: the movement of water and other materials, chiefly organics, from the interior to the exterior of the piece. These then volatilize and escape into the atmosphere as gases, causing weight loss and shrinkage in the piece (though there may be some initial expansion of the clay mineral itself). The changes are most pronounced at the relatively low temperatures used for terra-cotta (up to 800–900°C), the range at which much of the unglazed, non-kiln-fired pottery of prehistory was fired. The loss of water in the clay mineral structure brings about changes in the clay mineral itself, which lead to the formation of new minerals characteristic of high-temperature firings. At high temperatures—above 900–1000°C or so—additional changes in the form of sintering and vitrification, augmented by the action of impurities and inclusions in the clay mix, produce a glassy, nonporous ceramic body. The following sections describe each of these processes in turn.

4.2.1 Loss of Volatiles

Most of the weight loss and shrinkage in a clay body result from loss of water, including the remainder of the mechanically combined or pore water left in the clay after drying at ambient temperatures. This water is held on the surfaces of clay particles, but ions on the surfaces may also be hydrated with several water molecules. This surface-adsorbed water turns to vapor and is largely driven off by 200–300°C. If there is too much water (owing to incomplete drying) or if it is removed too fast (e.g., in very fine clays), hairline cracks may occur in firing or the piece may explode in the kiln.

As the temperature rises, the chemically combined water—the hydroxyls within the chemical composition of the clay, existing as interlayer or lattice water—begins to be lost. The temperature at which the hydroxyls are lost varies with rate of heating and type of clay mineral (fig. 4.2). Kaolinites, for example, lose most of their water rather abruptly between 400 and 525°C.

Smectites, on the other hand, because of their small particle size and ability to hold water and ions between their unit layers, have a good deal more surface-adsorbed water to lose initially. On heating, they give up a great deal of water at very low temperatures between 100 and 200°C, much of it being the interlayer water held between the silicate sheets. The water loss between 100 and 200°C, if graphed by weight loss of the clay, often shows a double peak. This may be attributable to the loss of two types of water: water of hydration of adsorbed ions on the surface of the particles, and water adsorbed onto the surface of the clay particles themselves (Grim 1968, 314).

Cracking and explosion from too rapid heating and removal of water in these fine, highly hydrated smectite clays are particular hazards. At higher temperatures most of the water lost is lattice water, the dehydroxylation occurring over a relatively broad range of roughly 300–800°C. The ions on the surface of smectite particles apparently are influential in dehydroxylation, with large numbers of polyvalent ions lowering the temperature of hydration. Smectites require less heat to achieve dehydration than do kaolinites. Illite clays lose much of their water between about 300 and 600°C, and they also experience considerable loss below 100°C.

Because much of the clay used for nonindustrial pottery is not in pure deposits but consists of several clay minerals mixed together, it is of some inter-

Figure 4.2 Weight loss of four clays with heating. The rapid increase in weight loss at about 400°C corresponds to dehydroxylation. After Norton 1970, fig. 15.4.

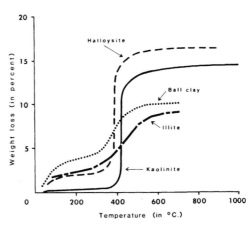

est to look at the dehydration behavior of the mixture. In general, it appears that mixing lowers the temperature at which the hydroxyl water is lost and also makes the loss more gradual, thus smoothing out the dehydration curve (Grim 1968, 349).

Besides water, a second component of the clay material volatilizes and contributes significantly to weight loss and shrinkage in firing. This is the organic material present in varying amounts in virtually all clays. The oxidation of carbon begins at 200°C or shortly above this temperature, when any carbon in the clay begins to burn out or oxidize as CO and CO_2. Clay briquettes fired to temperatures between 400 and 500°C are frequently blackened as the carbon particles move to the surfaces from the interior. The carbon usually is not effectively eliminated until temperatures above 600°C—usually about 750°C or more—are reached, and the atmosphere must contain free oxygen.

How long it takes to burn out the carbon depends on many factors: time and temperature of firing, the degree to which the atmosphere is oxidizing, the amount of carbon originally in the clay material; the fineness of the clay (hence the number and size of capillaries allowing carbon to move from the interior to the surfaces), and the specific clay mineral involved (e.g., smectites strongly retain organic material in their structure, and carbon is not readily given up in firing). Large amounts of carbon in a clay will cause greater shrinkage during firing as the organics are oxidized and burned out of the bulk volume. The incomplete oxidation of carbon in firing leads to the dark core often seen in the broken cross section of ceramics fired to relatively low temperatures for short periods or of very fine-textured pottery (fig. 4.3).

Besides water and organics, other impurities and inclusions may also volatilize in the temperature range of 500–800°C. Among these are carbonates, sulfates, and sulfides, occurring as calcite, dolomite, marcasite, pyrite or gypsum. Salts such as NaCl, Na_2CO_3, or $MgSO_4$ (Epsom salts) usually migrate to the surface of the clay piece during drying. On heating these decompose, releasing CO_2 and SO_2, further contributing to the weight loss. Chlorides in particular react with any iron present to form $FeCl_3$, which volatilizes readily at about 800°C.

The net effect of the breakdown and loss of organic matter, mechanically combined water, and carbonates and salts is continued weight loss and shrinkage of the clay body beyond the effects of drying. Both kinds of changes are negligible in a representative kaolin clay up to about 450–500°C but are significant at higher temperatures. Shrinkage occurs largely because the clay particles continue to draw together as pore water and then interlayer and lattice water are eliminated from the system. Shrinkage is accompanied by increasing density and decreasing porosity or absorption of the clay body as pores close (table 4.3). At higher temperatures, shrinkage increases as new minerals form and the clay body melts into a glassy phase.

Like drying shrinkage, firing shrinkage occurs in linear and volume dimensions. Also as in drying, the shrinkage frequently is differential, following the patterns caused by preferred orientation of the clay particles (see sec. 3.3.3); this orientation will in turn be exaggerated in the additional shrinkage during firing. The most pronounced particle orientation effects are seen in seams of wares cast in molds. Preferred orientation shrinkage effects will be exag-

Figure 4.3 Laboratory firing of Florida clay C-16 (see fig. 3.9), showing the relation of the thickness of carbon coring to the relative particle size distribution of the clay. Briquettes on the left are made of the natural clay; briquettes on the right are made of clay that has been sieved, with sand-sized particles coarser than 120 mesh removed. In the coarse clay, the carbon core is small, with diffuse edges, and has burned out after twenty minutes, while in the fine clay the core is large with relatively clear edges, and is sizable even after twenty-five minutes of firing at 500°C.

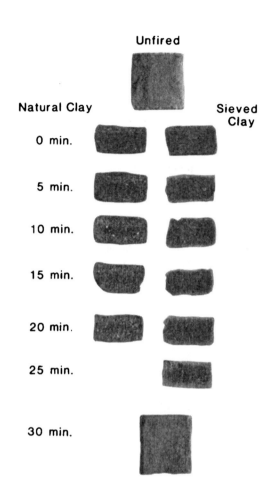

Table 4.3   Firing Shrinkage and Absorption of a Group of Pottery Clays

| Clay Type | Fired to Cone 04 (1060°C) | | Fired to Cone 4 (1186°C) | | Fired to Cone 9 (1280°C) | |
	% Shrinkage	% Absorption	% Shrinkage	% Absorption	% Shrinkage	% Absorption
Ohio red clay	11.5	3.9	12.5	0	Bloated	
Red clay	11.0	9.7	15.0	3.4	15.0	0
Stoneware clay	9.0	12.2	10.5	8.4	12.0	3.2
Stoneware clay	6.5	16.8	8.5	11.6	10.5	5.3
Common surface clay	10.0	1.5	Bloated		Fused	
Saggar clay	10.0	9.5	13.0	16.0	16.0	5.0
English ball clay	14.0	16.0	18.0	15.0	18.0	2.0
Fireclay	8.0	11.7	10.0	8.9	11.0	6.3
Florida kaolin	12.5	25.2	16.5	12.7	18.5	6.5
Georgia kaolin	8.0	29.6	9.0	26.9	12.0	22.9

Source: Rhodes 1973, 313.

gerated by the thermal gradient, or differences in temperature within the wall of a clay piece during firing. Dehydroxylation (loss of hydroxyls) is an endothermic reaction in which heat is necessary and is absorbed. As a result, not only is the interior of the clay cooler than the exterior surfaces, but dehydroxylation is completed more rapidly and shrinkage begins on the exterior while the interior is still expanding (fig. 4.4). If the preferred particle orientation exists primarily on the surfaces (e.g., as from burnishing), the cracking from shrinkage stresses could be especially severe.

Firing shrinkage and weight loss are measured while heating the clay to produce a constant rate of temperature increase. Linear thermal expansion may be measured continuously during firing by a recording dilatometer. Weight is measured by a thermogravimetric balance that monitors weight loss on heating (fig. 4.5). Alternatively, the clay pieces may be removed, carefully weighed and measured while still hot, then returned to the fire. In such a procedure the humidity of the weighing environment must be carefully controlled, because it can contribute to small weight changes in the fired piece. In most instances, the weight loss and shrinkage are noted as a function of temperature and graphed as such (see also sec. 13.2.3).

4.2.2   Changes in the Clay Minerals

At higher temperatures (above approximately 600°C), after the water of hydration is lost from the clay minerals, the clays undergo major alterations in their chemical and mineral structures. Most of these changes occur primarily at temperatures rarely, if ever, attained under the conditions associated with nonglazed ware bonfire firing, but some do begin earlier in the firing sequence.

Most work on thermal changes has been done on kaolin clays (fig. 4.6). When kaolinite is heated above approximately 500°C (Grim 1968, 304), the removal of the OH^{1-} groups results in an altered mineral called metakaolin ($Al_2O_3 \cdot 2SiO_2$). Metakaolin has a slightly disordered crystalline structure that is difficult to study by X-ray diffraction, but with electron diffraction the particles show a structure very similar to that of the original kaolinite. That the original structure may not be substantially lost is supported by the fact that metakaolin can sometimes be rehydrated back to kaolin and the hexagonal shape of the particles is preserved.

In smectite minerals, which have a three-layer structure, the loss of interlayer water may cause irreversible changes at lower temperatures than in kaolinite, which has a two-layer structure. Major dehydroxylation occurs at about 600°C, as shown by weight-loss curves.

At still higher temperatures, 900°C and above, the clay minerals lose all water and their lattice structure collapses irreversibly. If the firing is long enough, the clay minerals break down and form new silicates called high-temperature minerals because of their conditions of formation. In kaolins, at about 950°C metakaolin breaks down into an alumina-rich alteration product, spinel, plus free silica. This recrystallization is accompanied by a sharp increase in shrinkage. Above this temperature—between 1050 and 1275°C—spinel forms mullite ($3Al_2O_3 \cdot 2SiO_2$), which exists in needles or rodlike crystals. These mullite needles reinforce and strengthen the fired piece.

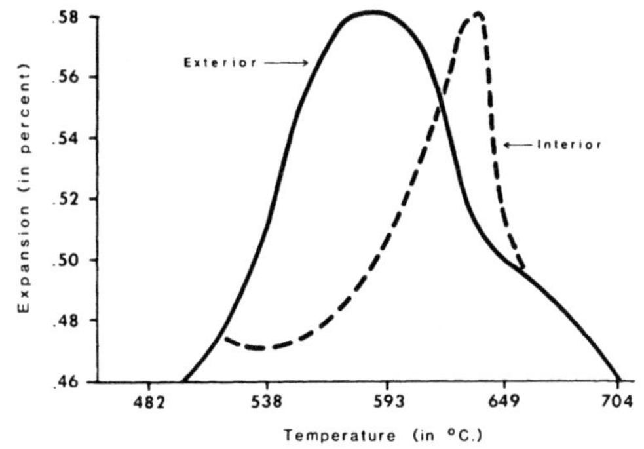

Figure 4.4 Thermal expansion of a white-ware heated in a periodic kiln at temperatures critical for the formation of preheating cracks, comparing expansion of the external surface (*solid line*) with interior core (*broken line*). While the outside expands, cracks form under tensile stresses and progress inward; they remain open as the interior continues to expand and stay open during the remainder of the firing because there are no compressive stresses to close them. Lawrence and West 1982, 146, 148, fig. 9-9.

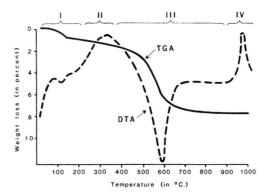

Figure 4.5 Differential thermal analysis (DTA) and thermogravimetric analysis (TGA) of a porcelain insulator body containing approximately 30% clay, heated at 20°C per minute: I—loss of adsorbed water; II—oxidation of organics; III—dehydroxylation, or loss of chemically combined water; IV—crystal formation. After Lawrence and West 1982, fig. 9-5.

Figure 4.6 Linear firing shrinkage and rate of shrinkage (per 100°C) curves for a kaolin clay. After Norton 1952, 129.

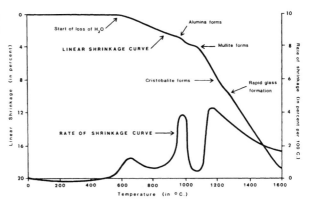

These considerations refer to alterations in clay minerals alone rather than to changes in triaxial bodies over mixtures of clays and other ingredients. It should be noted, however, that clay bodies for ceramic products usually contain substances (fluxes) to promote melting of the clay into a glass, which may begin at temperatures between 900 and 1100°C. Thus additional changes occurring in clay bodies at these temperatures, besides the mineral alterations, include accelerated shrinkage and decreased porosity as the material melts and forms a glass. At still higher temperatures, beginning above 1275°C and continuing to 1460°C, there is another sharp increase in shrinkage as cristobalite, sillimanite, and kyanite are formed. These minerals occur in nature as inclusions in metamorphic rocks, which have been subjected to intense heat and alteration during their formation. Impurities in the clays, especially K_2O and CaO, lower the temperatures at which these high-temperature changes occur (Johnson, Pask, and Moya 1982).

Smectites go through the same general transitions, but at different temperatures and with some variations influenced by the ionic substitutions common in these chemically variable clays (see Wahl 1965). The substitutions have the overall effect of lowering the temperatures at which the high-temperature minerals are formed as well as making smectites less refractory (less resistant to melting) than kaolins. The lattice structure of montmorillonites (Grim and Kulbicki 1961) is generally maintained until approximately 800–900°C. Above these temperatures, there seem to be two kinds of reactions a montmorillonite may undergo. In some clays, especially those with Al^{3+} ionic substitutions in the tetrahedral layer, spinel begins to form; in other montmorillonites (generally those low in iron), quartz rather than spinel develops. The order and temperature of appearance of high-temperature minerals such as mullite, cristobalite, and cordierite also vary in these two categories of montmorillonite. The presence of lithium, sodium, and potassium reduces the development of high-temperature minerals and also lowers the maximum temperatures to which they persist.

The structure of illite clays persists until 850°C or beyond, sometimes being identified at temperatures as high as 1000°C. Spinel appears at about 900–1000°C, and mullite, too, may occur at this low temperature.

High-temperature changes in clay minerals and clay bodies are studied by two primary methods. One of these is differential thermal analysis, or DTA, in which a sample of the clay is heated at a known rate together with samples of a thermally inert or unreactive material like alumina, which assumes the temperature of the furnace. The temperature differentials between the clay and the alumina reflect reactions and change within the clay, such as the conversion to metakaolin or mullite, as described above. Some of these reactions are exothermic (heat is given off by the reaction), while others are endothermic (heat is necessary for the reaction to take place and is absorbed). In most clays the loss of interlayer and lattice water is an endothermic reaction. For example, in kaolinite the reaction that occurs at roughly 600°C, loss of hydroxyls and formation of metakaolin, is endothermic, while the formation of spinel at 950°C is exothermic. The reactions are typically graphed from an arbitrary baseline as a function of the increasing furnace or kiln temperature (fig. 4.7; also fig. 4.5). Exothermic reactions are shown as upward curves and endothermic reactions as downward curves from the baseline, the distance from the base indicating the intensity of the reaction (see Johnson, Pask, and Moya 1982; Grim and Rowland 1942). The area under the peak is proportional to the latent heat of the reaction and can be used to evaluate it if the instrument is calibrated.

In addition to thermal analysis, another important method for studying clays at high temperatures is X-ray diffraction (see sec. 13.2.2), which allows investigation of the crystal structure, and changes in that structure, of the clays and of minerals formed from the clays by analysis of their atomic arrangements or lattices. Ideally, X-ray diffraction measurements are made while the sample is at a high temperature, but since most of the reactions stud-

Figure 4.7 Generalized differential thermal analysis (DTA) curves for clay minerals: *a*, kaolinite; *b*, halloysite; *c*, Na-montmorillonite; *d*, Ca-montmorillonite; *e*, vermiculite; *f*, sepiolite; *g*, palygorskite. Note low-temperature (100–200°C) endotherms corresponding to dehydroxylation of clays with quantities of water in their chemical structures (montmorillonite, vermiculite, sepiolite, and palygorskite. After Neumann 1977, fig. 20.

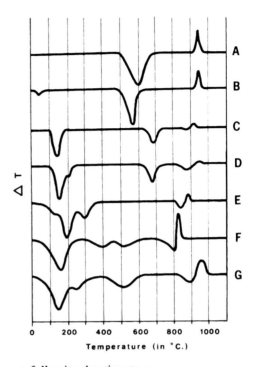

ied are irreversible, a room-temperature experiment following heating to a given temperature may be satisfactory. In situations where the particles are too small or too poorly crystalline for X-ray diffraction analysis, electron diffraction may be used instead, for example, in the study of metakaolin.

4.2.3 Changes in Inclusions and Impurities

Inclusions and impurities in any clay body play significant roles not only in the drying phase, as discussed in chapter 3, but also in all phases of firing. Inclusions may be naturally present in a clay or may be added by the potter as temper (sec. 14.1); but whatever their origin, they are important during firing in modifying the expansion, shrinkage, and microstructure of a clay body (see table 4.4). This discussion focuses on three major kinds of inclusions—quartz, feldspar, and lime—and their roles during moderate- and high-temperature phases of firing, particularly in melting and fusion.

The melting and fusion of a ceramic can be discussed in terms of sintering and vitrification. In sintering the surfaces of particles begin to stick to or fuse with other particle surfaces, and it may occur as a solid-state or liquid-phase reaction. In solid-state sintering, the surface diffusion of atoms between the particles forms a join or "neck" between them, and no melting or liquid phase is involved. A variety of complex processes accounts for the transfer of material between adjacent grains (Kingery, Bowen, and Uhlmann 1976, 469–79; Grimshaw 1971, 681–84; Anseau, Deletter, and Cambier 1981; Burke 1985), which usually results in shrinkage of the mass and in pores' changing shape (becoming more spherical) or being eliminated. The rate of sintering is more or less inversely proportional to particle size. In liquid-phase sintering the

Table 4.4   Percentage Changes in Volume of Tempered and Untempered Clays with Heating

Clay Type	Firing Temperature (°C)						
	200	400	600	800	1000	1200	1400
Plastic clay	+0.1	+0.3	+0.3	0.0	−4.3	−16.2	—
Clay plus 30% sand	+0.3	+0.5	+0.5	+0.8	−0.1	−4.3	—
Fireclay	+0.1	+0.2	+0.3	+0.4	0.0	−9.2	−14.0
Clay plus 20% grog	+0.1	+0.2	+0.4	+0.4	+0.1	−6.3	−9.5
Clay plus 40% grog	+0.2	+0.2	+0.5	+0.6	+0.4	−3.0	−6.2

Source: Grimshaw 1971, table XII-XII.
Note: Soaking time of two hours at each temperature.

fusion takes place when some constituents of the body (e.g., fluxes such as feldspars) begin to melt, forming a liquid. As sintering proceeds more of the solid melts, so that the particles draw closer together and the pores between them get smaller, giving rise to shrinkage, loss of porosity, and densification of the body. This shrinkage is enhanced by the surface tension forces of the glassy melt between the particles.

In vitrification a glassy phase forms as a result of continued heating and extension of liquid-phase sintering. In this process, defined as densification with the aid of a viscous liquid phase (Kingery, Bowen, and Uhlmann 1976, 490), the particles melt and form a bond for the body, pores are eliminated, the body becomes increasingly dense, and the mass shrinks considerably. If vitrification proceeds to an extreme of melting, the entire mass loses its form and may warp or slump under its own weight.

Sintering and vitrification begin earlier in very fine-textured materials than in coarse ones, even below the standard vitrification temperatures of the constituent minerals. This is true of very fine particles whatever their nature, including clays, feldspars, and quartz. It is an important point, not just in terms of high-temperature bodies and glazes of commercial or studio ceramics, but also for understanding the advantages of using very fine colloidal clays for slips. Besides feldspars, many naturally occurring materials or impurities in clays can act as fluxes in the body or in slips if they have extremely small particles. One of the most common of these is iron; very finely divided iron in a reduced state (ferrous oxide, FeO) may act as a flux at low temperatures between 800 and 900°C (see Grimshaw 1971, 275–97). Similar action may be caused by mica (see Arayaphong, McLaren, and Phelps 1984), boron, or lead minerals.

Inclusions are also important in developing use-related properties such as strength, thermal shock resistance, and porosity as well as in determining the color and hardness of the fired product. All of these functions are discussed elsewhere (chaps. 7 and 12), but the use-related mechanical properties will be briefly surveyed below with specific reference to the role of inclusions.

4.2.3.1   QUARTZ

The most common and abundant inclusion in most ceramic bodies—whether they are natural clays or triaxial bodies created by formulas (fig. 3.9)—is quartz, or free crystalline silica, SiO_2. Silica in its many forms is the earth's most stable and abundant natural mineral. Structurally, quartz is composed of

SiO_4 tetrahedrons, the same units that composed the silica layers of clays. In quartz, however, the tetrahedrons are arranged not in a sheetlike structure, but in spiral chains.

In the modern commercial or craft pottery business, silica may be referred to as potter's flint or sand, and often it is found as ground glass. Flint is very finely crystalline (micro- or cryptocrystalline) hydrated silica, containing 1% water in molecular form; it is less dense than sand, having very fine pores as a consequence of its cryptocrystalline structure. Silica thus has macrocrystalline (quartz or quartz sand) and cryptocrystalline (flint; also chert, chalcedony, agate, jasper) mineral forms that are important to potters; but a third class of silica—an amorphous form including organic, opaline, or biosilica—is occasionally found in pottery. Biosilica may occur in trees or grasses as phytoliths and may be freed by burning the plant. Alternatively, silica may be present in pottery as sponge spicules or diatoms (skeletons of siliceous organisms), both of which are often intermixed in fresh water or marine sedimentary clays (Borremans and Shaak 1986).

Silica or quartz is an important component of triaxial bodies, and it is for this use that its characteristics have been most thoroughly studied. It is important in determining the structural properties (shrinkage, porosity, strength) of clay bodies, but this function is influenced by particle size and crystallinity (whether the silica occurs as sand or microcrystalline flint; see Johnson 1976). It is also modified to some extent by the transformations quartz undergoes on heating. Although quartz is a refractory mineral—that is, it resists melting until 1710°C—during heating to high temperatures it undergoes three inversions, or changes in atomic structure and bonding. These inversions which occur at 573, 867–70, and 1250°C, have accompanying changes in related properties such as density and specific gravity.

The first inversion occurs rather rapidly at 573 ± 5°C and is a change from alpha to beta quartz. This transformation is accompanied by a structural change resulting in an expansion of the quartz grains, the expansion in volume being 2%, and the linear expansion 1.03%. This expansion of the particles of quartz in the clay body may not have any effect on the fired ware, however, because it occurs simultaneously with the removal of large amounts of water from the clay body (between 500 and 600°C) when the clay body is shrinking. In studies of thin sections of archaeological pottery from the New World, Shepard (1976, 29) noted no shattering of quartz grains that could be attributed to this inversion, perhaps in part because of the very rapid heating schedule used by the potters.

The second and third quartz inversions, which begin at 867 and 1250°C, lead to formation of tridymite from beta quartz and then to cristobalite from tridymite. These are very slow and sluggish reactions involving major rearrangements of the strongly bonded silica-oxygen tetrahedrons. Because these transformations take place slowly, the degree to which they occur in a clay body depends on how long the temperature is held at or above these critical points. Cristobalite stabilizes at 1470°C, but at that temperature not all tridymite or beta quartz will necessarily have turned to cristobalite unless the temperature has been held long enough. In fact, much of the cristobalite in fired clay bodies probably comes not from the quartz changes but from free SiO_2, which is liberated when mullite forms from the clay at 1050–1100°C (fig. 4.6). Most nonkiln firings do not even remotely approach the tridymite and cristobalite inversions and probably are too short for any significant formation even of tridymite. The alpha-beta quartz inversion, however, is well within the range of such firing technology.

At high temperatures these inversions are hastened by the presence of fluxes. Fluxes also cause the quartz particles to dissolve to form a siliceous glass, with a volume increase of 2.05%. The silica liquid undergoes very little thermal expansion with increasing temperatures, but the incompletely dissolved crystals have a large thermal expansion coefficient. On cooling, differential shrinkage causes stresses that may result in the cracking of large crystals (> 30 μm), creating microcracks in the clay body. Particles of 8 μm or less melt easily to form a glass. As the body cools, beta-cristobalite reverts to a lower temperature form, called alpha cristobalite, at a temperature between 200 and 270°C, accompanied by a volume contraction of approximately 2%. There is no reversion back to alpha quartz.

The role of quartz in enhancing desirable properties of fired clay bodies or eliminating undesirable ones has been the subject of numerous studies. Quartz reduces firing shrinkage, but unless it is of very small particle size or is present in very small amounts, it may also lessen fired strength, in part because of the expansion occurring with the alpha-beta inversion, but also because of the microcracking resulting from larger particles at high temperatures. Much of the influence of quartz in a clay body is a function of particle size; in potter's flints, approximately 50% of the material is below 30 μm.

4.2.3.2 FELDSPAR

A second important category of inclusions in ceramic bodies is feldspar. Feldspars, as discussed in section 2.2, are a large family of silicate rocks that constitute the most abundant mineral category in the earth's crust. These minerals occur primarily in granites and pegmatites, often with associations of mica, and they are in addition the primary parent materials of clay minerals. Feldspars are often present in small amounts in natural clays, especially primary clays, as a result of incomplete weathering.

Consisting primarily of SiO_2 tetrahedrons, the feldspars have significant substitutions of aluminum for the silicon atom in the center of the tetrahedrons, together with additional potassium, sodium, or calcium ions that maintain electrical neutrality. These latter substitutions give rise to the main categories of feldspars, the potash, soda, and lime feldspars. The feldspar family, in other words, consists of a continuum of aluminosilicate minerals, with graded compositions based on the proportions of three key elements: potassium (the resultant minerals being orthoclase and microcline), sodium (albite), and calcium (anorthite). These last two, the soda and lime feldspars, constitute a series called the plagioclases.

Rarely do other ions substitute for K^{1+}, Na^{1+}, or Ca^{2+} in the feldspars; iron, a common substitution in the clay mineral structure, never is part of the feldspar composition. Because the number of silicon ions replaced by these ions may vary to maintain balanced electrical charges, the proportion of silica varies in the several kinds of feldspars, potash feldspars having an average of 64.7% silica while the lime feldspars average only 42.8% (Cardew 1969, 44).

Table 4.5 Fluxing Action of Different Particle Sizes of Feldspar and Effects on Porosity of a China Clay

| Feldspar | | Porosity | | | | | |
| Size (mesh) | Amount (%) | | Firing Temperature (°C) | | | | |
		Unfired	1000	1100	1180	1280	1350
40	40	31.0	34.5	30.95	23.65	10.95	4.96
	20	36.6	40.0	37.15	30.0	18.45	14.21
100	40	32.85	36.5	30.8	17.1	6.6	1.4
	20	37.0	41.0	38.4	27.5	14.4	8.87
200	40	35.1	38.6	22.65	14.8	6.0	—
	20	38.05	41.55	33.6	23.7	10.5	7.11

Source: After Grimshaw 1971, table XII-XVI.

When subjected to the high temperatures of ceramic firing, feldspars do not undergo inversions of their atomic structure. Instead they melt, and feldspars are used in the ceramic industry as fluxes (see Schramm and Hall 1936). When finely ground (to 40 μm, or 0.04 mm), feldspars promote melting or sintering by virtue of three properties. First, most feldspars have a relatively low melting point or high fusibility: potash feldspars begin to melt at 1150°C, and soda feldspars melt at 1118°C. (Lime feldspar, being high in alumina [36.7%] and low in SiO_2, melts at a much higher temperature, 1550°C, but that temperature can be lowered if other feldspars are present or if limestone and quartz are added.) Second, feldspars are highly viscous on melting and form a thick, rather than thin and runny, liquid. Third, their very fine particles enhance their readiness to sinter and fuse. The net result is a dense body with reduced porosity (table 4.5).

Feldspars may be deliberately added to ceramic bodies, particularly potash or soda feldspars or nepheline syenite (a naturally occurring mineral with both potassium and sodium in its composition). Or crushed particles of feldspar-containing rock such as granite or basalt may be added. Rarely are these fine enough in particle size to have the fluxing action described above, however. Many primary clay deposits contain particles of unweathered or partly weathered feldspars as residual minerals, together with quartz. These materials combine in their natural state the three major components—clay, feldspar, and quartz—that are mixed artificially in triaxial bodies of commercial manufactures.

4.2.3.3 CALCIUM

A third important group of minerals in pottery is the calcium family (see Grimshaw 1971, 279–80), which most commonly occurs in various forms of calcium carbonate ($CaCO_3$), such as limestone, calcite, and shell, or as calcium sulfate, such as gypsum ($CaSO_4$). Lime or calcium may occur naturally in clays, and then the clay is described as calcareous or marly. Calcium may sometimes be added to clays, for example, in the form of animal bone ash or calcium triphosphate ($Ca_3[PO_4]_2$). Bone ash may compose 50% of the body of English bone china; the ash is made of finely ground, calcined ox bones and is responsible for the translucency of the ware (see Weyl 1941).

Calcium carbonate has a very distinctive property that affects its usefulness in fired clay bodies: calcite decomposes on firing at about 870°C. The exact temperature is a matter of disagreement: some researchers say it may occur at 850–900°C while others contend it may take place at as low as 650–750°C. That the argument exists highlights how time and atmosphere act in addition to temperature in governing firing behavior. In any case, when calcium decomposes it forms lime (CaO) and carbon dioxide gas (CO_2):

$$CaCO_3 \xrightarrow{650-900°C} CaO + CO_2 \uparrow .$$

The problem for pottery develops when calcareous clays fired to 850°C or above are cooled. CaO is hygroscopic—that is, it absorbs atmospheric moisture—and over time it picks up moisture from the air, forming quicklime ($Ca[OH]_2$) and releasing heat. This is accompanied by volume expansion, which sets up stresses in the surrounding clay body, causing cracking and spalling ("lime popping"). Most noticeable when the lime particles in the clay are comparatively large, the rehydration of the lime gives the fired ware a very low strength and in extreme cases may cause the entire body to crumble (see Rye 1976; Butterworth 1956).

Several solutions are possible (Laird and Worcester 1956). If the lime is present only in very fine particles, the rehydration and expansion tend to be less seriously damaging. In addition, the presence of salt in the clay can apparently prevent severe crumbling of the body (Rye 1976; Klemptner and Johnson 1986). A procedure called docking—wetting the newly fired and still hot vessels with water—can also prevent spalling (Klemptner and Johnson 1986). Alternatively, the clay may be fired in a reducing atmosphere, or oxidation fired to a temperature either below 700°C or above 1000°C. At temperatures over 1000°C, rehydration does not occur, since at these temperatures the calcium in most clays becomes a part of the liquid phase with sintering and vitrification. New calcium compounds are formed at these high temperatures, such as calcium silicates (wollastonite, $CaSiO_3$) or calcium ferrosilicates, depending on the composition. Melting of calcium compounds is accelerated in a reducing atmosphere and when the lime is in very fine particles (Tite and Maniatis 1975b; Maniatis et al. 1983).

4.2.4   Glaze Formation

Ceramic glazes are a particular kind of glass, a noncrystalline substance cooled rapidly ("supercooled") from a melt of earthy materials. When used as a glaze, this glass forms a highly viscous coating melted or fused at high temperatures onto a ceramic body; glazes cool and solidify without reforming a crystalline structure, and thus they retain some of the characteristics of a liquid. Glazes may be shiny or matte, translucent or opaque, colored or clear, thick or thin, and occasionally they may develop a crystalline structure (for general discussions of glazes, see Rhodes 1973; Nelson 1984, 190–263; Lawrence and West 1982, 173–99). Glazes and glasses have three components—network formers, network modifiers, and intermediates—each of which is important to the character of the final material (see Rhodes 1973, 88–94, 104–11).

Network formers create the largely unordered structure of the glass by combining oxygen atoms with certain cations, and by the arrangement of the resultant tetrahedrons. Although boron (B_2O_3) and phosphorus (P_2O_5) can meet these structural criteria, the most important of the network formers for glass and glazes is silica, SiO_2 (fig. 2.4).

Network modifiers are oxides that enter holes in the network of silica tetrahedrons. These oxides usually have larger ionic radii than silica and weaken the bonds in the network; they also have the important role of lowering the very high melting point of silica, which is normally 1710°C. Commonly acting as fluxes, these modifiers include Na_2O, K_2O, PbO, CaO, and MgO.

Intermediates are oxides that replace part of the silica and usually serve one or both of two functions. One function is to increase the viscosity (stiffness) of the glaze, which was originally lowered by adding fluxes. A glaze is melted in place on a body, so it must run, but it should not be too runny, and small amounts of alumina (often added as a ball clay) will give the requisite stiffness. A second function of intermediates is to strengthen the glaze in firing, for example, in reducing crazing. Al_2O_3, PbO, ZnO, ZrO_2, and CdO are common intermediates. Finally, a variety of metallic oxides, such as oxides of iron, copper, manganese, cobalt, and chromium, are added as colorants (see sec. 11.2.4), and organic materials may be used as binders to increase the strength of the raw glaze (Nelson 1984, 263).

Glazes may be applied to an unfired clay object and the piece finished in a single firing, but typically two firings are used. The first firing of the unglazed body is called the bisque or biscuit firing and is commonly done at temperatures of 900–1000°C. The ware is then cooled and the glaze is applied and refired in the glost firing. The bisque firing makes the piece stronger for dipping in the glaze and decorating, permits it to undergo most or all of its firing shrinkage, and leaves the body porous enough that the glaze adheres better. The glost firing may be done at about the same temperature as the bisque firing, or it may be higher or lower. Chinese glazed porcelains, for example, often had low-fired lead glazes applied to the high-fired biscuit porcelain body (Medley 1976, 14).

Glazes may be described and classified in many ways; for example, by their maturing temperature, their composition (chiefly with reference to the principal modifier), and the wares on which they may be used (see Hodges 1976, 48–51). They are frequently classified as high-temperature (or hard) and low-temperature (or soft), depending on whether they are fired below 1150–1200°C or above 1200–1250°C. High-fire glazes typically contain feldspars and/or alkaline earth minerals such as calcium carbonate (whiting), dolomite, or barium carbonate. Low-fire glazes (see Brody 1979, 75–89) either are alkaline in composition (containing borax or soda ash, for example) or are lead glazes, with lead as the principal flux; the soft, white tin glazes of majolicas are lead glazes with approximately 5% tin added as an opacifier. While low-temperature glazes can be used on high-fired (bisque) bodies, it is difficult or impossible to use a high-temperature glaze on a body with a low maturing temperature (such as an earthenware) because of the danger of overfiring and deformation. Bristol glazes, using zinc as a flux, were developed in England to eliminate the toxicity of lead-fluxed glazes. Slip glazes are high in iron and clay, which gives them their name; a material from prehistory that is often called a slip glaze is the unusual slip of highland Maya Plumbate pottery, which is partially vitrified (see Shepard 1948a).

Glazes may be compounded either from a variety of raw ingredients or from frits (see below), then mixed as liquids and applied to vessels in a number of ways, including dipping, pouring, splashing, painting, and spraying. Glazes made of raw materials are less expensive and are more resistant to chemical and mechanical attack. Some glazes are simpler to produce than others, however. A high-fired ash glaze may be created by dusting the surface with wood ash (or it may occur by the circulation of ash in the kiln atmosphere). Salt glazes are a type of noncompounded, once-fired alkali glaze created by throwing or shoveling salt (NaCl) into the kiln at temperatures of 1100–1250°C. The salt decomposes, with sodium acting as a flux when the ions make contact with the ingredients of the surfaces of the vessels, while the chlorine volatizes and escapes as a gas (Starkey 1977, 2):

$$2NaCl + H_2O \xrightarrow{\text{(heat)}} 2HCl \uparrow + Na_2O;$$

$$Na_2O + Al_2O_3 \cdot 4SiO_2 = Na_2O \cdot Al_2O_3 \cdot 4SiO_2.$$
$$\text{(soda)} \quad \text{(pot surface)} \quad\quad \text{(salt glaze)}$$

The result is a thin, mottled glaze with a pebbly texture often likened to orange peel.

Lead glazes may be applied by simply brushing the surface of a vessel with powdered lead oxide (called litharge) or galena (lead sulfide; PbS); they have the additional advantages of being easy to fit to the clay and firing with few flaws. It has been known since the nineteenth century, however, that they can be toxic both in application and in use (see Rhodes 1973, 82). For this reason, lead glazes are often compounded of frits (see Rhodes 1973, 196–200), which are basically premelted glazes: raw materials such as silica and a flux are melted together, cooled, and ground into a powder before being combined into a glaze mixture. Fritted glazes can be fired at lower temperatures and have fewer flaws than glazes compounded of raw materials, but they are more costly. The toxicity of the raw lead glaze compound is reduced by using purchased frits, but this does not significantly reduce the risk of lead poisoning if acidic substances (orange juice, wine, etc.) are stored or served in low-fired lead-glazed ceramics.

Besides being complex to compound, ceramic glazes can also be dangerous, because many of the ingredients are toxic (Brody 1979, 84–85; Nelson 1984, 210–23). For example, ash glazes are caustic and should not be stirred with the hands. The chlorine gas released in salt glazing is a threat not only to those stoking the kiln (they should wear masks, and the area should be well ventilated) but also to the environment, contributing to acid rain and deforestation in Westerwald, Germany, where famous salt-glazed stoneware is produced (Lowenstein 1986, 394). Finally, lead for lead glazes is particularly dangerous, both as a raw material in glaze preparation and as a possible poison in fired serving vessels.

The multitude of glaze recipes (table 4.6) found in the literature reflects the tremendous complexity of glazes and demonstrates that creating glazes for art and industrial ceramics requires a sophisticated understanding of chemistry. Glazing ceramics is difficult, and defects such as pinholes, crawling, bub-

Table 4.6   Glaze Recipes

1. Low-fire (cone 06) lead glaze, resistant to food acids
36.78 white lead
18.95 soda feldspar
9.78 gerstley borate
4.90 boric acid
6.80 kaolin
21.70 silica
0.83 zirconium oxide
2. Wood ash glaze, fired at cones 8–10
39.0 wood ash (mixed)
29.5 kona F4 feldspar
10.0 whiting
19.5 kaolin
2.0 bentonite
3. Mat glaze, fired at cones 10–12
40.0 potash feldspar
22.3 whiting
21.0 kaolin
16.7 silica
4.4 titanium oxide
4. Celadon glaze, fired at cones 8–10
79.5 potash feldspar
6.2 whiting
14.3 flint
2.0 red iron oxide

Source: Nelson 1984, 330.
Note: Amounts given by weight (percentage).

bling, crazing, and improper color development can arise from improper compounding, application, and firing (for general discussions of glaze flaws see Marquis 1952; Rhodes 1973; 241–49; Nelson 1984, 201–3; Hamer 1975, 77–85; Lawrence and West 1982; 189–91).

The variations in the glaze recipes also show how the sensitivity of glaze ingredients to changes in firing temperature and atmosphere can be used to create different textures and colors. The maturing temperature of a glaze is generally a function of the amount of silica relative to the amount of fluxes (Rhodes 1973, 164). In general, glazes have a firing temperature tolerance of about 30°C (Rhodes 1973, 124). A variety of low-, medium-, and high-temperature glazes have been developed, but firing at the wrong temperature—too high, for example—may cause the glaze to volatilize or run off the pot. Glazes fired too rapidly may develop bubbles; underfired glazes are generally rough to the touch and dull in appearance.

One of the principal concerns in firing glazes is fit—the dimensional adjustment of a glaze to a clay body—and this is particularly related to thermal expansion and shrinkage rates of the two materials (fig. 4.8). Unequal contraction rates in cooling can cause a variety of defects; crazing occurs when the glaze contracts more than the body and develops a network of surface cracks (fig. 4.9), and shivering occurs when the glaze contracts less, or more

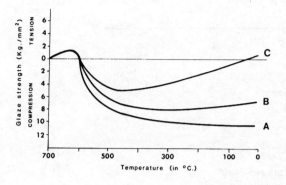

Figure 4.8 Stresses induced in glazes during cooling: *a*, the body has a significantly greater coefficient of expansion than the glaze, putting the glaze in high compression, which may cause it to peel; *b*, the body has a slightly higher coefficient of expansion than the glaze, reducing the stresses but leaving it in slight compression; *c*, the body and glaze are of comparable expansion, placing the glaze under tensile stress in cooling, which may lead to crazing. After Grimshaw 1971, fig. XII.6.

a   b

Figure 4.9 Crazing of a glaze under tensile stress: *a*, low stress; *b*, high stress. After Lawrence and West 1982, fig. 11-4.

slowly, and separates from the body. In general, if a glaze contracts very slightly more than the body after cooling, it compresses the body and so strengthens it.

4.3   Summary

4.3.1   The Thermal Reaction Sequence

Each clay mineral behaves in a unique way during firing, and the many kinds of clay bodies also behave distinctively, especially at high temperatures, depending upon their particular constituents. This variability is in part a consequence of the chemical composition of the clay materials and inclusions and also depends on the conditions of time, temperature, and atmosphere during firing. Nonetheless, despite these differences, it is possible to outline in a very general way the sequence of reactions and changes that takes place, with varying degrees of completion, in a clay body during heating (table 4.7).

Room temperature to 200°C. During this phase of heating, the last of the mechanically combined water (pore water, or water adsorbed onto the surfaces of the clay particles) is lost from the clay, disappearing as water vapor. In three-layer clays, such as smectites, a considerable degree of interlayer water may be lost as well. There is little to no shrinkage in this phase.

Table 4.7 Changes in Clays with Firing and Cooling Temperatures

Temperature (°C)	Change in Clay or Kiln
100–200	Clay begins to lose adsorbed water ("water-smoking period")
200–225	Alpha-beta conversion of cristobalite (on cooling after firing)
470	Lowest temperature at which a red glow can be seen in the dark
450–550	Kaolinite loses hydroxyls; metakaolin forms
500	Organic matter oxidized
550–625	Dull red glow, visible in daylight
550–650	Montmorillonite loses hydroxyls
573	Alpha-beta inversion of quartz
600–800	Micas lose hydroxyls
800	$FeCl_3$ volatilizes
870	$CaCO_3$ dissociates to CaO plus H_2O at or by this temperature; tridymite forms from beta quartz
950	Spinel forms; CaO reacts with clay forming calcium silicates (wollastonite)
960	Recrystallization of metakaolin begins (on cooling)
1000	Formation of calcium ferrosilicates; calcareous clays turn pale yellow or olive
1050	Light-yellow heat in kiln
1100	Mullite forms
1100–1200	Vitrification range of ball clays
1150	White heat in kiln
1160	K-feldspar begins to melt
1170	Na-feldspar (albite) begins to melt
1200	Gypsum dissociates
1250–90	Biscuit firing range for bone china; cristobalite forms from tridymite
1320–1450	Maturing range for hard porcelains
1470	Cristobalite stabilizes
1712	SiO_2 melts
2050	Al_2O_3 melts

Source: After Cardew 1969, app. 14.

200–400°C. At these low temperatures, organic matter present in the clay begins to oxidize. As oxidation proceeds, the organics migrate from the interior to the exterior of the clay, blackening the surfaces, before being driven off as CO_2.

450–600°C. Dehydroxylation or loss of chemically combined lattice water occurs in all clays. The loss takes place rather abruptly in kaolin and is followed by a structural transformation to the mineral metakaolin, with minor shrinkage and considerable increase in porosity. In illites and smectites, the water loss and shrinkage are more gradual.

573 ± 5°C. This is the temperature of the quartz inversion from the alpha, or low-temperature form, to the beta, or high-temperature form. The inversion occurs with a slight volume expansion of the mineral.

750–850°C. By the time this temperature range has been attained, most organic material present has been successfully burned out of the clay. With the removal of most lattice water from the clay minerals, kaolins and smectites begin to lose their characteristic crystalline structure. Calcium carbonate dissociates, changing to CaO and giving off CO_2 gas.

867–70°C. Beta quartz alters to tridymite.

950°C. The structure of most kaolins and smectites is irreversibly lost at this temperature, although that of illites may persist. With the loss of structure comes the formation of high-temperature alteration products of the clay minerals and pronounced shrinkage. Spinel is a product of the breakdown of metakaolin, accompanied by the release of SiO_2.

1050–1200°C. In this temperature range, spinel changes to needlelike crystals of mullite. Feldspars begin to melt, dissolving both the silica formed at the same time as the spinel and the quartz already present in the body. This initiates the glassy phase of the ceramic; pores begin to close, and porosity rapidly diminishes.

Above 1200°C. Porosity may increase as gases form in the melting body, and if there is no way for them to escape these gases can cause bloating. Tridymite changes to cristobalite, which stabilizes at 1470°C. Sillimanite, kyanite, and cordierite form as high-temperature mineral phases of the clay minerals.

4.3.2   The Fired Product: Stresses and Defects

The major concern in producing a fired ceramic is to achieve a product suitable for its intended use, and success always depends on both the materials used and the quality of the workmanship. "Suitability" may be judged by many criteria, artistic and functional. Because the concern here is with archaeological pottery, primarily utensils and containers that have a utilitarian purpose, for the present artistic and technical standards associated with firing to maturity will be ignored and the focus will be on functional attributes. Chief among the functional properties of interest here are strength, resistance to thermal stress, porosity, and freedom from defects (see chap. 7 for discussion of these properties and chap. 12 for details of their measurement).

Strength (see sec. 12.3.2) is perhaps the most complex of the use-related properties and in some ways may be considered a composite of them all. It refers to the integrity or durability of a ceramic—its resistance to breakage and its ability to perform whatever service is demanded of it without cracking, crumbling, warping, shattering, slumping, or otherwise failing. A strong vessel should be able to survive contact with hot fires or cold liquids, accidental blows, and other conditions of wear and tear.

Aside from the firing itself, the most important determinants of fired strength are textural and microstructural attributes (see sec. 12.2), including porosity. A strong ceramic is one with inclusions in a range of sizes and angular shapes. Although no specific quantity of inclusions can be specified for maximum strength, since this varies with individual bodies, it has been found that the optimum amount of quartz that may be added to strengthen a clay is 25% by weight (Robinson 1968a; Kennard and Williamson 1971). Very fine particles in the body enhance strength in relatively high-fired ware because they sinter and fuse more readily than do coarse ones, thus beginning vitrification and formation of a homogeneous glassy phase at lower temperatures.

The strength of a fired ware may be decreased by conditions contrary to those described above. Any inhomogeneities in the body—resulting from uneven drying, particle-orientation effects, thickness, shape, density—can cause stresses that may weaken the ceramic and increase the risk of cracking or failure in firing or use. Similarly, firing a body containing calcium carbonate to temperatures between 750 and 1000°C may weaken it because of the rehydration and expansion of CaO, unless the particles are extremely fine.

Thermal stress (see sec. 12.4) refers to the tensions that occur in a clay body, fired or unfired, when it is subjected to temperature changes (see Kingery 1955; Davidge and Tappin 1967; Hasselmann 1969; Crandall and Ging 1955; Chandler 1981). Thermal stresses of unfired clay materials were addressed in section 3.3.2; for example, exposure to cooling air currents, which may evaporate water from the surface too fast, can crack and warp the body. Thermal stress or shock may occur in firing a vessel in several circumstances: if it is subjected to firing without being preheated, if the temperature is raised too rapidly, or if cold air currents come into contact with the hot ware during firing or cooling.

Thermal stresses are of two kinds. One results from normal temperature changes, which cause minerals to expand on heating and contract on cooling. The other results from sudden or dramatic raising or lowering of the temperature and is known as thermal shock. When the ambient temperature is suddenly raised, for example, the clay body expands rapidly as water and other gases immediately volatilize and the clay constituents expand microscopically with heat. This expansion causes rapid compressive and tensile stresses that the body may not be able to accommodate instantly, and cracking or shattering result.

Clay bodies with high thermal shock resistance—good ability to withstand sudden temperature changes—are those whose components have very low rates of expansion or thermal expansion coefficients. In contemporary commercial ceramics, the wares with low thermal expansion include what are called ovenwares and flamewares (such as Corningware), which can be placed on a range or moved from a freezer to a hot oven without shattering from the abrupt temperature change. These wares are manufactured according to special formulas, usually including only small amounts of clay and quartz.

The reason for reducing these materials is that discontinuities in the expansion behavior of SiO_2—especially quartz and cristobalite—lead to stresses that can cause thermal shock breakage. The discontinuities of quartz (the alpha-beta transition) are above normal oven cooking temperatures, so the major problem in ovenware cracking is cristobalite, which undergoes a transition at 200–270°C. Thus materials that introduce quartz or induce formation of cristobalite in the body should be avoided if a ware is to resist thermal shock. The chemical formulas for such wares usually contain large amounts of cordierite (a magnesium aluminosilicate) or lithium minerals (e.g., spodumene), because these minerals have extremely low coefficients of thermal expansion (table 4.8; also Lawrence and West 1982, chap. 15). Another mineral com-

Table 4.8   Coefficients of Thermal Expansion of Some Ceramic Materials

Material	Coefficient of Expansion $\times 10^{-7}$
Alumina	81
Mullite	45
Silicon carbide	47
Electrical porcelain	60
Cordierite bodies	30
Steatite bodies	70
Dolomite bricks	110

Source: After Grimshaw 1971, table XII-X.

monly added to some ceramic manufactures to reduce expansion is steatite or talc (a hydrated magnesium silicate).

Although past and present nonindustrial village pottery may not be able to withstand such dramatic temperature transitions as modern wares—moving from freezer to hot oven—one of the fundamental uses of these vessels has always been cooking. Such usage often entails placing vessels directly on or in a fire with some confidence that they will not break. These traditional terra-cotta and earthenware pots typically are able to withstand this thermal shocking not because of their specially engineered chemical compositions, but because they are low-fired, porous, and coarse in texture (cf. Coble 1958). Because they are low-fired, they do not attain a rigid, glassy structure and can expand and contract as necessary. Also, their loose, open texture allows whatever expansion does occur to be accommodated by the pore spaces (see sec. 12.4.2.3). Furthermore, the pores permit any cracking that may take place from extending too far. Finally, people who are accustomed to eating beans cooked in earthenware pots claim they prefer the taste, and a porous jar allows stored water to cool by evaporation. Thus not being high-fired to a glassy, homogeneous phase increases the overall serviceability of these low-fired, porous wares.

By contrast, the object of commercial ceramic manufacture is to fire a clay to a temperature high enough to mature body and glazes and decrease porosity. Porosity is often reduced to 2%–3% or less in the bisque stage, and for some bodies it is desirable to have it less than 1% (table 4.9). Simultaneously, reducing the time and temperature of firing to a minimum saves fuel costs. Thus porosity is an important variable in determining the optimum firing range of a commercial clay body—that temperature interval in which both the curve of decreasing porosity and increasing firing shrinkage can be seen to level off (see Norton 1970, figs. 16.5, 16.6).

Aside from these and related considerations of the merits of porosity, what is considered a defect in a fired vessel is relatively constant regardless of firing technology or use (see McNabb and Duncan 1967). While most of the bonfire-fired terra-cottas or earthenwares common in prehistory would be considered underfired by the standards of the contemporary ceramics industry, owing to their inhomogeneous composition and porosity, they are suitable for their intended uses. One defect that occurred relatively infrequently is overfiring. Overfiring (to too high a temperature or for too long) can lead to excessive

Table 4.9   Porosity of Some Fired Ceramic Products

Product	Porosity (by volume %)
Stoneware	0.5–2.0
Hard porcelain bisque	3–9
Semiporcelain bisque	13–23
Chinaware bisque	2–11
Earthenware bodies	20–25
Tiles	3–18
Building bricks	10–35
Porous fireclay bricks	up to 60
Saggars	10–40

Source: After Grimshaw 1971, table XII-XVII.

melting, deformation, bloating, and a particular type of black coring, not the same as the carbon cores common in low-fired wares (see fig. 4.3 and sec. 11.2.1). Rather, in highly carbonaceous clays, some carbon may remain in the body even at extreme temperatures; when the glassy melt closes the exterior pores, any gases produced by this carbon, such as CO_2, are prevented from escaping. They then cause bloating and darken the body.

Cracking, the initial stage of failure or strain in a body, may originate from stresses during forming and drying, including preferred orientation, excessively rapid drying, differential shrinkage, and warping (see sec. 3.3). The cracks and strains may be invisible until the vessel is fired, then they may expand as the body shrinks farther or new cracks may begin to form (see fig. 3.6), causing breakage or final failure of the clay body. Dunting is a particular defect that results when too rapid cooling creates stresses as the constituents of the body contract at different rates.

4.3.3 Some Considerations of Firing Technology

A major objective in studying ancient pottery from a technological viewpoint is to understand firing technology. Many times these studies take the perspective of modern commercial ceramic standards and conditions as a basis for comprehending and evaluating the variables involved. Yet the conditions of much prehistoric, non-kiln-fired pottery manufacture are not directly parallel to those of modern industry.

In some senses it may be fair to say that a clay is a clay; that is, the behavior of a kaolinite clay mineral is the same whether the context is a village in Iraq in 6000 B.C. or a scientific laboratory in the twentieth century. The conditions for observing its behavior are very different, however. This point may be illustrated by considering, for example, the validity of comparative tests between a vessel of a "natural" clay containing a kaolinite component, formed by hand into a jar and fired in an open bonfire, and a test bar of a standard kaolinite clay mineral mixed with a measured amount of quartz of known purity and particle size and fired under regulated rates of heating in a controlled atmosphere.

The literature on clay mineralogy and ceramic engineering can provide a good deal of general theoretical and background information about the behavior of specific clay minerals under controlled conditions and can give an idea of the range of reactions that may be taking place in different situations. It cannot, however, always tell specifically what occurred in prehistoric firings, because for much of prehistory the parameters of resource selection, forming, firing, and distribution are largely unknown and may be approached only through cautious inference. Thus, while it is undeniably useful to understand the behavior of clays under regulated laboratory conditions of time, temperature, and atmosphere, these conditions rarely simulate the variable characteristics of nonindustrial pottery manufacture. For hand-built non-kiln-fired village pottery the conditions of production and the objectives of the entire operation may be very different from those of contemporary manufactures.

This caveat has several important ramifications. One is that the thermal and thermochemical behavior of clays or clay mixtures in a testing laboratory is described with respect to equilibrium conditions. That is, the slow rate of heating and the extended period of holding the materials at a specified temperature—sometimes for one hundred or even two hundred hours—usually allows completion of all mineral and chemical alterations or reactions occurring within the constituents of that system at that temperature. No further changes occur with time unless the conditions are changed—for example, if the temperature is raised. One important consequence of this equilibrium is that the thermal gradient within the material is eliminated during firing, as are the differences in degree of change between inner and outer portions of the final product. What is more important is that many of the quartz inversions (except the alpha-beta inversion), and other changes are very sluggish reactions that require long periods of sustained heat to occur to any significant degree.

In the time variable of firing and in the degree to which thermal changes will take place, most prehistoric pottery is therefore distinctly not comparable with testing conditions or even with commercial or art ceramics (see Chu 1968, 830). Studio or art pottery may be heated at a rate of 200°C per hour and held for twelve hours at the soaking temperature, but a real issue in the relationship of time and temperature is in the cost of fuel. It has been found commercially (Norton and Hodgdon 1931, cited in Norton 1970, 269–70) that increasing the firing time by a factor of ten permits a reduction of temperature to achieve maturity by 23°C. In fact, a fast rate of heating of 180°C/hr^{-1} and a holding time of one hour (maximum temperature not specified) permits development of satisfactory mechanical properties (Norton 1970, 270). Throughout much of prehistory and even in modern times, potters firing their wares in bonfires have heated them only a fraction as long as in commercial firings. Thus, it is debatable whether many of the changes, both desirable and undesirable, known to occur in laboratory ceramic bodies at equilibrium also take place in bonfire-fired terra-cottas.

Some of the changes in clay minerals—particularly those occurring at middle temperature ranges, such as structural changes resulting from loss of lattice water—have been found to be reversible or incomplete (Grim and Bradley 1948). This reversibility may exist if, after initial firing and cooling, the ceramic is held in a furnace at 200°C for fifty hours, for example. These are not the conditions under which the clays of ancient potsherds would be expected to regain their lattice structure and plasticity, however. Nonetheless, because much ancient pottery was not kiln fired for many hours (and thus did not undergo complete structural alteration through equilibrium) and because in most cases it was buried where there was some water percolation, the structural changes of firing may be reversible. This is important because it means the sherds can be tested by certain kinds of analysis, such as X-ray diffraction, that will identify the original clay mineral or minerals (Kingery 1974).

Some discrepancy in the relations of time and temperature thus can be seen to exist between the conditions of laboratory experimentation and commercial or craft pottery firing. This gap is still wider when it comes to comparing either of these firing conditions with those of nonkiln or bonfire firings. Although kilns evolved in the Old World, perhaps as early as the seventh millennium B.C., they were not widely used until much later; and in many areas of the Old World, in virtually all areas of the New World throughout prehistory, and in many areas of the world today, pottery has been successfully fired without kilns (see sec. 5.4).

Kilns allow control of the firing temperature, the rate of heating, and the atmosphere of firing, and they protect the vessels from contact with fuel, wind, and moisture. Pottery fired in the open or even in some simple kilns is frequently unevenly fired, showing fireclouds or other blemishes as evidence of contact with fuel, overfiring (warping, vitrified spots, color changes) because gusts of wind fanned the fire, or underfiring because of uneven distribution of fuel. Firings without kilns typically have a rapid and usually poorly controlled heating rate to a point determined by such necessarily imprecise cues as the color of the flame, the glow of the pots, the amount or color of the smoke, or even the amount of fuel available. Once the maximum temperature is reached, it is rarely held very long, if at all; more commonly no more fuel is added and the temperature begins to drop rapidly.

Not only are the time and temperature of bonfire firings poorly controlled, but so is the atmosphere. Instead of achieving fully oxidizing or reducing conditions, the atmosphere is more likely to fluctuate during firing. Thus variations may be expected as fresh fuel is added and consumed, as smoke is produced, as gases are released from the fuel and the pottery itself, and as wind gusts touch the fire, resulting in incomplete oxidation or reduction. At the end of the firing there may be intentional oxidation, caused, for example, by lifting ash or fuel residue to allow air to reach the pots, or intentional reduction, as from smothering the fire with dung or sawdust to blacken or smudge the surface.

In sum, whereas industrial or commercial firings or tests involve controlled parameters of temperature and atmosphere and long periods of soaking to approach equilibrium between components of the ceramic body, bonfire firings fall far short of such conditions. A temperature gradient exists in the clay between the surfaces and the core and, not inconceivably, from one side of the vessel to another. This should be borne in mind in interpreting observations on color, hardness, and other physical and mechanical properties of archaeological pottery collections (see chap. 12). The standards and values of the contemporary ceramic industry, while useful, should not be uncritically regarded as absolutes by anthropologists and archaeologists. The ethnographic record is full of incidents or anecdotes of people in nonindustrialized or non-urban areas who prefer water or stews from low-fired porous vessels; cooks who move pots from cool, damp earthen floors to the center of hot fires; potters who uncover their open-air-fired pottery to brisk breezes only minutes after the flames die down. These preferences and practices are unfamiliar to modern ceramists, but they do not imply that such makers or users are ignorant or incompetent. Rather, they represent a specific adaptive logic in which particular resources must meet particular needs. Scientists studying these pots and potters cannot overlook this logic, for it constitutes the entire context and rationale for investigating the relation between pottery and society.

4.4 References

Anseau, Deletter, and Cambier 1981
Arayaphong, McLaren, and Phelps 1984
Borremans and Shaak 1986
Brody 1979
Burke 1985
Burton 1906
Butterworth 1956
Cardew 1969
Chandler 1981
Chu 1968
Coble 1958
Crandall and Ging 1955
Davidge and Tappin 1967
Grim 1962, 1968
Grim and Bradley 1948
Grim and Kulbicki 1961
Grim and Rowland 1942
Grimshaw 1971
Hamer 1975
Hasselman 1969
Hodges 1976
Johnson 1976
Johnson, Pask, and Moya 1982
Kennard and Williamson 1971
Kingery 1955, 1974
Kingery, Bowen, and Uhlmann 1976
Klemptner and Johnson 1986
Laird and Worcester 1956
Lawrence and West 1982
Lowenstein 1986
McNabb and Duncan 1967
Maniatis et al. 1983
Marquis 1952
Medley 1976
Nelson 1984
Neumann 1977
Norton 1952, 1970
Norton and Hodgdon 1931
Rhodes 1973
Robinson 1968a
Rye 1976
Schramm and Hall 1936
Shepard 1948a, 1976
Staehelin 1965
Starkey 1977
Tite and Maniatis 1975b
Wahl 1965
Weyl 1941

PART 3

Pottery Manufacture and Use

A pot in order to be good should be a genuine expression of life. It implies sincerity on the part of the potter and truth in the conception and execution of the work.

B. Leach, *A Potter's Book*

Pottery Manufacturing Technology: An Ethnographic Overview   5

Pottery can be studied from a variety of viewpoints, anthropological and archaeological, technological and behavioral. Regardless of the questions asked or the analytical approaches employed, however, one should remember that pottery serves as both a utilitarian good and an economic livelihood and must be understood within its social and economic context, whether past or present. This chapter surveys the techniques and tools of traditional pottery manufacture as known through the ethnographic record.

5.1 Ethnographic Pottery Studies

Ceramic objects have served as utensils and containers in day-to-day activities for millennia, and in many parts of the world pottery water jars and cooking pots continue to be made and used in traditional ways. The number of communities in which pottery manufacture continues to flourish within the technological system is dwindling, however, as a consequence of the availability of durable metal and plastic containers. The popularity of these goods has reduced the demand for traditional pottery and the children of potters see little future in pottery making, so the craft is rapidly disappearing in many areas. As potters in Chalkis, Greece, reportedly commented, "The Nylon is eating us" (Matson 1973, 119).

It is fortunate that hundreds of accounts of pottery making document the manufacture and use of ceramic materials around the world. Although some are little more than commentaries on an intriguing bit of artisanship or notations on household goods, many are significant studies of the relation between technology and craft production as part of the broader social fabric.

Many ceramic studies owe their existence to the extensive ethnographic research carried out by cultural anthropologists in the twentieth century. A large number of detailed observations, however, come from accounts by explorers, military and religious personnel, colonial administrators, or even potters themselves who worked in non-Western societies, dating back to the mid-nineteenth century and in some cases considerably earlier. These studies and accounts (e.g., Picolpasso 1934; Brongniart 1844; Staehelin 1965; Bushell 1910) establish the corpus of data on pottery making in the period referred to as the "ethnographic present," and "modern potters" as used below refers to this broadly defined period.

The ethnographic present serves as a baseline against which information on pottery making in prehistoric times is customarily interpreted, a procedure anthropologists and archaeologists call ethnographic analogy. A major premise of archaeological research is that what is known about the past, in terms of both human behavior and the operations of cultural systems, is achieved by analogy with behaviors and systems in the present (see Gould and Watson 1982). While this is not the only avenue to interpreting archaeological remains, and though there are probably behaviors in the past and present that have no direct analogue, nonetheless ethnographic analogy is a fundamental part of interpretation and reasoning in all aspects of archaeology, including pottery studies.

Inextricably linked to analogical arguments in archaeology are the objectives and techniques of two related research endeavors: experimental archaeology and ethnoarchaeology. While it is not necessary to elaborate to any degree on either of these (see Donnan and Clewlow 1974; Gould 1978; Kramer 1979), it is important to note that both experimental archaeology and ethnoarchaeology are particularly important in ceramic studies; indeed, what may be the first ethnoarchaeological monograph was based on pottery (Thompson 1958). Experimental archaeology, as the rubric implies, involves the experimental manipulation of raw materials and tools of a particular archaeological context to try to replicate the conditions of their use or production or both. The procedures of ceramic ecology, with the collection and experimental testing of clays (sec. 10.2.3), can be included within this category. Ethnoarchaeology is the more encompassing term for the body of method, theory, and data underlying such analogical and experimental comparisons as archaeologists study the material culture of living peoples. Particularly interesting is the relation of manufacture and use of pots to the formation of archaeological sites (sec. 9.3; see also Nicholson and Patterson 1985a,b) and socioeconomic arrangements for producing and distributing pottery (chap. 6).

Because so many of the reconstructions of prehistory—especially chronological and intersite relationships—are based on ceramic data, this wide range of ethnoarchaeological concerns allows archaeologists to confront two major methodological issues that are essential to these interpretations but have not been adequately addressed. One is the way pottery moves from the context of use (Schiffer's [1976] "systemic context") to the archaeological record; the other concerns the nature and explanation of variability in prehistoric ceramics.

A summary of the full range of practices involved in all steps of pottery manufacture known in the ethnographic record is not possible here. Nonetheless, sampling the variety in these procedures will help establish a context for envisioning similar behavior in antiquity. This broad subject can be broken down into three areas: obtaining and preparing resources; forming, finishing, and decorating pottery vessels; and drying and firing.

5.2   Obtaining and Preparing Resources

5.2.1   Tools and Techniques

The most important resource in pottery manufacture is clay for the vessel body. In many areas large deposits of suitable clay are a prime determinant of where potters settle (see Nicklin 1979). Additional important resources are raw materials for "temper" (see sec. 14.1) as well as clays, pigments, and other substances used in slips, paints, or glazes. Finally, fuel for firing is critical to pottery manufacture (see secs. 5.4 and 6.1.3).

These materials may be obtained in a number of ways. Clay sources are sometimes open to all and widely shared, as among the Huichol (Weigand 1969, 35). In other areas individual potters, workshops, families, or communities may "own" the rights to mine or sell clay. At Bailén, Spain, for example, potting factories own specific deposits, and these are inherited through families along with the business (Curtis 1962, 491). Elsewhere potters may exploit "secret" locations that are not divulged to outsiders or competitors, as in Bangkok, Thailand (Graham 1922, 15) and in Izamal, Yucatán, Mexico (Thompson 1958, 66, citing Gaumer). Potters may use clay from a single source or employ different sources interchangeably (Fontana et al. 1962, 55; Weigand 1969, 35). The clay may be mined by the individual potter (or a relative or co-worker) as needed for each batch of pottery; several families may work cooperatively so it becomes a social occasion, as among the potters of Santa Clara Pueblo, New Mexico (LeFree 1975, 7–10); or mining may be carried out by individuals with no family ties to the potters, as in Deir el-Gharbi, Egypt (Nicholson and Patterson 1985b, 224–25).

The act of obtaining clay, or getting special kinds of clay, is often the focus of taboos or rituals. Among the Azera of Morobe Province, Papua New Guinea, for example (May and Tuckson 1982, 136), only married women who have not yet had children can gather clay, and then only at certain times. They must wear traditional dress while gathering clay, and they cannot smoke, chew betel, or speak pidgin; in addition, outsiders are forbidden to witness the activity. Among the Kwoma, in the Sepik River area of New Guinea, "A certain connection seems to exist between good blood, good health, good potter's clay (as long as it is wet), the human ability for procreation, the successful growing of yam tubers, and the religious meaning of sago starch on the one hand, and bad blood, sickness, common ground unsuitable for pottery work, etc. on the other hand" (May and Tuckson 1982, 221, citing Kaufman).

In general, large reserves of clay are not kept on hand except in large potting industries (see also Balfet 1965, 164): it is often difficult to store clay in quantity and protect it from rain or contamination. In hot, dry areas of Pakistan, potters may store prepared clay-temper mixtures for short periods in cool underground pits, which are advantageous under variable weather conditions or during especially hot times of the year (Rye and Evans 1976, 40, 45).

How far potters will travel to obtain their resources is highly variable. Arnold (1980, 149, 1985, 39–49) surveyed the ethnographic literature to quantify the areas within which potters acquire their clays, tempers, slips, and pigments and found interesting differences in distances traveled. In the 110 cases for which he found data on clay gathering, the distance from potting location to clay source varied from less than 1 km to 50 km. Of 31 cases detailing temper procurement, the range was from less than 1 km to 24 km; for slips and paints the distance ranged up to 800 km. He found that slips and paints were often acquired by trade rather than mined by the potters; since these materials are used in significantly smaller quantities than are clays and tempers, least-cost principles are less likely to be determinative. The general emphasis is on obtaining primary resources close to the working area, however, and the distance most frequently traveled for both clays and tempers is less than 1 km from the settlement (table 5.1). Arnold (1980, 149) labeled this the "preferred territory of exploitation." Because approximately 85% of the tabulated resources are obtained within 7 km of the potters' living or working areas, Arnold suggests this range as the resource area or catchment area for procuring their primary resources.

It is difficult to interpret these distance data, however, because no clear causal relationship can be reliably inferred between resource location and potting location (see Nicklin 1979, 442–43). Do potters establish themselves within a 5–7 km radius of resources? Or conversely, does a given settlement of potters choose to exploit only clays within a 5–7 km radius to achieve least cost? Can the location of suitable clays be used to predict the location of potters, or is the existence of potters a reliable predictor of the presence of suitable potting clays? Clearly, for prediction these relationships are oversimplified, and many other factors are involved: scale of production (see van der Leeuw 1977, 70–71), bulk and value of the goods produced, location of the market for the products (see sec. 6.3), and the presence of suitable fuel.

The locations of resources and of workshops may be most directly related at

Table 5.1 Distances between Potters and Their Clay, Temper, and Slip and Paint Resources

Distance (km)	Clay Source[a]	Temper Source[b]	Slip and Paint Sources[c]
<1	25	14	—
1–2	35	5	—
2–3	12	1	4[d]
3–5	11	6	6
5–10	15	4	3
10–15	3	—	4
15–25	7	1	2
25–50	2	—	6
>50	—	—	11
Totals	110	31	36

[a]From Arnold 1985, table 2.1. Some rounding of numbers and grouping error has resulted in minor distortions of his raw data.
[b]From Arnold 1985, table 2.2.
[c]From Arnold 1985, table 2.3.
[d]Three cases are given as distances ranging up to 2.5 km.

Figure 5.1 A brickyard in highland Guatemala. The plastic clay soils of the valley are excavated and mixed with water, then shaped in rectangular wooden molds to form bricks, which can be seen drying under cover in the foreground and to the right. In the background are the kiln and adjacent storage area.

the extremes of manufacturing scale or intensity (see sec. 6.2.2.1) and variable at intermediate levels. Potters in a large-scale industry may act on least-cost principles and establish manufacturing centers close to their resources so as to save time and labor in procurement and processing as well as to ensure a large supply of clays of known quality and performance. Clay may literally be obtained from the potter's own backyard: this is true of the utility pottery industry of Bailén, Spain (Curtis 1962, 491) and is especially common in the manufacture of heavy clay products such as bricks and roof tiles (fig. 5.1). Similarly, the *vendemaroi*, itinerant jar makers of Thrapsano, Crete, locate their workshops in fields where the three essential materials for pottery making—clay, fuel, and water—can be easily acquired (Voyatzoglou 1974, 18).

At the opposite end of the production scale, where pottery making is sporadic, pursued reluctantly when an accident necessitates replacing a water jar or cooking pot, potters may also be inclined to use whatever clay is handy rather than making a considerable effort to secure clays from a greater distance. For example, Fulani potters in Bé, North Cameroon, obtain clay from a pit only fifteen minutes' walk from the village (David and Hennig 1972, 5).

At intermediate scales of production the distance potters travel to obtain clays varies considerably. The Diola of southern Senegal, West Africa, manufacture pottery during the two or three months following their harvest season and obtain clay slightly more than 1.5 km from their compounds (Linares de Sapir 1969, 3). Potters travel as much as 10 or 15 miles for clay in parts of Nigeria (Nicklin 1979, 441, 445). At Santa Clara Pueblo, New Mexico, potters gather clay from pits between 3 and 4.5 miles from the pueblo, but the white kaolin for their paint is obtained from an undivulged source 100 miles distant (LeFree 1975, 7, 22). Similarly, the aromatic slip clay used by potters in Tonalá, Mexico, comes from 100 miles away (Díaz 1966, 141). In Melanesia the Amphlett Islanders obtain clay twice a year by canoe trips, the canoes returning from Fergusson Island laden with a ton or more of special clay used in making large, lightweight jars (Malinowski 1922, 283–84; Lauer 1970, 166). Among the Shipibo-Conibo of Peru, clays and other resources are also obtained by canoe, often involving repeated trips over minimum distances of 365 km up- or downriver; within these ranges, 84% of the potters' procurement decisions conform to least-effort expectations of travel distances (DeBoer 1984, 542–46).

Clays can sometimes be used in their natural state as dug from the ground, without modification. More typically, however, the clay has to be processed to make it suitable for use, and this usually requires either or both of two procedures: removing material from the clay or adding material to it.

Inclusions often must be removed from relatively coarse surface clays; this may simply entail picking foreign matter—rootlets, leaves, pebbles, and so forth—out of the clay by hand. The procedure may be considerably more complex, however, and involve drying the clay, then crushing, grinding, and winnowing or sieving it. Sieving may be done with baskets, or sieves may be constructed of palm ribs, rawhide punched with holes, perforated sheet metal, screens, or cloth. Levigation (mixing the clay with water and allowing the coarser particles to wash and settle out of the suspension) is usually done in relatively large, mass production industries; one enormous levigation tank used in the production of Arretine ware had a capacity of ten thousand gallons (see Peacock 1982, 54, 122). It is more common to find smaller containers for simply soaking and stirring clays and then evaporating, decanting, or screening them to eliminate impurities; these occur widely with smaller scales of production, as in Bailén, Spain (Curtis 1962, 491–92) or Chalkis, Greece (Matson 1973, 124–25). These cleaning procedures may be used with clays that are relatively coarse, stiff, and lean in their handling characteristics, or with those that contain quantities of organic matter or large fragments of minerals that can damage clay products under certain firing conditions (e.g., calcite or mica).

Other clays, especially those that are extremely fine textured and sticky, must have modifiers added to make them acceptable for pottery making. These added substances are commonly referred to by archaeologists as temper (also known as inclusions, aplastics, nonplastics, additives, modifiers, filler, aggregate, and grog; see sec. 14.1). Temper is considered highly (indeed probably excessively) important in archaeological studies, because the materials added are often distinctive of particular culture and time periods and are therefore useful in dating sites and tracing trade relationships. Among the most common additions are sand (quartz sand or volcanic sand), and crushed rock, shell, and potsherds. A seemingly limitless range of other modifying materials is known ethnographically and archaeologically, however: dung from a variety of animals (rabbit, donkey, horse, cattle; see London 1981);

sponge spicules (in Amazonian South America; Linné 1957, 156); animal blood (in arctic North America; Stimmell and Stromberg 1986, 248); and a variety of plant materials including fibers, silica, ash, cattail fuzz (Matson 1974b, 346), chaff from cultivated grains such as rice or wheat, and Spanish moss (*Tillandsia usneoides*) in some early southeastern United States pottery (Simpkins and Allard 1986). Clay itself may be a temper, since it is common for potters to mix clays of different colors and properties; this is known, for example, among the Shipibo-Conibo of Peru (DeBoer and Lathrap 1979), potters of old Cairo, Egypt (Matson 1975a, 133), Thrapsano, Crete (Voyatzoglou 1974), and widely throughout central Mexico, for example in Tzintzuntzan (Foster 1948a, 79–101; 1967, 41), Acatlán (Lackey 1981, 50), and Tonalá (Díaz 1966, 142).

Another substance used to modify clays' properties is salt (NaCl). Salt or salt water is often added to calcareous clays or clays tempered with calcareous materials (calcite or shell) in Pakistan (Rye and Evans 1976, 49, 91), Melanesia (Rye 1976), and the Near East (Matson 1971, 66–67). Salt appears to counteract the tendency of calcite to spall the surfaces of low-fired pottery (see sec. 4.2.3.3; Klemptner and Johnson 1986). It also changes the surface color to what may be a more desirable light or white color (Brooks et al. 1974, 52).

After the clay or clay-temper body has been made plastic by adding water, it is usually systematically manipulated, either by wedging, kneading with the hands, or foot treading (fig. 5.2). This arduous activity serves several purposes. It eliminates air pockets from the clay; it assures a uniform, homogeneous distribution of moisture and inclusions by locating and eliminating lumps (of clay or foreign matter) and by mixing wetter and drier portions of the mass; and it increases workability by ensuring that all clay particles are wet. Wedging is done by repeatedly slicing through the clay mass with a fine wire and recombining the segments or by slamming the clay onto a smooth, hard surface. Kneading involves movements similar to those used with bread dough: alternately pushing the mass with the heel of the hand and turning or folding it to present a new section. Foot trampling or treading is usually used to prepare extremely large batches of clay. In this process the clay is spread on a clean floor or in a pit and systematically trod, often by a young apprentice in the workshop. In modern factory operations, a pug mill or deairing pug mill (operating with the clay in a vacuum) accomplishes these tasks.

Although today's craft and industrial potters know that aging or souring a wet clay mass for a month or more improves its workability, there is little mention of systematic aging in the ethnographic literature except for overnight storage. Papago potters of Arizona, however, sometimes store their clay over the winter (Fontana et al. 1962, 57), and potters in Chamula, Mexico, may age clay as long as a year; pots of unaged clay are said to be inferior (Howry 1976, 79). Aging enhances workability by allowing the water to permeate the mass fully and wet the surfaces of each clay particle, thereby increasing plasticity. This process may be augmented by bacterial action or by adding small amounts of acidic substances.

Figure 5.2 Foot trampling clay in Nabuel, Tunisia. Photographed by Robert H. Johnston, reprinted from *Pots and Potters: Current Approaches in Ceramic Archaeology*, edited by Prudence M. Rice (Monograph 24, Institute of Archaeology, University of California, Los Angeles, 1985).

5.2.2 Ethnographic Examples

The procurement and preparation activities of potters vary irregularly along a continuum from very simple to highly complex, according to the time and effort devoted to cleaning the clay and modifying its properties. A number of points along this continuum can be illustrated.

The Kalinga potters of northern Luzon in the Philippines, for instance, expend little effort in obtaining and modifying clay before making their water jars and pots for cooking rice or meat (Longacre 1981, 54):

> All potters exploit the same clay source located just below the school. The clay contains an abundance of sand as a natural inclusion and no additional temper is added. . . . The clay requires no sifting or cleaning.
>
> The clay (*soka*) is carried in a basket to the vicinity of the potter's house. There the clay is pounded with a pestle (*salsal*) on a flat rock (*salsallan*). Small amounts of water are added during this process until the desired consistency is obtained (*tiplyon*). The potter then shapes a lump of the plastic clay into a truncated cone-shaped slab (*pokol*).

At this point the potter is ready to begin forming a pot.

Only slightly more attention is given to clay preparation by the potters of San Luis Jilotepeque, in the eastern highlands of Guatemala (Reina and Hill 1978, 165):

> Clays and pigment for painting are all found on a nearby cattle ranch. Although the clay for the vessels is free, the pigment . . . and the slip

clay . . . must be purchased. . . . After the potter gathers the clay, she carries it in net bags back to her home, where it is ground on a special deep metate [grinding stone] into a fine powder. This powder is placed in a pot with water and left to sit for five or six hours. The clay is then ready to be wedged on a workboard. No tempering material is added.

The wedged clay is then ready for making jars, basins, and pitchers.

Among the Ibibio of southeastern Nigeria, potters do little to clean or refine the clay, but they do add temper (Nicklin 1981b, 173):

Clay, *aduang*, is dug from pits and carried back by headload to the potter's home, which is usually within easy walking distance. . . . Clay from wet pits is allowed to drain and dry in a heap by the pit before being conveyed home. In the Eastern Nsit area of Etinan L.G.A. not all pottery-making extended families own clay pits, and those that are in this situation have to pay rent to the owners. In other places the potters have to buy their raw material from those who own the pits and dig it for sale.

Back at home the clay is mixed with substances called *nsiong* which improve the working qualities of the clay body, and reduce the incidence of firing breakage. Commonly a pounded potsherd grog is used, or a sandy filler obtained from decayed housewalls, or a combination of these. After sieving the additives with the aid of a conical basket, *nkitan*, they are thoroughly mixed with the clay, using a wooden pestle of the type used for pounding boiled yam, and also by trampling underfoot. This process is called *udige aduang*, and is maintained until the correct consistency, *aduang ndibiot*, of the clay body is achieved.

The Shipibo-Conibo of eastern Peru similarly expend comparatively little effort in cleaning their clays, but they manufacture jars and bowls from a complex series of "recipes" prescribing specific mixtures of three clays (black, red, and white) and three tempers (*caraipé* or plant silica, ground sherds, and sometimes wood ash) (DeBoer and Lathrap 1979, 110–11, 116–17):

The alluvial clays utilized in ceramic manufacture are usually obtained locally—within a few kilometers of the potter's village. At the clay bed, the clay is hand cleaned of large-sized vegetal and stone inclusions and is packed into loaves the size of volleyballs. The clay is transported back to the village and stored in this form.

The ratio of clay to temper volume ranges consistently between 2 and 3; however, the ways in which different clays and tempers are mixed depends on the kind of vessel to be made. Non-cooking ware—including jars, beer mugs, food bowls, and *shrania*—is ideally made from a mixture of equal parts of white and red clay tempered with two parts crushed sherd to one part *caraipé*. Cooking ware follows a more complicated recipe. In *ollas*, black clay tempered with two parts *caraipé* to one part crushed sherd is ideally used for the base and body of the vessel, while the neck is made from red clay tempered with reversed proportions of *caraipé* and sherd. These ideal rules or recipes for combining clays and tempers, however, are not always actualized.

The Seri, a group of nonagricultural people of coastal northwestern Mexico, exercise considerable care in preparing materials for pottery making. The initial steps for manufacture of a small jar by a potter named Maria have been described (Bowen and Moser 1968, 92–95):

> Either men or women will gather clay. On this occasion, Maria's husband brought . . . only slightly more than enough for the one vessel, which is the traditional custom.
>
> . . . The clay was placed in [a large sea] turtle shell and was crushed and ground with the mano [hand grinding stone]. When some of the clay had been pulverized she placed it in a shallow enameled metal bowl and winnowed the finer powder onto a cloth spread in front of her, a process called *koospX*. Then she replaced the heavier chunks remaining in the bowl back into the turtle shell and continued grinding.
>
> Maria next began grinding the rabbit dung which was to be the sole tempering agent for this clay. The dung of both jackrabbit and cottontail is used today, and in the past horse manure was sometimes added. . . . She proceeded to winnow the dung just as she had the clay. . . . [Clay and dung were then combined in the turtle shell until Maria] felt the mixture contained the correct proportion of each (about three parts clay to one part dung). . . .
>
> She soon began adding water to the clay and dung mixture. The Seri say that fresh water is always used because the salt in sea water would cause the pot to crumble. . . . Then she kneaded the mixture much as one kneads bread dough, in order to work the water into the clay. . . .
>
> Maria made two or three ropes of clay to test its coiling properties. At this stage in the manufacture the potter normally lets the mixture sit overnight to allow the water to soak into all of the clay particles.

Although the Seri (and many other potters) combine the temper with the dry clay and then add water to make the mixture plastic, many other potters add temper to wet clay, which may allow finer control of texture and plasticity. The potters of Chinautla, Guatemala, proceed in this manner (Reina and Hill 1978, 32–33):

> The three clays used in Chinautla are all fine-grained with inclusions of mica and moderate amounts of extremely fine sand. All are highly plastic and remarkably free of extraneous materials. . . .
>
> These clays are in privately owned deposits, so potters must purchase from the owners, who hire laborers to mine the clays. This is a hazardous occupation, especially in the white clay mine, where excavations reach a depth of forty-eight feet and cave-ins have caused several deaths. Because the clay beds in this mountainous region are accessible only by rugged footpaths, the clay must be taken home in baskets or in nets supported by tumplines. Thus a great amount of time and energy is expended obtaining clay. . . .
>
> The lumps of raw clay are stored on the hard-packed earth floor within the dark interior of the potter's house. . . . Without being aged, the clay lumps are broken down with a wooden mallet and left to dry through the day. Toward evening, the clay is gathered in an old

tinajera [a very large storage jar] and covered with water. By sunrise the next day, it has become a heavy workable mass.

Every potter wedges her own clay. This is a strenuous task. . . . The potter begins by taking several handfuls of the wet, sticky clay from the *tinajera;* she then places the clay on a broad, heavy, smooth board . . . well coated with an extremely fine pumice . . .; this prevents the wet clay from sticking to the board. If the clay is still too wet to work, dry powdered clay is added to hasten drying without sacrificing the clay's plasticity. Pumice . . . is used as temper. . . .

In general . . . eight to twelve pounds [of clay] are wedged at a time. The amount of pumice temper worked into the clay seldom exceeds 10 percent of the clay's weight. During the wedging, foreign matter—such as bits of wood, rootlets, pebbles, or vegetable material—is carefully searched out and removed. As successive amounts of clay are prepared, each is set out of the drying rays of the sun and covered with banana leaves, until a supply of wedged clay sufficient for the day's work has been accumulated.

In Pakistan, a variety of combinations of clay-preparation techniques and foot treading are employed. In Kharmathu (Rye and Evans 1976, 39–40), approximately 300 kg of clay is dug every three to four days by the potters at a deposit 5 km from the workshop and brought back by donkey. The clay is spread out in the courtyard to dry, large lumps are crushed with a shovel, and then the material is passed through a sheet-metal sieve with apertures about 1 cm in diameter. The clay body is prepared in a trough 15 cm deep, 1.7 m long, and 1 m wide. The trough is filled with dried clay, then enough water is added to make the clay plastic. After about fifteen minutes, salt is sprinkled over the clay and allowed to become moist, but it is not fully dissolved. Following this, a thick layer of sieved sand is spread over the clay and the potter treads the mixture, adding more sand as needed. After a short while, lumps of 7–8 kg of clay are removed and hand kneaded with more sand. The clay is then ready for use; portions that are not immediately worked on the wheels are stored in underground pits.

At Multan, Pakistan (Rye and Evans 1976, 90–91), a slightly different procedure is followed. Dried and crushed clay is weighed, then a specific quantity is spread on the ground in "a flat hollow conical pile," with water added to the central depression. The clay is left to absorb the water, and portions from the edges are moved to the center to be moistened. After a day, a weighed amount (usually 20% by weight) of sand is added to the wet clay and mixed by treading. The clay mass is kneaded and turned three times, each time for one and a half hours, then stored under wet sacking in a shady area of the workshop. For certain kinds of vessels, ½% to 1% of salt is added to the water mixed with the clay before the addition of sand.

One of the most elaborate systems of preparing clays is used in the manufacture of Chinese porcelains. According to an eighteenth-century description written by a master potter (Staehelin 1965, 22–26), the kaolin clay of Qimen, sixty miles northeast of the workshops of Jingdezhen in Jiangxi Province, was washed, crushed, and then rewashed several times. After cleaning it was strained through a sieve constructed of horsehair, then through a bag made of two thicknesses of silk. This purified clay was then formed into slabs that were air-dried before shipment and storage. It was apparently common for the clay workers in Qimen to adulterate the kaolin, however, so it was further washed and purified once it reached Jingdezhen.

5.3 Forming, Finishing, and Decorating

5.3.1 Forming: Tools and Techniques

The selection of resources and their combination into a workable mass is dictated in part by the shape or size of vessel intended and the method of forming it. Because many things can go wrong as a pot is being shaped, dried, and fired, a complex of beliefs, taboos, and rituals may surround potters and potting, especially where pottery is still used for cult objects or is important in ritual. Among the Huichol, for example, the water mixed with clay used to make a double-mouthed ceremonial vessel should come from the sacred caves where these vessels are frequently placed (Weigand 1969, 14). Huichol mothers also sometimes smear blood from the heart of a hummingbird on a young girl's wrist to enhance her skill at pottery making or at crafts in general (Weigand 1969, 31).

Among the Sepik River Kwoma in Papua New Guinea (May and Tuckson 1982, 218–20), where pottery cult objects are still used, clay is gathered only by fully initiated men and their wives; pots may be made only by married women who have borne two or three children or by men who have reached the third stage of initiation. Washing, loud conversation, wood chopping, sago cutting, and digging yams and taro are all forbidden during Kwoma pottery making; menstruating and pregnant women may not go near the clay, and neither sex may engage in intercourse. Among potters in the Chorotegan area of Costa Rica, women do not make pots during menstruation or for three months after giving birth (Stone 1950, 272). Pamunkey potters in Virginia do not like to have the process observed because they believe that if someone looks too hard at a pot in the making it will break (Stern 1951, 19).

Many techniques of constructing pots are known. These have been classified according to whether they are based on a single lump of clay or on successive additions, whether they are entirely manual or if tools are employed (Fewkes 1940, 1941), whether they are "primary" or "secondary" (Rye 1981), and whether or not rotational (centrifugal) force is employed in forming.

Six procedures, for the most part basic in vessel construction, are commonly identified: pinching and/or drawing, slab modeling, molding, casting, coiling, and throwing. A distinction is sometimes made between vessels that are "built" by hand (i.e., using pinching, drawing, modeling, or coiling) versus those that are thrown on a wheel, but for convenience all these techniques are grouped here as methods of constructing pottery. Frequently, several techniques are used in making a single vessel—what might be termed compound or composite forming methods. Compound manufacturing techniques are widespread, which makes it difficult to maintain a clear distinction between so-called primary and secondary procedures (Rye 1981, 62). In addition, in manufacturing a pot successive steps tend to obliterate evidence of earlier treatments. Thus, unless one has observed the actual forming, it can be a problem to specify the construction procedures, even from whole vessels. Rye (1981, 59–81; see also Balfet, Fauvet-Berthelot, and Monzon 1983, 57–67) notes the criteria by which most of the techniques discussed below can be identified on archaeological potsherds.

5.3.1.1 HAND BUILDING AND MOLDING

Pinching and drawing techniques are similar in that they manipulate a lump of clay into a vessel shape without adding more clay. Pinching consists of "opening" the lump of clay by inserting the thumb or fingers or both, then squeezing the clay between the thumb and fingers or between the fingers of both hands. Repeating this action around and over the entire lump thins and shapes it into the desired form. Pinching is often used for small, simple vessels that can be held in the hand or to form the bases of larger vessels that are built up by other methods.

Drawing is similar to pinching but is typically used on larger vessels and emphasizes vertical movement. A large lump of clay is placed on a support and opened by thrusting the thumbs, fingers, or fist into the center. The potter then simultaneously squeezes and pinches with an upward pulling or stretching movement to raise and thin the walls of the emerging vessel; a tool may be used to scrape the clay upward. Both pinching and drawing may be incorporated in an essentially equivalent technique sometimes called lump modeling.

In slab building (also called segmental modeling), a vessel is constructed from one or more slabs of clay that are rolled or patted flat and then joined into the desired shape. In modern craft pottery this technique is mainly used to create rectangular shapes, but it may also be used for cylinders or for building extremely large vessels. Morsel building (Fewkes 1940, 172; Stern 1951, 12–13), in which small lumps of clay are flattened and shaped then successively joined to build the vessel walls upward and around, is a variant of this method.

In molding or pressing, a section of clay, often preformed by patting or rolling into a "pancake," is pressed firmly into or over a prepared mold. Molds may be convex, with the clay applied on the exterior, or concave, with the clay fitted to the interior (fig. 5.3); they may form all (full molds) or part of the vessel body (most typically the base; see Reina and Hill 1978, 22); and they may be single units or made in two pieces (see Foster 1948b). Two-piece molds, in turn, may be used to form either the upper and lower halves of the vessel (as in Musazi, Pakistan; Rye and Evans 1976, 32–33, pls. 21–22), or to form two sides of a vessel, joined vertically, as in Los Pueblos, Mexico (Papousek 1981). Molds may be formed of plaster or fired clay; "ad hoc molds," however, are often created from large broken vessel fragments (as in fig. 5.3), baskets, or depressions in the ground.

To help the newly formed vessel separate from the mold, parting agents—powdered clay, ash, manure, pumice, or fine sand—are used to prevent sticking. It is somewhat easier to use concave molds, for during drying the clay will shrink away from the mold. With convex molds the potter must be careful to remove the mold before the formed clay shrinks too much (which will cause the piece to crack) but after the clay is firm enough not to slump of its

Figure 5.3 A woman belonging to a potter caste in Udaipur, Rajasthan, India, making griddles by paddling clay over the base of a water storage jar. The griddles are then dried in the top parts of jars that were damaged in firing or broken after primary use. Women in India do not use the wheel, and these griddles are virtually the only forms they make. Photograph by Carol Kramer.

own weight. The use of molds in vessel building is most clearly evidenced by the marks of seams at the juncture or edges of the mold. The technique may also be distinguished by a thin surface layer of parting agent or a contrast in textures between very smooth (mold side) and rough (scraped or beaten side) surfaces of the vessel.

Molds, especially concave molds, may be incised or carved with some sort of decoration, so that when the clay is firmly pressed into them the molded surface acquires the decoration in relief. This technique was used for much Samian ware (fig. 1.7; see Johns 1977a) and is typically associated with rapid manufacture of many highly standardized vessels (see Peacock 1982, 121, citing Goudineau).

A variant of molding is casting (or slip casting), but it is not known to what extent this technique might have been used, if at all, in antiquity. In slip casting a thin suspension of fine clay in water is carefully poured into molds (usually formed of plaster); it is allowed to stand for a short time while some of the water is absorbed into the plaster, then the excess slip is poured off and the piece dries in the mold. The potential for defects in cast ware is high, and many factors must be tightly controlled, especially the viscosity of the slip

Figure 5.4 Potter in Margaurites, Crete, adding a large coil segment at the top of a flowerpot. The join of the coil segments is just visible to the potter's left. The pot is formed on a pivoted turntable, turned by an assistant. Photograph by Lynnette Hesser.

and the rate of filling the molds (see Norton 1970, 101–29; Brody 1979, 27–39).

Coiling is a very common manufacturing technique whereby coils—ropes, rolls, or fillets of clay—are built up to establish the vessel circumference and gradually increase the height (Blandino 1984). The term coiling may refer to any of three variants: ring building, segmental coiling, or spiral coiling. In ring building individual rings of clay are laid in separate courses atop one another. Segmental or composite coiling is a variant of ring building in which each annular course is composed of several segments rather than a single rope of clay that measures the entire circumference of the pot (fig. 5.4). Spiral coiling refers to building a vessel from a spiraling rope of clay. Although the vessel is not usually formed of one enormously long continuous spiral, the coil is effectively continuous: a new rope of clay is spliced to the previous one and coiled around and upward in place of using a series of independent rings. Spiral coiling is usually used for the entire vessel; ring building and segmental coiling may be used either to form a whole pot or to build parts of vessels that are completed by other techniques such as pinching, modeling, molding, or throwing.

The coils are formed initially by squeezing or rolling the clay into long ropes or fillets whose diameter is usually two to three times the intended thickness of the vessel. Successive coils are applied to the exposed edge of the vessel wall, often overlapping slightly on the interior or exterior, and pinched to make a firm join. The oblique juncture formed by an overlap allows a stronger bond between the coils because the area for bonding is greater and more direct pressure can be applied than with a vertically placed coil. Continued squeezing, pinching, and drawing of each coil extends the wall beyond the original height (or diameter) of the coil itself (fig. 5.5). The junctions of the coils are usually obliterated by later finishing treatments, although on

Figure 5.5   (left) Potter in Chinautla, Guatemala, drawing up and smoothing a neck coil on a *tinaja*, or water jar. The body was partially dried before the neck was added. The vessel is formed on a board that permits turning the piece during manufacture.

Figure 5.6   (below) Coil fracture on a sherd of a vessel built by spiral coiling. Note the smooth edges where it was imperfectly bonded with another coil. Maximum exterior diameter, 13.2 cm.

some prehistoric pottery of the American Southwest the narrow coiled fillets were left as originally applied and pinched, forming the distinctive "corrugated" pottery ware (Gifford and Smith 1978).

Coiling can be easily identified as the technique used when the coils were poorly bonded. If, for example, the clay dried excessively before the next coil was applied, the join will not be strong, and the stresses of drying, firing, and use may further weaken these bonds. Hairline cracks and distinctive patterns of breakage may be evident along parallel planes, either horizontal or gently spiraling. The fractures themselves are usually relatively smooth and rounded (fig. 5.6), marking the upper edge of a coil that had another applied above it. Coiling is particularly well suited to building extremely large vessels, such as storage jars.

5.3.1.2   THROWING

Throwing is done on a potter's wheel (see sec. 5.3.1.3); because the wheel was never used in the pre-Columbian Western Hemisphere, this technique is confined to pottery of the Old World. The clay body prepared for throwing is generally softer and wetter than that used for hand building, partly because the lifting or drawing action used to raise the walls will not allow for a stiff, dry clay, but also because the air circulation during rotation leads to more rapid evaporation of the water and drying of the body. The clay is often somewhat finer textured as well, to avoid excessive abrasion of the potter's hands.

In throwing, a lump of clay is placed on the wheel with its mass carefully centered (fig. 5.7a); otherwise the pot will be asymmetrical and uneven in thickness. The clay is opened (fig. 5.7b) by inserting the thumbs or a fist into the center of the mass as it rotates. The vessel is shaped by lifting the clay (fig. 5.7c), aided by centrifugal force, with one hand inside and the other outside to draw the walls upward and outward, thinning them at the same time. The base may be trimmed with a tool (fig. 5.7d). A variant technique is throwing "from the hump," in which a very large lump of clay is centered on the wheel head and several vessels are thrown in succession from the clay at the top of the lump. Finished vessels are usually cut from the wheel with a wire or thread while the wheel is rotating or stationary (for an unusual variant of completing wheel-thrown bases, see Dumont 1952 and below).

Wheel-made pottery can usually be unambiguously detected because sherds exhibit "rilling"—rhythmic ridges and grooves that spiral around the vessel walls (fig. 5.8)—although these may be obliterated by careful smoothing of one or both surfaces. The undersides of the bases of wheel-thrown pots may also bear characteristic concentric striations (fig. 3.6) caused by removing the vessel while the wheel is still turning.

In jiggering (see Norton 1970, 143–44; Brody 1979, 57–59), a technique based on the wheel, clay is placed in or over a revolving mold, which shapes one surface, and a template is held against the clay (on either the interior or the exterior) to shape the other surface as the clay rotates. This is sometimes called jollying when the clay is placed inside a mold (Rhodes 1973, 307). Regardless of the specific terms, jiggering requires absolute centering of the mold and careful drying, especially if the clay is placed over the mold. The procedure is usually performed by hand, but in industry it is increasingly mechanized.

Vessels are frequently manufactured in separate stages by some combination of these constructional techniques. For example, vessels may be formed by molding the lower half and then coiling the upper portion; by throwing the body and adding a coil for the neck or rim; or by molding the base and throwing the body from coils, sometimes combined with beating, as in Musazi, Pakistan (Rye and Evans 1976, 32–34, pls. 18–26). There jars may be formed in two-part molds, the clay being pressed into the molds while rotating on a wheel; after a short drying period a coil of clay is applied to the opening in the top mold, and then this is thrown on the wheel to form the neck (Rye and Evans 1976, 33, pl. 22). Modeling or molding is frequently used to shape decorative or functional appendages such as handles, spouts, or supports for vessels formed by any of the other methods. Partially completed vessels or preforms may be set aside to dry briefly (as in fig. 5.3) while additional pots are begun, then the potter returns to the first pots and continues building by a different technique. In this procedure the potter must be careful that the edges of the preform do not dry excessively, and so the edges or the whole piece may be protected with cloth or leaves.

a

b

Figure 5.7 Throwing a pot on the wheel: *a*, centering the clay on the wheel; *b*, opening the lump of clay; *c*, lifting and thinning the walls; *d*, scraping to thin the base.

c

d

Figure 5.7 continued

Figure 5.8 "Rilling," the characteristic un- the interior or exterior (or both) of a wheel-
dulating ridges and striations running around thrown vessel.

5.3.1.3 SUPPORTS AND ROTATIONAL DEVICES

During all these operations, the soft, wet, plastic clay of the growing vessel
must be supported in some way, or it will slump. Small objects formed by
pinching can be held in the hand, but larger vessels are usually placed on some
surface that will accommodate their weight, shape, and the particular requirements of the forming technique. These supporting devices may be called pot
rests or bats (or batts), but a variety of particular forms have their own names
(see below). Vessels that will ultimately have flat bases may be formed on a
mat, a board (e.g., fig. 5.5), a clay disk, or the floor. Vessels with round or
pointed bases must be formed on supports or on pot rests that either shape the
base—such as a mold of some sort—or cradle a previously formed base, for

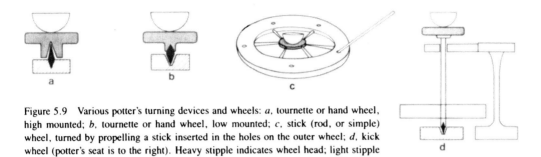

Figure 5.9   Various potter's turning devices and wheels: *a*, tournette or hand wheel, high mounted; *b*, tournette or hand wheel, low mounted; *c*, stick (rod, or simple) wheel, turned by propelling a stick inserted in the holes on the outer wheel; *d*, kick wheel (potter's seat is to the right). Heavy stipple indicates wheel head; light stipple indicates flywheel; black lozenge indicates bearing or pivot. After Lobert 1984, fig. 1.

example, large potsherds, baskets, bags, or rings of cloth, grasses, straw, twigs, or bark. Sometimes rings of bark, twigs, rope, or other firm materials are placed around the exterior of a finished pot during drying so it will not warp (see Matson 1974, 346).

Besides the building technique and the support given the vessel, one must consider how all sides of the vessel are given the potter's direct attention. The potter may either walk around the pot or, far more commonly, kneel or sit immobile and turn the pot during the work. Although it seems inefficient to keep the vessel fixed and have the potter walk around it, this procedure, called the orbiting technique (Reina and Hill 1978, 23; also Lothrop 1927) is not unknown. The clay is placed on the ground or on some other surface and is usually shaped by drawing, although coiling is also used. The potter, doubled over, moves slowly backward or sideways around the vessel as he or she works.

It is far more typical, however, to turn the clay during the process while the potter remains stationary, sitting, kneeling, or squatting. A variety of devices can be used to help move the vessel, and these also contribute to construction through the turning action. Three principles are involved: rotary motion, pivoting, and centrifugal force.

The simplest of these mobile devices are the great variety of pot supports or turntables that permit rotary motion but are not pivoted and do not supply centrifugal force. The large sherds used as concave molds, for example, will turn easily because of their curvature, and sometimes pottery saucers are used, as among the Aymara in Peru (Tschopik 1950) or the Pueblo Indians (the *puki;* Guthe 1925, 27–51). Several more specialized devices providing intermittent rotation—often at very high speeds—are found in the New World, including the *molde* of Coyotepec (Foster 1959), the pivoted convex basal mold of San Cristobal Totonicapán (Reina and Hill 1978, 79–80), the *parador* of Acatlán (Lackey 1981, 65), and the *kabal* of Yucatán (Thompson 1958, 76–81, 140–41; Brainerd 1958; Mercer 1897), which has been mistakenly termed a "primitive" potter's wheel. While most of the devices are turned with one hand, the *kabal*—a small disk or cylinder of wood—is usually turned by the potter's feet thus leaving both hands free for forming and shaping. In Nigeria an unpivoted turntable, *adiok,* used by the Ibibio, is turned with the hands rather than the feet (Nicklin 1981b).

Rotation, plus the advantage of a pivot to center the revolutions, is provided by a variety of turntable devices usually referred to as tournettes (fig. 5.9*a,b*).

The tournette typically consists of two stones with a pivot and socket (perhaps lubricated with oil) or a wooden board turning on a stick or pin that acts as a pivot. It is generally small and may be turned with the hands or with the feet (as in Kornos, Cyprus [Matson 1974, 345], or as with the *ladum* used by the Ogoni in Nigeria [Nicklin 1981b, 184]).

Although in form and in some aspects of use the tournette mimics the true potter's wheel, its small size and weight and its lack of a flywheel mean that it does not rotate with the sustained momentum and centrifugal force of the true wheel, and thus pottery is not thrown on it. It is often mislabeled a "slow wheel," but this term obscures the very real differences in operating principles between the two. Tournettes can, however, be rapidly rotated for short periods and may produce the same rilling seen on wheel-thrown pottery. This is also true of the *kabal,* which has been classed as a type of tournette, and the *molde;* as Foster (1959, 59) notes, the even, smooth spin of these devices can be attained only with large, heavy vessels.

The true potter's wheel developed in the Old World four to five millennia ago. Its age and antecedents are uncertain, although the evidence suggests it was in common use by the Middle Bronze Age (after ca. 2250 B.C.); it may have been preceded by a tournettelike mechanism (Johnston 1977, 206; see also Amiran and Shenhav 1984). In China it may have been in use during the first millennium B.C. The potter's wheel combines rotary motion and pivoting with centrifugal force, producing more-or-less continuous high-speed rotation. Critical factors in the use of the wheel for pottery building are the speed of the wheel, its momentum, and its steadiness or lack of oscillation. Momentum is important because the rotation is slowed by friction from the potter's hands on the clay. Two major types of potter's wheel are known: the stick wheel and the kick wheel (Lobert 1984).

The stick wheel (fig. 5.9c) or simple wheel has a large head and a short axle. There is no flywheel; the head itself has sufficient weight to maintain the momentum. The stick wheel, which may be made of stone, clay, or concrete, is rotated by inserting a stick into a hole in the top and turning it thirty or forty revolutions. This is enough to cause the apparatus to spin on its own for as much as five minutes without stopping. The stick-turning may be done by the potter (fig. 5.10) or by an assistant while the potter sits at the wheel and throws the pot from the centered lump of clay once the wheel is spinning. It is difficult to maintain continuous rotation with the stick wheel because it is impossible to turn it with the stick while the potter is working (though the wheel may also be hand turned).

The stick wheel is commonly used in India, where potters (Kumbhaars) have a myth about its origin:

> In ancient days the potters' wheel used to turn by itself. It was given by God. One day a man kicked it with his foot and it stopped turning. The potters then went to Shankar Bhagvaan and told him what had happened. He gave them a stick and said the wheel would have to be turned by using the stick. He also took off the waist string from the potters and said the pot would have to be cut from the wheel by that string. (Lynch 1979, 6–7)

Figure 5.10   A Muslim potter in Jhanwar, Rajasthan, India, turning a traditional stick wheel, interrupting the shaping of a large vessel used to make milk products such as yogurt. The walls are thrown on the wheel, then the base is paddled in from the bottom of the walls. Photograph by Carol Kramer.

The kick wheel, compound wheel, or double wheel (fig. 5.9d) consists of a wheel head and a flywheel joined by a vertical axle and mounted with separate bearings in such a way as to prevent oscillation. The apparatus may be raised to the level of a workbench or sunk into a pit. Either way, the potter sits at the level of the relatively small upper wheel, upon which he or she works the clay while kicking the lower flywheel. This lower flywheel is large and sometimes very heavy (as much as 150 pounds); the large size allows it to store energy supplied by kicking, release it as rotational motion, and maintain the rotational momentum without the upper wheel's being slowed by friction. The speed of rotation for shaping certain parts of the vessel (see Rye 1981, 74) is controlled by the rate at which the potter kicks the wheel. The advantage of the kick wheel is the constant rotation and the lack of interruption while an assistant (or the potter) sets the wheel revolving again. Because the kick wheel is a heavy and rather complex mechanism, unlike the portable stick wheel, it is usually permanent equipment and is typically associated with large-scale workshop production. In many instances, however, its speed and momentum are not fully utilized, the wheel being used more as a turntable (see Nicklin 1971, 36), as in the manufacture of moldmade jars in Musazi, Pakistan. Modern potter's wheels typically are electrically powered rather than kicked, but the principles are essentially the same.

All the devices used to rotate vessels—the pot rests, *kabal,* tournette, and wheel—may be employed throughout the process of manufacture, from construction, through finishing, to decoration.

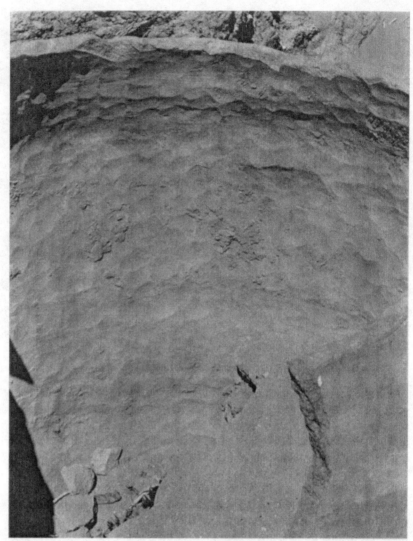

Figure 5.11   Characteristic dimpling showing the use of an anvil on the interior of a wine storage jar in the Moquegua valley, Peru. These jars, measuring as much as 9 feet deep and 4.5 feet in diameter, with walls more than 1 inch thick, were made by segmental coiling followed by paddle-and-anvil treatment to compact the paste and shape the walls.

5.3.2   Finishing: Tools and Techniques

Between the various stages of construction, or after steps are completed, the vessels may be partially dried, partially rewet, and subjected to a variety of finishing procedures. Some of these are considered secondary forming techniques; they may alter the dimensions of the vessel as well as the surface characteristics. Other techniques affect the surface alone. The most important of these finishing techniques are beating, scraping, and trimming, which essentially complete the forming process, and smoothing and texturing, which finish the surfaces.

Figure 5.12   The interior of a sherd showing the striations left by scraping with an uneven or serrated tool such as a shell.

Beating or paddling—repeatedly striking the clay with or without opposing pressure—is rarely a primary constructional process (cf. Solheim 1954, 305–7). Rather, the technique is employed on a roughly preformed vessel in the wet or nearly leather-hard stage to modify its shape, size, and surface characteristics and compact the paste. The most common kind of beating is the paddle and anvil technique (Fewkes 1941), in which a flat or concave stick or beater is used on one surface and a convex stone or clay anvil is opposed on the other surface (usually the interior), leaving a series of rounded impressions in the clay (fig. 5.11). Paddling or beating the surface has many significant effects on the final character of the vessel: it may improve the bonding of segments, obliterate coil marks or irregularities, thin the walls, compact the paste, smooth (or roughen; sec. 5.3.4.1) the surface, and alter or enlarge the contours of the vessel. Potters often employ several sizes, weights, or shapes of paddles in finishing a single vessel to vary the pressure or conform to its curvature (Scheans 1977, 13, 50; Ogan 1970, 87; Fontana et al. 1962, 65).

Paddling is perhaps most commonly associated with finishing coil-built vessels, but this is by no means exclusive. In parts of Pakistan and India, paddling is used on wheel-thrown jars to enlarge the vessel body (Rye and Evans 1976, pl. 26; see also Dumont 1952).

Scraping is often described as the most time-consuming step in pottery manufacture; it may be carried out several times to thin the walls and remove surface imperfections. Scraping is commonly used in finishing vessels shaped by coiling, molding, or pinching and is usually carried out before the vessel has completely dried, usually while the clay is still wet or at a soft leather-hard stage. Clay pastes having large inclusions usually exhibit linear scars or ridges where particles were dragged along the surface in scraping, showing the direction of movement of the scraping tool. If the tool is held perpendicular to the vessel surface and moved rapidly, the edge may leave a series of aligned shallow fractures and ridges in the clay perpendicular to its direction of movement. Scraping may be done with smooth-edged tools, such as pieces of cane, bamboo, gourd, bone, metal, or hard plastic similar to modern potter's ribs, or with a toothed or serrated device such as a shell or flaked stone tool or a sherd (fig. 5.12).

Trimming or fettling, usually associated with wheel-thrown or moldmade pottery, refers to cutting away excess clay and imperfections from the vessel when it is leather-hard. For example, the ridge where two halves of a mold joined may be trimmed away with a knife or other sharp tool.

Once the pottery vessel has attained its final shape and any irregularities have been eliminated, its surfaces are finished. This surface treatment may be cursory, or it may be time-consuming and precise; finishing may be the final treatment given the vessel before firing, or it may be a prelude to additional decoration. The major surface-finishing techniques are variants of either smoothing or texturing.

The vessel is smoothed to create a finer and more regular surface than results from forming. Smoothing is usually done with a soft, yielding tool such as cloth, leather, a bunch of grass, or the potter's hand. Alternatively, a hard tool may be rolled over the vessel to eliminate imperfections and even out the surface; in highland Guatemala, for example, corncobs, sticks, and wooden spools are used on the pot's surfaces (Reina and Hill 1978, 135, 165). Vessels are usually smoothed before they are completely dry, or they may be rewet before smoothing. Where the hand or fingers were used in smoothing still-plastic clay, the vessel usually has a distinctive appearance—extremely fine, shallow parallel striations with rounded edges. The final surface has a matte rather than a lustrous finish because the particles are not aligned or compacted; any luster is that natural to the clay.

In burnishing a surface is finished by rubbing back and forth with a smooth, hard object such as a pebble, bone, horn, or seeds. Compaction and reorientation of the fine clay particles (through plastic flow) give a surface luster. This compaction with each stroke of the burnishing tool creates the narrow parallel linear facets that are the telltale mark of the technique (fig. 5.13a); careless burnishing produces an irregular, streaky luster (fig. 5.13b) and incomplete coverage. Burnishing may be done on leather-hard or dry clay, but luster can be destroyed if the clay shrinks further. Except for clays with unusually low shrinkage or a high natural luster, the sheen will be retained only if the clay is burnished while dry.

Pattern burnishing creates a design by juxtaposing burnished (lustrous) and unburnished (matte) areas. A polished surface differs from a smoothed or burnished one primarily in care of execution: polishing is done on a dry surface and gives a uniform luster without the pronounced parallel facets produced by burnishing leather-hard clay.

Sometimes a formed vessel may be roughened, textured, or patterned, a common method of finishing vessels with utilitarian roles in cooking and transport (see sec. 7.3.5), in which case the surface treatment may be as much functional as decorative. Rough surfaces provide a better grip, for example, for carrying a heavy, wet vessel and may also improve heat transfer in cooking. Among the many techniques of surface patterning are brushing, striating, combing, stamping, impressing, and rouletting. Textured surfaces may also result more directly from the construction technique, as in the prehistoric coiled "corrugated" vessels of the American Southwest (McGregor 1941, 253–54; Gifford and Smith 1978), or from forming in a carved or otherwise patterned mold, or from beating with a patterned paddle. These roughening or texturing treatments may be applied to the entire surface of a vessel or to only a portion of the area, in which case they seem to be more decorative in nature.

a

Figure 5.13   Burnished surfaces: *a*, the parallel facets on
the surface of a burnished vessel marking the strokes of
a hard tool, which compacts the paste; *b*, the uneven,
streaky luster on a carelessly burnished and heavily fire-
clouded vessel with appliquéd decoration.

b

Figure 5.14   The overall surface texturing resulting from beating the surface of a vessel with a carved paddle while still wet.

In brushing, striating, and combing an irregular, toothed, or serrated tool is drawn over the surface, creating a series of shallow parallel marks. These treatments are often found on only part of the vessel—for example, the body of a jar, with the neck left smooth.

Brushing may be a type of smoothing; a handful of grass, straw, or other textured but pliant material is wiped over the surface. To affect the final appearance of the vessel and to leave visible traces, this must be done while the clay is still wet and plastic.

Striation means drawing a toothed or serrated hard-edged tool, such as a shell or chipped stone, across the surface of soft or leather-hard clay to create an overall effect of parallel scoring. The strokes are usually done in the same (or nearly the same) direction, creating a regular finish; sometimes the direction may be varied to create a herringbone pattern. Striating a vessel may also serve to scrape, thin, and even out the surface.

Combing is a more elaborate version of striating; the serrated tool may be applied only to particular areas of a vessel, or it may be manipulated to create patterns such as undulations, bands, or checkerboards.

Stamping, rouletting, and impressing are not always mutually distinguishable, and the terms may be at least partially interchangeable. Although these treatments may be used to decorate limited areas of a vessel, they may also be applied to the entire surface. Overall surface impressing or stamping may be done with corncobs, nets, the edges of shells, textiles, baskets or mats, and sticks or paddles that may be grooved, carved, or wrapped with cord. Thus the paddle-and-anvil technique of surface finishing may, if executed with a carved or wrapped paddle, also produce surface texturing (fig. 5.14).

Stamped and impressed surfaces were especially common in the east and southeast regions of the present United States during prehistoric periods (see, e.g., Broyles 1968), as well as in the present. In addition to the items mentioned above, Pamunkey potters of northeastern Virginia also used "thimbles, railroad seals, watch chains, buttons, the denticulated edge of fossil sharks' teeth, the fluted surface of a muskrat's tooth, the end of a key, a string of beads . . . [and] glass pieces with flower designs cut on them" (Stern 1951, 21).

5.3.3   Forming and Finishing: Ethnographic Examples

The ethnographic literature on pottery making provides abundant examples of the diverse procedures for constructing cooking pots and storage jars. Among the Papago of southern Arizona, for example, where pottery making is primarily a part-time occupation of middle-aged women, most vessels (except ashtrays, toys, etc.) are formed by a combination of convex molding, paddle and anvil, and coiling (Fontana et al. 1962, 58–79):

> [The potter] removes a fistful of wet clay from its container. This she puts on the cloth in front of her and begins to pat it into a bun. As soon as the ball of clay is round and flat, she adds ashes or dirt to the stone anvil with which she pats the bun, or to the mold, to prevent the clay from sticking to her hands. . . .
>
> The potter then places the bun over the base of the inverted pot that is being used as a mold. She may first put ashes on the base of the mold to prevent the bun from sticking to it, or she may use dirt, water, or, as one potter told us, nothing. . . .
>
> With the bun over the mold, the potter proceeds by using the stone anvil to pat the clay thin. She turns the mold in front of her from time to time. When the bun has been pressed over the base of the mold for a short distance by the use of the anvil, the potter then uses a wooden paddle (generally carved from mesquite or fashioned from a barrel stave) to spread it farther. . . .
>
> Then the potter wets her hands . . . and smooths the molded clay with her wet hands until the surface is quite shiny. She then lifts the clay from the mold and sets the new base upside down on a cloth on the ground, wrapping a second cloth around the rim as she does so. . . .
>
> After the base of the pot has dried to a leatherlike texture, the potter turns the base upright, setting it down in the center of a rag ring under a cloth. . . . [She wets her hand, smooths the base, and] then dips a curved wooden paddle into a pan of water, wets a stone anvil with it . . . and strikes against the rim of the base opposite the anvil with the paddle . . . to thin the wall of the base of the pot and increase its height.
>
> The potter then smooths off the rim with a moistened right hand and tears off a small handful of wet clay to make the first clay coil. . . . The length of clay rope is stuck to the rim of the base by placing four fingers behind it on the interior of the pot and pinching in and down against the coil in front of the fingers with the thumb. . . .
>
> When the coils for the body have been added they are made to blend into the base of the pot first by sealing the seam by hand where

the coils join the rim, and then by pounding smooth with the paddle-
and-anvil technique. . . .

When the pot has been brought to its desired form, it is allowed to
dry in the sun for a few minutes. Then the potter rubs over the entire
surface with a waterworn pebble or other smooth object.

In Guinhilaran, in the southern Philippines, both men and women make
pottery, but each sex makes different vessels and uses different techniques.
Men, for example, use a slabbing technique to make flowerpots (*maseteras*)
and large jars, both of which begin with a roughly cylindrical preform called a
mustra (Scheans 1977, 16–19):

> The basal pad, *buli*, is made by patting out a lump of clay on a
> square of newspaper placed on the potter's bench. The finished pad
> with its paper is then set on a square, footed wooden palette . . .
> [which is placed on a raised support. The potter forms a coil of clay
> and places it on a bench that is] sprinkled with fine wood ash, *abo*,
> so that when the coil is flattened it will not stick. . . . the coil is
> punched down with the ball of the palm, then spread across the board
> with the side of the hand. It is then patted flat and scraped, *nakaros*,
> with the fingers to even it and to find any unwanted inclusions. The
> slab, *tapi-tapi/lawas*, is next picked up and taken to the support
> where it is fitted around the edge of the *buli* by being bent into a tube
> on its narrow dimension. The long edges of the tube when they meet
> are overlapped and joined by finger smoothing. Next the base joint is
> scraped with the fingers as the potters walk around the support. . . .
> After the joints are finished, the potter hand paddles his piece in
> order to slightly flare out its upper portion. It is then finger scraped,
> hand paddled some more, and the joints reworked. . . . A final touch
> done by most potters is a smoothing of the lip with a wetted hand. . . .
> After a short drying period a bench coil is placed on top of the
> *mustra* lip. It is pinched and scraped into place, thickening the rim
> area. . . . When dry enough . . . paddling now is done with the
> wooden paddle and stone anvil and its purpose is to form and finish
> the completely built vessel. . . .
> After paddling, the lip is evened up and levelled by trimming . . .
> then smoothed down with the fingers and a wet cloth. . . . If the pot
> has the ordinary thickened belt rim, this will be finished either with a
> tool or by hand. The tool, *kias*, is a combination gauge and scraper.
> Its upper end rests on the lip and its lower end with its metal base
> marks the bottom of the rim. . . . The pot is then completed by pok-
> ing a hole into the wall near the base with the finger to serve as a
> drainage hole.

In Santa Apolonia, in the central highlands of Guatemala, ollas and jars are
made by the laborious "drawing" and "orbiting" processes (Reina and Hill
1978, 56–63; see also Arrott 1953):

> Forming a rounded clay column six to eight inches high by ten inches
> in diameter, the potter plunges her left hand into its center and, get-
> ting to her feet, models the clay into a cumbersome ring. Moving this
> ring to another . . . spot [sprinkled with dry clay], she straightens
> the walls and adjusts the ring to a uniform diameter by rotary pres-
> sure from within. Now, still upon her feet and stooping over, she

begins to move slowly backward in a clockwise motion, orbiting around the clay ring. . . . Her right-hand fingers now proceed gently, but with great firmness and speed, to drag the soft clay of the interior upward to form a steadily rising wall. . . . After circling backward two or three times around the work, the potter begins to shape and refine the walls. . . .

Work on the surface of the top half of the vessel now proceeds with the aid of a corncob. While continuing to move backward, the potter rolls the cob with gentle diagonal pressure upward from the heel of her right hand to her fingertips, leaving the imprint of its rough, pockmarked texture upon the clay. . . . [Then] she rolls a smooth, short, rounded stick about an inch and a quarter in diameter over the surface. The pockmarks disappear and the surface becomes more uniform. Finally the potter goes over the entire vessel with her wet hands, then smooths it with a folded wet cloth. . . .

Holding the soft clay at the [mouth] opening within the fold of a wet cloth or leaf held between thumb and forefinger of her right hand, she moves around the vessel rapidly to form the upturned rim.

At this stage . . . the potter leaves the half-completed vessel to dry in the sun for an hour or longer. . . . [Then] she will turn [it] over . . . and place it carefully on its rim upon the ground. This manipulation is difficult, for the vessel can still be easily distorted.

When she has inverted the vessel, the clay deliberately left within the ring when she began work . . . is still wet and pliable. Putting her left hand through the aperture to support the heavy clay from within, the potter shapes the curving walls of the bottom toward the diminishing space around her supporting hand. To extract her hand and complete the base, she uses a corncob to draw the clay toward the center, exerting pressure through the cob, slowly removing first her whole hand, then her fingers. Rolling and pressing the clay toward the center, the potter reduces the opening to a point where only one fingertip remains within the vessel. She withdraws this finger, raising a heavy flap of clay around the small opening that remains. This she rolls flat, incorporating it with the rest of the bottom, and the base is completed.

An unusual technique for making pottery is reported in Kokkulam, southern India. Potters combine throwing of the upper half of a vessel with two stages of paddling, which closes the base, thins the walls, and significantly increases the size of the lower half of the vessel (Dumont 1952, 81):

Several handfuls of clay previously prepared are flung upon the flat central part of the wheel, to form a large mass out of which several pots will be turned. The wheel is spun by a stick (or with the hands). Then, with both hands acting powerfully, the potter draws the clay up into a thick cylinder at the top of which the pot will be shaped. Hence, when the latter is removed, there is a large hole at the bottom. . . . It will be the first function of the subsequent beating to close that hole.

. . . after a short while, when the pots have been allowed to dry in the sun . . . the potter beats the pot between a round stone anvil, held inside with the left hand . . . and a hard-wood mallet, shaped like a pyramid surmounted by a cylindrical handle. . . . The pot is held between the left thigh and the right foot, and slightly turned from inside after each stroke with the mallet held in the right hand. Several phases should be distinguished in this process. . . . The potter himself . . . distinguishes two phases: first, closing the hole ("rent") at the bottom. . . . Then comes the polishing or "covering level," *neravi pudeippadu*, after watering the surface, with two phases, the first with perpendicular percussion, the second with oblique percussion to wipe out the traces of the first. . . . The latter is repeated after the pot has dried overnight. The process is thought to give more cohesion to the clay.

5.3.4 Surface Enhancement

Many decorative treatments can be applied to pottery. They may be differentiated as treatments that cover the entire surface versus those covering only particular parts; those applied before firing versus those applied afterward; plastic techniques versus applications of color; and additions to the surface as opposed to penetration of the surface.

For the present, decoration means embellishment of a vessel beyond the procedures used in forming the clay mass into the final vessel shape and finishing its overall surface. Certain surface treatments are left in a somewhat ambiguous status by this definition, however. For example, is an allover impressed treatment part of finishing, or is it decoration? One could perhaps argue that this treatment is functional and thereby sidestep the question, but this is not a satisfactory solution. Decoration may have a variety of functions, both utilitarian and symbolic (sec. 8.3.3). Furthermore, certain kinds of decoration may modify the shape rather than the surface of the vessel, and these secondary form characteristics may also enhance the utility of the piece.

Two categories of decorative treatments are distinguished here: those that displace or penetrate the surface, and those that involve additions to (or over) the surface. As was true of construction techniques, these decorative categories are not mutually exclusive, and frequently several kinds of decoration are superimposed or applied on different parts of the piece. Criteria for identifying these techniques on potsherds are discussed by Rye (1981, 89–94) and by Balfet, Fauvet-Berthelot, and Monzon (1983, 19–125).

5.3.4.1 SURFACE PENETRATION OR DISPLACEMENT

In displacement and penetration techniques embellishments are cut from or impressed into the surface. They may either remove or displace the clay, depending on how dry it is. Impressing is usually performed on wet clay, but cutting may be done on wet, leather-hard, or dry clay or even after firing.

Impressing and displacing techniques include simple impressing, stamping, rouletting, rocker stamping, and punctation. Impressing and stamping are similar to the techniques described above under finishing, but as decoration they embellish only part of the vessel rather than the total surface—as, for example, around the rim, neck, or shoulder or on an appliquéd fillet or flange.

The distinctions within this category depend on the object and method used to make the decoration. In simple impressing the imprint of a tool on the

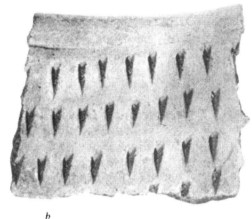

Figure 5.15 Punctation: *a*, with a hollow   made with a wedge-shaped tool.
tube, such as a reed; *b*, rows of punctations

clay surface creates a pattern; this may be a natural object such as shell, reeds, corncobs, or animal teeth or bones, or it may be a manufactured item such as a piece of mat, textile, or string. Impressing may also be done with a thumb, finger, or fingernail.

In stamping a tool (any of those mentioned above or a specially formed stamp) is used as a die to impress a repeated pattern of identical motifs. Stamping differs from simple impressing in the unitary rather than continuous character of the decoration.

In rouletting a cylindrical tool is rolled over the surface, leaving a continuous impressed design. Balfet, Fauvet-Berthelot, and Monzon (1983, 101) distinguish two variants of rouletting based on the size of the implement: *molette* (or roulette; 4 cm or less) and *rouleau* (roller; greater than 4 cm).

Rocker stamping is a combination of stamping and rouletting; a stamp (for example, a shell) is "walked" or moved over the surface by rocking from side to side, producing a distinctive irregular zigzag decoration. Rocker stamping is usually done with a convex tool or with the edge of an implement.

In punctation depressions are punched into wet clay, usually with a sharp or pointed instrument (fig. 5.15*a,b*), such as a stick, a hollow reed, an awl, or a finger or fingernail. This treatment is sometimes described as linear punctation if the depressions form lines. Punctation often (but not always) involves some displacement of the clay.

It is often difficult to determine the exact tool or pattern used in these decorative treatments because of indistinct or overlapping impressions, the rough texture of the clay, or surface wear. The motifs can frequently be discerned more clearly by covering the area with Plasticine and studying the positive cast.

Although impressing and cutting techniques both displace, penetrate, or remove material, in cutting operations the tool is drawn through the clay. The implement is moved along the surface rather than pressed perpendicularly into it. Cutting techniques fall into three major categories: incising, carving, and perforating. Most may be executed when the clay is plastic or leather-hard; some may be done when the clay is dry, and some after firing.

Incising—cutting lines into the surface of a vessel with a pointed implement—is one of the most variable of the decorative techniques. The appearance of incised decoration depends on the state of the clay (wet, leather-hard, dry, fired), the texture of the paste, the size and shape of the instrument, the angle at which the instrument is held, the pressure used, and the direction the tool is moved.

Based on these sources of variation, incised decoration may be further described by several terms (see Shepard 1976, 195–203); for example, in terms of the tool used to create the design. Fine incising is done with a sharp-pointed instrument and creates lines that are narrow, generally deep, and have a V-shaped cross section. Groove-incising may be done with an instrument that has a broader round or pointed tip, and the lines are broad and shallow; sometimes it may be done by a gougelike tool, held either perpendicular to the surface or at an angle.

Incised decoration may also be described in terms of when it is done, as preslip, postslip, or postfire. Preslip and postslip incising can easily be distinguished by whether the lines penetrate the slip or are covered by it. Postfiring incising may be difficult to discern from dry paste prefire incising (fig. 5.16a), because both cause fine chipping of the clay or slip at the margins of the lines, creating a ragged appearance; incising wet or leather-hard paste leaves a clean line, sometimes with a raised margin from displacement of the clay (fig. 5.16b). Balfet, Fauvet-Berthelot, and Monzon (1983, 91, 95) distinguish prefiring incising on wet clay (incision) from incising on dry or fired clay, which they term engraving.

Variations on the incising technique include gadrooning, combing, and sgraffito. In gadrooning broad grooves are subsequently modified by modeling or carving, forming segments that often give round vessels a squash- or melonlike appearance. Combing is done with an implement that has multiple points, creating groups of parallel striations. Sgraffito is a technique of incising through a slip, and the whole is then covered with a glaze and fired; the cut lines contrast in color with the areas covered by both slip and glaze.

In carving a series of cuts remove clay from the vessel to create a design. Different kinds of carving are distinguished by the amount of clay eliminated and how it is removed. Simple carving is the cutting or gouging out areas of clay, usually wet or leather-hard, to create a decorative pattern. Planorelief carving, champlevé, and excising, on the other hand, refer to cutting out clay as the background for a design, which then stands in low relief. The surface—often slipped—is typically cut or scraped away when the clay is dry or even after firing (fig. 5.16c). Of the three, excision is sometimes distinguished as involving only shallow scraping. Flat carving and modeled carving are usually executed in a leather-hard state, with the clay being deeply cut away, and then the design is further embellished by fine incising or modeling (or both) of the raised portions. Much of the carved black-and-red pottery of the Pueblo Indians in the American Southwest is of this type (e.g., LeFree 1975, 52–56, pls. 2–6). Chamfering is slicing away regular sections of the clay wall to create vertical or horizontal planels, often stepped. Fluting creates one or more shallow, broad grooves or channels in the clay, running either around the piece or vertically (usually as multiple contiguous flutes). Like gadrooning, vertical flutes often create melonlike forms (see LeFree 1975, pl. 13).

a

b

c

Figure 5.16   Incising and excising: *a*, postslip fine incising, done when the vessel was dry or nearly dry; note the fine chipping of the edges of the lines; *b*, fine incising done while the clay was still relatively wet; note the displacement of the clay along some of the lines, especially in the upper left; *c*, postslip (and possibly postfire) fine incising and excising.

Perforating and piercing refer to cutting through the entire vessel wall and removing portions of the clay, creating a pattern by a series of holes. The clay is usually plastic or leather-hard when this is done. Such containers may be more decorative than functional, as in the lustrous blackware produced in Coyotepec, Mexico, for use as dried flower containers and lampshades (Whitaker and Whitaker 1978, figs. 74 and 75).

5.3.4.2   ADDITIONS TO THE SURFACE
A great variety of techniques may be employed to decorate a vessel by additions to or over the surface; they include joining formed clay elements to the vessel and applying treatments that alter its color. Any of them may be

combined with each other or with the impressing and cutting techniques discussed above.

5.3.4.2.1 Joins to the Surface. Decorative techniques based on joining include attaching small appliqués or modeled or molded elements and adding decorative inlays. Appliqué refers to the application of small, shaped pieces of clay to the surface of the vessel (e.g., fig. 5.13*b*), including fillets, pellets, spikes, flanges, and other attachments. For best results the clay of vessel and appliqué should be at roughly the same state of wetness, either leather-hard or plastic. The surface of the vessel where the appliqué is to rest may be rewet and roughened, or the appliqué may be joined by luting, in which a small amount of fluid clay slurry or slip is used to promote adhesion.

Instead of these small elements, the appliqués may be large and complex modeled attachments that are not only ornamental but also functional. Vessel supports (feet or bases) and handles may be elaborately shaped, often in natural or animal effigy forms, and attached to the vessel. These elements may be shaped and modeled by hand or formed in molds.

Decoration may also be achieved by inlay, in which small fragments of some nonceramic material, usually stone, are pressed into the clay to form a decorative pattern. Some jars made in Portugal, Spain, and Tunisia have inlays of small feldspathic rock fragments (see, e.g., Balfet, Fauvet-Berthelot, and Monzon 1983, 124–25).

5.3.4.2.2 Color Additions: Painting. In a second major category of additions to a pottery vessel, color is the essential ingredient. There are two major types of surface coloration: those applied to only a portion of the total area, and those that coat the entire surface. A third way to alter vessel color is in firing, and firing variations can be elaborations on the other techniques.

The most common method of coloring the surface is to paint with a colorant or pigment. Pigment is the inclusive term for the coloring material, while paint refers to the action of applying a pigment rather than to a specific kind of material. Pigments may be organic or inorganic and may be applied either before or after firing the vessel, although organic pigments frequently oxidize and disappear in firing. The substance generally adheres better if the surface is dry when it is applied. Decoration painted in two colors is sometimes described as bichrome; painting with three or more colors is polychrome decoration.

Most pigments used on pottery are mixtures of colorants, fine clay, water, and a binder. Clays slow the settling of the particles in the mixture and enhance the flow and adhesion of the pigment. Painting may be done with a brush made of animal hair or fur, vegetable fibers, or feathers.

Colorants (see sec. 11.1) are chemical elements that contribute color to a mixture; for unglazed, low-fired pottery, only three colorants that are naturally found in abundance (in oxide form) can survive the temperatures of firing: iron, manganese, and carbon. A much wider range of metallic elements, usually commercially manufactured preparations, is used in compounding glazes to give a broader range of colors.

Organic carbon, occurring in a variety of forms from powdered charcoal to plant extracts, can produce only a black or gray color and is typically applied after firing. Nicobar potters, for example, apply strips of unripe coconut husks to the sides and rim of fired pots while they are still hot to create black stripes; the husks are then wiped over the entire interior and exterior surfaces, imparting a light copper color (Man 1894, 25). A similar technique is reported for the Ibibio of Nigeria (Nicklin 1981b, 177). Organic material may be used before firing, either as pigment or as a binder mixed with other materials. Potters in the Nicoya peninsula of Costa Rica add sour orange juice to their pigment to increase its adhesion to the vessel surfaces (Stone 1950, 272). To make black pigment, Papago potters in Arizona boil mesquite bark and add mesquite resin to the solution; this is painted onto the pots after firing, and the vessels are then reheated briefly (Fontana et al. 1962, 77–78).

An unusual and nontraditional pigment is employed by the Seri of northwestern Mexico, who paint their pottery either before or after firing with commercial laundry bluing (Bowen and Moser 1968, 91).

Several unusual kinds of painted decoration are known. Slip trailing or barbotine is the application of a thick mixture of clay and water to the surface of a vessel, often creating a raised design. Glaze painting, in which painted pigments vitrify into a glass during firing, was known in antiquity in the Southwestern United States (Shepard 1942a, 1965; DeAtley 1986) and in the ancient Near East (Steinberg and Kamilli 1984).

Certain colorants may be applied to pottery after firing to highlight particular areas of a design. Among the Gisiga of Cameroons, kaolin is rubbed into grooved decorations (David and Hennig 1972, 6). Graphite is used traditionally as a painted pigment by contemporary Phalaborwa potters in South Africa (van der Merwe and Scully 1971, 194), and in prehistoric times it was used as a painted pigment or slip in some areas of the New World; also, cinnabar (mercuric sulfide) was occasionally rubbed into incised lines, particularly on black-slipped pottery.

In resist painting (Shepard 1976, 206–12) a temporary protective coat is applied over portions of the vessel surface, color is applied to the remainder, and the protective coating is removed (usually during firing). The background color is typically black and is often achieved by postfire smudging of the vessel; the protective coating is usually something organic—such as wax—that will be removed by heat but not distort the underlying color. The decoration is relatively simple—wavy lines, dots, or irregular blobs—and of a sort that is easier to paint on (with the coating) than to paint around with a background colorant (see Shepard 1976, fig. 17).

5.3.4.2.3 Color Additions: Slips and Glazes. Color additions that coat the entire vessel surface are described as slips or as glazes, depending on their composition and the temperatures at which they fire to maturity.

A slip is a fluid suspension of clay (and/or other materials) in water that is applied before firing to form a thin coating. Slips may also be called engobes, but this term tends to be used primarily with reference to high-fired ceramics, to designate a slip applied under a glaze. Engobes are intended to alter the color of the vessels and are usually white; their ingredients are selected to ensure low shrinkage and good fit with the vessel body (see Rhodes 1973, 250–54).

Slips are usually a different color than the body of a vessel, and if distinctively colored they may be applied for that reason alone. White or extremely light-colored slips may, however, serve a function similar to the engobes of glazed pottery in providing a smooth, clean surface for subsequent painted decoration and translucent slipping, as in the case of Classic Maya polychromes (see Rice 1985). If the clays are the same color as the paste, they may be extremely difficult to distinguish from unslipped, smoothed surfaces without a microscope or hand lens to reveal textural differences.

Slips exhibit considerable variation in color, quality, luster, and thickness, depending on the type of clay mineral present, the particle-size range, the kinds and amounts of adsorbed ions, and the degree of dispersion (flocculation vs. deflocculation) of the particles in the suspension (see chap. 2). Of these, perhaps the most important is the kind of clay mineral present, for all the others are affected by this. Some of the most distinctive slips in antiquity—for example, the slips of Greek figured ware and Roman Samian ware—have been composed of fine-textured illite clays (see sec. 2.3.4.1.3). There is, however, no minimum percentage of clay content required to create a slip. In Santa Apolonia, Guatemala, for instance, cooking pots are covered with a thin sliplike paste of talc before slipping with a clay fluid (Reina and Hill 1978, 63); a similar sliplike coating of *tez* (a mixed talc and chlorite mineral) is used on tortilla griddles in nearby Mixco (Arnold 1978, 341). In these coatings the talc acts like Teflon to prevent substances from sticking to the surfaces.

Slips may be applied by any of three techniques. Dipping a vessel in the slip gives uniform coverage, filling all holes, grooves, and irregularities in the surface. The vessel should be slipped in this manner while there is still some moisture in the body. Pouring is used for vessels too large to be dipped or for vessels to be slipped only on the interior. Because of rapid absorption of the moisture in the slip, the pot must be turned smoothly and rapidly during pouring or the slip will be very uneven. Slips may also be wiped onto the surface of a vessel with a cloth, a pad of grass or animal fur, or the potter's hands. Wiping frequently gives uneven coverage and may leave fine grooves in the direction the slip was wiped over the surface.

Slips may be applied over previous decoration, such as incising, or various kinds of decoration—painting or incising—may be executed over or through the slipped surface (fig. 5.16*a,c*). Some slips have a high natural luster (a function of the type of clay mineral used), but most are burnished or polished with a stone to compact and orient the particles and impart a luster.

In slipping pottery the greatest problems occur in drying and firing: the slip and clay body may shrink differentially, so that the slip adheres poorly. For this reason, slips on low-fired pottery are usually applied to completely dried wares, often immediately before firing, and carefully burnished for better adhesion. If the slip and body have very different coefficients of expansion, the slip may craze or flake during or after firing. Some slips may actually be "tempered": whether this is to improve fit (as in some Maya slips; Shepard 1962, 253) or to enhance the cooling properties of water jars, as suggested by potters in northwestern Pakistan (Rye and Evans 1976, 53), is not always clear. In addition, if the slip is fired to too high a temperature, firing shrinkage may destroy its luster. The uneven compaction of the clay particles in careless burnishing occasionally results in slight color differences between burnished and unburnished areas; this is especially true in areas of fireclouding.

Slips, especially thin slips, may be applied in several coats, as at Santa Clara Pueblo, New Mexico (LeFree 1975, 40), for better coverage of the body. Santa Clara potters enhance the bonding qualities of their slip by adding an organic glue or adhesive: after burnishing the two coats of slip, they coat the pottery with grease, allow it to penetrate, then polish the vessels with a chamois cloth before firing (LeFree 1975, 40–44).

Three additional terms are fairly common in the literature to designate coatings that are variants of slips. The terms self-slip and floated surface are sometimes used for finely textured surfaces that appear to be slipped with the same material that constitutes the clay body. The presence of a distinct slip is difficult to determine, and in some cases this effect could result simply from carefully wiping the surfaces with a wet hand, which brings the finest particles of the paste to the surface and orients them. Finally, a wash usually refers to a separate postfire coating of the surfaces; this may be a pigment or a lime-based stucco and may subsequently be painted. The major distinction between a wash and a slip is that a slip is applied before firing and a wash is applied after firing.

A glaze is a coating of glass melted in place and thus fused with the surface of a vessel (see sec. 4.2.4). Glazes are applied for the same reasons as slips— to add color or texture and to reduce permeability. They are, however, very different from slips because they are high fired and glassy, they make the surface completely impermeable, and they are compositionally complex (see Rhodes 1973; Lawrence and West 1982).

The primary constituent of glazes is silica; a variety of substances called fluxes are added to lower the melting point, and metallic oxides are added as colorants (see sec. 11.2.4). The flux may be added as ashes (forming an ash glaze, in which potassium and soda are principal fluxing agents), and the ashes of wood, grasses, leaves, or other vegetal material (see Leach 1976, 159–63) may be components of the glaze. An example is the *khār*, or sintered plant ash, manufactured by Pakistani potters as a glaze constituent (Rye and Evans 1976, 180–85). The earliest glazes manufactured in Egypt, China, and the Near East were probably of this alkaline ash type (Rhodes 1973, 82–83).

The ingredients for the glazes used by traditional potters very often come from nontraditional sources. In Quetta, Pakistan, for example, the silica for the glaze comes from glass cullet, waste products of window-glass cutting or broken bottles purchased from the bazaar; manganese comes from the crushed cores of old dry-cell batteries also purchased there (these batteries also contribute aluminum and zinc); and copper is obtained from copper scale, produced by heating sheet copper to red heat, quenching it in cold water, and then scraping off the black fire scale (Rye and Evans 1976, 74).

Organic materials such as gums or sugars are sometimes added as binders to toughen glazes for overpainting (as in majolicas) and to protect them against accidental damage during drying, stacking in storage, or handling while setting the kiln. For example, the manufacturers of Talavera-style pottery in Puebla, Mexico, add honey to the glaze as a binder (Whitaker and Whitaker

1978, pl. 3). In Quetta, Pakistan, flour and water are boiled for several hours, making a thick binder solution to which the glaze ingredients are added (Rye and Evans 1976, 74).

5.4 Drying and Firing

Drying a formed pottery vessel typically takes several days or even weeks. If a piece is dried too rapidly or if drying is incomplete, flaws may develop (see sec. 3.3.3) that can destroy the product, either during the drying itself or later in firing. For this reason, drying of the vessels is usually carefully monitored. Firing, too, has great potential for disaster, and potters select their firing times and materials with care. In Chinautla, passersby do not look at pottery during its firing, because of the widespread belief that the "evil eye" will cause an unsuccessful firing and make pottery turn black (Reina 1966, 272).

5.4.1   Tools and Techniques

Vessels manufactured of relatively coarse pastes can often be placed in direct sunlight, where they dry quickly without cracking. Sun-drying is especially common for quick-drying the surfaces of vessels before burnishing or decorating. For example, a Nasioi potter on the island of Bougainville dries her pots in the sun for six hours before smoothing, and then for a week more before firing (Ogan 1970, 88). Some potters in the Philippines dry their vessels in the sun for only one day after forming (Solheim 1952, 33). Vessels constructed of finer and denser pastes or with thicker walls usually must be dried more carefully and slowly, and they may be placed in the shade for all or part of the time. Pamunkey (Virginia) potters dry their pots indoors on benches or shelves in their houses or in the smokehouse for not less than a week (Stern 1951, 26).

The time needed for drying is closely related to weather (see Arnold 1985, 65–70): in cool or rainy climates or seasons vessels take longer to dry, and potters in cold climates also risk having frost damage their wares. In such areas pots may be dried indoors in the workshop, sometimes near the kilns to benefit from their warmth. In addition to such environmental determinants, drying time may be highly variable (table 5.2) because of idiosyncratic or situational factors. For example, vessels may be left to dry as long as necessary for enough to accumulate for a firing.

Where pottery is fired without kilns, pots are often warmed slightly immediately before firing. This both ensures that all moisture is out of the clay before firing and minimizes thermal stress when the pots are first placed on the fire. Preheating is thus at least a partial equivalent of the early water-smoking stage of dehydration in commercial ceramic firing (see chap. 4). It is most common to find preheating arrangements in cool or damp climates or seasons, when pottery is often dried indoors. In Chinautla, Guatemala, for example, pottery to be fired in the late afternoon is brought outside early in the morning to warm in the sunlight (Reina and Hill 1978, 39). Pamunkey (Virginia) pot-

Table 5.2   Vessel Drying Customs in Sixty-one Ethnographic Situations

Drying Custom	Number of Cases
Time	
<1 day–2 days	13
2–5 days	17
Up to 1 week	14
1–2 weeks	9
2–4 weeks	6
1 month or more	2
Total	61
Location[a]	
In sun	14
Outside (general)	3
Shade or partial shade	10
Inside	16
Total	43

Source: After Arnold 1985, table 3.1.

[a]Some societies noted two locations of drying, while for others no location was given.

ters start bonfires in their yards and place the pots to be fired near the blaze, turning them and gradually moving them closer until they are too hot to handle, when they are lifted onto the fire (Stern 1951, 27). One of the most elaborate warming procedures is used by potters in Santa Apolonia, Guatemala, who preheat the vessels in their houses for as much as twelve hours before firing by placing the pots on a wooden rack suspended four to five feet above a slow-burning fire (Reina and Hill 1978, 63).

Pottery is fired by two fundamental techniques: with and without a kiln. Although kilns were widely used throughout the Old World in antiquity, in the New World they had a very restricted distribution, primarily in highland and Gulf coastal Mexico (Payne 1982; Santley 1982), until the arrival of Europeans and European technology in the early sixteenth century. Kilns probably were an early response to three needs of potters: more control over products, higher firing temperatures, and more economical use of fuel.

5.4.1.1   NONKILN FIRING

Firing without kilns is called the open firing, bonfire, or clamp method. Firings done by this technique are always short and generally achieve relatively low temperatures. Although procedures for open firing of pottery vary, they share certain general characteristics. A bed of fuel (often fairly slow burning) is prepared on the ground, the pottery to be fired is placed over the fuel, and more fuel (the same kind that constitutes the original bed or else a faster-burning kind, such as grass, or a mixture) is placed around and on top of the pottery. A single pot may be fired this way, or a large arrangement of several hundred carefully placed pots several feet high may constitute the firing (fig. 5.17). The fuel is ignited, usually begining with the lower layer (fig 5.18a), additional fuel is added (fig. 5.18b), and after a short while the fuel burns itself out and the firing is over. Pots may be removed almost immediately or allowed to cool before being taken from the ashes (fig. 5.18c).

Figure 5.17 Potters in Gogunda, Rajasthan, India, rushing to begin a firing of various sizes and shapes of cooking pots before the rains start during the monsoon season. Many of these firings involve 800 to 1,000 vessels at a time. Note how fuel is inserted into the mouths of vessels encircling the base of the open setting. Once the firing has commenced, sawdust and a layer of ashy earth are placed over the pots to create a smudged blackware. Pots are removed from the pile the day after firing. Photograph by Carol Kramer.

This basic procedure varies from place to place, depending on the nature of the potting craft and the local resources. In some areas large chunks of fuel, sherds, metal, or other protective devices such as basins or grates may be arranged around the vessels to constitute a rudimentary "kiln" (e.g., the potters of Santa Clara; LeFree 1975, 58–60). Another kind of protective device—a sort of cross between a kiln and a saggar—is the *mapú ëite*, a bottomless vessel used by Shipibo-Conibo potters to fire small vessels (DeBoer and Lathrap 1979, 120). The fuel used is highly variable, including wood, cattle or sheep dung, bark, brush, branches (sometimes pruned from cultivated trees), charcoal, coal, palm fronds, straw, bamboo, coconut husks, and agricultural by-products (corncobs or cornstalks, sugarcane) are among the common materials used to fire pots. The duration of firing is also highly variable. Although clamp firings usually last only a few hours, they sometimes take up to eight hours, as among the Pamunkey of Virginia (Stern 1951). On the other hand, they may last only fifteen to twenty minutes, as in some parts of Nigeria (Nicklin 1981a, 348) and Cameroons (David and Hennig 1972, 6), the South-

a

b

c

Figure 5.18   A bonfire firing of water jars in the courtyard of potters in Chinautla, Guatemala: *a,* Pots are placed over a layer of pine bark and dung, which has been ignited with a few coals. *b,* When the pots begin to turn black, the pile is covered with straw, which burns very rapidly (the firewood to the left is for cooking, not for firing pottery). *c,* The thick layer of ash after firing is gingerly poked away soon after firing, and pots are exposed to the air while still hot (at the time this photograph was taken, there was still a dull red glow to be seen in the center of the pile of pots and ash).

western United States (Shepard 1976, table 3), and the Philippines (Scheans 1977, 45; Longacre 1981, 60).

The disadvantages of this type of short, open firing are many. The major one is that the pots are not completely protected either from contact with the fuel or from drafts. For this reason, open firings are almost never used for glazed ware (but cf. Reina and Hill 1978, 86, for an example from Guatemala). Not only are the fired pots usually marked by fireclouds, but the rapid temperature changes (as well as shifts in the position of the fuel as it burns) can easily crack, dent, or over- or underfire the vessels. In addition, although the maximum firing temperatures are sometimes fairly high, soaking times are nonexistent or extremely short, the heat is generally very uneven, and much heat is lost to the atmosphere through radiation and convection.

Despite these difficulties, open firing is a satisfactory economic solution for nonindustrial potters, and for millennia the technique has provided a means of producing useful low-fired unglazed wares for cooking and storage. The short firing is possible because the clays are often rather coarse textured and thus less subject to thermal shock. In addition, preheating the pots decreases the risk of thermal shock from the characteristically rapid temperature increase. If pots are not preheated before firing, the same effect may be created by lighting the upper layer of fuel first; because most of the heat is dissipated to the atmosphere, the heat that does reach the pots effectively preheats them. Generally, the slow-burning fuel underneath the pottery provides most of the heat for cooking the pots; the quicker-burning fuel around the sides and top also fires them, and it creates a covering blanket of ash that holds in the heat from below and protects the hot pots from the wind. The method is comparatively cheap and does not require the heavy capital investment needed to construct and maintain a kiln.

Windy conditions are a serious problem in firing pottery by the bonfire method, and potters may schedule their firings for times of the day when the wind is calmest, such as in the early morning or late afternoon. A gust of wind can cause the temperature to drop as much as 246°C (500°F; Reina and Hill 1978, 24). Strong winds can also damage kiln firings, however; a typhoon in Japan ruined several kiln loads there (Leach 1976, 195). Humidity and rainfall are also crucial factors, and many part-time potters practice their craft only in the dry season to avoid the difficulties rain causes in drying and firing their pots. A variety of signs may be used to predict rainfall or success in firing during the rainy season. Potters in Chinautla look at the position of the moon or the behavior of vultures: if vultures "make a blowing noise while flying by, it is a sign that there will be rain, which prevents the firing of the pottery: but if they whistle, the weather will be favorable for firing" (Reina 1966, 92). Many potters recognize that firing losses (see sec. 6.1.3) in the rainy season are generally much higher than in the dry season. Normal dampness of the soil may be compensated for by preheating the firing area to dry it or by placing a layer of sand over the ground before laying the bed of fuel.

The heavy smoke that results from firing pots, either in open fires or in kilns, is frequently a problem (Lynch 1979, 5), and partly for this reason potters' quarters, workshops, or firing areas may be on the outskirts of populated areas or downwind according to the prevailing winds.

Temperatures attained by open firings generally range between 600 and 850°C, but there is considerable variation. Although Cardew (1969, 11) claims that a minumum temperature of 550°C must be attained to make serviceable pottery, because of the chemical and physical constraints of clay structures (see chap. 4) it is doubtful that such an absolute minimum temperature can reliably be specified. The most striking characteristic of open firings is the extremely rapid rise in temperature. Temperatures of 900°C or higher are not

Figure 5.19   The rapid schedules of three Pueblo firings of smudged ware: *a, b,* adding dung and juniper chips; *c,* smothering the fire with powdered manure; *d,* removing protective sheets of tin; *e,* bonfire heap covered with ashes for additional smudging. After Shepard 1976, fig. 6.

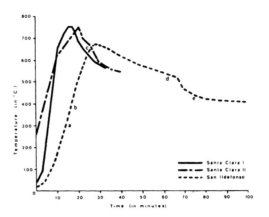

uncommon and can be reached within twenty minutes in the American Southwest (fig. 5.19; Shepard 1976, fig. 5 and table 3; see also Colton 1951) and Nigeria (Nicklin 1981a, 352, fig. 32:2). Maximum temperatures are usually attained at or just after the fuel covering the pile of pots has been consumed; following this the temperature declines, rapidly at first and then more slowly. Measured temperatures of open firings may vary with the measurement techniques used, and relatively few ethnographic pyrometric studies have been done at all. The measurements may be based on optical pyrometers, pyrometric cones, or thermoelectric pyrometers (thermocouples) (see Nicklin 1981a).

The maximum temperature attained, the time necessary to reach it, and the duration of high-temperature burning are all functions of the kinds of fuel used and its size, quantity, and position in the firing (see Shepard 1976, 77–91). Hardwoods burn hotter and longer than softwoods and generally with the preferred cleaner flame, though the resins in pine can contribute to high temperatures. Temperatures of 900°C or more have been attained in open firings with dung, coal, and juniper wood in the American Southwest (Shepard 1976, fig. 4) and with palm fronds in Nigeria (Nicklin 1981a, 352).

The rate of combustion is affected by the ratio of the surface area to the weight of the fuel, because this determines the availability of oxygen. Slow combustion occurs with large pieces of fuel, such as logs, while rapid combustion occurs with finer matter such as wood chips, shavings, or grass. For this reason the slow-burning fuel is usually placed under the stack of vessels; quick-burning fuel, such as grass, placed around the sides will fire rapidly because of the abundant surface area available to oxygen, and it deposits an insulating layer of ash over the vessels that helps retard convective heat loss. Dung cakes placed on top of the pots will also enhance the heat-enclosing kilnlike effect. There is some variability in the rate of burning of dung— Shepard (1976, 77) considers it to be fast burning, while potters in Pakistan regard it as slow burning (Rye and Evans 1976, 165)—and this doubtless varies from species to species (see Winterhalder, Larsen, and Thomas 1974 for a discussion of dung as fuel for cooking fires).

Potters usually use color—either the color of the fired clay or the glow of the hot pots (e.g., red heat is visible in daylight at 550–625°C)—to determine when the firing is complete, and they often allow the pots little time to cool after maximum temperature has been attained. Indeed, pots are frequently uncovered or removed from the hot coals at measured temperatures above 600°C (Shepard 1976, 85; Nicklin 1981a, 356). This enhances color development and may, if temperatures are sufficiently high, help oxidize fireclouds. An important point in pyrometric studies of bonfire firings is whether, given the extremely short firing times, the measured temperatures are actually attained by the vessels themselves (which exhibit a thermal gradient within the walls) or whether they are simply the temperatures within the bonfire surrounding the pots (see Nicklin 1981a).

An interesting variant of open firings is smudging, where the pottery is blackened, usually at the completion of the firing, by covering the pile of pots with fine material such as powdered manure or sawdust. This material closes off the supply of oxygen to the ware so that carbon is deposited on the surfaces and in the pores. In Santa Clara, the famous polished blackwares are created by adding manure when the fire has reached its maximum heat, after which the temperature drops; the pots are left for thirty to ninety minutes before being removed from the remains of the fire (LeFree 1975, 63–65).

5.4.1.2   KILN FIRING

Higher firing temperatures and more complete heating of the pots are achieved with kilns, enclosed chambers for containing and channeling combustion in the firing of ceramic materials. Kilns are constructed of refractory material, usually brick, which is able to withstand the stresses of continual expansion and contraction in firing and cooling; kilns may sometimes be partly or entirely of stone, however, as in Peru (fig. 5.20) and Pereuela, Spain (Peacock 1982, 21). Kilns developed fairly rapidly in the Near East, with a double-chamber vertical downdraft kiln known from the late seventh millennium (Majidzadeh 1975–77, 217). In China the oldest known kilns at Banpo may be as early as the middle fifth millennium and are of both vertical and horizontal types (fig. 1.5; Shangraw 1977, 388). Three basic types of kilns can be identified: pit kilns, updraft kilns, and downdraft kilns (see Rhodes 1968; Leach 1976, 178–97; Cardew 1969, 170–212; Nelson 1984, 21–24).

Pit kilns may be considered functionally intermediate between open firings and updraft kilns in that they involve enclosures but the fuel is usually spread around and between the pots rather than being concentrated in a separate area (Rye and Evans [1976, 164–66] call this the "mixed firing" technique). Pit kilns (fig. 5.21) typically consist of an excavated area of earth surrounded on three or four sides by low walls of mud or mud brick (or the wall of the potter's house). Fuel is placed below and above the pots in the kiln, and then the assembly is fired in much the same way as are open firings. Because the heat is partially contained, however, pit kilns may achieve higher temperatures and sustain them longer than do completely open bonfires (see, e.g., Shepard 1976, fig. 4). In addition, the kiln may be constructed on a slight slope for better draft, as in bank kilns. Although temperatures may be within the range required for successful firing of glazed wares, the pots are too close to the fuel for this, and pit kilns are generally used for nonglazed firings. Most of the advantages and disadvantages of open firings also hold true for pit kilns.

Figure 5.20 A large round updraft kiln at Yahuay, an abandoned winery in the Moquegua valley of Peru. The lower exterior portion is reinforced with rounded river stones, while the major construction is of adobe brick. The three openings for introducing firewood into the chamber are not visible in the photograph. Note buttresses left and left center and the cracks near the top of the structure.

Figure 5.21 Open pit kiln (clamp) at Musazi, Pakistan: a, cross section; b, plan—circle indicates size of large water jar for comparison. After Rye and Evans 1976, fig. 7.

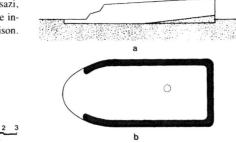

Updraft kilns are simple enclosed firing chambers in which the heat moves upward from underneath the pots and then is vented outward. These kilns are usually cylindrical for pottery firings (fig. 5.20) but square or rectangular for firing bricks. Fuel is fed through openings in the side of the kiln or through a firebox below and forward of the firing chamber (fig. 5.22). Early updraft kilns were often bank kilns, dug into the side of a hill or embankment with the firebox at the lower level, the firing chamber immediately adjacent, and a vent or chimney leading up and outside. In freestanding updraft kilns a slotted platform may act as the floor of the chamber to allow the flames to penetrate from the firebox up to the pots. Heat and gases escape through the top of the kiln, either by a chimney or through an open top with a temporary covering.

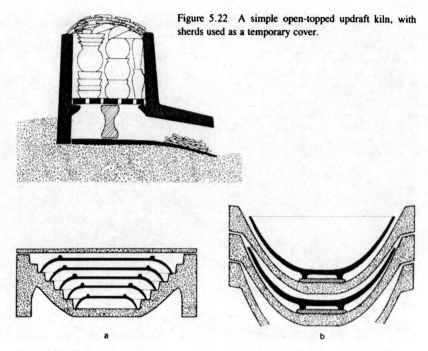

Figure 5.22   A simple open-topped updraft kiln, with sherds used as a temporary cover.

a   b

Figure 5.23   Two versions of saggars (or "setters") from China. After Medley 1976, 109.

While many types of complex updraft kilns exist, simple ones used by traditional potters usually have open tops through which the kiln is loaded for each firing, with the setter often standing on lower tiers of pots to position the successive layers. The opening may be closed by placing a layer of large sherds over the vessels to be fired, or a temporary domed roof may be created by setting bricks in a series of courses angled inward until the top is almost sealed. Pots are often placed inside protective containers called saggars or seggars (fig. 5.23), and for glost firings the glazed wares may be carefully separated by small tripods called stilts or props so that they do not touch each other and mar the glaze. The maximum temperature these kilns attain is usually 900 to 1000°C.

Although updraft kilns have numerous advantages over open firings in terms of containing and sustaining the heat, there are several disadvantages. As in open firings or pit kilns, a considerable amount of heat escapes unused through the top of the kiln. Also, hot spots or conduits of heat ("chimneys") are often created by the placement of vessels in the kiln, so that parts of the load are overfired and other parts are underfired. In addition, there is danger of thermal shock to vessels at the bottom of the kiln load, which receive the direct heat of the fire.

Downdraft kilns differ from updraft kilns in the location of the vessels to be fired relative to the movement of the flames and heat of combustion. Whereas in updraft kilns the heat moves upward through the kiln load, in downdraft kilns it is deflected from direct contact with the pots by a bag-wall and forced to travel upward in the kiln. It then passes down through the chamber holding pots and is vented outward through an exterior chimney assembly, which also

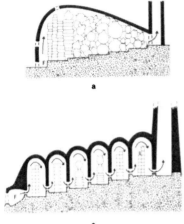

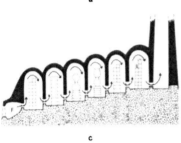

Figure 5.24 Kilns: *a*, *b*, large, single-chamber climbing bank kiln similar to those used at Jingdezhen (*a*, after Nelson 1984, fig. 24; *b*, after Leach 1976, 183); *c*, Longquan (Lung-chu'an, China) multichamber climbing kiln (after Medley 1976, 148, and Nelson 1984, fig. 25); *d*, plan of ruins of Old Karatsu multichamber climbing kiln, dating to the sixteenth to seventeenth century (after Mikami 1979, fig. 166). F indicates firebox.

provides most of the draft. The advantages of downdraft kilns are many. A major feature is that more of the heat of combustion is used because the downward draft through the kiln counters convective heat loss. Also, the downward currents discourage "chimneys" of intense heating within the kiln.

Tunnel, bank, or climbing kilns, which are used in many parts of the Far East including Japan, Korea, and China, may operate on updraft or downdraft principles. Climbing kilns consist of a long, tunnellike chamber or a series of linked kiln chambers built on a slope; the gradient provides the draft for combustion (fig. 5.24). Firing takes place at the bottom of the slope, with fuel supplemented at points along its extent. Exterior openings in the kilns permit setting pots, adding fuel and admitting air, and viewing the vessels as they fire. In multichambered kilns, such as the semicontinuous downdraft kiln, the heat and flames enter each chamber at its base, are deflected upward, then circulate down through the pots, out at the rear base, and into the next chamber (see Leach 1976, 186). Extremely large kilns may have as many as twenty chambers and take two weeks to fire (Leach 1976, 186).

Kilns represent a major advance toward ensuring success in firing pots, the most dangerous final step of the potter's enterprise. By protecting the vessels from drafts and providing a boundary to enclose the heat, these structures permit higher and better-controlled temperatures, control of atmosphere, and more efficient use of fuel. But kilns do not completely remove the element of chance from a firing. As Leach (1976, 195–96) describes it,

> The firing is the climax of the potter's labour, and in a wood-fired kiln of any size it is a long and exhausting process. Weeks and months of work are at stake. Any one of a dozen things may go wrong. Wood may be damp, flues may get choked, bungs of saggars fall, shelves give way and alter the draughts, packing may have been too greedily close, or for sheer exhaustion, one may have snatched an hour's

sleep, handing over control to someone else and thereby altering the rhythm of the stoking. At white heat things begin to move, to warp and to bend, the roar of combustion takes on a deeper note—the heavy domes crack and tongues of white flame dart out here and there, the four-minute stokes fill the kiln shed with bursts of dense black smoke and fire. . . . a big kiln firing has the aspect of a battle-field where men test themselves to the utmost against odds.

Thus despite the security they provide, kilns are not without their problems. They represent a substantial capital investment for potters, one that needs constant maintenance and repair. Kilns and their components constantly expand and shrink with firing and cooling, and under these stresses they may develop cracks or flaws that can be lethal to a load of pottery. They must be very carefully designed to make maximum use of prevailing winds, available heat, draft, and space for setting pots to ensure even heating. Even so, kilns experience pronounced thermal gradients from top to bottom and center to sides that will affect the firing of the pots. The rhythm of stoking the kiln during firing also changes the atmosphere, from oxidizing just before stoking to reducing just after fuel is added (Rye and Evans 1976, 167). Experienced kiln setters and stokers understand these variations and carefully load the chamber keeping them in mind. Indeed, at large pottery factories, such as in the Chinese porcelain industry, setting and firing the kilns were carried out by specialists, apart from the process of creating the vessels.

The use of fuel in kilns is not as efficient as might be expected. A large proportion of the energy produced is used just to heat the kiln structure itself; small kilns have a particularly unfavorable ratio of heat distribution with respect to pots versus structure, but even in large kilns it has been estimated that 30% to 40% of the heat is lost (Cardew 1969, 182) through radiation, convection, and conduction. The situation is far more serious for open firings. It has been estimated that in open cooking fires only 10% of the energy potential of wood is actually used (National Academy of Sciences 1980, 28); doubtless a comparable figure obtains for bonfire pottery firings, and this is improved only slightly by the ash layer insulation.

These figures are of no little concern, because fuel is the most expensive of potters' raw materials (see sec. 6.1.3.2) and, next to labor, represents their greatest expenditure. But firewood is becoming increasingly scarce, driving up its price and forcing either a search for fuel alternatives, changed firing strategies, relocation of manufacturing areas, or abandonment of potting as an economic pursuit. The shortage of firewood in highland Mexico, for example, has resulted in a variety of solutions: potters in Acatlán, Puebla, use lower-quality fuel such as cactus and automobile tires to fire their wares (Lackey 1981, 59–60); some potters in Chamula, Chiapas, buy tracts of woodland for a reliable fuel supply or have abandoned their craft altogether (Howry 1976); in Los Pueblos, Michoacán, potters fire with sawdust or tires or drive as much as eighty kilometers to obtain wood (Papousek 1981, 84–85, 114). Elsewhere the situation is much the same; in Bombay, for example, potters fire with lint from a cotton factory (Lynch 1979, 8). The firewood shortage is not solely a modern problem, however. In the ancient Near East political and social unrest may have contributed to a shortage of fuel early in the

first millennium A.D., leading to reduced firing temperature of pottery at Seleucia (Matson 1971, 74). And in China the staggering rate of consumption
inevitably gave rise to a scarcity of firewood around Jingdezhen, forcing porcelain manufacturers to go three-hundred miles for wood by the eighteenth
century (Staehelin 1965, 38).

5.4.1.3 POSTFIRING TREATMENTS

A variety of postfiring treatments are applied to pottery, either to improve appearance, seal surfaces to decrease permeability, or perhaps to increase
strength. In Papua New Guinea, for example, Azera pots may be treated by a
procedure similar to docking (although it is not clear if the paste contains calcite): river water is poured into pots hot from the fire and stirred until it evaporates (May and Tuckson 1982, 138).

Most commonly, these postfiring treatments involve applying a variety of
organic materials to the pot while it is still hot (table 5.3; Arnold 1985, 140).
In West Africa, potters boil the pods of the locust tree in water and then splash
this liquid on pots while they are still red hot from firing to coat the surface
and close the pores; coal tar is sometimes used for the same purpose (Cardew
1985, 37). Ibibio potters of Nigeria treat water pots with resin from the
avocado pear tree to give a "superficially glaze-like appearance" (Nicklin
1981b, 177).

The use of tree resins is widespread. The Shipibo-Conibo of eastern Peru
apply two resins to their pottery, one for "lending a glaze-like slip to white-
slipped surfaces" and the other to waterproof the interior of vessels that will
contain liquids (DeBoer and Lathrap 1979, 115). Resinous coatings are also
applied by potters in the Philippines (Foster 1956; Longacre 1981, 60) and
Ethiopia (Messing 1957).

Food substances are also commonly applied to pots after firing and before
use. In Ethiopia milk may be poured into new pots and swirled around until
they cool (Messing 1957); presumably the scalded milk seals the interior surface. Potters of Santa Apolonia, Guatemala, coat their slipped pots after firing
with *agua de masa,* the liquid left after soaking corn in limewater to make

Table 5.3 Postfire Coatings and Treatments for Pottery

Substance	Location or Group
Milk	Ethiopia
Coconut milk	Philippines, Panaeati Island
Agua de masa (limewater)	Santa Apolonia, Guatemala
Manioc juice	Caribs, Brazil
Pawpaws, yams, bananas, boiled	Papua New Guinea
Sago flour and hot water	Papua New Guinea
Banana or passion-vine leaves, rubbed on	Papua New Guinea
Locust-tree beans, boiled	West Africa
Beeswax	Sarayacu Quichua, Ecuador
Mangrove bark, boiled	Papua New Guinea
Resin, avocado pear tree	Ibibio, Nigeria
Resins, various	Philippines, Ethiopia, Papua New Guinea, Shipibo-Conibo (Peru), Sarayacu Quichua (Ecuador)

Source: For references, see text and Arnold 1985, 140.

tortillas; the residue left on the pots is rubbed to a high polish (Reina and Hill 1978, 63). In Papua New Guinea a variety of things may be done to new pots (May and Tuckson 1982, 49, 139, 174): they may be sealed by boiling paw-paws, yams, or ripe cooking bananas in them, by splashing on a solution of sago flour and hot water, by rubbing their surfaces with banana leaves or passion-vine leaves, or by coating them with a milky tree resin also used to caulk boats; traditionally a new cooking pot must be covered with the blood of a pig before it can be used.

5.4.2 Ethnographic Examples

One of the simplest procedures of open or bonfire firing is practiced by the Hopi Indians of Arizona (Colton 1951, 73–74):

> To fire pottery the Hopi women . . . first build a fire of juniper chips to dry out the ground. This is to be sure that moisture will not con-dense on her pots to be absorbed by the clay and cause breakage. Around this fire the potter will place her batch of pots which may number from one to twenty-four, depending on their size. They are warmed and the last trace of water removed from the clay. Later when the fire has burned down, the potter will cover the ground with blocks of sheep dung and these, in turn, covered by sandstone frag-ments the size of a fist, thus building a platform. . . .
>
> On the platform the Hopi potter will build a mound of pots a foot or more high and about a foot and a half in diameter. This mound she covers with large sherds for protection from contact with the fuel. Over the sherds she builds a kiln [sic] of dry sheep dung from some corral—chunks about six inches across—with which she completely covers the mound. Sometimes she sprinkles a little coal on the dung to increase the temperature.
>
> The dung covering the pottery catches fire from the remains of the preliminary wood fire, smoking violently until the whole mass bursts into flame. For about an hour it burns furiously, but dying down gradually leaves a mass of tough gray ashes covering the pottery. A Hopi potter does not remove her pots until four or more hours after the fire starts. In fact she usually does not remove them from the kiln until they are cool enough to handle easily.

In Guinhilaran, Philippines, firing is also by the open or bonfire method, but many more pots may be fired at a time. In one firing that was described, there were over three hundred pots in the pile (Scheans 1977, 19–20):

> The firing piles themselves are composed of lines of supporting rocks or broken flower pots averaging 1' in height and almost any combustible material that is, ideally, both cheap and available. The largest set of support rocks that we measured covered an area of 3 by 8 meters. It had five rows of rocks across its narrow dimension. Wood is presently favored as the material to be laid across the sup-ports to build the floor of the pile. . . . After the floor is built the pottery is laid in on its side and the firing can begin.
>
> [After placing the pots on the prepared floor] the pile was then lit

by pushing burning sugar cane leaves and cogon [a type of grass] between the supports at the upwind end. This was repeated the length of the pile. Then cogon was heaped on the pile starting at the upwind end. After this was completed, the two men doing the firing stood by and tended the fire by adding more cogon and moving bunches of it around to insure even heating. After fifty minutes, one flower-pot was pulled and judged to be completely fired. Shortly after, small holes were poked into the bottom of the pile to increase its draft. By this time the floor of the pile had burned through and the pile had slumped. . . . After one and one-half hours the base of the pile was a mass of brightly glowing embers but no attempt was made to take pieces out. Guinhilaran potters prefer to leave the pile to cool overnight and to remove their wares the next morning.

Potters in Kharmathu, Pakistan, fire with an elaborately set pit kiln placed on a slope at the far edge of their village. The slope gives the kiln a strong updraft (Rye and Evans 1976, 41):

The width of the pit across the hillside is 3.7 m and the length of the pit from front to back up the hillside is 4.6 m. The perimeter of the pit has been built up with earth to provide a low wall (*bannā*). The maximum depth of the pit from the level of the top of the walls to the lowest floor level is approximately 1 m. . . . The narrow end of the pit (*durrā*, "firemouth") is filled with rounded pieces of rock about 15 cm in diameter to provide a passage of air to the front of the setting. . . .

After sweeping off the floor of the kiln, the next stage of setting is to place a layer of straw (from the mustard seed plant . . .) on the floor of the pit. Twigs from an unidentified scrub bush, which grows wild around Kharmathu, are mixed with the straw. . . . This base layer of twigs and straw is trampled down to a final thickness of about 25 cm. The next layer consists of mixed wood (*lakrī*) scraps . . . from 5–10 cm diameter and about 1 m long. . . . Dung cakes (*gohā*) are packed between the rows of wood.

The vessels are then placed on top of these two base layers of fuel. Larger pots are set at the bottom and smaller vessels between, or on top of the larger, with all vessels set upside down. When all the vessels are placed in position, a layer of what straw (*nār*) about 15 cm thick is spread over the pots. . . .

Broken pieces of dung (*pāh*) are then used to form another layer over the straw. The layer of dung pieces is only about 8 to 10 cm thick. This completes the setting: the final setting is approximately level with the top of the perimeter walls of the pit kiln.

The potters start the firing . . . by lighting a small fire of twigs at the front or firemouth end of the kiln. The fuel is consumed in 8–10 hours depending on climatic conditions and the fired vessels can be removed every 24 hours after the firing commences.

At Vounaria, Greece, potters use simple cylindrical updraft kilns with a conical vaulted roof and fire about once a week during their working season from April to October (Matson 1972, 218–20):

The potters are skilled in loading their kilns so that they effectively use the space, so that there is little damage from the simultaneous firing of unglazed and glazed ware, and so that the flames and hot gases of combustion can flow freely around the kiln load in ways that will result in quite a uniform heat distribution. . . . Water jars (*vikes*) are first placed in the kiln to a depth of about 0.6 m. Above them are stamnes [amphoralike jars] which, if this is their second firing, have glazed interiors and a glazed exterior shoulder and rim zone. Vikes are again used to top the load. Thus the glazed ware is to some degree protected from the direct impingement of the flames, and may possibly be exposed to a slightly lower firing temperature. . . . The ware is usually stacked in the kiln upside down to prevent ash accumulation in the vessels and, for the glazed ware, to maintain a thick glaze on and near the rim as well. Roof tiles are used as dividers and supports in loading the kiln, as also are large sherds from broken pieces. A kiln load of medium-sized and small vessels consists of about 700 pieces. . . .

The firing begins very slowly, which is normal good ceramic practice. Throughout the 7–10 hours of the operation, fuel is added constantly in short pieces. . . . The fuel used at Vounaria varies according to what is available and how much it costs. The generally preferred fuel is *verga,* prunings from the vineyards, for the vine clippings burn well and do not build up a bulky mass of glowing slow-burning charcoal. . . .

The end of the firing is determined in Vounaria by the kiln color of the pottery in the bisque firing, or by the quality of the glaze in the glost firing. Often glazed and unglazed ware are fired together. When the incandescent pottery looks "white" in the kiln, the proper temperature has been reached and the firing is finished. Judging from laboratory experiments, this will be at about 900° plus or minus 50°. . . . The kiln is then allowed to cool from two to four days, depending upon its size, the exterior temperature, and the immediate need for the fired ware to supply a trucker who has come to purchase it.

5.5   References

Amiran and Shenhav 1984
Arnold 1978, 1980, 1985
Arrott 1953
Balfet 1965
Balfet, Fauvet-Berthelot, and
    Monzon 1983
Blandino 1984
Bowen and Moser 1968
Brainerd 1958
Brody 1979
Brongniart 1844
Brooks et al. 1974
Broyles 1968
Bushell 1910
Cardew 1969, 1985
Colton 1951

Curtis 1962
David and Hennig 1972
DeAtley 1986
DeBoer 1984
DeBoer and Lathrap 1979
Díaz 1966
Donnan and Clewlow 1974
Dumont 1952
Fewkes 1940, 1941
Fontana et al. 1962
Foster 1948a,b, 1956, 1959, 1967
Gifford and Smith 1978
Gould 1978
Gould and Watson 1982
Graham 1922
Guthe 1925

Howry 1976
Johns 1977a
Johnston 1977
Klemptner and Johnson 1986
Kramer 1979
Lackey 1981
Lauer 1970
Lawrence and West 1982
Leach 1976
LeFree 1975
Linares de Sapir 1969
Linné 1957
Lobert 1984
London 1981
Longacre 1981
Lothrop 1927
Lynch 1979
McGregor 1941
Majidzadeh 1975–77
Malinowski 1922
Man 1894
Matson 1971, 1972, 1973, 1974,
    1975a
May and Tuckson 1982
Medley 1976
Mercer 1897
Messing 1957
Mikami 1979
National Academy of Sciences 1980
Nelson 1984
Nicholson and Patterson 1985a,b
Nicklin 1971, 1979, 1981a,b
Norton 1970

Ogan 1970
Papousek 1981
Payne 1982
Peacock 1982
Picolpasso 1934
Reina 1966
Reina and Hill 1978
Rhodes 1968, 1973
Rice 1985
Rye 1976, 1981
Rye and Evans 1976
Santley 1982
Scheans 1977
Schiffer 1976
Shangraw 1977
Shepard 1942a, 1962, 1965, 1976
Simpkins and Allard 1986
Solheim 1952, 1954
Staehelin 1965
Steinberg and Kamilli 1984
Stern 1951
Stimmell and Stromberg 1986
Stone 1950
Thompson 1958
Tschopik 1950
van der Leeuw 1977
van der Merwe and Scully 1971
Voyatzoglou 1974
Weigand 1969
Whitaker and Whitaker 1978
Winterhalder, Larsen, and Thomas
    1974

6 Pottery Economics: Perspectives on Production and Distribution

Although ethnography provides abundant information on the wide range of techniques used in pot manufacture, the same is not true of its organization. Pottery production—the socioeconomic arrangements involved in practicing the craft as opposed to the mechanics of building a pot—has not been comprehensively addressed. This is unfortunate, because without a broad set of comparative data concerning how, where, or by whom pottery is produced, distributed, and used, archaeological reconstructions of these patterns are on shaky ground.

This chapter addresses the production and distribution of pottery from an organizational and economic viewpoint; functional and stylistic perspectives are taken up in succeeding chapters. The emphasis is on the range of production and distribution arrangements, their interrelation, and the relevance of these data for reconstructing such behavior in prehistory.

6.1 Anthropology and Commodity Production

Questions about pottery production are at the forefront of much archaeological research into ceramic materials, but unlike many other areas of pottery studies, there is very little theoretical work on contemporary pottery production that archaeologists can draw upon in interpreting their data. Ethnographers have devoted a great deal of attention to manufacture: the techniques or procedures of making pottery, including collection of resources, the building, decorating, and firing of clay objects, and the associated tools (chap. 5). But manufacture is only one aspect of the economics of pottery. As an economic activity, pottery production is woven into the fabric of the broader social and political context within which manufacturing decisions are made and is closely tied to patterns of distribution and consumption.

For much of prehistory and continuing to the present in many parts of the world, the production of ceramic objects—traditional household utensils, roof or floor tiles, bricks, flowerpots, tourist items—exemplified what is called cottage or domestic industry (Muller 1984) or simple commodity production. Much of it takes place in urban areas (see, e.g., Lynch 1979), but a greater proportion occurs in rural locations that are tied to larger urban or regional political economies.

6.1.1 Economic Anthropological Literature

Little attention has been given to rural nonagricultural commodity production in the economic anthropology literature (cf. Cook 1984), and thus there is a dearth of models for archaeologists trying to understand prehistoric pottery production. Most of the formulations by which archaeologists have attempted to characterize pottery (and other craft) production arrangements since Neolithic times are legacies of European economic histories, which have had at least three important consequences for economic archaeological studies.

One is that most quasi-evolutionary schemes in economic archaeology posit a direct progression from individual household production for "own use" through workshops to factory organization, with special variants in particular situations, such as medieval guilds. These schemes were borrowed from economists' efforts to understand the transformations occurring during the Industrial Revolution in Europe and have been extended, often uncritically, outside their original space/time framework to include prehistoric contexts.

A second legacy of European economic histories is a focus on the relation between craft production and agriculture (see also Dow 1985). Most of the prehistoric societies in which commodity production has received any attention at all were agrarian, and there has been an implicit and explicit tendency to emphasize maximization/marginalist concerns in hypotheses about individual producers' decision making. This reflects a vision of a relatively simple inverse relation between agricultural holdings and income or craft output and income (Chayanov 1966, 40).

Third, the literature on economic development, to which archaeologists might turn for a broader temporal perspective on economics and economic change, has emphasized agricultural rather than commodity production. Where traditional peasant industries have received attention, the emphasis is on modernizing them so they can be incorporated into the capitalist—and often tourist-oriented—economy (sec. 15.1). The consequence has been to relegate

> to an unimportant role the traditional and small-scale industries in the process of development. Instead, manufacturing development is essentially seen as a transformation process from traditional to modern, from rural to urban and from agrarian to industrial. . . . Small-scale production has been taken to mean inefficient and backward; large-scale production has become synonymous with the efficient and modern. Moreover, the consumer is characterized as preferring

standardized products, while traditional goods are believed to be inferior and easily replaced by factory goods. (Ho and Huddle 1976, 232)

These approaches shed little if any light on prehistoric commodity production in general or pottery production in particular, and the negative ramifications are considerable. One problem is that models and concepts of modern economics may be inappropriately extended to prehistoric situations. Examples include the perpetuation of a strict rural/urban dichotomy and the uncritical application of central place theory. Significant questions can be raised concerning the connection between production in the rural and urban sectors, and about extending into prehistory today's economic relationships, which are predicated on world market systems, rapid communication and transportation, and tourism.

Another problem is that the development literature, with its emphasis on modernization, obscures the value and role of traditional craft items and their labor-intensive productive arrangements in the day-to-day livelihood and broader ethos of many societies. In the case of pottery, attempts to modernize the rural industries have included efforts to make them less labor intensive and more capital intensive by, for example, introducing the potter's wheel and kilns into communities where pottery is traditionally hand built and fired in open fires (Foster 1962, 143–44). The potters' refusal to adopt these modern capital-intensive technologies has sometimes been interpreted as reflecting a conservative basic personality structure or as backwardness (see sec. 15.2.1).

6.1.2   Concepts in the Study of Production

The relation between archaeological and ethnographic studies of the economics of pottery has been limited by the lack of common analytical units and behavioral concepts that can be addressed by both disciplines. Many concepts or units either are not shared in the analysis of pottery or are virtually unmeasurable archaeologically. These include the taxonomic units or types archaeologists work with (see sec. 9.1), the idea of craft specialization, and the concepts of reciprocity, redistribution, and marketing, to name only a few.

Archaeologists need ethnographic studies of pottery production to provide a context for understanding the behavior and decisions involved in four aspects of the production process in antiquity: scale of production, mode of production, variability in products, and, of course—given the longitudinal perspective of archaeology—changes (both long and short term) in any of these. The scale of production refers to how much pottery was produced and what kind; production level or scale is obviously closely tied to manufacturing technology as well as to distribution and use—that is, to the "market" for the pottery. The mode of production likewise addresses manufacturing technology, but it is more specifically oriented toward labor and organizational arrangements, including who is engaged in production (males, females, young, old, families, clans) and where they work (e.g., households, workshops); distributional questions have also been incorporated, for example, in recognition of the role of middlemen traders or entrepreneurs.

For archaeologists, perhaps the most important conjoining of mode and scale of production is in the concept of specialization (sec. 6.2.3). In discussing pottery production, very often the question addressed is whether the activity was an economic or craft specialization—that is, Was it restricted to a few skilled producers? This issue seeks to place pottery production within the more general process of economic differentiation of complex societies, a process that involves—among other things—commoditization, or the production of goods for exchange and use by others (Hart 1982, 40–41). The existence of craft specialists is difficult to determine archaeologically, however, and the criteria by which ethnographers recognize economic specialists are not entirely amenable to archaeological application.

To study pottery production in prehistory one needs to identify and quantify its inputs (labor and resources) and its outputs (the pottery products). These objectives have been pursued on several levels and by various approaches, the most common being to identify the techniques used in pottery manufacture and where it was produced. Understanding the prehistoric socioeconomic organization of production also demands attention to both scale and mode of production; archaeologists' efforts have most frequently been directed toward specialization or have at least assumed that specialization existed. In general, however, the organization of production has not been heavily investigated archaeologically.

In the absence of satisfactory concepts and "middle-range theory" spanning the gap between economic anthropology theory and the empirical realities of the archaeological data base, archaeologists have pursued production arrangements indirectly. That is, they have not looked at the quantitative labor and resource inputs but have instead examined the patterns of variability within the output—the ceramic products themselves. For example, quantitative variation in a qualitative attribute, style, has provided the basis for some interpretations of mode of production in prehistory (see chap. 8), while amounts of pottery produced and its quantifiable attributes have been used to infer both scale and mode.

These investigations of variability have been undertaken as a means of understanding the scale and mode of production and thereby the existence of economic specialization within a prehistoric society. It is unfortunate that ethnoarchaeologists have obtained little or no comparable data on ceramic variability, other than stylistic, against which archaeological observations could be measured. Until such data are gathered, the finer points of full-time versus part-time specialization and degree of centralized control of production are likely to be unanswered, and the whole subject of scale and mode of pottery production will have to be treated in very general and simplistic terms. On the other hand, it is difficult to evaluate whether the lack of attention to such matters in the ethnographic literature reflects overall inattention to variables of commodity production in general or indicates that these matters are idealized constructs with little empirical reality.

The focus on output, that is, on the pottery products, is partly a consequence of the lack of middle-range theoretical constructs that would allow direct testing of economic theory. It also reflects the lack of abundant evidence for clearly defined workshops and capital investment in manufacturing technology in many parts of the world throughout much of prehistory. Given these inadequacies, closer scrutiny of the ceramic products is a pragmatic—if somewhat unsatisfactory—solution providing an alternative to a dubious deductive strategy grounded in negative evidence. Attention to the pottery products encourages, in areas where these restrictions hold, using behavioral information encoded in the pottery to draw inferences about production. A major difficulty with this approach is that equivalent attention to coded economic (as opposed to stylistic, e.g.) behavior has not been evident in ethnographic and ethnoarchaeological studies, thus precluding any insightful interchange of ideas and conclusions.

6.1.3 Ethnographic Overview: A Focus on Firing

In any study of the economics of pottery making, the overwhelming conclusion to be drawn is that traditional potters in all parts of the world are at or near the bottom of the socioeconomic scale (see Foster 1965b; also Hodges 1974, 35; Nicholson and Patterson 1985a, 59). Only in a few areas are potters and their work held in any appreciable local esteem, and that is usually where skilled women potters contribute the major household income or earn significantly extra (see Stone 1950, 278; Crossland and Posnansky 1978, 82; Reina and Hill 1978, 21) or where individuals produce for a tourist market and are considered artists (e.g., Lackey 1981, 38). Most traditional potters seem to live in a precarious economic state, their expenditures equaling or exceeding income, with limited opportunity to amass any extra income and improve their life-style. This situation is made even more tenuous by the overall declining market for traditional pottery (cf. Stone 1950, 278) as the utensils produced by potters are rapidly being replaced by more durable metals and plastics (see chap. 15). Where potters labor in workshops run by entrepreneurs, the economic situation is often worse: in the Liloan factories in the Philippines, the drop in prices and the reduced market resulted in a dramatic decline in the potters' income, but that of the entrepreneur stayed essentially the same (Scheans 1977, 65).

Seeing more promise of education and financial success in other activities, especially in the cities, younger generations are not entering pottery making (Lackey 1981, 126; Nicholson and Patterson 1985b, 236–37). Because children often are an important source of labor as well as heirs to the family business, in many cases this means that the craft is gradually disappearing. When potters themselves strive for some degree of upward mobility, this often means becoming a dealer rather than a manufacturer of pottery (see Papousek 1981; Scheans 1977, 21–22). As David and Hennig (1972, 25) comment about the Fulani, "the hallmark of a successful potter is to have stopped potting."

Initially it might seem that pottery making has the potential for being, if not lucrative, at least minimally secure. The raw materials for making pots are often obtainable at no cost, and potters may make many of their own manufacturing tools, such as paddles, anvils, bricks for kilns, and so forth. Also, in many traditional communities pottery objects are still household necessities. But the utensils themselves are given low monetary (or exchange) value, and the time that goes into their creation—apart from the cost of the raw materials—is not adequately compensated. Two additional factors are probably responsible for much of the low economic return: the high loss rate in firing and the high cost of fuel.

6.1.3.1 FIRING LOSS RATES

Firing is the climactic step in pottery manufacture, and it is a crucial one, because if it is not done properly, or if the wind and rain do not cooperate, the vessels being fired may be lost (see sec. 5.4). The loss may be only one pot or it may be several hundred, and it can represent the work of anywhere from several days to several months, depending on the frequency and volume of firing. A cross-cultural look at firing loss rates is instructive (table 6.1) and suggests that high rates of loss are not atypical, regardless of the firing technique. Open or bonfire firings seem to be the most variable, with loss rates ranging from zero to 100% among Hopi potters in the Southwestern United States (Colton 1951, 75). The estimated loss in pit kilns averages between 25% and 50% in Pakistan (Rye and Evans 1976, 36, 41, 54, 62), and this rate is commonly higher in the rainy season.

It might be expected from these data that large piles of wasters would be abundant at prehistoric sites, but this is not always the case, because potters

Table 6.1   Rates of Firing Loss with Different Kinds of Firings

Type of Firing	Place	Firing Loss	Reference
Open	Huichol, Mexico	25%, 100%[a,b]	Weigand 1969, 43
Open	Hopi, Southwestern U.S.	0%–100% in firings of 4–20 pots	Colton 1951, 75
Open	Fulani, Africa	13 of 16 pots cracked	David and Hennig 1972, 24
Open	Mixco, Guatemala	10% of *comales*[b]	Reina and Hill 1978, 44
Open	Chinautla, Guatemala	5%–10%	Reina 1966, 55
"Mixed"	Pakistan	<2%[b]	Rye and Evans 1976, 60
Shallow pit	Diola, Africa	11 of 179 destroyed, 8 kept for dry storage	Linares de Sapir 1969, 7
Shallow pit	Seri, Mexico	10%[b]	Bowen and Moser 1968, 115
Pit kiln	Pakistan	up to 50%	Rye and Evans 1976, 62
Pit kiln	Pakistan	25% of 400; 50% not uncommon[b]	Rye and Evans 1976, 41
Updraft	Ticul, Yucatán, Mexico	12%	Stark 1985, 174 (citing Hurd 1976)
Updraft	Tepakan, Campeche, Mexico	20%	Stark 1985, 174 (citing Hurd 1976)
Updraft	Coyotepec, Oaxaca, Mexico	20%	Van de Velde and Van de Velde 1939, 34
Slope	Philippines	18 of 148 jars	Scheans 1977, 64

Note: Rates are usually higher in the rainy season.
   [a]Firing loss occasionally viewed as witchcraft or punishment. Only two observations.
   [b]Figure is an estimate.

diligently repair or recycle their materials. Vessels that show only minor cracking from firing will usually be repaired, often by covering over the crack with clay or other pasty material to seal it. Among the Diola of Senegal, cracked pots that cannot be used for holding liquids are kept for dry storage, and those damaged beyond repair are crushed for sherd temper (Linares de Sapir 1969, 7). In general, the adage "Use it up, wear it out, make it do, or do without" describes well how potters recycle their firing accidents, as detailed in this vignette on Afghan potters (Rye and Evans 1976, 122–23, translated from Demont and Centlivres 1967, 57):

> Pieces damaged during firing are sold "as is" if not too badly deformed, or repaired with a sort of cement. The potter himself uses broken pieces to close the mouth of the kiln. In some cases he crushes sherds to add to the clay as temper. In his workshop, damaged pieces or the bottoms of jars serve as receptacles for slip and other materials. Waste clay removed during vessel manufacture is put in the bottom of a broken bowl or base of a jug, which then is used as a mold. Other fragments are used as scrapers or polishers. In general, all artisans have fragments of jars or jugs in their workshops for storing the water they use in their work. . . . During the rainy season, the garden paths are covered with sherds reduced to the size of gravel. Gardeners employ jars with broken necks as watering cans. Fragments of pottery are even used for intimate purposes.

6.1.3.2 FUEL COSTS

Firing loss is all the more serious because fuel is usually the highest—often the only—expense incurred in pottery manufacture, and it is consumed in enormous quantities. The porcelain kilns of Jingdezhen reportedly used 180 loads of firewood at 133 pounds each, and in earlier times 240 loads were burned, with 20 more consumed in the rainy months (Staehelin 1965, 38). Potters of the eighteenth- and nineteenth-century Staffordshire kilns used three tons of coal per ton of clay, while an experimental Romano-British kiln burned ten units of wood per unit of clay (Peacock 1982, 25). The ratios are somewhat more favorable for firing in Pakistan, ranging between 2:1 and 3:1, and open pit kilns may actually be more efficient (in terms of fuel consumption, insulation, and air supply) than enclosed kilns (Rye and Evans 1976, 165). Nonetheless, in view of the enormous quantities of fuel consumed in firing pottery, it is doubtless significant that the earliest technological developments in pottery making in the Near East, China, and the New World were kilns—structures designed to contain combustion and conserve heat.

Wood seems to be the preferred fuel for firing, both among modern studio potters (Cardew 1969, 171; Leach 1976, 179) and among traditional potters past and present. Indeed, the well-known porcelain factory at Sèvres, France, still fires with wood (Leach 1976, 179). Wood, however, is an extremely scarce resource worldwide, and this is especially a problem in underdeveloped countries in the tropics. In most of these areas wood is still the primary fuel for cooking and heating; it has been estimated that 1.5 billion people in developing countries obtain 90% or more of their energy requirements from wood or wood products (National Academy of Sciences 1980, vii). Unfortunately, these areas represent the last reserves of many of the world's hardwood forests, but unchecked development and population growth are rapidly decimating them through lumber exporting, ranching, and farming. In recognition of these pressures, there is an increasing need for reforestation with fast-growing "firewood" crops (National Academy of Sciences 1980).

Fuel is scarce and expensive, and potters must balance these expenditures against the tremendous but unavoidable risk of losing the vessels and the income they represent in firing accidents. The costs (and losses) can be reduced if the potter or an assistant collects the fuel rather than purchasing it; this, however, may reduce production time and thus the potential profits. (The same relationship of time/cost/profit holds for collecting versus purchasing clay; see also Beals 1975, appendixes 10, 11, and 14, for data on time, labor, and cash alternatives in pottery production in Santa María Atzompa, Oaxaca, Mexico,) Another twist on the fuel problem comes from Westerwald, Germany, where the disappearance of forests plus the environmental damage caused by the emission of HCl from the salt-glazing furnaces have required that potters fire with different fuels and retrofit their kilns with gas-scrubbing systems. This expensive equipment has forced many potters out of the business (Lowenstein 1986, 394).

While problems of increasing costs and decreasing fuel supplies are described for many areas, the most detailed ethnographic study of the relation between fuel costs and pottery production decisions deals with several communities ("Los Pueblos") in highland Mexico (Papousek 1981, 86–87, 114–15). For example, potters in Santiago can obtain wood for firing from either of two sources, each with advantages and disadvantages that must be weighed. Scrap wood from the sawmill at El Oro is closer (25 km away) and cheaper, but since it is fresh wood it is of lower quality; a three-ton truckload will supply only enough for 5.2 firings. Furthermore, it is often not available. Fuel from Ciudad Hidalgo, on the other hand, is dry wood, so a similar quantity (three-ton truckload) supplies enough for 7 firings, but Ciudad Hidalgo is 85 km from Santiago. Table 6.2 shows the detailed costs of various arrangements of bringing firewood for the second (glaze or glost) firing of vessels in Santiago in 1976. The cost of wood for this firing ranged between 67 and 129 pesos; these figures do not include the costs of the first firing or the glaze materials themselves. Although the cost of the wood from Ciudad Hidalgo was determined (by the ethnographer; potters reportedly do not make such calculations) to be 15 pesos more per kiln load, potters prefer it because it is of better quality and there is greater assurance that it will be available.

Earlier, in 1967, comparable costs were 50 pesos for fuel and 5 pesos for glaze materials. With the sale of a kiln load of pots at 162.5 pesos, the net profit per kiln load was 107.5 pesos, and net income was approximately 10–12 pesos per week (Papousek 1981, 56–57). Equivalent income figures for 1976 are not available; the net profit on a kiln load is estimated to be 700–1,200 pesos (Papousek 1981, 123), but the weekly income of potters, and a translation of this figure into the inflated pesos of 1976, is not given.

What is clear, however, is that fuel constitutes an increasingly burdensome portion of the costs of producing pottery in Los Pueblos, resulting in an ever narrower margin between profit and loss. Potters cope with this uncertainty by selling pots that are only partially fired or even unfired, a situation that is

Table 6.2   Comparison of Santiago Prices of Fresh Wood from El Oro with Prices of Dry Wood from Ciudad
Hidalgo, 1976 (in Pesos)

Origin of the Wood	Price per Three-Ton Truckload			Price per Kiln Load		
		In Santiago			In Santiago	
	In Place of Origin	Brought by Oneself[a]	Delivered by Others[b]	In Place of Origin	Brought by Oneself	Delivered by Others[b]
El Oro (fresh; enough for 5.2 firings)	300	350	600	58	67	115
Ciudad Hidalgo (dry; enough for 7 firings)	450	575	900	64	82	129

Source: Papousek 1981, 86.

[a]Price includes three tons of wood, plus expenses for one helper and for gas (the latter two adding 50 pesos to the cost of wood from El Oro and 125 pesos to the cost of wood from Ciudad Hidalgo).

[b]Price includes three tons of wood plus expenses for two helpers and transportation (the latter two adding 300 pesos to the cost of wood from El Oro and 450 pesos to the cost of wood from Ciudad Hidalgo).

highly profitable to the middlemen traders in pottery. Pots that have been given the first firing but are unglazed can be sold for 50% to 60% more than unfired pots; those that have been glazed and given a second firing sell for 100% to 200% more than unfired pots (Papousek 1981, 114). Regardless of the selling price, about one-third of the increases was already spent on fuel (as well as glaze for the second firing).

Seen in a broader light, the potters' decisions concerning fuel alternatives in Los Pueblos are commonplace: they reflect a need to balance cost, distance, and quality. It is interesting that in many areas of the world, especially on the fringes of large urban markets, potters have effected a symbiosis with other industries, especially agriculture, in order to obtain nontraditional fuels. Thus not only does agriculture often produce the primary contents of pottery vessels, but its by-products are a major source of raw materials for manufacturing them. Although dung is probably the agricultural by-product most widely used for firing, other agricultural and industrial materials include cotton lint in Bombay (Lynch 1979, 8), pruned olive branches in Spain (Curtis 1962, 496), wood shavings and sawdust in Los Pueblos, Mexico (Papousek 1981), tires, cornstalks, and sugarcane in Acatlán, Mexico (Lackey 1981, 59–60), and vineyard cuttings and the sludge from pressing olives in Greece (Matson 1972, 219).

6.2   Issues in the Study of Pottery Production

Studying the economics of pottery—its production, distribution, and use—requires attention to where the pottery was produced and how its production was organized. In studies of ethnographic communities and for much of the historical period, neither of these questions may pose much difficulty, since a variety of records attest to the present or past location of pottery manufacturing sites and in some cases to the organization of production as well. In prehistoric times, however, these issues are not so straightforward: questions concerning the location of manufacturing sites, the types of wares produced there, and the organization of production, while interrelated, pose their own difficulties for analysis and interpretation. Until production locations are known, studies of distribution cannot fruitfully proceed.

6.2.1   Location of Production

The location of pottery production has generally been investigated by two very different approaches. One of these is to note the spatial distributions of resources, ceramic styles, or artifacts related to ceramic production (table 6.3; see also Stark 1985). The second, far more technically sophisticated, is based on the analytical methods of provenience studies (see chap. 13 and sec. 14.2).

One clue to the sites of prehistoric pottery manufacture is the location of contemporary potting communities; the premise is that they tend to be relatively near clay resources (see sec. 5.2). Another clue archaeologists use is the spatial occurrence of ceramic styles. The "criterion of relative abundance" suggests that the pottery was probably manufactured in the region where it is most frequently found and was moved out from that location by trade. The general assumption is that at most sites the bulk of the pottery used was made locally. This approach, which harks back to early Americanist anthropological concepts of "culture areas" and "age-area hypotheses," is not particularly illuminating. Nonetheless, is has formed the basis for many archaeological reconstructions of economic relationships and chronologies, as well as other processes such as conquest or the spread of religion that may be indicated by the areal distribution of horizon styles of pottery and many other categories of artifacts.

Ethnographic data reveal that the location of pottery-making communities is governed by a number of factors (see Nicklin 1979, 449–51), of which proximity to resources and proximity to markets (in the sense of consumers rather than formal marketplaces) are perhaps the most important. Neither of these can be given absolute primacy, however. In Pakistan there was no clear evidence that workshops were established near clays of unusual quality; in fact, Rye and Evans (1976, 127) concluded that the workshop location may be

Table 6.3   Data Useful for Inferring Locations (Communities, Sites, or Individual Workplaces) of Ancient Pottery Production

Proximity to high-quality clay resources
Location near modern potting communities
Presence of kilns
Presence of burned soil areas—red soil, ash deposits, thermally altered rock
Presence of kiln furniture—stilts, props, saggars
Presence of firing wasters
Presence of pottery-making tools—wheels, molds, polishing stones, etc.
Stashes of raw materials—clay, temper, mixtures of clay and temper
Quantities of unfired vessels
Quantities of identical vessels (style, shape)
High frequency of locally made vessels
High frequency of different types of vessels

Note: No single one of these criteria is necessary or sufficient to prove production locations, nor do any of them necessarily indicate anything about the organization of production.

chosen first and that whatever clays are nearby may be used. Potters' perceptions of the suitability of clays and their utilization in a viable craft may also be governed more by sociopolitical considerations and trade alliances than by the reality of the geophysical environment. A more complex and perplexing situation obtains for the siting of the Roman Samian industries (Peacock 1982, 117–20). Arezzo, the most famous town producing this ware, is 250 km by mountain road from Rome, whereas other manufacturing areas were closer and were served by coastal transport. Furthermore, the wide distribution of production sites throughout Gaul suggests that a specific clay was not crucial to workshop location.

A confounding factor to be taken into account in areas of intensive manufacture of pottery over a long period is exhaustion of resources, especially clays and fuels. Potters in Cologne in Roman times used clay from Frechen, only 15 km away, but later the mines were exhausted, and now clay is obtained from up to several hundred kilometers away (Hancock 1984, 210). The manufacture of Chinese porcelains is particularly telling (Staehelin 1965, 38): for centuries porcelain was made from the famous white kaolin clays in Jiangxi Province, but by the seventeenth century that clay source was exhausted and potters had to import clay from 60 miles away. A similar situation existed with fuels: after deforestation of the surrounding hillsides, wood for firing the kilns had to be brought as much as 300 miles.

There is no simple formula to predict the presence or pinpoint the location of potting communities merely by the occurrence of high-quality clays, principles of least cost aside. Furthermore, identifying the geographical site of production and locating the geological sources of the clays used in manufacture are two distinct research objectives. Nonetheless, these considerations, together with other environmental factors relating to craft and agricultural production (see sec. 10.2.3; Arnold 1975a, 1985) can at the very least provide a starting point for identifying likely areas for further investigation.

A more precise and useful effort to identify sites of prehistoric manufacture involves noting the locations of tools and equipment used in making pottery or concentrations of raw materials and finished pottery products at a site (e.g., Kardos et al. 1985). Such data are invaluable, for they provide information not only on the locations of manufacture but on the actual techniques, and they give clues to organization as well. For example, piles of raw clay, paints, tempering materials, or mixed clay plus temper, the occurrence of turntables, wheels, molds, burnishing and scraping tools, saggars or other kiln furniture, and the presence of kilns all are useful and largely unambiguous indications of past pottery manufacture. The archaeological visibility of potting households or workshops has been addressed in ethnoarchaeological studies in Chiapas, Mexico (Deal 1983, 97–111) and in Egypt (Nicholson and Patterson 1985a). Table 6.4 compares how frequently several archaeological indicators of pottery making occur in potting households versus nonpotting households in two Chiapas communities.

Problems arise about the survival through time of some of these indicators at a site, however. Unconsolidated clays and pigments may erode or be dispersed during the hundreds or thousands of years of postoccupational weathering or reuse of a site. Many of the tools used in finishing pottery are made of perishable materials (gourd rind, bamboo, cane, leaves) and there-

Figure 6.1   A potter's kiln shed in Ticul, Yucatán, Mexico, showing piles of wasters and stacks of saggars (*left*) in front of the kiln.

Table 6.4   Comparison of Potting and Nonpotting Households in Aguacatenango and Chanal, Mexico

	Potting Households	Nonpotting Households
Number of households with stored clay	25 (78%) of 32	0
Number of households with stored temper	22 (69%) of 32	X[a]
Number of households with smoothing stones	14 (42%) of 32	0
Average number of metates per household	2.1 ($n = 28$)	1.4 ($n = 22$)
Average number of local vessels per household	36.8 ($n = 25$)	26.2 ($n = 24$)
Average number of types of pots per household	7.1 ($n = 25$)	5.2 ($n = 24$)

Source: After Deal 1983, 97–111.

[a]Temper is occasionally present in Aguacatenango nonpotting households; people collected it and exchanged it for pottery in nearby Amatenango (Deal 1983, 110).

fore will survive only in exceptional circumstances. Over much of the world, pottery manufacture was carried out without wheels or turntables, and even where these were used they were often made of wood and were thus perishable; similarly, much pottery was fired without kilns. Piles of unfired vessels may indicate manufacturing in a given area; they are fragile and unlikely to have been moved far from their locus of fabrication, but on the other hand they can easily disintegrate in wet conditions.

Accumulations of wasters—misfired or overfired sherds and vessels (see Johns 1977b)—may also be useful evidence (fig. 6.1), because firing, especially bonfire firing, produces a relatively high percentage of damaged or unusable pieces. Wasters may be difficult to identify, however, since sherds or broken vessels may be reused in open firing (see Stark 1985, 174–76).

By far the most complex and exciting methodological advances in locating source areas of pottery production have come from provenience studies (sec. 14.2). Provenience (or provenance) studies seek the origin (the geographical source or provenience) of particular artifacts, whether pottery or stone or some other material. In these analyses the composition of a set of artifacts is determined by sensitive mineralogical and chemical techniques (chap. 13) to obtain a "fingerprint" unique to that composition and hence to the geological source. The same procedures are used to characterize resources available in the geographical region of interest. Finally, the physicochemical data on the artifacts and the resource samples are compared by complex mathematical techniques to search for similarities and differences (see Bishop, Rands, and Holley 1982).

While provenience studies may be able to identify the kinds of clay used in a particular kind of pottery, that is, the geological correlates of manufacture, they do not provide information on the cultural or socioeconomic context, such as the locations of workshops within a settlement system. This, of course, is dependent on other kinds of data, such as those outlined above (deposits of raw materials at a site, kilns, wasters, etc.).

6.2.2   Organization of Production

The ideal situation in investigating structure of ancient pottery production is, of course, to know the source of the clay used as well as the location (by workshop materials, wasters, and/or kilns) of the pottery making. In many cases, however, some or all of this information is unavailable. In such situations, within a certain range of behavioral variation, one can make some observations. The two variables most important in understanding the organization of ceramic production are the scale and the mode of production.

6.2.2.1   SCALE OF PRODUCTION

Scale of production refers to levels of labor and resources used and quantity of output. These matters can be approached initially and largely intuitively in terms of the general level of societal complexity. At one extreme, large, complex societies with high population densities are likely to have complex and specialized arrangements for producing a variety of agricultural and nonagricultural commodities as well as for distributing them. The size of the population necessitates some relatively constant rate of providing goods to serve continuously in a variety of utilitarian and specialized functions. At the other extreme, in small villages that are not strongly integrated into broader regional economies, craft production may be pursued primarily for "own use" or for irregular household exchange and consumption: production may be sporadic, on a seasonal or ad hoc replacement basis. The former increases the likelihood of archaeologically visible indications of pottery production, conducted by more-or-less full-time workers who have spatially segregated activity areas and technological investments in their craft. Simple household production, on the other hand, is likely to be archaeologically invisible or incapable of detailed quantitative investigation as a result of low output, informal organization, and lack of specialized tools and workspace.

These two examples are extremes, of course, and between them is a wide range of production arrangements that have had little or no systematic analysis in prehistoric contexts (cf. Peacock 1982). They do, however, call attention to another important aspect of scale of production—level of demand. Household production involves a close relation between consumer demand and producer output; in some cases producer and consumer may be the same individual. Demand is likely to be low and intermittent, and production rates may vary according to the financial circumstances of individual households. Both, therefore, are stochastic and unpredictable, and neither input (labor, resources) nor output is quantitatively large. In production for a large society, however, there is relatively constant demand from a large and dense population of consumers with varied needs. It is important to distinguish between what might be termed general and specific demand, or between independent and attached producers (Earle 1981, 230), since this can be expected to affect the quantity and character of the output. A related consideration is the role of pottery in communitywide ceremonies or fiestas, which is a major determinant of the seasonal volume and rhythm of production in several areas (Reina and Hill 1978, 249; Lynch 1979, 5–6; Howry 1976, 210).

The scale or level of commodity production is thus an important aspect of production structure. It involves the demand for the product—the density and complexity of social statuses, roles, and utilitarian needs within the population of consumers that forms the market for the commodity. These factors, while significant, can be approached archaeologically only by inference. More empirical and quantitative observations can be applied to the scale of production, but in many periods and places these data may not all be available. Critical questions concern the number of producing areas (e.g., workshops), their degree of nucleation, their size (spatial extent, the number of workers they may have occupied, and rate of output), and the kind, amount, and size of facilities at the working areas (kilns, drying space, etc.).

Also significant—but requiring different kinds of supporting data—are the variety of products turned out and the quantities of each type. While evidence concerning the former might be gleaned from wasters, the latter will be difficult to ascertain except by estimating the volume of individual firing loads or by extrapolating from frequencies of wares of form categories recovered in residential middens or other deposits. Questions about the rate of production are not likely to be answered by this latter method, however, given the generally poor level of fine chronological control at archaeological sites. Similarly, assessments of full-time versus part-time manufacture, or seasonal versus year-round production, will very likely be beyond direct archaeological investigation. In general, the ethnographic literature indicates a high frequency of part-time and seasonal production cycles among potters, even in areas with many large, specialized workshops.

6.2.2.2   MODE OF PRODUCTION

Study of the mode of pottery production is based on interrelated determinations of how the pottery is made, who makes it, and for whom it is made. Pertinent questions thus relate to manufacturing technology, the role and status of producers, the integration between tasks, the organization of producing units and their relation to the overall economic organization, and the relation between producers and consuming groups.

How pottery is made is a question that largely concerns the kind and level of manufacturing technology. With prehistoric pottery, one can search for traces of procedures on the sherds or vessels (e.g., coil fractures, rilling, etc.), or indications may be found "on the ground"—for example, ancient tools or other equipment such as kilns, wheels, or molds.

The extent to which the manufacturing procedures discussed in chapter 5 can be identified on archaeological pottery is variable (see Rye 1977, 1981, 46–89). In general, a great deal can be reconstructed from whole vessels and from sherds, in part because of the additive process of creating vessels out of clay and in part because of the nature of clay itself. Much depends, however, on the size of the sherds available and what parts of the vessels they represent. A variety of physicochemical analytical procedures—many of them highly complex—are discussed below in part 4.

Labor-intensive and capital-intensive modes of production can be differentiated by the role items such as kilns and wheels play in manufacturing. These devices permit rapid production of large quantities of virtually identical products, that is, mass production, but they require substantial investments of money and space—usually permanent workshops—for efficient use (see below). Distinctions between labor intensity and capital intensity may be evidenced by pottery-making tools at archaeological sites.

Other signs of how pottery making was organized are more ephemeral. For example, the internal organization of production includes the size, composition, and integration of the groups that execute particular tasks—such as obtaining and preparing resources, forming, finishing, decorating, firing, and distributing. These issues, more commonly phrased in terms of horizontal, vertical, or functional divisions of labor—and indeed the question whether such task differentiation existed as part of the productive process—may prove impossible to investigate archaeologically in many situations (see Nicholson and Patterson 1985a, b for an ethnoarchaeological example).

Determining who made prehistoric pottery largely depends on understanding the demographic and socioeconomic position of potters in the society, including whether pottery is made by virtually anyone or is effectively limited, by any number of social sanctions, to small numbers of producers. Relevant questions concern the age and sex (Barbour 1976) of potters and whether pottery manufacture is practiced by particular families, clans, or castes. This latter may be shown in some archaeological situations by architectural differentiation, for example, if there is a wardlike or barriolike clustering of residence-cum-production loci (Millon 1970), evidenced by any of the locational or abundance criteria noted above. The individual identities of manufacturers can sometimes be determined if they have signed their wares—molds or final finished vessels—either by name or by workshop affiliation, as

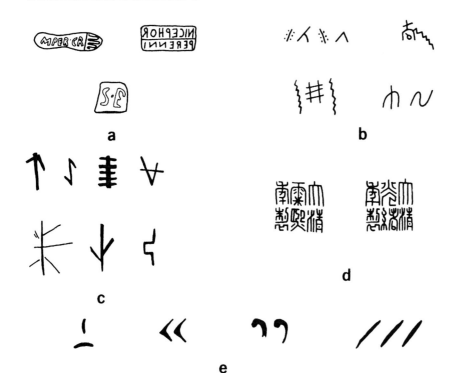

Figure 6.2   Potter's marks and stamps (not to scale): *a,* Arretine stamps (after Peacock 1981, fig. 61); *b,* Yangshao pottery marks from Banpo, China (after Cheung 1983, fig. 12.1); *c,* multisign "inscriptions" on pottery from Tepe Yahya, Iran (after Potts 1981, fig. 2); *d,* Chinese porcelain marks (*left,* K'ang-hsi, 1662–1722; *right,* Kuang-hsu, 1875–1908; after Medley 1976); *e,* marks on Moche pots from Peru (after Donnan 1978, fig. 3i,l,n,q).

in examples of Greek (Beazley 1945; von Bothmer 1985) and Roman (Johns 1963; Hartley 1966; Dickinson and Hartley 1971) pottery, or made distinguishing marks on it (fig. 6.2; Man 1894, 26; Donnan 1971; Arnold 1972; Potts 1981; Gill 1981). Individual potters may also be identifiable by stylistic attributes (Hill 1977; Hardin 1977). Indeed, decoration itself may serve as a potter's mark, as in the Philippines, where the number of painted bands identifies a particular potter's output in a communal kiln load (Scheans 1977, 65).

6.2.3   Models of Production and Specialization

Several models have been developed to describe the organization of pottery production. These generally posit categories of increasing complexity based on examples drawn from the ethnographic record (Balfet 1965, 162–63; van der Leeuw 1977, 1984; Peacock 1981, 1982; Rice 1981; Redman and Myers 1981, 289–90), with the exclusion of itinerant potters (see Asboe 1946; Voyatzoglou 1974; Linné 1965, 21). The variables differentiating the categories include frequency and seasonality of production; number of workers; age, sex, status, and relationships of the workers; degree of labor division; kind and extent of investment in special space or tools; variability in raw materials and products; and size and proximity of consuming groups.

Two very similar schemes (van der Leeuw 1977, 1984; Peacock 1981, 1982, 8–10) suggest that the following four modes of production may be important in prehistoric contexts:

1. Household production. Also known as the domestic mode of production (DMP), pottery manufacture is occasional and primarily for own use, typically in the hands of women, and characterized by simple technology (see Balfet 1965, 162). It is often stressed that this type of extensive production system is oriented toward self-sufficiency, with little opportunity for intensification. The Kalinga of the Philippines are an example of a society in which every household produces its own pottery (Longacre 1981, 1985).

2. Household industry. Production is somewhat more continuous, but it still involves only a simple technology with little investment in capital equipment and is likely to be in the hands of women. Described as "potting for profit" (Peacock 1982, 8), the household industry can be seen to represent the beginnings of commoditization (Hart 1982): pottery not only has use value but acquires exchange value as well and is made for someone outside the immediate environment. Pottery manufacture frequently is an important source of supplemental household income for women (see Fontana et al. 1968, 24; David and Hennig 1972; Stone 1950) and often is found in areas with relatively poor agricultural potential. Much of today's production that falls into the category of household industry is oriented toward the tourist market (see sec. 15.1), as in Chinautla, Guatemala (Reina and Hill 1978, 253–72), Santa Clara, New Mexico (LeFree 1975), and lowland Peru (Lathrap 1976).

3. Individual workshop industry. Production is typically in the hands of men, who have a significant capital investment (kilns, wheels) in the enterprise and derive their major livelihood from it. Workshops are usually isolated, and distribution may be by rather "rudimentary" marketing systems (Peacock 1982, 9, 31).

4. Nucleated workshops (see Peacock 1981, 190–91, 1982, 9). These represent a "clustered industrial complex" in which pottery manufacture is a major economic activity, practiced by males with extensive technological investment. Production may be seasonal, but because of competition it is usually year-round; products are fairly standardized and of high quality. Marketing is often a distinct economic specialization, typically integrated with urban market economies, and often relies heavily on the activity of middlemen traders (see Papousek 1981). Also referred to as "village industry," "domestic industry," or "dispersed manufactory," these units may be in urban areas (Lynch 1979; Thompson 1984) but are especially notable as features of rural regions, as at Djerba, Tunisia (e.g., Johnston 1984) or Deir el-Gharbi, Egypt (Nicholson and Patterson 1985b).

Workshops, whether individual or nucleated, often have explicit division of labor: they include a thrower, several individuals who prepare the clay for throwing or finish the vessels, and young assistants who tread the clay, turn the wheel, and perform other tasks (e.g., see Scheans 1977, 59). In addition, the workshop structure is typically divided into special activity areas (fig. 6.3) for mixing clays, storing and drying clays and other supplies such as firewood (fig. 6.4), forming and drying pots, and for kilns.

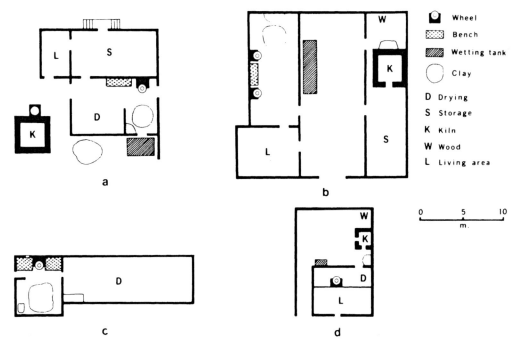

Figure 6.3 Workshop plans: *a*, Orei, Euboea, Greece (after Peacock 1982, fig. 11-1); *b*, Viana do Alentejo, Portugal (after Peacock 1982, fig. 11-2); *c*, Deir el-Gharbi, Egypt (after Nicholson and Patterson 1985a, 55); *d*, Saõ Pedro do Corval, Portugal (after Peacock 1982, fig. 11-3).

Figure 6.4 The interior courtyard of a potter's workshop in Antigua, Guatemala. Firewood is stacked to the left, freshly made pots dry in the sun in the background, and a sleeping dog sprawls on the crushed clay spread on the floor of the patio.

Several other categories of production organization may also be identified. Large-scale industry or factory organization makes use of mechanically powered technology and developed only during the Industrial Revolution. The manufactory (Peacock 1981, 1982, 9–10; also Annis 1985, 243) is an arrangement based essentially on the workshop, in which a large number of people work under the direction of a supervisor; production may involve an "assembly line" of individually specialized tasks, or the same person may execute all steps of the production sequence. The production of Arretine Samian ware is given as an example of a manufactory (Peacock 1981, 122), whereas Gaulish Samian ware was probably produced by a more dispersed workshop arrangement (Peacock 1981, 192, 1982, 127). In addition, production may be organized through estate and military systems, as it was in the Roman economy (Peacock 1982, 10–11), which emphasized manufacture of bricks and tiles rather than pottery and probably paralleled various types of workshop organization.

Finally, Peacock (1982, 13) suggests that municipal or state authorities may exercise some control over production. This situation, like that of estate and military workshops, may be interpreted as involving what Earle (1981, 230) called "attached" specialist producers. Attached specialists may be associated with a particular interest group that can in some way manipulate production and demand, for example, elite entrepreneurs or other supervisory authorities controlling the manufacture of ritually or functionally specialized products. Independent specialists, on the other hand—those producing a range of products for general consumers—may operate largely without specific directives or intervention other than local preferences and needs, although taxation or tribute demands may be important to the scale of their production efforts.

For interpreting production in antiquity, these schemes raise several problems. One is that the descriptions of these production modes also incorporate statements on the distribution of the product. For example, the household industry and workshop categories are described in terms of orientation toward a market economy and profit motivation. Although these relationships are significant in illuminating how the producing unit functions, they contribute to confusion in explicitly defining production in a prehistoric context because they overextend the definition. Is it necessary to identify markets in order to identify a workshop mode of production?

If production were treated alone, strictly independent of distribution, one could see that, rather than a continuum of five or more categories, there are basically two kinds of production arrangements, household and workshop, differentiated by where the work takes place, the manufacturing technology used, and factors of scale (personnel, production rate or intensity, and volume). The variations—which primarily exist in the workshop mode—are further based on scale (size and intensity) as well as on degree of integration with urban centers, presence of outside control, and role (if any) of entrepreneurs.

Of the major production categories (omitting factories as exclusively post-Industrial Revolution), (1) and (2) and to some extent (3) are likely to leave little trace archaeologically because of lack of material technological investment (see Deal 1983, 97–111), low intensity of activity, and isolated or dispersed geographical distribution. Their existence and location would have to

Table 6.5   Characteristics of Pottery Making in Two Mexican Towns

	Household Production (Chanal)	Village Industry (Amatenango)
Frequency	Occasional/part-time	Part-/full-time
Organization	Work separately	Assembly line within extended family or guild
Market	Home use; intracommunity	Local or regional
Seasonality	Dry season	Year-round
Division of labor	None	Considerable
Manufacturing technology	Hand, small tools	Hand, small tools
Firing technology	Open fire	Open fire
Time per vessel	<20 minutes	>30 minutes
Raw materials		
Clay	Black and red; local (<1 km)	Black, white, yellow; local (<1 km)
Temper	Calcite; distant (2–8 km)	Calcite; local three types of sand; local
Fuel	Pine kindling, oak bark; local	Pine kindling, oak bark, cypress; distant (>5 km)
Pigments	Not used	Distant (purchased)
Smoothing stones	Local	Distant (8–60 km)
Investments	Time only	Cash for pigments and transportation
Range of functional types	Narrow	Wide
Range of wares	Unslipped only	Slipped (red and white) and unslipped
Role of men[a]	None	Gather firewood, help with firing, help with marketing

Source: After Deal 1983, table 17.   [a]Women are the potters in both communities.

be identified largely by spatial occurrence of the products (the "criterion of abundance," above), by proximity to desirable resources, or both. Category (4) is today clearly associated with urban marketing economies, and category (3) may be associated with rural or peripheral urban industries too; the extent to which these latter could be identified in prehistory is questionable (see Nicholson and Patterson 1985b). Furthermore, distinguishing attached from independent producers and determining the participation of entrepreneurs, who are hypothesized to play an important role in various levels of production, is also problematic because they cannot be detected archaeologically.

It is somewhat difficult to place various community-based specializations into this scheme. In the highlands of Mexico and Guatemala entire communities produce a single craft item such as pottery, baskets, grinding stones, or leather goods, exchanging the products within a bounded "solar marketing system" (see Smith 1974, 176–77; Nash 1966); production may be by men or women and is usually part time and seasonal. These systems seem to fall into Peacock's (1982, 103) category of "rural nucleated industries," which commonly specialize in a single widely distributed product, but in Mesoamerica the potters are usually (though not always) women rather than men, and these systems do not consist of workshops with major technological investments. They are closer to the characteristics of the household industry, suggesting that a great deal of variability exists within this category (table 6.5). Similar community-based craft concentration is described in Ghana, where villages restrict themselves to manufacture of particular wares or forms: pots for palm wine at one, spindle whorls at another, and utility wares at a third (Crossland and Posnansky 1978, 88). Comparable situations are described for the southern Andes of Peru (Tschopik 1950, 215) as well as for Melanesia (see Lauer 1970; Ellen and Glover 1974).

Part of the problem is the tendency to associate females with one kind of productive mode (households and minimal technological investment) and males with another (workshops and the use of wheels and kilns). The differences between the two modes are not always defined by gender or by technology, however. In 1950 in the northern Nicoya peninsula of Costa Rica, for example, some of the female potters working in their homes practiced a system that was close to the "manufactory" described by Peacock. In this system of "peonage" some women (the "peons") go to the homes of other potters in the same village and work (for pay) for half a day either molding or finishing the vessels; the owner of the house prepares the clay for them and then dries and fires the vessels herself (Stone 1950, 278). In another situation, in Chucuito, Peru, household production is in the hands of males, who are assisted by their wives or female relatives and work without wheel or kiln; it was not noted whether these potters were full- or part-time producers (Tschopik 1950), but most probably they worked part-time.

Finally, within all these categories save (1), household production, questions can be raised concerning the role of specialization. In economic specialization a particular occupation is restricted to a relatively small number of skilled practitioners who make it their primary livelihood. The qualifier "relatively" is important here, for the number of producers must be compared with the total output and the total market.

Ethnographically, defining or identifying specialist production has not been a consuming concern in pottery studies, and indeed the criteria used for recognizing economic specialists of any kind are very different from those used archaeologically. Among the significant elements are the proportion of time devoted to the specialty, the amount of subsistence (or income) gained from it, the existence of a native title or name for the occupation, and the receipt of some remuneration for the product (Tatje and Naroll 1973).

For archaeologists this subject has been important because, despite the operational problems of identifying specialists in prehistory, economic specialization in production and distribution is generally acknowledged to be a concomitant of large, complex, highly differentiated societies and to depend on other intensive production arrangements, for example, in agriculture (Dow 1985). It is an adaptive response, in part to the different needs and requirements of a large, heterogeneous society, but also to the differential distribution of productive resources in the physical environment (Rice 1981).

Dealing with specialization in prehistory raises several problems, including determining whether specialization exists, when and how it developed, and its degree (full or part time). Specialization has clear implications for the kinds of developmental typologies discussed above, and just as there are few widely agreed-upon criteria for defining or recognizing those particular organizational arrangements in prehistory, there is little consensus on how to identify the existence of specialists in commodity production (see Evans 1978, 115, for one example). If workshops can be identified the issue is relatively straight-forward, but in the absence of workshops—that is, in cases corresponding to village industry ("dispersed manufactories") and perhaps even household industries in the typology discussed above—the archaeological visibility is low and the entire matter is likely to be far more ambiguous.

Part of the difficulty lies in defining what *is* specialization. As Muller (1984, 490–92) has pointed out, considerable confusion arises because ar-chaeologists fail to distinguish between site specialization and producer spe-cialization. In site specialization localities have limited functions or intensive production activity; their existence may be determined by fortuitous environ-mental factors such as good fishing, fertile soils, mineral deposits, and so forth.

Site specialization does not necessarily imply producer specialization, however, which is defined by the time individuals devote to an activity as a part of gaining their livelihoods. Producer specialization, in turn, does not refer to division of labor by sex within a society, such as the occasional situa-tion in which men make large, heavy wares while women make smaller pots (see Scheans 1977, 95–96). Nor does it pertain to skill of execution (e.g., Balfet's [1965, 163] "elementary specialization"). Rather, producer spe-cialization designates the allocation of labor (or a labor force) in a particular economic pursuit. It is one aspect of broader patterns of socioeconomic inten-sification, entailing increasing labor input (intensification proper), differen-tiation of skills (diversification), and output (see, e.g., Kaiser 1984, 12, 293–94).

Producer specialization is usually described in terms of intensiveness as part time or full time, but this is a blurry distinction even ethnographically. Full-time specialization itself has two connotations: that an individual makes pottery year-round (Arnold 1985, 18) or that an individual follows no eco-nomic pursuit other than pottery making. The seasonal aspect of many eco-nomic activities, including pottery making, makes this nebulous distinction even murkier. Potters may concentrate their potting during the most favorable weather (e.g., the warm or dry season) and produce at a different *rate*—only sporadically or with very reduced output—during cold or rainy periods. In addition, potters often also have landholdings, and they may work their farms during the agricultural season and make pottery during the off-season. The employment of assistants in workshops may also vary seasonally for the same reasons. To call any of these individuals "part-time specialists" is somehow misleading. For example, in 1905 in the famous porcelain center of Jingdezhen, China, production was highly seasonal, since most of the 104 workshops and kilns in the town employed summer help: "During this busy season, when every kiln is perhaps employing an average of 100 to 200 men, the population of Ching-tê Chên [Jingdezhen] rises to about 400,000, but of this nearly, if not quite, half are labourers drawn from a wide area of country . . . who only come for the season, live in rows of barracks-like sheds, and do not bring their families with them" (W. J. Clennell, *Journey in the Interior of Kiangsi*, quoted in Hobson 1976, 155). One may question how an understanding of producer specialization is advanced by distinguishing these Chinese workers as part-time versus full-time specialists.

Aside from these problems of differentiating part-time and full-time specialization by seasonal factors or production rate, the differences are even more difficult to discern in prehistoric contexts. It is likely that full-time specialized personnel—those who produce at a relatively constant rate year-round—may be distinctive only of state-level societies (see Muller 1984, 493), primarily present in areas with sizable and dense (urban) populations to establish a constant demand. In smaller, nonstratified societies, full-time specialization incorporates some risk during times of economic stress or famine, since there is less provision for political redistribution of goods (Hayden and Cannon 1984, 341).

The widespread positive correlation between levels of "craft specialization," levels of societal complexity, and agricultural intensification (Dow 1985) suggests some additional aspects of pottery production to consider. In agricultural studies, a distinction is made between intensification and specialization. Intensification refers to raising the yield per unit of land or labor and may be achieved by increasing the frequency of cropping, the technological investment, or the labor input. Specialization is a particular kind of intensification, focusing on a single crop or a small number of crops.

This distinction is also useful with respect to pottery production, particularly in archaeological contexts, because it separates issues of labor from those of output. Intensification increases the output per unit of time or labor, and may be achieved by changing production from part time to full time, increasing the number of producers, or using more efficient manufacturing techniques (molds or the wheel). Production may also be increased by focusing on a single class of product, that is, by specialization. Specialization may occur when certain households, barrios, workshops, or communities concentrate on manufacturing particular functional, formal, or decorative categories of pottery. It may arise without intensification proper if it does not increase production. Either intensification or specialization may involve diversification through task or product differentiation, such as "assembly-line techniques," whereby different individuals are responsible for separate tasks or products.

Agricultural studies suggest that both approaches to intensification—increasing frequency of production events and increasing yield per event—may occur simultaneously, but there is a tendency to favor the latter. In the evolution of the different kinds of pottery production organizations discussed above, it is likely that the same would be true. In part such an emphasis on increasing yield may be due to the constraints imposed by climate and by the scheduling of pottery making vis-à-vis agriculture (see Arnold 1985). While "full-time specialization" in pottery may not be widespread in prehistory and may be restricted to situations of conspicuous urbanization, a variety of forms of intensification may be found, including greater technological or labor investment and "specialization" in the narrower sense of concentration on particular products. Such arrangements may characterize a broader ranger of levels of socioeconomic complexity, population density, and production scheduling, and they have the additional advantage of being more amenable to archaeological investigation.

In sum, while "site specialization" seems to be a useful concept for studying some aspects of craft production in archaeological contexts, "producer specialization" seems to fall within the broader category of intensification processes, which requires further subdivision to be useful archaeologically. It may also be appropriate to hypothesize a third kind of specialization, "resource specialization": selective employment of particular resources in pottery manufacture. An example is the production of glaze paint pottery in the Rio Grande area of New Mexico, which was made possible by the availability and control of an essential material (lead ores for the paint) as well as superior clays for the body and slip, and which led to specialized production of the ware as a trade commodity (Shepard 1965, 86).

Distinguishing resource specialization from other categories is potentially important for interpreting the results of provenience analyses (sec. 14.2), which can isolate particular pottery resource groupings by their geochemical composition but cannot identify either users or production sites. Pottery production may involve any of three kinds of specialization—locus, personnel, and resource—and all three certainly can occur simultaneously. But it is also possible for one to occur without the others.

An important point in these distinctions is the relation between site specialization and agricultural productivity, because modern pottery manufacturing communities are often in urban fringe areas with very poor agricultural potential. This suggests that the impetus toward community specialization in pottery making at the household level—which is not infrequently associated with poverty and a need for supplemental income—may be the inadequacy of the agricultural subsistence base in these regions (see Arnold 1985, 198–99; but cf. Cook 1984, 20–21). The extent to which this contemporary correlation may reach into prehistory has not been satisfactorily explored.

6.3   Distribution and Exchange

6.3.1   Ethnographic Overview

The means by which pottery reaches its users are as many and varied as the means by which it is produced. It is self-evident that, as Renfrew (1977b, 9) observed, "a high level of production by a number of craft specialists in a limited area cannot be easily sustained without a highly organized means of distributing the product and without a large constituency of customers." Nonetheless, impressive volumes of production can occur, and considerable distances can be traveled, without nucleated workshops, kiln and wheel technology, or professional merchants (e.g., Loughlin 1977, 88).

Traditionally, distributional behavior in ethnographic and modern peasant societies is described in terms of three categories: reciprocity, redistribution, and exchange (see Polanyi 1957; Sahlins 1972; Earle 1977; Hodder 1978, 199–211).

Reciprocity is the movement of goods, usually between individuals, based on more-or-less symmetrical or equal relationships. Reciprocity is sometimes categorized according to the social distance of the participants (Hodder 1978, 203) as generalized reciprocity (e.g., hospitality, care of the elderly), balanced (socially mandated gift exchanges, bride-price, etc.), or negative (taking place between relatively distant partners and perhaps involving haggling). The material transactions may be significant in these interactions, but in general the social and symbolic aspects are more so.

Redistribution has, in theory, two critical components: pooling of goods and centrality. In its idealized form, redistribution usually takes place in relatively formalized relationships, often within or between groups, in which goods are accumulated, moved appropriatively to a center, and then reallocated. In practice, however, much redistribution may take place without any centralized direction or location, either within or between production locales, from family activities to regional fairs. Four types of redistributional institutions have been identified (Earle 1977, 215): leveling mechanisms (e.g., potlatching); domestic household pooling and sharing; share-out (allocation on the basis of cooperative effort such as hunting); and mobilization, or appropriation of goods and services by and for a separate entity, often involving several communities (tribute, corvée labor). The first three of these are common at all societal levels, whereas mobilization exists only in hierarchical (ranked or stratified) societies (Earle 1977, 216).

The term exchange is sometimes used in a general sense for any process by which goods are moved and change hands in return for some other good, service, or intangible. More specifically, however, exchange refers to market or marketplace exchange; marketplaces may be periodic (including fairs) or fixed, and they may or may not be administered or involve supply-and-demand price mechanisms. Such price mechanisms are extremely rare in prehistory; since in general much of the theory of market exchange is based on modern industrial and capitalist systems, it is of questionable value in understanding prehistoric societies. As distinct from reciprocity and redistribution, market exchange is impersonal and is not focused primarily on the social relationships between individuals. The definitions and origins of formal market arrangements are poorly understood; the mechanisms may be internal to the socioeconomic system, reflecting demand and production of surpluses, or they may be external, deriving from the redistribution of goods acquired through long-distance trade or produced within ecologically or socio-ethnically bounded groups (Hodder 1978, 209–11).

All three of these terms are sometimes lumped under the rubric "trade." In general, however, trade is usually limited to appropriational processes in which distance and transport are significant and in which there is often some relatively formal and permanent relationship between the partners as individuals or official agencies.

Reciprocity and redistribution are idealized categories of exchange behavior. With respect to the actual mechanics of the transactions, one fairly simple scheme outlines five arrangements (fig. 6.5) whereby pottery (or any other good) may change hands from producer to user (Renfrew 1977b, 9–10):

1. The consumer travels to the potter. In this case, potters do not actively seek out consumers for their wares but produce on commission or consignment (Howry 1976; Scheans 1977, 46) or for the occasional purchaser who needs to replace a household vessel. Examples of this type of production include the Njemps potters of Africa (Hodder 1979a), and the Siuai (Oliver 1955).

2. The potter travels to the consumers. In this situation the potter (or a member of the production unit, often kin) carries the pottery—on his or her back, by donkey or cart (fig. 6.6), or by truck or canoe—to the consumers, acting as an itinerant vendor. Examples include Papago potters (Fontana et al.

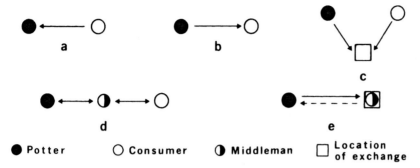

Figure 6.5   Model of pottery distribution relationships: *a*, consumer travels to potter; *b*, potter travels to consumer; *c*, both potter and consumer travel to a third location; *d*, pottery is exchanged through a middleman; *e*, potter takes goods to a central redistributive agency.

Figure 6.6   A rural Muslim potter and his wife travel with a bullock cart loaded with pots for sale in western Rajasthan, India. They sell along the road, but primarily in small villages and towns where few pottery shops are found. Photograph by Carol Kramer.

1962, 23), potters of the Amphlett Islands (Lauer 1970, 1971), and potters of the Nicoya peninsula of Costa Rica (Stone 1950).

The movement of pottery in both arrangements (1) and (2) may be through gift giving or other processes of reciprocal social obligations, may represent redistribution, or may be more impersonal exchange.

3. Both potter and consumer travel to a third location, which is often a market or fair but may be simply a convenient street corner or other area where there are large numbers of passersby. Potters (or members of potting families) acting in this role in Guatemala are referred to as vendors (Reina and Hill 1978, 207–9), and they are most active in local markets. There they sell directly to local consumers or to merchants who carry the pottery farther away in secondary distribution to other locations. A similar situation is described for periodic markets in rural Yoruba areas (Hodder 1962, 116, quoted in

Figure 6.7   A pottery stall in the main market in Guatemala City, where pottery vessels from all over the highlands can be found. This stall sells a variety of glazed and unglazed cooking wares (basins, flat griddles or *comales*, drink- ing mugs) as well as the more elaborate tourist- oriented white-slipped "urban ware" visible to the woman's left: vases, *angelitos*, candelabra. The glazed and unglazed vessels with faces are braziers.

Renfrew 1977b, 11). These exchange activities are generally impersonal and may exhibit aspects of negative reciprocity discussed above.

4. The potter turns over the goods to a third party (a wholesaler or middle- man) who interacts with consumers (see below). This interaction usually takes place at a market and may be in the vicinity of the potting community or some distance from it. In Guatemala, two types of middle traders are known: *regatones* may be male or female and operate permanent stalls in regional (rather than local) markets (fig. 6.7); *comerciantes* are itinerant merchants who travel throughout a relatively broad area, either on foot or with motorized transport, and sell to individuals or *regatones* at more distant markets (Reina and Hill 1978, 207, 215).

As Foster (1965b, 56) notes, high-quality pottery may travel 150 miles in primary distribution and then even farther in secondary distribution. In many areas of the world where road systems are poorly developed, travel by foot may still be the most effective marketing scheme; it has been estimated that in Ghana, only 2% of an annual production of ninety thousand vessels was trans- ported by road (Crossland and Posnansky 1978, 87). Occasionally a particular merchant can act as a monopolist in buying from potters and extending credit to them, as in the case of Don Asunción in Mexico (Papousek 1981, 79–82, 100–105).

5. The potter takes his goods to "some central agency which assigns him goods in exchange," a statement of the idealized process of redistribution. The extent to which pottery vessels are directly exchanged for other goods through a central administrative office receives little if any confirmation in the ethnographic record. The case of a monopolist merchant such as Don Asunción may be a parallel; the example cited by Renfrew (1977b, 14)—Inca storage jars at Huánuco Pampa (Morris 1974)—may represent state-controlled production but does not necessarily imply redistribution.

The actual form of the exchange transaction and the value of the goods are highly variable in these five schemes, but in many areas the sale of pots is an important source of supplemental income as well as a source of otherwise-unobtainable financial freedom for women (Fontana et al. 1962; Stone 1950). Where consumers travel to the potters, the prices of pots are relatively stable (Hodder 1979a, 17), without the inflationary effect of distance. In many situations of household production and sales, the stability of prices may be a consequence of informal price fixing or social sanctions against competitive pricing and underselling, as among the potters of Santa Clara, New Mexico (Le Free 1975, 68) and Matti, Philippines (Scheans 1977, 46).

Exchange may also involve bartering pottery or exchanging it for other goods, usually food. For example, the Papago in the American Southwest traded pottery for flour, salt, sugar, coffee, beans, or corn as well as cash (Fontana et al. 1962, 22–23). Similarly, at Begho, Ghana, West Africa, "plantains, cocoyam, palm nuts and dried cassava . . . are made available at [the potters'] doorsteps; cowries and gold dust were also used in exchange before modern currency" (Crossland and Posnansky 1978, 87). This system is not restricted to the irregular commerce associated with household production: workshop potters of Vounaria, Greece, exchange their wares for wheat (Matson 1972, 220; see also Miller 1981, 224).

Although distance and supply are probably most influential in determining the cost of vessels, other mechanisms operate as well, though not always consistently. A slip, glaze, or decoration is usually presumed to confer additional value to a pot (e.g., Feinman, Upham, and Lightfoot 1981; see also Hardin 1977, 115), partly because of labor and partly because of the expense of materials. Among the potters of Los Pueblos this principle holds: the presence of a glaze firing is a major determinant of the cost of pots to merchants (Papousek 1981, 84, 114–15). At Begho, Ghana, however, the presence or absence of a slip does not influence the cost of a pot (Crossland and Posnansky 1978, 88). Quality certainly plays a role too: in Nigeria, Ibibio consumers acknowledge that Igbo pots are better than their own and last longer in use, and they are therefore willing to pay as much as 50% more for them (Nicklin 1981b, 183). Seasonal factors are also likely to influence supply and hence price.

All of these systems of interaction—the reciprocity, redistribution, and exchange models and the typology of exchange transactions—are heuristics, or idealized categories of behavior. As in many applications of behavioral constructs to actual situations, a number of cautions may be registered.

First, any combination of these arrangements may occur in a single society.

For example, in the Baringo district of Kenya either potter or consumer may travel to the other (Hodder 1979a, 11–12); in Papagueria, Arizona, there has been a gradual change from potters' acting as traveling vendors to their selling their pots from their homes (Fontana et al. 1962, 22–24). The inflationary economy of recent decades has placed a premium on flexible selling strategies, as documented among full-time potters in the Philippines (Scheans 1977, 103):

> Most of the San Nicholas potters prefer to retail their wares whenever possible in order to maximize their gains in a market that they know is subject to rapid fluctuations of supply and demand. Indeed, some will even take their wares to hawk in distant towns in order to receive the highest price. Others will barter their stock for whatever their family might need. Rice, of course, is a preferred item in bartering. Because of this they try to barter for it before the time of harvest since rice prices are the highest then and bartering is based on the volume capacity of the item to be traded. If they cannot do that they will advance the pots and be paid at harvest time an agreed amount plus interest.

No single behavioral category can describe an entire economy because of the simultaneous existence of multiple distributive arrangements.

Second, exchange networks, whether local or long distance, are important not only in supplying necessary goods and economic relationships, but in maintaining information flow and social relationships (see DeBoer and Lathrap 1979, 115–16; Spriggs and Miller 1979, 28), including political and kinship alliances and even enmities. An interesting example comes from the Yanomamö of Venezuela: one group, the Momaribowei-teri, claimed they neither knew how to make pots nor had suitable clays and obtained their pots from a group they were allied with, trading them on to a third allied group, the Kaobawa. When the alliance with the potting group faltered, the Momaribowei-teri suddenly "remembered" how to make pots and "discovered" suitable clays nearby and so maintained their alliance with the Kaobawa (Nicklin 1979, 450, citing Chagnon 1968, 100–101). Related to this alliance maintenance, it should be noted that the boundaries between social or cultural (ethnic, political, tribal) categories or environmental zones may not hinder exchange (Reina and Hill 1978, 216; Hodder 1977, 269); indeed, the different specializations may foster economic interactions. Material exchanges will also vary between centralized and noncentralized societies (Hodder 1978, 211–34).

Third, entrepreneurs (individuals who intervene to change the patterns of production and distribution [Schumpeter 1961, 78]) or a centralized authority may be significant in these processes. Middlemen and entrepreneurs today play a very important part in the activities of commodity production, marketing, and pricing. This is particularly evident in the status of powerful individuals who have accumulated sufficient wealth to own trucks, thereby dominating distribution and, by extension, production as well (Papousek 1981). Obviously trucking could not have played a part in prehistory, but other kinds of entrepreneurs could have figured significantly, especially in large, complex societies. The role of an institutionalized merchant class, such as the *pochteca* of Aztec Mexico, or other long-distance traders may be analogous, both by virtue of controlling distribution and by their access to knowledge about a broader world and its affairs (see also Helms 1979, 33–34).

6.3.2 Archaeological Approaches and Models of Distribution

The distribution sphere of pottery economics has received considerably more archaeological study than has production. This is no doubt because archaeologists have traditionally devoted a good deal of attention to commodity exchange in general as a prime mover in models of sociopolitical evolution. Most of the work on prehistoric exchange has been with long-distance trade and has involved primarily a single commodity. That commodity is usually an item that can be easily traced to a particular source or source region, such as obsidian, jade and other semiprecious stones, certain kinds of fauna or animal products, soapstone (chlorite), metals, or highly distinctive decorative styles of pottery. In many cases, because of the distances involved or the relative scarcity of the commodity itself, there is an implicit or explicit understanding that the items being traded are elite. A number of models drawn from network analysis and locational geography have been developed to describe these long-distance distributional systems (e.g., Renfrew 1977a). Less common are studies of the distribution of locally produced coarse pottery or other nonelite commodities within the region surrounding the locus of manufacture (e.g., see Hodder 1974c; Loughlin 1977; Brisbane 1981; Arnold 1981).

Archaeological studies of the economic process of pottery distribution begin, like those of virtually any other commodity, by examining the spatial disposition of the categories of interest, including presence/absence as well as relative frequencies. As with production, in distribution a large number of variables need to be investigated: the range of movement of the commodity, the amount exchanged, the time span involved, the direction and intensity of flows, the degree of centralization of distribution, and the overall complexity of the system (Plog 1977, 129).

These variables, and the relation between interaction processes and distance implied by the spatial occurrence of a particular item such as pottery, can be examined by means of three kinds of data. These are (Hodder 1974b, 175) the percentage of the item in the total assemblage at each site (probably most suitable for voluminous categories of artifacts, such as pottery); the density of sites having the item within concentric bands around the source; and the number of sites with the item as a percentage of all contemporaneous sites in that concentric band. Regardless of which method is used, investigating distribution in prehistory requires an archaeological sampling strategy of survey and excavation that includes a broad range of sizes, locations, and kinds of sites (see Plog 1977, 132–33). Without such coverage the intensity and centralization of the distributional process are likely to be misjudged. With respect to pottery, its fragility and patterns of reuse may make it hard to resolve these issues (see sec. 9.3).

Clearly, to study the economic processes and behaviors of pottery distribution, one must first understand its production. Absolutely essential is infor-

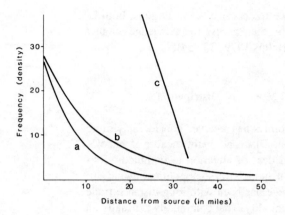

Figure 6.8 "Fall-off curves" for Savernake pottery, showing frequency of occurrence (density) of the ware as a function of distance from the production center: *a*, density or frequency of sites bearing Savernake pottery in zones around the production center; *b*, Savernake pottery as a percentage of all pottery at sites around the center; *c*, percentage of all sites in each zone possessing Savernake pottery. The steep gradient of all three curves is commonly found in fall-off curves for the distribution of coarse, bulky objects. After Orton 1980, fig. 4.9.

mation regarding the source of an item or the locus of production. This information is frequently difficult to ascertain, but without data on the location, mode, and scale of production, it is impossible to move beyond a simple description of an item's spatial occurrence.

Another problem is that frequency of occurrence of pottery categories, if based on numbers of sherds rather than on estimates of the number of whole vessels (see sec. 9.2), will vary with the differential breakage rates of the pottery (Hodder 1980, 153; Orton 1980, 156–67), confounding estimates of exchange intensity and centralization. Finally, because pottery is cheap, bulky, and fragile, it is apt to circulate in different patterns than other commodities.

Simply describing the coordinates of spatial occurrence of pottery or any other commodity is not equivalent to understanding the processes or mechanisms by which it was distributed, however. Assuming that the sources of production or distribution have been identified, those studying exchange processes usually proceed by graphing the frequency of that commodity as a function of distance from the source. Such fall-off or decay models (fig. 6.8) graph a decline in interaction (distribution) as effective distance from the source of supply increases (the so-called friction effect of distance). A number of studies have compared the shapes of the curves obtained by different transformations of the data, both prehistoric and modern, to discern the variables that act significantly on their form (Hodder 1974b; Hodder and Orton 1976; Renfrew 1977a).

Several important conclusions have resulted from these studies. One is that different exchange processes may produce substantially the same spatial disposition of artifacts, giving identically shaped curves. In other words, reciprocity and redistribution of archaeological materials cannot be distinguished in fall-off curves (Hodder and Orton 1976).

A second important point is that there are two major classes of curves that reflect different categories of items being exchanged (Hodder 1974b, 179–82; Orton 1980, 121). Goods with high value and less bulk will have relatively broader areal distributions and hence flatter curves (their frequency declines more slowly with distance). Bulky, low-value goods, on the other hand, typically exhibit a high frequency near their source and then a sharp fall-off in frequency with distance beyond what may represent a day's journey to the source of supply. This type of localized distribution curve, which is likely to

Figure 6.9 "Fall-off curves" for Oxfordshire color-coated pottery, showing percentage of the ware as a function of distance from the production source: *a*, sites obtaining pottery by water transport, indicating a slow rate of fall-off; *b*, sites obtaining pottery by overland transport, showing a rapid decline in frequency with distance. After Orton 1980, fig. 4.11.

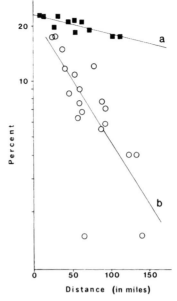

be typical for utilitarian pottery, is said to represent supply-zone behavior (see Renfrew, Dixon, and Cann 1968, 327). Differences between the two may be a function of mode of transport, however (fig. 6.9). A third kind of curve, exhibiting a "plateau and kink" structure, may illustrate the exchange of items within and across boundaries (Hodder 1980, 152).

Finally, the gradient of the fall-off curve will vary with the demographic characteristics of the region in question (Hodder 1974b, 173). The fall-off (or decline in frequency with distance) is less sharp in urban areas than in rural areas and in larger centers than in smaller ones.

Questions of pottery distribution are closely related to questions of scale and mode of production (as seen above), specifically with reference to how much is produced and the distance between producers and consumers. Several factors have been identified that affect the distance a given commodity can be expected to move in exchange transactions (Renfrew 1977a, 77), and these are of particular interest in ceramic studies. Two of the most significant are the transportability of the product and its effective life.

The transportability of a ceramic object is a ratio of the value of the item to its weight and to the breakage rate in transit (Renfrew 1977a, 77; see also sec. 7.2.4). This property is clearly related to the distance vessels travel. Most utilitarian pottery vessels have comparatively low transportability, although it might be enhanced if their transport also took advantage of their function as containers: the contents would increase their value. Modern tourist pottery, which is miniaturized, is outside the realm of these observations (sec. 15.1.1).

Other considerations weigh in the transportability factor, however, and underscore the relation mode and scale of production have to distribution. Peacock (1982, 99), for example, has pointed out that urban nucleated potting industries produce a much greater variety of wares than individual workshops, and these generally travel much greater distances, while rural nucleated industries often specialize in a single widely distributed product. Some clues to this situation emerge when we consider the relation between agriculture and the need for bulk containers (Riley 1981, 136): rural rather than urban areas are likely to provide the demand for large containers for storing and distributing agricultural produce.

It is also important to consider access to transportation. Ease of distribution and profitability may be responsible for a regional division of labor (specialization in forms) in Los Pueblos, Mexico (Papousek 1981, 6–7): heavy but relatively costly large vessels are produced some distance from roads, whereas small pots (which are cheaper individually and therefore must be sold in larger quantities to make a profit) are manufactured closer to roads to promote distribution and commercial success.

A second factor in exchange distance is the use life or effective life of the item, which involves frequency of use, breakage rate in use (both of these relate to the mechanical properties of a ceramic), patterns of reuse or discard after breakage, loss-recovery rate, and patterns of deliberate burial (see also sec. 9.3). These considerations make it clear that the bulk of utilitarian pottery will not move far from its locus of manufacture, and distribution curves, assuming production areas can be identified, are likely to reveal supply-zone behavior. At the same time, production sites are likely to be closer to the consuming markets for much these same reasons, as well as because of the generally widespread occurrence of clays suitable for pottery making. Supply-zone curves for domestic or utilitarian pottery doubtless represent both of these mechanisms.

Certain exceptionally strong or highly valued ceramic items may, however, act as prestige goods, which have been found to travel farther and have a more gentle gradient in their fall-off curves. Prestige goods in general, whether ceramics or other commodities, are likely to exhibit these distributional characteristics in part because usually only a restricted number of people can have or afford the item, and in part because the items may be exchangeable only for a restricted class of items that are also scarce or prestige goods (Renfrew 1977a, 76–77). It is possible, however, to get a distorted curve in which low-value goods (such as pottery) exhibit high-value curves because they are obtained in connection with long-distance special-purpose travels, as in the case of Marigat pottery in the Baringo District of Kenya (Hodder 1979a, 19, fig. 7).

Social and demographic factors provide additional complications that argue against simple relationships between levels of trade and distance. Where pottery is not strictly speaking a commodity and its manufacture is purely a household replacement activity, trade plays little or no role in spatial disposition of the wares. Among the Fulani, for example, pottery stays in the same quarter of the village in which it was manufactured and "rarely travels more than 200 meters between producer and consumer" (David and Hennig 1972, 21). And among the Shipibo-Conibo it was found in a census of twenty-five households that only 4% of 325 vessels were manufactured outside that household (DeBoer 1984, 354). Migration is yet another complicating factor in attempting to assess the presence and level of trade from distributional data alone. In societies with relatively unstable membership—for example, women (potters) moving in and out on the basis of marriage or other relationships—it may be difficult to distinguish traded vessels from locally manufactured vessels of nonlocal styles (David and Hennig 1972, 27; see also Phillipson 1974, cited in Hodder 1978, 259).

6.4 Variability in Ceramic Products

Because in many prehistoric contexts the nature of the archaeological record does not accommodate direct investigation of the scale and mode of production, these arrangements have to be approached indirectly. Archaeologists could turn to other criteria, for example, those used ethnographically, such as the amount of time spent practicing the craft, receipt of payment for the product, and so forth, but of course these have no potential for direct archaeological measurement. Instead, archaeologists have most frequently turned to various procedures based on variations in the output—pottery vessels or fragments. The idea is that variability in pottery encodes information on the strategies of production (Rice 1981) in much the same way as pottery decoration can be viewed as a stylistic code reflecting other structural—primarily social—behavior involved in production and use (see chap. 8). Looked at another way (Redman 1978a, 173), production is a process of variety generation, whereas "consumption" (purchase and use) is variety selection; together these create cultural patterns distinctive of different sociocultural arrangements.

The underlying principle in this inferential process is that variability in the three components or kinds of specialization—locus, personnel (intensification), and resource—is reduced or regularized in different productive modes. This means that fewer craftspersons use selected resources and produce more vessels for a larger corpus of consumers; simultaneously, the time and labor investment will be diminished so that all steps of manufacture will be routinized. In other words, there is a gradual development toward locus, personnel, and/or resource specialization. What is not clear is whether there is a tendency for one to happen first, or for differences in them between household and workshop production. Variations in resource selection, processing, forming, finishing, and firing will diminish in response to considerations that are referred to in modern manufacturing as cost effectiveness and quality control, leading to more uniform or standardized products. Unfortunately, the degree of product standardization in household versus workshop industries has not yet been investigated ethnographically so as to test these propositions.

A related idea is "technological styles" (Lechtman 1977): experience and custom combine to establish a body of information and practice governing the manufacture of pottery vessels, from choice of resources to procedures of shaping and firing, resulting in a characteristic final product with a unique range of properties. (Rye's [1981, 5] comment that "Technological traditions are recognized from high correlations between process sequences" is also relevant here.) This final product will ultimately be one favored by consumers; producers may alter their procedures to conform to the preferences of specific consuming groups and thus maintain a market (Crossland and Posnansky 1978, 88).

Studies of variability in pottery as well as other artifacts owe their primary debt to Clarke (1968), one of the first archaeologists to provide explicit and thorough treatments of both the description and interpretation of patterns of artifact variability. The major concepts around which studies of pottery variability have been organized are standardization and diversity. These concepts reflect two ways of systematizing the dimensions of variability in the ceramic

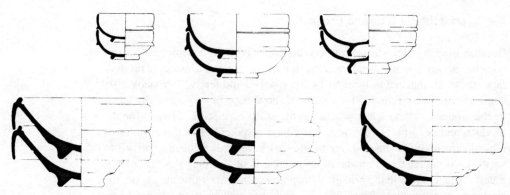

Figure 6.10   Stacking of Roman provincial bowls, aided by flanges and ridges on the outside. After Röttlander 1968, fig. 7.

products of a society so they can be interpreted within a broader framework of ideas concerning socioeconomic systems.

Standardization refers to a reduction of variability and has implications for all the economic spheres in which a commodity participates: production, distribution, and use. Standardization can be considered in terms of all aspects of the pottery manufacturing process, including resource selection, processing, forming, finishing, and firing as well as the organizational aspects (scale and mode). Highly standardized products imply that production is carried out by individuals utilizing a limited range of materials and somewhat formalized or routinized techniques that result in virtually identical products, such as mass production or the use of molds (see Peacock 1982, 121–22, citing Goudineau 1968, for a discussion of this in production of Arretine Samian pottery). Standardization of production does not necessarily mean that only one kind of pottery is made and used in a community; it indicates rather that little heterogeneity in composition and appearance (form and style) is evident within each category of pottery.

In terms of distribution, standardization may be most important to ease of movement: standard-sized vessels, especially those that stack or nest well (fig. 6.10), may be easier to transport in quantity and thus have a wider distribution (see Rathje, Gregory, and Wiseman 1978, 171; Rottländer 1967, 1968; Whittlesey 1974). Bowls of standard sizes may also imply standardized units of measure (Rottländer 1967, 1968), which may in turn be important for the distribution of their contents (e.g., Wright and Johnson 1975).

With respect to consumption or use, standardization of composition, technomorphological properties, and decorative styles is likely to significantly affect the utility and popularity of certain vessel classes, governing their actual use functions as well as their rate of replacement and entry into the archaeological record.

Diversity is a concept borrowed from population ecology, where it is used to describe the structure of an ecological community in terms of the number, size, and proportion of constituent species (see Pielou 1974). In archaeological assemblages, diversity means variability not in the properties of individual sherds but in the numbers and frequencies of different categories of pottery, which may be taxonomic units, form classes, decorative styles, and so forth.

Diversity is a statistical measure akin to "variance," which summarizes the kind and amount of variation around a mean; in this case the "mean" is the constitution of an assemblage. The variation is described in terms of two components: richness, or the number of categories present, and evenness, the distribution of individuals within the categories.

There is some disagreement on how diversity measures can be interpreted in ecology, and as in other situations where a concept from one discipline is transferred into another, there is danger of misapplication in anthropological and archaeological studies. An additional problem is sample size: a large total number of vessels or sherds is required if the calculations are to be meaningful. Otherwise, as in any sampling procedure, rare categories may be underrepresented, distorting the picture. Finally, there is the problem of assessing whether differences in diversity indexes are statistically and behaviorally significant. These problems aside, the potential of diversity measures for ceramic studies has still not been fully realized (Rice 1984a). Among the possible interpretive frameworks are access to resources; patterns of distribution; and assemblage variability between time periods, sites, or subcomplexes (e.g., functional or status). The general view in ecology is that more complex communities exhibit greater diversity, and this may be true of archaeological assemblages as well.

Although there has been little explicit use of the concepts of standardization and diversity in archaeology until recently, in studies of pottery production they have been used in efforts to understand specialization (Rice 1981, 1984a; Toll 1981); diversity has also been employed in studies of pottery styles (see sec. 8.3.3) and to characterize the assemblages of households of different socioeconomic statuses (Deal 1983, 269–309; Rice 1984a). In addressing specialized production, the premise is that a small number of skilled producers manufacturing pottery will adhere to a greater or lesser extent to principles of cost effectiveness, quality control, and mass production, leading to homogeneity or standardization of the products. The attributes relating to technology will be less variable where there are few choices available in selecting and processing resources and in firing the products, in the interest of cost effectiveness and quality control. Attributes of form will also be less variable where molds or other devices are used used for forming and shaping uniform vessels and there is an otherwise restricted range of techniques and economical motions to produce quantities of pottery per unit of labor input. Again, considerations of cost effectiveness and quality control will be important.

Attributes of decoration or "style" are less likely to conform to these principles, however, because they are responsive to a broader set of social, ideological, and aesthetic concerns that may not be influenced by economic controls at all (see sec. 8.3.3; Adams 1979; Rice 1984b). On the other hand, standardization may be envisioned in terms of gestures and brushstrokes and the efficiency of execution of a design, as it has been in the American Southwest (Hagstrum 1985). Stylistic attributes may be standardized, or instead they may be greatly elaborated, with increased variation and diversity.

Different production arrangements may exist for different categories of pottery (see Vince 1981; Brisbane 1981). That is, so-called elite wares—products with high value, special function, low consumption, or restricted distribution—may participate in all spheres of economic activity (production, distribution, and use) in a very different way than utilitarian wares (those with low value, high consumption, and wide circulation). Standardization and mass production may be encountered in the latter, whereas the former may be more vulnerable to the changing preferences of entrepreneurial or administrative authorities and thus more variable. Differences in labor intensity may also distinguish these two categories (Feinman, Upham, and Lightfoot 1981).

Although these procedures for measuring variability do not directly address scale and mode of production, they are efforts to utilize more fully the enormous quantity of information about pottery production that is encoded in a sherd. Hypotheses about standardization and diversity should thus be sensitive to output variations of household versus workshop production. In addition, they should be suitable for assessing variability in the kinds of specialization associated with each mode: locus, personnel, and resource. These propositions concerning standardization, diversity, and specialized craft production have only begun to be tested, however, and it is not yet known how well they conform to ethnographic reality or retrodict prehistoric arrangements. This can come only from ethnographic testing, but to date there has been little effort to employ standardization and diversity measurements in ethnographic research on ceramic production.

6.5 Summary and Conclusions

Surprisingly little ethnographic research has addressed pottery economics, so it is difficult to formulate congruences between the data of prehistory and the ethnographic record. Enough has been accomplished, however, to require some cautions about applying the observations and models outlined above.

First, much of the information available on contemporary pottery economics concerns the relation between potters and modern nontraditional market economies, which are often tied into international tourism (see chap. 15). Care must be taken in using these data as analogies to prehistoric situations, particularly in areas distant from urban centers.

Second, the full range of any society's production, distribution, and consumption relations cannot be reliably characterized by a single product, so those described for pottery do not necessarily hold true for other sectors and goods in the economy.

Third, the models of production and distribution described here are heuristic categories. In real life the arrangements will differ from community to community or potter to potter; any given area might exhibit workshop and household production side by side and have consumers traveling to some potters while other potters market their wares through middlemen.

Fourth, the tendency to confuse place with process must be avoided. This is evident, for example, in a failure to distinguish between market and marketplace, site specialization and producer specialization, and spatial distribution (occurrence) and distributional mechanisms of exchange.

Fifth, it must be recognized that much economic behavior is informal and sporadic; for example, various kinds of redistribution or household production. Such behavior, if not invisible archaeologically, is at least hard to isolate and verify.

Sixth, these constraints make the study of pottery production, specifically, a tenuous proposition. The absence of abundant workshop evidence in many areas and a lack of middle-range theory to bridge the gap between archaeology and ethnography render matters all the more difficult. The total picture of pottery economics is very much conditioned by the scale of production, and many of the variables of scale are largely invisible in the archaeological record. Thus, while the presence of pottery in an area indicates that pottery production or distribution, or both, was carried out relatively nearby, understanding the organization and scale of those activities often depends on an indirect strategy of studying the ceramic products (or fragments of the products) rather than directly examining the producing units themselves.

Object- or product-oriented ethnoarchaeological research is fairly common in some aspects of pottery style analysis (see chap. 8); the motifs and structures of pottery designs are seen as encoded behavioral information that can be used to infer social and cultural processes. But similar models have not yet been developed for explicitly interpreting the behavioral information encoded in the technological variables of pottery in terms of pottery function (chap. 7) or production organization. Given the frequency with which an output- or product-based strategy must be adopted by archaeologists studying pottery production, it is all the more imperative to have a variety of comparable studies of the ceramic manufactures of contemporary potters.

6.6   References

Adams 1979
Annis 1985
Arnold 1981
Arnold 1972, 1975a, 1985
Asboe 1946
Balfet 1965
Barbour 1976
Beals 1975
Beazley 1945
Bishop, Rands, and Holley 1982
Bowen and Moser 1968
Brisbane 1981
Cardew 1969
Chagnon 1968
Chayanov 1966
Cheung 1983
Clarke 1968
Colton 1951
Cook 1984
Crossland and Posnansky 1978
Curtis 1962
David and Hennig 1972
Deal 1983

DeBoer 1984
DeBoer and Lathrap 1979
Demont and Centlivres 1967
Dickinson and Hartley 1971
Donnan 1971, 1978
Dow 1985
Earle 1977, 1981
Ellen and Glover 1974
Evans 1978
Feinman, Upham, and Lightfoot 1981
Fontana et al. 1962
Foster 1962, 1965b
Gill 1981
Goudineau 1968
Hagstrum 1985
Hancock 1984
Hardin 1977
Hart 1982
Hartley 1966
Hayden and Cannon 1984
Helms 1979
Hill 1977

Ho and Huddle 1976
Hobson 1976
Hodder 1962
Hodder 1974b, c, 1977, 1978, 1979a, 1980
Hodder and Orton 1976
Hodges 1974
Howry 1976
Hurd 1976
Johns 1963, 1977b
Johnston, 1984
Kaiser 1984
Kardos et al. 1985
Lackey 1981
Lathrap 1976
Lauer 1970, 1971
Leach 1976
Lechtman 1977
LeFree 1975
Linares de Sapir 1969
Linné 1965
Longacre 1981, 1985
Loughlin 1977
Lowenstein 1986
Lynch 1979
Man 1894
Matson 1972
Medley 1976
Miller 1981
Millon 1970
Morris 1974
Muller 1984
Nash 1966
National Academy of Sciences 1980
Nicholson and Patterson 1985a, b
Nicklin 1979, 1981b
Oliver 1955
Orton 1980
Papousek 1981

Peacock 1981, 1982
Phillipson 1974
Pielou 1974
Plog 1977
Polanyi 1957
Potts 1981
Rathje, Gregory, and Wiseman 1978
Redman 1978a
Redman and Myers 1981
Reina 1966
Reina and Hill 1978
Renfrew 1977a, b
Renfrew, Dixon, and Cann 1968
Rice 1981, 1984a, b
Riley 1981
Rottländer 1967, 1968
Rye 1977, 1981
Rye and Evans 1976
Sahlins 1972
Scheans 1977
Schumpeter 1961
Shepard 1965
Smith 1974
Spriggs and Miller 1979
Staehelin 1965
Stark 1985
Stone 1950
Tatje and Naroll 1973
Thompson 1984
Toll 1981
Tschopik 1950
van der Leeuw 1977, 1984
Van de Velde and Van de Velde 1939
Vince 1981
Von Bothmer.1985
Voyatzoglou 1974
Weigand 1969
Whittlesey 1974
Wright and Johnson 1975

Vessel Function: Form, Technology, and Use

7

Objects fashioned wholly or in part from clay have served a wide variety of human needs past and present, from sewer pipe to spacecraft insulation. But the broadest and most fundamental use of clay has been in containers—pottery vessels. Pottery containers may be used for carrying liquids, storing dry substances, or heating contents over a fire. Each use places different demands on the vessel, and so its suitability for a particular task depends on its design, in an engineering as well as an artistic sense.

This chapter treats pottery vessels serving as containers, whose morphotechnological characteristics—their attributes of shape and technology—are closely related to their suitability for a particular activity. Other clay objects such as toys, candlesticks, roof tiles, figurines, tools for certain tasks (e.g., spinning), and containers such as burial urns, flower vases, chamber pots, cache vessels, and other special-use ceramics are excluded because the vessel itself rather than its morphotechnological properties is of primary concern.

The discussion of form, technology, and function is based on the decisions potters make to modify properties toward particular kinds of uses. Real-life production behavior involves complex decision making in the face of uncertainty regarding variables and outcomes; it aims to minimize risk and accommodate any number of tangible and intangible considerations. Choices may be rational, but they are not always clear-cut. Thus the principles and relationships outlined here do not constitute rigid recipes for pottery making; rather, they form a hypothetical menu from which various selections may be strategically combined according to particular requirements and needs to create durable and pleasing wares.

7.1 Vessel Function

Ceramic vessels have served a variety of nonculinary purposes for ten thousand years or so, but it is in domestic and culinary roles that their functions as

207

containers can be addressed most broadly and comparatively, both through time and over a wide geographical area. In these activities the full spectrum of cultural and technological factors underlying the choices involved in manufacturing a vessel is brought into play.

7.1.1.   Kinds of Vessel Functions

In their general role as containers, ceramic vessels are tools (see Braun 1983); they are a subset of a broader category of material or technological devices called facilities (Wagner 1960; cf. Oswalt 1973; Lustig-Arecco 1975). Facilities contain or restrain the movement of their contents and include such things as corrals, granaries, and baskets as well as pottery. Facilities are not necessarily passive containers; they may increase the usefulness of their contents by prolonging their life span as well as by allowing different kinds of energy to transform or transport the contents. Thus the functions of domestic ceramic containers take place in three broad realms: storage, transformation or processing, and transfer or transport.

These uses can be broken down into the kinds of storage, processing, and transport that may be involved, permitting a broader understanding of the use-controlled requirements of the containers and the characteristics of design that will accommodate them. Many issues enter into the relation of design to function: (1) whether the contents are liquid or dry; (2) whether the contents are hot or cold (or whether heat is to be applied to them in use); (3) frequency of transactions, that is, access or movement of goods into or out of the container; (4) duration of episodes of use (especially in storage); and (5) distance (in transfer). Other concerns include whether a hand or utensil must be put into the container, whether the activity/function is tended (watched, manipulated) or unattended, and the volume of the goods being stored, processed, or moved. Figure 7.1 diagrams these considerations in the three main categories of use—storage, processing, and transfer.

The main disadvantage of pottery is its fragility: pots are easily broken if dropped or accidentally struck. Aside from this vulnerability to mischance, however, vessels of fired clay are well suited to a variety of functions. For storage, they are longer lasting and more durable than other kinds of containers, such as baskets or gourds, and more suitable for holding liquids. Similarly, they are more resistant to destruction by rodents or insects, as well as to moisture, than these other kinds of containers, and they can be sealed to prevent vermin from damaging their contents. In processing activities such as mixing, soaking, and grinding as well as in domestic and industrial activities involving heat, such as cooking, pottery again has advantages over other containers. Pots can hold liquid contents, they can be set directly into a fire without being destroyed, and their rigidity allows them to withstand considerable agitation of the contents without damage or deformation. Transfer may be over short distances, as in presenting or serving (and eating) food, or long distances, where the vessels have an implicit storage function. For long-distance movement, pottery is in principle likely to be preferred only for carrying liquids; for dry goods, baskets function as well and have the advantage of being nonfragile and lightweight.

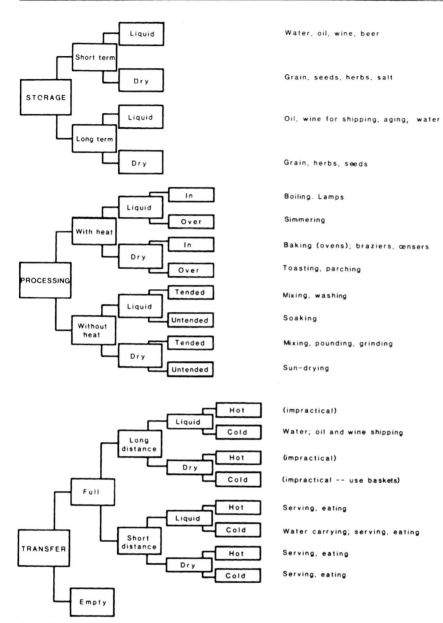

Figure 7.1 Categories of vessel use.

Each category of vessel use requires a different combination of attributes of form and composition to achieve a product that meets its special needs. But many vessels have multiple uses; for example, the same vessel may be employed for carrying water and storing it or for preparing food and eating it. Thus vessel designs must accommodate the sometimes conflicting demands of different uses, within the limits imposed by the resources available.

Many of the problems of understanding vessel functions, particularly for archaeologists, relate to definitions. Established categories of vessel forms and uses, such as cookpot and storage jar, are often vague and overlapping, so that forms and functions are inextricably linked in terminology. Of interest here are vessels whose morphotechnological properties are in large part crucial to their containment functions. They are frequently described in the archaeological literature as utilitarian, functional, domestic, subsistence, coarseware, or plainware categories of pottery. None of these terms is entirely accurate, however.

All pottery has some function or utility; the terms utilitarian and functional are usually used for contrast with elite, ceremonial, nonutilitarian, display, or special-purpose pottery. Elite pottery is usually found in smaller quantities than utilitarian pottery and is typically more finely made and more elaborately decorated (labor intensive). But even pottery for cooking and serving food may also function in display, testifying to the potter's skill in providing utensils and adornment for her home (e.g., Balfet 1965, 163). Fortunately, the tendency for archaeologists to see pottery decoration and style as lacking function is quickly disappearing (see chap. 8).

The terms domestic and subsistence are also unsatisfactory for this pottery, though they are less objectionable than the others. Pottery containers may have had a variety of quasi-industrial or manufacturing roles; for example, in salt making (Charlton 1969), dairying, or metallurgy (as molds or tuyeres), in addition to serving as pipes or lamps. These would have had similar technological or morphological requirements, since all are used over a fire to contain liquids, yet these are not direct subsistence uses. One can make functional inferences from the ceramic properties, with only a small shift of analytical perspective from domestic to nondomestic arenas.

Perhaps a better term for the pottery containers of interest here is technomic—relating primarily to technological and economic realms (Binford 1962a). Utilitarian or technomic pottery constitutes the bulk of the pottery recovered from archaeological sites as well as most of the utensils inventoried in ethnographic surveys.

7.1.2   Determining Vessel Function

Pottery containers come in all shapes and sizes, and each food item or occasion of preparation may have its own vessel or set of vessels in a well-equipped household. In ethnographic situations, determining their functions is a relatively simple matter of asking questions and recording observations (see also sec. 9.3.1.1). This vessel is used for boiling beans, that one is for carrying water, this one is for drinking, that one for storing grain, those others for community beer-making festivities, boiling rice, toasting manioc cakes, simmering sauces, grinding condiments, and so forth. In archaeological contexts, however, the matter is not so simple. Archaeologists have used a variety of observations or strategies to permit some general statement about the uses of the vessels they recover in excavation.

One kind of data consists of written records, such as documents, inventories, and ethnohistorical accounts; painted and sculptural art, such as that of the Near East (Porada 1984) or the Maya (Benson 1974), may also show pottery vessels in household or ritual use.

A second and more traditional basis for hypotheses about function is the archaeological context of recovery. If a pot is found in a burial or a cache, or on a living surface in association with a cooking fire or with its contents intact, the function of that vessel—at least at the time it became a part of the archaeological record—is fairly clear. The availability and reliability of this kind of information are consequences of the strategy employed in excavating any site rather than the skill of the ceramic analyst, however, and so will not be further treated here. Moreover, such an approach is of little use in dealing with the enormous volume of broken pottery recovered from midden debris or other ambiguous contexts.

A third approach to ascertaining prehistoric vessel function is through ethnographic analogy, experimental archaeological studies, and inference (see chap. 5). Analogy and inference are applied to problems of pottery function in three typical ways: on the basis of form, through technological characteristics and experimental usage, and by the presence/absence and location of decoration.

Finally, a variety of analytical procedures can be used to examine residues on or in the walls and pores of vessels, thereby determining their contents and uses.

7.2   Vessel Form: Relating Form and Function

One of the most long-standing but nonetheless inexplicit relationships in the field of ceramic studies is that between the form of a vessel and its function. Just as a chipped stone tool with a point and a long sharp edge will often be called a knife by analogy to the shape and usage of modern knives, so a low, open ceramic vessel will be called a bowl by analogy to the bowls in modern kitchens. The differences between this bowl and another vessel that by the same reasoning might be categorized as a jar are not always well understood and are often contradictory, but they provide a descriptive and predictive framework for establishing what a particular class of prehistoric vessels look like and how they may have been used.

Although the form/function relationship can be subsumed under a broader statement of interactions between morphology, or structural characteristics, and functional roles—an interaction that is also evident throughout the biological sciences, for example—in ceramics this linkage has not been thoroughly explored. Most of the attempts to deal with the issue have done little more than decry the ambiguity or regionality of terms used for vessel shapes. Examples of such exotic regional terms are aryballus, tecomate, pithos, krater, and mortarium, used in South America, Mesoamerica, the Near East, Greece, and Britain, respectively. Though these terms are specific and precise, they may not convey any information to an audience outside those immediate areas.

The application of more familiar or generic terms such as bowl and jar introduces a different set of problems. One is that these terms tend to ascribe a particular function without clear indications that such was the vessel's intended use. Terms such as storage jar, cooking pot, and serving bowl leave little doubt as to their supposed use, but they reinforce the implicit association of form and function: each of these binomial terms combines a use category with a shape category.

Another problem with familiar terms is their subjectivity. In the absence of explicit criteria, it is often difficult to distinguish between a bowl and a basin, or between a jar and a vase. As a result, these common terms—which carry significant weight in describing the appearance of the vessels in question and inferring their use—are often useless and imprecise. Still another difficulty is that many complex vessel shapes defy labeling by these familiar terms.

7.2.1 Anatomy of a Vessel

Any ceramic vessel form can be described or characterized in a number of ways, usually with explicit or implicit reference to particular parts and their proportions. Most simply, a vessel has three essential components: orifice, body, and base (fig. 7.2a). These are significant in terms of the construction, function, and possible decoration of the vessel, and their relative proportions determine its overall shape category.

The body of a vessel (sometimes called the belly) may be defined as the portion between the orifice and base that includes the maximum diameter of the vessel or the region of greatest enclosed volume. Figure 7.2b and d show forms in which the maximum diameter is at or near the midpoint of the height of the vessel. Figure 7.2c shows a vessel with the maximum diameter at the orifice; this does not pose an identification problem, however, because the body is still that portion of the vessel whose walls enclose the greatest volume between orifice and base.

The orifice, or mouth opening, of a vessel is subject to a great deal of elaboration, much of which is functional. One of its most important characteristics is its relation to the maximum diameter of the vessel. If it is equal to or greater than the maximum diameter (fig. 7.2a, c), it is described as an unrestricted orifice. If it is less than the maximum diameter, it is called a restricted orifice. On a restricted form, with the maximum diameter below the orifice of the vessel, the region between the point of maximum diameter and the orifice or neck is the shoulder or upper body of the vessel (fig. 7.2d). Sometimes the point of maximum diameter alone may be called the shoulder. The area between the point of maximum diameter and the base is the lower body.

Not all vessels have such simple contours, however; often they have complex shapes set off by curves or angles, especially at the orifice. Also, the orifice may be raised and extended into a neck or collar, which affects the proportions of the vessel. A neck is a restriction of the opening of the vessel (fig. 7.2e, f), beginning above the point of maximum diameter of the body, that is, at some point on the shoulder (see also Shepard 1976, 230, for discussion of independent restricted vessels). A collar, on the other hand, usually begins at the point of maximum diameter (or at a slight restriction very close to it), and does not significantly reduce the orifice opening relative to the diameter of the body (fig. 7.2g, h). Collars typically join the body at an angle, while necks may join with a curve or an angle (see below). Either the base of the neck or collar or its point of maximum restriction may be called the throat.

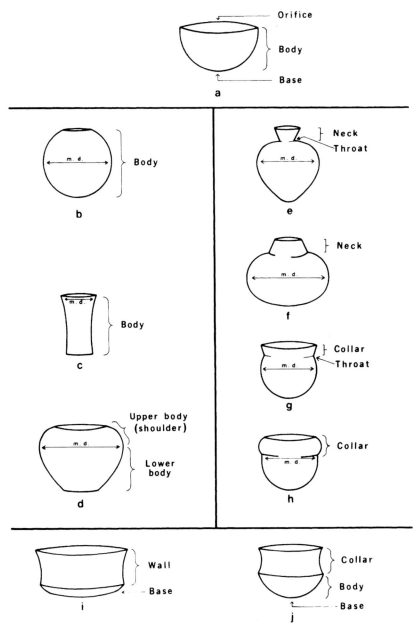

Figure 7.2 Major subdivisions of pottery vessel shapes: *a*, divisions of a simple vessel; *b–d*, vessel body; *e–h*, neck, collar, and throat; *i, j*, base and body on composite forms (m.d. = maximum diameter).

The third region of a vessel is the base, sometimes called the foot. The base is the underside of a vessel, touching the surface it rests on during normal use. Although this is self-evident for flat-based vessels (fig. 7.2*c, d*), for round-based vessels it is hard to distinguish the base from the side. The juncture may be marked by a slight change in curvature between the side walls and the

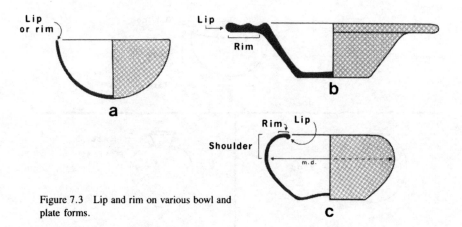

Figure 7.3   Lip and rim on various bowl and plate forms.

underside or base (fig. 7.2*k*), or a distinct angle may differentiate them (fig. 7.2*i*). In the latter case, even though the entire lower portion does not touch the surface, it is still called the base. A problem arises if the proportions of the vessel are changed (e.g., compare fig. 7.2*i* with 7.2*j*), altering the definitions of components.

The three vessel zones—orifice (including neck or collar), body, and base—may be elaborated, but because these modifications do not distort the primary shapes of the vessels or their proportions, they can be thought of as secondary form variations. They often have important utilitarian as well as decorative functions, however, and secondary does not imply insignificant.

The orifice, for example, whether restricted, unrestricted, necked, or collared, may be described in terms of two secondary form characteristics, the lip and the rim (fig. 7.3). These two terms are often used interchangeably, because the point where one ends and the other begins is not always clear. The lip itself is easy to identify, being the edge or margin of the mouth of the vessel; it may also be described as the edge of the rim of the vessel. The lip is thus a part of the rim, but precisely defining and differentiating the two is a bit more difficult. The rim is easily distinguished only when it is articulated—set off by a curve or an angle from the wall or neck of the vessel (fig. 7.3*b*, *c*). Where such a change exists, the rim is the area between the change of orientation of the lip (the margin) and the side or neck of the vessel. A direct rim (e.g., figs. 7.2*a, c* and 7.3*a*), in contrast, has no change of orientation between the wall or neck and the lip, and the lip and rim are equivalent.

An additional category of secondary form or shape attributes includes flanges or ridges and appendages. Flanges and ridges are bands or projections that extend out from the vessel wall (e.g., fig. 6.9), differing in degree of projection (flanges are greater than ridges). They are usually added to the wall of a fully shaped vessel rather than being part of the wall and its contours, and most typically (though by no means always) they run around the circumference. Appendages or attachments are primarily of three kinds: vessel supports (also called feet) applied to the base; handles applied to the body, neck, or collar; and spouts applied to the orifice, neck, collar, or body.

Each of the primary and secondary anatomical zones or features described

above—neck, collar, rim, lip, wall, base, flange, supports, handle, spout—
may be further identified by a series of terms that describe the particular appearance of the feature or its relation to other features. In other words, each of
these zones or features may be considered an attribute or variable of a vessel
and described more specifically in terms of the possible states or conditions in
which it may appear (see, e.g., Redman 1978a, fig. 8.6). Particular kinds of
rims or bases or flanges—not simply their presence or absence—may be of
functional, stylistic, chronological, and social/ethnic significance in distinguishing the makers and users of different kinds of ceramic vessels. Because
the variations of orifices and rims are usually given chronological and cultural
significance, archaeological ceramic reports typically devote a great deal of
space to illustrations in cross section, called profiles (as, e.g., in fig. 7.3a–c).

7.2.2   Description of Form

Vessel components and their proportions provide the basis of several descriptive systems for overall forms. One is a simple use-oriented system similar to
that applied to modern culinary apparatus; another includes classifications
based on solid geometry. The categorizations discussed here are explicitly restricted to shape; more general discussion of pottery classification is found in
section 9.1.

7.2.2.1   INFERRED USE CLASSIFICATIONS
Pottery manufactured and used in contemporary communities may be classified according to categories recognized and applied by its makers and users.
These ethnosemantic or folk classifications (sec. 9.1.2) are based on complex
consideration of size, shape, and customary use, and they often emphasize
functional attachments such as handles or spouts (Kempton 1981, 46).

Similar use classifications are known from historical documents (e.g., pro-
bate inventories), which list vessels by name as well as by function, but many
of these names—pipkin, for example—are no longer in modern use. There
have been several attempts to standardize and clarify vessel-shape terminology (e.g., Fournier 1981, with concordances of terms in English, Spanish,
and French; Balfet, Fauvet-Berthelot, and Monzon 1983; Castillo Tejero and
Litvak 1968; Theuvenin, Bullen, and Sanoja 1970). A number of non-English
terms for shape or use have entered the English-speaking literature on pottery;
for example, cazuela and olla are common in the southwestern and southeastern archaeological literature. Other vessel category names seem to be virtually universal—at least in English—and though they have important functional implications, their definitions are remarkably imprecise.

Although functional attachments are important in categorizing vessels, use-
related classifications of vessel shapes by anthropologists and archaeologists
are most frequently based on ratios of height to maximum diameter and on
kind or size of orifice (e.g., Smith 1955, 4; Millett 1979a, 37; Longacre 1981,
54; Henrickson and McDonald 1983, 631–36; Kempton 1981, 46). The
height of a vessel includes the body plus any neck or collar but usually does
not include basal supports. The diameter is the maximum diameter of either

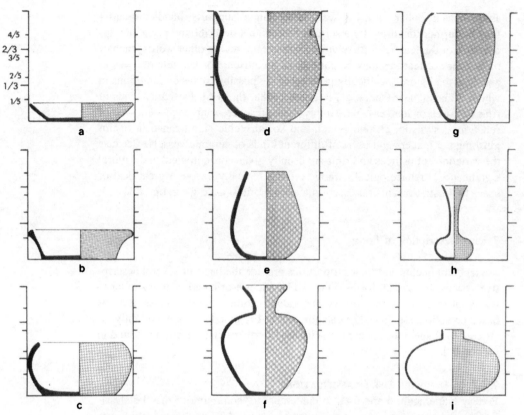

Figure 7.4 Vessel proportions (as ratio of height to diameter) and shape categories: *a*, plate; *b*, dish; *c*, bowl; *d*, bowl; *e*, vase; *f*, jar; *g*, neckless jar with diameter approximately 70% of height, which could be classed as a vase; *h*, *florero*, with a restricted orifice, which could be classed as a jar; *i*, jar with height 66% of diameter, which would be classed as a bowl but for the neck.

the body or the orifice (in an unrestricted form), excluding appendages such as handles, spouts, or supports.

One of these classificatory schemes (Smith 1955; Sabloff 1975, 23), used rather commonly among Mesoamerican archaeologists, includes five vessel forms: plate, dish, bowl, jar, and vase. Plates and dishes are both shallow forms with unrestricted orifices. A plate (fig. 7.4*a*) has a height less than one-fifth its maximum diameter; a dish (fig. 7.4*b*) is slightly deeper, having a height more than one-fifth but less than one-third of its maximum diameter. A bowl (fig. 7.4*c*, *d*) may have a restricted or an unrestricted orifice and is deeper still, its height varying from one-third the maximum diameter of the vessel up to equal to the diameter. An important modification of this relatively standard definition is that bowls may have collars, but they do not have necks.

It is in identifying jars that definitional issues become inconsistent and difficult to put into practice in this scheme. A jar (fig. 7.4*f*) is a necked (and therefore restricted) vessel with its height greater than its maximum diameter (see also Shepard 1976, fig. 21*k*–*q*). If this definition is taken strictly, however, it becomes very difficult to classify any number of forms known ethnographically or archaeologically. For example, figure 7.4*g*, a common large jar form in the southeastern United States, would not be called a jar because it has no neck. The vessel in figure 7.4*i,* considered a jar form in the Southwestern United States, would be a bowl (its height is over one-third the maximum diameter but not equal to it) had not the "no neck" qualifier been added here to the definition of a bowl. If jars must have necks, then there can be no neckless jars, however, and what are the vessels in figure 7.4*g* and *e?*

Alternative terms for these vessels are vase, flagon, and beaker. A vase (fig. 7.4*e*) is a restricted or unrestricted vessel with a height greater than its maximum diameter. Vases may or may not have restricted orifices, but their heights must be greater than their diameters. Can vases have necks? If they cannot, then figure 7.4*h* (a *florero* in Mexico) is not a vase; if they can, then how might necked vases be differentiated from necked jars? Useful alternative terms are flagon, "a vessel with a neck very narrow in comparison with its height and girth," and beaker, "a vessel whose height is greater than its rim diameter; and which is of suitable size and shape for drinking from" (Millett 1979a, 37).

The principle of classifying vessel shapes by ratios of height to diameter is clearly a good one, and further utility could be built into these systems by expanding the principles to include additional ratios of body to neck height and overall vessel size or volume. Some problems remain, however. For example, a scattergram of the relation between height and rim diameter in 250 complete Romano-British vessels showed that flagons, jars, dishes, and bowls could be easily separated, but beakers could not be clearly differentiated from jars (Millett 1979a, 37 and fig. 12).

An alternative classification has been used on historical period pottery of the eastern United States (Beaudry et al. 1983) and divides vessels into flatware (such as plates) and hollowware (those that enclose their contents). Absolute size or volume criteria are used to differentiate many of the categories. By this scheme a saucer can be distinguished from a plate and a dish by absolute diameter: a saucer is less than seven inches across, while a plate is seven to ten inches and a dish is greater than ten inches. Similarly, a cup can be differentiated from a drinking pot by volume: a cup has a capacity of less than a pint, while a drinking pot holds from one pint to two quarts. The names as well as the uses of these historical period vessels were known (a nicety rarely granted prehistoric archaeologists), but even without this advantage the scheme provides a basis for standardizing a number of common terms in both ethnographic and archaeological literature, such as mug, bottle, pitcher, jug, and basin.

At first glance it seems desirable to have some agreement and standardization of form terminology, particularly for the almost universal but disturbingly vague categories of bowl and jar. Specialized shapes occur virtually everywhere, however, and often have unusual features of proportion, size, or appendages. There is no reason these localized vessel form classes—for example, a juglet or a canteen—should be forced into attempts to create a standard or universal scheme of vessel categorization.

7.2.2.2 VESSEL CONTOUR CLASSIFICATIONS

Another system or set of systems of shape classification is based on vessel contours and proportions and eschews quasi-functional terms such as jar and

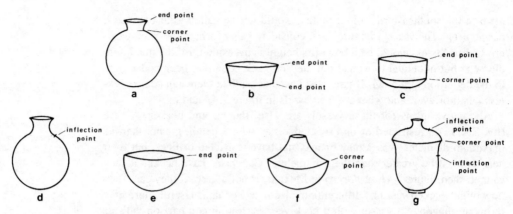

Figure 7.5   Characteristic points of a vessel profile.

bowl (Shepard 1976, 225–36). Shapes are differentiated by "characteristic points" of curvature or angling of the vessel contour; structural terms, principally orifice characteristics; and reference to geometric solids and surfaces. These classificatory organizations can be either used separately or combined into a single construct.

With regard to the first criterion, four "characteristic points" determine the contours of a vessel silhouette or vertical section (Shepard 1976, 226). For example, end points (fig. 7.5*a, b*) are the points at the top and bottom of the wall silhouette, marked at the mouth and base; tangent points are points where the tangent of curvature of body or neck or both is vertical. Two of these characteristic points are of particular interest, the corner (or angle) point and the inflection point. A corner point (fig. 7.5*c,f*) is an abrupt change in the orientation of a vessel wall, or a distinct angle in the joining of vessel parts such as neck and body. The join of wall to base acts as a corner point only if the base rises to join the body; otherwise it is simply an end point. An inflection point is the point on the vessel silhouette marking the change of direction of curvature of two parts of the vessel (fig. 7.5*d*); it lies between two points of vertical tangency.

Corner and inflection points provide a basis for the structural classification of vessel contours (Shepard 1976, 231–32), which may be described as simple, composite, inflected, and complex shapes. Vessels with simple contours or silhouettes have a smooth, uninterrupted straight or curving wall; they lack angle and inflection points (fig. 7.5*b,e*). Composite silhouette vessels have a single corner point (fig. 7.5*a,c,f*), and inflected vessels have a single inflection point (fig. 7.5*d*). Complex contoured vessels have two or more corner points or inflection points or one or more of each (fig. 7.5*g*). Bowls may be described within any of these categories. Necked vessels cannot be simple; they are always either composite, inflected, or complex, while collared vessels may be composite or complex.

Vessel contours may also be described by several mathematical procedures that make them amenable to coding or statistical treatment. One such scheme is based on measurements along a series of horizontal "slices" cutting the circumference, while another uses a grid superimposed over the vessel profile (Shennan and Wilcock 1975, cited in Orton 1980, 40–42).

7.2.2.3   GEOMETRIC OR VOLUME CLASSIFICATIONS

Other approaches to classifying vessel shapes are based on volume or geometry. These classifications make reference to geometric shapes: three solids (sphere, ellipsoid, and ovaloid) and three surfaces (cylinder, cone, and hyperboloid), the latter having no defined end points or dimensions (fig. 7.6). These shape classifications may be used for restricted or unrestricted vessel forms; the orifices of any of these forms may have a neck or collar added,

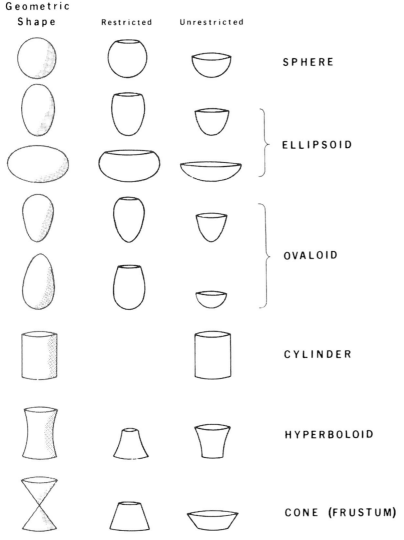

Figure 7.6   Geometric solids and surfaces as references for vessel shape description; sections of these shapes may combine with sections of other shapes to form necks, collars, or bases of composite or complex vessel forms. After Shepard 1976, figs. 23 and 24.

which is itself a section of a geometric form. Thus not only simple but also composite and complex vessel shapes can be described by their geometric equivalents.

The hyperboloid gives rise to vessel or neck contours that curve inward or outward, while out- or in-slanting walls represent sections of cones. Cylinders are always unrestricted forms. Spherical forms are often called globular, especially jar bodies. The ovaloid is the closest approximation to forms sometimes described as pyriform or pear shaped. The low ellipsoid form—the ellipsoid with its long axis in the horizontal plane—is usually thought of as having greater width than a sphere, but a cross-sectional cut through such a vessel at its maximum diameter would yield a circle, not an ellipse. With low, unrestricted bowl or dish forms, it is often difficult to determine which of the convex forms is represented: sphere, oval, or ellipse. In such cases it may be clearer simply to label the form semispherical or subspherical than to specify a particular geometric solid.

The analogies between vessel shapes and geometric solids or surfaces provide a basis for describing vessel forms. One such scheme (Castillo Tejero and Litvak 1968) assigns numerical values to the basic silhouette and to reference points on the silhouettes (fig. 7.7), points that roughly correspond to Shepard's characteristic points. For example, a round-sided bowl with a flat base would be coded 1 : 1 – 3 by this scheme.

Most vessel forms can be described as sections or combinations of the geometric forms discussed above (plus a rectangular solid and minus the ovaloid), and this provides a basis for calculating vessel volumes or capacities. For example, the pithoi at Myrtos, Crete, are large storage jars that can be thought of as consisting of two truncated cones. Inserting the vessel dimensions into the formula for the volume of a truncated cone lets us compute the average storage capacity of these vessels at that settlement, eighty-nine liters (Warren 1972, 144).

A more complex scheme describes vessel shapes by a numerical code (Ericson and Stickel 1973). This code incorporates both the geometric form(s) involved and the appropriate measurements (in millimeters) of the vessel used in the volumetric formulas (radius, diameter, height, etc.), together with the mean wall thickness. For example, a round-sided bowl with a flat base would be considered a truncated hemisphere (H) with a spherical segment (SS) removed from the base. Assuming this vessel has a radius of 20 cm (200 mm) and a thickness of 7 mm, and the removed segment has a truncated radius of 18 cm (180 mm) and a height of 3 cm (30 mm), its shape would be expressed by the descriptive code as H 200 (SS 180/30). A complex vessel shape—for example, the same hemispherical bowl with a high collar—would be described as a hemisphere (H) missing a segment (SS) for its flat base, combined with a cylinder (C). The cylinder has a radius of 12 cm (120 mm) and a height of 10 cm (100 mm); the hemisphere has a 12 cm (120 mm) radius; and the segment has a truncated radius of 6.5 cm (65 mm) and a height of 3.5 cm (35 mm); average wall thickness is 8 mm. The code description of this vessel is C 120/100—H 120 (SS 65/35). These dimensions can then be substituted in the appropriate formulas (table 7.1), in order to calculate the volume or capacity of the vessel.

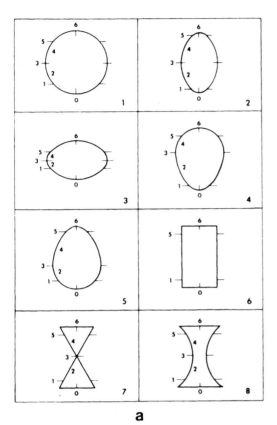

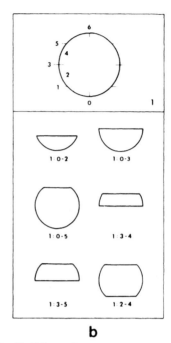

a   **b**

Figure 7.7   Reference points and line seg-   segments of a circle. After Castillo Tejero and
ments for describing vessel shapes: *a*, different   Litvak 1968, 12, 15.
basic shapes; *b*, vessel shapes described by

Table 7.1   Formulas for Calculating Volumes of Geometric Shapes

Sphere	$V_s = \frac{4}{3}\pi r^3$
Hemisphere	$V_H = \frac{2}{3}\pi r^3$
Spherical segment	$V_{ss} = \pi r^2(r - h/3)$
Ellipse	$V_e = \frac{4}{3}\pi abc$
Cylinder	$V_c = \pi r^2 h$
Cone	$V_k = (\pi r^2 h)/3$
Frustum	$\pi h(r_1^2 + r_1 r_2 + r_2^2)/3$

Note: r = radius a = vertical axis
    r_1 = radius of base b = larger horizontal axis
    r_2 = radius of truncation c = smaller horizontal axis
    h = height π = 3.141

A more accurate, though tedious, method for estimating the volume of a
vessel is the "summed cylinders" method (fig. 7.8), whereby the vessel is envisioned as divided horizontally into a series of equal slices. The interior diameter of the vessel is measured from mouth to base for each of these slices,
the measurements representing, in effect, the diameters of a series of thin cyl-

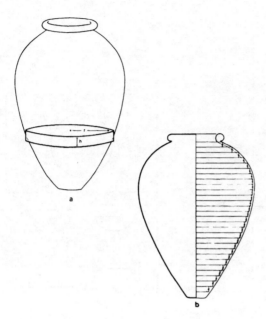

Figure 7.8   The "summed cylinders" method of estimating the volume of a vessel. The vessel is divided into a series of equal horizontal slides or thin cylinders, the volume of each cylinder is calculated by the formula given, and then these are summed to give an estimate of the total volume of the vessel.

$$V_v = \left(\sum_{i=1}^{n} r_i^2 \right) \pi h$$

inders. Stacked one on top of another, these cylinders encompass the entire vessel (cf. Nelson 1985, 312–13). By calculating the volume of each cylinder ($V = \pi r^2 h$) and summing the resultant figures, the volume of the vessel is determined in either cubic centimeters or cubic inches. Cubic centimeters translate directly into liters; in the case of cubic inches, $57.75 \text{ in}^3 = 1$ quart, and $231 \text{ in}^3 = 1$ gallon. Obviously, the narrower the intervals of measurement, the more accurate the total volume estimate.

7.2.3   Reconstructing Form from Sherds

Archaeologists face an additional problem in studying the function of pottery containers recovered from their excavations: most are broken and incomplete rather than whole pots. If whole vessels were smashed in place either at the time of deposition or shortly thereafter, the pieces can usually be glued back together and for study purposes the vessel is as good as new (or better, because the fractured edges allow examination of paste variables). Too often, however, the pottery remains are incomplete fragments, and it may or may not be possible to determine the form of the original pot.

Rim sherds provide the most information for assessing the size and shape of a vessel. By fitting the curve of a rim sherd to a standard diameter-measurement template, typically marked off in centimeter units, one can calculate the orifice diameter (fig. 7.9). Care must be taken to ensure that the lip of the sherd forms a plane matching that of the orifice of the original vessel and that these both correspond to the plane of the rim-diameter chart (see Joukowsky 1980, 423).

The easiest way to do this is to hold the sherd so the lip is at eye level. A horizontal plane can be envisioned by tilting the sherd until three points along the uppermost edge—one at each end of the sherd and one in the middle—are

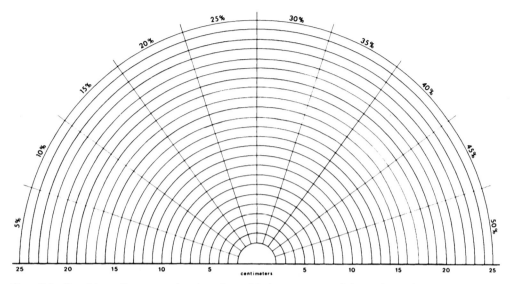

Figure 7.9   Template used to measure the orifice radius of a sherd and estimate (in 5%

intervals) the percentage of the total vessel
orifice circumference present.

aligned horizontally. At the same time, the angle of the wall or neck against
the vertical can be determined and, if the template has been appropriately
marked, the percentage of the total rim circumference can be estimated.
These procedures establish the mouth diameter and wall orientation of the
vessel; depending on the size of the sherd, they may also establish vessel
height and maximum diameter. The base form or diameter cannot be determined unless the vessel fragment includes part of the base.

A common problem in this procedure arises from asymmetry: the rim may
be uneven either vertically or horizontally, making it difficult to establish the
precise orientation and diameter of the sherd. In addition, there may be considerable difference in diameter estimates from individual to individual (see
DeBoer 1980), and an alternative procedure using a curve-measuring device
similar to a lens gauge has been proposed (Plog 1985).

Base sherds are often less informative than rim sherds (cf. Franken 1971);
they provide evidence of the type of base used, and perhaps its diameter, as
well as the orientation of the wall to the base. As with rim sherds, further
information on vessel height or maximum diameter depends on the size of the
sherd. Base sherds may be more accurate than rims in predicting the total
number of vessels in an assemblage, however (Franken 1971, 250; see also
sec. 9.2.2), or in classifying general shape categories (Froese 1985, 239).

Body sherds are, on the whole, the most difficult to work with. This is unfortunate, because most archaeological ceramic collections consist primarily
of body sherds; for most vessels, far more sherds result from breakage of the
body, which has a greater surface area, than from the proportionately smaller
rim and base regions. Very often it is extremely hard to determine whether the
sherd came from the top or bottom of the body, much less suggest the vessel's
size and shape. This problem may be lessened if flanges, ridges, decoration
orientations, handles, or other appendages occur on the sherds. Sometimes

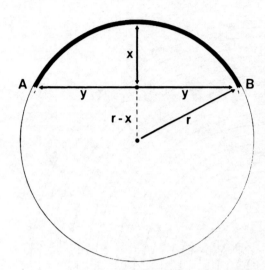

Figure 7.10   Formula for calculating radius and circumference from a chord; r = radius (unknown); y = half length of chord (or $AB/2$); x = height from chord to interior surface. Where only body sherds are available for calculating vessel diameters or circumference, the measurements available and desired are those of a right triangle whose sides are y, r, and $r-x$. By the Pythagorean theorem, the square of the hypotenuse of a right triangle (r) is equal to the sum of the squares of its other sides (y and $r-x$). This equation can be solved for r using $r = (y + x)/2x$, with the calculated value then substituted in the formula for calculating the circumference of a circle ($C = 2\pi r$).

there are other indications of the sherd's location and orientation: marks of surface treatment (scraping, burnishing), drips of paint, smooth breaks from coil fractures, or finger ridges (rilling) from throwing.

If the body sherd can be oriented to vertical and horizontal planes by these procedures, some idea of its position on the vessel can be gleaned. With vessels that are approximately spherical, the radius and circumference can be estimated from a sherd (see Greer 1977; Landon 1959) by measuring the chord (the straight line between the ends of the interior curvature of the sherd) in the horizontal plane (fig. 7.10). First the radius is calculated using the formula: $r = y^2 + x^2/2x$. Here, y is half the length of the chord, x is the depth or height from the chord line to the concave interior surface (a segment of the radius), and r is the unknown radius of the circle. The value of r is then substituted in the formula for the circumference of a circle: $C = 2\pi r$.

The figure that results from these computations is the circumference of the vessel in a horizontal plane that cuts its body in the region represented by the broken fragment. This is not necessarily the maximum diameter of the vessel unless it can be determined that the sherd came from the widest portion of the vessel and the proper orientation of the sherd can be ascertained. Estimates of vertical dimensions (e.g., height of the vessel) cannot be made using the formula for the circumference of a circle unless it can be determined that the vessel was spherical.

7.2.4   Use-Related Properties: Capacity, Stability, Accessibility, and Transportability

No one-to-one correlation exists between variables of use and form; neither variable set perfectly predicts the other, and clearly their relationship is one of multivariate causality. In addition, many vessels serve multiple functions, so a ceramic product may have been a compromise to meet a variety of needs (see sec. 9.3.1 and chap. 12). In trying to understand the relation between use and form there is danger of overdeterminacy, and care must be taken not to overrationalize the decisions potters made in designing their products. Despite these limitations, it is possible to suggest advantages and disadvantages, or inducements and constraints, that may have been factors in design decisions (see Ericson, Read, and Burke 1972; Braun 1980; Smith 1983; Hally 1986).

Four major use-related properties of ceramic containers are directly related to form or shape: capacity, stability, accessibility of contents, and transportability or ease of movement. Several other, more specific properties bear on use as well.

Capacity depends upon the shape and size of the vessel. It can thus be calculated directly from several common vessel measurements and is expressed in some volumetric unit such as cubic centimeters (cc), cups, liters, or gallons (one liter is 1,000 cc; one cup is roughly 240 cc). The relation between use and capacity of a vessel (see also sec. 9.3.1.1) can be conceived in terms of the kind of material the vessel contains (liquid or dry), the amount, the length of time it is to be contained, the number of anticipated users of the material during that time (Nelson 1981, 109–11), and microenvironmental factors such as availability of water or other necessities (see Arnold 1985, 145–47). Vessels may also be made in sizes that suggest standard units of volume or multiples of such units (e.g., Turner and Lofgren 1966; Rottländer 1967).

The stability of a vessel refers to its resistance to tipping or being upset, determined by shape, proportion, center of gravity, and breadth of the base. The center of gravity is the point of balance of the vessel and is a function of mass, shape, and weight. Vessels that are taller than they are broad, or that have a high shoulder (fig. 7.5g), will have a high center of gravity; such containers, like those with a narrow or curving base, are unstable. Unstable vessels include, for example, very tall, narrow cylinders and jars or vases with unusually high and heavy necks or collars (e.g., fig. 1.2). Although instability might appear to be undesirable, it is advantageous in certain situations such as tilting a vessel to pour the contents. Stable vessels generally have broad, flat bases and a low center of gravity; they are often described as low or "squat" (e.g., fig. 7.4i).

As Shepard (1976, 238) points out, a vessel is in stable equilibrium if its center of gravity must be raised to tip it. To enhance the stability of tall vessels, the shoulder thus is often placed low—the shape may be a low ellipsoid or ovaloid—lowering the center of gravity. Vessel supports may increase stability if they broaden the area where the vessel rests on the surface, but they may also raise the center of gravity. There is no single measure of stability. The best indicators might be the position of the center of gravity and the ratio of base to height.

The accessibility of the contents of a vessel—better stated, perhaps, as access to its interior—is determined by the orifice. If a vessel has a sharply restricted orifice, such as a narrow neck, it is hard to get at the contents because of the angle of access. Similarly, reaching into an especially large and deep vessel requires a certain effort. By contrast, a shallow, unrestricted bowl or dish permits immediate access. A neck or collar does not normally hinder access; rather, it is the restriction of the orifice—either at the rim or at the throat—that does so. An extremely *high* neck might have the same result, but it will also be an advantage in accurately pouring liquid. No measure of ease of access exists at present; a possibility might be some ratio of orifice diameter to maximum diameter with height, or a ratio of height to diameter.

Transportability or ease of moving a vessel is a consequence of form, primarily its size, weight, and quality that may be called "graspability," "hold," or "purchase," related to moving the vessel in difficult circumstances. Such circumstances might include handling a vessel that is hot or holds hot contents, that is heavy and difficult to support or carry, or that is wet and may slip (see also sec. 7.3). The shape characteristics affecting hold are not so much the primary form characteristics as the secondary ones, such as handles or flanges that provide grip or leverage, prevent slipping, and protect against high temperatures. A large base or supports might provide the same advantage in handling a hot vessel. Ease of movement appears to be a purely qualitative and subjective property with no suitable indicator or measure except the presence of relevant secondary forms or other attributes.

Besides these use-related properties of shape, several attributes are specific to particular uses. Durability of ceramic vessels may be equated with the technological property of "resistance to mechanical stress" (see sec. 7.3.2 and 12.3) and also related to wall thickness and shape. As Rye (1981, 27) has pointed out, "cookpots" usually do not have sharp angles, which would cause uneven heating and thermal stress over the fire. Instead, they typically have smooth contours and are simple or "inflected" rather than composite or complex (cf. Woods 1986). Thus, for one particular kind of vessel use, fragility can be related to shape.

Another form- and use-related property is weight: this depends on size and wall thickness and is particularly important to the transfer function, especially when the contents are liquid.

Finally, closure or containment security (Braun 1980) is related to the storage function, indicating how tightly a vessel can be closed or covered to prevent spillage or other loss of the contents.

7.3   Composition and Properties: Relating Technology to Use

Clearly, it is not solely form that determines a vessel's suitability for particular uses. Designing a durable and appropriate vessel for a given function begins much earlier, with the selection and manipulation of the raw materials (see chaps. 2–4). The use of different clays and tempers for different form or function classes of pottery is widely known ethnographically (Stone 1950, 270; DeBoer and Lathrap 1979, 116; Arnold 1978, 367; cf. Rye and Evans 1976, 126–27; see also chap. 5). Thus the chemistry, mineralogy, granulometry, and relative amounts of clays and particular inclusions that may be present are the basis of variability in the use-related properties of any ceramic. These may be modified throughout the manufacturing process by the potter's skill or lack of skill in preparing the clay, forming the vessel, and drying and firing it. Together the resources and manufacturing procedures can be directed toward the pragmatic goal of creating a useful pot.

Four properties or clusters of properties can be described as use-related characteristics that derive from composition, forming, and firing of a vessel.

These properties are thickness, resistance to mechanical stress, thermal behavior, and permeability/porosity/density (see also chap. 12). Surface treatment, though not directly related to composition, represents a fifth realm of
decision making that affects vessel use.

All these properties are influenced by decisions the potter makes at some
point in the manufacturing process, and so to some degree they are all manip-
ulable. The fundamental decision is what clay to use, a de facto choice often
based on proximity (see secs. 5.2 and 6.2.1). For those properties most directly dependent on the raw materials, especially the clay—particularly mechanical stress resistance—freedom is severely limited once this choice is
made. Because there may be a scarcity of clays suited to special purposes,
other decisions—choices about temper, form, thickness, and so forth—can
be seen as accommodation strategies that in part modify the raw clay material
toward the desired use of the pot. Potters in Pakistan, for example, select clay
near their workshops; if it is not suitable for particular uses, they prefer to
modify its characteristics rather than to obtain better clay from farther away
(Rye and Evans 1976, 126–27).

7.3.1 Thickness

The thickness of the vessel walls is related to the size of the container and its
intended use, but it also depends on the properties—especially the green (or
unfired) strength—of the clay being used (see sec. 3.3.3). During the shaping
of the wet clay, the walls serve as a structural support: like the walls of a
house, they rest upon a foundation (the base) and support a heavy superstructure—shoulder, neck, collar, rim, flanges, handles, spouts, and so forth. This
superstructure is also composed of wet, heavy clay, and if the walls and foundation are not strong enough to support it, the vessel may slump or warp during drying. Furthermore, the intended appearance and function of the vessel
may dictate that some of these upper parts be thickened to enhance their
strength in use, for example, at the rim (discussed above) or where handles
are attached; and these thicker areas can cause further stress during drying.
Thus the walls have to be strong enough to see the vessel safely through this
stage of the manufacturing process. In general, larger vessels require thicker
walls for structural support, and this often calls for more temper (sec. 14.1) to
reinforce the clay.

There must be continual compromise in design, then, between the advantages and disadvantages of thick walls in drying and during use. For storage,
thick walls or a thick base may be desirable to increase stability and keep
moisture in or out of the vessel. In processing, thick walls are likely to be
stronger and more resistant to sharp blows during pounding, stirring, or mixing. Thick walls are likely to be a disadvantage for cooking, however (cf.
Henrickson and McDonald 1983, 631): thin walls conduct heat better (see
sec. 12.4), cooking food faster and saving fuel. In addition, thin walls increase thermal shock resistance (see sec. 7.3.3). In transfer functions, thick
walls slow the conduction of heat from the contents, keeping the outside
cooler, and also increase strength; however, thick-walled vessels are heavy.

These considerations may influence various steps of manufacture, such as how long the vessel is beaten with paddle and anvil to thin and consolidate the walls.

The need for thick walls can often be avoided by manipulating the paste composition. Pastes can be given high green and fired strength either through their natural particle-size distribution or by adding temper in appropriate kinds, sizes, shapes, and amounts. These pastes then can be shaped into thin-walled, lightweight, but very durable containers. One example of such a clay composition is that used by the potters of Chinautla, Guatemala, for their *ti-najas*, or water-carrying jars. The clay contains diatoms, and the temper is a pumiceous volcanic ash (Rice 1976a, 1978a); both of these inclusions, by their lightness and angularity, permit the manufacture of jars that were held in great esteem in the highlands for their thin walls, light weight, and durability.

7.3.2   Resistance to Mechanical Stress

A vessel's resistance to mechanical stress depends largely on its hardness and strength. These properties are closely related and can be described in many ways, but primarily they refer to the ability to tolerate various stresses (sec. 12.3.2): resistance to breakage (lack of brittleness), penetration (stiffness), shattering or failure (integrity), and deformation (e.g., by compression).

Like thickness, hardness and strength are important to vessel viability in both the unfired (green) and fired states. Unlike thickness, however, both these properties have a more direct relation to composition, and also to firing as the final modifier of the clay's components. Hardness and strength are related to the kind, size, shape, and proportions of the clay and inclusions in a ceramic (see chaps. 3, 4, and 12). Firing can be manipulated to modify this relationship, because in general vessels that are fired to higher temperatures, or that have a period of reducing atmosphere during firing, will be harder. Thus better-fired vessels are more resistant to mechanical stress, but strength and hardness are complex properties that also relate to other characteristics (sec. 12.3), and all can be tied to function.

Little can be said about how hardness and strength relate to use, because it is difficult to conceive of circumstances where a soft, weak vessel would be an advantage. In other words, hardness and strength are virtually always desirable. Even for storage, where vessels undergo little movement, a hard, durable vessel is best. It is probably in processing and transfer, however, that strength and hardness are most important. In processing the contents of a vessel may be stirred, pounded, or ground, mechanically stressing the vessel and causing cracking, pitting, abrasion, and eventual breakage. Cooking can produce thermal stresses as well as mechanical ones (stirring the contents, placing the vessel in the fire). Transfer activities probably pose the greatest threat, since vessels frequently break as they are carried, and in this type of use mechanical strength is most valuable.

7.3.3   Thermal Behavior

Reactions to thermal changes are important for the cooking and serving functions of ceramic containers or for any activity where heat is applied to a vessel

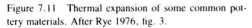

Figure 7.11   Thermal expansion of some common pottery materials. After Rye 1976, fig. 3.

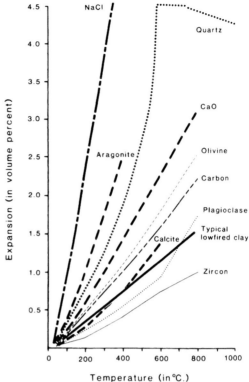

or its contents. One of the thermal reactions of a ceramic is thermal stress, strain caused by uneven or unequal reactions to heat over the vessel body (sec. 12.4). Thermal stresses arise as a vessel and its contents are heated, but they may actually be more severe in cooling because tensile stresses develop on the exterior, especially when the vessel is resting on a colder surface (Amberg and Hartsook 1946, 451).

One way to manipulate thermal properties and reduce stresses is to decrease wall thickness: thinner walls lessen the thermal gradient and hence the stress (see Van Vlack 1964, 117–65; Lawrence and West 1982, 226). Stresses can also be reduced by modifying the vessel shape to eliminate angles.

A major determinant (or modifier) of resistance to thermal stress is the composition of the ceramic, particularly the inclusions present or added, because certain materials have lower coefficients of thermal expansion than others (see sec. 4.2.3). It has been suggested that because of the importance of cooking pots in household assemblages, adaptation to thermal stress is the most important determinant of vessel composition, while other considerations are subsidiary (Rye 1976, 119). The optimal solution in the manufacture of vessels intended for use with heat would be to have inclusions (temper) with coefficients similar to or less than that of the clay (fig. 7.11). Among such inclusions are grog (crushed sherds), calcite, crushed burned shell, zircon, rutile, feldspar, augite, and hornblende (Rye 1976, 116–17). Talc, which is used commercially in making saggars (Cardew 1969, 75, 159), is useful for increasing thermal shock resistance in amounts up to about 10% (Burnham and Tuttle 1945; Lawrence and West 1982, 224). In Uganda, some potters traditionally add asbestos-containing talc as temper in their cooking pots and report that it "lengthens the life of the article, seemingly reducing the incidence of cracking on repeated domestic use" (Wilson 1973, 301). Yet another way to improve resistance to thermal stress is to increase porosity, since pores provide an elasticity in the body that allows for sudden expansion of the materials. This alternative has its drawbacks, however, because repeated heating and cooling of porous materials causes them to gradually lose strength and suffer thermal fatigue (see sec. 12.4.2.3; also Lawrence and West 1982, 216–26). In lieu of these other alternatives, in northwestern Pakistan the bases of cooking pots are periodically coated with a mixture of clay and sand to insulate the pot from thermal shock (Rye and Evans 1976, 25).

Some of these propositions concerning the relation between composition and thermal stress have been tested against the ethnographic record in the Southwestern United States (Plog 1980, 86–87). The results show that although potters may recognize how different kinds and sizes of temper affect the functional suitability of their products, some of their behaviors run counter to prediction, at least with regard to thermal properties. Potters may use coarse temper to make vessels more porous, particularly for storing water, and clays intended for cooking vessels are often given special temper, but the Mohave use grog temper (with low thermal expansion) for all but their cooking wares. Both the Hopi and the Mohave use sandstone temper for cooking pots, while the Yuma use granite, but relative particle sizes are not specified. In Yucatán, crystalline calcite temper is most frequently used for cooking vessels, while attapulgite clay is generally used for water jars, but this differentiation is not strictly followed (Thompson 1958, 113); in Tabasco, coarser sand is used for cooking pots.

Perhaps the most complex series of adjustments is made by Shipibo-Conibo potters in Peru: different clay and temper combinations are used not only for different vessel functions (cooking versus noncooking) but also for different parts of cooking vessels (DeBoer and Lathrap 1979, 116–17). For example, ideally the bases of ollas are made of black clay tempered with two parts *caraipé* (plant silica ash) and one part grog, while the neck is made of red clay tempered with reversed proportions of *caraipé* and grog. In practice the composition is variable, although cooking vessels depart less from standard recipes than do eating and serving wares (DeBoer 1984, 540), perhaps because of thermal considerations.

7.3.4 Permeability/Porosity/Density

Three related properties, determined by composition and manufacturing, affect vessel use: permeability, porosity, and density. These properties are by no means equivalent (see sec. 12.2), but they are sufficiently related in their constraints or actions that they can be discussed together.

Permeability refers to the penetration of moisture into the vessel wall by means of pores opening into either its exterior or its interior surface. The permeation may be outward seepage of a liquid contained in the vessel or the penetration of exterior moisture from the atmosphere or the resting surface. Permeability is reduced by modifying the interior or exterior surface of the vessel, or both, to increase its density or make it act as a barrier to penetration. A glaze (sec. 4.2.4) is the best guarantee of impermeability, but in areas of the world where glazes were not and are not used by traditional potters (e.g., much of the Western Hemisphere), applying a slip or even burnishing the surface can reduce permeability to some degree (Henrickson and McDonald 1983, 633; Birmingham 1975). Vitrification of the body also reduces both permeability and overall porosity.

Porosity refers to the presence of pores or spaces within the wall (see sec. 12.2), which allows liquid to move through the wall once it has penetrated either surface. Density, the weight of an object per unit volume, may be considered in some senses the inverse of porosity: a dense paste may be at least partly describable as low in porosity. Porosity and density are largely manipulated by the steps of initial clay preparation, the amount, size, and shape of inclusions present in the paste, and the care exercised in wedging.

The relation between porosity/permeability and use is complex. Excessive porosity and permeability are not desirable in vessels used for long-term storage, particularly of liquids. Nonetheless, high porosity characterizes non-vitrified vessels, especially earthenwares: Jōmon pots were found to lose about 10% of their contents overnight (Kidder 1968, 14), and some Corinthian amphorae were permeable in nine to thirty-one minutes (Vandiver and Koehler 1986, 204). For relatively short water storage, porosity is often an advantage: evaporation on the exterior cools the water, making it taste fresher. After a time, however, minerals in the water seal the pores so the pot loses its effectiveness as a cooler, and it may then be switched to some other use such as cooking (Fontana et al. 1962, 80). Raised bases or supports on unglazed pottery may keep a leaky, porous serving or processing vessel from direct contact with a surface.

In cooking vessels, some porosity may reduce thermal stress, as described above. It has been suggested that for vessels used in cooking at temperatures of 300–500°C, the optimum pore size is 7–9 mm, based on the size and density of packing of the mineral grains (Rye 1976, 114). Increasing porosity may be a more appropriate strategy for dealing with thermal shock in vessels used for toasting or parching than for vessels used to hold and cook liquids for any length of time, however, because of seepage. If liquids are boiled in porous vessels, they will seep through and rapidly evaporate. This volatilization could cause the vessel to crack, but the danger can be reduced through some of the technical strategies of manufacturing discussed above. With respect to vessel shape, the absence of corners or angles prevents moisture from collecting, and thin walls let water convert to steam rapidly without buildup in the body.

The ethnographic record provides many instances in which porous vessels are given postfiring treatments—typically interior coatings of lime water, resin, vegetal material, or some other substance—before use in storing, processing (cooking), or transferring liquids (see sec. 5.4.1.3; also Reina and Hill 1978, 245; Fontana et al. 1962, 80). These treatments reduce permeability, and in cooking vessels they do not decrease the usefulness of porosity in reducing thermal stress. The charred or incompletely oxidized organic material remaining in the walls of low-fired vessels may serve similar purposes, acting to reduce porosity, increase the strength of very coarse or sandy pastes, and serve as a charcoal filter.

7.3.5 Surface Treatment

Although surface treatment is not directly related to composition and technology, the surface may be modified in producing a vessel (secs. 5.3.2 and 5.3.4.1), helping reduce permeability in vessels intended for use in storage and processing. Glazes (sec. 4.2.4) are the most extreme example, but even slipped or burnished surfaces can somewhat retard the penetration of liquids by creating a dense surface of fine and compacted particles. Slips and glazes often cover the interiors of bowls and jars and extend over the lip and partway down the exterior shoulder or neck; this lessens the penetration of drips and splashes in the vessel walls and makes cleaning easier.

Surface treatment is also important to transfer: a rough surface provides a more secure grip. The classic illustration is a water jar: heavy and wet, it is slippery and difficult to grasp. With roughened surfaces, however, it can more easily be lifted and carried. A number of roughening procedures can be used: striated or combed surfaces are common on large jars from prehistoric Mesoamerica; in the eastern United States a variety of impressed or stamped surface treatments are known—cord, net, corncob, checked, complicated, and so forth (see fig. 5.14); in the Southwestern United States "corrugated" surfaces may serve the same function.

Finally, surface treatment is an important modifier of the thermal properties of vessels: an uneven exterior has more surface area to absorb heat from a fire (Herron 1986) or to evaporate a liquid, as in salt making (Charlton 1969, 75). Thus the surface roughening treatments discussed above—striating, check-stamping, corrugation—also enhance the properties of cooking vessels. Such vessels might have been used for both cooking and transfer; determining what functions they might have served involves studying other properties such as form, thickness, composition, or some of the direct indicators of vessel use discussed below.

7.4 Direct Evidence of Use

Vessel shape and manufacturing technology give archaeologists an indirect basis for hypotheses about vessel use, or at least suggestions about the functions for which a vessel was particularly well suited. More direct indications of use are also sometimes available.

Context of recovery may or may not provide evidence on the functions of ceramic vessels. A bowl holding jade beads found under a Maya stela, a jar filled with seeds in a Southwestern pueblo, smashed effigies beneath the east side of a Florida burial mound—these give clear indications of use at the time the vessel was deposited, or removed from "systemic" to "archaeological" context (Schiffer 1976). Vessels typically have multiple uses during their life spans, however (see sec. 9.3.1.1), so that their archaeological context is merely their final resting place rather than an accurate indicator of how their use life was spent. For example, one may ask if a vessel was manufactured specifically for a burial or a cache, and whether such usage was its sole function from the start of its existence. Or were some of these vessels used in other domestic activities before being placed in this special deposit (see Bray 1982)?

Several direct lines of evidence on the functions of ancient vessels have been developed. Most investigate the processing and storage activities in which pottery containers may have been used. Significantly, these procedures could also be applied to pottery from ethnographic contexts as an aid to building models for archaeological interpretation.

7.4.1   Identification of Contents

One type of evidence on the functions of ancient vessels is the contents they originally held. This evidence is useful not only for cooking vessels, where charring sometimes preserves the contents, but also increasingly for storage vessels as well. The techniques of identification are particularly appropriate for unglazed vessels, which are usually permeable and porous and are therefore likely to retain residues. The materials sought in these analyses include phosphate, pollen, salts, and organic substances such as resins, gums, carbohydrates (sugars and starches), and, more commonly, animal fats and vegetable oils. For fats and oils the typical methods of analysis include infrared absorption, mass spectrography, gas chromatography, and, less frequently, proton magnetic resonance spectrometry (Beck, Fellows, and MacKennan 1974), all of which identify specific fatty acids, lipids, cholesterol, triglycerides, and other components of organic materials.

The results of these analyses must be interpreted with some caution. Because ceramic vessels are usually recovered from some sort of soil matrix, the substance of interest must be carefully measured both in the vessel and in the burial environment. This will eliminate the possibility that concentrations of the substance come from the postuse depositional environment rather than the use itself. Examination of concentration gradients—either from interior to exterior in the vessel wall or from the mouth to the base of the vessel—may aid in resolving this question and others. In addition, some organic materials may degrade or otherwise alter through time, making their analysis somewhat questionable (see Bowyer 1972, 331; Rottländer and Schlichtherle 1983, 36). It is also possible that substances detected by this procedure may have been added to reduce the permeability of the vessels (see secs. 5.4.1.3 and 7.3.4), rather than constituting stored or processed contents.

The phosphate (P_2O_5) content of a pot can be analyzed to determine whether the vessel held organic material. Phosphorus is an essential element for metabolism of all living things; it occurs naturally in all soils (including clays) and is concentrated in areas of dense or prolonged human or animal occupation (e.g., houses or animal pens). In one study, experiments revealed that even when fired in the temperature range of 600–800°C, kaolin clays still have phosphate permanently bound to them; binding diminishes above 800°C

(Duma 1972). A number of unglazed pots found in burials dating from the Neolithic period through the sixteenth century were analyzed, with phosphate measured in three locations: in the earthen contents of the vessels, in the vessel walls, and in the surrounding earth. Enrichment of the phosphate content in all these areas, particularly on a gradient of increase from the mouth to the base of the vessels (though not through the vessel walls), was taken as evidence that the pots had originally contained organic material (Duma 1972). The possibility that they may have absorbed additional phosphate from an enriched surface (e.g., a house floor) was not addressed, however.

Specific organic contents of vessels have been identified through a variety of techniques. Visual examination and infrared absorption suggested that the charred material on the interior and exterior of an Indian pot from Massachusetts probably was a sugar (Clancy 1961), perhaps from boiling maple sap. Similar charred encrustations on vessels from the Juntunen site, in the upper Great Lakes area of the United States, were hypothesized (without chemical analysis) to result from cooking fish (McPherron 1967, 47).

Gas chromatography is particularly well suited to identifying organic materials such as oils and resins (see Mills and White 1977) and requires only a small sample of material (ca. 3–5 mg). The contents of amphorae, used widely in the ancient Mediterranean wine and olive oil trade (see Will 1977; Vandiver and Koehler 1986) were analyzed by chromatography to detect traces of olive oil in their pores (Condamin et al. 1976). Three groups of specimens were used (dates and proveniences were not reported), and ancient olive oil was positively identified in one. Fatty acids were concentrated in a gradient through the sherd walls, declining from the interior surface to the exterior. Chromatographic analysis used on the contents of various jars and pots from early Bronze Age Crete suggested that one tub had been used in processing animal material, perhaps wool (Bowyer 1972). The contents of Neolithic and Roman period vessels have been analyzed and showed evidence of milk, butter, olive oil, fish, pig, and mustard seed (Rottländer and Schlichtherle 1983, 37). Marine animal fat, possibly seal, has been identified as a brown, flaky residue in some South African cooking pots (Patrick, de Koning, and Smith 1985). Finally, a highly oxidized pine resin was identified in a Byzantine storage jar from Israel, possibly intended for use in caulking, waterproofing, or preparing an unguent (Shackley 1982).

7.4.2 Use Wear

Another source of inferences about vessel use comes from use-wear studies. Damage to the vessel surfaces is most likely to occur during processing, such as in stirring, scraping, mixing, grinding, or pounding the contents. Performed repeatedly, these actions can scar the interior surfaces (see Chernela 1969; Griffiths 1978; Bray 1982; Hally 1983b). Areas most likely to show wear are the interior base, the interior sides (especially below the rim), and the exterior base.

Use wear on vessel interiors causes attrition of the slip or surface, or both, leaving striations, pitting, or patchy abraded areas. These may be very faint

Figure 7.12   The interior of a fragment of a large jar from northern Georgia, showing a band of pitting thought to be caused by chemical action of solutions used in food preparation. Photograph reproduced with permission from David J. Hally, "Use Alteration of Pottery Vessel Surfaces: An Important Source of Evidence for the Identification of Vessel Function," *North American Archaeologist* 4, No. 1 (1983): 3–26, fig. 6c; © Baywood Publishing Company.

or distinct and substantial, removing the slip and exposing the underlying paste (fig. 7.12). Interior surfaces may also be finely scarred or abraded by scouring clean with sand. On the exterior, wear on the base may indicate that the vessel was scraped against its resting surface, for example, in turning a vessel during mixing.

These indications of wear may be difficult to see on excavated ceramics if the surfaces are badly eroded. Further, because the patterns are extremely localized, it is difficult to carry out use-wear analysis on sherds; sizable collections of complete pots yield much more reliable inferences.

7.4.3   Fireclouding and Sooting

The presence and location of soot deposits and fireclouds on the exterior sides and base of a vessel are clear indications of use in cooking or other activities involving fire. To take advantage of these observations, care must be taken not to remove soot residue when the sherds are cleaned in the field or laboratory.

Soot is a by-product of fuel combustion, composed of carbon and resins. Not only is soot on a vessel evidence that the vessel was used with fire, but the location of the soot tells how it was used (Hally 1983b, 7–10). If the soot occurs primarily on the sides of a vessel, from the base up to or near the maximum diameter, the vessel was probably set in the fire. Soot is deposited as a combustion product at the edges of the flames, and vessels used this way usually also have an oxidized area in the center of the base, which was set into the fire (fig. 7.13*a*). Vessels that lack such an oxidized zone and instead have soot deposits on the base (and also the sides) were probably suspended over the fire rather than set into it (fig. 7.13*b*). These vessels may have been used for simmering or frying; vessels placed in the fire were probably used for boiling. The blackening of the pots by smoke and soot also would have increased their heat retention somewhat.

Resins, one of the components of soot, are more abundant in softwoods such as pine than in hardwoods. Systematic study of soot deposits is a recent

Figure 7.13   Examples of sooting on vessel exteriors: *a,* soot and fire blackening occur around the sides of the vessel while the base is lighter and more oxidized, indicating it was placed in a fire; *b,* soot deposits on both the base and sides of a pot, indicating it was placed above the fire (these "shoe form" or "boot shaped" pots from southern Peru may have been suspended by the handles over a cooking fire and are typically found in burials).

endeavor, and it remains to be seen how the deposits may vary in regions where there are different kinds of firewood.

7.5   Summary: Form, Technology, and Use

The relation between vessel use, morphology, and technology has been investigated and described by several comparisons of ethnographic, archaeological, and technological data (Howard 1981, table 1.1; Smith 1983, 1985; Henrickson and McDonald 1983). Using ethnographic samples from the American Southwest and from West Africa, Smith (1983, table 42) found that ten out of eighteen form/function relationships could find support in the literature. These include the findings that vessels used in both cooking and processing have larger orifices than those used for storage, but duration of storage has no effect on orifice diameter; vessels used for long-term storage have greater volumes than those used for short-term storage; vessels used for transporting liquids have smaller orifices than those used for other purposes; vessels used for transport over small distances have greater volumes than those carried over large distances; vessels used for cooking and heating have greater volumes than those used for eating; and serving and eating vessels tend to have their greatest diameter at the rim (they are unrestricted forms).

Many of the predicted relationships between form, technology, and function have been found to be somewhat equivocal (Plog 1980, 86–87; Smith 1983, 221; Henrickson and McDonald 1983, 632–34; Miller 1985, 60–62). These findings cast some doubt on Rye's (1976, 119) hypothesis that in preparing clay for pottery making the primary consideration is "to give suitable physical properties for cooking pots and for other purposes vessels are either also suitable or are modified subsequent to firing." A pottery vessel is a product of a set of decisions about shape and use that are not necessarily given equal weight and do not always adhere to the principles of modern materials science. Ceramic attributes relate to several behavior complexes, including scale of manufacture, and no single variable of form, composition, or use can be reliably predicted from any other. Vessel forms within an assemblage may exhibit a great deal of redundancy and a lack of secondary attributes (spouts, etc.) that aid in efficient performance of their intended tasks or—for archaeologists—as clues to their function (Miller 1985, 62–67). In addition, multiple uses of pots and reuse after they have outlived their primary functions (sec. 9.3.1.1) render ethnographic data sets even more complex.

Despite these cautions, the relation of form, function, and technology may be summarized in a simplified, idealized way (table 7.2). Empirically observed deviations from the ideal will occur because these relationships refer to general shapes and uses (cooking, storing), while specific uses (cooking beans, storing wine) may place more specific constraints on variability (e.g., in secondary form characteristics). One approach to understanding the causes and patterns of such departures from the ideal is to begin with function, consider what shape and compositional characteristics favor certain uses. Another is through form: what activities may be accommodated by particular shapes and their constraints?

7.5.1 Vessel Functions

Vessels may vary depending on whether they are intended for long- or short-term storage, how frequently their contents are used, and the nature of their contents (liquid or dry). Vessels used for long-term storage or needing infrequent access are generally large and when full are too heavy for easy movement. A survey of ethnographic data suggests that liquid storage vessels may be more variable in shape than dry storage vessels; liquid storage vessels are relatively taller as an aid to pouring, while long-term dry storage vessels are relatively short and squat (Henrickson and McDonald 1983, 632–33; cf. Birmingham 1975, 371). Contrary to expectations, they do not necessarily have restricted orifices and necks to prevent loss of contents or for easier covering and closing of the mouth (Henrickson and McDonald 1983, 633).

Vessels intended for cooking would be expected to make efficient use of the heat from the cooking fire, but they also exhibit characteristics suited to particular modes of cooking, and this doubtless accounts for the wide range of shapes in cooking pots, past and present (fig. 7.14; also fig. 7.13). They are generally likely to have rounded rather than angled contours (cf. Woods 1986), to avoid thermal damage, and also because the rounded contours permit greater exposure of the vessel base, walls, and contents to the heat. They can also be expected to be relatively thin walled, to conduct heat better and reduce the thermal gradient between the surfaces (cf. Henrickson and McDonald 1983, 631, who note thick walls in their ethnographic sample). Further, they are likely to be coarse textured, porous, and tempered with materials that have low coefficients of thermal expansion (calcined shell, crushed potsherd) to accommodate thermal stress.

Table 7.2 Predicted Archaeological Correlates of Vessel Function

Functional Category	Shape	Material	Surface Treatment and Decoration	Depositional Context	Frequency	Clues
Storage vessels	Restricted forms, orifice modified for pouring or closure; appendages for suspension or movement (tipping)	Variable (possible concern for low porosity)	Variable for display or messages; slip or glaze to reduce permeability	Dwellings (sometimes set into ground); trash middens	Low (low replacement); may be reuse of broken or old vessels	Residues of stored goods in pores
Cooking pots	Rounded, conical, globular, unrestricted; generally lacking angles	Coarse and porous, thin walls, thermal shock resistant	Little to none; surface roughening for handling ease	Dwellings, trash middens; rarely in special deposits (e.g., burials)	High (frequent replacement)	Patterns of exterior sooting or blackening; burned contents
Food preparation (without heat)	Unrestricted forms, simple shapes	Emphasis on mechanical strength; relatively coarse, dense	Variable; generally low	Dwellings, trash middens	Moderate?	Internal wear; abrasion or pitting
Serving	Unrestricted for easy access; often with handles; flat bases or supports for stability	May be fine	Generally high, for display or symbolic roles	Dwellings, trash middens, special deposits (burials, caches)	High (frequent use and replacement)	Sizes correspond to individual servings or group size
Transport	Convenient for stacking; handles; lightweight; restricted orifice	Emphasis on mechanical strength; dense, hard	Variable, generally low; slip or glaze to reduce permeability	Trash middens, nondomestic (market) areas	Variable	Uniform size or multiple units of size; residues of contents

Source: After Howard 1981, table 1.1.

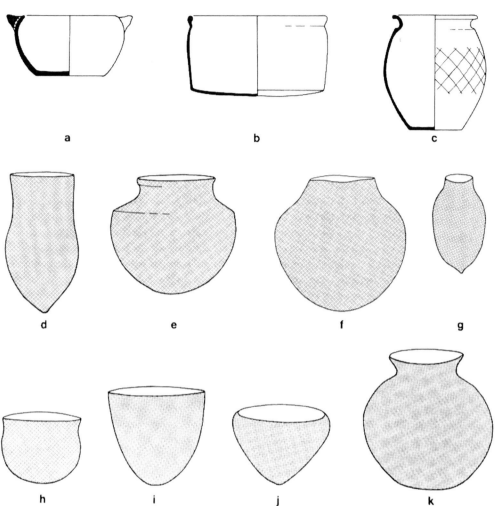

Figure 7.14   Variations in cooking pot shapes, ancient and contemporary: *a*, olla from modern Jocotán, Guatemala (height ca. 16.5 cm; after Reina and Hill 1978; fig. 45a); *b*, thirteenth-century cooking pot from Gloucester, England (diameter ca. 40 cm; after Vince 1977, fig. 2, no. 4); *c*, black-burnished ware from Roman Britain (after Orton 1980, fig. 2.2); *d–k*, modern cooking pots from three provinces in Papua New Guinea—*d*, Madang Province (height 37 cm; after May and Tuckson 1982, fig. 8–44); *e*, Madang Province (height 29 cm; after May and Tuckson 1982, fig. 1.5); *f*, Madang Province (height 19 cm; after May and Tuckson 1982, fig. 1.6); *g*, Madang Province (after May and Tuckson 1982, fig. 8.40); *h*, Mailu Island, Central Province (height 22 cm; after May and Tuckson 1982, fig. 3.5); *i*, Morobe Province after May and Tuckson 1982, fig. 1.8); *j*, Morobe Province (height 27 cm; after May and Tuckson 1982, fig. 6.23); *k*, Morobe Province (height 34 cm; May and Tuckson 1982, fig. 1.7).

Boiling seems to be or to have been the most common aboriginal cooking technique in a variety of culture areas (Lischka 1978, 229; Hally 1983b; Solheim 1965, 257; see also Linton 1944), so many characteristics of form of cooking vessels may be adapted to this pattern of use. The vessels are likely to have a relatively open orifice for adding and removing food, but a slight constriction or a low neck helps prevent boiling over and reduces evaporation. Although it might be expected that cooking vessels used for boiling would be relatively deep to conserve heat, one survey of the ethnographic data suggested an emphasis on short, squat shapes (Henrickson and McDonald 1983, 631). Vessels used for simmering or frying may be more open and have flatter bases, intended to be raised slightly above the fire rather than set in it; they are more dishlike than bowllike. Utensils for drying, toasting, or parching—such as griddles or *comales*—are usually nearly flat with little to no rim curvature, because spillage is not a concern.

Vessels for serving and eating are likely to vary greatly in size depending on the number of people partaking (Henrickson and McDonald 1983, 632, 634). They are usually open for easy access and perhaps visibility of the food; they may have a flat base or supports for stability. Secondary form variations are likely to be elaborate: flanges and handles can be for decorative display as well as for grasping a hot vessel as it is carried or passed around; spouts aid in serving liquids and preventing spills. Another aid in handling a vessel filled with hot liquid may be thick walls, which conduct less heat from the contents to the outside. The surfaces may be finished by burnishing or slipping to reduce permeability. Furthermore, because vessels for serving and eating are usually used in company, they may display fine surface finishing and elaborate decoration (see chap. 8).

Another important consideration in the transfer function is the weight of the vessel when it is full. This is especially pertinent for jars used to carry water, because water weighs approximately 8.3 pounds per gallon. The capacity of water transport jars may be relatively limited, varying between 2 and 4.5 gallons, with full weights of 18 to 35 pounds, before exceeding the maximum weight for convenient carrying (see, e.g., Reina and Hill 1978, 241–43). Corinthian amphorae would have weighed from 60 to 190 pounds and very likely had to be rolled to the ships or other transport (Vandiver and Koehler 1986, 202–3).

Storage and transfer raise additional issues that cannot be conveniently related to domestic or subsistence functions. Vessels may be used for long-distance movement of goods, perhaps in tribute or in trade, for example, the Mediterranean amphorae or the transatlantic shipment of so-called olive jars from Europe to the colonial New World. Such vessels serve for both storage and transfer, and both tight closure and easy handling are likely to be important. Thick walls may be a disadvantage because of weight, but they may add stability and strength. On the other hand, the empty vessels themselves may be moved or traded; a wide-ranging pottery trade is known ethnographically (sec. 6.3). Either way, there would be a premium on being able to move more vessels per trip. Shallow, unrestricted forms can often be easily stacked or nested when empty (Whittlesey 1974, 108) and thus conveniently moved over considerable distances, particularly if they are relatively lightweight. Stackability depends on form and may be improved by lateral flanges or ridges (fig. 6.9; see Rottländer 1968). Large-necked jars probably were too bulky for trading unless it was the contents—wine, olive oil, honey, and such—that were important.

7.5.2   Vessel Forms

The characteristic of vessel form most specifically modified or adapted to distinct uses is the orifice. Of special interest is whether the orifice is restricted or unrestricted and whether or not it has a neck or collar.

An unrestricted orifice permits easy access to the contents, as discussed above, and the hands or a utensil can be used for mixing or stirring. Unrestricted vessels are an advantage not only in getting the contents out, but also in putting materials in. This makes them suitable for holding goods that will be used frequently, or for very temporary storage. The open orifice also shows the contents, which might be important in serving from a dish or plate, for example. A slip over the mouth and rim area makes cleaning easier.

A restricted orifice, on the other hand, is principally useful for keeping the contents, especially liquids, inside. It can prevent spills during serving and processing, and in cooking pots it retards evaporation of the contents during prolonged heating. In addition, for storage vessels, a restricted orifice can be easily closed with a lid or stopper. Smaller orifices suggest infrequent access or relatively longer periods before the contents are needed.

A neck is a special adaptation of a restricted orifice for containing liquids or for particular storage and transfer functions. A water jar, for example, has a narrow neck to prevent the water from spilling while being carried and to control pouring. A tall, flaring neck acts much like a spout and also serves as a funnel in filling the vessel. A wide-necked vessel may be more appropriate for storing goods that are sometimes poured out and sometimes scooped out. Dry goods—grain, seeds, and such—might be readily stored in such a vessel, though water, oil, or other liquids might certainly be ladled out as well. In all these situations it is not the diameter of the mouth opening itself, but rather the diameter at the maximum constriction of the neck—the throat—that determines the accessibility of the contents.

A final orifice modification with functional significance is the rim or lip form. Whether on a restricted or unrestricted vessel, with or without a neck, a modification of the lip can be not only decorative but useful. Because the mouth of a vessel is subject to much of the movement involved in reaching the contents, thickening the lip with a bolster or flange strengthens the rim against breakage from an accidental blow (see, e.g., Dinsdale, Camm, and Wilkinson 1967, 374–86). This may, however, reduce resistance to thermal shock (Amberg and Hartsook 1946, 450, 452). The lip form may also be a modification for lifting the vessel (e.g., a labial flange on a bowl), or it may make pouring easier. Lip extensions on jar necks make it easier to fit the vessel with a lid or stopper. An interior ridge, for example, is a resting place—a lid seat—for a cover within the vessel mouth, while an exterior lip extension may allow a cloth or skin cover to be tied beneath the flange with a cord—especially common in long-term storage (Henrickson and McDonald 1983, 632).

The base of a vessel is important to stability during any use: storage, processing, or transfer. Broad, flat bases generally are most stable, but certain activities may favor other shapes. Because a flat base joins the vessel wall at an angle, this shape may not be most efficient for cooking because of thermal differentials. Instead, a raised foot or concave base (Amberg and Hartsook 1946, 451) or a round or conical form might be more suitable. Although rounded or pointed bases must be positioned over the cooking fire by some sort of suspension or support, their contours expose a greater surface area to the flames—the base as well as the sides of the vessel—for more efficient heating. For certain kinds of mixing an indented or annular base might offer less resistance and friction as the vessel is turned. Finally, a concave base may be found on water jars that are carried on the head.

Appendages or attachments may serve a variety of purposes; particularly, handles are not necessarily intended for lifting or carrying vessels, especially large ones. Instead, they may be used to attach covers or for maneuvering and tilting vessels to pour out the contents.

7.6 References

Amberg and Hartsook 1946
Arnold 1978, 1985
Balfet 1965
Balfet, Fauvet-Berthelot, and
   Monzon 1983
Beaudry et al. 1983
Beck, Fellows, and MacKennan
   1974
Benson 1974
Binford 1962a
Birmingham 1975
Bowyer 1972
Braun 1980, 1983
Bray 1982
Burnham and Tuttle 1945
Cardew 1969
Castillo Tejero and Litvak 1968
Charlton 1969
Chernela 1969
Clancy 1961
Condamin et al. 1976
DeBoer 1980, 1984
DeBoer and Lathrap 1979
Dinsdale, Camm, and Wilkinson
   1967
Duma 1972
Ericson, Read, and Burke 1972
Ericson and Stickel 1973
Fontana et al. 1962
Fournier 1981
Franken 1971
Froese 1985
Greer 1977
Griffiths 1978

Hally 1983b, 1986
Henrickson and McDonald 1983
Herron 1986
Howard 1981
Joukowsky 1980
Kempton 1981
Kidder 1968
Landon 1959
Lawrence and West 1982
Linton 1944
Lischka 1978
Longacre 1981
Lustig-Arecco 1975
McPherron 1967
May and Tuckson 1982
Miller 1985
Millett 1979a
Mills and White 1977
Nelson 1981, 1985
Orton 1980
Oswalt 1973
Patrick, de Koning, and Smith 1985
Plog 1980, 1985
Porada 1984
Redman 1978a
Reina and Hill 1978
Rice 1976a, 1978a
Rottländer 1967, 1968
Rottländer and Schlichtherle 1983
Rye 1976, 1981
Rye and Evans 1976
Sabloff 1975
Schiffer 1976
Shackley 1982

Shennan and Wilcock 1975
Shepard 1976
Smith 1983, 1985
Smith 1955
Solheim 1965
Stone 1950
Theuvenin, Bullen, and Sanoja 1970
Turner and Lofgren 1966
Vandiver and Koehler 1986

Van Vlack 1964
Vince 1977
Wagner 1960
Warren 1972
Whittlesey 1974
Will 1977
Wilson 1973
Woods 1986

8 Pottery Decorative Styles and Stylistic Analysis

Not only can clay objects be made in a limitless variety of shapes, their surfaces can also be manipulated in many ways to alter the texture, color, and overall appearance of the formed piece. The characteristic patterns of pottery embellishment define decorative styles, and the analysis of these styles is the foundation for anthropological and archaeological inferences about social and economic interactions, artistic communication, and the dating of prehistoric sites.

This chapter outlines some of the approaches to decorative style and stylistic analysis that have been employed in the study of pottery and suggests some problems. As noted in chapter 7, it is clear that the finished surfaces of pottery vessels are not "merely" decorative but have a multitude of functions.

8.1   What Is Style?

Style is a complex concept that is applied in a number of disciplines and is difficult to define with precision. The term is perhaps used most frequently in the arts and literature, where it has two primary meanings: a manner or mode of expression (as distinct from the content or ideas expressed), and the distinction, originality, and character of that expression. In anthropology and archaeology, however, especially with respect to ceramic studies, this separation of content and execution (or technique) in definitions of style has not been maintained; indeed, there has been emphasis on the former.

Virtually all definitions of style in anthropology stress communication and information transfer. Styles are generally considered visual representations, specific to particular contexts of time and place, that at the least transmit information about the identity of the society that produced the style and about the situation or location where it appears. Styles may be thought of as culturally structured or "standardized" in some senses: their components are se-

244

lected from within a relatively narrow body of interrelated technical, thematic, and aesthetic alternatives and combined by a set of rules. All of these are, by group consensus, peculiar to a given cultural system.

This standardization does not imply rigid conformity or homogeneity, however. Styles are open rather than closed systems of expression, constantly receiving and transmitting new information. Variations exist within them because there is usually a range of alternatives from which choices can be made and some flexibility in their application. In addition, several styles or style variants may be appropriate to particular behavioral contexts. Thus the degree of free or idiosyncratic variation that exists within styles is also culturally significant.

Anthropologists and archaeologists use the term style primarily to mean decorative style, that is, the surface embellishment of an object. Other style realms, such as technological styles, which encompass the techniques of manufacture and execution (see Lechtman 1977), are also important but have not yet been systematically investigated in pottery studies.

For archaeologists, styles—especially pottery styles—have long been important in reconstructing the histories and cultural relation of peoples who occupied archaeological sites. Although other artifacts such as architecture, lithics, or textiles are important in these efforts, pottery has played a premier role. This is no doubt partially because of its ubiquity at archaeological sites, but it also reflects the fact that pottery making is an additive technology. That is, the steps of making and decorating pottery create a cumulative record of the choices and procedures the potter selects throughout the process of manufacture. The greater the evidence of choices, the greater the potential for unraveling the complexities of stylistic behavior.

Archaeologists have tended to avoid explicit definitions of style, however, and so style often has been effectively either undefined or defined negatively, relegated to the status of an ambiguous residual category for aspects of artifact variability that could not be explained in terms of other attribute subsystems or agencies (such as function or raw material). Since the 1960s, style has taken on increasing importance among archaeologists who seek to explain variability in the archaeological record in terms other than the simple chronicle of events (e.g., Weissner 1984). Despite this amplified role, the concept of style (and its derivatives, such as stylistic behavior or analysis) is still being employed with little effort at precise definition. The most detailed treatments of the concept have sought to explicate the relation between stylistic and functional variation in artifacts, though occasionally with contradictory conclusions (see Dunnell 1978; Sackett 1977).

8.1.1   Origins of Styles

Specific origins or causes of stylistic behavior in human groups are nearly impossible to pinpoint. Distinctive styles of architecture and art, including ceramics, are associated with the development of civilizations, standing as symbols of a powerful state organization, but it cannot be claimed that these are the earliest art styles in human history. The Paleolithic art of western Europe (Leroi-Gourhan 1968; Conkey 1978) exists as a powerful medium of expression that amply qualifies as a style (or as several styles), even though there is no consensus on its interpretation.

A number of hypotheses have been advanced to account for the development of styles and their maintenance within particular societies. These have called attention to social, psychological, and environmental factors and include some of the following variables: technical evolution, historical diffusion, settlement patterns, child-rearing practices, presence of sex-specific social groups, wish fulfillment, and environmental pressures (see Fischer 1961; Wolfe 1969).

Psychological factors of individual personality structure, creativity, and perception also intervene, as well as physical attributes such as motor skills (e.g., Hill 1977) or age, which are important in the origin and transmission of styles. Styles are not fixed, static entities: they also have dynamic and personal elements that are particularly important in any long-term perspective. Within a community's style, then, individual microstylistic variants may be highly distinctive. Societies differ, however, in how much departure they permit from the norms of their particular traditions and in the acceptable sources of such innovation, whether very personal experiences (e.g., dreams; see Bunzel 1972, 54–55) or contacts with other communities. Insights into the psychological and social factors underlying individual creative impulses and their effects on stylistic change in pottery come from ethnographic contexts in a number of areas: tropical Peru (Lathrap 1983), highland Guatemala (Reina 1963), the Southwestern United States (Marriott 1948), and Africa (Thompson 1969).

Archaeologists have shied away from many of these considerations and rarely try to address individual style variations in pottery or other materials. This is unfortunate but understandable, because to deal with individual styles in prehistoric contexts requires not only isolating significant variables of the general style from other aspects of variability (use, manufacturing technique, etc.) but confidently recognizing individual variations between artisans. Individuals can sometimes be satisfactorily differentiated in prehistory if their output was copious or extremely distinctive, or of course if they signed their work, as did the Greek vase painters or Arretine moldmakers, for example. Complex painted styles may provide the best opportunity to discriminate individual artists, because there are more steps in their execution and hence greater opportunity for idiosyncratic and perhaps unconscious variation (see Hardin 1977; Hill 1977). Otherwise, heuristic categories such as "microstyles" (J. Muller 1977) or the "analytical individual" (Redman 1977) may be the smallest constellation of stylistic consistencies that can be reliably isolated in prehistoric contexts. Although these do not necessarily correspond to the work of a single individual, their high level of similarity may reflect task or production units.

8.1.2   Terminology of Styles

Besides the difficulty of defining styles per se, a wide variety of terms are used to describe particular kinds of styles as well as some of the specific com-

Figure 8.1   Interior of a Macaracas polychrome (A.D. 700–800) pedestal plate from Panama, depicting a saurian figure with human attributes. The vessel is painted in red (*hatching*), bluish purple (*stipple*), and black on white. After Cooke 1985, 33.

Figure 8.2   The design configuration of a black-and-white vessel from the El Morro Valley, New Mexico. After Redman 1978a, fig. 4.3.

ponents or analytical units of styles. Styles are often described by common, though by no means intuitively comprehended, expressions such as representational, naturalistic, realistic, abstract, iconic, or geometric. The first three—representational, naturalistic, and realistic—refer to styles that constitute pictures of things portrayed more or less accurately, with emphasis on form (fig. 8.1). The last three—abstract, iconic, and geometric (e.g., fig. 8.2)—are applied to styles in which the subject has been reduced to a selection of particular features regarded in some way (usually in symbolic content) as essential or basic; the full visual character is not elaborated.

A different set of terms calls attention to the relative degrees of realism in art and art styles. Although two-dimensional art rarely is truly realistic, representational forms (e.g., of animals) differ in how much the parts of the design are distorted to fit the space (Holm 1982). Configurative designs try to achieve an essentially realistic likeness with little distortion. At the other extreme are distributive designs, which sacrifice a realistic image to a *horror*

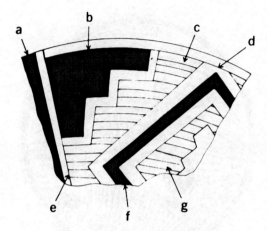

Figure 8.3 (left) Some of the individual design elements found in the vessel shown in figure 8.2: *a*, single straight band, touches rim; *b*, single solid step; *c*, obliquely hatched, straight-based, merging, isosceles triangles; *d*, single rim line, does not touch rim; *e*, single straight line, touches rim; *f*, single solid angle band; *g*, single obliquely hatched step.

Figure 8.4 (below) Some common basic elements (*a*) and their combination into motifs (*b*). After Washburn 1977, fig. 10.

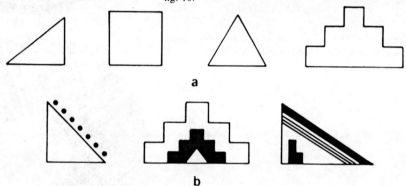

vacui, a need to fill a given space completely, so that the relationship of the parts is greatly distorted. Expansive designs fall in the middle: there is some distortion in the image but less insistence on filling all the available space. Whatever term is used to describe a style, it is evident that an important part of the concept concerns the characteristic way the artist defines the space to be decorated and the way that space is filled.

Besides the descriptive terms for various styles, another vocabulary is employed for the components used to create the design and fill the design space (see Friedrich 1970; Hardin 1983): element, motif, configuration, basic unit, layout, and structure.

An element is the smallest self-contained component of a design that is manipulated or moved around as a single unit (fig. 8.3). It may correspond to a single stroke of a painter's brush or cut of an incising tool or to several such steps. Defining these smallest units of design has always been problematic; though they need not be the irreducible minimum of design (a single brushstroke, for example) it becomes difficult to separate them from larger, more inclusive design units once they are conceived as composite.

Design motifs are fixed combinations of elements that are used to form larger components of the decoration (fig. 8.4). They are usually large or complex enough to fill major portions of the design space, and they may occur in groups rather than singly. For example, a diagonal incised line may constitute a design element; these diagonal incised lines may be combined as hachures within the motif of an incised triangle.

The design configuration refers to the way the decorative motifs are arranged to fill a spatial division, constituting a visual complex that is essentially recognized as "the design." A row of incised triangles, for example, may constitute the design configuration of a particular area of a vessel. It may be the only decoration on the vessel, or it may be combined with other motifs and configurations. Configurations may be relatively complex, involving various subdivisions of the design space.

The basic unit of a design is the conceptual category the artist uses to fill in the design space; it equates in a general way with what the artist envisions as the primary constituents of the design. Basic units are in essence the most immediately recognizable components of a design, and so may be easily borrowed or imitated from artist to artist. The basic unit may correspond to different design levels in different communities—it may equate with design elements, with motifs, or with configurations—although it is perhaps easier to envision it in terms of the larger units of motifs and configurations. Basic units are categories in the mind of the artisan and thus may be difficult to work with in prehistoric contexts without too much subjective inference.

Other important terms address the arrangement of the decoration—its elements and motifs—on the vessel; that is, the decorative layout or structure (fig. 8.5). Layout or structure refers to where the decoration appears on the surface area—whether the area is subdivided and bounded (and if so, how), the symmetry and balance of the decoration, the amount of space covered, and the placement and relation of different elements, motifs, or configurations (fig. 8.6). The location of decoration in general or of different kinds of decoration has clear associations with how a vessel is both viewed and used, as discussed earlier, but design layout is usually studied with the object of relating it to other structural patterns in the society.

8.1.3 Analysis and Interpretation of Decorative Styles in Pottery

A satisfactory definition of the concept of style is only one step in analyzing decoration on pottery or other items of material culture. Another consideration is the relation between the pottery decoration and the society that produced it, a concern that is frequently dichotomized into questions concerning only the form or the visual qualities of the decorative style as opposed to its meaning or content (see Schapiro 1953; Silver 1979).

The formal qualities of styles are encompassed by the terms discussed above, which concern particular elements, motifs, configurations, and decorative layouts. The so-called traditional approach to analysis of pottery styles focuses on identifying these, grouping vessels or sherds into classes or types by the presence/absence of certain stylistic features. These categories are then used for reconstructing local and regional site sequences through seriational arguments of relative similarities and inferences of gradual stylistic change (see sec. 14.1; also Willey and Sabloff 1980, 71–73, 84–100). The geographical distributions of particular elements, motifs, and styles on pottery

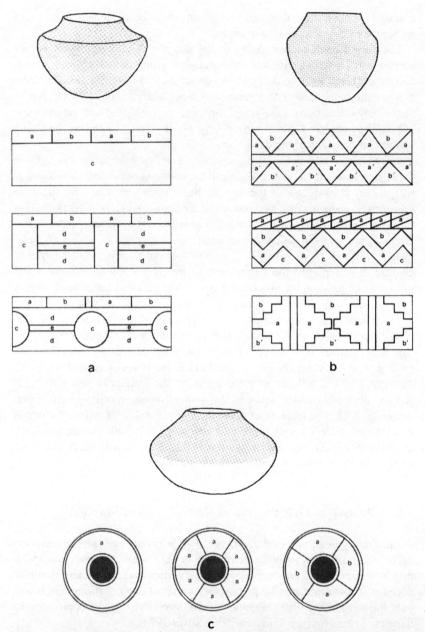

Figure 8.5 Modern Pueblo (Southwestern United States) jars and their design arrangements. Area of design on vessel is shown by stipple; small letters within zones indicate particular designs and their repetition: *a*, Zuñi— jars have two contiguous units of decoration, neck and body, and clear distinctions as to the designs that belong in each (after Bunzel 1972, plates III*a*, II*a,b,c*); *b*, Acoma—although the jars are nearly the same shape as Zuñi jars, the entire jar is a single design space and is covered with elaborate motifs emphasizing the diagonal (see also fig. 1.10) (after Bunzel 1972, plates XI*f*, XIII*a*, XII*d,* XIII*b; c,* Hopi— the shallow, squat jars are decorated on the upper shoulder, presenting a ring-shaped field that can be viewed in its entirety in painting and use. (after Bunzel 1972, plates XV*a*, XVI*a,b,c*).

Figure 8.6 Structural and design elements on a Susa (Iraq) beaker. After Hole 1984, fig. 2.

STRUCTURAL
ELEMENTS

DESIGN
ELEMENTS

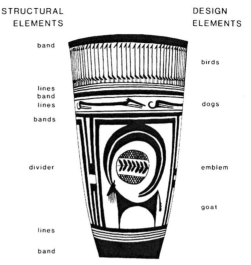

band

birds

lines
band
lines

dogs

bands

divider

emblem

goat

lines

band

also permit hypotheses about contacts between sites or regions. Where the areal spread of a style is especially extensive within a relatively brief period, it is often referred to as a horizon style (see Willey and Phillips 1958, 31–33). Comparatively little effort is made to uncover the specific mechanisms underlying this spread, however, or the processes involved in the stylistic changes used in dating sites.

Those studying the meaning or content of styles address the many ways art expresses deep-seated characteristics or beliefs of the society that produced it. The meaning of a style can be construed on several levels, of course; two rather straightforward types of content interpretation go beyond the strictly visual aspects of the style. Thus at one level of meaning style is seen as a reflection of aesthetic preferences, conscious or unconscious; at another, style is considered to mirror significant features of the natural and social environment. Particularly useful in societies whose art (ceramic or other) is rather strongly representational, these approaches frequently address the art's natural, mythological, or iconographic themes (e.g., fig. 1.10; Mera 1937; Pyne 1976; Bankes 1980; Proulx 1968; Thompson 1969; Coe 1978; Lathrap 1973).

Some of the most complex approaches to pottery stylistic analysis deal with a third level of meaning. In such approaches the content of styles—both visual images and spatial arrangements—is seen as a symbolic code reinforcing social and cosmological structures, beliefs, and values. Decorative styles are thus a kind of visual communication that reproduces the principles and relationships by which a community structures and organizes its perceptions of the cosmos and of social realities—consciously or unconsciously—so as to order experience into coherent categories (Munn 1966).

This view of decorative styles emphasizes their information content and communication function. Numerous variants of this general perspective have been applied to pottery analysis by archaeologists and ethnoarchaeologists, addressing sociocultural matters ranging from interpersonal contacts to ethnicity to social structure to cosmology. Hypotheses vary concerning the source and intent of information contained in the decorative style; that is, whether it stems from conscious or unconscious selection by the artists; they also vary on the nature of the intended audience and on how the pottery is meant to be used or displayed. Because one may question to what extent the hypotheses of stylistic communication exist purely within the explanatory framework of anthropological/archaeological reconstructions, some of the information functions of pottery decorative styles may be intentional, active, and direct while others may be inferred, passive, and indirect.

Although it is difficult to categorize the many kinds of stylistic analysis of pottery decoration and their interpretations, three major approaches can almost be considered schools: design element analysis, symmetry analysis, and design structure analysis. Other avenues of investigation focus more explicitly on the intended information content and meaning and on the symbolic role of the decoration.

None of these approaches is exclusive, however, and a good deal of cross-fertilization of ideas and procedures occurs between them all. Most analyses of pottery decoration and decorative styles have used painted pottery. Few if any address in any essential way the significance of color per se as opposed to texture or form (see Sahlins 1976) or the implications of incising as a decorative technique that emphasizes boundaries (see Douglas 1966, 121–22). Thus they are not limited to painted designs and can as easily be applied to impressed (e.g., Broyles 1968; Irwin 1974; Saunders 1986) or incised pottery decoration.

8.2 Design Elements and Interaction

Design element analyses typically attempt to isolate the individual elements of pottery design and explain their spatial occurrence in terms of the social behavior of the makers and users of the pottery. This approach to pottery stylistic analysis was developed in the early 1960s as archaeologists tried to expand the inferential potential of pottery beyond merely dating sites. Its theoretical basis is the proposition that the similarity (or comparative frequencies) of design elements between groups will be proportional to the direction and intensity of social interaction between members of those groups.

This proposition is generally referred to as the interaction hypothesis or the social interaction theory; it is also named for two of its earliest and best-known exponents—the Deetz-Longacre hypothesis. Regardless of the label, the central concept has been investigated in a variety of ways. The interactions of interest may be between members of different social subgroups (clans, families, residence compounds) within a single community or site or between different sites or communities. This hypothesis may also be used to compare such interaction patterns as they change through time.

More specifically, these interaction analyses have been used to measure similarity of design element occurrences between two social organizational units (between-group similarity; Longacre 1964, 1970), the homogeneity of element occurrence within a particular group (within-group homogeneity; Whallon 1968), and the associations of elements between different styles within or between groups (Deetz 1965; Whallon 1968). These uses are closely interrelated and are often combined to infer degree of relationship from pre-

Figure 8.7 Designs on Arikara pottery handles used in one of the early interaction studies. After Deetz 1965, fig. 23.

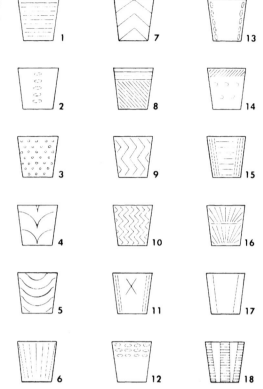

historic material. Most of these studies have been carried out in the culture area where the approach was pioneered, the Southwestern United States, but several have been undertaken in other regions, including the northeastern region of the United States (Whallon 1968; Engelbrecht 1978), Mesoamerica (Plog 1976; Pyne 1976), and the Near East (Johnson 1973; LeBlanc and Watson 1973).

Briefly summarized, this procedure begins with compiling all the design elements appearing on the pottery of interest (fig. 8.7). The frequency of occurrence of each element in the pottery assemblage associated with each group or subgroup is tabulated. These frequencies may simply be compared directly, or a statistic may be calculated to express the similarity of the pottery of each group to that of every other group. The covariation of similarity coefficients with distances between sites may be measured, if distance is a concern. Because these studies can involve comparing a hundred or more elements on several thousand sherds, computerized multivariate statistical procedures have been invoked.

Design element analyses are interpreted within a context of postulates about historical or social reality for which the interaction hypothesis is believed to be a valid test, such as descent and residence rules, frequency of intermarriage, and intensity of religious or economic contacts between groups. When the comparisons are through time rather than between geographical areas, the object may be to look at the effects of warfare, subsistence shifts, or acculturative changes, for example, on patterns of social interaction as measured by stylistic similarities. Recent studies have attempted to correlate frequencies of decorative elements and variation in design systems with individual work groups, aging of potters, and seasonal changes (Graves 1981, 1985). Because of these foci of inference, the design-element approach has also been called "ceramic sociology" and "ethnic iconography" (Sackett 1977, 376, 377).

Design element analysis has been carried out for two decades and has received enormous criticism in several reviews (see, e.g., Watson 1977; Plog 1978; Hodder 1981; Washburn and Ahlstrom 1982). Some of the criticism is directed toward the interaction hypothesis, while some is leveled at the use of design elements in ceramic style analysis. Because these criticisms have provided the foundation for many of the later approaches to ceramic stylistic analysis, they are discussed here in some detail.

8.2.1 Critiques of the Interaction Theory

Criticisms of the social interaction theory are directed primarily toward two issues, and the validity of the objections depends in part on how the interaction proposition is stated. One criticism concerns whether styles primarily reflect social relationships or whether they are equally (and confoundingly) responsive to other phenomena such as ecological factors or belief systems. The second focuses on the explicit statement of the interaction hypothesis, which claims a direct correlation between the degree of stylistic similarity and the intensity of social interaction.

With respect to the first objection, it can be noted that styles, whether in ceramic decoration or in some other class of material culture, can reflect social interactions, but they need not do so necessarily or exclusively. The Hopi and Hopi-Tewa Pueblos live in three contiguous villages but have different languages, religions, and social patterns; nonetheless they manufacture identical pottery (Stanislawski 1978, 225–26). In contrast, in the Baringo District of western Kenya, considerable stylistic isolation is observed in some categories of material culture despite a long history of easy intertribal communication and movement across tribal boundaries (Hodder 1977). Clearly, physical proximity and potential or actual social interaction are not determinative of stylistic similarities. Different kinds of interaction in varying circumstances may evoke dissimilar stylistic responses or degrees of response in different categories of material culture. Unfortunately, there is little understanding about the variability in those responses.

The second criticism of the theoretical underpinnings of the social interaction hypothesis—that there is a positive correlation between the degree of stylistic similarity and the direction and intensity of social interaction—is much broader than the first, more complex, and more damaging to the entire practice of element analysis. The objections concern the legitimacy of the particular assumptions that underlie this research and the corresponding validity of the interpretations drawn from them. These critiques have been elaborated by cultural anthropologists, many of whom have conducted studies of pottery manufacture, decoration, and use in modern communities and have discovered flaws in the "ceramic sociological" approach. Most serious among the difficulties are oversimplified assumptions and inattention to confounding factors in human behavior. These problems fall into four distinct subject areas: inferences about descent and residence; patterns of learning; archaeological record formation (the relationship of manufacture, use, and refuse disposal); and the role of other mechanisms in the spatial movement of pottery vessels. A fifth concern is the frequent lack of control over the time dimension, since stylistic variability may be primarily temporal in nature, but as this is not specifically a criticism of the interaction hypothesis, it will not be treated further here.

Design element studies initially carried out with prehistoric pottery in the Southwestern United States were based on ethnographic analogy, which retrodicted the matrilineal descent and general matrilocal residence among contemporary Pueblo Indians into the archaeological past. The substance of the major critique of this assumption was that residence rules as identified by anthropologists are largely idealized analytical constructs that are not unvarying within communities; the likelihood of finding a community that is purely matrilocal in residence is very slim (Allen and Richardson 1971).

In conjunction with the hypothesis of matrilineality/matrilocality, the early Southwestern design element studies assumed that the potters were all female and that they learned techniques of manufacture and decoration from their mothers (Bunzel 1972, 54). Since this work, numerous studies have investigated learning patterns and sources of inspiration for decoration on pottery and other objects. In the Hopi and Hopi-Tewa Pueblo villages, for example, four teaching patterns have been found to be most common—mother/daughter; mother-in-law/daughter-in-law; aunt/niece of different clans; and neighbor/neighbor—and eight other teaching situations have also been observed (Stanislawski 1978, 219; Stanislawski and Stanislawski 1978, 66–73). Studies of craft learning carried out as part of the Coxoh (Maya) Ethnoarchaeological Project in three communities in the Maya highlands identified six learning modes—family-centered (nuclear family), corporate (residential), kin-extensive, minimally structured, formal schooling, and specialist (Hayden and Cannon 1984, 330–41)—of which only the first three relate to kinship or residential organization. Investigations of patterns of learning the designs and techniques used in painting cloth and pottery in Peru emphasize that residence proximity and economic and artistic cooperation, irrespective of actual kin ties, promote stylistic transmission (Roe 1980; Lathrap 1983). The Coxoh project study of the kin-extensive mode of learning reached similar conclusions and emphasized cooperative socioeconomic relationships between households as well as the frequency of the craft activity. In this case, however, the stylistic variables of pottery were not painted decorations but body shapes in cooking vessels (table 8.1), which, for technological and other reasons (secs. 7.3 and 7.5), are apt to exhibit a very restricted range of variability in the first place.

The correlations proposed in the interaction hypothesis have also been criticized from the point of view of archaeological record formation. That is, it may be questioned whether the location of archaeological recovery of pottery—particularly broken fragments—directly reflects the location of its manufacture and use. This is partly a question of scale of production and distribution of the ware, as discussed in chapter 7. In addition, though, the spa-

Table 8.1 Olla Form Variants Produced in Potting Households in Chanal, Mexico

Household ID number	Spheroid	Ellipsoid	Pointed Ovaloid	Round Ovaloid	Cylindrical	Hyperboloid
3		x	x			
4	x		x			
6		x				
7[a]	x		x	x		
9		x	x			
10		x				
13	x	x	x	x	x	
14[a]		x	x			
15[b]	x	x		x	x	
16		x				
17				x		x
19		x				
20		x	x			
22		x		x		
24		x				
25[a]		x	x	x	x	
27		x				
28		x	x	x		
29	x	x				
30		x				
31[a]		x	x	x	x	
37		x	x	x		
41				x		
43	x	x		x		
45[a]	x	x	x		x	
48[b]	x	x	x	x		
53		x		x		
Totals (*N* = 27 households)	8	23	13	13	5	1

Source: After Hayden and Cannon 1984, table 8.   [b]Three potters in household.
  [a]Two potters in household.

tial dislocations caused by discard and recycling of broken vessels (sec. 9.3.2) may disrupt the inferred relation between local manufacture and use and thus weaken the underlying premise of the interaction hypothesis. Within or around a site, broken vessels may be left more or less in place, or they may be swept outside into areas of general refuse disposal, which may then be modified further as old or new areas are incorporated into the living space.

Finally, the disposition of pottery styles within and between sites may be a consequence of other similarities, differences, or social arrangements among the inhabitants besides interaction intensity. For example, different kinds of pottery may be made for men and for women (e.g., Crossland and Posnansky 1978, 89), or different styles of decoration may be applied to marketed wares and to those intended for the potter's own use (e.g., Balfet 1965, 166).

Also, pottery may have been traded widely through a region. To be sure, such distributions do reflect interactions at some level (i.e., socioeconomic), but they are not of the sort that can indicate social organization, residence, marriage rules, or patterns of learning within the family. The relative frequencies of the traded pottery at a site or sites may register social interactions such as intermarriage or ritual activity, but on the other hand they may be equally or more sensitive to scale of production and distance from the manufacturing center. It is therefore necessary to have some sort of control over the manufacturing provenience of the pottery in question (see Plog 1976, 256–59, 1980, 54–76).

8.2.2   Critiques of the Element Analysis Method

The second broad area of criticism of the ceramic sociological studies is methodological, questioning whether design elements are sensitive to the kinds of interactions being proposed and what procedures are appropriate. Three specific problem areas have been raised: defining elements, sample size, and the statistics used.

How to define the design elements and construct a typology of them is a particularly vexing issue. In most analyses the criteria have been vague and subjective, making it difficult to evaluate the success of the studies or replicate their results because of interanalyst variation (e.g., Plog 1978, 159). Longacre's (1964, 163) elements were chosen as "the smallest units or elements of design that would be nonconsciously selected [by the potter] based upon learning patterns," while Deetz (1965, 46) defined a stylistic attribute as "one which results from a choice on the part of the manufacturer from a number of possibilities, made to produce a certain effect." Thus one definition of elements seeks unconscious selections while the other looks for conscious choices (i.e., basic units) to be reflected in the units measured; there is, however, no way to objectively verify either viewpoint. In many studies the procedures used in defining and measuring elements were simply not clearly spelled out. An additional problem is that analysts disagree on what constitutes an element: what is an element to one person may be a motif or an attribute to another, and the procedures of element analysis have also been used on design motifs (e.g., Pyne 1976).

A second methodological criticism concerns sample size. Most of the ceramic sociological studies have explored a wide range of stylistic variability encompassing different motifs, types, and forms as they vary with location or time period (table 8.2). For this reason a large enough number of sherds or

Table 8.2   Sample Sizes and Contexts in Design Element Analyses

Study and Study Area	Number of Sherds	Number of Elements or Attributes	Number of Sites	Number of Important Areal or Temporal Divisions
Hill 1970 (Broken K, Southwestern U.S.)	2,849	53	1	
Longacre 1964 (Carter Ranch, Southwestern U.S.)	4,160	175	1	39 rooms
Cronin 1962 (Southwestern U.S.)	2,188	45	7	
Plog 1980 (Southwestern U.S. restudy)	3,110	12	5	
	1,177		22	
Deetz 1965 (Arikara)	2,000	200	2	3 time periods
Engelbrecht 1978 (New York)	8,500	5	28	4 periods

whole vessels must be analyzed from each unit of comparative interest. With regard to sherds, some type of minimum number of vessels (MNV) estimates rather than individual sherd counts should be used, because differential vessel breakage and recovery may inflate the number of elements tabulated (see sec. 9.2.2).

No guidelines have been offered on minimum sample sizes. One early study (Tuggle 1970) suggested that if samples are smaller than 75–100 cases per locus of interest (a site, room, etc.), the statistical calculations of similarity or correlation will not be reliable. Reexamination of this finding with a different data set yielded contradictory results, suggesting that noncontemporaneity of sites in the sample may cause spurious results and that issues of sample size should be considered site by site (Plog 1978, 157–58).

A related matter is the statistical procedures used in calculating similarity and in comparing sites or other provenience units. The methods include simple visual comparison of actual frequencies (Deetz 1965) as well as low-level statistical manipulations for measuring how attribute occurrence covaries with provenience—for example, N-by-N contingency tables (Pyne 1976; Leblanc and Watson 1973) or calculation of the Brainerd-Robinson similarity coefficient (Freeman 1962; Cronin 1962). More complex multivariate statistical procedures have been employed to form groupings of similar provenience units (i.e., residence units) or similar element/attribute categories. These include simple linear regression (Freeman and Brown 1964) or multiple regression (Longacre 1964). For more complex data sets, a matrix of similarity (or other correlational) coefficients (see Plog 1976, 259–62) may be used as a basis for factor analysis (Hill 1970) or cluster analysis (Plog 1978, 169–71) of the data.

The problems in applying some of these multivariate statistical models have been discussed in some detail (Plog 1978, 166–77), calling attention to errors caused by the inappropriateness of the models' assumptions to the data (size of sample, randomness of samples, intercorrelation of variables), or apparent arbitrariness in determining significant and nonsignificant results. In the case of this particular criticism, the problems lie not with the aesthetics of the element analysis per se, but with the lack of familiarity with the statistical transformations involved in interpreting large multivariate data sets.

8.3 Alternative Approaches to Style

The criticisms of design element analyses have been discussed in some detail because in many ways this body of data, which has been considerably augmented, reworked, and modified over the past two decades, forms the basis for a "new generation" of ceramic stylistic analyses. The growth of the design element methodology has involved not only negative criticism but also positive recommendations for improvements. Some of these have been suggested in the preceding review: for example, the need for controls on sample size and on the temporal dimension in order to make valid comparisons.

Concern with defining design elements as emically and socially meaningful units is being replaced by an effort to deal with variability within and between

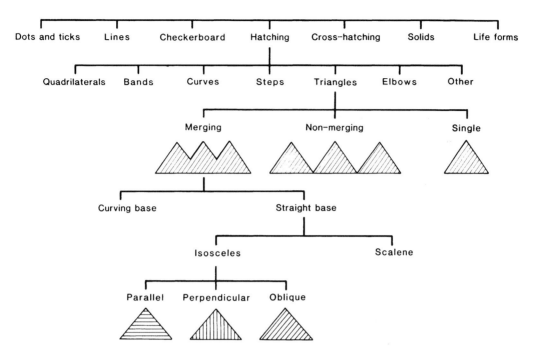

Figure 8.8 Master chart for coding design elements or portions of elements used in analysis of El Morro Valley (New Mexico) pottery. Different levels in the hierarchy represent individual potter's decisions and levels of cultural patterning in overall designs. The figure shows decisions leading to obliquely hatched straight-based merging isosceles triangles (see also fig. 8.2). After Redman 1977, fig. 4.5.

elements, as, for example, with the attributes of designs (Deetz 1965; Redman 1978a, 175; Plog 1980). Attributes are measurable characteristics of elements or of motifs and include features with clear alternative states, such as line width and frequency, techniques of filling in spaces, presence of appended forms, and so forth (fig. 8.8). These may be further identified within a hierarchy as primary and secondary attributes (or primary and secondary forms) on the basis of their order of execution and prominence within the design (Plog 1980, 53, fig. 4.4; Friedrich 1970, 335).

The distinction between primary and secondary elements reflects another approach in stylistic analysis that has grown out of the ceramic sociology studies and that concerns the recognition of a hierarchy of procedures or decisions that artisans follow. This point has been made on several occasions (Friedrich 1970, 342; Plog 1982; Roe 1980) but has been most extensively elaborated by Redman (1977, 1978a). At Cibola (Southwestern United States), a hierarchical list of 203 formal decorative (fig. 8.8), and technological attributes, hypothesized to be the potter's basic units, was developed to test the interaction hypothesis at the site. The stated advantage of this procedure is that evidence of cultural patterning can be sought at a variety of levels of the hierarchy—at the level of attributes, elements, or motifs. The limitations of a hierarchical approach to design description have been discussed with respect to Southwestern United States pottery, and a nonhierarchical approach based on "schema" (configurations) was proposed as an alternative (Jernigan 1986).

Another development in stylistic studies is the increasing awareness of the relation of decorative units and styles to vessel form. Ethnoarchaeological studies of pottery manufacture have shown that potters may be explicit in associating specific design motifs and arrangements with particular vessel forms (Friedrich 1970, 335; Stanislawski 1978, 215). Subsequently this observation was explored in the archaeological record and found to hold true there as well (Plog 1980, 112–13; LeBlanc and Watson 1973). Nonetheless, systematic incorporation of this principle into design element analysis was belated. Covariation of design with vessel form is clearly significant to the interaction hypothesis, which interprets the spatial distribution of design frequencies as indicating intensity of contacts between different groups characterized materially by their stylistic distinctiveness. The importance of this relationship is illustrated by the hypothetical instance of a site including a storeroom full of broken storage jars. These jars, decorated differently from serving bowls or other vessels, might mistakenly be considered the products of a completely different group of people than pottery from other areas of the site (Watson 1977, 388).

Finally, there is much greater awareness of the inadequacy of anthropologists' and archaeologists' understanding of style—both how to define it and its transmission and change. It is in response to these deficiencies that a second generation of scholars of style has evolved, their attention devoted to stylistic analysis of pottery as well as other materials. Some of these more recent studies are still "ceramic sociological" in emphasis and fall within the purview of the interaction hypothesis, while others frame their concerns more broadly.

8.3.1 Symmetry Analysis

One approach to pottery design and style that emerged in the late 1970s is pattern analysis or symmetry analysis. The pioneering treatise on this approach was written decades earlier by Shepard (1948b), and a brief note suggesting its potential had appeared some years before that (Brainerd 1942). Symmetry analysis is based on the principles underlying descriptions of the three-dimensional crystalline structure of atoms (Shubnikov and Koptsik 1974; Buerger and Lukesh 1937, cited in Shepard 1976, 268). The approach uses a standard set of terms for describing the property of symmetry with respect to the spatial position of geometrical figures and their movement across a line or around a point axis. The location, shape, and size of the decorated area on the vessel are not of primary interest.

Symmetry analysis of ceramic decoration involves identifying and describing a design pattern—any design with regularly repeated parts. The process begins by first identifying the basic unit or fundamental part of the design. This represents "the unique part of the pattern from which the entire composition can be generated" (Shepard 1976, 268) and may be either a motif or an element in conventional terminology. The next step is to determine the motion by which that part is repeated on the vessel or the transfor-

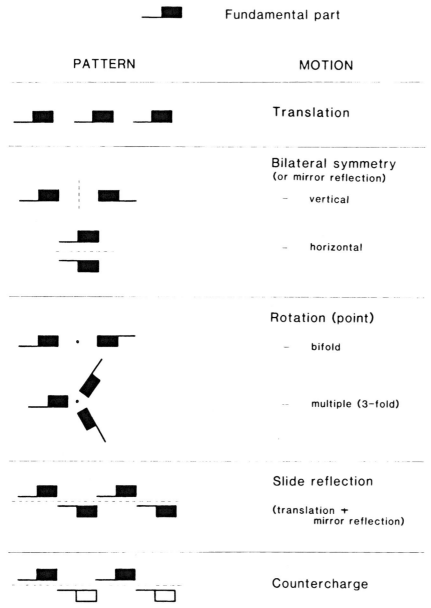

Figure 8.9 Symmetry classes and kinds of   patterns from the fundamental part illustrated.
motion involved in producing different design

mation by which it is moved and superimposed upon itself around a real or imaginary point or line to form the design. If a design is composed of only one nonrepeated fundamental part, it is said to be asymmetrical.

There are four kinds of movement, and thus four classes of symmetry may be defined (fig. 8.9): translation, bilateral, rotation, and slide reflection. Translation is the simple serial repetition of the element or part along a straight line with no change in its orientation. Bilateral symmetry (also called reflec-

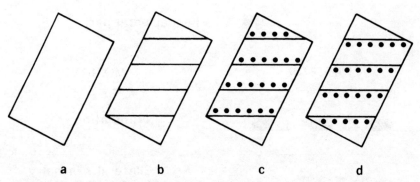

a   b   c   d

Figure 8.10   Change in design symmetry by addition of embellishments: *a*, rectangular element; *b*, motif—element filled with horizontal hatching; both the design structure and the motif have identical class 200 bifold rotational symmetry; *c*, adding dots to motif *b*, means that the figure can no longer be rotated 180° (as in *d*) and still remain the same design. The symmetry of the design featuring repetition of these units is translation (class 100). After Washburn 1977, fig. 12.

tion or mirror reflection) refers to the repetition of an element as though it were reflected across a mirror plane. The plane may be vertical, horizontal, or diagonal in orientation. Rotational symmetry refers to the motion of rotating the design unit around a point. Most typically this occurs as bifold rotational symmetry, with a rotation of 180°, so that the elements essentially oppose each other; interestingly enough, however, this pattern does not commonly occur in nature as a source to be imitated. Rotational symmetry may also occur in multiple (threefold, fourfold, and sixfold) forms as well. The final motion category is slide or glide reflection, which combines reflection and translation.

All the decorations involving these motions can be described with respect to single or multiple points or axes. Where movement is around a single point, the design is referred to as finite. Movements repeated along a straight line yield a one-dimensional infinite pattern, more commonly called a band pattern (e.g., fig. 8.6, top). A pattern repeated in two directions is a two-dimensional infinite design. Band designs may involve any type of movement of decorative units, though perhaps translation and bifold rotation are most common. Two-dimensional infinite or allover decorations may involve any symmetry movements except translation. Decoration on pottery surfaces is, of course, always executed in only two dimensions, even though those surfaces may have a pronounced curvature. Similarly, the decoration is not truly infinite because it is limited by the vessel dimensions.

It should also be noted that symmetry may be imperfect, because of careless execution, asymmetrical curvature of the surface, or deliberate intent. For example, adding embellishments may alter the symmetry (fig. 8.10), or one side of a figure may be solid while the other is filled with hachure. In painted designs where the size and shape of parts repeat through any of these motions but the colors alternate in some way, the pattern is said to have color reversal or countercharge.

Pattern or symmetry analysis has been used to describe pottery decoration primarily in the Southwestern United States (Washburn 1977, 1978; Zaslow

1977; Zaslow and Dittert 1976), and it has also been used in Mesoamerica, particularly for comparing the designs in this area with those of the Southwest (Brainerd 1942; Shepard 1948b; Zaslow 1981). Neolithic Greek and Aegean pottery has also been described with respect to pattern symmetry (Washburn 1983), as has early pottery from Ban Chiang, Thailand (Van Esterik 1979).

One of the stated advantages of pattern or symmetry analysis in pottery decoration studies is the objectivity in classifying and describing designs arising from the use of mathematical terms to describe the juxtaposition of fundamental parts of the design as opposed to descriptive terms such as herringbone or chevron. The decoration can be described by a notational system that employs either numerical or alphabetical designators or some combination of the two. For example, Washburn (1978, 110) describes a positional notation involving prefixes, superscripts, and subscripts on a basic three-digit system. A "Class $1\text{-}2^{2}00$" pattern translates into a one-dimensional infinite design with two rotations around the principal axis (bifold rotation) and countercharge between figures along that axis. In plain English, this design consists of two rows of opposed right triangles, one triangle being solid black, the other hatched. Zaslow (1981, 11), on the other hand, uses alphabetic designators to describe, for example, a "pgg" symmetry class common in the Southwest, "where glide lines alternate with rows of two-fold axes." The lack of agreement on the descriptive notations in this approach and the tendency for the vocabulary to be rather cumbersome may be stumbling blocks in its use.

Interpretations of the symmetry patterns of pottery design have generally been undertaken within the overall framework of the interaction hypothesis, in much the same way as design element analysis. The idea is that particular symmetry patterns are characteristic of particular societies not because of the potters' conscious recognition of the motions or movements involved in their design repetitions, but because of preferences and a repertoire of design alternatives shared and handed down from generation to generation. Symmetry patterns are thus sensitive to time and space in the same way that styles are. Brainerd (1942, 165), for example, noted that the Pueblo Indians of the Southwestern United States and the Maya had different symmetries in their designs, even though the motifs were similar: the Pueblos seemed to employ bifold rotation more commonly, whereas in Mesoamerica slide reflection predominated. Even within the Southwestern United States, however, different symmetry systems are characteristic of particular subareas (Washburn 1978).

Although it seems that different cultures have different decorative systems when described by their symmetry or pattern mathematics, it is less clear what these differences may mean. They have been interpreted in the context of changing social organizational and interactional factors, but these are not formulated around specific sociocultural features such as residence rules as were the earlier ceramic sociological design element studies. Instead, the broader matters addressed have included indigenous versus introduced stylistic change (Washburn 1983), identification of production and marketing relationships (Washburn 1983), and prolonged long-distance trade relationships (Zaslow 1981).

A lack of consensus is evident concerning the behavior of patterns as opposed to styles and motifs where contacts between cultures are hypothesized.

It is not clear, for example, how readily patterns or symmetry relationships will be transmitted and integrated into local styles compared with similar transmission of motifs. Brainerd (1942, 165) suggests that in comparing two regions, if a motif can be originally associated with a particular symmetry system in one area, its presence in a system with different symmetry principles suggests that it was added to that system from its original area. Zaslow (1981, 39), however, suggests that if a design is copied from one area into another the pattern will spread as the artist deciphers basic construction principles through visual recognition, but the embellishment is likely to be in the local style.

The symmetry approach is still relatively new, and it is not possible to specify the situations in which patterns will or will not be transferred. Nor has it been subjected to extensive ethnoarchaeological testing as has the design element approach. Thus far, however, the tendency has been to argue that in situations of geographical proximity or known contacts, similarities between areas bespeak some transfer of ideas concerning symmetry.

Recent applications of symmetry analysis to pottery designs have endeavored to make intersite comparisons more objective and systematic by using multivariate statistical procedures such as multidimensional scaling (Washburn and Matson 1985). Symmetry analysis is also complementary to a nonhierarchical approach to design called "schema analysis" (Jernigan 1986, 17). In addition, the procedures and interpretations of symmetry analysis are increasingly being linked to those of a third viewpoint in pottery stylistic analysis. which has been developed ethnoarchaeologically. By calling attention to the role of symmetry in the structure of designs, symmetry analysis may gradually fall within the more general approach emphasizing design structure.

8.3.2   Design Structure Analysis

Interest in the structure or spatial arrangement of the designs on pottery or other decorated objects is not new: it is part of virtually all approaches to art and style. In pottery analysis specifically, although layouts and structures were discussed and illustrated by Bunzel (1972, 13–48) and Shepard (1976, 259–305), the elaboration of these discussions in the 1970s can be seen as a response to questions about the methods and interpretations of ceramic sociologists testing the interaction hypothesis. For archaeologists, the seminal paper on design structure was an analysis of the painted decoration on pottery of a small Mexican village, San José, in the Department of Michoacán (Friedrich 1970).

This approach sees design structure as the cognitive system, or body of organized knowledge, that underlies a particular style and through which the style is produced by artists. The design components are referred to as elements and configurations and may be categorized as either primary or secondary (fig. 8.11). These are united with a hierarchy of spatial divisions in this cognitive system, the result being described in terms of four features: definition of the area to be decorated, that is, the deocrative problem (fig. 8.12), identification of the basic units of decoration, classification of the basic units, and identification of the rules by which the basic units are used to solve the

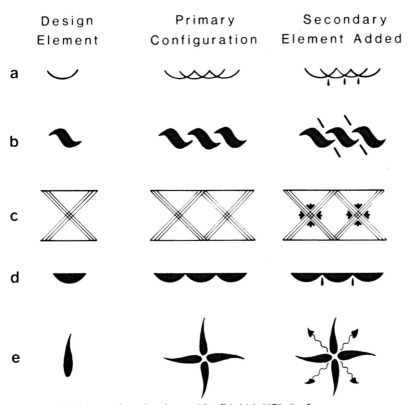

Figure 8.11   Design configuration classes. After Friedrich 1970, fig. 2.

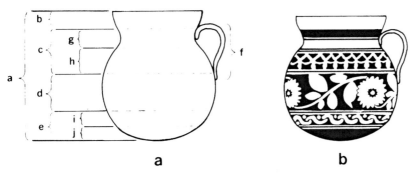

a

b

Figure 8.12   The system of spatial divisions underlying the painted decoration on Tarascan (Mexico) ollas: *a*, named parts of exterior (*a–f*, major divisions; *g–j*, subdivisions); *b*, painted designs on a Tarascan olla, showing different designs in each division and subdivision. After Hardin 1984, figs. 1, 2.

decorative problem (Hardin 1983, 9). Because this approach was developed by ethnoarchaeologists, it has benefited from the complementary joining of the analysts' observations with informants' verbal information on how basic units are classified and the rules for combining them in decorating a vessel. Not only has this provided a fuller picture of the "design grammar" underlying stylistic structure, but it has suggested specific features of artists' interactions and executions that are relevant to the ceramic sociological studies.

One of the tenets of the social interaction theory of pottery decoration is that stylistic similarity (as indicated by sharing of elements) reflects the intensity of interaction between various groups of people, whether they are potters or members of different kin groups, residence units, or communities. In the design structure approach, although actual elements and configurations (motifs) are studied, they are not seen as useful indicators of interaction intensity because they are too easily copied and exchanged when there is even minimal contact between artists. Instead it is their structure (the spatial relation on a vessel) that relates to community identifications and standards; they may be shared more directly by birth cohorts than by kin or work groups (see Graves 1985), and because they are community specific they can aid in differentiating individual locations of manufacture (see Hole 1984). Friedrich's early work suggested three particular aspects of design structure that indicate such identifications: (1) organization of the spatial divisions (especially the presence and location of boundary markers in the design); (2) classification of design elements and configurations (as primary or secondary); and (3) the manipulation or function of particular elements within configurations (Friedrich 1970, 338–39).

Patterns of interaction within the community of potters can be discerned more readily if the individual potters or work groups develop distinctive substyles, as did one such group in San José, Mexico. The conclusion, however, is that "the success of any attempt to reconstruct interaction patterns depends upon the extent to which the artisans who produced the archaeological style were actually interested in the designs they painted" (Friedrich 1970, 342).

Study of the pottery manufactured in Quinua, a small community in highland Peru, combined symmetry analysis with a structural approach and amplified many of these observations (Arnold 1983, 1984). The structural relations evident in the design on four classes of vessels clearly reflect differences among the communities producing them. This supports the notion that because design structures are more closely identified with producing groups than are elements, they are more stable indicators of interactions than elements, which transfer readily. Second, the symmetry patterns and spatial locations of decoration on the pottery are hypothesized to correspond to principles of social organization and environmental utilization that are part of the broader cultural and ecological relationships in Quinua.

8.3.3   Information, Diversity, and Symbols

The three approaches to style analysis above are content or meaning oriented, either supporting or opposing the tenets of the social interaction hypothesis. Interaction is largely an ex post facto explanatory framework constructed by archaeologists to interpret the spatial disposition of similar stylistic manifestations. By this view the communication role of styles is incidental: styles reflect group affiliations, but there is little presumption of deliberate intent by the manufacturers of pottery to send overt messages to those who see it being used.

Another approach to the content analysis of styles stresses a more active role in communication and sometimes addresses the actual information being communicated within the society itself. In this information theory (or symbolic functionalist) approach, the traditional dichotomy between style and function is opposed; instead, it is posited that styles in any category of artifacts have important functions in information exchange. Styles send messages of social, political, and economic group affiliation that are known and recognized by the person displaying the message and by the person intended to receive it (Wobst 1977; see also Weissner 1984). The need for such messages arises as societies grow larger and more complex, with an increasing need for the members to convey information about themselves to others who may be physically or socially distant. The messages should be readily apparent visually and capable of being decoded by their audience. Furthermore, they may be independent of the actual context of use of the medium, although clearly that context is important in establishing why the message is sent at all.

According to Wobst (1977, 327–28), style or stylistic behavior has three major functions. One is to make social interactions more predictable by providing immediate visual information about the participants, thereby reducing stress. Items of clothing, headdresses, insignia, and objects carried or displayed all bear information about status or group affiliation that would otherwise be unknown or difficult to elicit. A second function is that over the long term, as societies become more complex, styles reinforce social differentiation by symbolizing group (rank, status) affiliation and enhancing within-group solidarity. Third, and closely related to this, stylistic behavior is important in signifying and maintaining the boundaries between groups by visual messages of within-group solidarity. These stylistic functions are served most fully in three situations: in relatively large social groups, in interactions over some distance (physical or social), and when the artifacts bearing the stylistic messages have high visibility.

These symbolic functionalist analyses of the informational role of decorative styles in a variety of material categories have pursued two closely related interpretations. One concerns the content or substance of the message (usually with reference to iconography), and the other addresses the context or situation in which the message is being sent. Both viewpoints have been investigated ethnographically, and the perspectives can be rather easily transferred to archaeological settings.

A series of studies of the role of material culture styles in boundary identification and maintenance is provided by Hodder (1977, 1979b, 1982) in the Baringo District of Kenya. Different categories of material culture—pottery, calabashes, clothing, ornaments, hairstyles, weapons—may play different roles in group identification, or they may not function in that sense at all. Only when they do call attention to boundaries can they be expected to carry stylistic messages. The need to support social relations and order will change through time, but as Hodder (1979b, 450) observes, the role of artifact styles in symbolizing group identity is especially significant when tensions exist between groups. These tensions may be institutionalized, as in the relations between males and females within a society, or they may be acute situational strains, as in warfare. The stresses may also stem from broader environmental relationships and economic competition, with ramifications in social relations.

Because the message functions of styles are fulfilled to varying degrees on different types of material objects, it is important to consider how they apply to pottery and pottery styles. Although pottery may serve in the most mundane tasks, such as cooking and food storage, it also may be used in culturally significant or emotionally charged situations, for example, religious ritual, mortuary activity, and a variety of ceremonies involving food. Its portability is an advantage in transitions from familiar to unfamiliar or sacred to profane contexts or in situations of changing visibility. Thus pottery may be employed in public or private contexts: it may be highly visible or it may be virtually unnoticed. Its household display functions may be simply for adornment, testifying to the skill of the potter (Balfet 1965, 163); in more public contexts of use the messages may or may not change.

Several studies of the potential message functions of pottery are instructive. An analysis of 178 vessels from five Shipibo-Conibo (Peru) settlements revealed that vessels used in public, especially on festive occasions, exhibited relatively high stylistic diversity, while those used within household compounds exhibited low diversity in their border designs (DeBoer and Moore 1982). The rim decoration on public vessels thus did not seem to symbolize compound identity, but rather was a message of ostentatious display. This did not match the expectation that clear stylistic messages would be sent across boundaries by means of greater consistency (less diversity) in publicly used vessels. The authors note that the larger and more visible designs on the bodies of vessels may behave differently and fulfill expectations; the alternative is that rim designs are not intended to convey messages in such feast encounters (see Braun 1985 for an example of measurement of stylistic diversity relating more directly to the interaction hypothesis).

Less ambiguous is the symbolic information carried by pottery decoration in specific contexts of use among the Azande of southern Sudan (Braithwaite 1982). In Azande society there is a pronounced separation, social and physical, between male and female activities. Pottery is made by men but owned and used by women, who cook food and serve it to men. These food transactions are significant occasions in which the social order is transcended or violated: boundaries between opposed male and female categories must be publicly crossed. The decoration on vessels used in this context acts as a ritual marker or message acknowledging the symbolic ambiguity and concern engendered by this breach of the accepted social order. Men's drinking cups, on the other hand, which do not publicly pass between men's and women's hands, are left undecorated. So too are the chief's eating utensils, because the chief eats alone—an unsettling observation in view of archaeologists' frequent assumptions concerning decoration and social status. The decoration on non-pottery items is increasing among the Azande (Braithwaite 1982, 87), and this may be an expression of concern over the gradual erosion of the traditional cultural order, which strictly opposes men and women and young and old.

A final example comes from a community in Puebla, Mexico, where locally made and decorated domestic pottery is either red, black, or black on red. Black pots are valued and particularly associated with ceremonies honoring the dead, except that pottery for dead children is quite different. Although made by the same potters who make ordinary domestic wares, the miniature vessels for children are decorated by outsiders who come into the community once a year to paint the pots with pink and blue flowers (Kaplan and Levine 1981, 878). Just as children are outside the boundaries of the fully adult world, so too is the pottery associated with them outside traditional decorative systems, and indeed the painting is done by individuals from outside the physical boundaries of the community.

Within these contexts, then, analysis of stylistic behavior of pottery within the unidimensional view of the interaction hypothesis can be seen as painfully simplistic. It has already been noted that distinct motifs and elements may be associated with specific vessel forms used in different activities. In addition, it is entirely possible that in some societies pottery decoration may transmit important messages while in others it does not, just as some societies have certain elite pottery items with restricted distribution while other societies show no clear evidence of prestige styles. In other words, pottery may symbolize affiliation and maintain boundaries, but it also may not. Thus that identical pottery styles are produced in the three contiguous Hopi and Hopi-Tewa Pueblo communities (Stanislawski 1978) suggests that pottery is not important in symbolizing group identity in this area; such affiliations and boundaries are demarcated through other kinds of behavior. The same may hold true for the Shipibo-Conibo rim designs (DeBoer and Moore 1982).

The role of variability or diversity within decorative styles in these situations has barely begun to be studied, but Hardin (1984, 592–600) has suggested four barriers to precise replication of designs (i.e., sources of decorative variability). These barriers include communication differentials (lack of visual access), decoding differentials (idiosyncratic analysis of design), stylistic screens (modification and reinterpretation), and style boundaries (change through time).

The variable roles of information transfer give rise to additional problems in interpreting social interaction as measured by the stability or borrowing of motifs and symmetry patterns. Certain aspects of style—colors, structures, symmetry relations—may be more or less involved in the message and information exchange functions and therefore more or less likely to alter in differing circumstances of interaction between pottery producers.

8.4   Summary: Additional Considerations and Problems

Pottery styles and stylistic analyses are complex, and there are no simple ways to interpret them. Several problems have been mentioned above in connection with the various approaches to stylistic analysis, and efforts have recently been made to reconcile the interaction and information exchange theories (Hill 1985), but it is worthwhile to isolate these and others for further discussion. In general, the difficulties with stylistic analysis of pottery fall into two areas: problems of method and problems of interpretation.

8.4.1   Problems of Method

Apart from objections to the interaction hypothesis itself, many critiques have challenged the validity of the procedures used in stylistic studies. Some of these focus on design element analysis and the difficulty of distinguishing elements from motifs. One solution to this problem has been to use design attributes, while another is to use design symmetry or structure. All these alternatives may be equally difficult to apply to archaeological pottery, however, for reasons of sample size, fragmentation, and provenience. Archaeological pottery typically exists only as fragments; whole vessels (e.g., from burials) are readily found in museums, often in sizable collections, but these may lack precise provenience information, thereby weakening the inferences to be drawn from them. In addition, the criteria applied in selecting objects for museum collections may result in a distorted sample of pottery shape and size (sec. 15.1.1).

The assumptions that accompany stylistic analysis are another source of methodological problems. Some of these are based on statistical models and tests applied to the data and usually involve questions of sample size, randomness, independence, and level of measurement. These include the regression and factor analyses applied to some of the design element analyses (Plog 1978, 169–77), as well as the use of diversity indexes in studies of style and production (Rice 1984a). Another category of methodological assumptions concerns the formation of the archaeological record, such as the use and discard of pottery. Many processes alter the condition of an activity area between ancient times and archaeological excavation (Schiffer 1976) and must be taken into account in quantitative assessments of stylistic exchange and interaction.

Ethnographic and ethnoarchaeological studies have long been at the forefront of stylistic analyses of pottery and have led to closer examination of many of the assumptions archaeologists make. One such questionable assumption, with immediate repercussions for the interaction hypothesis, concerns learning patterns: ethnoarchaeological studies in the Southwest reveal that patterns of learning and design transmission (Stanislawski 1978; Stanislawski and Stanislawski 1978) are more complex than archaeologists originally expected.

Another problem relates to the fact that archaeologists often concentrate on vessel rim and lip variations as sensitive indicators of individual or group-specific styles. The data on rims are equivocal, however (see also Froese 1985; Miller 1985, 42–44, 149). Work in Thailand (Solheim 1984, 98–100) and among the Papago in the American Southwest (Fontana et al. 1962, 65) suggests that rim details receive little conscious or systematic attention from potters, whereas in Deir el-Gharbi and Ballâs, Egypt, there was considerable consistency in the rims on wheel-thrown jars produced by individual potters (Lacovara 1985, 58; Nicholson and Patterson 1985a, 58, 1985b, 234). Sometimes rim variations are efforts to cater to consumer preferences (Kaplan and Levine 1981, 880; Birmingham 1975, 382).

8.4.2   Problems of Interpretation

Problems of interpretation in stylistic analysis of pottery largely spring from an incomplete understanding of the nature of styles in general. These are magnified exponentially in prehistoric contexts by the difficulty of inferring nonmaterial culture—social relations and concepts of meaning—from material remains. Included are such interrelated matters as how styles are produced, how they are transmitted, and how they change.

Questions concerning how styles are produced subsume patterns of learning as well as distinctions between individual and group styles. Archaeologically, it is difficult if not impossible to discern the products of individual artists of exceptional creativity among the general range of variability within an assemblage (see contributions in Hill and Gunn 1977). On the assemblage level itself, anthropologists and archaeologists have until recently had great difficulty escaping the normative view of culture, which sees culture as a collection of ideas and behaviors that are equally shared or participated in by members of a given society. The greater attention to variability within particular styles that has emerged in the literature points to several new directions in analysis and interpretation. These include efforts to identify individual artisans by idiosyncratic features of execution and attempts to differentiate the styles of communities by characteristic features of layout and composition.

There are no definite answers about the rates at which styles change, for this is likely to vary with period and area. On a particularistic level, among the factors involved in stylistic transmission and change are the size of the social networks involved and the intensity of the artistic communication between practitioners (see Friedrich 1970, 342; Lathrap 1983, 39); it has also been suggested that designs have different adaptive significance and that the more strongly adaptive the design the more slowly it will change (Graves 1981, 307–8). Stylistic change is also likely to fluctuate and suffer lags as a consequence of social and geographic distance. Its reconstruction from the archaeological record will be hindered if different kinds of decoration characterize different sizes of pots and if these are replaced at different rates, perhaps reflecting the age of the potters (Graves 1985; Linares de Sapir 1969, 9; see also sec. 9.3.1).

Structurally, a broader look at stylistic change through time in medieval Nubia (Adams 1979) called attention to the lack of clear stylistic change in pottery produced and used during periods of dramatic cultural change. This is a sobering observation in light of traditional archaeological methods that periodize sites and regions according to disjunctions in ceramic styles and forms. A similar view of the nature of change in some variables of pottery technology, form, and style (Rice 1984b) is that, at least in the Maya area, technology and form adhere to a "sine wave model" of change through time, whereas stylistic or decorative variables are less predictable.

The reasons for this unpredictable behavior are also difficult to understand but clearly relate to the fact that styles are imbued with content and meaning. Decorative elements and motifs and their arrangements have a significance beyond their chemical compositions or the angles and curves they define. Thus it is important to distinguish whether styles and motifs are changing or expanding in popularity as opposed to the movement of actual pots bearing the decoration. The one involves a spread of ideas and symbols (which may or may not involve the simultaneous diffusion of associated meanings), while the other may be simply a consequence of economic exchange. Part of the meaning of decoration is iconographic: specific motifs are painted or incised on pottery because they represent deities or are symbols of concepts and beliefs widely recognized in the society (e.g., fig. 1.10) and because they may relate to the specific uses of the vessels. Other interpretations of the meaning of decoration are directed outward socially rather than iconographically, calling attention to how decoration sends messages about group affiliation. These several levels of meaning and interpretation give rise to a continuum of complexity in decorative styles and interpretations; more complex styles can send more messages and be interpreted on more levels (see Van Esterik 1979).

In discussing meaning, however, it is important to bear in mind the caution suggested in ethnoarchaeological studies of decoration about the difference between what informants say they do and what they actually do. Informants may ascribe a particular meaning to an element or motif or acknowledge a significant role of a particular color or structure or number in their belief system, but this admission does not ensure an unvarying association in the decorative system. Bunzel (1972, 20–23), for example, notes that among the Zuñi the number four is prominent in literary and ceremonial traditions, and potters expressed a preference for four designs on their painted vessels. Nonetheless, in actual execution three seemed to be the most popular number of repetitions of a design (or divisions of the design space). In pottery decoration as in other aspects of culture, there may be wide disparities between the ideal and the reality of behavior.

Ultimately, these uncertainties and unresolved questions reflect the fact that style is not well defined or understood, for pottery or any other medium. The relation between stylistic attributes (elements, motifs, symmetry, structure) of pottery decoration and other behavioral or social structural variables merits considerably more ethnographic and archaeological attention.

8.5   References

Adams 1979
Allen and Richardson 1971
Arnold 1983, 1984
Balfet 1965
Bankes 1980
Birmingham 1975
Brainerd 1942
Braithwaite 1982
Braun 1985
Broyles 1968
Buerger and Lukesh 1937
Bunzel 1972
Coe 1978
Conkey 1978
Cooke 1985
Cronin 1962
Crossland and Posnansky 1978
DeBoer and Moore 1982
Deetz 1965
Douglas 1966

Dunnell 1978
Englebrecht 1978
Fischer 1961
Fontana et al. 1962
Freeman 1962
Freeman and Brown 1964
Friedrich 1970
Froese 1985
Graves 1981, 1985
Hardin 1977, 1983, 1984
Hayden and Cannon 1984
Hill 1970, 1977, 1985
Hill and Gunn 1977
Hodder 1977, 1979b, 1981, 1982
Hole 1984
Holm 1982
Irwin 1974
Jernigan 1986
Johnson 1973
Kaplan and Levine 1981

Lacovara 1985
Lathrap 1973, 1983
LeBlanc and Watson 1973
Lechtman 1977
Leroi-Gourhan 1968
Linares de Sapir 1969
Longacre 1964, 1970
Marriott 1948
Mera 1937
Miller 1985
Muller, J. 1977
Munn 1966
Nicholson and Patterson 1985a,b
Plog 1976, 1978, 1980, 1982
Proulx 1968
Pyne 1976
Redman 1977, 1978a
Reina 1963
Rice 1984a, b
Roe 1980
Sackett 1977
Sahlins 1976
Saunders 1986

Schapiro 1953
Schiffer 1976
Shepard 1948b, 1976
Shubnikov and Koptsik 1974
Silver 1979
Solheim 1984
Stanislawski 1978
Stanislawski and Stanislawski 1978
Thompson 1969
Tuggle 1970
Van Esterik 1979
Washburn 1977, 1978, 1983
Washburn and Ahlstrom 1982
Washburn and Matson 1985
Watson 1977
Weissner 1984
Whallon 1968
Willey and Phillips 1958
Willey and Sabloff 1980
Wobst 1977
Wolfe 1969
Zaslow 1977, 1981
Zaslow and Dittert 1976

9 Special Topics in Archaeological, Ethnoarchaeological, and Ethnographic Pottery Studies

Pottery vessels primarily serve as containers for storage, processing, and transfer (see chap. 7), but they also constitute an exceedingly useful data base for archaeologists, who use sherds to date sites, trace trade patterns, understand social and economic relationships, and so forth. Most of these interpretations, which contribute significant insights into prehistoric culture processes, are based on ethnographic and ethnoarchaeological observations concerning pottery manufacture, use, and distribution among present-day peoples. The kinds, quantities, sizes, and appearance of vessels in use in individual houses and communities—and by extension at archaeological sites— are related to a complex set of considerations that extend beyond simple factors of form and function. This chapter addresses some more specialized methodological and interpretive concerns relating to how pottery helps us understand ancient people and cultures. Three important issues are treated: pottery classification, pottery quantification, and the composition of ceramic assemblages and processes of archaeological record (site) formation.

9.1 Pottery Classification

Phrased most simply, classification is the grouping of similar entities. Not only is it fundamental to all scientific disciplines, it lies at the core of human conceptualization of the real world by identifying, organizing, and naming different kinds of things: for example, distinguishing between members of the categories human, dog, tree, and stone. The object of a classification is to create groups whose members are very similar (high within-group homogeneity) while the groups themselves are very dissimilar (low between-group homogeneity). The principle is that the similarity of entities within groups does not occur by chance but reflects something inherently significant in their nature. In the case of pottery, groups are usually based on certain common features of material, technique, and style, and their significance is interpreted culturally.

Different kinds of groupings—which also represent different levels of classification—may be distinguished. Technically, for example, the process of classification is somewhat different in creating groups for a new and previously unclassified set of materials (an activity called categorization) as opposed to assigning individual objects to established classes (a process of identification) previously defined by certain criteria or properties of their members.

The characteristics of the entities to be classified or identified are usually called attributes. An attribute is a property, characteristic, feature, or variable of an entity; in the case of pottery, attributes that are commonly of interest include color, thickness, inclusions, hardness, form, and so on. An attribute state is usually an artifact's specific value or score on a particular attribute; for example, the states or values of the attribute "color" may be red, black, white, or brown, and values for the attribute "hardness" may be 1.5, 4.0, 6.5. (The terms attribute and attribute state are sometimes employed interchangeably, however, with attribute occasionally referring to the state or value of a particular variable; see Doran and Hodson (1975, 99.)

In classifying pottery, anthropologists and archaeologists commonly approach their subject matter from two directions. Devised (or formal or scientific) classification has a long history, while ethnotaxonomic or folk classification is only now beginning to receive attention. There is some overlap among the concepts and objectives of these two positions, however, so they are not mutually exclusive.

9.1.1 Devised Classifications

The most typical approach to archaeological data is devised, formal, or scientific classifications, which are created by the analyst. Although many schemes have been developed for grouping similar sites, artifacts, and cultures in conjunction with a variety of archaeological objectives, these activities are comprehended by the more general purposes of classifications within all scientific disciplines. Formal classifications structure the domains of inquiry of scientific disciplines by furnishing a system for describing and naming the objects of study within a science; fostering communication within a science through shared terminology and nomenclature; permitting predictions about the relation of the classified items to other objects studied within the science; and serving as extensions of and empirical justification for concepts used within the body of theory of that science (Blashfield and Draguns 1976, 574). Classification is not the final goal of any science; it is a basic procedure by which a discipline and its data are structured. Within archaeology, its long-standing importance is reflected in the fact that major stages in the history of archaeology in the Americas, stages spanning approximately one hundred years, have been termed the classificatory-descriptive and classificatory-historical periods (Willey and Sabloff 1980, 34–180) because of the emphasis on these operations for describing and organizing archaeological data.

The object of most classificatory operations in archaeology is to create types, and variations in the definition of a type arise from different positions on how they are created (see Hill and Evans 1972; Cowgill 1982). According to one position, types consist of (and are based on) attributes of artifacts: thus types may be simply defined as nonrandom attribute clusters (Spaulding 1953b, 1982). An alternative view sees types as clusters of items (Hodson 1982) and defines a type as a group or class of items that is internally cohesive and can be separated from other groups by one or more discontinuities in attribute states (Whallon and Brown 1982, xvii). This object-based position is not totally opposed to the attribute-based definition, however, because types still depend on several attributes (and hence indirectly on their associations) rather than on a single attribute. Attributes may be (and often are) employed hierarchically rather than simultaneously to create types within a collection (see Whallon 1972).

Different types with different meanings arise from the particular attributes that determine the group divisions. Although it is often claimed that to be valid classifications should account for all attributes, this is patently impossible; no matter how many attributes are considered in any classification system, the number that theoretically exist is infinite (see Hill and Evans 1972, 250–51). Selecting different kinds of attributes in constructing a classification leads to different kinds of types—for example, morphological, historical-index, functional, and cultural (Steward 1954).

Attributes themselves have often been classified by their role or utility in a devised classification. For example, attributes of archaeological pottery may be described as intrinsic, including an object's composition, shape, and decoration, or extrinsic, such as its date, provenience, and function as assigned by the archaeologist (Gardin 1980, 65–68). Attributes can also be ranked as key, essential, and inessential variables (Clarke 1968, 71) according to their significance and utility within a particular devised classification scheme.

Groups, classes, and types are sometimes distinguished at different stages of classification (see Dunnell 1971). A group consists of actual objects, such as potsherds, and exists in the phenomenological or empirical realm. Classes and types, however, represent verbal models or descriptions of objects and are ideational. A class may be further described as a "generic term referring to any division of materials into groupings based on similarities and differences" and may be based on single attributes, whereas a type is a formal conceptual (or abstract) unit based on "a consistent patterning of attributes of the materials" (Hill and Evans 1972, 233). This differentiation between the empirical (group) and the conceptual (class and type) is highlighted by a distinction between classification and typology: "A classification is no more than a set (or sets) of empirical groupings established for convenience. A typology, however, is a theoretically oriented classification that is directed toward the solution of some problem or problems" (Kluckhohn 1960, cited in Gifford 1960, 346; see also Gardin 1980, 63).

One can distinguish different kinds of classifications by noting, for example, whether the criteria for describing classes are equivalent and unordered, nonequivalent and ordered, or hierarchical (fig. 9.1; see Dunnell 1971, 70). In the ideational realm, creating equivalent units is sometimes called paradigmatic classification. An example in pottery analysis is categorizing vessels by certain features such as form: bowl, jar, plate, and cup are equiva-

Figure 9.1 Model of different methods for ordering objects and events by classification versus grouping procedures. After Dunnell 1971, fig. 9.

		FIELD	
		PHENOMENOLOGICAL (GROUPING)	IDEATIONAL (CLASSIFICATION)
UNIT RELATIONSHIPS	EQUIVALENT	Statistical clusters	Paradigmatic classification
	HIERARCHICAL	Numerical taxonomy	Taxonomic classification

lent, unordered dimensions (attribute states) of form, and the procedure yields a morphological type. An ordered or hierarchical structure of categories, on the other hand, is the basis for taxonomic classification, which specifies inclusion relations and is exemplified in pottery studies by the type-variety system (sec. 9.1.3.1). Taxonomic classification is sometimes more broadly defined simply as creating types (Rouse 1960, 315–17), as opposed to analytic classification, which analyzes attributes to isolate and describe modes (Rouse 1960, 313–15).

Modes are certain attributes the analyst judges to reflect communitywide standards for manufacturing and using the ancient artifacts. As defined by Rouse (1960, 313; see also Taylor 1948, 129–30), a mode is "any standard, concept, or custom which governs the behavior of artisans of a community, which they hand down from generation to generation." Not all attributes of the artifacts represent modes as originally defined, however; for example, attributes pertaining to the chemical or mineralogical composition of the raw material would not be considered modes. Two types of modes have been discerned, both inherent in the data: conceptual modes relate to the style or form of the object, such as red slips or tripodal supports, while procedural modes relate to manufacture and include, for example, particular kinds of temper or the use of molds or coiling techniques (see Rouse 1960, 315). Modes represent efforts to achieve some isomorphism between categories of devised classifications and those of the ancient makers and users of the pottery—that is, to replicate ancient folk classifications.

9.1.2   Folk Classifications

Folk classifications group and name entities according to native, as opposed to scientific, categories. They may use a variety of characteristics, singly or in combination, and it is not always easy to penetrate their structure, as seen in the following ancient Chinese classification of animals:

> Animals are divided into (a) those that belong to the Emperor, (b) embalmed ones, (c) those that are trained, (d) suckling pigs, (e) mermaids, (f) fabulous ones, (g) stray dogs, (h) those that are included in this classification, (i) those that tremble as if they were mad, (j) innumerable ones, (k) those drawn with a very fine camel's hair

brush, (l) others, (m) those that have just broken a flower vase, and (n) those that resemble flies from a distance. (Borges, *Other Inquisitions: 1937–1952*, quoted in Aldenderfer and Blashfield 1984, 7)

Native classifications for pottery vessels, while not as complex as the Chinese animal classification, have long been carefully recorded as a traditional point of ethnographic research into pottery manufacture. It is instructive to look at these classifications, because archaeologists have frequently aspired to replicate folk categories.

In surveying the native terms for pottery vessels gathered by researchers working in pottery-making societies, one sees that the most striking cross-cultural feature is that terms are almost invariably based on projected use. That is, rather than being categorized by attributes traditionally deemed significant by archaeologists, such as surface treatment, color, paste composition, or decoration, pots are named primarily for general functions such as cooking, storage, or serving. These classes of vessels are commonly given particularistic modifiers referring to the size of the pot or its intended contents. The Tarahumara of Mexico, for example, call all pots *sekori* and distinguish three functional classes: pots to eat from, pots for parching corn, and small pots (called *sekori ranara*, the modifier being a term usually used to refer to one's children) (Pastron 1974, 103). At Manumanu, Papua New Guinea, vessels are given four names: *uro* or cooking pots, *hodu* or water vessels, *nau* or dishes, and *tohe* or sago storage vessels (Groves 1960, 10).

As these relatively simple classifications suggest, vessel names often combine several dimensions simultaneously: size, shape, specific functions, and contents. Differently named sizes of vessels often have very different functions (e.g., Linares de Sapir, 1969, 8). Among the Fulani in Cameroon, for example, 84% of the classified pots in the households studied were "jars with short necks and everted rims . . . [that] come in five named sizes": (in decreasing order) *loonde* or *ngiiramwal, fayande gaari* (named for sorghum), *defruunde, hakoore* (named for a sauce), and a miniature *julduude* or ablution jar (David and Hennig 1972, 8–12). Among the Kalinga in the Philippines, rice cooking vessels and vegetable/meat cooking vessels are differentiated lexically, although some of the size terms overlap; in other aspects of the folk classification there is clear differentiation of vessel types and names by both size and contents (table 9.1).

The Shipibo-Conibo of Peru, in contrast, name vessels by general shape

Table 9.1 Size-Function Terms for Kalinga Vessels

Use	General Term	Size	
		Small	Large
Rice cooking	Ittoyom	Oggatit	Lallangan
Vegetable/meat cooking	Oppaya	Oggatit	Lallangan (oggan)
Water jar	Immosso	Im-immosso	
Water basin	Pannogan		
Wine jar		Volnay	Amuto
Pot cover	Su-kong		Chong-chong

Source: After Longacre 1981, 53.

categories, adding modifiers to denote size subsets, and though different sizes have different functions there seems to be little specificity in naming as to their intended contents. Cooking pots or ollas are called *kënti* and are distinguished by size as *ani* (large, used for beer), *anitami* (medium, used for meals), and *vacu* (small, for medicines). Similarly, jars (*chomo*) and beer mugs (*kënpo*) come in three sizes, but food bowls (*këncha*) and *shrania* exhibit less standardized size ranges (DeBoer and Lathrap 1979, 105–10).

Many investigators who have elicited vessel terminology express some dismay that such categories are so little evident to (or replicable by) outsiders. The attributes that anthropologists and archaeologists commonly focus on— overall shape, rim and lip variations, base, decoration—may or may not co-vary significantly in native classifications (see, e.g., Weigand 1969, 13). For example, in Kathmandu a great deal of variation exists both within and between classes:

> in terms of actual measurement the three classes [of liquid storage jars] could overlap quite considerably whereupon I was told that it was a combination of shape and size; when I pressed further in attempting to identify the precise shape variations concerned, i.e., flat or round base, rim forms, nothing could be selected as a permanent and identifying shape characteristic of one or another. However, the fact remains that all agreed instantly on names for any given pot. (Birmingham 1975, 384)

Potters in Kathmandu claimed that many of the minor variations of rim form and decoration were efforts to cater to customers' preferences (Birmingham 1975, 382).

On a more optimistic note, precise measurements or ratios of vessel sizes and proportions may sometimes correlate with shape classifications, and this augurs well for traditional archaeological practice. Kalinga rice cooking pots can be distinguished from vegetable and meat cooking pots, for example, by a relatively more restricted aperture, steeper rim angles, and a lower ratio of aperture to height (Longacre 1981, 54).

Given the relative flexibility of criteria for ethnographic vessel terminology—based chiefly on size, shape, and contents or use—it is perhaps not surprising that when any of these features change the vessel names may change too. The names, in other words, are situation specific; in the terminology of devised classifications, they are phenomenological, empirical, and pragmatic group identifiers based on use rather than ideational, conceptual, or analytical classes based on abstract similarity relations. For example, in Papua New Guinea, cooking pots (*uro*) and water vessels (*tohe*) are given different names after the rims are accidentally broken off (Groves 1960, 14n); among the Kalinga, if a rice or meat/vegetable cooking pot becomes worn out or cracked and is transferred to use in toasting, it ceases to be an *ittoyom* or an *oppaya* and instead is called a *linga*. Elsewhere, if the contents or use of an intact vessel varies, so does the name: the large ollalike Huichol pot called a *šáalei*[h] is primarily used for brewing corn beer for ceremonial occasions, but if it is used for other purposes it may sometimes by referred to as a *kašuhéla*[h] (=cazuela; a term often interchangeable with *šáalei*[h]), whereas if it is used for water storage it becomes a *ya'é*, a water-storage vessel (Weigand 1969, 16,

22). Among the Fulani, the largest storage vessel is called *loonde* when it is used for water storage in a compound courtyard and *ngiiramwal* when it is used for dry storage within the hut (David and Hennig 1972, 8).

Although records of society-specific names for pottery vessels have traditionally been of ethnographic interest, intensive studies of taxonomic systems of pottery have been rather rare. Attention to native terms and folk classifications is part of ethnotaxonomy, a major focus of the relatively recent field of inquiry sometimes called ethnoscience. Ethnoscience addresses the structuring of cognitive domains—the boundaries and terms used by some group of people in organizing their surroundings (see Ellen 1979). The primary domains explored from ethnoscientific perspectives have included botanical and faunal classes, disease categories, and color systems (for reviews see Sturtevant 1964; Werner 1972).

Two recent studies in pottery ethnotaxonomy examined the folk classification of vessels in highland Mexico from different perspectives. Their findings are important for understanding the nature of pottery classification among traditional societies, and the implications of these classifications are relevant to certain objectives of archaeological taxonomy (see also Miller 1985).

The problem addressed in one study (Kempton 1981) is that of defining boundaries or disjunctions between categories based on continuous variation. A model of "prototypes and graded extensions" is proposed for certain categories of material such as pottery, where dimensions of variability are not as highly structured by biological, genetic, or social factors as are, for example, kinship, plant, and animal domains. This model holds that individuals identify categories of things both by means of prototypes, which can be considered typical or ideal examples of a particular object, such as a jar, and by extending the concept to other objects that are not ideal or prototype jars but still are "basically" jars (as opposed to bowls, for example). Graded extensions acknowledge that within the attributes or dimensions by which a prototype is recognized, inevitable variations broaden the category beyond the ideal.

This model was applied in Tlaxcala, Mexico, by eliciting classifications of drawings of variable pottery shapes (fig. 9.2). Although the informants' verbal definitions of vessel categories typically mentioned specific functions and the presence or absence of certain features (such as handles), their gestures and drawings stressed shape, particularly width-to-height ratio (or "fatness") and neck position (Kempton 1981, 36, 39–40).

Vessel definitions (both prototypes and extensions of definitions) varied with the age, sex, occupation, and socioeconomic status of the informant. For example, although males and females had generally the same prototypes, they extended these definitions beyond the ideal in different ways. Males gave more weight (less extension) to shape, while females gave more weight to attachments such as handles, which are important functionally (Kempton 1981, 127). Similarly, although one might intuitively hypothesize that potters themselves would have more names for vessel categories or use more restricted category definitions, this did not appear to be so. Instead, like female informants, they gave more weight to function and attachments and less to overall shape in classifying the vessel drawings (Kempton 1981, 123, 138).

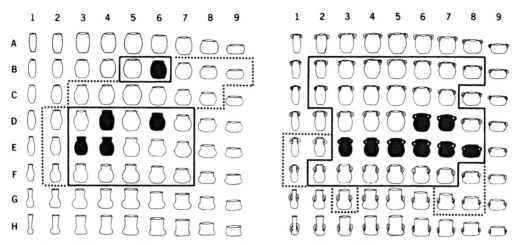

Figure 9.2   "Olla" as a vessel shape category identified by a young Mexican woman. Focal category members are solid colored; simple members are enclosed by a solid line; peripheral members are enclosed by a dotted line. After Kempton 1981, fig. 3.3.

Figure 9.3   Multidimensional scaling plot of ninety-four features of twenty-five black-on-red glazed pottery types from Puebla, Mexico. The types are identified by number, and the groups obtained by cluster analysis are circled. The two major dimensions of scaling are open/closed forms (axis I) and multiple/nonmultiple handles (see text). After Kaplan and Levine 1981, fig. 3.

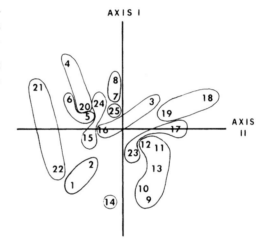

Another study of folk classifications of pottery was based on both features (attributes) and type names elicited from eighty-five potters and assistants in Puebla, Mexico (Kaplan and Levine 1981). Cluster analysis and multidimensional scaling were used in interpreting the results, revealing the structure of the taxonomy both by analogy with hierarchical devised classifications and by creating a "cognitive map" of the features organizing cultural perceptions of the pottery. The nonmetric multidimensional scaling procedure was based on the relative similarities of the twenty-five identified categories or types of pots in this study. The similarity of the types is represented by their positions on a two-dimensional scaling plot, whose dimensions are interpretable in terms of known cultural categories that structure thinking and behavior in the society.

In the scaling plot of the Puebla pottery (fig. 9.3), the two primary features that differentiated the types are axis I, restrictedness or nonrestrictedness of the form, and axis II, the presence of multiple or nonmultiple (one or none) handles (Kaplan and Levine 1981, 876), findings that closely parallel those cited above. The first axis, differentiating open and closed forms, parallels several other dichotomies or oppositions within the pottery and in the culture itself. For example, the types on the right side of the plot are associated with open forms; with red colors, black-on-red designs, or no decoration; and with life, daytime, heat, and femaleness. The left side of the diagram is associated with closed forms, black colors or black-on-red decoration, and death, night, cold, and maleness.

9.1.3   Issues in Archaeological Pottery Classification

9.1.3.1   DESCRIPTIVE AND CHRONOLOGICAL SYSTEMATICS

The history of classification schemes in American archaeology illuminates some of the broader issues and controversies surrounding the use of formal or devised classifications in the discipline and efforts to relate them to actual or hypothetical native systems. Although stylistic descriptions and comparisons of pottery were important during the late nineteenth and early twentieth centuries, fairly elaborate schemes of pottery classification began to be developed for descriptive or chronological-comparative purposes in the 1920s and 1930s in the Southwestern United States. The formal procedures for identifying, describing, and naming types elucidated during this period established the foundation for many of the modern concepts concerning pottery typology.

One of the first statements of what constitutes a type was offered by the Pecos (New Mexico) Conference in 1927: types were defined as "the totality of characteristics which make a given ceramic group different from all others" (Kidder 1931, 21–22), a position essentially aligned with what is now known as the attribute-cluster position. This conference also developed the binomial system for naming pottery types (Kidder 1927, 490), analogous to the biological system of binomial nomenclature, whereby type names combine a geographical place (e.g., Tularosa or Jeddito) with a technically descriptive term referring to surface treatment or color (black-on-white, polychrome, plain, etc.). An unfortunate by-product of this procedure was the tendency to draw implicit analogies between the spread of pottery traits through time and space and biological reproductive patterns, for example, by identifying "ancestral types."

Perhaps the most elaborate and widely used formal scheme for archaeological pottery classification is the type-variety system, developed in North America in the late 1950s primarily as a systematic framework for creating, describing, and naming widely comparable historical-index classificatory units. The system is an outgrowth of three articles describing concepts and methods: the first (Wheat, Gifford, and Wasley 1958) describing the ceramic variety as a unit in the Southwest; a later transference of this system to the eastern United States, together with elaboration of the type concept, which was composed of a number of related varieties (Phillips 1958); and finally, further synthesis of the type-variety concept and sorting and naming procedures as applied to Maya pottery (Smith, Willey, and Gifford 1960; Gifford 1960).

The type-variety system is a hierarchical system of classification in which varieties are the smallest unit recognized and are subsumed within types: for example, an incised type may have a groove-incised and a fine-incised variety. One or more types may be subsumed within a ceramic group (cf. Colton 1953), which is usually formed on the basis of similar surface treatments—for example, a red-slipped ceramic group—and may include a number of different decorative types, such as incised, appliquéd, and polychrome painted, within red-slipped wares.

Subsequent elaborations of the type-variety approach and applications to Maya pottery (Willey, Culbert, and Adams 1967; Gifford 1976) led to development of higher, more inclusive levels in this taxonomic hierarchy and a concern with broader questions of integration and interpretation (see sec. 9.1.3.4).

9.1.3.2 Are Types "Real" or "Artificial"?

In the late 1940s and early 1950s, a series of disputes erupted in the field of archaeological classification concerning whether types are inherent in the data and merely recognized by analysts or whether they are artificial units imposed on the data. A key publication was Ford's (1953) "Measurements of Some Prehistoric Design Developments in the Southeastern States," which argued that pottery types were analytical constructs created by the archaeologist as tools for chronology building and, more important, for achieving an understanding of culture change. The position had actually been established somewhat earlier (Ford 1938), and indeed a classic statement of this creationist view had been made in 1946, some years before the Ford monograph, by J. O. Brew, who argued that

> We must classify our material in all ways that will produce for us useful information. . . . We need more rather than fewer classifications, different classifications, always new classifications, to meet new needs. We must not be satisfied with a single classification of a group of artifacts or of a cultural development, for that way lies dogma and defeat. (Brew 1946, 65)

The position that archaeologists' types were created analytical constructs was challenged implicitly in a review of Ford's monograph (Spaulding 1953a), but the manifesto of Spaulding's opposing stand was published separately as "Statistical Techniques for the Discovery of Artifact Types" (Spaulding 1953b). Types are said to be attribute associations inherent in a data set that archaeologists can discover through statistical correlation techniques. This view of types as real and inherent in the data had been articulated earlier in one form or another by several scholars (e.g., Taylor 1948, 130; Krieger 1944) and continued to be popular with archaeologists in subsequent decades, particularly as quantitative techniques gained emphasis in archaeology in the 1960s.

A key interpretation of types based on the discovery position is that because types are thought to be culturally and historically real, they therefore reflect the ideas and values of the ancient people who made and used the artifacts: "Each type should approximate as closely as possible that combination of mechanical and aesthetic executions which formed a definite structural pattern in the minds of a number of workers, who attained this pattern with varying degrees of success and interpretation" (Krieger 1944, 278). In other words, archaeologists' types should reproduce folk classifications and represent the artisan's "mental template" for creating the artifact. A mental template is "the idea . . . from which the craftsman makes the object. The form of the artifact is a close approximation of this template, and variations in a group of similar objects reflect variations in the ideas which produce them" (Deetz 1967, 45–46; but see Kempton 1981 and sec. 9.1.2).

The importance of this issue in typological debates led to considerable efforts to cloak devised (artificial) classifications in folk clothing. For example, the type-variety system was extended beyond its original chronological-comparative goals by developing normative or ethnosemantic interpretations of the units in conformance with the desire to view types as culturally real (e.g., Sabloff and Smith 1972). The ceramic variety was held to reflect

> minor ceramic differences [which] were the result of work produced within the confines of relatively small social groups or by individual potters who indulged preferences as to the locale where temper or clay must be gathered or who were able to give vent to artistic flairs and so on. . . . Varieties are apt to reflect "individual and small social group variation" . . . while the type portrays a combination of a number of pottery traits that were acceptable not only to the potter but to most others adhering to a given culture pattern. (Gifford 1960, 343)

In addition, it was advocated that the type-variety system of taxonomic classification be combined with modal analysis (analytical classification) for added interpretive power in culturally real terms (e.g., Sabloff and Smith 1969).

It was observed belatedly that the question whether types are real or artificial is poorly phrased (Hill and Evans 1972, 261). Any artifact class formed by associating two or more attributes—whether these associations are determined statistically or by eyeball sorting—can be considered to represent patterned behavior on the part of prehistoric peoples. But this patterning may or may not correspond to explicitly held notions (i.e., mental templates) concerning the artifacts. In addition, as has been seen, folk classifications are much too fluid and context based to be accommodated within the constraints of archaeological data recovery and inference systems. Besides these issues, it is also relevant to ask how the archaeologist can verify whether the devised categories correspond to native classes.

Attribute associations are empirically real, discoverable, and verifiable, and this is important whether types are considered to be clusters of attributes or clusters of objects. The more significant issue concerns the archaeologist's choice of the attributes used to seek associations. Because it is impossible to consider all attributes of any entity, some selection has to be made, and it is that choice that governs the nature of the resultant classes. Furthermore, because the types formed are an artifact of the attribute selection process, it is pointless to argue whether a single classification is the best or only one for a particular data set. Attributes are selected either because they pertain to a particular problem or based on some consensus concerning their role within a given classificatory scheme (e.g., the type-variety system). Although for certain purposes it may be desirable to achieve some correspondence between devised and folk classifications of archaeological pottery, this is not the only criterion for the utility of a classificatory system.

9.1.3.3 STATISTICAL APPROACHES TO CLASSIFICATION

Taking their cue from Spaulding's (1953b) work, archaeologists gradually began to investigate quantitative approaches for bringing order out of their data. Many factors were responsible for this interest. The objectivity of statistical methods and the growing availability of computers at archaeological research stations enhanced the appeal of these techniques. In addition, the increasingly rigorous methodological focus of archaeology as a whole, plus the attention to a much wider range of attributes in artifact collections as classifications began to be expected to do more than date sites, contributed to a need for more sophisticated systems for investigating the structure of such complex data sets.

Although Spaulding's work emphasized that types were discovered by correlating attributes, subsequent quantitatively derived classifications were not invariably interpreted in the vein of types inherent in the data. In the late 1960s and early 1970s, numerical taxonomic (Sokal and Sneath 1963) and multivariate statistical techniques gained increasing attention among archaeologists for classifying large data sets by similarities and differences in many attributes simultaneously. These classifications were usually regarded as created rather than discovered types (e.g., see Hodson 1982). One approach was to use factor, or principal components, analysis (Christenson and Read 1977) to extract major underlying dimensions of variability in the data, dimensions thought to be measured imperfectly and nonindependently by the original attributes.

More commonly, the technique of cluster analysis (Hodson 1969; Aldenderfer and Blashfield 1984) has been employed. Cluster analysis is a multivariate statistical procedure that groups entities by their similarity on a large number of attributes. Although there are several variants of the technique, the output is usually a treelike graph (a dendrogram; see fig. 14.1) showing successive linkages of similar entities.

Verifying the quality of the classifications resulting from these procedures—determining which is "best" for the data—is problematic. The choice of attributes and specific procedures is critical, for different classifications can result from different techniques. Although the methods replicate to some degree the archaeologist's actual artifact sorting (in which several attributes are considered simultaneously), they do not always accurately reproduce archaeological classifications of real data sets. One procedure that did replicate archaeologists' classifications of a sample pottery collection was association analysis (Whallon 1972), which divides the collection by individual attributes (rather than total similarity, as in cluster analysis). This and related procedures, however, have been interpreted (Whallon 1982, 127) from the position that classifications are inherent within the data sets and can be discovered statistically.

Much of the appeal of statistical approaches to pottery classification is that they offer solutions to the difficult and sometimes arbitrary procedure of drawing boundaries around classes—identifying discontinuities in what appear to be continuous variables. Pottery can be described with respect to a large number of attributes, but only some are qualitative (or noncontinuous). With qualitative variables it is easy enough to determine classes: color, for example, is a qualitative variable, and the boundaries between attribute states of black, white, and red pottery seem clear (see chap. 11), as do categories of inclusions, such as limestone, shell, volcanic ash, and quartz sand. But there are subtle shades or gradations of color and mixtures of inclusions, so that overlapping categories, continuous variables (size, diameter, thickness), and other boundary issues force the classifier to make difficult decisions about lumping or splitting classes. Computer programs that permit hierarchical rankings of attributes (Whallon 1972) or consider mixed-level (qualitative and quantitative) data in groupings (Rice and Saffer 1982) may be useful in this regard. The question is still, however, one of fuzzy boundaries: How much variability can exist within a class before it should be divided? The answer depends on the purpose of the classification. As has been remarked, a homogeneous group is merely one that has not yet attracted the attention of an investigator (Benfer 1975, 246).

Although the statistical procedures used to identify types within this approach to classification are themselves of considerable interest, what are more significant culturally are the interpretations of the types discovered. Traditionally, types have been viewed as intrinsically present in the data and therefore as cultural realities constituting fundamental observations or "basic data." Argued to an extreme, this viewpoint can lead to the questionable interpretation of a particular classificatory scheme as the only possible one for the data and thus as the best and most meaningful one (Hill and Evans 1972, 235–38).

9.1.3.4 What Is the Purpose of Classification?

Despite the appeal of the view that types are inherent and real, some still believe types are analytical and descriptive constructs devised by archaeologists specifically to determine the structure of variability in their data and to investigate particular problems. This view gained strength with the changes in archaeological method and theory in the 1960s and the concomitant rejection of normative orientations in favor of deductivist and positivist models (see Binford 1965; Hill and Evans 1972). In addition, with the increased precision of chronometric dating techniques, the need to direct pottery typologies solely toward chronology building diminished, as did the often rigidly classificatory schemes associated with this objective.

As archaeology has developed research goals other than chronology and comparison, new aims of pottery analysis have emerged, including function, production, residence patterns, and socioeconomic relations, and these have put a premium on innovative approaches to classification and on problem-oriented typologies. A number of investigators have developed their own classification schemes to answer particular problems (e.g., Redman 1978a), and many of these have been based on vessel forms (morphological types). Curiously, despite the accelerating interest in pottery paste composition and provenience (see chap. 13 and sec. 14.2), there has been little effort to develop what might be called technological types.

The type-variety system of pottery typology includes a level of classification that has some potential in this regard—the ware concept. Wares have long been used informally in archaeological ceramic studies in the Southwestern United States and Mesoamerica, and they seem to continue as the primary unit (rather than types) in Europe and the classical area. Wares have been identified based on a large number of attributes, including function (e.g., kitchenware), decoration (black-figured ware), paste composition or texture (coarse ware), color (Fine Orange ware), surface treatment or color (glazed ware, Plumbate ware), form (beaker ware), firing technology (earthenware), time period (Iron Age wares), and geographical location (Derbyshire wares). Although in these largely informal uses the members of ware categories may share characteristics of color, firing, method of construction, composition, and so forth, as indicated by the ware name, their fundamental defining criteria are aspects of composition, manufacturing technology, or surface treatment. In the terminology discussed above (sec. 9.1.1), wares are paradigmatic classes, and they correspond to procedural modes in analytical classifications.

Surface-treatment attributes (presence or absence of a slip or glaze, luster, color, etc.) are closely aligned with the attribute emphasis of the traditional type-variety system classification procedures, and thus they make it relatively easy to integrate wares into the hierarchy of units. Variables of paste composition (and manufacturing technology) are more difficult to place in this hierarchy, but they are also significant because they allow inferences about pottery production technique, organization, location, and trade distribution patterns—objectives that are aligned more closely with current archaeological goals than with chronology building (Rice 1976b).

Systematic incorporation of technological data into classification systems (e.g., through the ware concept) would be a significant extension of classificatory procedures (see Shepard 1976, 310–14; Rice 1982). This, however, is a formidable task for several reasons, chiefly because it is often difficult to interpret technological properties or identify composition without extensive laboratory analysis (see chap. 13). Other units that would have the same effect of bringing in data on manufacture include the concepts of technological style (see Lechtman 1977) and ceramic school (Smith 1962, 1175), though the latter is concerned more with decorative comparisons and similarities.

9.1.3.5 SUMMARY

Some of the problems in the literature on archaeological and ceramic classification are common to classifications in general. One example is boundaries: all classifications, by definition, require putting objects into one category or another. Any artificiality in archaeological classifications arises not from the nature of the type concept itself or from the need to impose boundaries, but from the conflation of decisions made by the analyst. These decisions are shaped not only by the inescapable need to select a limited number of attributes for the classification, but also by uncertainty about whether the excavated collection represents the full range of pottery at the site, adequately and without bias. In addition, types focus on attribute norms within the collection, but variations—such as might be caused by changes in the mental template through time or by new manufacturing techniques—are rarely incorporated systematically (although the use of varieties in the type-variety system has this potential).

In this vein it is also pertinent to remember that though artifacts function simultaneously in different realms—social, functional, and ideational (see Binford 1962a, 1965)—attributes (or states) may be more narrowly focused. Thus different sets of attributes will be more or less informative depending on the cultural realm, process, or function under investigation. Types based on primarily functional or morphological or technological variables will crosscut standard devised or folk classifications but still represent valid associations of attributes.

In sum, most archaeological pottery typologies are devised classifications, elaborated during the past fifty to sixty years primarily to standardize descriptions of artifacts, develop chronologies, and help with intersite comparisons. These goals have largely been met within the discipline, and with the development of new methods—especially chronometric dating techniques—and new theoretical orientations during the past twenty years or so, the objectives of archaeology have changed substantially. Archaeological pottery research has benefited extensively from these developments, with growing interest in compositional analysis, ethnoarchaeological studies, and so forth. Yet classificatory systems for pottery have not kept pace with these developments, and the procedures still in use are by and large the ones devised long ago for chronology building. New typologies have been developed ad hoc for particular problems, especially stylistic and morphological/functional ones. There has, however, been little systematic effort to broadly evaluate pottery classification procedures in general, or to integrate newer morphological classifications (or others involving technological attributes) into more traditional devised typological schemes.

A prominent thread running through the interpretations of archaeological classifications has been the need to reconcile devised (artificial) classifications with inherent folk classifications purportedly discoverable in the data. Relatively recent ethnotaxonomic data call into question how far this objective is feasible. These studies demonstrate that the heterogeneity of a society is reflected in the heterogeneity of its categorizations; pottery vessels may be classified (named) differently depending on the age, sex, status, and occupation of the classifier. More important, they are also categorized by their size, age, contents, function, and location of use—mostly information the archaeologist is unlikely to have. Overall shape is less important to folk classification than are vessel proportions and size or, sometimes, particular features of secondary shape variation that have functional significance.

9.2 Pottery Quantification

Like classification, pottery quantification is of concern to anthropologists and particularly to archaeologists for a variety of descriptive, inferential, and comparative purposes. For example, it may be desirable to know what proportion of the excavated material from a site represents serving wares versus cooking pots, or how much was imported rather than locally made, or whether site A had more pottery of type X than did site B. Such quantitative questions are important in studies of vessel function or of economic activities such as production and trade and in estimating the extent and duration of occupation at a site. At the heart of quantitative studies of pottery are relatively simple tabulations of quantities of material in different ceramic categories (types or forms) from various sites or parts of sites.

These quantitative questions in archaeological pottery studies, whether phrased in terms of absolute quantities or of relative amounts such as proportions or percentages, are deceptively simple, however. The difficulty is that more often than not fragments are recovered rather than whole pots, and these fragments must somehow be translated into numbers of whole vessels. Yet this is only part of the problem, because in addition to estimating how many pots are represented, it is also important to know what proportion of the site was excavated to yield the pottery being studied. Thus archaeological pottery quantification has two major components: sampling and counting vessels.

9.2.1 Sampling

Methodological issues of archaeological site sampling are beyond the scope of the present work (see Redman 1974; Mueller 1975b), but the subsampling of excavated artifact collections for a variety of purposes in pottery analysis is well within its purview. Some general issues of sampling in reconstructing pottery assemblages and site usage are considered here; more specialized issues of sampling for physicochemical analysis are addressed further in chapters 10 (sec. 10.3.2.2) and 13 (sec. 13.1).

The most important consideration at the start of a ceramic analysis is how the pottery was recovered in the field, a consideration over which the analyst may or may not have control. Of specific interest are the way the excavation units were selected and the techniques by which they were excavated.

To take the latter issue first, excavation technique is important in maintaining comparable conditions of recovery from one excavation to another. The primary technique in question is screening, for screening only some portions of an excavated site would result in differential recovery of particularly fine fragments of pottery and other materials (see Keighley 1973), and quantitative comparisons would then be skewed.

An archaeological pottery collection almost never represents all the pottery from an entire site, because rarely is a site completely excavated. Instead, the pottery is usually a sample of the total population. The excavated areas may have been chosen in any number of ways: by purposive or judgmental selection to explore some specific aspect of the site, such as a particular structure or zone; by haphazard or grab sampling for logistic convenience or to satisfy some nonscientific criterion; or by a probabilistic sampling strategy. In this last procedure the total area of the site is divided into equal units, and then individual units are selected for excavation by a method in which each one has a known probability of being chosen. Examples of such probability sampling strategies are simple random, stratified, and systematic sampling (see Mueller 1975b; Redman 1974; for a general discussion of sampling see Cochran 1963).

Each of these strategies has some practical merits, depending on the overall project goals, but they also have ramifications for pottery analysis and its objectives. If all that is desired is a quantitative description of the pottery from excavated portions of the site, sample selection is not highly significant. But if the object is to draw some conclusions about the pottery at the site as a whole from the smaller amount of excavated material—that is, to generalize from the sample to the population—this is a different matter entirely. Inferring the characteristics of the population from a sample is a matter of inferential statistics, and there must be some assurance that the sample fairly represents the range of variability within the characteristics of the population. Such generalizations can be made only if excavation units are selected by a probabilistic sampling procedure, because the other sample selection methods have a greater risk of imposing known or unknown biases on the data recovered.

A related point is that excavated artifact samples from archaeological sites are cluster samples (Vescelius 1960; Mueller 1975a). That is, the probabilistic excavation sampling strategy by which the artifacts, in this case pottery sherds, are recovered does not yield a sample from an identified population (a sampling frame) of itemized sherds, since the artifactual population of a site cannot be known in advance of excavation. Instead, the sample of pottery is recovered from an identified population of horizontal and vertical spatial units of the site, and these contain groups (or clusters) of many items such as sherds. Thus the artifacts themselves are not sampled independently and directly by excavation, but rather constitute clusters of items that proceed fortuitously from the actual sample units (see Cowgill 1964). This distinction has further implications for calculating the characteristics of the population of artifacts at the site from the excavated sample (see Vescelius 1960), should that be the object of the analysis.

The quantitative analysis of archaeological pottery may stop with simple recording of counts (and weights) of sherds falling into certain categories, whether types, wares (fabrics), or shape classes. Sometimes, however, particularly with extremely large collections, it is impossible to completely analyze all the sherds recovered, and in such cases the collection has to be subsampled. In these situations the artifacts do become the individual itemized units of subsequent sampling activities; however, unless the entire site has been excavated, it is usually important to remember that the artifacts are originally cluster samples representing spatial contexts.

It is impossible to know beforehand what materials can be safely ignored or discarded in collection sampling (the so-called sampling paradox), yet such decisions often must be made to save time, personnel, and cost. In such situations, the object of subsampling should be to acquire a sufficiently large representation of rare categories. Collection sampling usually requires stratification of the collection—by context or classificatory units (see Benfer 1975), by rare versus abundant categories within the original spatial clusters (see Cowgill 1964), or by some combination of these.

9.2.2 Counts, Weights, and Vessel Equivalents

Although quantification of archaeological pottery can simply mean measuring how much material is present, its most common goal is to determine how many vessels were represented in a particular deposit. The simplest and most traditional way to achieve the first of these goals is counting or weighing the sherds from the excavation units; determining the number of vessels involves more complex data transformations (for a review see Deal 1983, 251–67).

Counts may be made by simply tabulating the individual sherds from all excavation units, but this effectively considers each sherd to represent a different vessel. In many cases two or more sherds can be joined together or cross-mended; counting the joined pieces as single sherds thus more closely reflects the actual number of individual vessels than does simply counting all sherds. Counts of sherds can be reported as before- or after-mending totals, the latter indicating a maximum number of vessels. Both measures generally overestimate the number of vessels at a site, however. A variation of sherd counts is sherd ratios, usually calculated as number of sherds per unit of excavation volume.

Sherd counts may be misleading as estimates of numbers of whole vessels because there is no simple relation between a vessel's size or shape and the number of sherds it breaks into: large vessels typically break into more pieces than small vessels; thin-walled pots may break into more sherds than thick-walled pots; and low-fired pieces may break into more fragments than high-fired objects. The vessels that break into more sherds or are subject to more disturbance (see Kirkby and Kirkby 1976, 237; Solheim 1984, 101; also Deal 1983, 201–2) or weathering (Reid 1984) in middens after discard will be overrepresented in a particular excavation unit.

For these reasons, sherd weight (Baumhoff and Heizer 1959; Solheim 1960; Chase 1985) has sometimes been touted as a more accurate quantitative indicator. Sherd weights will effectively standardize the data for differences caused by large versus small sherd sizes or thickness, which may result from differences in disturbance and comminution in certain areas of a site. It is frequently recommended that both sherd counts and weights be recorded to compensate for the inadequacies of each measure (table 9.2).

Sherd weight totals may be modified by adjusting for thickness (Hulthén 1974). In this time-consuming procedure, the sherd collection is sorted into different thickness categories, which are weighed separately. The gross weight

Table 9.2   Percentages of Sherds by Weight and Count from a Test Pit at Site 17, Fiji

Classes of Sherds	Depth in Inches								
	6	12	18	24	30	36	42	48	74
Plain									
Percentage weight	79.0	80.0	81.0	82.5	76.5	74.5	47.5	49.5	45.0
Percentage by count	89.0	90.0	91.0	90.0	89.0	82.0	60.0	60.0	60.0
Number of sherds/oz.	7.5	8.0	7.0	8.0	8.0	9.0	8.0	7.0	6.0
Incised									
Percentage weight	17.0	16.0	14.0	10.5	10.0	3.5	0.5	—	—
Percentage by count	9.0	7.5	4.5	5.0	4.0	1.0	0.3	—	—
Number of sherds/oz.	4.0	3.0	2.0	3.0	3.0	4.0	4.0	—	—
Relief									
Percentage weight	4.0	4.0	5.0	7.0	13.5	22.0	52.0	50.5	55.5
Percentage by count	2.0	2.5	5.0	5.0	7.0	16.0	39.5	40.0	34.0
Number of sherds/oz.	5.0	4.0	6.5	5.0	4.0	7.0	4.0	4.0	3.0

Source: After Deal 1983, table 33. The data in Deal's table were taken from Gifford 1976, tables 17 and 18.

of each group is then multiplied or divided by the necessary factor to achieve a standard weight, and an estimate of the number of vessels.

Sherd weight data can be converted to individual vessel estimates by at least two procedures. One requires that the sherd collection be separated into form or type categories (see sec. 7.2.3) for weighing, and a whole or reconstructable vessel must be present for each category. Weighing the whole vessel and then dividing the sherd weight totals by this figure gives some idea of the numbers of vessels for each category and for the collection as a whole. Closer estimates are possible if this procedure is combined with estimates of the numbers of individual vessels based on rims, bases, handles, or other distinctive features.

A second weight-based procedure estimates proportions of vessel categories by comparing size classes using the assumption that the weight of a vessel is proportional to its surface (times thickness). Vessels are sorted into size categories, total category weights are determined, and the average body diameter is estimated for each category (Baumhoff and Heizer 1959, 312). For example, if large vessels have an average radius of nine inches and small vessels have an average radius of two inches, then the ratio of the weights can be given by the formula for ratios of their surface areas: $4\pi(9)^2 = 20$. Thus the larger vessels are twenty times as heavy as smaller ones, and the weight totals for vessels in the large class should be divided by twenty to estimate the proportion of large and small vessels in the whole collection (Baumhoff and Heizer 1959, 312). This procedure assumes spherical shapes.

Another approach to vessel quantification is to calculate vessel equivalents or estimated vessel equivalents (EVEs), and this may be accomplished by several means (see Orton 1982). Calculating minimum number of vessels (MNV) or number of inferred vessels (NIV) is analogous to the zooarchaeological procedure of determining minimum numbers of individuals (MNI) of faunal species, and for pottery two methods have been proposed (Millett 1979b, 77–78). One is the subjective assessment and grouping of all sherds that definitely do, or at least might, represent a single vessel. This procedure may be fairly useful, but it lacks replicability and tends to underestimate the number of vessels actually present.

Several related procedures are based on counts and measurement of rim sherds, bases, or handles. Rim equivalents, for example, may be calculated from the lengths (or percentages) of rims of a particular type of pot, which then may be divided by the mean rim diameter (Egloff 1973); similarly, the length of the arc of the rim sherd can be divided by the total rim circumference (DeBoer 1974, 340; see also Plog 1985). The easiest way to carry out these measurements is with a diameter template that shows both radius in centimeters and percentage of the total orifice circumference (fig. 7.9). A combination of these procedures may be used to calculate estimated vessel equivalents: the total rim equivalents and base equivalents are added together, and the total is divided by two (Orton 1980, 166).

The disadvantage of these techniques is that they ignore body sherds and are difficult to use with extremely small rim fragments, for which diameter measurements are unobtainable. It is also important to consider the possibility of differential preservation of rim sherds, which are curved, sometimes thinned, and relatively more fragile (see chaps. 7 and 12 [sec. 12.4.2.4]), than bases, which are often thickened and therefore stronger. Additional problems are posed by the original issues of sampling areas of a site and the relation of those areas to patterns of use, discard, and postdepositional fragmentation of pottery.

9.3 Assemblage Composition and Site Formation Processes

The many uses of pottery vessels for storage, processing, transfer, and display raise questions concerning the numbers and kinds of utensils that constitute the ceramic assemblages at household, site, and community levels in prehistoric contexts. The broken pottery fragments that archaeologists recover in their excavations were originally intact vessels serving a variety of uses in daily life. These vessels constitute a ceramic assemblage, a collection of artifacts that are associated temporally and contextually at a particular site. Although archaeologists usually treat ceramic assemblages (or subassemblages) in terms of the total sherd collection from a site, ethnographic studies of individual household pottery inventories permit some generalizations about use, discard, and replacement that are significant for understanding the formation of the archaeological record.

9.3.1 Ceramic Assemblages

Ethnographic and ethnoarchaeological investigations of pottery assemblages have generally focused on ceramic censuses, or the numbers of pots in individual households, and on the use life or longevity of the censused vessels. These data have been borrowed and adapted, implicitly and explicitly, by archaeologists in a variety of approaches to the assemblages of historical and prehistoric sites.

9.3.1.1 ETHNOGRAPHIC CERAMIC CENSUSES
Ceramic censuses usually document the numbers of pots in the households in an ethnographic community. Observed or elicited information in these censuses ideally should include the native name for the vessel (see sec. 9.1.2), its dimensions (including volume), use(s), age, maker or source, decoration (if any), frequency and location of use, and anything significant or unusual about it. It is also useful to obtain a count of nonceramic (metal, china, plastic, wood, or basketry) containers in use in the households as alternatives or replacements for traditional clay pots (see Deal 1983, 140–43).

   Much of this information is typically missing from ethnographic accounts, and the most common category of information is simply a count of the number of vessels in a household. Partial ceramic censuses are available for households in Tzintzuntzan, Mexico (Foster 1960), Fulani and Gisiga households in Bé, Cameroon (David and Hennig 1972, 17–21), Conibo households in Peru (DeBoer 1974; DeBoer and Lathrap 1979, 122–23), and the communities of Dangtalan and Dalupa in the Philippines (Longacre 1985). These censuses

Table 9.3   Recycled Uses of Damaged Pots or Sherds

Hopi-Tewa, Arizona[a]	*Pakistan (cont.)*
Building into window or door frames of houses	Liquid receptacles
Chinking walls or bread ovens	Molds
Tools in pottery manufacture	Scrapers in pottery manufacture
Protecting pots in firing	Placing in paths in rainy season
Placing in shrines	Watering plants
Divining the future	"Intimate purposes"
Templates for copying designs	
Grinding for temper	*Thailand*[f]
	Animal feeders
Huichol, Mexico[b]	Frying pans
Animal feeders	Dry storage
Wax melting, candle dipping	Water troughs
Lids	Children's playthings
Dustpans	Pot stands
Ladles or scoops	Games
Shipibo-Conibo, Peru[c]	*Chanal and Aguacatenango, Mexico*[g]
Grinding for temper	Pot lids
Pot supports	Cutting boards
Griddles over fire	Mixing
Chicken roosts	Trash removal
"Kilns"	Nests for fowls
	Feeders
Fulani, Cameroon[d]	Seedling protectors
Animal feeders (sheep and goats)	Watering plants
Tools for pottery manufacture	Paving material
Cooking tripods	Chinking walls
	Storage containers
Pakistan[e]	Toys
Kiln construction	Bathwater containers
Grinding for temper	

[a]Stanislawski 1978, 221–22.
[b]Weigand 1969, 23–24.
[c]DeBoer and Lathrap 1979, 111, 125, 127.
[d]David and Hennig 1972, 21.

[e]Rye and Evans 1976, 123.
[f]Solheim 1965, 259, 1984, 100.
[g]Deal 1983, 176–79.

(table 9.3), plus other data (Weigand 1969, 28–29; Nelson 1981, 112), suggest a range in number of pots per household from three to seventy-five; the average number of pots in the households in these communities varies between nine and fifty-seven.

The number of pots in any given household within a community is likely to relate to several factors. One seemingly significant variable in predicting inventory size is the number of persons in the household, but what is more meaningful is age-grade composition (number of children versus adults). Each generation has different eating habits and nutritional requirements, necessitating different kinds of pots (see Nelson 1981, 109–12). The socioeconomic status of the household is also significant in determining both the absolute number of pottery vessels (David and Hennig 1972, 17; Miller 1985, 74; Longacre 1985, 337; cf. DeBoer and Lathrap 1979, 124) and the kinds of vessels, which relates to dietary variety as well as to the ability to acquire modern industrially produced containers of metal or plastic or nonlocal vessels (Deal 1983, 148–53).

In addition, the average number of vessels or kinds of vessels per household may differ between communities in a region—for example, in potting households as opposed to nonpotting households, or in potting versus nonpotting communities. Variations in kinds and numbers of vessels may be seasonal or related to environmental features, such as proximity to water sources and the need to store water during a dry season. These relationships—which also pertain to other household occupations or activities, such as dairying—have not yet been investigated systematically.

Simple logic, plus abundant modern ethnographic data, indicate that certain primary activities have to be carried out in all households, such as cooking, storing, and carrying. Though the specifics of these activities may vary— cooking may involve boiling, frying, baking, or toasting many different kinds of foods—these general needs and functions persist. Census data from some communities for which such observations are available (table 9.4) show a considerable range in the composition of household vessel assemblages. Of the 12,518 vessels tabulated in 291 households in 10 communities, most (4,758, or 38.0%) were used for cooking, while much smaller numbers (435, or 3.5%) were used for storing goods. The percentage of the individual assemblages that constituted cooking vessels ranged from 25.9% (Shipibo) to 87% (Dangtalan Kalinga), while the range of storage vessels was from 2% (San Mateo Ixtatán) to 30.8% (Conibo). Households in Chanal and Aguacatenango, Mexico, did not use any pottery vessels specifically for storage, but used containers of perishable materials, plastic, or metal (Deal 1983, 165, 166).

Serving vessels were relatively rare in these assemblages, accounting for 544 vessels (4.3% of the total), while 3,841 (30.7%) functioned in "other" activities. With respect to the serving vessels, the data for three communities (San Mateo Ixtatán, and Dalupa and Dangtalan Kalinga) lacked tabulations for this functional category; for the remaining seven communities, percentages ranged from 8.1% (Chanal) to 40.9% (Shipibo). The high frequency in this latter group is explainable in light of traditional hospitality guidelines, which dictate serving guests from new, unused beer mugs (DeBoer and Lathrap 1979, 124).

These ethnographic data suggest certain cautions in inferring the composition and functions of vessel assemblages in archaeological contexts. One problem is the redundancy of vessel forms within individual assemblages and their multifunctional character. Many vessels, for example, in Bé, Cameroon, and Metepec, Mexico, are described as being "cooking/storage" vessels; they are tabulated here in the storage category, but this dual usage is probably very common (see sec. 9.1.2) and is important for archaeologists seeking to ascribe functions to archaeological pots. Similarly, in Chanal and Aguacatenango, Mexico, vessels were not specifically identified as storage vessels, but while the vessels were themselves being stored they often held a variety of foods, dry goods, and other supplies (Deal 1983, 167).

Another problem concerns the context of these ethnographic observations: they come from pottery-making societies in the 1960s and 1970s. One might

Table 9.4   Some Ethnographic Pottery Censuses

| | Cameroon | | | | Philippines | | | | Peru | | | |
| | Fulani[a] | | Gisiga[a] | | Dangtalan[b] | | Dalupa[b] | | Conibo[c] | | Shipibo[d] | |
Vessel Type	N	Years[i]	N	Years[m]	N[n]	Years	N[o]	Years	N	Years	N[p]	Years
Cooking pots General												
Large					268	13.0–13.8	33	3.5–5.4	10	1.0	18	
Small/ medium	180	2.6	20		303	4.2–4.6	255	9.0	30	.8–1.5	25	
Storage	81[f]	10–13	26[g]		52	8.2	87	7.2	37	1.0–2.2	48	
Bowls	33	2.7	8						30	.47	45	
Other serving									8[w]	.25	23[x]	
Other	19	4.2	3		33		14		5		7	
Total pots	313		57		656		389		120		166	
Mean per house	20.9		9.5		13.4		8.8		17.1		15.1	
Median age		5.4								.96		
N households	15		6		49		44		7		11	
N potters	7		2						9		13	

[a] David and Hennig 1972, table 3.
[b] Longacre 1985, tables 1–3.
[c] DeBoer 1974, 338.
[d] DeBoer and Lathrap 1979, 122–23.
[e] Nelson 1981, 115.
[f] Reina and Hill 1978, 246–47.
[g] Pastron 1974, 108–9.
[h] Weigand 1969, 29.
[i] Kirkpatrick 1978, 49.

[j] Deal 1983, table 1.
[k] Deal 1983, table 1.
[l] Median.
[m] Ages not given because of recent arrival of Gisiga in village.
[n] 1979–80.
[o] 1981.
[p] Excludes those made for sale.
[q] Mean.

well ask to what extent they are comparable to nonpottery making communities, where pottery may be less available and more costly. A related question is whether these assemblage data are valid for prehistoric times before the advent of plastics and metal containers. David and Hennig (1972, 21) suggest that in precolonial times the Fulani may have had twice as many clay pots as they do now. Significantly, it is serving and storage vessels that occur in low frequencies in these censused communities. Modern substitutes are adopted far more readily for these functional categories than for cooking, where traditional diets and taste preferences require traditional clay vessels (see sec. 15.2.2).

On the one hand, therefore, it might be appropriate to view the ethnographic assemblage data as a baseline or minimum number of vessels estimate; on the other, it is possible that before plastics were available some household containers may have been made of wood, basketry, or leather, and thus the relative numbers of pottery versus other containers may not be too severely distorted.

Many ceramic censuses have aimed to determine pottery use life, that is, how long a vessel is used before being damaged or broken and discarded. A

Table 9.4 (*continued*)

Vessel Type	Guatemala				Mexico									
	San Mateo I[c]		Zunil[f]		Tarahumara[g]		Huichol[h]		Metepec[i]		Chanal[j]		Aguacatenango[k]	
	N[q]	Years	N	Years	N	Years	N	Years	N	Years	N	Years	N	Years
Cooking pots														
General	22.6 (2–50)		6		3	1–2	8		89		1885		2435	
Large			1				11							
Small/ medium			4				15							
Storage	3.7		1		1	3–5	2		70[l]		343[u]		389[v]	
Bowls			3						33					
Other serving			2				13		90[y]		269		505	
Other	30.4		2				13		24		836		937	
Total pots	2907		19[z]				62		306		3333		4266	
Mean per house	57				7–8[aa]		12		51		62.9		85.3	
Median age N households	51		1		10		5[bb]		6		53		50	
N potters														

[l]34 vessels called "cooking-storage vessels."
[u]12 vessels called "cooking-storage vessels."
[v]70 ollas are called cooking and storage vessels.
[u]No storage vessels noted, but water jars are tabulated here as storage.
[z]No storage vessels, but water jars tabulated here as storage.

[u]Beer mugs.
[v]Beer mugs.
[y]Variety of beverage mugs and pitchers.
[z]All vessels newly purchased for setting up a new household.
[aa]Range is up to 19.
[bb]Ranchos—extended family residences with 4–42 members.

tremendous disparity can be noted from area to area; some vessels may survive only three to six months before discard, while others endure ten to fifteen or even twenty years. Honeypots used for importing honey at Bé, Cameroon, were more than thirty years old (David and Hennig 1972, 13), a "fiesta pot" in Tzintzuntzan, Mexico, was about forty or fifty years old (Foster 1960, 607), and a large Huichol, Mexico, cooking olla may have been seventy years old (Weigand 1969, 33).

The notion of an average life span for pottery is therefore misleading; nonetheless, estimates of the longevity of cooking pots in regular use have ranged anywhere between three months (Irwin 1977, 291, cited in Longacre 1985, 336) to one year (Foster 1960, 608; DeBoer 1974, 341), up to two to ten years (Longacre 1985, 339; David and Hennig 1972, 19). Foster's estimate was based on kiln-fired, glazed pottery produced at Tzintzuntzan, Mexico, and he suggests that low-fired, unglazed pottery may have a shorter use life of only six months (Foster 1960, 608). The data from other communities for which use life is available for unglazed wares do not bear out this supposition, however. A longitudinal study of pottery assemblages in two communities in the

Philippines, for example, revealed that over a four- to five-year period more than one-third of the original total of 720 vessels survived; 291 pots were broken, and 137 were sold, bartered, or given away (Longacre 1985, 339–40).

As might be expected, many factors affect breakage rates and hence use life of utilitarian pottery (Foster 1960, 608). Some of these are technological concerns, principally the strength of the ware as it relates to composition, forming technique, wall thickness, overall shape, and firing (see secs. 3.3.3, 4.3.2, 7.3.2, and 12.3). In Mesoamerica, for example, the microstructural requirements of thermal stress resistance and the flat, platelike shape of traditional tortilla griddles (*comales*) make them extremely fragile (see Weigand 1969, 24–25). In northern Peru, the ollas used for brewing *chicha* (maize beer) last only two months if used once a week, and a mixture of clay and dung is smeared on the outside of the pots to make them last longer (Bankes 1985, 275–76).

The size and weight of the vessel are also important determinants of longevity and are closely related to another factor: frequency of use (fig. 9.4; see Deal 1983, 155–56; DeBoer 1985; Graves 1985, 23). Small or medium-sized, easily portable pots such as water-carrying jars or serving/eating vessels are likely to be broken relatively quickly because they are used and moved frequently, perhaps several times a day. Large, heavy vessels that are rarely if ever moved, such as water-storage jars set into the floor or ceremonial cooking

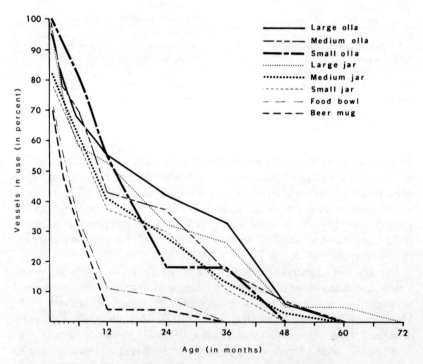

Figure 9.4 "Survivorship curves" for eight major Shipibo-Conibo (Peru) vessel forms. Note long use life of large jars and large ollas and very short use life of small serving vessels such as food bowls and beer mugs. After De-Boer and Lathrap 1979, fig. 4.5.

pots, have a longer life span. Mode or context of use is still another factor that involves exposure to thermal stresses and the weakening resulting from repeated cycling in and out of heat (see sec. 12.4.1). It also relates to the proximity of vessels to activity areas or to the movement of children or domestic animals such as dogs, pigs, and chickens, especially if the pots are used on the floor rather than on tables (see Weigand 1969, 24; Longacre 1981, 63–64). Other considerations include practices in caring for vessels, including cleaning and storage.

In addition, the cost of pottery is important (Foster 1960, 608): where pottery is inexpensive and easily obtained, carelessness in its use may be the norm. This obviously relates to weight and size: large, heavy vessels require more time, skill, and raw material in manufacture. Finally, breakage is not the only reason a pot is removed from its original use: pots may be replaced (or recycled) because they are old and sour, changing the taste of the food cooked in them.

Ethnographic and ethnoarchaeological studies dealing with kinds and quantities of pottery on the assemblage level call attention to the multitude of variables relating to the composition of a household assemblage. The complex relationships between form, function (chap. 7), and ceramic assemblage content and variability can be summarized in part by several cautionary observations:

1. Vessel shapes and uses are not independent of ceramic resources.
2. Vessel shapes and their uses are culturally prescribed.
3. Potters' decisions on resources and shapes are not completely free choices.
4. Some container functions can be performed with different shapes of pots.
5. Some pots have multiple functions.
6. Some pots may be used for functions not originally intended.
7. The same vessel shape can occur in several sizes, each with different functions.
8. The need for increased vessel volume can be met either by using more pots or by using larger pots.
9. Larger households may have either more pots or larger pots than smaller households.

Additional significant concerns for pottery assemblage composition include age-grade makeup of the household; context of vessel use; socioeconomic or ethnic status of the household (as measured by land owned or farmed, participation in religious/political office, or possession of modern cash goods and conveniences); dietary patterns or foodways—kinds of foods eaten, methods of preparation, meal scheduling; environmental data (seasonal availability of water, particular foods, etc.); and level of economic specialization (Is the community one of pottery specialists?).

Of five primary ceramic variables—shape, size, function, composition, and number of vessels—no single one is a consistent and reliable predictor of another. An interaction effect is involved in use-related variables of form whereby a number of factors may counterbalance each other.

9.3.1.2 ARCHAEOLOGICAL APPROACHES TO ASSEMBLAGES

Several recent archaeological studies have focused on the relations between form, function, and assemblage composition (see Braun 1980; Nelson 1981; Turner and Lofgren 1966; Smith 1983, 1985; Shapiro 1984; Hally 1983a, 1986). These studies are largely based on a complex series of arguments—for example, that there is a rank order of frequency of vessel shape categories in households or sites and that this ordering varies inversely with extremes of size and secondary functional attributes (hence degree of functional specialization) of the vessels. The relative frequencies are held to be informative about many aspects of ceramic-related behavior at a site, including kinds and numbers of activities, number of people, duration of use, and relative status of occupants. Not all of these are equally useful in explaining the variability in ceramic frequencies, but given other lines of evidence, some may be rejected and others supported.

Relative frequencies of vessel forms provide a basis for distinguishing primary, secondary, and tertiary morphological categories and associated functions in archaeological pottery assemblages. In one of these studies (Braun 1980, 216), primary vessel forms were medium-sized plain bowls and medium-mouthed necked jars, hypothesized to have served in secure containment, processing, and consumption. Secondary forms included medium-mouthed intermediate- and recurvate-restricted jars and bowls, considered to have served in nonsecure containment and in moderately high-volume secure containment and consumption. Tertiary and peripheral form categories consist of forms extreme in orifice diameter or size or both. Varying frequencies of primary, tertiary, and peripheral forms in the nineteen assemblages analyzed were related to specialization of activities and permanence of occupation at the sites from which the assemblages were recovered (see also Shapiro 1984).

Although archaeological efforts to reconstruct complete pottery assemblages are gaining interest, attendant difficulties must be recognized and confronted. The primary problem is that archaeologists usually have to begin with reviews of ethnographic data, in which the function is already specified (it is an independent variable) and the shape and technological properties (which effectively constitute dependent variables) are often incompletely described. In analyzing prehistoric specimens, however, archaeologists essentially have to work backward, retrofitting their technological and shape data (archaeologists' independent variables) into retrodictive tests of hypotheses of vessel function (function then becoming a dependent variable). Such transformations are empirically and methodologically specious for several reasons. The relationships between form and function in these studies constitute theories to be tested rather than empirical givens. In addition, shape, composition, firing, and such, are consequences of many constraints on the potter's behavior (see chaps. 5, 7, 12), not simply dependent variables reflecting or predicting the vessel's intended use.

Furthermore, the inferential problems caused by real-world determinants of assemblage variability (sec. 9.3.1.1) are of course multiplied for prehistory, because archaeologists rarely excavate entire sites and therefore rarely have access to an entire ceramic assemblage representing the full range of socioeconomic status at a site. Moreover, in many areas assemblages may be expected to vary depending upon whether a site was permanently or only seasonally occupied (e.g., Braun 1980; Plog 1980; Shapiro 1983, 1984).

Reconstructions of archaeological ceramic assemblages and functions are thus fraught with uncertainty, because variability may be explained by status, function, size, ethnicity, and a whole host of complex factors. Although knowledge of these factors can be used to retrodict the composition of a ceramic assemblage in a particular censused ethnographic household (e.g., Nelson 1981), they cannot so easily be used to predict the individual ceramic vessels in an unknown archaeological situation or draw precisely the same conclusions from their presence. Determining the specific functions of each vessel is of course even further removed from certitude.

The problem is that variability of vessel forms may be tied not to specific activities but to more general ones. That is, common or primary vessel forms are often sufficiently nonspecialized in size and shape (and probably also technological characteristics) that each could have served reasonably well in a variety of activities. They represent adaptation through generalization rather than through specialization: a strategy for satisfying a number of needs adequately rather than a single function optimally. For example, a single vessel may function for processing, cooking, and serving, and another may be used for carrying, processing, and storage, rather than there being a separate vessel form for each activity.

In this light it is useful for archaeologists to calculate and compare the relative percentages of different vessel forms for individual households or individual sites. The bulk of the assemblages may or may not comprise basic vessel forms. The variability and diversity of formal and functional categories in these assemblages can be expected to vary not only with the considerations of use, activity, and status identified above, but also with the specialization of ceramic production in the society, the possible existence of resources with special properties, and probably also with the level of sociocultural complexity in general. Complex societies can be expected to have a greater number of social or ethnic segments or statuses, each of which may have its own special container-related needs and activities, particularly dietary, and modes of satisfying them (see Otto 1975). Societies at lower levels of complexity—either in sociopolitical, economic, or demographic parameters or in ceramic production organization—are likely to have a smaller range of vessel form categories, fewer specialized forms, more overlapping of functions, and greater emphasis on the primary all-purpose or multifunctional forms.

9.3.2 Site Formation Processes

One of the less common but nonetheless significant archaeological applications of ceramic assemblage studies is in reconstructing site formation processes. An important objective of archaeological research in the past twenty or twenty-five years has been to understand the transformation artifacts undergo as they move from active use within a prehistoric or historical community (their systemic context; Schiffer 1976) to final abandonment and discard (the archaeological context). This is known as the study of archaeological site formation processes, and because pottery constitutes such a large proportion of the artifactual material recovered at archaeological sites, its behavior in site formation processes has come under increasing scrutiny.

Within this general realm archaeologists have employed census and use-life data provided by ethnographic and ethnoarchaeological investigations to explore specific objectives, such as calculating the length (or permanence) of occupation and the population of a site. These objectives require many separate determinations concerning pottery use, and each of these in turn involves a number of assumptions that may or may not be realistic. Some of the quantitative problems of reconstructing demography via potsherds have already been highlighted (Grove and Buge 1978), and the procedure bears further consideration.

In general, calculating the length (permanence) of occupation or the population of a site on the basis of the pottery recovered in excavation requires some or all of the following information: (1) the proportion of the site excavated; (2) contemporaneity, or the number of households at the site that were occupied at any given time; (3) the number of whole vessels at the site; (4) the number of whole pots per household; (5) the rate of replacement of broken pots; and (6) the number of persons per household.

Information on items 1 and to some extent 2 are matters of archaeological research design strategy and are therefore outside the scope of attention here, except to note concerns about randomization processes in selecting excavation units and cautions on generalizing from a sample to a population (see sec. 9.2.1). Estimates of item 3 are calculated from the sherds recovered in excavation, and this may be done on the basis of total sherd counts, rim and base counts, sherd weights, or a variety of more complex procedures using combinations of these measures, depending on the nature of the collection (see sec. 9.2.2).

Item 4, the number of whole pots per household or the composition of the household assemblage, is highly variable, as outlined above (sec. 9.3.1.1 and tables 9.3 and 9.4). Although every household has to meet more or less similar needs for food preparation, cooking, eating, and storage, the ways these needs are met by means of pottery can vary considerably, depending on household size, composition, socioeconomic status, and other factors, including—especially in modern times—the substitution of containers made of other materials, such as wood, plastic, or metal. Because size and composition of the household may be one of the elements sought in the investigation, a certain circularity is introduced if this element is used to predict assemblage size.

Item 5, the rate of replacement of broken pots, might seem to be a relatively straightforward matter of householders' producing (or purchasing) a new pot whenever one cracks or breaks. Instead, however, it is a complex and decidedly not straightforward process involving production, use, and discard (recycling) of the pottery. Most of the studies of this issue were initially undertaken to investigate whether the broken pottery fragments recovered as refuse at archaeological sites (middens, etc.) were sufficiently short-lived to be considered contemporaneous with the occupation of that site. It was found that the longevity of pots in regular use (used at least every few days) varied generally from less than one year to about five years (see sec. 9.3.1.1); thus except for very large pots the assumption is generally safe, at least within the range of precision of virtually all archaeological dating techniques.

The data available on patterns of refuse disposal are ambiguous: some reports support the idea that pottery is disposed of fairly close to where it was used and ultimately broken or damaged, while others suggest fairly wide dispersal. Tzeltal discard patterns in Mexico were studied carefully, and it was noted that damaged items often were stored for future use, especially along walls, patio edges, or on roofs (Deal 1983, 193–96). In Thailand, distribution of refuse has been related to patterns of storage within households, with prestige wares such as porcelains and celadons being stored in sleeping areas, away from traffic (Solheim 1984, 100). Sweeping concentrates sherds in midden areas at the peripheries of household compounds (see DeBoer and Lathrap 1979, 128–33; Deal 1983, 197), but sherds may be found anywhere from five or ten meters (Pastron 1974, 108–9) to one hundred meters (Weigand 1969, 24, 26) from residences. Distinct differences in sherd frequencies and sizes as a result of comminution along pathways as opposed to normal refuse deposits (DeBoer and Lathrap 1979, 133 and n. 14; see also Solheim 1984, 102) and other problems of sherd taphonomy (Reid 1984), add to problems of quantifying sherd materials (see also sec. 9.2.2).

Few data are available on the actual rate of replacement of broken vessels within households. Understanding this process requires data on the interval between breakage and replacement or, failing that, on the rate or intensity of production and the levels of sale or gift giving within potters' households. Potters themselves are often vague about this subject; they replace broken household vessels out of their regular production without thinking about it. Among the ten households studied among the Tarahumara of Mexico, two to four cooking pots are made each year, a large storage pot is made every other year, and the replacement rate is two or three pots a year (Pastron 1974, 101–2). Among the Huichol in Mexico, roughly 1% to 10% of the assemblage is broken each year (Weigand 1969, 25). In Chanal, Mexico, an average of 33.3 vessels were replaced in 30 households (Deal 1983, table 23). In Bé, Cameroon, an average of 3.14 pots per year (or 15%) per household are broken and enter the archaeological record, necessitating approximately 360 pots per year for replacements (David and Hennig 1972, 20–21).

The replacement rate of pottery is by no means equivalent to the production rate, however, nor is it a constant one-for-one exchange (see Longacre 1985, 344–45). A shortfall between the need for replacement pots and those produced locally may be overcome by importing pots manufactured outside the community (David and Hennig 1972, 21). Conversely, not all pots produced in the community may end up there. In communities in the Philippines, 19% of the originally inventoried vessels were given away, sold, or bartered over a five-year period (Longacre 1985, 340), although it is not known what proportion of these may have actually left the community.

Damaged vessels may or may not be removed from active service. Cracked vessels may be repaired and continue in their primary uses, but many times they are recycled into a variety of secondary uses (see DeBoer and Lathrap

Table 9.5   Proportions of Vessels in Ethnographic Censuses Used in Various Activities

Census Location	Cooking	Storage	Serving	Number of Pots[a]	Number of Households
Fulani	57% (150)	25.9% (81)[b]	10.5% (33)	313	15
Dangtalan	87% (571)	7.9% (52)		656	49
Dalupa	74% (288)	22.3% (87)		389	44
Conibo	33.3% (40)	30.8% (37)	31.6% (38)	120	7
Shipibo	25.9% (43)	28.9% (48)	40.9% (68)	166	11
San Mateo Ixtatán	56% (1,628)	2% (58)		2,907	51
Huichol	54.8% (34)	3.2% (2)	21.0% (13)	62	5
Metepec	29.1% (89)	22.9% (70)[b]	40.2% (123)	306	6
Chanal	56.5% (1,885)	10.3% (343)[c]	8.0% (269)	3,333	53
Aguacatenango	57.1% (2,435)	9.1% (389)[c]	11.8% (505)	4,266	50

Sources: See table 9.4.

[a]Total number of pots counted; excludes those given as "other" in table 9.4.

[b]Some vessels were originally given combined cooking and storage functions; these are all tabulated here as storage.

[c]No storage vessels were specifically noted, but water jars were tabulated here as storage vessels.

1979, 125, 127). Some of these secondary services are beyond the concern of the archaeologist in estimating site occupation duration or size from culinary assemblages (e.g., the fragments are used as planters, feeders for animals, scoops, etc.; see table 9.5), but in other uses—for example, as griddles or in the common switch from liquid to dry storage with age—they are essentially being recycled into new primary activities in the absence of production of new vessels. In Chanal and Aguacatenango, Mexico, 21% of the household inventories were reused vessels (thirteen to eighteen vessels per household), with potters tending to reuse vessels more frequently than nonpotters in Chanal (Deal 1983, 179).

Another very common method of recycling broken vessels leaves no trace in the archaeological record—sherds may be ground into temper for use in pottery manufacture (see also sec. 14.1). This frequently involves destroying sherds from ancient middens (Stanislawski 1978, 222; DeBoer and Lathrap 1979, 111), but more typically the sherds used are modern manufactures. No estimates are available for the number of sherds or vessels used this way or for how much sherd counts or weights might be distorted as estimates of total numbers of vessels.

It might be added that these concerns of vessel recycling and replacement are of considerable interest to archaeologists not only for assemblage reconstruction, but also for seriational dating of sites. Differential and unpredictable rates of replacement of vessels, different use lives, and recycling all create problems for archaeological assumptions underlying seriation, such as the assumption of regular change through time. They therefore can give the impression of different populations rather than processes of developmental change (see David 1972; Hatch, Whittington, and Dyke 1982).

Item 6, the number of persons per household, is another complex issue that has been approached archaeologically in several ways. The most common approaches are to use ethnographic or ethnohistoric estimates of household composition, which can sometimes be projected back into prehistory; at other times estimates may be based on abstractions from worldwide ethnographic samples correlating household size with floor area of dwellings (Naroll 1962).

Less frequently, household size estimates have been based on ceramic data, specifically vessel volume capacities. In one such study household size was estimated by ratios of cooking-jar capacity to serving-bowl capacity (Turner and Lofgren 1966); the underlying assumption was that a cooking pot represented a household unit of food preparation, used to prepare a certain number of serving bowlfuls of food to feed the particular number of persons in that household. Comparisons were made between the capacities of three different types of vessels—ladles, individual serving bowls, and cooking jars—in archaeological collections representing Western Pueblo sites in northwestern Arizona. Ladles were found to have a mean capacity of 360 cc (approximately one and a half cups), while bowls had a mean capacity of 691 cc or two ladles; cooking jars had a bimodal distribution, with peaks above and below 8,000 cc (Turner and Lofgren 1966, 124–25). The sizes of households estimated by the jar-to-bowl ratios ranged between 4.4 and 5.1 persons; these could then be multiplied by numbers of rooms at individual Pueblo sites to yield estimates of the total site population (Turner and Lofgren 1966, 129–30; see also Nelson 1981).

Elsewhere, individual household size has been ignored in favor of directly estimating total site population from ethnographic data on breakage/replacement rates, a suggestion originally proposed by Foster (1960, 606). One study introduced these data into a computer simulation program to reconstruct the processes of deposition leading to the pottery assemblage recovered in probabilistic sampling excavations at the McKeithen site, a Weeden Island period site in northern Florida (Kohler 1978). The ceramic census and breakage/replacement rates came from the Fulani of Cameroon (David 1972; David and Hennig 1972), translated into an average inventory of 30 vessels per household, with breakage rates of 0.138 per year for utilitarian vessels and 0.056 for "elite" vessels. These figures were combined with sherd weight totals from the McKeithen site in a simulation of population changes over six hundred years of occupation. As simulated through the combined weight data and breakage rates, population at the site probably did not exceed 300–400 individuals, leading to the conclusion that the McKeithen site probably never reached a chiefdom level of social organization (Kohler 1978, 12). This issue was important for understanding not only the sociopolitical organization at the site but also questions of pottery production (Cordell 1984; Rice and Cordell 1986).

In other areas, permanence of site occupation rather than population has been investigated by pottery (e.g., Braun 1980). One such study (Shapiro 1984) was based on the assumption that the relative frequency and size of storage jars correlate with year-round (rather than seasonal) occupation and the need for permanent storage. Of four small late Mississippian sites in the Georgia piedmont, the largest had both the highest frequency and largest sizes of jars presumed to be used for storage, in conformance with test implications. This site is believed to have been occupied year-round, as suggested by the pottery as well as other independent lines of evidence. The other sites are interpreted as having varying degrees of semipermanent or transitory settlement.

9.4   References

Aldenderfer and Blashfield 1984
Bankes 1985
Baumhoff and Heizer 1959
Benfer 1975
Binford 1962a, 1965
Birmingham 1975
Blashfield and Draguns 1976
Braun 1980
Brew 1946
Chase 1985
Christenson and Read 1977
Clarke 1968
Cochran 1963
Colton 1953
Cordell 1984
Cowgill 1964, 1982
David 1972
David and Hennig 1972
Deal 1983
DeBoer 1974, 1985
DeBoer and Lathrap 1979
Deetz 1967
Doran and Hodson 1975
Dunnell 1971
Egloff 1973
Ellen 1979
Ford 1938, 1953
Foster 1960
Gardin 1980
Gifford 1960, 1976
Graves 1985
Grove and Buge 1978
Groves 1960
Hally 1983a, 1986
Hatch, Whittington, and Dyke 1982
Hill and Evans 1972
Hodson 1969, 1982
Hulthén 1974
Irwin 1977
Kaplan and Levine 1981
Keighley 1973
Kempton 1981
Kidder 1927, 1931
Kirkby and Kirkby 1976
Kirkpatrick 1978
Kluckhohn 1960

Kohler 1978
Krieger 1944
Lechtman 1977
Linares de Sapir 1969
Longacre 1981, 1985
Miller 1985
Millett 1979b
Mueller 1975a,b
Naroll 1962
Nelson 1981
Orton 1980, 1982
Otto 1975
Pastron 1974
Phillips 1958
Plog 1980, 1985
Redman 1974, 1978a
Reid 1984
Reina and Hill 1978
Rice 1976b, 1982
Rice and Cordell 1986
Rice and Saffer 1982
Rouse 1960
Rye and Evans 1976
Sabloff and Smith 1969, 1972
Schiffer 1976
Shapiro 1983, 1984
Shepard 1976
Smith 1983, 1985
Smith, Willey, and Gifford 1960
Smith 1962
Sokal and Sneath 1963
Solheim 1960, 1965, 1984
Spaulding 1953a,b, 1982
Stanislawski 1978
Steward 1954
Sturtevant 1964
Taylor 1948
Turner and Lofgren 1966
Vescelius 1960
Weigand 1969
Werner 1972
Whallon 1972, 1982
Whallon and Brown 1982
Wheat, Gifford, and Wasley 1958
Willey, Culbert, and Adams 1967
Willey and Sabloff 1980

Characterization Studies of Pottery

To make of unstable clay quick to fall to pieces or to crack, a solid and water-tight pottery there must have been a scientific attitude, an alert and sustained interest in knowledge for its own sake.

Claude Lévi-Strauss, *The Savage Mind*

Ceramic Characterization: An Introduction 10

The analysis of formed and fired ceramic materials—whether ancient or modern, whole or in fragments—usually begins with a description of the ceramic and its many properties, referred to as characterization. In modern industrial ceramic production, characterization studies are carried out for quality control, maintenance of performance standards, research and development, and reproducibility. In archaeological studies other objectives are at the fore, particularly inferring how the ceramic might have been used (chap. 12) and determining the location and techniques involved in its manufacture (chap. 14).

This chapter provides an introduction to the objectives and concepts of ceramic characterization, together with a summary of the properties measured and how the results may be interpreted. The methods discussed in chapters 11–14 are used to analyze physical, mechanical, thermal, structural, mineralogical, and chemical properties of ceramic materials. They can be used to characterize ethnographic vessels, archaeological pottery, or test tiles manufactured in the laboratory from clays collected in the field.

10.1 Characterization

Characterization is the qualitative and quantitative description of the composition and structure of a ceramic so as to evaluate its properties and uses and permit reproduction of the material (Hench 1971, 1). Numerous features of a ceramic can be the focus of characterization studies, including mineralogical composition, chemical composition, microstructure, and surface traits (Hench 1971, 2–3; Hench and Gould 1971). The methods chosen to study these features may be simple or complex, qualitative or quantitative, but they all describe the properties by objective, precise, and replicable standards. Their precision and replicability varies, of course, with some techniques being highly precise and accurate (see chap. 13 for specific comparisons) and others still incorporating elements of subjectivity. Nonetheless, the tests discussed in this chapter and subsequent ones permit the evaluation of ceramic materials in terms relatively free of the aesthetic or qualitative judgments common to art historical appraisals. More important, they yield a data base that can be used to relate the properties of the raw materials—such as plasticity, hardness, color, and chemical makeup—to human behavior and decision making in pottery production and use.

The precision and replicability of these procedures confers a number of advantages aside from reducing the subjective element. One advantage is that they allow definition of units of measurement or comparison that are standardized and independent of the context of observation. A pot that would be seen as hard and well fired in one cultural region may be considered relatively soft and poorly fired in another; describing it as having a Mohs' hardness of 4.0 and having been well oxidized at firing temperatures between 800°C and 850°C eliminates the ambiguity of these qualitative terms.

A related advantage is that with removal of the contextual limitations, characterization procedures can be used to compare archaeological, ethnographic, and industrial or commercial ceramic materials. This confers a tremendous potential in geographic areas where known continuities exist between historical pottery-manufacturing communities and prehistoric settlements, because the procedures allow investigation of long-term changes and similarities between manufacturing traditions.

Finally, because the results of these analyses are often expressed at the ordinal or interval levels of measurement, a variety of statistical manipulations can be employed in their interpretation. The statistical methods, like the characterization procedures themselves, range from relatively simple operations, such as tests of significance, to sophisticated multivariate techniques such as cluster analysis. These in turn allow evaluation of hypotheses about similarities, differences, patterns, or changes in large, complex ceramic data sets.

10.2 Technological Ceramic Studies

Most of the physicochemical characterization studies of pottery are undertaken within what has traditionally been called ceramic technology: the analysis and description of physical (broadly construed), mineralogical, and chemical properties of ceramic materials, both raw and fired, in order to understand their manufacture and use. Characterization studies of pottery thus apply the techniques of engineering and the natural or physical sciences to archaeological and ethnographic materials. With respect to archaeological data, at least, these approaches fall into the broader category of multidisciplinary research known as archaeometry. Coined as the name for the chief journal in the field, which began publication in 1958, archaeometry means using the methods of physics and chemistry to study many categories of artifactual data—stone, metal, and glass, as well as pottery. The status the field enjoys at present reflects a long history of slowly developing interest in the composition of artifacts (see, e.g., Matson 1952; Meschel 1978).

10.2.1 Historical Background

Application of the techniques of chemistry, physics, geology, and materials science to archaeological artifacts can be traced back to the late eighteenth century. Although many of the earliest investigations of the chemical composition of ancient artifacts were directed toward metals (see Caley 1951 for a review), a few focused on glass and pottery, materials typically originating in the classical area. M. H. Klaproth is usually cited (Caley 1949, 120; Bishop, Harbottle, and Sayre 1982, 272; Meschel 1978, 7) as the pioneer in this subject, for his work on the colors of ancient Italian glass tesserae. Chemical analysis of pottery goes back to the mid-nineteenth century, with study of the composition of the pottery of Nineveh (Layard 1853) as well as Faraday's finding lead in Roman pottery glazes (Meschel 1978, 7). Later in the nineteenth century, Richards (1895) studied the chemical composition of some Athenian pottery to determine its origin, laying the groundwork for contemporary provenience studies (Bishop, Harbottle, and Sayre 1982, 272).

Microscopic and mineralogical investigations of ancient pottery go back to the late nineteenth century and owe a great deal to the observations of Anatole Bamps. Bamps discussed the value of microscopic analyses of pottery in a paper presented at the Fifth International Congress of Americanists (1883), where he noted that red and black colors of different pots and colored layers in cross sections of individual vessels represented degrees of oxidation in firing rather than different clays. In addition, his early report called attention to mineral study for what is now called provenience analysis, as he noted the importance of combining mineral and chemical investigations. The role of mineral identifications in provenience studies also received an early impetus from the work of Nordenskiöld (1893) who—like Bamps—used petrographic thin sectioning to study aboriginal pottery. He applied the technique to sherds from Mesa Verde (Colorado) and also evaluated the possible sources of local clays and tempering materials.

Detailed descriptions of the technology of contemporary and ancient pottery manufacture generally appeared as short notes in regional publications, but several were more ambitious undertakings. Brongniart's early *Traité des arts céramiques* (1844) is a classic, as is Franchet's *Céramique primitive* (1911).

The late 1920s through the 1940s saw the founding of modern ceramic technological studies. Significant contributions during this period include Hawley's (1929, 1930) investigation of the chemical composition of black pigments in pottery of the Southwestern United States; the extensive technological, chemical, and petrographic studies of Anna O. Shepard at Pecos (1936), the La Plata District (1939), and the Rio Grande valley (1942a) in the Southwest and at San Jose, British Honduras (1942b), and Kaminaljuyú, Guatemala (1946), in Mesoamerica; the technological studies of F. R. Matson at Seleucia on the Tigris in the Near East (1939) and at the Younge site in Michigan (1937); early use of petrography at Troy (Felts 1942) and in Haiti (Horton and Berman 1941); early application of heavy mineral analysis in England (Wallis and Evens 1934); and spectrographic studies of early Chinese and Egyptian glass (Ritchie 1937; Farnsworth and Ritchie 1938). During this period, several analytical instruments also were developed that came to be of great significance in ceramic and other artifact studies. Electron microscopes were invented in the 1930s, and it was also during this time that X-ray diffraction came to be a reliable technique for investigating mineral structures. X-ray diffraction revealed that clays were crystalline substances, and X-ray radiogra-

phy showed promise as an investigative technique in archaeology (Titterington 1933; Drier 1939).

These same decades saw considerable effort to standardize the methods of
analysis and several published descriptions of archaeological pottery, for example, March's *Standards of Pottery Description* (1934). Indeed, Shepard's
"The Technology of Pecos Pottery" (1936) can be seen as constituting a first
draft of her later text, *Ceramics for the Archaeologist* (1976), first published
in 1956 and reprinted eight times. Several pioneering steps in systematizing
ceramic analysis in the Americas can be credited to the Museum of Anthropology at the University of Michigan. In 1928 Carl E. Guthe established the
Ceramic Repository for the Eastern United States there, and Michigan also
published March's (1934) guidelines for pottery description. In addition, the
first of a series of conferences on ceramic technology was organized and held
at the Museum of Anthropology of the University of Michigan in 1938: the
Conference of Archaeological Technology in Ceramics, sponsored by the National Research Council and attended by eleven conferees (Shepard and
Horton 1939). The second and third such conferences were sponsored by the
Wenner-Gren Foundation for Anthropological Research (Viking Fund) and
were held in 1961 at Burg Wartenstein, Austria (Matson, ed., 1965), and in
1981 in Lhee, the Netherlands (van der Leeuw and Pritchard 1984).

In the late 1950s and early 1960s, physicochemical analyses of pottery appeared with increasing frequency. Massive analytical programs were undertaken at major research institutions on both sides of the Atlantic, the Oxford
Laboratory for Archaeology and the History of Art focusing on optical emission spectroscopy while Brookhaven National Laboratory utilized neutron activation analysis (see Bieber et al. 1976, 59). Among the earliest subjects of
concentrated effort in physicochemical analysis, at these laboratories and
others, was Greek pottery, investigated by both mineralogical (Farnsworth
1964) and spectrochemical (e.g., Hofmann 1962; Catling, Blin-Stoyle, and
Richards 1961) techniques, although Far Eastern (Young and Whitmore 1957)
and European (e.g., Richards 1959; Musty and Thomas 1962) wares were examined as well. Perhaps the greatest stimulus to the later growth of chemical
analytical research was the application of neutron activation analysis, with its
high sensitivity and precision, to ceramic artifacts (Sayre and Dodson 1957;
Sayre, Murrenhoff, and Weick 1958; Emeleus 1960; Emeleus and Simpson
1960). The results from over twenty thousand of these neutron activation
analyses, primarily on Mesoamerican and eastern Mediterranean ceramics
and clays, are now stored in a data bank at a new research facility at the
Smithsonian Institution in Washington, D.C. (Beck 1984).

It was also during the 1950s that the application of physicochemical analyses to the broad range of archaeological artifacts gained widespread interest.
In 1950 the first of a series of symposia on archaeological chemistry was held
at the annual meeting of the American Chemical Society. The proceedings of
six of these symposia, all with ceramic-related research significantly represented, have been published (Caley 1951; Levey 1967; Brill 1971; Beck 1974;
Carter 1978; Lambert 1984). Similar interest in application of research techniques to historical and prehistoric topics has been manifest in the fields of
geology (Rapp 1977; Rapp and Gifford 1985; Kempe and Harvey 1983, xiii)

and, more recently, in ceramic engineering, with the establishment of a new publication series entitled Ceramics and Civilization (Kingery 1985), by the American Ceramic Society.

Apart from the meetings sponsored by professional societies, a very long and distinguished series of summary articles and compendiums, extending from the 1960s through the 1980s, treat—in whole or in part—the relation between the natural sciences and archaeological pottery (Aitken 1961, 16–24; Hall 1963 [in Pyddoke 1963]; Matson 1963 [in Brothwell and Higgs 1963]; Peacock 1970; Peacock, ed., 1977; Tite 1972, 208, 224–30, 314–28; Frierman 1980; Goffer 1980, 108–66; Olin and Franklin 1981; Howard and Morris 1981; Olin 1982; Williams 1983 [in Kempe and Harvey 1983]; Hughes 1981; Rice, ed., 1984; Orphanides 1985).

10.2.2 Technological Properties

Physical properties are significant descriptive characteristics of both raw materials (clays or clay/temper mixtures) and fired clay objects. Physical properties of unfired clay pastes include color, texture, plasticity, shrinkage, and strength. The physical properties of fired ceramic materials, most broadly conceived, are those that provide evidence of manufacture (surface or internal imperfections, dark coring, firing shrinkage, estimates of firing temperature) and those that characterize the appearance or functional capabilities of the finished piece. Among these latter are color (chap. 11) and mechanical, structural, and thermal properties such as porosity, hardness, texture or microstructure, strength, and thermal stress resistance (chap. 12).

Mineralogical properties or composition (sec. 13.2) constitute a more homogeneous set of variables than do physical properties. The mineral constituents of a ceramic include the specific clay mineral or minerals of the fabric as well as the larger or clastic grains naturally present in the clay or added as temper. Not only the identity of these added minerals but their physical characteristics, quantities, and associations are frequently important for determining sources of production of nonlocal wares. The mineral properties of a ceramic—the kinds, quantities, sizes, and shapes of individual mineral phases— are related to virtually all the physical properties, not just to texture and porosity but also to hardness, color, and strength. This is true not only of the large or clastic grains but of smaller grains as well, and the clay minerals themselves also contribute to these properties.

The chemical properties (sec. 13.3) of ceramic materials typically are discussed in terms of major, minor, and trace constituents. Major constituents usually include SiO_2, Al_2O_3, and iron, the principal chemical components of the clay fraction as well as of many of the clastics commonly occurring in a ceramic paste. Minor and trace elements usually occur in combinations and amounts that are more distinctive of individual clays or clay/temper combinations. It is the elements occurring in these tiny amounts, measured in parts per million or billion, that typically are the focus of chemical analysis.

It goes without saying, of course, that the chemistry of a ceramic is directly related to its mineralogy. Chemical analysis generally measures the elements or compounds in the ceramic material as a whole, that is, as clay plus temper, rather than within a specific mineral fraction. The same element may occur as an oxide or a compound in several minerals within a single pottery fabric, and the bulk chemical composition is thus a sum of all those occurrences. For this reason there is usually no attempt at achieving a one-to-one correspondence between the presence or amount of one particular element, oxide, or compound and the occurrence of a single mineral in the mixture.

Certain mineralogical and chemical comparisons may also provide a basis for inferring locations of production of particular vessel categories (sec. 14.2). Because of the technical precision required to detect and measure elements occurring as a few parts per billion of a larger matrix, analyses of trace or minor chemical constituents are often prohibitively expensive. Where these analyses have been carefully applied to clearly defined problems, however, the results have been exciting and justify the enormous cost (see chaps. 13 and 14).

10.2.3   Ceramic Ecology

The inferential potential of analyses of the physical, mineralogical, and chemical properties of a ceramic in illuminating the process of its manufacture can be enhanced if samples of raw materials—clays, tempers, and pigments—are available for analysis and comparison with the fired pieces. This procedure is one way of addressing the alternative possibilities mentioned above in trying to determine what choices potters made. Collecting and testing the raw materials used in pottery making is the focus of a research perspective closely related to ceramic technology, referred to as ceramic ecology (Matson 1965).

Ceramic ecology is a contextual approach to ceramic analysis that seeks to place technical data into both an ecological and a sociocultural frame of reference by relating the technological properties of the local resources to the production and use of the ceramic products. Ceramic ecology, like general cultural ecology, begins with studying the ceramic environment—local resources used in pottery making—as well as with describing the ecological and climatological features that might impinge on potters.

The resources most obviously of interest are clay, tempering materials (see sec. 14.1), and pigments for paints, slips, and glazes. Understanding the ceramic environment begins with studying the local geology and is predicated on recognizing not only the kinds of geological deposits (rocks and sediments) in the area and their ages, but also local hydrological conditions (drainage, flooding, stream cutting) and soils. In geologically active regions, it will be useful to have some idea of the history of volcanic eruptions or earthquakes. Fuel availability is also of considerable importance to ceramic manufacture (see secs. 5.4.1 and 6.1.3.2), and some idea of vegetation history, especially ancient or modern deforestation and reforestation, is essential.

Collecting clay, temper, and pigment resources, experimenting with these materials in the laboratory, and comparing them with the pottery of interest help define the effective or operational ceramic environment: the range of ceramic resources that were/are probably recognized and used by potters, past and present. Experimenting with these resources in the laboratory permits some insights into the characteristics of the clays, their working properties, and their limitations. This then begins to shed light on potters' choices in selecting, modifying, and working with particular clays. In addition, selecting the appropriate techniques of technological analysis and interpreting the results require an understanding of the local soils, geology, and hydrology.

The second aspect of studying the ceramic environment, investigating climatic conditions in the area of interest, has only recently received systematic attention. Meteorological factors are only indirectly relevant to interpretation of technological analyses, given that clays are relatively ubiquitous, and there are very few inhabited areas worldwide where pottery could not be made at all because of environmental factors. Weather is not a determining factor for pottery specialization (cf. Arnold 1985), but it is important to the scale of production and specialization within pottery making.

Certain weather-related conditions favor pottery making as an economic activity; particularly important are moderate to warm temperatures and a moderate to dry climate. Over much of the world these temperature and rainfall conditions vary seasonally with wet/dry or cold/warm portions of the year. Pottery is usually made in the warmer and drier seasons for ease, comfort, and more successful results. Arnold (1985, 61–77, table 3-2) tabulated data on manufacture and firing of pottery in forty-seven communities or cultures and identified a number of weather-related problems or limitations in scheduling pottery production (table 10.1).

Most attention is given to the constraints posed by rain, but dry weather or water shortages may also limit certain aspects of technology, such as levigating clays and wheel-throwing pots, which take more water (McGovern 1986, 44). One of the most significant ways seasonality affects pottery making as an economic activity concerns how the seasonal scheduling of agriculture (Arnold 1985, 99–108) relates to production specialization (see sec. 6.2.3). The annual rhythm of production also may vary with religious and festival cycles (e.g., Lynch 1979, 6; Miller 1985, 84–85), which of course are often governed by seasonal change and the agricultural cycle.

Table 10.1   Weather-Related Limitations on Pottery Making

Rainy season
Digging clay (mines may collapse or be flooded)
Too wet or cold to work comfortably
Drying pottery
  Takes too long
  Pots need protection
Firing pottery
  Wind, rain, dampness, snow, frost
  Greater losses
  Fuel is wet
  More fuel required, so costs increase
Conflicting demands (of agricultural activities)

Dry season
Pots dry too fast (cracking)
Greater demands for water vessels

Source: After Arnold 1985, table 3.2.

Extreme climatological features, such as excessive cold, rainfall, or wind, can place constraints on the manufacturing process, for example, by affecting the plasticity of raw clays and the drying and firing of finished vessels (see Arnold 1975b, 1985, 61–98). Cold weather makes it unpleasant to work with wet clay, and frost can crack incompletely dried pots, thus destroying the fruits of several hours or even weeks of labor. Heavy rainfall (absolute amounts and seasonality) and wind are of interest over the long term because they can cause erosion of the landscape, which in turn will affect the continuing exposure of clay deposits that potters may use. Rainfall is particularly disruptive when it is heavily seasonal (e.g., India's monsoons; Lynch 1979, 6), but it can create difficulties at all stages of the manufacturing process, as detailed by Papousek (1981, 58) for highland Mexico:

> Especially during the summer rains, excavating the clay was impossible, while transport became difficult because of the impassability of the roads and footpaths. Drying, milling, sifting and—if there was a lack of space inside—storing the clay were also impossible. Nor could [the pottery] be dried or decorated. As a result, the potter, because of a lack of material, could not occupy himself with preparing [clay], moulding or glazing.
> Finally, firing the kilns was generally impossible during rainfall. First of all, most of the kilns were open at the top. . . . Secondly, the fuel was wet and thus unusable. Thirdly, during rain the lower part of the kiln, where the fire was made and which was dug out of the ground, filled up with water. During the rainy season, the water stayed in the kiln for weeks.

The ideal solution to these problems is roofed storage and working areas that will keep rain away from clay, freshly formed vessels, fuel, and kilns, but for economic reasons this is not always practicable.

Observing and measuring meteorological conditions is fairly straightforward in areas of modern ceramic manufacture. For inferred loci of prehistoric pottery manufacture, however, these conditions can only be broadly retrodicted from present meteorological data or paleoclimatic reconstructions (e.g., by pollen diagrams). One of the few explicitly ceramic ecological studies is that by Arnold (1975a) in the Ayacucho basin of the Peruvian Andes. He relates the development of a tradition of pottery craft specialization near the site of Wari from prehistoric to modern times to low rainfall, a heavily eroded landscape, and the general inhospitability of the area for subsistence agriculture. Similar conditions obtained for continuity of ceramic production in the northern valley of Guatemala, in the Guatemalan highlands (Arnold 1978; Rice 1978a).

Apart from analyses of the ceramic resources and environment, further ceramic ecological investigation procedures are directly feasible only in a modern ethnographic setting. These include studying behavior patterns in pottery making (e.g., by age or sex), tools used, social organization, patterns of learning, and seasonal (or similar) rhythms of production (see chap. 5). In prehistoric contexts these behaviors can only be inferred by general or specific analogies with ethnographically known pottery-making communities, which of course renders them vulnerable to the same problems that beset other applications of analogue reasoning in archaeology.

The final step of a ceramic ecological investigation is relating the accumulated data on the environmental and sociotechnological factors of pottery making to the broader role of pottery in a culture. This includes such features as economic organization (local and long-distance trade arrangements), kinship structure, settlement patterns, demographic factors, ceremonial or ritual activities, and so forth.

Pottery manufacture, like any other productive technology, represents a point where a cultural system interacts directly with the environmental system. Although it is difficult to make the range of ceramic ecological procedures fully operational in prehistoric research contexts, a ceramic ecological approach provides a broader perspective on the role of pottery in a culture from archaeological, technological, and ethnographic viewpoints. No longer does pottery represent simply a convenient means of dating sites and tracing trade patterns, a category of useful containers, or a clever craft item to sell to tourists. Instead, ceramic ecology can be linked with ceramic technology to show pottery production as one of many patterned ways of exploiting particular environments and as one of a variety of economic adjustments in a network of productive relations in a society. Ceramic ecology emphasizes the potter's role as an active and controlling agent in the procedures of pottery manufacture (resource selection, forming techniques, firing strategies) as these are revealed through technological analyses of both ancient and modern pottery.

10.3   Research Design Considerations

10.3.1   Identifying Problems

In ceramic characterization studies, as in any research endeavor, it is important first to define the problem, then to select methods and samples in light of the particular questions to be answered. All too often, unfortunately, the reverse is done: a collection of sherds or a piece of equipment is the starting point, and a research question is formulated in accordance with the capabilities of what is at hand or the answers already found.

It is impossible and indeed totally undesirable to try to catalog ceramic research problems and the methods appropriate to their solution. But these are surveyed extensively in succeeding chapters, either in discussion of the individual characterization methods (in chaps. 11–13) or in terms of particular kinds of cultural research questions (chap. 14). Perhaps the reasons for carrying out technological or characterization studies of pottery were best articulated by Shepard (1936, 389) in the opening words of her study of Pecos pottery:

> The immediate purposes of a ceramic technological investigation are to identify the materials and locate their sources, to study the indications of workmanship, and to describe properties by reference to exact, impersonal standards. There are two ultimate aims in the interpretation of technological data. The first is to trace the history of the potter's craft; the second is to recover more accurately and in greater detail than is possible by other methods the evidence which pottery preserves of cultural development, contacts, and influences.

Technological properties of pottery—the physical, mineralogical, and chemical characteristics of ceramic materials—constitute an irreducible minimum of detail on individual ceramic objects. For this reason, technological information can be employed in solving a broad variety of questions. Technological data are independent of other common categorizations of pottery used by archaeologists, such as styles, type classes, or shape categories, yet they can be used for comparing such groupings or creating new ones. In combination with ceramic ecology, ceramic technology can, for example, characterize properties of both resources and pottery and permit comparisons between pottery and resources as well as between prehistoric and contemporary pottery. Furthermore, these objectives can be achieved on broken fragments as well as intact vessels. The techniques provide a basis for understanding many questions about manufacturing techniques, history of technology, production organization, functional relationships between specific resource manufacturing combinations, and patterns of local, regional, or extraregional distributions of pottery. These are the fundamental research problems of ceramic technological (and ecological) analysis.

10.3.2   Selecting a Sample

Most archaeological investigations yield enormous quantities of potsherds, but because of cost and time not all can be given complete individual characterization. It thus falls to the archaeologist (or anthropologist studying contemporary manufactures) to select a sample for analysis. Given the high cost of many of the physicochemical analysis methods, their remarkable sensitivity to infinitesimal amounts of particular elements in the specimens, and archaeologists' general preoccupation with sampling issues in the field (Mueller 1975b; Redman 1974), it seems logical to expect that great attention would be paid to sampling sherd collections or clays for archaeometric analysis. Sadly, this is not the case, and there are few adequate treatments of the subject (among the most useful being Shackley 1975, 23–36; Rye 1981, 6–8, 12–13; Bishop, Rands, and Holley 1982, 278–80).

Although sampling sherd collections specially for physicochemical analysis has received little attention, there has been considerable discussion of quantitative analysis of large sherd collections (Solheim 1960; Cowgill 1964; Keighley 1973) and formalized field and laboratory procedures for recording ceramic data (see, e.g., Bennett 1974; Peacock, ed., 1977; Redman 1978a; Joukowsky 1978, 1982; Sedgwick, Fossey, and Attas 1980; David 1982; Fossey, Sedgwick, and Attas 1982; Anderson-Stojanovic 1982). Many of these studies were carried out in conjunction with mineralogical or chemical characterization projects, and the suggestions for what information to record, and in what way, are applicable beyond the immediate concerns of the individual projects.

If the archaeologist envisions that physicochemical investigations will be part of the postexcavation analyses, a ceramic technologist, archaeometrist, or someone skilled in physical and chemical analysis of pottery and clays should be consulted before the fieldwork begins to discuss objectives, methods, and limitations, with particular attention to contamination that can occur

by standard procedures of washing, drying, cataloging, and conserving artifacts. Ideally, the consultant should be in the field for a significant portion of
the fieldwork so as to be familiar with the excavation contexts and geological
situation.

Any investigation of ceramic technology at an archaeological site or region, or in an ethnographic setting, is most fruitfully conducted within the
perspectives of ceramic ecology. This means it is essential to search out deposits and sample them so as to compare the pottery of interest with the properties of local clays. At the same time, sources of possible tempering agents,
pigments, and other important pottery constituents (glazes, mineral coatings)
should be found and sampled as well.

10.3.2.1 SAMPLING RESOURCES

Sampling clays and other resources in a region poses two problems: locating
them and obtaining clean samples (see Talbott 1984 for a general discussion).

The easiest way to locate suitable clays and other resources is to ask local
informants. If there are contemporary communities of traditional potters in
the area (Rye 1981, 14–15; Rice 1978a, 433–44), or craft potters who work
with natural clays, they may be willing to tell where they get their materials.
Elderly residents in rural areas may remember former potters and know where
they obtained their clays; workers in modern farming or construction—excavating for house foundations, laying sewer pipe, and so forth—may also
have encountered clays or clayey soils.

It is also advisable to consult soil and geological maps of the region to learn
about local hydrological patterns, soils and subsoils, and variations in geological deposits. These maps are rarely satisfactory for archaeological location purposes, however, because they typically are not at a fine scale; in addition, geological maps may record only commercially valuable clay deposits,
and soil charts may have been created by recording differences in standing
vegetation. Nonetheless, it may be useful to travel along river or stream
courses, lakeshores, or estuaries looking for outcrops or bluffs with clayey
deposits exposed. The area within a radius of about 7 km from the site of
interest should be given greatest attention, since this appears to be the zone
where potters most commonly procure primary resources (see sec. 5.2).

Within the site itself, excavators should take special care with unusual
earthy deposits in the debris within rooms or yards (Jeancon 1923, 36–37;
Southward and Kamilli 1983), since these may indicate deposits of potter's
clays. In addition, clays or clayey soils within or underlying cultural deposits
also should be noted. Depending on the situation, it may be helpful to test
with a soil auger to determine the location or extent of buried clay deposits
(see Shackley 1975, 24–29).

Because of space, cost, and distance, it is often useful to carry out preliminary tests of the workability of a clay at the deposit before bringing it back to
the laboratory. A small pinch of wet clay (or dry clay with water added) can be
squeezed, rolled into a rope, and twisted to get some idea of workability (see
sec. 3.2.2). A deposit that is extremely coarse and sandy or mealy and cracks
under slight pressure is not likely to have been suitable for potting and is
probably not worth careful sampling.

Table 10.2   A Clay Sample Recording Form

SAMPLE #: ———

DATE: ———

COLLECTOR/RECORDER:

COLLECTION LOCATION:

THICKNESS OF DEPOSIT:

FORM AND EXTENT OF DEPOSIT:

HOW EXPOSED:

CHARACTERISTICS IN SITU:

MATERIAL OVERLYING:

MATERIAL UNDERLYING:

SURROUNDING NATURAL FEATURES:

CULTURAL FEATURES:

AMOUNT SAMPLED:

OTHER REMARKS:

For all clay deposits sampled, as well as other materials, a standardized reporting form should be used to record essential information. This should include data on the deposits underlying and overlying the clay, the color and texture of the material, how the deposit was exposed, the thickness of the deposit, kind and degree of known or probable contamination (such as rootlets), and so forth (see table 10.2).

In taking a sample of a clay, it is most important to avoid contaminating it with soil or other materials, a serious impediment to sensitive chemical analyses. If the deposit is in an outcrop, stream bank, or some other more or less vertical exposure, its face should be carefully scraped with a clean trowel back to a depth of at least 10 cm. This will reduce surface contamination and expose a fresh area for sampling. Where there is a horizontal exposure, the same guideline applies. In auger testing, the continual danger of contamination from the coring procedure is a serious disadvantage. In all situations, it is advisable to take multiple samples of the material both vertically and horizontally (see Talbott 1984, 1048–49), because there may be natural compositional variations owing to the original conditions of deposition.

The amount of material sampled often depends on conditions of exposure and the logistics of transportation. While the actual sample necessary for mineral or chemical analysis is tiny—only a few grams at most—it is useful to have much greater quantities for tests of workability, plasticity, firing, and so forth. In addition, to try to achieve some representativeness for chemical characterization, a larger amount of the material is usually prepared and then repeatedly subsampled (see below). Finally, given the volatile political situation in many areas of the world, it may be impossible (or at least expensive) to return later to collect more of the material. To bring soils into the United States from foreign areas, it is necessary to have an import permit from the United States Department of Agriculture.

A sample of approximately 5 kg, the equivalent of a bucketful, is usually satisfactory. The clay should be removed with a clean shovel, trowel, or auger, with special care to avoid contamination with surface soil or other foreign matter, then placed in clean plastic bag and immediately sealed and labeled with an identification name or number, or both, keyed to the recording form. Double bagging is advisable, with the label placed between the two bags rather than inside with the clay.

10.3.2.2 SAMPLING SHERD COLLECTIONS

Many of these same considerations apply in selecting a sample of sherds from a larger collection (see also sec. 9.2.1). There is an enormous range of recognized variation in visible characteristics, and it is extremely difficult to break down a collection into a much smaller number of sherds that represent the variations in the entire collection (see Cowgill 1964).

The best starting point is the identification of a problem, and this is where the sample selection procedure is relevant. Whatever the research problem— and many are addressed in the succeeding chapters—the categories of archaeological pottery from which the sample will be drawn are generally those traditionally used in archaeology (see sec. 9.1): types, decorative classes, shape classes, and wares, as well as chronological and regional variations. However, it is useful to be aware of broader criteria for categorizing pottery that are based on attributes more relevant to technological and archaeometric investigations. These include hardness, porosity, shaping techniques, and firing.

Although the greatest proportion of the sample should be weighted toward the sherds judged to be "typical," the extremes of variation should also be included. These variants might represent extremely early or late examples or unusual contexts. More commonly, however, they may be variations in the state of some attribute, in which case the prevailing direction of the variations from the norm (toward over- rather than underfiring or toward darker rather than lighter colors) will itself be informative. In addition, it may be useful to include a selection of the "exotics"—rare or atypical sherds or presumed nonlocal items at the site—as a basis for comparison.

The emphasis on understanding the range of variability in human behavior and artifacts (see Clarke 1968) is part of a general rejection of normative approaches in anthropology, but it has a special significance in ceramic characterization studies:

> The classificatory and control devices used by potters in the past have usually been far less precise than our facilities for analyzing their results. Materials that vary widely according to our physical and chemical measurements may have been considered identical or interchangeable. Methods of measurement were also less sensitive.

Materials for blending, for example, were often calculated by volume rather than weight. Potters using clay and sand mixes might judge that "two handfuls of sand is enough for this much clay." Although our measurements might determine that the proportion of sand varies between 20 and 45 percent, this variability might be viewed by the potter as within the normal range; he would consider a body with 20 percent sand identical to one with 45 percent sand. Similarly, firing temperatures, whether in open firings or kilns, can vary not only between firings and within settings, but over parts of a single vessel by as much as 400°C. The same latitude applies to the shapes of vessels; the criteria used by a potter to judge that two vessels are the "same" may be difficult or impossible to reconstruct. Thus, the parameters for defining a technological tradition cannot be specified until the range of variations encompassed within the tradition can be differentiated from characteristics that are outside the "normal" range. (Rye 1981, 27–28)

It is also useful to select sherds representing a range of areas on the vessel, including the rim, body, and appendages (supports, handles, spouts, etc.), particularly if vessel form is not the primary attribute guiding sample selection. This provides an additional bit of information on the sherds themselves that may prove useful in interpreting differences in physicochemical properties. In addition, it is possible that the composition of different vessel parts may vary (see sec. 5.2).

Given that virtually all the technological characterization methods are directed toward analysis of the fabric or paste of the ceramic, a small corner should be broken off all sherds in the preliminary stages of investigation. This permits examination of the paste in a fresh cross section as well as preliminary sorting (under a hand lens or binocular microscope, if available) into categories by such attributes as paste constituents, color, hardness, and texture.

Whatever the archaeological problem and classification scheme used for the sherds, some more general guidelines can be offered for selecting samples for characterization analysis. The sherds chosen should be as large as possible: it is extremely useful to be able to break them into smaller fragments for refiring tests, porosity tests, and strength measurements as well as the many kinds of mineralogical and chemical tests requiring that a gram or so of the specimen be cut or crushed.

Not only should the sherds be large, but many should be chosen. The more sherds in the sample, the greater the likelihood that they will provide an accurate picture of the total range of variability in the collection. There is one rather significant difficulty in this, however: in trying to select a sample of large sherds that proportionally reflects the existence of some attribute in the population, one should remember that sherds have different breakage rates (see sec. 9.2). Sherds of lower-fired wares are apt to break more easily and thus to be present in smaller sizes but proportionally greater quantities in the assemblage.

The sherds selected for characterization should also have well-preserved surfaces, with little or no evidence of erosion, encrustation, discoloration, or mineralization. Although the surfaces of sherds are routinely removed before chemical analysis as a precaution against contamination, it is impossible to know to what extent damp soils and groundwater may have permeated porous low-fired pottery and altered its chemical or mineral content (e.g., see Courtois 1976; Franklin and Vitali 1985; Freestone, Meeks, and Middleton 1985). Such rehydration, which is most likely to occur in environments with high permanent humidity and relatively stable temperatures, can affect a variety of properties and analyses including cation exchange, alteration of iron oxides, differential thermal analysis, X-ray diffraction, magnetic dating, and firing-temperature determinations.

It is also useful to have stylistic information preserved on the sherd surfaces, particularly if decorative style was not the primary basis for sample selection, as a further aid in interpreting the results of characterization study. As noted elsewhere (Bishop, Rands, and Holley 1982, 279–80), a sherd sampled for chemical (or other) analysis becomes a special resource, and it is wise to select sherds that preserve maximum cultural information.

In addition, sherds should be selected from well-documented archaeological contexts, that is, from carefully excavated locations with unambiguous cultural significance. They should ideally be from sealed stratigraphic contexts (pits, burials, storage areas, etc.), from deposits of known date, and from units that can be clearly identified or differentiated as to status and residential, ethnic, or functional associations. These are ideal conditions, and frequently the pragmatics of archaeological excavations do not permit satisfying them all. An important possible exception is in the application of these techniques to the enormous collections of artifacts already lying in storage in the world's museums. These collections are frequently shunned because they were excavated decades ago, before today's more rigorous standards of scientific procedure. Although the exact date and provenience of these sherds may be unknown, they often are from easily identifiable types, forms, or wares and may be considered relatively expendable for examination by some of the more damaging methods (requiring that sherds be cut or broken). If these materials have been glued or painted in reconstruction of vessels or exposed to chemicals for cleaning, preservation, or fumigation, chemical analysis is not advised.

Finally, the decision must be made whether the sherds or vessels can be damaged in obtaining a sample for analysis. Some techniques of chemical analysis require only a few micrograms of sample, which can be obtained from an inconspicuous area at the base of a whole vessel, allowing exhibit-quality objects to remain effectively undamaged. Other techniques, however, particularly the petrographic methods, require that slices several millimeters thick be removed from the specimen or that several grams be crushed. Techniques for examining physical properties such as strength or porosity, or refiring tests, require that fairly large (and sometimes multiple) samples of standard size be cut from the sherd, and this much damage may preclude applying them to any but the most expendable of undecorated wares.

Selecting the sherds for analysis is usually best accomplished through some preliminary sorting procedure where variations are observed and noted. Sorting may be done either by visual inspection or under a binocular microscope. It is usually a good practice to begin with a very large preliminary sample and then sample further within that assemblage as the steps of the analysis proceed; it is also best to begin with the simplest techniques or properties for characterization and work up to more complex and costly ones. In other words, there should be a constant interaction between successive levels of analysis and selection of sherds for additional study, always using earlier findings as guidelines for later procedures.

10.3.2.3 SAMPLING FOR ANALYSIS

The final step in sampling, and one of the most critical, is usually carried out at the last stages of the investigation, if researchers decide to determine the chemical composition of some component of a set of sherds. This requires, first, understanding the methods of analysis—the sample size and configuration needed, the elements they can determine, and their accuracy (see sec. 13.3). In some cases it also requires that a sample of the sherd be removed for analysis, and this entails special problems in sample preparation and extraction.

Sherds must be cleaned of contamination on surfaces and edges. This is usually accomplished by scraping with a noncontaminating drill or burr, commonly sapphire, tungsten carbide, or diamond. The sample itself may be obtained by breaking off a section (with clean pliers) and crushing in an agate mortar or by drilling into the core of the sherd (or the base of exhibit vessels) with the clean bit of a noncontaminating drill. Drill bits vary in size down to very small diameters, so it is possible to extract small amounts of material even from very thin sherds. It is advisable to sample the sherds in more than one place to get a more representative selection of material, and to obtain a considerably larger quantity than is actually required by the technique. The separate samples may be analyzed individually or mixed together in a clean vial or crucible and then subsampled for analysis. The usual method for subsampling is to heap the fine powder into a pile, quarter it, and select one quarter, then to repeat this procedure until the material has been reduced to the amount needed.

The analytical techniques that measure elements in amounts as tiny as parts per million or billion are extremely sensitive to slight compositional variations caused by contaminants, by natural inhomogeneities in the raw material and in the final product, or by careless sampling. Because the object of these trace element analyses is to determine meaningful compositional differences in sherds, and sometimes to compare them with raw materials to determine their place of manufacture or provenience, it is extremely important that the compositional differences determined for the sherds reflect real differences in raw materials and not errors introduced by contamination or sampling. Considerable attention has been devoted in the literature to avoiding contamination during sample extraction and preparation (Reeves and Brooks 1978, 14–15; Carriveau 1980; Attas, Fossey, and Yaffe 1984) as well as to issues of analytical precision and quantification (see Bishop, Harbottle, and Sayre 1982). Although the research objectives also require a whole conflation of assumptions (treated at length in sec. 14.2), here it is important to deal further with the sampling issue.

The most important question is sample size, and a look at some of the literature on sampling rocks and particulate matter for chemical analysis (e.g., Kleeman 1967; Shotton and Hendry 1979, 82; DeBruin et al. 1976;

Bromund, Bower, and Smith 1976; Shackley 1975, 24–25; Reeves and Brooks 1978, 5–6) places less emphasis on the frequency of the clastics and more on grain size in sample selection. The larger the average (sometimes the maximum) size of the grains in the material to be analyzed, the larger the sample must be to represent the whole—a tiny amount might register chemical aberrancies such as unusual grains that would not reflect the overall composition.

The amount of material required is directly proportional to grain size, and several scholars have recommended that for material with average particle sizes of less than 5 mm (which certainly applies to virtually all pottery), and even with inclusions of 1 mm, a sample of 1 kg should be crushed, mixed, and subsampled to ensure true representativeness (Shackley 1975, 24; Reeves and Brooks 1978, 5; Shotton and Hendry 1979, 82). It is immediately obvious that sherd samples for chemical analysis never approach that amount, more typically being on the order of several micrograms. The question that should be asked—but has not yet been investigated in any depth—is whether the usual sampling procedure for archaeological trace element analyses of pottery, involving such tiny quantities of material, really gives an accurate picture of the chemical composition of the individual sherds, the wares they represent, or the raw materials from which they were manufactured. Recognition of these potential problems with sampling has led to an alternative practice: separating coarse and fine fractions and analyzing them individually (e.g., Fillières, Harbottle, and Sayre 1984).

Until these questions of sampling are resolved and realistic guidelines for sampling coarsely crystalline archaeological materials such as pottery have been proposed, it is wise to take a conservative approach to trace element analysis of pottery. The technique is extremely expensive, and it requires many assumptions to use it to infer the origins of pottery. While trace chemical analyses of very fine-paste, ostensibly untempered wares can be pursued with considerable promise of success, applying these procedures to coarse wares or sandy pastes is probably ill advised, and petrographic techniques will yield far more useful information about composition and resource origins.

Above all, it is important to remember that a sample is part of a larger entity or population (see sec. 9.2.1). In virtually any sampling situation, and particularly with clay deposits and archaeological sherd collections, it is not known precisely what constitutes the population. That is, the full extent of clay beds and their variability can rarely be comprehended, because they extend for indeterminate horizontal and vertical distances beneath the surface of the earth. Similarly, because archaeological sites are never excavated in their entirety, the true population of ceramic vessels at a site is never known. An excavated sherd and vessel collection is itself a sample of the site; the collection may or may not be a fair representation of the complete ancient assemblage, and it is better considered as the available population rather than the true population. Consequently it is impossible to know if the sample selected from the collection is proportional to any existing reality in prehistoric times. The nightmarish ramifications of these considerations for interpretation of ceramic data have been virtually ignored, although similar problems for archaeological data in general have been treated at length (Binford 1964; Mueller 1975b).

10.3.3 Selecting Methods of Analysis

Technological analyses and characterization should begin with simple methods of observation rather than with the more complex and costly ones (Hench 1971, 3–4). These can be relatively quickly and easily applied to large collections of ceramic materials to sort out significant categories and aberrant specimens. A low-power hand lens and a pair of snub-nosed pliers for breaking fresh cross sections of sherds are often enough for preliminary sorting by color and texture. Scratching the surface with a fingernail or a penknife, or tapping sherds against a hard surface, suffices for rough sorting by hardness.

These simple techniques provide a quick scan for determining the range of variability of the collection on a number of characteristics. They also serve as a background for selecting an appropriate smaller sample for the more specialized and expensive physicochemical techniques often employed in ceramic technological analyses, particularly in identifying production areas and in studying trade. Whether the focus is on the wares thought to be more "typical" of the collection or on the unusual specimens, it is important to have a frame of reference incorporating the variability of the entire collection in order to establish a context for interpreting the analytical results.

If more detailed information on the composition of the pottery is needed, then selection from the variety of instrumental physicochemical techniques for mineralogical and chemical characterization (chap. 13) is warranted. Each of these techniques, however, provides very different kinds of data, and the suitability of each method depends on the geological setting where the resources were obtained and on the questions being asked. Mineral and chemical analyses, for example, are both extremely informative, but they tell very different things about the ceramic. In general the most productive strategy is to combine mineral and chemical methods rather than relying strictly on one or the other. The more complex and sophisticated the method of analysis, the more difficult it is to interpret the results in behavioral terms because of the problems of translating mineral and chemical data into human decisions about pottery production and trade.

This interpretational leap is easier when one examines physical properties of ceramics, which include a broad range of characteristics that relate rather closely to the procedures of selecting and preparing resources and forming and firing a vessel, and to the vessel's final appearance and use. As such they can be considered to reflect more directly the choices potters make from a range of alternatives. For other properties the choices and decisions of the potter are not free, being effectively ordained by cultural patterns or traditions; for example, where the use of a particular clay source is explicitly part of a potting community's self-identification, as in Chinautla, Guatemala (Reina and Hill 1978, 236–38).

Particular minerals may be used to modify physical properties, as in adding attapulgite clay as temper (Arnold 1971) or adding salt to a calcareous clay to prevent lime popping (Rye 1976), or for specific decorative objectives, as in applying graphite or cinnabar. Pigments—for paints and slips—usually are particular chemical compounds (usually found as minerals) such as oxides of iron, manganese, or copper. In high-fired vitrified wares, and in wares with glazed surfaces, the chemical composition is critical because adding certain compounds (or minerals) lowers the melting point of the mixture and promotes vitrification.

Determining the relation between the mineral constituents of a ceramic and the decisions of traditional potters is not straightforward. Whether it is a matter of free choice or conditioned by *costumbre* (custom), the selection of clay and temper (and also pigment) resources rarely means explicitly differentiating one mineral from another; rather, it involves recognizing that a mineral confers some desirable property. In this regard potters are often highly discriminatory about which clays or tempers are acceptable (Arnold 1971). Similarly, the chemical composition of a low-fired earthenware body is a consequence of the choice of clay and temper and their properties rather than the product of specific known chemical formulas.

10.4 Interpreting Technological and Characterization Studies

Interpreting the significance of quantitative and qualitative physicochemical characterizations of ceramic materials and variations between classes of pottery being analyzed is an independent procedure that is not contingent upon the technique itself. Several cautions are in order.

One caution is that characterization studies can bestow a false sense of precision. The selection and testing of materials in ceramic engineering research are considerably more standardized than they are in nonindustrialized pottery manufacture (see sec. 4.3; also Rye 1981, 27–28); thus the purity of the ceramic materials being tested and the experimental conditions are far more controlled. Many of these tests confer the additional advantage of precise measurement of variables in units such as microns or milligrams. It should be remembered, however, that the socioeconomic concepts that anthropologists and archaeologists may be investigating through pottery samples are rarely if ever formulated with comparable precision, nor can they be experimentally controlled with similar exactitude. Thus, although particular tests and measurements may be statistically significant or significant with respect to engineering standards, they may not be behaviorally significant within the past or present cultural context of the investigation.

Another caution is that though the technological tests allow objective description of pottery remains, the researcher must exercise care in interpreting the results. Subjective judgments of vessels as "poorly" made, for example, are best avoided. At the very least they must be carefully phrased within a narrow comparative framework relative to the specific context under investigation. Vessels that to twentieth-century eyes may seem coarse, porous, and underfired may have been carefully crafted to accommodate the peculiar properties of the resources locally available as well as to meet certain use requirements (e.g., in cooking or storage; see sec. 7.5).

Finally, significant differences in the kinds, sizes, or quantities of particular materials between two or more vessel categories (forms, decorative classes, etc.) may represent conscious choices made by the potter and may corroborate structural or physical principles of engineering, mineralogy, or chemistry.

They cannot necessarily be assumed to represent such decisions, however, unless alternative possibilities (and chance alone) can be eliminated. Association between variables, in ceramics as in other areas, is simply a statement of relation between those variables and does not automatically reflect human intent: correlation does not prove causation.

Characterization tests must be interpreted within some sort of a broader framework by which technological properties are viewed as manifestations of nonrandom occurrence or deliberate human action, and that action in turn must be seen within a cultural or historical context involving the production, distribution, and use of ceramic materials. This interpretational transition is not easy. Although the technical instrumentation of materials analysis has advanced to extreme sophistication, there has not been a corresponding development of what is called "middle-range theory" to bridge the gap between technological data and sociocultural theories, a body of relational statements that will allow analysts to take advantage of the technological precision. Nonetheless, the transition from the technological to the cultural is a basic and unavoidable research responsibility in the analysis of ceramic materials.

There are, of course, a variety of ways of making this transition, and many of them are interrelated. Ceramic ecology is a restatement of earlier ideas on the relation of cultural interpretations of technical data—for example, the concept of "techniculture" (Osgood 1951). R. H. Thompson borrowed this concept in his study of continuities between ancient and modern Maya pottery in Yucatán, noting (1958, 6) that the "technical and ecological factors which condition the properties, source, and availability of raw materials define a specific range of possibilities for the manufacture of any class of artifacts." Many of the criteria for defining this range of technological possibilities come from the various natural and physical sciences; these provide the basis for investigating such properties as plasticity, strength, shrinkage, and vitrification point. The technical observations and measurements from any artifact must be linked to inferences about human behavior involved in its production and use, however, and this is the "technicultural" objective of analyses of material culture. Thompson (1958, 7) uses pottery as an example:

> Basic to the interpretation of ceramic evidence is the generalization that clay becomes plastic when mixed with water. But the significance of this generalization to a specific type of archaeological ceramics is obscured unless the technological data are rephrased to emphasize some use which man makes of this plastic property. This shift in emphasis from the purely technical property to the use to which man puts it introduces cultural factor. The generalization then becomes a technicultural combination, technical data in a cultural frame of reference.

A similar point of view exists in the ceramic engineering literature: "Data taking alone is not valid characterization regardless of how sophisticated the technique may be—correlation of the data with properties and behavior is essential for characterization to be meaningful" (Hench 1971, 4).

A complementary interpretation is offered by Lechtman (1977). Arguing that technologies represent activities or "performances" carried out in culturally prescribed ways, she feels that anthropologists and archaeologists should exploit this information to study technological styles:

> The culturally accepted rules of the performance are embodied in the events that led to the production of the artifact. We should be able to "read" those events, if not all of them at least those of a technical nature, through laboratory study of the materials that make up the artifacts in question. The history of the manipulation of those materials is locked into their physical and chemical structure: the methods of material science can interpret that technological history. (Lechtman 1977, 14)

Technological styles incorporate materials and behavior: they represent a society's interactions with its environment, relating to specific patterns of exploiting particular kinds of materials in agreed-upon ways. Like other kinds of styles, they are a means of communicating information; as such, they are symbolic systems that contain messages about the society that manufactures and uses the items (see sec. 8.3.3). Those messages, of course, cannot be interpreted with reference to technology alone, but they are clarified within the broader context of the society, its cosmological structures, ritual behavior, overall productive systems, relations with neighboring areas, and other kinds of symbolic codes expressed in a variety of material categories.

10.5   References

Aitken 1961
Anderson-Stojanovic 1982
Arnold 1971, 1975a,b, 1978, 1985
Attas, Fossey, and Yaffe 1984
Bamps 1883
Beck 1974, 1984
Bennett 1974
Bieber et al. 1976
Binford 1964
Bishop, Harbottle, and Sayre 1982
Bishop, Rands, and Holley 1982
Brill 1971
Bromund, Bower, and Smith 1976
Brongniart 1844
Brothwell and Higgs 1963
Caley 1949, 1951
Carriveau 1980
Carter 1978
Catling, Blin-Stoyle, and Richards 1961
Clarke 1968
Courtois 1976
Cowgill 1964
David 1982
DeBruin et al. 1976

Drier 1939
Emeleus 1960
Emeleus and Simpson 1960
Farnsworth 1964
Farnsworth and Ritchie 1938
Felts 1942
Fillières, Harbottle, and Sayre 1984
Fossey, Sedgwick, and Attas 1982
Franchet 1911
Franklin and Vitali 1985
Freestone, Meeks, and Middleton 1985
Frierman 1980
Goffer 1980
Hall 1963
Hawley 1929, 1930
Hench 1971
Hench and Gould 1971
Hofmann 1962
Horton and Berman 1941
Howard and Morris 1981
Hughes 1981
Jeancon 1923
Joukowsky 1978, 1982
Keighley 1973

Kempe and Harvey 1983
Kingery 1985
Kleeman 1967
Lambert 1984
Layard 1853
Lechtman 1977
Levey 1967
Lynch 1979
McGovern 1986
March 1934
Matson 1937, 1939, 1952, 1963,
    1965
Matson, ed., 1965
Meschel 1978
Miller 1985
Mueller 1975b
Musty and Thomas 1962
Nordenskiöld 1893
Olin 1982
Olin and Franklin 1981
Orphanides 1985
Osgood 1951
Papousek 1981
Peacock 1970
Peacock, ed., 1977
Pyddoke 1963
Rapp 1977
Rapp and Gifford 1985

Redman 1974, 1978a
Reeves and Brooks 1978
Reina and Hill 1978
Rice 1978a
Rice, ed., 1984
Richards 1959
Richards 1895
Ritchie 1937
Rye 1976, 1981
Sayre and Dodson 1957
Sayre, Murrenhoff, and Weick 1958
Sedgwick, Fossey, and Attas 1980
Shackley 1975
Shepard 1936, 1939, 1942a,b,
    1946, 1976
Shepard and Horton 1939
Shotton and Hendry 1979
Solheim 1960
Southward and Kamilli 1983
Talbott 1984
Thompson 1958
Tite 1972
Titterington 1933
van der Leeuw and Pritchard 1984
Wallis and Evens 1934
Williams 1983
Young and Whitmore 1957

The Color of Ceramic Materials

11

The analysis, classification, and description of pottery, whether complete vessels or vessel fragments, frequently use color as a key variable in differentiating categories. These categories are then usually assigned some significance in cultural, temporal, or technological terms. Color is one ceramic property that permits easy visual differentiation, and indeed it is important in both aesthetic and technical senses, for the color of a ceramic can tell us about the raw materials used and the way it was fired.

11.1 Human Perception of Color

Color is not an inherent property of an object but a function of the light from it that reaches the human eye. What the eye perceives as color is a particular form of electromagnetic energy traveling within a certain range of vibration rates, known as the visible spectrum, which includes wavelengths of 400 (violet) to 700 (red) micrometers (fig. 11.1). Vibrations beyond this range, such as microwaves and radio waves, cannot be seen, nor can shorter waves of electromagnetic energy such as X rays or gamma rays. Objects that appear transparent, such as glass and glazes, are registered by the color (energy) of the light that passes through them, while opaque objects are seen as the color of the light reflected, all other wavelengths being absorbed.

The perception of color may be linked, consciously or unconsciously, to attributes independent of electromagnetic energy, as is evident in efforts to elicit folk classifications or measurements of colors. For example, Mexican potters could not match clay colors with standard charts (the Munsell charts; see sec. 11.3) because the charts "lacked the features of wetness, texture, and smell that they considered essential in judging 'color'" (Kaplan 1985, 358). The use of color on pottery (and other categories of material culture) often highlights fundamental aspects of the structure of belief or worldview of a

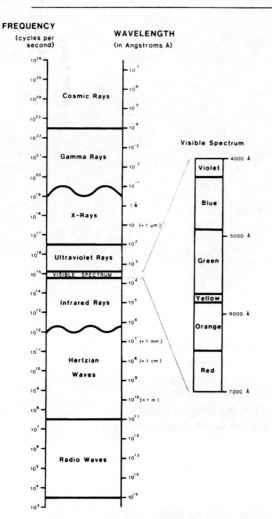

FREQUENCY
(cycles per
second)

WAVELENGTH
(in Angstroms, Å)

Figure 11.1   The electromagnetic spectrum, divided into regions on the basis of use and mode of detection. The visible spectrum ranges between 4,000 and 7,000 Ångstrom units (1 Å = 1 × 10⁻⁸ cm).

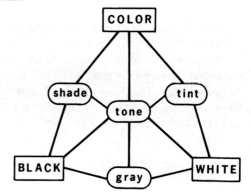

Figure 11.2   Color terms based on mixing with white or black.

people. For example, in Puebla, Mexico, distinctions between red and black colors in general—red associated with life, day, and hot and black with death, night, and cold—are extended to distinctions in the use of the pottery of different colors (sec. 9.1.2; Kaplan and Levine 1981, 876–78; for an Indian example, see Miller 1985, 142–48).

Color variations are often described by terms denoting various degrees of lightness, darkness, or saturation of the color (fig. 11.2). For example, colors mixed with black create dusky shades, while light, clear colors mixed with white are termed tints. Tones are mixtures of colors plus black and white.

Research into the cultural and biophysical context of color perception has led to the conclusion that there are eleven basic perceptual categories, the discrimination of which can be traced in the development of most languages (i.e., the "color encoding sequence," fig. 11.3; see Berlin and Kay 1969). The earliest color terms identified in languages are the oppositions of black and white, with red appearing next, frequently as an opposition or contrast to black or to white or to black and white together (see Sahlins 1976). The next stages of terminological evolution discriminate blue/green and yellow, fol-

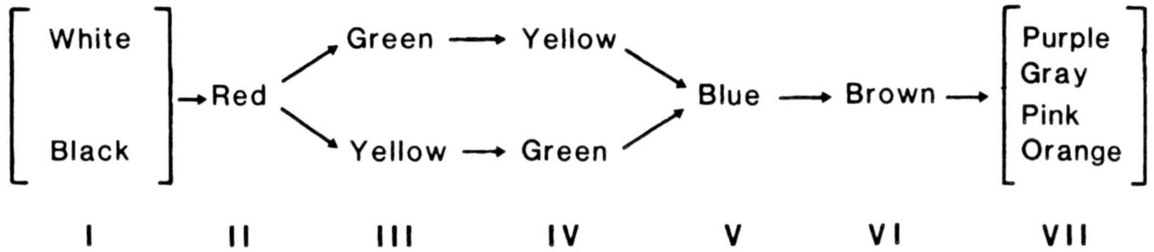

Figure 11.3   The "color encoding sequence," showing the basic color categories perceived by humans and the order in which specific terms for these categories develop in most languages. After Baines 1985, fig. 1.

lowed by brown, purple, pink, and orange. It should be noted that this sequence refers to the developmental sequence of color terms, not to the use of pigments themselves in various types of artistic expression (e.g., see Baines 1985, 285). In unglazed pottery decoration, black, white, and red are certainly the most common colors, probably because they are easy to obtain from common minerals or firing procedures and afford pleasant contrasting and complementary effects.

11.2   Source of the Property and Its Variability

The color of a fired clay piece is a consequence of several variables, of which two are most important. One is the size, amount, and distribution of impurities, chiefly iron and organic material, present in the raw clay; the second concerns the time, temperature, and atmosphere of the original firing. The colors of low-fired natural clays will thus be limited to white, black, orange-red, or some mixture of these colors (various shades of cream, brown, or gray). Although some iron minerals are yellowish in the natural state (e.g., hydrous ferric oxides, such as goethite and limonite), on firing they lose their water and are changed to ferric oxides, yielding a red color. Colors such as pure yellow, blue, and green are virtually impossible to achieve on low-fired pottery except by special additives (usually added to high-fired clays or glazes) or as postfiring pigments.

In an unfired clay, the kind and amount of iron compounds and organic matter (and the oxidation state of the iron) also determine its color, but in general raw clay color is not an accurate predictor of fired clay color. If a clay is completely free of these two classes of impurities, it will usually be white in the raw state and white or cream when fired. White clays (often called china clays) are thus comparatively uncommon and are likely to be accorded special value, both prehistorically and in modern ceramic production.

Organic material in a raw clay makes it gray, black, or dark brown, depending on the amount present. Iron in a raw clay will contribute a red, yellow, or brown color if it is oxidized or ferric, as in hematite, limonite, or goethite. If, however, the iron is in a reduced state, as in waterlogged clays, the deposit may be gray, black, or bluish. Thus it is difficult if not impossible to know whether a dark brown or black color is the result of iron or organic matter or both in the raw clay; nor is it possible to specify whether the clay will fire to a cream, brown, or reddish color. The complex interrelation between the fired color of a clay and the color of the original raw material can be seen in table 11.1.

Table 11.1   Relation between Fired and Unfired Colors of Clays

Fired Color	Raw Color
White	White, gray, black
Light brown ("buff")	Cream, yellow, gray, black, brown, gray-brown
Red, brown	Yellow, red, brown, gray, black
Dark gray, black	All colors

Source: After Shepard 1976, 17.

11.2.1   Organic Matter

The primary determinant of the final color of a low-fired clay is the presence of iron, but this element does not begin to play an active role until any organic matter present in the clay has been oxidized and eliminated. The amount of carbonaceous material (humus, rootlets, fibers) in clays is highly variable, depending on the way the clay was deposited; surface clays and some sedimentary clays often contain considerable quantities (see chap. 2 and sec. 3.4.2).

When a clay containing organic matter is heated, the carbon begins to char and oxidize. Carbon is eliminated from the interior to the surface of the clay piece as it gradually decomposes and is burned off in the form of CO_2 gas. Organic matter in the interior is gradually removed as this process continues under elevated temperatures and in an oxidizing atmosphere. At temperatures of 300–500°C, depending on the amount of organic matter present and the fineness of the clay, the surfaces of the clay piece may have a pronounced black color as the carbon is moved to the surfaces before being burned off. Carbon will burn out of fine clays more slowly than coarse clays because of the more restricted pore space within which oxidation and movement of the particles can occur. In addition, certain kinds of clays, especially the three-layer expanding lattice clays (e.g., smectites or montmorillonite) tend to bind carbon fairly easily and strongly within their chemical structure and to give it up slowly on heating.

Significant quantities of organic matter in a fired clay piece are usually signaled by a dark core in a freshly broken cross section through the wall (see fig. 4.3). This core may be a thin gray streak or a pronounced black band occupying most of the wall section. Its presence can result either from large amounts of organic matter originally present in the raw clay, or from deposition of carbonaceous material during firing, or from some combination of the two. This core should not be confused with the black coring also noted in high-fired bricks, in which rapid firing leads to vitrification and pores on the surfaces close before the organic material on the interiors has burned out. The gases from the organics as well as other impurities can lead to bloating (see Kingery, Bowen, and Uhlmann 1976, 503–4).

If the dark core is present in the center of the wall and the portions of the cross section underlying the surfaces are lighter colored, this usually means that the organic material was present in the raw clay and not completely removed in firing. In other words, the conditions of firing—the duration, temperature, and atmosphere—were not such that the carbon could be oxidized and burned out of the clay. The firing conditions necessary to burn out carbonaceous material vary from clay to clay, depending on the amount originally present, the fineness of the clay body (fig. 4.3), and the kind of clay mineral present. A coarse clay will lose small quantities of organic matter even in relatively rapid, low-temperature firings, while a very fine montmorillonitic clay with large amounts of organic matter may retain some carbon coring even after firing to 800 °C.

Sometimes the dark organic matter visible in cross section is present at or just below the surfaces rather than in the center. This feature, especially when combined with a black surface, usually indicates smudging, a firing practice in which an open fire or bonfire is smothered with a dense layer of fine organic matter such as sawdust or manure so that no oxygen reaches the pots and carbon is deposited on the surface and in the pores.

The atmosphere of firing has a great effect on color development through the abundance or scarcity of oxygen. In a fully oxidizing atmosphere, the carbonaceous matter can be readily burned out of the clay beginning at low temperatures, because there is abundant free oxygen in the atmosphere to combine with the carbon. It is important to remember that in open or mixed firings (sec. 5.4) the firing atmosphere is generally highly variable and is rarely completely oxidizing because of the proximity of the fuel and the prevalence of combustion products in the air. Even in kilns, changes in oxidation can be caused by the rhythm of stoking, though these are less pronounced than in open firings. Sometimes a very complex record of fluctuations in the firing atmosphere is registered by darker and lighter layers in the clay cross section, which reflect varying degrees of oxidation of organic matter in the clay.

11.2.2 Iron Compounds

Once the organic matter has been largely oxidized and eliminated, the color development of iron compounds in the clay begins. The final fired color depends upon the chemical state of the iron (determinable by Mössbauer spectroscopy; see sec. 13.3.2.7): fully oxidized or ferric iron (e.g., hematite, Fe_2O_3) produces red or reddish brown, while iron in the ferrous state (as in sulfides, carbonates, and silicates) or ferrous-ferric state (magnetite, Fe_3O_4) occurs more rarely and produces gray, bluish, greenish, or gray-brown (see Hess and Perlman 1974). Iron cannot exist in a fully oxidized state while there is still considerable organic material in the clay.

The full color development of iron in an oxidizing atmosphere occurs with increasing temperature of firing up to approximately 900–950°C. The color also depends on the amount of iron compounds present: in general, other things being equal, iron oxides in amounts of 1% will contribute a yellowish tone to the fired clay, 1.5–3% will cause light brown or orange, and 3% or more red (Shepard 1976, 150). It is important, however, to note that the color of a fired iron-bearing clay will also relate to the distribution of the iron, which in turn is a function of the particle size of the clay. The finer the clay, the greater the surface area and the more finely particulate the iron required to cover this area. The total amount of iron in a clay may include small nodules of magnetite, pyrite, hematite, or other iron-rich minerals rather than being evenly distributed as fine particulate matter, and this would affect its contribution to the overall color of the piece. Shepard (1976, 16, citing Ries 1927, 260), for example, notes that two clays of nearly the same fired color had very different quantities of iron: one had 3.12% ferric oxide while the other had 12.4%.

Iron compounds may act as fluxes at high temperatures, especially when they are finely particulate, or are exposed to a reducing or very incompletely oxidizing atmosphere. In such situations, the red color may change from red to brown to blackish as the formation of a glassy phase inhibits continued oxidation and has the effect of a reducing atmosphere. An example of this on prehistoric Mesoamerican pottery is the fine ferruginous slip of Plumbate ware, an Early Postclassic ware manufactured in southern Guatemala, which has an iridescent gray slip that is partially vitrified (Shepard 1948a). A similar situation may exist with "Northern Black Polished Ware" of Iron Age India, in which X-ray photoelectron spectroscopy, scanning electron microscopy, and X-ray diffraction showed that the glossy "bronze metallic" black slip may be due to sintering of an iron-rich biotite layer on the surface (Gillies and Urch 1983, 38–41). The red colors of ferric oxides are generally not stable if fired to temperatures above 1000°C (Norton 1970, 217).

11.2.3   Other Colorants

Besides iron and carbon, materials such as lime may contribute to the color of fired clays if they are present in significant quantities. These changes usually take place at moderately high temperatures, about 800°C and above. For example, once $CaCO_3$ has decomposed, the CaO may react with clay to form calcium silicates (wollastonite) with pale yellow or white colors. At high temperatures, above 1000°C, lime may also react with iron to form calcium ferrosilicates, suppressing the red color and contributing to a yellow or olive-greenish tone.

Manganese may be present as reddish-brown or blackish-brown flecks or nodules in clays, particularly those from swampy areas. It is rarely found in sufficient quantities (ca. 10% or more) as a natural constituent of clays to cause an overall black color in the paste, but nodules or concretions may be ground and mixed with a binder for use as a paint (see Shepard 1976, 40–42).

Magnetite (Fe_3O_4) may be used for a black pigment if it is not allowed to oxidize in firing (Shepard 1976, 39).

Titanium, present either as TiO_2 or as titanate of iron, may contribute a light tan or cream color in iron-free clays.

Sulfides (pyrites, marcasite), sulfates (gypsum), and chlorides may also influence the color of fired clays. As soluble salts, these materials migrate through the capillaries of the wares as they dry and concentrate on the surfaces, forming a brownish or whitish scum or efflorescence that looks like a white slip after firing. The location of the salt scum will tell which areas of the vessel were uppermost (exposed to air) in drying and contrast with surface areas that may have been scraped in further finishing (see Franken 1971, 236).

In addition, various sulfide and carbonate minerals provide pigments that are unstable if heated but are useful for postfire painting of ceramics. Copper carbonates (malachite and azurite) will yield blues or greens, for example, and in Mesoamerica a distinctive pigment called Maya Blue was obtained either by adding indigo to an attapulgite clay (van Olphen 1966; see Shepard and Pollock 1977, 81–87, for a review), or by using a naturally blue montmorillonite clay (Littman 1980). Dark purplish-red could be obtained from cinnabar (mercuric sulfide, HgS) or specular hematite (which could also be fired), and yellows from goethite or limonite.

11.2.4 Glaze Colorants

The colors of glazes on high-fired pottery result from a more complex series of chemical processes involving a broader range of elements. Coloring agents in glazes are primarily the so-called transition elements—titanium, vanadium, chromium, manganese, iron, cobalt, nickel, and copper (Grimshaw 1971, 910). These have incompletely filled electron shells in their atomic structures, and their ability to produce color is linked to the absorption of part of the radiant energy of light by electrons that jump between shells. The color can also be traced to the presence of the ion in multiple valence states, such as iron in the ferrous-ferric state, which is dark brown or black. Finally, some ions that produce characteristic colors, such as copper, chromium, and manganese, are called chromophores.

The transition elements have ionic radii intermediate between sodium and silica, and so they may either form or modify the glaze structure (see sec. 4.2.4). Depending on their role—which is in turn related to the composition of the glaze and the presence of other oxides as modifiers and intermediaries as well as on the firing temperature and atmosphere—individual elements can give rise to very different colors (table 11.2). In general, a broader range of colors can be attained at lower temperatures (e.g., below 1125°C), because at higher temperatures many of the elements are unstable and volatilize.

Colorants are added to glaze preparations in two ways. Finely ground metallic oxides (from carbonates or salts) of the transition elements may be used; carbonates seem to be most commonly employed because they naturally occur

Table 11.2 Color Development from Adding Colorants to Glazes

Colorant	Oxidizing Atmosphere	Reducing Atmosphere
Iron	Tan, yellow, brown; green with copper	Gray, blue, green (celadon), red
Copper	Green; blue-green (with cobalt or alkaline formula)	Red to reddish purple
Cobalt	Blue	Blue
Manganese	Purple, purplish blue, black	Brown
Tin	Opaque white	Volatilizes
Nickel	Gray or brown	Gray or gray-brown
Chromium	Green	Yellow; turquoise with cobalt

Source: After Rye 1981, 47; Rhodes 1973, 317–18.

Note: Any of these colors will vary depending on the presence of other colorants in the glaze (see Rhodes 1973, 218), as well as the overall composition of the glaze (lead versus alkaline, for example) and firing temperature.

in fine particle sizes. Commercially prepared stains are also common; these are often combinations of oxides purchased from color companies (see Norton 1970, 214–16). Strong colorants such as cobalt may be added in amounts as low as a fraction of a percent, while as much as 5%–6% or even 10% of other weaker materials may be added (see Rhodes 1973, 215, 317–18). Glazed wares may also be colored by specially prepared underglaze pigments, which are very finely ground and contain little flux in their composition. They are, as the name implies, painted on a vessel before the glaze is applied, and because they do not flow as the glaze melts, they allow for fine detail in decoration (see Brody 1979, 89–92; Rhodes 1973, 255–58).

Iron is often added as hematite, the ferric oxide (Fe_2O_3); depending upon the composition of the glaze and firing characteristics, it can yield colors from cream through brown to black and even green. In lead glazes, for instance, iron yields warm tones of tan, yellowish brown, amber, and reddish brown, while in alkaline glazes iron is responsible for cooler tones in the same range. In a lead glaze with tin oxide present, the iron creates mottled cream colors. If large amounts are present (7% or more), the glaze colors will be dark brown or black. In a reducing atmosphere (and with the presence of barium) an iron-bearing composition results in the cool grayish-green glaze colors of celadon (Rhodes 1973, 266; Vandiver and Kingery 1984), the jadelike stoneware that dates from the beginning of the second millennium A.D. in China and was widely copied in Japan and Korea.

Copper is a versatile glaze colorant, readily available from copper salts or the carbonate minerals malachite and azurite, and needing to be added in amounts of 2%–5% to create the desired color. Copper glazes were probably the earliest to be used in antiquity, both in the Near East and in China. In a reducing atmosphere the color is a deep red or reddish-brown (often called oxblood, or *sang-de-boeuf*); copper is probably the best source of a high-fired red color, which is difficult to create at high temperatures. Oxidizing conditions give copper a blue or green color. In high-alkaline (Na or K) glazes copper is a distinctive turquoise, and the presence of barium and boron will also give rise to bluish or greenish tones. Added to lead glazes, copper usually results in a green color, but since it increases the release of lead it is not an appropriate glaze for tableware. Copper itself is volatile above approximately 1225°C.

Cobalt, which began to be used by the Persians in the ninth century and the Chinese in the fourteenth century A.D., is the most stable of the colorants, varying little with changes in temperature and atmosphere of firing or with composition of the glaze. It is also an extremely strong colorant, with amounts as little as 0.25% giving rise to a definite blue color. Manganese with cobalt will contribute a purplish tone, and iron, chromium, or copper will give bluish-greens. Cobalt yields variable and blotchy colors above approximately 1250°C.

Chromium yields a highly variable range of colors, including red, yellow, pink, brown, and green, depending on the composition of the glaze and the firing temperature. In low-lead glazes lacking zinc it yields a green color; with zinc it is brown. In low-fired lead glazes with low aluminum, chromium will give an orange or red color, whereas at higher temperatures it is brown or green; the presence of sodium gives rise to yellow, and adding tin makes the glaze pink or maroon. Usually added in amounts ranging between 0.5% and 5%, chromium is volatile above approximately 1190°C.

Manganese, available as manganese dioxide or pyrolusite, is usually added in amounts of 2%–6%. It is a weak colorant, yielding a plum or bluish-purple in alkaline glazes and a softer purple in lead glazes; in the presence of iron it is black. At temperatures above about 1200°C or in reduction, manganese yields brown.

A variety of additional elements are used as colorants in glazes. Titanium (in rutile or ilmenite) gives rise to brown, or it may instead be added for textural interest (mottling, speckling, opaque, or crystalline glazes). Nickel is used for green or brown. Uranium, although largely unavailable since World War II with the development of the nuclear weapons industry, earlier was used commonly for yellow, red, or coral colors. Several elements are most typically added by commercially prepared stains: these include cadmium and selenium for reds, vanadium and antimony for yellow, and gold for pink, red, or purple. Some of these are undesirable for a variety of reasons: cadmium and selenium are toxic on tableware, for example; antimony is unstable above approximately 1135°C; and gold (and also platinum) is prohibitively expensive.

11.3 Measuring Color

Although the wavelengths of the electromagnetic spectrum can be measured by a spectrophotometer to determine colors precisely, pottery colors are most commonly measured or classified by a series of standard samples. Among the systems used by archaeologists in the study of pottery have been Ridgway's (1912) system, consisting of 1,115 named colors used to describe the colors of birds, and the Maerz and Paul (1950) *Dictionary of Color,* presenting 7,000 color samples (see March 1934, 26–27; Colton 1953, 32–36; Shepard 1936, 430–32). The most common system is the Munsell color system, developed by Alfred H. Munsell, a Boston artist and art teacher, between 1900 and 1912 (Nickerson 1948, 51). A similar system, the Ostwald system, is not widely known or used in archaeological studies (Nickerson 1948).

The Munsell (Munsell Color Company 1975) system standardizes color specifications by organizing three variables of color—hue, intensity, and saturation—into a three-dimensional "color solid" that approximates an irregular cylinder (fig. 11.4). In this figure, hues represent named colors, that is, the dominant wavelengths in the color spectrum, and extend around the circumference of the solid. The complementary pigment colors (pairs of colors that give neutral grays or black when equally mixed) are on opposite sides of the cylinder: blue is opposite orange, red opposite green, and yellow opposite violet. The central axis of the figure thus represents the region of neutral colors and is graduated from black at one end to white at the other end along the vertical dimension. Extending out from this central axis along the radii of the cylinder, the hues vary in chroma (saturation, strength, or purity), from black or gray near the central axis to a clear pure color at the exterior "surface" of the cylinder. The hues and chromas also vary in value (intensity, brilliance, or

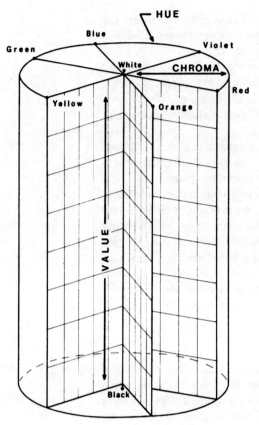

Figure 11.4 The model of a "color solid," simplified into a cylindrical shape, from which the Munsell color charts are drawn.

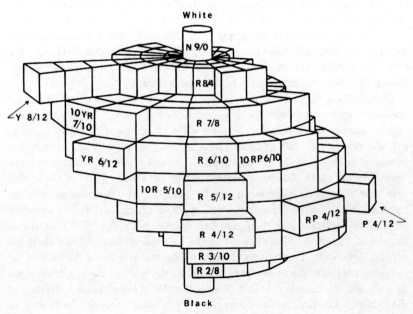

Figure 11.5 A representation of the three-dimensional model of the Munsell color system. After Nickerson 1948, fig. 6.

lightness) along the vertical dimensions of the cylinder, with dark colors at one end and lighter colors at the other.

For graphic representation and application, the individual vertical sections surrounding the axis of the Munsell color cylinder are identified by their hues or wavelengths, as red (R), yellow red (YR), yellow (Y), and so forth (fig. 11.5). These are further subdivided into individual hue-constant "charts" that radiate around the central axis and are coded by numerical prefixes such as 10R, 7.5R, 5R, 2.5R, 10YR, 7.5YR. Each of these charts or spectral subdivisions displays a series of vertical and horizontal color gradations of value and chroma indicated by numbers from 0 to 10 (or higher). For achromatic colors (pure grays, white, and black), the designation N (neutral) replaces the hue.

The Munsell charts include virtually all colors in the visible spectrum and can be used to specify colors of any variety of materials, including textiles and paints. For unglazed pottery a portion of the red and yellow spectrum is commonly used. These selected charts are referred to as the Munsell Soil Color Charts and are sold by the Munsell Company as a package of seven panels with 199 color chips designed for use by scientists interested in classifying the colors of natural soils and soil products. The soil color package includes the following hue charts—10R, 2.5YR, 5YR, 7.5YR, 10YR, 2.5YR, and 5Y—plus a separate chart for neutral gray. Additional charts extend the color range to darker and purer reds, for example, or "gley," covering greenish and bluish grays. Charts covering clear blues, greens, and yellows are normally not of interest in unglazed pottery studies, though they are useful for identifying glaze colors.

Munsell colors are designated by alphanumeric codes that give the hue identifier (or page of the chart) first, then value and chroma separated by a slash. For example, a color described as 5YR 6/8 has a hue of medium reddish yellow, medium-high value or brightness, and high purity or chroma. A color of 5YR 3/4, while representing the same hue, is a darker and grayer (browner) tone, lower in value and chroma.

Besides the numeric notations, the Munsell charts give verbal color names and modifiers for specific description of the hues (e.g., see fig. 11.6b). These terms, in combination with the alphanumeric notations, are more informative than, and thus preferable to, the descriptive terms used formerly, which in Mesoamerican ceramics, at least, included dubious descriptors such as "Mouse Brown," "Avellaneous," and "Vinaceous Tawny" with reference to the terminology of the Ridgway system.

Recorded or published Munsell color measurements should include both the alphanumeric notation and the verbal description. In some instances the Munsell verbal category is not very satisfactory; for example, an enormously wide range of distinguishable colors is included in "yellowish red" or "very pale brown," and it is likely that in these situations more information on the actual color will be conveyed by using nonstandard terms such as orange, cream, and so forth. The term "buff" is not recommended, since there is a wide variation in the actual colors (from tan to brown to orange to cream) denoted by this vague category.

Often an exact match cannot be found between a specimen and the Munsell

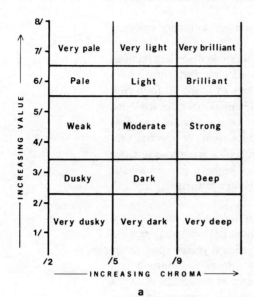

Figure 11.6   The Munsell soil color charts: *a*, a system of modifiers for color names (after Shepard 1976, 110); *b*, the Munsell soil color book opened to hue chart 5YR. *a* shows color chips varying in value and chroma; *b* shows names for the various colors on the chart (after Munsell Color Company 1975).

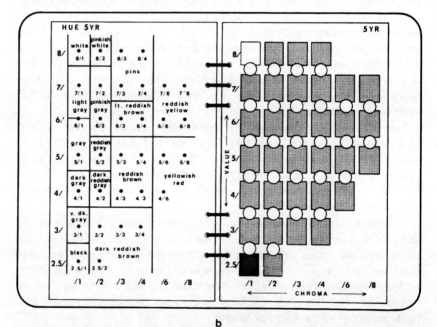

charts because of the gaps in specific hue, chroma, and value illustrations on each chart. In such situations, more specific designations are attained by interpolation with decimals, usually by distinguishing the approximate value and chroma positions on one hue chart and then comparing between charts if necessary. For example, a color may be found to be 10YR 7.5/4.5 by interpolating between values of 7 and 8 and chroma of 4 and 5 on the 10YR chart. It may also be necessary to interpolate between hues—for example, 9YR 7.5/4.5. It is generally difficult to achieve reliable interpolations smaller than a half-step (0.5 or so) between illustrated chromas and values. The Munsell charts usually come with page-sized cards of gray and black cardboard with windows cut out of the centers. These can be used to mask out the confusion of multiple colors when trying to decide the best match between pairs of values and chromas.

In conducting a series of color measurements on a collection, it is important that all measurements be made by the same person to eliminate individual variations in color perception. In addition, all measurements should be made under the same lighting, with light hitting the specimens and the color chips at the same angle. The quality of the light can cause variations in the color readings, but these can be minimized if the conditions are standardized—for example, if all recordings are made in the same room. Lighting conditions in the field may be less than satisfactory, but direct sunlight should be avoided. In reporting color measurements, the lighting at the time of measurement should be noted.

Color measurements should be made on both exterior and interior surfaces of a sherd or vessel, as well as on a freshly broken cross section if possible. In the cross section, the presence and thickness of any dark coring should also be noted. For large collections it is generally most informative to record both the typical color or color range of the material and the extreme variations in hue, value, or chroma.

11.4   Estimating Firing Conditions from Color

The changes in color development of low-fired pottery, which are evident in relative degrees of oxidation of carbon and iron, provide a basis for very general assessments of the conditions under which the pottery was fired. These are not precise estimates with respect to time, temperature, or atmosphere, however, and a number of more precise techniques are available for determining firing temperature in particular (see sec. 14.3).

Low figures for value and chroma measurements give a clue to the amount of free carbon present in the sherds. Although this alone does not tell whether the carbon was initially present or deposited during firing, the presence of a dark gray (low chroma and value) color indicates incomplete oxidation: either an atmosphere with insufficient oxygen or a short period and/or low temperatures of firing.

Higher value and chroma designations indicate greater oxidation, less organic matter initially present in the clay, or both. Chroma is more apt to reflect the increasing development of the color of whatever iron is present, although of course the relative amounts of iron are primarily indicated by the hue designation. Hodges (1976, 196) notes that chroma varies with the breakdown of clay minerals at temperatures beyond 850°C, and the change in hue from Y to R reflects the degree to which limonite is dehydrated to hematite.

In attempting to interpret the original firing conditions from prehistoric sherds, it is useful to analyze separately the variations in value, chroma, and hue within a given collection, because each dimension tells something different about the original clay and the firing conditions. It is useful to know, for example, whether the greatest variability occurs in hue or in chroma or in value. It is also important that these comparisons be based on sherds that either are from the same ware or represent the same or similar clays, because variations in quantities of impurities affect color development. Two strategies are appropriate in this regard: laboratory firing experiments carried out on clays collected from the locale of interest (sec. 10.3.2) and refiring experiments with fragments broken from sherds of the ancient pottery.

Firing experiments with local clays are usually conducted in electric kilns in a fully oxidizing atmosphere. Draw trials (removing test tiles or briquettes at a series of increasing time intervals) will establish the relation of firing time and temperature to a variety of physical properties including color development, shrinkage, weight loss, hardness, porosity, dark coring, and so forth (see fig. 4.3). An alternative strategy is based on a thermal gradient furnace (Matson 1975b), which raises the temperature continuously along a gradient from front to back of the kiln in a single firing rather than in a series of independent steps in multiple firings. Regardless of which procedure is used, firing local clays provides a view of the range of colors attainable, whether the clays are primarily red- or white-firing, and of their refractoriness or tendency to vitrify at relatively low temperatures. This provides a background for comparing the colors of prehistoric pottery, within which the prehistoric firing strategies can be interpreted (see, e.g., Matson 1971). Test firings with various tempers can also tell much about color development as well as mechanical properties (see Rye 1976, 123–26).

Interpretation of original firing conditions is also aided by refiring fragments of sherds in an oxidizing atmosphere at a series of temperature intervals (e.g., intervals of 100°C) or at a single sufficiently high temperature and for long enough that most of the organic material can be eliminated and the colors from any iron allowed to develop fully. Thirty minutes at a temperature between 800 and 850°C is usually satisfactory. Refiring samples of sherds of a large variety of wares (whether different pastes, forms, or decorative categories) establishes a general picture of the variability in the kinds of clays the prehistoric potters used: Did they select primarily red-, brown-, or white-firing clays? Once this is known, other questions can be investigated (see Shepard 1976, 104–7). Were particular kinds of clays selected for different forms or decorative categories? Were different firing practices used for different categories of wares? For example, if two kinds of pottery are brown, is this because the same clay or the same firing was used for both, or was one incompletely oxidized while the other naturally attained a brown color with full oxidation? Is a dark core easily removed, or is it retained after refiring? Some of these relationships are summarized in table 11.3.

Although a variety of conclusions are suggested by color measurements and assessment of changes in color with refiring, these should be understood within the context of the firing technology, which for nonkiln firings is highly variable (see sec. 5.4). Because of nonuniform rates of heating caused by kinds and placement of fuel and by drafts, the colors of vessels from a single kiln load are apt to vary considerably according to the temperatures to which they were subjected (see sec. 14.3). Thus, on the one hand it could be argued that standardized measurement of color of non-kiln-fired sherds represents

Table 11.3   Relation between Fired Color and Original Firing Conditions

Color		Probable Firing	Comment
Surface	Core		
Clear colors; identical throughout cross section		Relatively well oxidized	No evidence of original state of the clay with respect to carbon content; any color development is due to the presence of iron.
Brown	Brown	Incompletely to relatively well oxidized	May be lightly smoked or smudged paste, or color may be due to iron in ferric state. Refiring in oxidation will clear colors.
Clear or light gray	Light to dark gray	Incomplete oxidation	Probably a carbonaceous clay that was not sufficiently fired to oxidize organics and allow color development of any iron present. Refire.
Light gray	Light gray	Incomplete oxidation or reduction	
Dark gray or black	Dark gray or black	Reduced or smudged	May be highly carbonaceous clay or heavily smudged.
Dark gray or black	Light gray	Smudged	Carbon deposited on surfaces during or at the end of firing; lighter core indicates it was not an organic clay. Refiring may clarify colors.
White	White	Uncertain	May be clay lacking both iron and organics. Refire in oxidation to note color development, if any.

false precision, because the original conditions through which the colors were developed were uncontrolled and highly variable. On the other hand, careful investigation of the dimensions of that variability can tell much about aboriginal firing practices. For this reason the colors of a collection of sherds are usually described both by the measurement deemed average or most common and by their range of variations. For example, the color of a particular category of pottery may be reported in the Munsell system as "5YR 7/6, varying to 5/4, 8/7; 7.5YR 6/5."

Finally, it is important to note the possible sources of color alteration during use and in the postdepositional environment. Pottery vessels used in or over cooking fires are exposed to smoke, soot, and charring, which deposit carbon on the surfaces and in the exterior pores (fig. 7.3). Pots used for storage may be stained or build up residues, such as salts, depending on the substance stored, and processing activities may abrade and discolor the slip, decoration, or surface finish. Postuse or postdeposition processes may alter the color of vessels: accidental burning in house or field fires can oxidize pots or deposit carbon; acid soils and contact with rootlets can cause leaching or staining; and soluble salts or carbonates in the burial environment may leave encrustations or efflorescences of a white scum on the surfaces.

11.5   References

Baines 1985
Berlin and Kay 1969
Brody 1979
Colton 1953

Franken 1971
Gillies and Urch 1983
Grimshaw 1971
Hess and Perlman 1974

Hodges 1976
Kaplan 1985
Kaplan and Levine 1981
Kingery, Bowen, and Uhlmann 1976
Littman 1980
Maerz and Paul 1950
March 1934
Matson 1963, 1971, 1975b
Miller 1985
Munsell Color Company 1975
Nickerson 1948

Norton 1970
Rhodes 1973
Ridgway 1912
Ries 1927
Rye 1976, 1981
Sahlins 1976
Shepard 1936, 1948a, 1976
Shepard and Pollock 1977
Vandiver and Kingery 1984
Van Olphen 1966

Physical, Mechanical, and Thermal Properties of Pottery

12

Pottery analysis is frequently directed toward the properties influencing the original use of the vessel—its ability to contain liquids, to bear loads, to survive sudden heating and cooling, and to withstand impact. These physical, mechanical, and thermal ceramic properties provide information not only on use, but also on the manufacture of the object and the nature of the raw materials. The importance of these characteristics is recognized in some of the earliest discussions of procedures for analyzing and describing archaeological pottery (Colton 1953; March 1934; Shepard 1936, 433–37).

Some though not all of these properties can be readily measured by relatively simple procedures involving little equipment or special training; others require the specialized techniques and instruments of the physical and materials sciences. Irrespective of the equipment used, these techniques permit objective, as opposed to subjective, measurement and description of important characteristics of a ceramic by precise and reproducible standards. Among the characteristics of interest are hardness, strength, microstructure, including porosity, and thermal properties, including thermal stress resistance (see Bronitsky 1986 for a review).

Two cautions should be observed in interpreting these properties in archaeological pottery. First, although there may be a correlation between certain properties of the ceramic and the requirements of certain uses, for example, between thermal expansion coefficients and cooking, this does not necessarily mean the relationship was consciously invoked as the vessel was built. Second, because of a variety of processes relating to primary use, secondary or recycled use, and natural and cultural phenomena operating during the hundreds or thousands of years since discard, the physical, mechanical, and thermal properties of an excavated sherd may be different from those of the newly fired pot. What are measured are the properties that exist after years of use and postdepositional alteration; they are "remnant," "residual," or apparent properties that can be used to estimate the ancient parameters but are not necessarily equivalent to them.

12.1 Microstructure

The use-related properties of a ceramic are a function of its internal structure, which has two aspects: the arrangement of atoms within the components of a ceramic (see chap. 2) and the arrangements of these components with respect to each other. The latter is important in the study of the physical, material, and thermal properties of archaeological pottery, because pottery has several constituents. In engineering terms pottery can be described as a material consisting of more than one phase. A phase is "any part of a system which is physically homogeneous and bounded by a surface, and that is mechanically separable from other parts of the system" under specified conditions of pressure, temperature, and composition (Kingery 1960, 248).

Phases in ceramics thus include individual grains, glassy material, and pores. The relationships among phases are important because they are constantly changing with the chemical and physical state of the ceramic on firing and cooling. During these stages the system changes to minimize the free energy in the system and approach thermodynamic equilibrium at given conditions of temperature, pressure, and composition. True equilibrium, however, is rarely attained in real ceramic bodies, even high-fired wares, because the reactions involved take time. Phase diagrams (Levin, Robbins, and McMurdie 1964; Kingery, Bowen, and Uhlmann 1976, 265–319; Roth, Negas, and Cook 1983) are graphic representations of the number, amount, and composition of all phases present, as determined experimentally (fig. 12.1).

This complex arrangement of phases in a ceramic is termed its microstructure: the internal arrangement of crystalline and amorphous materials, voids (pores), and the boundaries between them in a polycrystalline and (usually) polyphasic medium. Microstructure is generally discussed in terms of four aspects: composition, texture, structure, and surface characteristics (Wolkodoff, Ferreira, and Weaver 1968, 297). Composition refers to the nature of the crystalline and noncrystalline (glassy) phases and the pores. Texture is a function of the size, shape, and orientation of phases, while structure refers to the arrangement of the phases. Surface characteristics include all these features as they are visible on ground, polished, and fractured surfaces in sections or replicas. The amounts of the various phases present in a ceramic are usually measured by areal or lineal point counts (see sec. 13.2.1.3) of a prepared section in a microscope (Kingery, Bowen, and Uhlmann 1976, 526–28). Estimates of quantities of inclusions are frequently compared with prepared standards, either diagrams (fig. 12.2) or actual mixtures of clays and different amounts of sizes of inclusions.

In low-fired pottery, the primary determinants of microstructure are the raw materials and fabricating technique (including firing), and to some extent the phase changes involved in sintering, whereas in high-fired ceramics the equilibrium relations among different phases and the changes resulting from vitrification and high-temperature mineral formation are much more important.

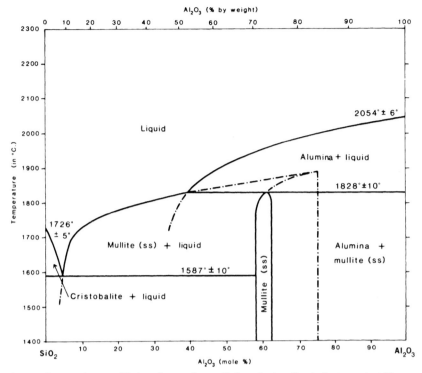

Figure 12.1   A phase equilibrium diagram for the system $Al_2O_3 \cdot SiO_2$, showing changes in liquid and solid components as a function of temperature. Solid line indicates stable equilibrium; broken line indicates metastable extension of liquidus and solidus lines for mullite; ss = solid solution. After Kingery, Bowen, and Uhlmann 1976, fig. 7.28.

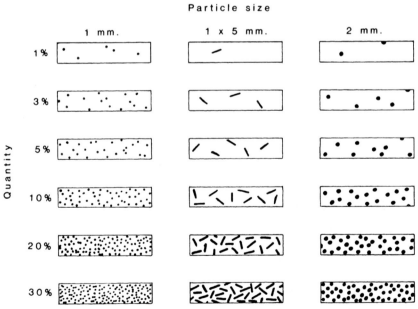

Figure 12.2   Comparison chart for estimating various quantities of different sizes and shapes of particles in a sherd cross section.

The microstructural characteristics of a ceramic underlie virtually all its use-related properties: for traditional pottery vessels the most important are porosity, hardness, and strength. These properties, in turn, affect the durability and serviceability of the ware in storage, processing, and transfer. The special character of ceramic objects as containers—their ability to hold liquids and to withstand sharp temperature changes—is conferred by features of microstructure.

12.2   Porosity

Virtually all ceramic materials contain pores or voids, spaces existing between or within the solid particles. Pores constitute one of the important phases of a ceramic as phase is defined above; that is, they are homogeneous, bounded, and separable from other phases.

Pores may be characterized by their size, shape, and position in the ceramic as either closed (sealed) or open to the exterior surface. Open pores have been further divided (fig. 12.3) into pocket pores, which often have a narrow aperture or neck; micropores, which are too small to contain liquid under normal pressure; loop pores, two interconnected pores; channel pores, which connect two pores or a pore and the surface; continuous pores, which extend from one surface to the other; and blind-alley pores, which extend from the surface without other connections (Grimshaw 1971, 417, 419, after Washburn 1921, 918; see also Brewer 1964, 91–93). Closed or sealed pores may occur naturally in the body of the ceramic without any exterior connections, or they may develop during heating as open pores become sealed through shrinkage and vitrification.

The size and shape of pores are influenced by the size and shape of particles in the clay body and their arrangements. Open pores may be formed from the packing of individual grains in the body, the escape of water or gases during firing, and the cracks that develop during drying and firing, with concomitant shrinkage or expansion (Grimshaw 1971, 419). In traditional pottery these processes may be increased by the burnout of organic material in the clay or the decomposition of carbonates.

Pores are usually irregular in shape, but different forms are characteristic of different kinds of particles and ceramic materials. For example, isolated spherical pores will be found in high-fired fine-textured products such as porcelain; fibers, seeds, and other macrobotanicals present accidentally or inten-

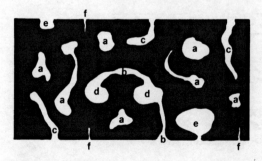

Figure 12.3   Various kinds of pores: *a*, closed pores; *b*, channel pores; *c*, blind-alley pores; *d*, loop pores; *e*, pocket pores; *f*, micropores. After Washburn 1921, 918, and Grimshaw 1971, fig. VII.21.

tionally in low-fired pottery usually burn out, leaving voids that are "casts" of the original (see Reid 1984). Pores in high-fired industrial and commercial ceramics are frequently so tiny that they can be measured only in micrometers (see, e.g., Grimshaw 1971, 426, 427); the larger pores in low-fired pottery, in contrast, can often be seen and measured with the naked eye.

The volume of pores within a ceramic determines its porosity. Among the factors influencing porosity are the size, shape, grading, and packing of particles, the specific constituents of the clay-body mix, and the treatment to which the material was subjected during manufacture. Porosity of a vessel can also be affected by the porosity of inclusions: if individual grains are porous, they will contribute to the porosity of the body (Grimshaw 1971, 420).

Before firing, almost all porosity exists as open pores; during the early part of the firing sequence porosity increases as organic matter and volatiles are burned out of the system. Porosity reaches a maximum at about 800°C and may be maintained at well above 30% until temperatures as high as 1000°C are reached (table 4.8; Grimshaw 1971, 816). In general, however, above 800°C porosity declines as the mass starts shrinking, a process accelerated by vitrification (see sec. 4.2.3.1). Many open pores are eliminated or transformed into closed pores; open pores are usually eliminated when porosity is reduced to about 5%, and the volume fraction of closed pores increases (Kingery, Bowen, and Uhlmann 1976, 521). Changes in the pore structure—in average pore size and in the homogeneity or distribution of pore sizes—can be graphed against firing temperature or against the rate of rise of firing temperature, and these provide one basis for inferring original firing temperature (Sanders 1973; Morariu, Bogdan, and Ardelean 1977; Magetti 1982; see also sec. 14.3.1).

Porosity affects a wide range of properties of a ceramic (see sec. 7.3.4), including strength (sec. 12.3.2), resistance to spalling, conductivity (sec. 12.4.2.3), resistance to mechanical and chemical erosion, refractoriness, vacuum tightness, and surface availability for catalytic reactions (Kingery, Bowen, and Uhlmann 1976, 518, 521; Grimshaw 1971, 420–21). In addition, high porosity can contribute to high thermal insulation: the air space resists the passage of heat, especially if the voids are discontinuous.

Porosity is usually described as either true or apparent. True porosity (also called total porosity) refers to the total proportion of the bulk volume occupied by pores and includes pores that are open to the exterior as well as interior or "closed" pore space. Apparent porosity includes only the larger open pores connecting to the surfaces and excludes closed pores and micropores. Apparent porosity is often related to absorption (which is, however, a weight rather than a volume measure).

A related property is permeability, the rate at which a liquid or air passes through the ceramic from one surface to the other. Permeability depends on the kind, size, number, and distribution of pores, the presence of cracks and flaws, differences in pressure and temperature on each side of the piece, and—because permeability measures the rate of movement of air or liquid—the thickness of the piece, nature of the fluid, and duration of the test (Grimshaw 1971, 436). Although clearly related to porosity, permeability is strictly a function of the various types of open pores and does not register the presence of closed pores. For this reason a clay object covered on one or both surfaces with a slip or glaze, which limits the penetration of a liquid into the pores, could be porous but at the same time relatively impermeable, particularly with an impervious glaze.

In determining the porosity of a ceramic, the shape, size, and number of pores are of interest as well as their volume. The shape and size of pores are measured by a variety of microscopic methods, including standard and polished thin sections and electron microscopy (see secs. 13.2.1 and 13.4.1). Although thin sections of heterogeneous, crystalline materials have problems with "pullouts" of grains (see Kingery, Bowen, and Uhlmann 1976, 530), they have the advantage of allowing a view of the range of sizes, shapes, orientations, and positions relative to other phases in the ceramic. The volume of pore space can be estimated through point counts or areal analyses, done more easily with the newer automatic integrating microscopes.

Direct measurement of volume porosity is restricted to apparent porosity (or absorption) rather than total porosity, since absorption methods cannot gain access to the sealed pores. For this reason, total porosity is calculated in terms of density. The bulk or apparent density is a ratio of total weight to external volume and is thus a function of both total porosity and true density. Because sealed pores often make up a portion of the volume, true density is the total weight divided by the total volume of solids. The formula for calculating total porosity is expressed as a ratio of bulk density (d_b) to true density (d_t):

$$P_t = \frac{d_t - d_b}{d_t} = 1 - \frac{d_b}{d_t}.$$

The total porosity of commercial ceramic articles varies from less than 1% to as much as 90%. For example, earthenwares (most directly comparable to archaeological pottery) vary from 20% to 25%, stonewares from 0.5% to 2.0%, and bricks from 3% to 73% porosity, but 12% to 30% is the typical value (Grimshaw 1971, 820).

Apparent porosity is usually measured by liquid immersion, water absorption, or mercury intrusion porosimetry techniques. In all these procedures, test samples of the ceramic are thoroughly dried in a drying oven at 105–10°C and then weighed (W_1). In the liquid immersion method, the dried test piece is placed in a vacuum chamber and evacuated, then enough liquid is introduced to cover it. The liquid permeates the pores under vacuum conditions, and the piece is then removed and reweighed (W_2). Its weight when immersed in liquid is also determined (W_3). The percentage of apparent volume porosity is then determined by the following equation:

$$P_A = \frac{W_2 - W_1}{W_2 - W_3} \times 100.$$

The water absorption method is a variant of the liquid immersion technique, except that instead of using a vacuum, the dried and weighed (W_1) piece is placed in a suitable container, covered with water, and boiled for five hours. At the end of that time the container is removed from the heat and the piece is cooled to room temperature while still immersed in water. When cool it is removed, wiped dry of surface water, and reweighed (W_2).

In the mercury intrusion porosimetry method, mercury is forced into the pores of the piece under pressure. The higher the pressure required the smaller the pores of the piece, so the technique gives an estimate of the distribution of open pores according to volume (see Grimshaw 1971, 426; Whittemore and Halsey 1983; also Sanders 1973 and Morariu, Bogdan, and Ardelean 1977 for archaeological applications).

Additional methods for measuring porosity use replicas of a ceramic surface (Heimann 1977) or study the movement of a solution sensitive to ultraviolet light through the pores of the ceramic (Crandall and Ging 1955, 47; Davidge and Tappin 1967, 409; Tankersley and Meinhart 1982).

The distribution of pore volume according to some measure of pore size yields much more information than a simple parameter such as apparent porosity and is often used in studies of ceramic processing. Such information may be presented as a cumulative graph showing the proportion of pores smaller or larger than a given pore size (e.g., fig. 14.3).

The techniques of materials science have increasingly been used to determine the porosity and permeability of traditional pottery (e.g., Vandiver and Koehler 1986). The object of these applications is to understand the use-related properties of the ceramic and infer something about the compositional and manufacturing design decisions it represents. In drawing these inferences it is important to recognize several differences between low-fired traditional pottery and the high-fired commercial ceramics more commonly tested by these methods.

One is that a given degree of porosity may or may not have been desired in the pottery product (see sec. 7.3.4). Traditional potters today frequently coat their pots with a variety of organic substances, such as grease or resins, before use to reduce permeability (see sec. 5.4.1.3), and it is not known how well these coatings might survive deposition to be registered in porosity analyses. In addition, a porous vessel or sherd may be buried for hundreds or thousands of years, during which substances may be deposited or crystallized in the vessel pores (e.g., salts or various minerals), reducing its porosity (see Magetti 1982; Courtois 1976; also Franklin and Vitali 1985). What is being measured in archaeometric analyses, therefore, is neither true porosity nor apparent porosity, but "residual" or estimated porosity, which may or may not have been characteristic of the vessel at the time of use.

Second, Grimshaw (1971, 438) has noted that permeability, and therefore the apparent porosity it measures, can vary in different parts of a commercial ceramic body because of fissures, holes, and inhomogeneities. These irregularities are even more likely to be present in traditional hand-built pottery; and because permeability is often used as a measure of apparent porosity in unglazed (and probably even in some slipped) pottery, this known variability casts further doubt on the significance of the measurement. Further variations in porosity/permeability of hand-built pottery may result from the actual techniques of manufacture, which devote greater attention to stroking, thinning, scraping, or burnishing certain areas of the vessel (e.g., a rim) and may be expected to alter their porosity. In addition, the highly variable conditions of open firings (and even of some unsophisticated kilns) suggest that vessels will vary in many physical properties as a consequence of fluctuations in firing temperature and atmosphere, which can affect shrinkage and hence porosity from one side of the vessel to the other. These factors should be recognized in selecting sherds for measurement of porosity.

12.3   Hardness and Strength

One of the most important use-related properties of any material—metal, ceramic, wood, or whatever—is its durability or ability to withstand mechanical stresses during normal use (see sec. 7.3). Metals, for example, are malleable and ductile; they absorb forces and will distort their shape to some degree before rupturing. Ceramics, however, react differently. Although wet clays are highly plastic and can distort without failure in response to a variety of forces that crush or stretch them, fired ceramic materials are generally rigid and brittle.

Materials scientists have devoted considerable attention to the performance characteristics of commercial ceramics, and these approaches are increasingly being used to understand the durability or failure of ancient vessels. Although most of the technical materials literature treats high-fired industrial ceramics and bricks, the tests also provide a variety of data, concepts, and techniques that can, with care, be applied to prehistoric pottery.

Two closely related performance properties of fired ceramics are hardness and strength.

12.3.1   Hardness

One way of assessing the durability or serviceability of a ceramic material is to determine its hardness. As Shepard (1976, 113) points out, hardness has many meanings, including resistance to penetration, abrasion, scratching, and crushing. Hardness is also related to the stiffness or the coefficient of elasticity of a material, an aspect treated in more detail below as the property of "strength." Although both terms, hardness and strength, refer to a material's resistance to mechanical deformation, hardness denotes deformations affecting the surface while strength is a measure of the response to stresses involving the entire body.

Like color, the hardness of fired clays depends on a combination of variables, the most important being the conditions of firing, kinds of impurities present, microstructural features, and surface treatment.

The hardness of a given clay generally increases with the temperature of firing, ceteris paribus. Hardness will also be affected by the firing atmosphere: an atmosphere of reduction (or even severely limited oxidation) for some interval during the firing will harden the fired piece. This occurs because under reducing conditions iron compounds react with silica to produce a flux, thus bringing about sintering (see sec. 4.2.3) and a hard, glassy phase at a lower temperature than usual.

Impurities in the clay increase the fired hardness if they act as fluxes and lower the temperature at which sintering begins; sintering and subsequent vitrification result in a hard, glassy body that resists surface deformation. Besides compounds of iron, which cause sintering under reducing conditions, a variety of compounds of alkali metals, including sodium and potassium, may act as fluxes. Other impurities, such as salts, may lower the surface hardness if they concentrate on the surfaces of the piece as a soft, scummy residue.

Microstructural features influencing hardness include grain size and the porosity of the fired piece. Finer-grained, relatively nonporous materials will provide greater resistance to penetration, abrasion, and crushing and thus be generally harder and more durable than coarse, porous materials.

Finally, various surface treatments of a clay piece can affect its hardness. Burnishing, for example, will compact and smooth the particles on the surfaces and make the surfaces harder and more resistant to abrasion. Similarly, a coating of a different material, such as a slip or glaze, intended to be harder, more resilient, and more resistant to abrasion than the clay body, may be applied.

The hardness of archaeological pottery has long been informally assessed in the field by a variety of impressionistic but nonetheless useful observations. Listening for a "clink" when sherds are tapped against each other or against a stone or metal object is a time-honored technique of distinguishing relatively hard and "soft" pottery. Similarly, when a sherd is broken, the way it fractures can give some idea of hardness: a hard sherd may be difficult to break and may fracture·with a snap, leaving clean edges, while a softer sherd may break more easily with a crumbly or "friable" fracture edge.

These techniques are too imprecise to provide any quantitative measure of hardness, however, and for such determinations a variety of laboratory methods have been developed (see Bowie and Simpson 1977, 138–49). These measure three dimensions of surface hardness: resistance to penetration, resistance to abrasion, and "scratch hardness," which is in some senses a combination of the other two.

The penetration or indentation methods of measuring hardness include the Brinnell, Knoop, and Vickers techniques (see Grimshaw 1971, 866–69, for a general discussion of indentation methods). These tests are all similar in that a static load is gradually applied to a polished specimen; hardness is calculated by dividing the applied load (force) by the area of the surface indentation on the specimen as measured under a microscope. The primary difference between the methods is that the Brinnell test uses a steel ball, which leaves a circular indentation, while the Knoop and Vickers tests use a pyramidal diamond point, which leaves a square indentation.

Abrasion or abradability hardness tests measure debris removed from a specimen that has been either tumbled, ground, or blasted with a harder material (Grimshaw 1971, 869–70).

Perhaps the most familiar hardness testing procedure used by archaeologists is the Mohs' mineral hardness scale, devised by an Austrian mineralogist, Friedrich Mohs, in 1822. This scale uses a series of minerals of increasing hardness, ranked from 1 to 10 (see table 12.1), talc being the softest and diamond the hardest. Mohs' test measures scratch hardness, or the ease with

Table 12.1   Mohs' Hardness Scale and Substitutes

Hardness Number	Mohs' Mineral	Substitute
1	Talc	
2	Gypsum (selenite)	
2.5		Fingernail
3	Calcite	Copper wire
3.5		Celestite
4	Fluorite	
4.5		Window glass; chabazite
5	Apatite	
5.5		Blade of pocketknife; willemite
6	Orthoclase	
6.5		File; vesuvianite
7	Quartz	
8	Topaz	
9	Sapphire; corundum	
10	Diamond	

Source: Substitutes after Grimshaw 1971, table XIII-III; March 1934, 20.

which the minerals will produce an indentation or scratch when drawn over the surface of a specimen. One advantage of Mohs' test is that it can be readily interpreted in terms reflecting the actual use and serviceability of a pot. The testing procedure is analogous to stirring or scraping, which abrades the interiors of vessels and the surfaces of serving pieces (see Norton 1970, 199). Few actual uses of pots lead to indentation or penetration, the resistance to which is measured by the Brinnell test and related techniques.

Mohs' test is performed under a binocular microscope, beginning with minerals at the harder end of the scale and moving toward softer minerals. The hardness value of the test specimen is recorded as the hardness of the mineral that will just produce a visible scratch; if the ceramic is harder than the test mineral, the "streak" visible on the specimen's surface comes from the abraded mineral. Hardness values frequently are interpolated between two minerals, so that a given specimen may be judged to have a hardness of 4.5 if apatite, with a hardness of 5, scratches its surface but fluorite, hardness 4, does not. Non-kiln-fired pottery commonly ranges between 3 and 5 in hardness (see Shepard 1976, 114), but values of 2 and 7 are not unknown.

Interpreting the results of hardness tests requires a good deal of caution, partly because the surfaces of pottery—especially hand-built, non-kiln-fired pottery—are likely to be highly variable, but also because the results of different tests may not correlate well with each other. Grimshaw (1971, 866, also 856–57), for example, notes that indentation tests are associated with the hardness of the mineral components of a composite (crystalline) material, whereas abrasion tests measure the strength of the bonds holding the grains together. Similarly, scratch hardness is not likely to be useful on rough surfaces, because the movement of the mineral will tend to tear out individual grains rather than actually penetrate the surface (Shepard 1976, 116).

Mohs' scale has a number of advantages for archaeologists. The kit of minerals is readily available from scientific supply companies and is easy to use with minimal equipment. In addition, there are several convenient substitutes or approximations for particular values in the scale: a fingernail, for example, averages 2 or 2.5, copper wire is 3, window glass is 4.5, and a pocketknife is about 6 (see also Peacock 1977, 30).

Nevertheless, some cautions should be heeded in applying Mohs' scale to archaeological specimens. First, the same person should do all measurements, because the pressure applied in drawing the minerals over the specimens will vary from individual to individual. Second, the test is not likely to be reliable on extremely rough ("sandy") ceramics. Third, both surfaces of a sherd should be measured, and it should be clearly noted whether the hardness value is that of the clay body or an overlying slip or glaze.

In addition, several problems are inherent in the scale itself. One is that the minerals in the kits usually vary in the sharpness of their points, and hence in their propensity to cut. Second, the mineral set represents an ordinal rather than a ratio or interval scale—the differences between any two values are relative and unequal rather than quantitatively equal (see also March 1934, 20, for an effort to develop a scale with values intermediate between those of the Mohs' scale minerals). Thus there is very little difference in microhardness between minerals 3 (calcite) and 4 (fluorite) in the scale, but a great difference between 6 (orthoclase) and 7 (quartz) (see Shepard 1976, 15; Grimshaw 1971, 869). For this reason, although hardness is a quantitative measure, it cannot be used with statistics designed for interval scales, such as calculation of a mean. Instead, the descriptive measures common to ordinal scales, such as modal and median values, must be used to characterize the hardness of a collection.

The greatest difficulties arise in interpreting the results of hardness measurements. Hardness is typically interpreted in terms of firing technology, with greater hardness taken to indicate higher firing temperatures (see also sec. 14.3.1). Although this relationship generally holds true, inferences of firing technology from hardness measurements are reliable only within the context of a known series of related clays or sherds of identical composition. In other words, differences in hardness between red paste pottery and white paste pottery cannot be confidently attributed to differences in firing temperatures unless the effect of firing temperature on local red- and white-firing clays has previously been determined by independent experimentation (e.g., firing and refiring tests, described above). It is partly for this reason that it is useful to conduct firing experiments with local clays to test this relationship. As Shepard (1976, 114) has noted, "if identity of paste can be established for a series of sherds, then variations in hardness will reflect differences in firing conditions, but uniformity of hardness does not prove identical firing temperature when pots differ in composition."

12.3.2 Strength

Besides hardness, which treats the surface of a ceramic, the durability or strength of the body as a whole is of considerable interest. The strength of a fired ceramic is a function of many properties: its composition, physical properties, method of forming, conditions of drying and firing, thermal conditions of use, and other conditions to which it may have been subjected (Grimshaw 1971, 871). Correspondingly, strength may be defined operationally in several ways, largely in terms of its ability to withstand various stresses without rupturing, fracturing, deforming, or abrading (Grimshaw 1971, 832).

Strength is usually analyzed in terms of resistance to the various mechanical stresses (stress = applied force per unit area) that may act upon materials. In response to applied stresses, a material deforms or strains, strain being defined as the change in dimension per unit dimension. At low stresses the strains in most solids are proportional to the stresses and are reversible; the material is said to exhibit elastic behavior. Too much stress will exceed the material's elastic limit, which is the maximum stress that can be withstood without permanent distortion. Metals are able to respond to such heavy stresses by accommodating through plastic deformation or absorbing the force by distorting shape. Ceramics, on the other hand, are brittle and experience fracture and, ultimately, breakage without plastic deformation. This type of response is partly a consequence of the types of atomic bonding in ceramic materials: their mixed covalent/ionic bonds are rigid and strongly directional and allow little or no plastic flow, in contrast to the responses of materials with metallic bonding (Grimshaw 1971, 836, 837).

Two quantitative measures or "intrinsic properties" of ceramic materials are related to strength assessments: the modulus of elasticity and Poisson's ratio. The modulus of elasticity, or Young's modulus, is a measure of a ceramic's ability to resist mechanical stress without deformation or failure. Symbolized as E, it is measured as the ratio of stress to strain derived from the change in dimension of the specimen under applied force (see Grimshaw 1971, 864). Poisson's ratio is a measure of the relation between strains occurring in perpendicular directions: for example, as a piece is being "stretched" the longitudinal strain of elongation is accompanied by transverse strains, in a direction perpendicular to the elogation. Poisson's ratio or μ is thus a ratio of lateral to longitudinal strains (Grimshaw 1971, 839).

Six kinds of stresses have been analyzed (fig. 12.4): tensile, shear, compressive, transverse, torsional, and impact stresses (Grimshaw 1971, 832–34, 842–55). The response of the material to each of these can be measured in different ways, so one can calculate the strength of the material in resisting each (e.g., tensile strength, compressive strength, etc.) as well as identify particular characteristics of the resulting fracture pattern after failure. In general it is impossible to apply one type of stress without others, and virtually all failure results from either tensile or shear stresses, regardless of how the forces are applied. Additionally, most of these stresses play a significant role not only in mechanical performance, but in thermal behavior as well (see sec. 12.4.2).

Tensile stress (fig. 12.4b) results when tension or elongation forces are applied to a material, tending to pull it apart across a plane at right angles to the direction of the force. The linear relation of stress and strain is given by E, that is, Young's modulus or the modulus of elasticity. Tensile stress is calculated as the amount of force applied divided by the area of cross section of the piece in the plane at which fracturing occurs. Tensile strength is the tensile

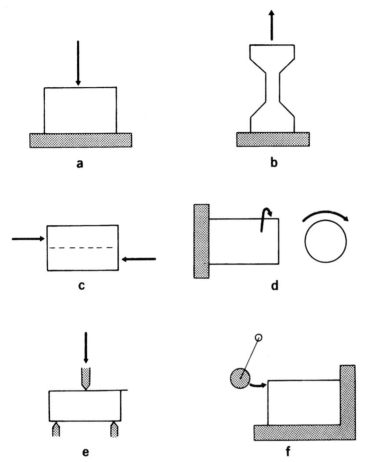

Figure 12.4 The principal methods of apply-   shear; *d,* torsion; *e,* transverse; *f,* impact.
ing stress: *a,* compression; *b,* tension; *c,*   After Grimshaw 1971, fig. XIII.1.

stress at which fracturing occurs. In testing tensile strength, the result should be independent of the size and shape of the piece, and special shapes need to be used to ensure this (Grimshaw 1971, 857–58), which often causes problems in testing archaeological specimens. In general, ceramics are weaker in tension than under other kinds of stresses, but because fired ceramics are rarely subjected to tensile forces alone during use, the testing procedure is primarily applied to green (unfired) ware (see sec. 3.3.3). Tensile stresses are especially significant during cooling, however (see Kingery 1955, 12), and tensile strength is an extremely important property of ceramic glazes, preventing them from crazing on cooling. It is important to note that as tensile forces act on a material in one direction, compressive strains develop at right angles to the direction of force.

Shear stresses (fig. 12.4c) occur when one part of the body is made to slip or slide relative to another part. Wet unfired clays have low resistance to shear;

the shear strain that develops is part of their plasticity, and their failure (cracking) ultimately occurs because their limit of strain is exceeded. Shear results from two noncolinear stresses applied in opposite directions, and tensile forces develop at an angle of approximately 45° to the shearing force, leading to fracturing. The relation between stress and strain during shearing is summarized by a constant known as the modulus of rigidity, E_R (Grimshaw 1971, 839).

Compressive stress (fig. 12.4a) occurs when a crushing force is applied to a material, as in load-bearing structures such as brick walls. Also, glazes may compress the underlying body as they shrink in cooling. These stresses strengthen the ware up to a certain point, but beyond it the glazes will craze or crawl (see fig. 4.7). Compressive stress/strain relationships, as in the case of tensile stresses, are expressed by E. Failure under compressive forces is usually evidenced as a shear fracture occurring at an angle of approximately 45° to the direction of force. The compressive strength of ceramics is roughly four times greater than its tensile strength (Kingery 1955, 12). Testing for compressive strength is closely tied to the rate at which the stress is applied as well as to the shape and particle size of the object being tested (Grimshaw 1971, 859). Fracture lines usually follow the flaws and cracks inherent in the material, with large grains acting as barriers. Test pieces should be at least ten times the maximum dimension of the largest grains present in the material, and small test pieces often give a larger scatter of values because of compositional heterogeneity.

Transverse or flexural stress (fig. 12.4e) is an applied force that causes bending of the material. The bending strength of a ceramic is approximately twice the tensile strength (Davidge and Tappin 1967, 417). Measurement of transverse strength (also known as the modulus of rupture, or T) is fairly straightforward: the test piece, which must be flat, is supported at one or more points (usually it is rested upon two or more points), then downward force is applied to the upper surface. The lower layers, bending down between the supports, are thus in tension, and fracture begins by tensile failure at the lower surface and moves into the interior of the body. Calculation of the modulus of rupture takes into consideration the length (l), width (b), and thickness (t) of the piece at a given force (W), according to the following formula (Grimshaw 1971, 861): $T = 3Wl/2bt^2$.

Torsional stresses (fig. 12.4d) are twisting or rotational forces applied to a material and may occur when different parts of a material are subjected to forces in different directions. The strain is basically one of shear and is marked by a characteristic S-shaped fracture.

Impact stresses (fig. 12.4f) occur when force is applied suddenly and with momentum, as in a sharp blow. The breaking stress is generally one that if applied slowly would not cause failure, but because there is not time enough for the body to yield, local strains can be very large, causing the test piece to fail. Brittle bodies such as ceramics cannot transmit the energy fast enough to disperse it throughout the body. The direction of the stress is determined by the direction of momentum of the impact, and the initial fracture is caused by tensile stress (Grimshaw 1971, 843).

Most of the mechanical performance tests measuring the response of a ceramic to various types of stresses are at least partially dependent upon the size and shape of the test piece; this is particularly true of the transverse, torsional, impact, and compression tests (see Grimshaw 1971, 844). For example, the engineering literature on simulated service testing of tableware with various design attributes has examined the rims of vessels as an important source of fracturing leading to failure or breakage. One study (Dinsdale, Camm, and Wilkinson 1967, 374–86) found that chipping resistance varied closely with thickness and profile or cross-sectional shape: thicker pieces and pieces with flat or squared cross sections had greater resistance than thinner pieces and those with pointed and/or rounded contours.

These relationships may also be important in assessing the serviceability of archaeological ceramic vessels, which are likely to be subject to impact or bending stresses. Strength testing of prehistoric pottery may yield a wide scatter of values because of its inhomogeneities, curvature, and fragmentary nature (limiting sample size). The testing procedures (e.g., American Society of Testing Materials standards) generally recommend testing multiple specimens, uniform in size and thickness; for example, for transverse breaking strength it is recommended that ten specimens be tested. Any test values varying more than 15% from the average should be discarded, and if more than two are discarded the test should be repeated.

For archaeological pottery, larger samples or broader tolerances may be necessary, depending on the circumstances. Shepard (1936, 434–35) manufactured over one hundred clay test pieces and fired them to temperatures comparable to those used for Pueblo pottery in order to test the effects of shape and thickness on transverse breaking strength. She found that in those test samples both thickness and curvature had negligible effects on strength, the thickness variants differing less than 15% from the group average and curved pieces only 5% from flat pieces.

More significantly, the local stresses are also a function of the microstructure of the pottery, specifically the kinds and sizes of crystals in the material, the degree of porosity, and the presence of flaws and microcracks. Fracture of brittle materials like ceramics generally starts at preexisting flaws or microcracks. These concentrate the stress at their tips, and when this local stress exceeds a critical value, the microcrack starts to grow. When it is large enough, this crack propagation process becomes catastrophic (under constant load) and the piece fractures. The fracture strength of the material therefore depends on the sizes and orientations of these preexisting flaws and on how subsequent crack propagation takes place once the critical stress is exceeded as well as on inherent properties of the material.

Most of the testing in the materials industry has involved high-fired (vitrified) ceramics or materials that are relatively homogeneous in composition, particularly whitewares, porcelains, and bricks. Lower-fired vessels are clearly less durable, at least in comparison with normal commercially fired tableware. In one test identical sets of earthenware service pieces, differing only in firing (normal fired versus "easy fired") were used for four weeks in an industrial canteen. At the conclusion of the test, 68.6% of the easy-fired pieces had suffered damage, with a damage:use ratio of 1:9, while 28.9% of the normal-fired earthenware suffered damage and had a damage:use ratio of 1:54 (Dinsdale, Camm, and Wilkinson 1967, 402–3).

Phase relationships between constituents are also important with respect to the durability of low-fired, heterogeneous archaeological pottery, because the kinds and sizes of grains have many crucial effects (see Bronitsky and Hamer 1986, 94–96, for an example). The boundaries of contact planes between phases (grains) can be a source of weakness, and the crystals themselves have cleavages and fracture planes that will vary in strength at different temperatures. In addition, the strength of multiphase ceramics decreases significantly with increasing grain size (Chu 1968, 853; see also Kirchner 1979, 8). Generally, smaller grain size contributes to greater bending strength and higher resistance to crack initiation.

These relationships are especially important in the case of preexisting boundary stresses between phases with different thermal expansion coefficients (see below). They are also particularly significant with respect to the quartz inclusions in porcelain (Robinson 1968b, 550–51; Warshaw and Seider 1968), because of the inversions quartz undergoes at high temperatures and again on cooling (see sec. 4.2.3.1). These quartz problems probably are minimal in low-fired archaeological pottery, in part because only the low-temperature alpha-beta inversion is likely to take place, and it occurs, at least on heating, while there is still considerable porosity in the vessel to absorb the stresses.

It is also known that strength decreases with increasing porosity, because "pores act as brittle phases of zero strength" (Chu 1968, 852). Pores of the appropriate shape and orientation can be viewed as stress concentrators, and even small volume fractions of porosity (e.g., 10%) in a brittle ceramic can reduce strength by as much as half (Hasselman and Fulrath 1968, 345). Different forces seem to affect the relation of porosity to strength in vitrified and in crystalline low-fired ceramics. Vitrification and the formation of a glassy phase can increase the strength of a piece because the glasses in ceramics are more elastic and can tolerate greater deformation without rupture than the crystalline materials (Grimshaw 1971, 836, 894). On the other hand, pores make a ceramic less brittle, because as a phase of a material they lower the elastic modulus of the whole (Kingery 1960, 598).

Porosity has an important effect on strength largely through its influence on the development and propagation of microcracks in the ceramic. Cracks may be present in the ceramic as a result of internal stresses during drying or firing, the latter including crystal phase transformations or differential thermal expansions or contractions between phases (Chu 1968, 854). Some of the pores themselves may act as flaws. Cracks and flaws in the microstructure can also arise from surface imperfections and the mechanics of forming, and these are likely to penetrate well into the body (Stokes 1968, 380). This factor is of considerable significance in hand-built wares, in which both surface and internal flaws can result from coiling, molding, scraping, burnishing, and so forth.

Given that flaws, weaknesses, and cracks are inherent in the body of a ceramic, the question becomes one of understanding the characteristics that contribute to or restrain the propagation of cracks. Pores reduce strength in a vitrified ware by acting as flaws to initiate cracks, but in a crystalline ceramic, especially one that is subjected to thermal stresses or already contains critical flaws, porosity can increase serviceability to a certain extent. Rounded pores blunt the crack or, like the individual crystals, interrupt its path, causing the crack front to lose its planarity and preventing its continuation. Glassy bodies often lack these irregularities, so cracks can travel unimpeded through the material. Experiments with single-phase noncrystalline glass materials having low porosity showed that the effect of spherical porosity on strength can be divided into three regions based on the relative sizes of the cracks and the pores; the least decline in strength occurred when the pores were considerably smaller than the flaws (Hasselman and Fulrath 1968, 372–73). This same relation can be expected in multicrystalline materials.

12.4 Thermal Properties and Stresses

The behavior of a clay material at a series of uniform temperatures or under conditions of temperature change is of considerable interest, because heat is a significant component in the manufacture and in many applications of ceramics. Their refractoriness, or ability to withstand extremely high temperatures, has contributed to the wide range of uses of ceramics, from ancient and modern cooking to jet engines.

The thermal behavior of a ceramic is of concern in two situations: in the initial firing of the clay and in use of the fired vessel with heat. In both situations heat causes most of the individual constituents or phases of the ceramic to expand, and on cooling they contract. This expansion and contraction of individual phases within the body can create stresses, particularly when the phases are contiguous and their common boundaries restrict free expansion or contraction. It is the response of the body to these thermal stresses that interests ceramists.

Thermal stresses and restraints on free thermal expansion commonly arise out of two circumstances that are generally not independent. One is a change in the ambient or uniform temperature of the material, for example, a change from room temperature to 250°C. The separate crystalline components expand at different rates and constrain each other within the finite bounds of the ceramic body, setting up stresses that can cause fracturing and eventual failure. The second situation, usually occurring along with the first, involves a temperature gradient within the body of the ceramic, so that exterior surfaces may be hotter or cooler than the interior vessel walls or one side may be hotter or cooler than the other. Again, the components of the body heat or contract at different rates, being constrained by adjacent grains or phases. Compressive and tensional stresses arise in these circumstances, exacerbating the tendency to fracture. For example, when a ceramic is heated the surfaces become hotter than the interior, resulting in compressive stresses on the surfaces and tensile stresses on the interior. On cooling the reverse is true, with more rapid contraction on the surfaces causing tensile stresses (e.g., those that result in dunting; see sec. 12.4.1), while the interiors suffer compressional stress (Kingery 1955, 4). Shear and transverse stresses may also be present. Stresses are generally greater with rapid cooling than with slow cooling.

12.4.1   Thermal Properties

Two "intrinsic" materials properties of ceramics are important to understanding their thermal behavior: the coefficient of thermal expansion and thermal conductivity.

The coefficient of thermal expansion, either length (α) or volume (β), is a measure of the increase that accompanies the heating of a material. It is expressed as the amount of change per unit per degree Celsius. In solids the volume expansion is approximately three times the linear expansion. Materials expand because as heat energy is applied, the vibrational movements of the constituent atoms or ions increase in amplitude, expanding the crystal lattice. The expansion may exert considerable pressure: for example, the expansional pressure of MgO on heating from room temperature to 100°C is 70,000 pounds per square inch (Lawrence and West 1982, 219). The expansion coefficient is a function of the temperature: very rapid increases at low temperatures gradually level off with higher temperature, although the temperature range over which this occurs varies among different minerals (see Kingery, Bowen, and Uhlmann 1976, 591–95). The thermal expansion of some materials is reversible—contraction occurs on cooling, and with subsequent reheating the expansion will recur—but in other cases the volume change may be permanent.

Most ceramics—particularly those of anthropological and archaeological interest—are composite, mostly crystalline materials, and so it is difficult to determine precisely the expansion of the body. Although the thermal expansion of a mass approximates the average of its constituent phases, individual mineral grains may have different coefficients of expansion in different crystallographic directions (Grimshaw 1971, 790).

Thermal conductivity or k refers to the rate or ease with which heat passes through a substance under a particular temperature gradient. The transmission of heat through a solid body is a sort of three-dimensional analogue of the propagation of a wave pulse along a tightly stretched string when it is plucked; the vibrational states of the atoms act like the modes of vibration of the string. If the body is homogeneous on a scale smaller than the wavelengths, the waves are easily transmitted, but grain boundaries, pores, compositional variations, and such can interfere with and scatter the waves, reducing the transmission of heat. In general, ceramics—especially those that are multiphasic, crystalline, and porous—are poor conductors; they transmit heat slowly (compared with metals, for example), and thus thermal gradients are easy to establish within the piece (Lawrence and West 1982, fig. 9.9). On the other hand, poor thermal conductivity means high thermal resistance, and ceramics can therefore be good thermal insulators.

Thermal conductivity is influenced by a variety of factors (Grimshaw 1971, 934–46), the most significant being the composition of the ceramic and its microstructure. Different degrees of thermal conductivity are desirable for different purposes; refractory bricks, for example, should have low thermal conductivity, to provide better insulation in kilns and not lose heat, whereas saggars and cooking pots should have high conductivity to transmit heat rapidly to their contents (Grimshaw 1971, 939).

The practical consequences of these ceramic properties of thermal expansion and conductivity occur as temperature changes during firing and use with heat. Thermal stresses may arise because the components of a ceramic body cannot expand or contract freely as the ambient temperature changes, either because of inhomogeneity in the body or because of thermal gradients. Thermal shock is extreme thermal stress caused by a sudden and severe temperature change. Thus an important property of ceramic materials is their thermal stress resistance—that is, their resistance to weakening, fracture, or spalling under conditions causing thermal stress or shock (Kingery 1955, 3).

In practice, it is usually thermal shock resistance that is measured: the maximum sudden temperature change the ceramic can withstand without cracking or weakening (Crandall and Ging 1955, 44). Thermal shock results from tensile stresses developing because of temperature gradients through the body and differences in thermal expansion of its components. When these stresses exceed the strength of the body, fracturing occurs. Thermal shock resistance can be measured by quenching specimens in water from successively higher temperatures and then measuring some relevant physical property, such as fracture strength. At some temperature a sudden change takes place, such as a drop in strength or even a fracture. The temperature drop, Δt_f, bringing this about is taken as a measure of thermal shock resistance. The various properties that influence resistance to the initiation of fracture, for instance, are illustrated with the following approximate equation:

$$\Delta t_f \approx R' = \frac{kS_t\,(1 - \mu)}{E \cdot \alpha}\,.$$

In this equation R' is the "thermal stress resistance factor," k is the thermal conductivity of the material, S_t is the tensile strength, μ is Poisson's ratio, α is the coefficient of thermal expansion, and E is the modulus of elasticity (see Kingery 1955; also Davidge and Tappin 1967, 407; Crandall and Ging 1955; Grimshaw 1971, 949).

Some thermal stress can bring about complete failure of the ceramic without the suddenness of thermal shocking. A significant category in much ceramic use is cumulative thermal fatigue, the delayed failure of a ceramic caused by gradual weakening through repeated cycles of thermal stressing. Another kind of thermal stress failure is dunting, the cracking that occurs either while ware is cooling from its original firing (especially if it is cooled too rapidly) or from expansion of quartz between 400 and 600°C on reheating bisque ware (Lawrence and West 1982, 287). Dunting cracks typically occur at the rim of vessels as a result of tensile stresses (Rye 1981, 114).

Thermal shock resistance has been tested in a variety of ways. In each, some method of establishing a temperature gradient is used (e.g., by quenching; see Davidge and Tappin 1967) and some property is measured to detect the onset of failure (Coble and Kingery 1955). One test measures thermal expansion (Coble and Kingery 1955). Another procedure uses simulated service tests, which subject a large batch of identical pieces to testing conditions simulating those of actual use. The latter procedure is especially useful for testing how shape affects thermal stress resistance.

12.4.2   Factors Influencing Thermal Stress Resistance

The susceptibility or resistance of a ceramic body to thermal stresses is conditioned by a number of factors (see Grimshaw 1971, 948–49; Kingery 1955, 6, 8). Some can be manipulated during manufacture by modifying either composition or design, whereas others are largely fixed, constrained by the nature of ceramic materials in general. The significant variables of thermal stress resistance can be divided into four major categories: the intrinsic material properties of ceramics (expressed in the equation for calculating shock resistance); factors relating to the temperatures at which the observations take place; microstructural features of the ceramic body; and design features of the shaped ceramic piece.

12.4.2.1   INTRINSIC PROPERTIES

Many of the major factors influencing thermal shock resistance are those intrinsic properties incorporated as variables into the equation for predicting this behavior (sec. 12.4.1). These include modulus of elasticity, Poisson's ratio, strength, thermal conductivity, and thermal expansion coefficient. The modulus of elasticity (E) cannot be manipulated to increase thermal stress resistance; ceramic materials generally have high moduli of elasticity, and hence their susceptibility to thermal failure occurs partly because under the mechanical deformations accompanying thermal changes they respond by creating large stresses, which cause cracking. The quantity $E/(1-\mu)$ is a measure of these stresses. Similarly, Poisson's ratio (μ) is a measure of elastic response and, like the modulus of elasticity, cannot be controlled by potters. The strength of a body can be modified considerably by compositional and microstructural alterations, yielding high tensile strengths and greater resistance to thermal shock (see below; cf. Lawrence and West 1982, 219).

The coefficient of expansion (α) controls the magnitudes of the thermally generated deformations. Furthermore, the expansion coefficients of the individual components are significant because of the danger of "thermal dimensional mismatch," a condition in which the differential expansion of some minerals creates large internal stresses that exceed the body's ability to withstand it. High coefficients of thermal expansion will contribute to low resistance to thermal shock. For example, in modern ceramics used in cooking, ovenwares have thermal expansions from 2.2 to 4.5×10^{-6} per °C, while flamewares (designed for use directly over heat) have even lower expansion coefficients below 2.0×10^{-6} per °C (Norton 1970, 357–58). Thermal expansion is important to the potter primarily in selecting materials to be added to the clay as aggregate or temper (sec. 14.1): ideally the additives should have low coefficients of thermal expansion or coefficients that match those of the fired clay as closely as possible (see sec. 7.3.3; also Lawrence and West 1982, 223; Rye 1976, 116–17; Bronitsky and Hamer 1986, 96–97).

The relation between clay and temper as it applies to thermal behavior, however, is complicated. Robinson (1968b, 550–51) points out that because mineral additions "dilute" the concentration of a clay in a given body, they also diminish the thermal mismatch that occurs in the body during the critical dehydroxylation stage of firing, thereby reducing cracking. On the other hand, because most of the materials in polycrystalline ceramics are anistropic (varying in their properties in different crystallographic directions), "anistropic thermal contraction on cooling from the fabrication temperature leads to the development of internal residual stresses" (Stokes 1968, 381).

Thermal conductivity is also a factor in resistance to thermal stress. Because ceramic materials generally are not good conductors, they transmit heat slowly and are prone to develop strong thermal gradients. Thus high thermal conductivity will increase thermal stress resistance, and characteristics that increase conductivity will also reduce thermal stress. The chief of these that can be manipulated by the potter is porosity (see sec. 12.2 and 12.4.2.3). High thermal conductivity is especially desirable for reducing stresses during cooling (Kingery 1955, 11).

12.4.2.2 TEMPERATURE

The rate of temperature change greatly affects susceptibility to thermal stress. Indeed, it is a sudden temperature change that causes the severe reaction known as thermal shocking. Slow temperature changes minimize thermal gradients in the body and allow for gradual transfer of heat without excessive stress. Absolute temperature differences in heating and cooling are also important, not only in the establishment of thermal gradients but especially in their effect on the expansion of individual constituents of the body.

12.4.2.3 MICROSTRUCTURE

Microstructural features are perhaps most important to thermal stress resistance, in large part because they can be controlled by the manufacturer. The chief microstructural properties of interest are particle size and porosity.

Fine-grained materials have more grain boundaries than coarser bodies, so they have greater thermal resistance and lower conductivity; they slow the transfer of heat through a body and are likely to give rise to thermal gradients. On the other hand, smaller grain size (and decreased porosity) increases the fracture strength of polycrystalline ceramics (Stokes 1968, 381). Also, the smaller the particles the less the effect of thermal mismatch on some important constituents of ceramic bodies, such as quartz (Robinson 1968b, 550–51). This finding, however, generally pertains to high-temperature firings, where the quartz inversions can be particularly serious.

Porosity is of considerable significance in the thermal stress resistance of a ceramic, but its role is highly complex and sometimes equivocal (see Coble and Kingery 1955, 33–34, for a review of studies; also Buessem 1955). Porosity affects the overall thermal expansion and conductivity of a body, and pores will also halt cracks that originate from thermal stresses. Increased porosity in a body reduces thermal expansion because voids interrupt the linear and volume continuities between the components (Grimshaw 1971, 791, table XII-VII): crystals can expand into voids without exerting pressure on surrounding grains. This is doubtless an important reason why the expansion of quartz and other constituents of low-fired bodies creates little stress: the voids absorb the strains.

Thermal conductivity is affected by porosity, because the kinds and sizes of pores will determine how rapidly heat moves through them by convection and radiation. Thermal conductivity of a homogeneous body may be decreased by high porosity if the pores are closed, because air insulates better than solids. For example, Coble and Kingery (1955, 37) note that in their experimental firings the specimens with 50% porosity had about one-sixth the conductivity of dense samples; thermal stress resistance of specimens with 50% porosity was about one-third that of dense samples. Thus a material with many small closed pores will be a good insulator (Grimshaw 1971, 936, 947); it will conduct heat more slowly, but it will maintain thermal gradients, decreasing thermal stress resistance. On the other hand, large, open, and connected pores will increase thermal conductivity because they permit hot gases to pass throughout the body (Grimshaw 1971, 420–41, 937), reducing thermal gradients and increasing thermal stress resistance. Pores may also prolong the serviceability of ceramic wares under thermal stress because they inhibit the propagation of cracks and fractures that form them (discussed above). On the other hand, porosity may help bring about the gradual weakening and loss of strength characteristic of cumulative thermal fatigue (Lawrence and West 1982, 225–26).

Two approaches have been used to design bodies with compositional and microstructural characteristics that promote thermal shock resistance (Kingery, Bowen, and Uhlmann 1976, 828). One is based on thermoelastic theory and focuses on the initiation of fractures (Buessem 1955; Davidge and Tappin 1967): fracture initiation can be reduced in bodies having high tensile strength, high thermal conductivity, low modulus of elasticity, and low thermal expansion. The second approach is to reduce the propensity toward fracture propagation (Hasselman 1963; for a theory unifying both approaches, see Hasselman 1969), and this quality is enhanced by characteristics opposite to those reducing fracture initiation. A high modulus of elasticity, low strength, and irregularities in the microstructure (such as pores) that concentrate rather than disperse stresses will all decrease crack propagation in ceramic bodies. Reduced propensity for crack propagation, which is especially important in refractory materials, further depends on the length of the initial crack, and the strength of the piece itself varies inversely with crack length. Because of the numerous and contrasting variables affecting each property, it is difficult to design a body composition that will simultaneously resist both initiation and propagation of cracks under thermal stresses. Furthermore, experimental results often exhibit a marked scatter as the sum of deviations of each variable, hindering easy interpretation (Coble and Kingery 1955, 36–37).

12.4.2.4 SHAPE AND DESIGN

Ceramic design must consider not only composition, however, but also size, shape, thickness, and surface finish, all of which are important in thermal stress resistance.

Two features of surface finish are primary: evenness of the surface and the presence of a glaze. It is extremely important that ceramic materials subject to heating have smooth surfaces. Minor surface imperfections and cracks introduced by shaping cannot be completely eliminated by surface treatment and will be propagated below the surface with heating and cooling (Stokes 1968, 380). With repeated temperature change their cumulative effect will be to reduce strength, though this may be minimized by factors of porosity. Burnishing or applying a slip may reduce this problem.

A glaze may either increase or decrease a ceramic body's resistance to thermal stress, depending on the degree of mismatch between the expansion coefficients of the two materials (see Kingery 1955, 11–12; Grimshaw 1971, 954; Lawrence and West 1982, 179–85; Rhodes 1973, 241–43). On heating, the critical stresses are in the interior and are either shear or tensile, whereas on cooling they are tensile surface stresses (Kingery 1955, 12). These tensile stresses, if severe, will lead to crazing of the cooled glaze (see fig. 4.7). However, a glaze may act as a buffer on the body, decreasing the rate of heating and cooling at the surface and hence the thermal shock or stress on the body. Furthermore, if thermal expansion differs greatly between the glaze and body, it may increase the compressive stress on the body. An engobe, intermediate in thermal expansion between the body and the glaze, may solve this problem (Grimshaw 1971, 954). It has been found that glazes with about 10% lower expansion than the body of the ceramic will provide a slight surface compression on the body and will actually increase its strength (Kingery, Bowen, and Uhlmann 1976, 610; Lawrence and West 1982, 182; Rhodes 1973, 242).

The thickness of a ceramic object will also affect its resistance to thermal stress. In general, thinner pieces are more resistant than thicker pieces (Van Vlack 1964, 117–65; Brody 1979, 11), because the increased conductance (conductivity divided by thickness) resulting from thinner walls reduces the thermal gradient. Regardless of the absolute dimensions of vessel walls, it is advantageous for the piece to be of uniform thickness, because thicker areas have a more pronounced gradient than thinner ones and localize maximum stresses on heating and cooling (Kingery 1955, 10). Similar thermal stresses will arise at any corners or edges of a piece that is not rounded.

Several studies have investigated the relation between the size and shape of test vessels and their thermal fracture characteristics (e.g., Baroody, Simons, and Duckworth 1955; Crandall and Ging 1955; see also the relation between shape and mechanical strength, sec. 12.3.2). The larger the vessel, for example, the thicker the walls are apt to be and the greater the thermal stresses (Kingery 1955, 9). Simulated service testing has provided a basis for investigating the relation between shape and thermal stress resistance (Burnham and Tuttle 1945; Amberg and Hartsook 1946). In one test (Amberg and Hartsook 1946), the vessels that survived the experimental conditions of thermal abuse were those with more gently rounded contours (see also Rye 1981, 27) and a raised base (preventing direct contact with the heat source). Similarly, variable thickness of the vessel walls can cause stresses because of interior thermal gradients: edges, corners, and thickened areas are particularly vulnerable to thermal fracturing. For example, a form with a thickened "bead lip" reacted poorly to heating in one simulated use test, but a raised foot was found to be an advantage (Amberg and Hartsook 1946).

12.5 References

Amberg and Hartsook 1946
Baroody, Simons, and Duckworth 1955
Bowie and Simpson 1977
Brewer 1964
Brody 1979
Bronitsky 1986
Bronitsky and Hamer 1986
Buessem 1955
Burnham and Tuttle 1945
Chu 1968
Coble and Kingery 1955
Colton 1953
Courtois 1976
Crandall and Ging 1955
Davidge and Tappin 1967
Dinsdale, Camm, and Wilkinson 1967
Franklin and Vitali 1985
Grimshaw 1971
Hasselman 1963, 1969
Hasselman and Fulrath 1968
Heimann 1977
Kingery 1955, 1960
Kingery, Bowen, and Uhlmann 1976
Kirchner 1979

Lawrence and West 1982
Levin, Robbins, and McMurdie 1964
Magetti 1982
March 1934
Morariu, Bogdan, and Ardelean 1977
Norton 1970
Peacock 1977
Reid 1984
Rhodes 1973
Robinson 1968b
Roth, Negas, and Cook 1983
Rye 1976, 1981
Sanders 1973
Shepard 1936, 1976
Stokes 1968
Tankersley and Meinhart 1982
Vandiver and Koehler 1986
Van Vlack 1964
Warshaw and Seider 1968
Washburn 1921
Whittemore and Halsey 1983
Wolkodoff, Ferreira, and Weaver 1968

Mineralogical and Chemical Characterization of Pottery 13

Although mechanical, structural, and thermal properties of ceramics have been used sporadically—but increasingly—to characterize archaeological and ethnographic vessels, the more commonly used techniques focus on the mineralogical and chemical constituents of the ceramic. This chapter summarizes the·primary methods used in mineralogical and chemical characterization, their underlying principles, and some special considerations in applying these methods to archaeological pottery. More extensive discussion of their use with archaeological problems such as temper identification, provenience study, firing temperature determinations, and authentication can be found in chapter 14.

13.1 Objectives and Sampling: Additional Considerations

Two issues merit significant attention at the start of a mineralogical or chemical characterization project. One is that the objectives of the analysis must be defined so they can be translated into chemical and mineral terms; the other is that the requirements of sample selection for each technique must be understood. Although these issues were covered in detail in chapter 10 and are treated briefly below within discussion of the individual methods, it is useful to reiterate some of the preliminary considerations guiding ceramic characterization.

An important first question is whether to characterize paste, inclusions, slip, paint, or glaze—whether the surface of a specimen or the body is of interest and whether point or bulk analyses are needed. Techniques capable of one kind of analysis cannot always be used for the other. For example, the bulk chemical composition of the body of a ceramic, even an unslipped or unglazed one, cannot be analyzed by a technique sensitive only to constituents within a few microns below the surface without using a ground powder sample of the body. This could be difficult in situations where extensive leaching, corrosion, or other alteration of the ceramic surface may have occurred in the depositional environment (see Courtois 1976; Franklin and Vitali 1985; Hancock 1985; Freestone, Meeks, and Middleton 1985).

Additional questions concern whether to determine the mineral (crystalline) or the chemical element composition of a body (for glazes, usually only element determinations are made). Although it is self-evident that mineralogical and chemical techniques address different properties of the ceramic, this has important ramifications for structuring ceramic research. It is usually advisable to undertake a mineral analysis before a chemical study, unless very specific questions have been raised about chemical composition. If questions about composition are phrased in more general terms, mineralogical examination will usually indicate whether chemical analysis is necessary, and if so what kind; especially with low-fired pottery, mineral analysis also provides a great deal of information on structure and texture. Once this is settled, one must decide whether to determine the presence of a single mineral or element (or compound) or a large number. Finally, the physicochemical objectives must be set forth: a qualitative (by presence/absence) or quantitative (actual amount) characterization of each mineral or element (or both) in the specimen.

All these questions and others relate to the cultural problems under consideration, which may be, for example, ones of technology, such as determining how a particular ceramic or an attribute of it was created. This usually involves determining the presence or absence of a particular constituent: for example, whether lead is present in a glaze, or a particular type of feldspar is in the body, or manganese is in a paint. It may also involve assessing the temperature at which a ceramic was fired, determining whether a particular constituent was naturally present in the clay or added by the potter, or identifying where an object was manufactured.

Mineralogical characterization, as applied to pottery, is oriented toward quantitative and qualitative description of its mineral components. Typically this focuses on the larger crystalline components of the paste or fabric, which may be inclusions naturally present in the clay or added as temper (see sec. 14.1). Identifying the specific clay mineral or minerals composing the matrix is often problematic, as discussed below; it generally requires more complicated instruments and entails a narrower range of conditions for making such determinations for a given specimen. The most widely used mineralogical methods in ceramic characterization are petrographic analysis and X-ray diffraction, though various thermal analyses and certain other procedures are also employed from time to time.

Chemical analysis is oriented toward identifying the chemical elements (or their compounds) constituting the ceramic. These may be major elements (or their oxides) such as SiO_2, Al_2O_3, FeO, or elements present only in minor or trace amounts. If the chemical analysis is performed on a bulk sample of pottery, the analysis will provide no information on how a particular element became a part of the ceramic—whether it is a constituent of the clay or an added inclusion. Some methods can analyze a particular tiny area or point of the ceramic body; this is useful, for example, in comparing the composition of the body of a ceramic with that of a slip, glaze, paint, or inclusion. Common methods of chemical characterization of ceramics are optical emission spectroscopy, X-ray fluorescence, electron microprobe analysis, and neutron activation analysis. Some of these methods, such as neutron activation analysis, are extremely costly, ranging well over four hundred dollars per sample.

A further issue in deciding between the individual techniques of mineralogical and chemical characterization is how to prepare the specimen for analysis, usually phrased in terms of whether the technique is destructive, though this is a somewhat misleading concept. More significant is whether the technique requires damage to the specimen, largely by removing a small to sizable sample for analysis. The sampling rarely if ever destroys the entire object, but most techniques do necessitate removing a portion of the ceramic material (see chap. 10).

Once a sample has been removed, if necessary, it is useful to know whether it will be destroyed or can be reused in subsequent analyses. In mineral methods, for example, petrographic thin sectioning requires removing a rather large slice of the vessel, usually a few millimeters thick and 1–3 cm long. Once the section is prepared, however, it can be retained as a permanent record of the ceramic and examined repeatedly. Heavy mineral analysis requires crushing several grams of the ceramic and separating various mineral fractions. Some chemical methods, such as X-ray fluorescence, can analyze very small artifacts without removing a sample, and the milliprobe can be used even on large and bulky objects. Most chemical methods, however, require that a sample be removed from the specimen for analysis; for neutron activation analysis the necessary quantity of material is so tiny that it can be drilled from an inconspicuous area, so the method is effectively nondestructive.

The analytical techniques themselves raise important questions of sensitivity, accuracy, time, and cost (table 13.1; see also Rankin 1971, 30; Hall 1963, 170–72; Orphanides 1985). These issues are best investigated in consultation with a physicist, chemist, or materials scientist trained in the analytical procedures and limitations of the techniques themselves. More specifically, for each method used or contemplated, the following questions should be answered:

1. Does the method provide information on the surface of the sample or on the bulk composition? Is it a point analysis of a small area?

2. Is the technique destructive or damaging, and to what degree?

3. How much sample material is required? Can it be reused?

4. What kind of sample preparation is required? Are special techniques or equipment necessary? Who will prepare the samples?

5. Are the instruments available to perform the analyses? Are there experienced operators? What sort of backlog or priority system controls access to the equipment?

6. What is the cost of the analysis? What is the cost per sample? Do charges include the use of the instrument, the operator's time, sample preparation, data reduction, and extra analyses for clarification should they be necessary?

7. How much time is involved? How long does it take to analyze one sample? The entire data set? How long until final results will be available? Should delays be anticipated?

Table 13.1　Comparison of Some Common Methods of Physicochemical Analysis

	X-Ray Diffraction	Optical Emission Spectrometry	X-Ray Fluorescence	Atomic Absorption Spectrometry
Sample size and preparation	2–20 mg, powdered	5–100 mg, powdered and mixed	100 mg–2 g, powdered and mixed, or whole artifact	10 mg–1 g, powdered and mixed
Destructiveness	Sample reusable	Sample destroyed	None or sample reusable	Sample destroyed
Area analyzed	Bulk composition	Bulk composition	Surface of whole specimen; bulk composition with powder	Bulk composition
Components analyzed	Crystalline minerals only	30–40 metallic elements	80 elements, $Z>12$	50 elements (not rare earths or nonmetals)
Concentration range	Major, minor (>1%)	Major, minor, trace (to 100 ppm)	Major, minor, trace (50 ppm–100%)	Major, minor, trace (10 ppm–10%)
Accuracy and precision	Semiquantitative	Low to moderate (10%)	High (2%–5%); problems with geometry of sample (whole)	High (2%)
Cost	Moderate	Low	Low to moderate	Low
Speed	Automatic photographic recording	Manual photographic recording; rapid multielement analyses	Rapid multielement analyses; automatic sample changing, recording	Manual, automatic recording; slow multielement analyses
Typical uses and applications	Clay minerals, inclusions, high-temperature minerals in glazes	Ceramic body, slip, glaze, paint	Ceramic body or surface coatings (slip, glaze, paint)	Ceramic body, glaze, slip

Note: See also Orphanides 1985, 80; Meschel 1978, 14–15.

8. What is the sensitivity of the equipment? What elements can be reliably detected and at what level?)

9. What is the accuracy of the equipment (in quantitative analyses)? How are ambiguities resolved? What kinds of standards and calibrations are used?

10. What are the limitations of the technique (in sample size, elements analyzable, accuracy, etc.)?

11. What kind of data transformations are necessary? Are the raw data provided, or are they given multivariate statistical reductions (if necessary) for conversion to quantitative form? Who performs these? Is this charged separately?

12. What precautions should the archaeologist take in excavating, handling, or transporting the artifact?

13. Is accuracy required, or is precision sufficient? (Because many problems involve only comparison among sets of specimens, relative, not absolute, quantities may be all that are needed. The extra expense in absolute calibrations and standards [for accuracy] may not be necessary.)

After these points have been treated, the cultural objectives are primary issues in characterization studies of traditional pottery, since they require the anthropologist or archaeologist to translate pottery manufacturing behavior into physicochemical terms.

Table 13.1   *(cont.)*

Neutron Activation	PIXE	Mössbauer	X-Ray Photoelectric Spectroscopy	Microprobe
50–100 mg, powdered, pressed into a pellet, or whole	Few mg, cut section or powdered pellet	Whole or powdered	Ca. 1 mg, cut section or powder	Few g, cut and polished section
Sample destroyed	Slight	None	Slight	Sample reusable
Bulk composition	Point analysis or bulk composition	Bulk composition	Bulk composition	Point, surface
75 elements	Elements with $Z>13$ (poor on Na)	Elements with Mössbauer effect (Fe, Ni, Al, Zn)	Elements with $Z>10$ (except hydrogen and helium)	Elements with $Z>12$
Major, minor, trace, ultratrace (ppb–100%)	Major, minor, trace	—	Major, minor	Major, minor, trace (>100 ppm)
1%–5%	5%	Nonquantitative	Semiquantitative	Good; problems with sample geometry
Very high	High	Moderate	High	High
Automatic sample changing and recording; rapid multielement analyses	Automatic; multielement analyses	Slow	Rapid multielement analyses	Rapid, versatile
Ceramic body, raw materials; slip, glaze	Ceramic body (focused beam point analysis), inclusions, slip, paint	Generally limited to iron (e.g., the Fe_2O_3/FeO ratio)	Bulk composition; can detect carbon	Bulk and point analyses; also texture, firing changes, phase relationships

Optimally, characterizing a ceramic involves both mineral and chemical methods (Peacock 1970, 381), because each set of techniques yields information the other cannot provide. While chemical methods such as neutron activation give extremely sensitive and thorough analyses of the trace constituents of the material, they provide no data on how the elements are distributed, that is, on the structure of the fabric that is so vital to understanding its use-related properties. Although this may not be very important with extremely fine pastes, it certainly is with coarse-textured, low-fired pottery. In addition, ceramics with widely dissimilar mineralogy and textural characteristics could have generally similar chemical compositions.

13.2   Mineralogical Analysis

Mineralogical analysis of pottery is done to determine its mineral constituents, both in the clay matrix and in the coarser particulate matter. As defined earlier (sec. 2.1), a mineral is a homogeneous, inorganic solid with a definite chemical composition and atomic ordering; that is, it is a crystalline solid. The chemical composition of a mineral—which, though definite, may vary and is fixed only within limits—is important in characterization and is treated further in section 13.3. For characterizing pottery by its mineralogy, however, the other components of the definition are important—that is, that minerals are homogeneous solids with a regular arrangement of atoms. Although minerals can be identified by a very large number of attributes, the techniques used in pottery studies ultimately depend on properties determined by the atomic ordering. The most common techniques are based on the optical characteristics of minerals visible under a microscope (petrography), their behavior when bombarded by X rays (X-ray diffraction), and their behavior when heated (thermal analyses).

13.2.1   Petrographic Characterization

The principal method of identifying minerals in archaeological pottery studies is petrographic analysis. Petrographic techniques are borrowed from geology, where they are used to describe and classify rocks, usually through study with a special microscope. Petrography is closely related to petrology, a broader field that deals with the origin, occurrence, structure, and history of rocks (Blatt 1982, 548) and includes chemical as well as optical characterizations. Applying these techniques to ceramic materials (Frechette 1971; Hodges 1963; Williams 1983) is justified by the concept of ceramic materials as artificial stone (see Bamps 1883, 278). Pottery may be compared to metamorphosed sedimentary rocks: "the fabric of a sherd consists principally of clastic grains held in a clay matrix, both partially altered during firing" (Williams 1983, 302).

In petrographic analysis, minerals are identified by their optical properties, that is, their characteristics as observed in a microscope when a beam of light is passed through them (see Kerr 1977; Phillips 1971; Muir 1977). Understanding these properties requires understanding the optical properties of mineral crystals as well as the characteristics of light as it is utilized by a special microscope called a petrographic or polarizing microscope.

13.2.1.1   SOME PRINCIPLES OF OPTICAL CRYSTALLOGRAPHY
A crystal may be defined as "a solid body bounded by plane natural surfaces, which are the external expression of a regular internal arrangement of constituent atoms or ions" (Mason and Berry 1968, 12) or as "a regular arrangement of atoms that repeats itself indefinitely in three dimensions" (Mason and Berry 1968, 21). Crystals are described and differentiated by different aspects of internal and external morphology; the most important relate the faces or external planes of the crystal to each other by imaginary lines in three-dimensional space. These imaginary lines, called axes of reference, are symbolized as a, b, and c. Any plane can be defined by its intersection of each of these lines, and mineral crystals are classified by the relation of the angles between individual faces of the crystal as they crosscut these planes. The faces themselves reflect the internal atomic structure of the mineral and the strength of bonding between atoms in different directions. This is particularly evident in minerals with layered structures, in which bonding is strong within layers but weak between layers, giving rise to platy or sheet structure. The tendency for minerals to break along planes of weak bonding is called cleavage.

The atomic arrangements (spacing and strength of bonding) along these crystallographic axes give rise to differences in observable properties of the mineral along the axes. For petrographic study, one of the most important properties is transmission of light, and minerals may be classified as isotropic or anisotropic. Isotropic (iso = equal; tropic = turn, rotate, mix) minerals have equivalent atomic arrangements as viewed along all three axes, and so light is propagated in the same way (at the same velocity) in all directions when it passes through them. In anisotropic minerals the view of the crystal or atomic structure varies among the three crystallographic axes, giving rise to different properties—including the propagation of light—in each direction.

Petrographic methods identify minerals by their behavior in a polarizing microscope, where they are subjected to transmitted light (light that is passed through the mineral, as opposed to incident light, which is used merely to illuminate the surface in ordinary binocular microscopes). Light is a form of radiant energy that can be measured either as quanta (photons) or as waves; the latter are important in petrography. According to the transverse wave theory of light, unpolarized light comprises waves of energy vibrating in all planes through the line of propagation or transmission.

Light can be polarized or modified so that it vibrates in only a single plane. The polarizing microscope accomplishes this by two filtering devices that restrict the planes in which light can vibrate, thus controlling the properties of light passing through a mineral and permitting characterization of the mineral by its effects on the further transmission of that light. These filters were developed out of work done in the early 1800s by William Nicol, who used a prism made of two pieces of clear calcite cemented together to polarize light into a single plane. Although modern microscopes substitute polyvinyl filters for calcite prisms, these polarizing devices are still referred to as "nicols" after their inventor.

13.2.1.2 THE POLARIZING MICROSCOPE

Most petrographic microscopes constitute some variation of the arrangement shown in figure 13.1. Light passes through the lower nicol or polarizer, which polarizes it so it vibrates in only a single plane through the direction of propagation, usually referred to as the north-south plane. Thus, viewed along the direction of propagation, the light transmitted to the mineral is vibrating in a single direction. The section to be studied is held in place on a horizontal rotating stage that can be turned 360° while light from the polarizer passes through it. The specimen may be viewed through several centerable objective lens systems, which magnify (e.g., 10×, 25×, 40×) and resolve the image. From the objective lens, the light passes through the second polarizing filter, called the upper nicol or analyzer, which permits only passage of light vibrating in a plane perpendicular to that of the lower nicol, that is, in an east-west plane. The analyzer can be moved in and out of position: when the analyzer is in position, a situation called "crossed nicols," the field as seen through the lenses in the ocular or eyepiece is black, because the north-south light from the lower polarizer is absorbed by the analyzer, which passes only east-west

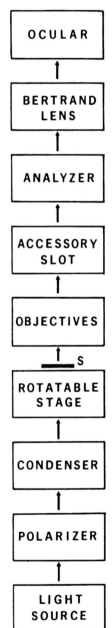

Figure 13.1   Schematic diagram of a petrographic microscope: S = specimen.

light. Provision is sometimes made for the polarizer to rotate, so that intermediate situations can be examined.

Petrographic microscopes also include several devices that can modify light transmission in different ways. These include an iris diaphragm and condenser, between the polarizer and the stage, that adjust and concentrate the illumination; various accessory plates such as a quartz wedge, gypsum plate, and mica plate between the objectives and analyzer; and the auxiliary Amici-Bertrand lens, between the analyzer and ocular. Most of these are used in some combination to identify minerals and their optical orientations by the unusual light patterns, called interference figures, formed on the back lens of the objective with convergent or conoscopic illumination.

The behavior of polarized light passing through crystals is most useful in identifying the very large body of anisotropic (rather than isotropic) minerals. Anisotropic crystals in effect divide the polarized light into two rays according to its inherent vibration directions, a "fast" and a "slow" ray, having unequal velocities. The difference in velocity between the two of them is called retardation.

In plane-polarized light (analyzer out of position, or "uncrossed nicols") the minerals in a ceramic material may be identified or characterized by a number of properties. Color is very important: minerals with significant quantities of coloring elements such as iron, magnesium, and chromium will appear brown, green, red, pink, yellow, or light blue in plane-polarized light. These colors result from the property of pleochroism, the differential absorption of light vibrating in different directions as it passes through the mineral. In other words, as the stage is rotated and the light is altered by different atomic arrangements along the different crystallographic directions of the mineral, the mineral changes color. Pleochroism is usually described as weak to strong depending on the degree of color change. Commonly occurring pleochroic minerals include biotite mica, hornblende, tourmaline, hypersthene, and augite. Although the clay matrix of a pottery thin section may not be clearly pleochroic, it usually appears reddish brown or gray because of the very common presence of iron or organics in the clay.

Another useful identifying property that can be measured in unpolarized (for isotropic crystals) or plane-polarized (for anisotropic crystals) light is the refractive index of minerals, which refers to the bending or refraction of the light as it passes from one material into another, for example, from air into a mineral or from a mineral into any surrounding medium. As the light bends it no longer follows its original path, and its velocity changes. The refractive index of a mineral is the ratio of the velocity of light in air to its velocity in the mineral. The difference between the refractive index of the mineral and that of a surrounding liquid is visualized through the apparent relief (positive or negative; weak or strong) of individual grains. By using liquids of known refractive indexes, that of the mineral can be measured. In anisotropic minerals, because light travels through the mineral at different velocities along different crystallographic axes, the refractive indexes of the fast ray and the slow ray differ, with velocity inversely proportional to refractive index.

Under crossed nicols, minerals may be characterized by the difference in refractive index between the fast and slow ray, measured by the birefringence of the mineral. Also referred to loosely as interference colors, the effect of birefringence of minerals under crossed nicols is a spectrum of colors ranging from gray to red and violet and iridescent white. Minerals with very low birefringence are gray or pale yellow under crossed nicols, while those that are slightly higher are bright blue or red. With greater birefringence the color spectrum is repeated in increasingly paler or higher orders, until minerals with extremely high birefringence, such as calcite, appear as a distinctive "high-order white" that is opalescent and "twinkly." Differences in birefringence are frequently apparent between the body and surface of vessels in thin section and provide evidence for the presence of slips; the birefringence of clays is eliminated, however, if the firing was sufficient to destroy the clay's crystalline structure. The interference colors of a mineral are also strongly affected by its thickness, and thus it is important to have thin sections made in a correct, uniform thickness (0.03 mm).

13.2.1.3   PETROGRAPHIC METHODS
Petrographic analyses are usually accomplished by study of thin sections or by study of individual grains.

13.2.1.3.1   Petrographic Thin Sections. Thin sections of ceramic materials are slices taken from a sherd or fired clay briquette. Low-fired pottery usually has to be impregnated with a bonding substance such as an epoxy resin or a thermoplastic cement (e.g., Lakeside 70), often in a vacuum, to consolidate its friable texture (see Taylor 1960; Meinholz 1983). Affixed to a glass slide, the section is ground on a lap with successively finer abrasives to a uniform thickness of 0.03 mm and covered with a thin cover glass. The proper thickness is determined when quartz grains are a characteristic pale yellow and feldspars are gray or white under crossed nicols.

Thin sections of pottery (fig. 13.2) are useful because they allow identification of different kinds of minerals, their abundances and associations, particle orientations, void size, shapes and locations, surface treatments (compaction or slipping), and alterations owing to firing (cracking) or postdepositional factors (recrystallization). Among the most useful characterization features are granulometrics: description of the size (Folk 1966), sorting, shape, and percentage of inclusions of different kinds in the fabric and the skewness and kurtosis of these distributions (see Peacock 1971; Hodder 1974a). Many of these features have rather complex measurement procedures. Grain shape is identified by the properties of roundness (smoothness of the outline) and sphericity (surface area), usually by comparison with visual charts (fig. 13.3; see also Shackley 1975, 44–51). The percentage of inclusions is usually determined by some variant of point counting or modal analysis (Chayes 1956), whereby grains of different minerals are counted and measured over traverses (made using a mechanical stage device allowing perpendicular movement of the slide) along the length and width of the section. The traditional method measures along two sets of lines perpendicular to each other; other methods have used random grain selection (Peacock 1971), and more recently a modified procedure of systematic sampling along linear transects has been suggested, together with tests of the accuracy of different sampling fractions (fig. 13.4; Middleton, Freestone, and Leese 1985; Wandibba 1982).

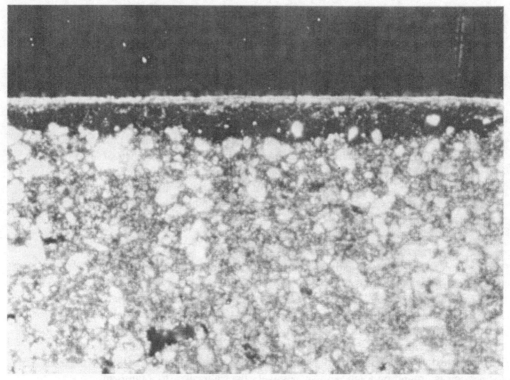

Figure 13.2   Photomicrograph of a thin section of pottery taken at low power (40×) magnification. The vessel has a marly paste, and the bright white particles are calcite. The surface of the sherd shows two layers distinguished by their birefringence, and these represent an opaque white slip covered with a thin, translucent red slip.

	High sphericity	Low sphericity
High roundness	⬭	⬭
Low roundness	⬭	⬭

Figure 13.3   The relation between high and low sphericity and roundness (angularity) of grains.

Most thin sections are made parallel to the vertical axis of the vessel (i.e., perpendicular to the plane of the orifice); in coiled vessels these sections sometimes show slight differences in composition or orientation of particles between coils or joins of the coils themselves. For different purposes, different orientations of the section of the vessel may be useful. Sections taken on planes parallel to the orifice, or even flat sections parallel to the surface, may be desirable, for example, to study inclusions with elongated or platy shapes (mica, sponge spicules, etc.). These materials often have a preferred orientation in the vessel as a result of shaping by coiling, thinning, and smoothing. It

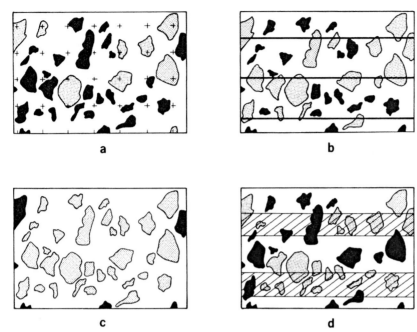

Figure 13.4 Comparison of different methods of counting grains in a microscope: Stippling indicates grains that are counted; black grains are not counted: *a*, point count; *b*, line count; *c*, area count; *d*, "ribbon" count. After Middleton, Freestone, and Leese 1985, fig. 3.

should be noted that individual clay platelets almost never can be identified under even high-power objective lenses in petrographic microscopes.

13.2.1.3.2 Grain Identifications. Individual mineral grains (L. Muller 1977) are usually studied as grain mounts, and several procedures may be involved. Mineral fragments may be recovered from the sherd either by crushing it or by simply poking the mineral grain out of the fabric; mineral separation of clays may be accomplished by sieving or by chemical methods. The grains are then crushed (rather than ground) to about 0.1 mm. The fragments are usually mounted temporarily on glass slides in immersion oils with known refractive indexes, though permanent mounts can also be made. Grain mounts cannot be used to study associations of minerals and their sizes and shapes, but if relatively few minerals are of interest the method is very useful. Grain mounts can also be used to study fragments of glasses and glazes; the refractive index of the sample is generally proportional to its lead content. In addition, the method is fairly fast and requires little sample preparation.

One of the most common individual grain studies is analysis of heavy or accessory minerals (Peacock 1967)—high-density or detrital minerals occurring as tiny grains in small quantities (less than 1%) in sedimentary, metamorphic, and volcanic environments. They are usually highly colored (black, green, brown) owing to iron, magnesium, chromium, and such in their chemical compositions. In heavy-mineral analysis a pottery sample of usually 20 to 30 g is finely crushed and sieved, then the sample is mixed with a liquid of a high specific gravity, such as bromoform (SG = 2.89). The light minerals, such as quartz, feldspars, calcite, mica, and clay, "float" on the surface of the liquid, while the heavy minerals sink to the bottom of the container (or they may be separated by centrifuge; see Williams 1979). After the two fractions are separated, the heavy minerals are cleaned and mounted on slides for study. Estimates of the total number of heavy mineral grains necessary for reliable characterization of archaeological pottery has ranged from 150–200 (Williams 1977, 168) to 250–500 (Williams 1983, 305), up to as many as 1,500 grains (Brewer 1964, 104).

Heavy-mineral analysis is especially useful in the study of very coarse sandy (high-quartz) pastes, particularly when the object is to determine the source of the raw materials used in manufacture (see sec. 14.2). In thin section such sherds are likely to reveal little beyond quantities of clear quartz grains in a matrix of clay. Although the size, shape, and possible alteration of the quartz may be useful for characterization, in an environment of sandy clays and soils these data are not sufficient to determine where the ware was produced. Because sands (whether sedimentary or volcanic) usually contain suites of heavy minerals characteristic of the original parent deposit (see Blatt 1982, 169), separating these minerals from a coarse sandy paste sherd can be useful in distinguishing original raw materials as well as suggesting possible locations of the deposits.

In general the petrographic methods, particularly thin sectioning, are probably the most useful for characterizing the broadest range of low-fired pottery. Petrography is inexpensive, so it can be used on a large number of specimens; the technique can provide useful information on the pottery fabric with minimal training of the analyst; it can identify not only the kinds of minerals present but their sizes, shapes, orientations, and interrelation; it provides information on slips, paints, surface treatments, and voids in or on the ceramic; and the thin section itself forms a permanent record that can be analyzed repeatedly. Heavy-mineral analysis, while particularly useful for coarse sandy pastes, must destroy fairly large amounts of sherd to obtain a sample sufficient for study.

13.2.2   X-Ray Diffraction

X-ray diffraction (XRD) analysis (Zussman 1977) is a method of ceramic characterization based on identifying minerals by their crystalline structure. The method therefore is most appropriately used on crystalline solids, although noncrystalline or amorphous materials such as glass or glazes can also be studied (Gould 1971, 165–66). The crystalline structure of minerals is a function of the regular or periodic spacing and arrangement of their constituent atoms and can be thought of as a regular array of planes or layers of atoms. Each mineral has a unique chemical composition and structure and thus a unique atomic lattice arrangement. X-ray diffraction was first used for mineral analysis in 1912 by a German physicist, von Laue (Cullity 1967, 78).

In X-ray diffraction analysis, X rays are produced when electrons bombard a target made of one of several elements (copper, molybdenum, iron, chromium). These rays, after suitable filtering, are monochromatic—that is, they

Figure 13.5 One method of mounting film (the van Arkel mounting) in a camera for X-ray powder diffraction, and the resultant lines on the exposed film: S = specimen. After Zussman 1977, fig. 4.

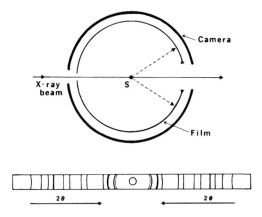

have a sharply defined wavelength between 0.5 and 2.5 Å—and their wavelength is closely similar to the spacings of lattice planes in mineral crystals. The X rays are aimed onto a specimen, and the specimen's successive atomic planes then "reflect" or diffract the X rays; diffraction refers to the coherent scattering of waves and the constructive interference among them that occurs only along certain directions. The diffracted X rays are then picked up by a detector.

Whenever the paths of these diffracted X rays are in phase, that is, whenever their wavelengths are synchronized (differing either by θ or by a whole number of wavelengths), an X-ray intensity maximum or peak is produced. It is at this point that the Bragg equation is satisfied: $n\lambda = 2d \sin \theta$. The Bragg equation states that for maximum diffraction intensity, the difference between the paths of the rays must be a whole number (n) of wavelengths (λ). In the identification of unknown minerals, the Bragg equation is solved for d, the interplanar spacing, from the observation of maximum intensities at particular measured angles of diffraction (θ) and knowledge of the wavelength. The series of intensity maxima that result from a measurement is called the diffraction pattern, and thus in X-ray diffraction analysis minerals are identified by their distinctive and characteristic lattice spacings.

Two methods of X-ray diffraction are common: the powder photography (camera) method and the diffractometer method. These differ in the apparatus used as well as in sample preparation, but both require finely ground or powdered samples.

The powder photography method has three variants, the most common being the Debye-Scherer camera method. A sample of 2–5 mg is finely ground (to less than 240 mesh) and formed into a thin (less than 0.3 mm) rod either by mixing the powder with a gum, inserting the powder into a capillary tube, or coating a fiber with Vaseline and rolling it in the powder. This sample is then placed in the center of a special cylindrical camera (fig. 13.5) that has an X-ray sensitive film arranged around its circumference. The X-ray beam is aligned by passing through a collimator and directed on the sample, which rotates during exposure. Because the mineral grains are randomly arranged in the sample rod, the X rays are diffracted in the form of concentric cones of scattered waves. These are recorded simultaneously on the strip of film as a

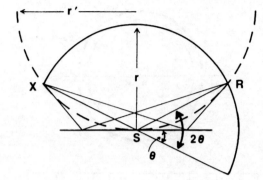

Figure 13.6   (*left*) Geometry of an X-ray diffractometer: X = source of X rays; S = specimen; R = receiving slit; r = radius of goniometer; r′ = radius of focusing circle at Bragg angle θ. After Zussman 1977, fig. 11.

Figure 13.7   (*below*) X-ray diffraction pattern of an unordered mixture of one-third each of quartz (Q), kaolinite (K), and illite (I). Differences in peak height among the three minerals result from the combined effects of differences in crystal structures and orientation of grains on the glass slide holding the material. Peaks occur when the Bragg equation is satisfied, that is, when $n = 2d \sin \theta$. After Blatt 1982, fig. 3-8.

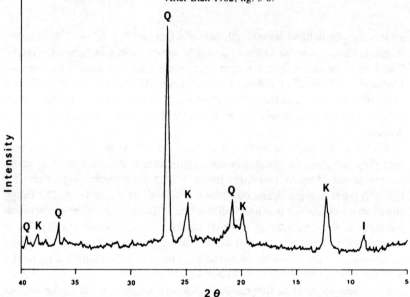

series of concentric arcs of varying width and blackness. After the film is developed, measuring the positions of the line reveals the angle of diffraction, and the intensity (determined subjectively or by a microphotometer) is proportional to the quantity of the mineral.

In the diffractometer method (fig. 13.6), approximately 20 mg of powdered material is placed on a glass slide inserted in the diffractometer apparatus. The X-ray source remains stationary while the sample rotates through an angle θ and the detector (counter) revolves about the center of the sample through an angle 2θ. The equality of angles of incidence and diffraction the Bragg equation requires is maintained. The diffracted intensity is recorded on a paper chart (fig. 13.7) by a recording device. Compared with the camera method, the diffractometer measures a relatively small range of the total number of diffraction angles. Both methods analyze only the surface of the sample; in addition, in both there is a danger of preferred orientation of the particles, meaning that certain interplanar arrangements of the crystal may never meet the Bragg criterion and so will not be recorded in the diffraction pattern. On the other hand, the diffractometer method measures line position (angle of diffraction) and intensity more directly and in a single operation, making it somewhat more accurate for quantitative determinations. The diffractometer also provides better resolution of closely spaced diffraction lines.

Sets of standard X-ray powder diffraction patterns have been published as reference materials by the Joint Committee on Chemical Analysis by Powder Diffraction; these are available both in book form and as computer input, and automatic search and identification computer programs exist. Indeed, some automated commercial X-ray diffraction equipment is now sold with the file and computer programs built in, giving an automatic mineral identification facility.

X-ray diffraction of aboriginal pottery—especially low-fired pottery—has to be approached with some caution, because although the method is eminently appropriate for certain objectives, it is difficult to apply in all situations. First, pottery is usually a very complex substance mineralogically, frequently consisting of a very large number of minerals, including mixtures of different clay minerals plus clastics such as quartz, feldspar, calcite, and a variety of accessories. Because of this complexity, and because most minerals give multiple diffraction peaks, the diffraction pattern of a typical ceramic (and an unfired natural clay; see Bradley 1964) can yield a bewildering skein of peaks that are nearly impossible to identify. Clay minerals themselves are particularly difficult to analyze; imperfections in the crystalline structure affect their diffraction characteristics, and special cameras and techniques are often necessary (Grim 1968, 126–64). X-ray diffraction is thus more useful for discerning the presence of a small number of minerals in a clay or a fired ceramic than for complete mineral characterization. The automatic mineral identification described above, however, is greatly improving this situation.

A second consideration is that X-ray diffraction is really only semiquantitative because the many correction factors preclude a direct relation between peak area (or line intensity) and quantity. Third, X-ray diffraction does not provide any information on whether given minerals might be naturally present in the clay or added as temper (Rice 1974). Information on mineral size and shape can be obtained indirectly (Gould 1971, 166–67), but in general petrography furnishes more reliable data on size, shape, alteration, and associations.

Finally, X-ray diffraction is one of the few mineral methods with the potential to identify the clay mineral constituents, but this potential cannot always be realized. Clays lose their crystalline structure—and hence their ability to diffract X rays—upon dehydroxylation at firing temperatures of approximately 500–600°C and above. There is some evidence, however, that this process may be reversible (Grim and Bradley 1948; Kingery 1974; Magetti 1982, 129). Thus pottery fired to low temperatures (below 800°C) or for very short durations (or both) may rehydrate during postuse burial and regain its crystalline structure, permitting X-ray identification of the clay mineral constituents, provided the rehydration has produced large enough crystals. X-ray diffraction lines begin to broaden as the crystal diameter decreases to below about 0.5 μm, and for crystals as small as 20 nm the lines are so broad they are useless.

Nonetheless, much non-kiln-fired pottery is fired at temperatures between roughly 650 and 900°C (see sec. 5.4), making rehydration moot. In these situations X-ray diffraction may be most useful for study of high-fired pottery: clay minerals then can be identified by the high-temperature minerals, such as mullite and tridymite, that form at temperatures over approximately 900°C (see chap. 4). If the pottery was not originally fired to high temperatures, it can be refired in the laboratory and then analyzed by X-ray diffraction. The same is true of clays, which can be experimentally fired to high temperatures. In either case it is important to quench the sample rapidly after firing to avoid the inversion of high-temperature minerals to low-temperature phases.

13.2.3   Thermal Analysis

Petrographic and X-ray diffraction methods are generally best suited to identifying and describing clastic inclusions in pottery and are not oriented toward the clay minerals of the matrix. Clay minerals can be successfully characterized by a series of analytic methods that focus on thermal behavior (see also chap. 4). These methods, which include differential thermal analysis, thermogravimetric analysis, differential thermogravimetric analysis, thermal expansion analysis, and evolved gas analysis, are based on the fact that individual clay minerals react differently and characteristically when they are heated or cooled at controlled rates (see Ware 1971; Neumann 1977; Mackenzie 1964). Among the variable reactions are changes in volume, weight, and heat content, and in theory any of these may constitute a basis for distinguishing one clay mineral from another.

In practice, however, there are considerable difficulties in using thermal methods to characterize complex mixtures such as natural clays and pottery. The constituents may have overlapping and contrasting reactions, especially if they are slow to occur, making it difficult to separate and identify individual minerals by their thermal behavior alone. For example, the quartz alpha-beta inversion at 573°C, the dehydroxylation of montmorillonite at 600°C, and the beginning of the calcite dissociation may all overlap. Thus it is usually better to use thermal techniques to characterize a known mineral than to try to identify the constituent(s) in an unknown polycrystalline material such as a clay or pottery. In addition, it is often advisable to combine thermal methods with one or more other techniques. For archaeological pottery, thermal methods have been most often applied in archaeothermoetric studies—efforts to determine original firing temperatures (see sec. 14.3.4).

Differential thermal analysis, or DTA, for example, is based on measurement of changes in the temperature of clays heated experimentally to temperatures of 1000 to 1300°C. When a clay is heated, it undergoes a series of changes in which heat is either given off (exothermic reactions) or absorbed (endothermic reactions). Exothermic reactions include those driven by chemical reactivity, in which new chemical combinations are formed (especially at elevated temperatures); endothermic reactions include those of decomposition (e.g., dehydroxylation), at which point the crystal structure is lost, and the alpha-beta inversion of quartz.

Figure 13.8 Differential thermal analysis (DTA) curves
of illite showing effects of different schedules of heating
and intervals before analysis: *a*, untreated clay; *b*, heated
to 600°C for 3 hrs, analysis after standing 2 hrs; *c*, heated
600°C 1 hr, standing 1 day; *d*, heated 600°C 1 hr, standing
70 days; *e*, heated 800°C 1 hr, standing 13 days: *f*, heated
800°C 1 hr, standing 70 days; *g*, heated 800°C 1 hr, standing 147 days; *h*, heated 800°C 1 hr, standing 275 days.
After Grim 1968, fig. 9-30.

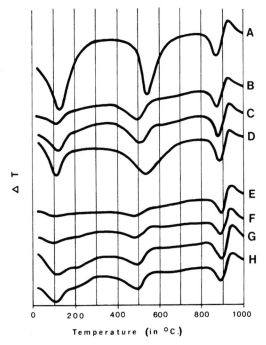

In differential thermal analysis, a sample of about 100 g of powdered clay
or sherd is heated at a controlled rate in an electric furnace, together with a
thermally inert material (e.g., calcined Al_2O_3). Each material is placed in a
specimen holder, and one end of a differential thermocouple is embedded in
each. During heating, the temperature of the inert substance increases evenly
with the heating temperature of the oven, while the temperature of the clay
increases or decreases depending on the reactions taking place. The differences in temperature between the sample and the inert material are measured
by the thermocouple and recorded on a continuous curve plotting temperature
differences as a function of furnace temperature. Conventionally, these are
shown as upward (exothermic) or downward (endothermic) deflections from
the baseline of the curve (see figs. 4.4 and 4.6). The height and width of these
deflections gives some idea of the intensity and duration of the reactions.

Interpreting differential thermal curves is complex for known materials,
and for unknowns it is formidable. The curves for individual clay minerals
can vary considerably from one sample to another (fig. 13.8) depending on
the degree of crystallinity, particle size, mixing with other materials, rate of
heating, interval between heating and analysis, sample thickness, thermal
conductivity, and symmetry of the heating arrangement (see Grim 1968,
292–95; Spiel et al. 1945; Ware 1971, 284–90, 296–97). These factors can
affect the temperature at which reactions occur (very small particle size, slow
heating rate, and poor crystallinity will lower the temperature), change the
width of the reaction peaks (a slower heating rate broadens the peak), and
alter the intensity of the reaction (very small particle size will decrease the
reaction, and the presence of other materials may increase it). As a result,
interpreting DTA curves for natural clays, which include complex mixtures of

clay minerals, organics, and clastic minerals having their own thermal reactions, can be highly problematic. DTA was used to investigate the black color of Etruscan bucchero: an exothermic peak between 450 and 500°C corresponded to the oxidation of carbonaceous material from the clay (Francaviglia, Minardi, and Palmieri 1975, 225–26; see also Flamini and de Lorenzo Flamini 1985). Clay minerals of archaeological pottery may be determinable at lower temperatures if they have rehydrated during burial (Grim and Bradley 1948; Kingery 1974; see also Enriquez, Danon, and Beltrao 1979).

Thermogravimetric analysis measures changes in weight when a sample is heated to approximately 1000°C. Several procedures may be used to record these changes: the sample may be heated at a series of temperatures, cooled, and weighed, or the sample may be heated at a continuous rate and weighed while still hot, either by removing it from the oven or with a device that records changes in weight within the furnace itself.

The changes in clay minerals that affect weight are, of course, dehydration at low temperature, reactions of dehydroxylation involving the loss of water at 500–700°C, and decomposition of calcite at 700–900°C. Thermogravimetric analysis in the 500–700°C range produces a cumulative dehydration curve, plotting loss of weight as a function of firing temperature (see chap. 4). Thus it is important that the humidity of the ambient air be controlled while samples are being moved for weighing (see Ware 1971, 277–80 for additional sources of error). Differential thermogravimetric analysis (also called dynamic differential calorimetry) measures differences in weight per unit time measured against temperature.

As with differential thermal analysis, interpreting these gravimetric results is difficult if not impossible with complex mineral mixtures. In many natural clays, or in pottery, for example, the weight change will reflect not only water loss but the removal of organic matter and the decomposition of carbonates and sulfates into CO_2 and SO_2 (a process registered by evolved gas analysis); the oxidation of divalent iron or manganese, on the other hand, would cause an increase in weight (Grim 1968, 283).

The same processes in clays that cause fluctuations in the temperature and weight with heating also cause changes in volume. Thermal expansion analysis characterizes clays by dimensional changes with changing temperature and is usually studied from about 100–200°C up to 500–800°C, depending on the clay mineral (see Grim 1968, fig. 9–20). At high temperatures the mass contracts, and there is loss of lattice water, sintering, and vitrification. A specimen is placed in a dilatometer assembly heated at a controlled rate in an electric furnace. In a common form of apparatus, the sample supports a fused silica rod connected to a transducer, which converts changes in the length of the clay to electrical impulses and plots the changes as a function of change in temperature. In this apparatus it is the differential expansion relative to the fused silica that is measured.

13.2.4　Other Methods of Mineral Identification

Besides these sophisticated and highly instrumented methods, a number of relatively simple techniques can show the presence of specific minerals in a clay or fired ceramic (see, e.g., Peacock 1977, 30–32, for a key to identification of inclusions). These are generally nonquantitative, however, and therefore indicate only presence/absence. Montmorillonite clays, for example, if allowed to rest five minutes in a saturated aqueous solution of benzidine, will turn blue (Shepard 1976, 153).

If a clay or sherd is crushed and sieved, individual mineral grains may be separated and identified by characteristic properties such as luster, color, and cleavage, familiar to mineralogists and listed in most mineral texts (e.g., Mason and Berry 1968). Some identifying properties are even simpler to investigate, however, requiring no training in mineralogy and only minimal equipment. For example, the characteristic colored streak left on a white porcelain "streak plate" will identify certain minerals such as hematite (red streak) or limonite (yellow streak). Similarly, the property of ferrimagnetism will cause particles of magnetite to adhere to a magnet moved over the sample grains.

Carbonates in raw or fired (at less than 750°C) clays are easily identified by their characteristic dissolution and effervescence when acid is added. Hydrochloric acid at room temperature will make calcium carbonate (limestone or calcite) in a clay or sherd effervesce, and magnesium carbonate (dolomite) effervesces in warm hydrochloric acid. Staining can also be used to identify carbonate minerals in hand specimens or thin sections (Dickson 1966). An organic reagent, titan yellow, can be added to determine the presence of magnesium: with only 5% or more magnesium in the material, the solution turns pink, whereas if only calcium is present the solution remains yellow (Shepard 1976, 381). A similar staining technique can be used to distinguish feldspars of different compositions (Bailey and Stevens 1960).

The presence of salt (NaCl) in a sherd may be of interest, since it may have been added to calcareous clays (see Rye 1976) or deposited in the ceramic during or after use. Fragments of pottery may be soaked in small amounts of distilled water for 24 hours and then removed. A few drops of silver nitrate ($AgNO_3$) added to the water will form a white precipitate of AgCl if salt was leached from the sherd, making the water cloudy. The addition of salt to a clay before firing cannot be determined by this method if the pottery was fired to 800°C, because at that temperature the salt reacts with other constituents and at higher temperatures chlorine volatilizes. In such situations the addition of salt to the clay can sometimes be determined in petrographic thin sections because the salt reacts with calcareous fragments, leaving a yellow "reaction rim"; cubic voids are not reliable indicators of salt (Woods 1986, 166–67; cf. Rye 1976).

13.3 Chemical Analysis

Determining the chemical composition of a ceramic material, ancient or modern, is an important analytic objective. Although chemical analysis of ancient pottery and glass is part of a general and long-standing interest in archaeological chemistry (sec. 10.2.1), it is during the past twenty-five years that the techniques have become extremely popular in archaeology. This is in large part because advances in instrumentation have increased the accuracy and speed of these techniques, neutron activation analysis being the outstanding example. Studying the chemical composition of a ceramic can provide important information on its origin and fabrication, but it is important to remember that the chemical data do not identify the sources of the elements within the body or their relation to each other. For this reason, chemical analysis and mineralogical study together may give optimal characterization.

In chemical analysis of pottery, as with other materials, the object may be either qualitative or quantitative; the latter involves additional considerations of sample selection and preparation. Chemical constituents are frequently categorized as present in major, minor, and trace amounts. Major elements, present in pottery in amounts of 2% or more, include silica, alumina, oxygen, and frequently also calcium, iron, and potassium. Minor constituents are present in amounts between 0.1% and 2% and may include any or all of the following: calcium, iron, potassium, titanium, magnesium, manganese, sodium, chromium, and nickel. Trace elements are present in very small quantities of less than 0.1% and are usually measured in parts per million (ppm) or parts per billion (ppb). The term ultratrace is sometimes used for elements in quantities less than 1 ppm. Trace and ultratrace elements include geochemically rare elements such as cesium, rubidium, vanadium, uranium, tantalum, scandium, lithium, gold, selenium, antimony, strontium, cobalt, and the rare earth or lanthanide series (atomic numbers 57–71). Because the kinds and amounts of trace elements are so uniquely characteristic of individual clays and clay products, they, together with the minor elements, have formed the basis for most provenience analyses of pottery (sec. 14.2), which are carried out by many of the techniques described below.

It is extremely important, when analyzing chemical elements present in such small amounts, to be very careful in sample preparation to avoid contamination and assure representativeness. No sherd (or rock) is of uniform composition. If a particular sherd or clay were sampled and analyzed repeatedly, the determined quantities of chemical elements it contains would vary owing to both "natural" or geochemical causes and to random statistical variations in counting and detection.

In addition, the techniques of analysis themselves vary in their ability to detect and measure certain constituents. Techniques may be evaluated for sensitivity, precision, and accuracy (see Bishop, Rands, and Holley 1982, 289–90; Orphanides 1985). Sensitivity refers to the limits of detection of the technique. Although it is usually expressed in terms of the ability to detect relative quantities of minor, trace, or ultratrace elements, sensitivity may also be expressed as the lowest atomic numbers of elements that can be analyzed. Precision refers to the reproducibility of the analytic procedures of detection, counting, weighing, and so forth. The accuracy of a technique describes how close the result is to the true figure and is of concern in quantitative determinations. It depends, among other things, on the calibration of the experimental measurements with reference standards and their compositions. Accuracy and precision are often expressed as percentages, stating that the measurement of a particular element or set of elements by a given technique is accurate, for example, within ± 5%.

In sum, the chemical composition of a sherd of a particular type of pottery made from a particular resource or combination of resources can be expected to differ slightly from that of another sherd of the same type and raw material(s); but the composition also varies among samples taken from a single sherd. This internal variability is a particular problem with coarse paste pottery, where textural and mineral inhomogeneities can make representative chemical sampling a serious concern (see sec. 10.3.2.3; also Kleeman 1967 and Reeves and Brooks 1978, 4–6, 13–19, for discussion of sampling procedures and problems in chemical analyses).

The quantity of chemical elements in a sample may be determined by a number of measurements, including the weight of compounds formed, volume of solutions used, and wavelength and intensity of radiation absorbed or emitted. The first two are the basis of the classical methods of chemical analysis; the last are involved in the physical methods of chemical analysis.

13.3.1   Classical Methods

Until fairly recently in the history of chemistry, the elemental constituents of a substance were determined qualitatively and quantitatively by their distinctive chemical reactions under specified test conditions. A certain amount of the unknown substance is brought into solution, and then individual components are identified by their behavior when specific reagents (substances taking part in chemical reactions and used to detect other substances), such as acids or alkalis, are added. Because the materials are in solution, these methods are called "wet" chemistry.

Such classical or wet methods measure the products of these chemical reactions by their weight (gravimetric methods) or volume (volumetric methods). In gravimetric methods, analysis is based on mass: the reagent unites with individual elements to create new compounds that form precipitates (insoluble solids formed by chemical reactions between solutions), and these are then filtered out, dried, and weighed. The element quantity in the sample is determined from the weight of this new compound. In volumetric methods, the reagent is added in known quantities until the element of interest is entirely transformed into the intended compound. The amount of the element in the sample is calculated from the total volume of reagent used.

Wet chemistry is useful primarily for quantitative analysis of major and minor elements in an unknown compound and for identifying nonmetallic elements (carbon, sulfur, nitrogen, and phosphorus and their oxides). No expensive equipment is needed, a major advantage of the techniques; disadvantages are that large samples (1g or more) are usually required, the techniques are damaging or destructive and time consuming, and elements present in trace amounts are difficult to determine.

Shepard (1976, 387–90) and Hawley (1929) describe microchemical procedures for identifying iron, manganese, copper, and mercury, which are important constituents of pre- and postfire pigments applied to pottery.

13.3.2   Physical Methods

The classical methods of analysis are used infrequently in archaeological applications, having been supplanted by the physical methods (see Zussman, ed., 1977). They do not involve chemical reactions between known and unknown constituents but are based on detectable changes in the elements when energy is introduced into them, for example, by heating or by bombarding them with X rays, electrons, or neutrons. Atoms respond either by emitting detectable levels of resultant energy (in the form of visible light or X rays, gamma rays, etc.) or by absorbing some of the introduced energy. The wavelength of the emitted or absorbed radiation is characteristic of each chemical element and forms the basis for identifying it in an unknown specimen (see Goffer 1980, 31–53).

The chemical characterization methods employing these properties are called spectroscopic or spectrometric techniques because they analyze the electromagnetic spectrum of radiant energy. Most of the methods used in analyzing artifacts, especially pottery, are variants of emission spectrometry, meaning that they measure the wavelength of the energy emitted by the sample to determine the kind and quantity of elements present. These techniques include optical emission spectroscopy, X-ray fluorescence, electron microprobe, neutron activation analysis, and X-ray photoelectron spectroscopy. Methods of absorption spectroscopy useful in archaeological analysis are atomic absorption, Mössbauer spectroscopy, and infrared spectroscopy (little used in pottery studies).

13.3.2.1 OPTICAL EMISSION SPECTROSCOPY

In optical emission spectrometry (Ahrens and Taylor 1961), or OES, a sample is volatilized in a flame or an electric arc. The thermal energy excites the outer electrons of atoms, and when they return to the ground state they release energy. This energy is visible as near ultraviolet and visible light, emitted with well-defined wavelengths characteristic of the particular element excited. The light of various wavelengths is dispersed by a quartz prism or diffraction grating (the latter giving higher resolution) and detected by a photographic plate, on which the individual wavelengths appear as a series of black lines, or with a slit and photomultiplier. A quantitative analysis is obtained from the intensity of the light emitted, which is in turn deduced from the blackness of the lines on the film (with a densitometer) or from the photomultiplier output.

The method requires some damage to the artifact, in that approximately 5–100 mg of powdered sample is used in the analysis and the sample is destroyed. Optical emission spectrometry can be used to measure between thirty and forty (mainly metallic) elements in major, minor, and trace quantities (down to approximately 100 ppm), with an accuracy of approximately 10%.

The advantages of the method are that it is widely available and rapid and only small amounts of the material must be removed for analysis. Because it can use very small samples, it can easily be employed to study the body of a ceramic as well as the constituents of slip, glaze, or paints. Optical emission spectrometry was one of the first techniques to be widely used in the compositional studies of Oriental pottery (Ritchie 1937), Egyptian glass (Farnsworth and Ritchie 1938), and Mediterranean pottery (Catling, Blin-Stoyle, and Richards 1961).

The disadvantages of optical emission spectrometry are that it has a relatively low precision (of only ± 10%), and it can be cumbersome if many elements are present because of the need to interpret complex spectral data. Furthermore, because of problems in calibrating data for absolute quantitative determinations, it is better viewed as a semiquantitative technique.

The method has declined in use in recent years, since other techniques (such as X-ray fluorescence) are more sensitive and accurate. New refinements using plasma (ionized gases) and laser beams to vaporize samples may lead to a revival of interest in the method.

13.3.2.2 X-RAY FLUORESCENCE SPECTROSCOPY

In X-ray fluorescence analysis (Bertin 1978; Norrish and Chappell 1977), or XRF, a specimen is irradiated with primary X rays from an X-ray tube or from radioactive sources (fig. 13.9). These X rays displace electrons from the inner orbits of the constituent atoms, and these energy levels are filled by electrons from the outer levels. The energy released in this process is emitted as secondary or fluorescent X rays with wavelengths ranging from 0.1 to 50 Å. The secondary X rays are analyzed either through diffraction by a crystal, after passing through a collimator, or with a semiconductor detector and multichannel analyzer. The result in either case is a graph showing the intensity of the X rays (i.e., peaks) as a function of energy or wavelength. Each individual element has a series of wavelengths at which it emits secondary X rays and hence has multiple peaks in its spectrum. The constituent elements of an unknown compound are thus identified by their wavelengths, while quantitative determinations are based on the X-ray intensities, using a series of calibrations or corrections.

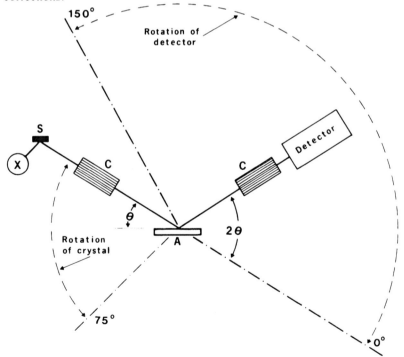

Figure 13.9 Geometry of an X-ray fluorescence spectrometer: X = X-ray tube; S = specimen; C = collimator; A = analyzer crystal. After Olsen 1975, fig. 12.8.

Samples for X-ray fluorescence analysis can be prepared in several ways. If the artifact is small the entire object can be inserted into the apparatus rather than removing a sample, thus making the method completely nondestructive. Otherwise a small sample (100 mg up to 2 g) of the pottery must be removed and ground into a fine powder; this material is usually mixed with a flux and fused into a glass bead.

An important consideration in sample selection and preparation for X-ray fluorescence analysis is that the method analyzes only the surface (the low-energy X-ray beam penetrates only 20–200 μm below the surface) of the sample. This makes the procedure useful for characterizing surface coatings such as glazes, slips, or paints, but because the beam may analyze an area 1 cm in diameter, care must be taken to include only the material of interest. For characterizing pottery pastes, the sample should be ground and prepared in a bead.

X-ray fluorescence analysis is useful for investigating about eighty elements present in major, minor, and trace quantities (see Norrish and Chappell 1977, 258–62 for discussion of sensitivity to individual elements). The elements that can be usefully analyzed by the instrument are those above atomic number 12 (magnesium; cf. Goffer 1980, 47) on the periodic chart; elements with atomic numbers down to 9 can be detected, but with difficulty, because they emit X rays with low energies (long wavelengths) that are absorbed by air. It is useful for elements that are not analyzable by neutron activation analysis, for example (such as magnesium and titanium), and for elements such as potassium and calcium it may be more precise (Bishop, Rands, and Holley 1982, 292).

X-ray fluorescence spectrometry is widely available, relatively low in cost, and may be nondestructive for very small artifacts (for others it requires slight damage for sample removal). The technique has relatively high precision (usually better than ± 5%), and for large numbers of samples it can be fully automated. For certain kinds of investigations, the surface focus of XRF is particularly useful. Identifying individual elements by their X-ray peaks is relatively straightforward compared with some other techniques.

The principal disadvantage of X-ray fluorescence analysis is that quantitative measurements are extremely sensitive to the thickness and shape of the specimen. Also, the method may slightly discolor the specimen surface, though this usually disappears after a short time. For certain applications the beam width may be a disadvantage, since it does not represent a point analysis as do other methods (e.g., microprobe).

X-ray fluorescence analysis can be done by energy-dispersive or nondispersive methods (Bishop, Rands, and Holley 1982, 291; Tite 1972, 269; Goffer 1980, 47); confusingly, these are also called respectively wavelength-dispersive and energy-dispersive methods (Kempe and Templeman 1983, 44). Conventional energy (or wavelength) dispersive XRF uses a crystal spectrometer and detector. In the crystal spectrometer the secondary X rays are collimated into a beam falling on a flat, perfect crystal of lithium fluoride, quartz, or a similar substance. The diffracted beam is passed into a suitably positioned scintillation or proportional counter (see Norrish and Chappell 1971, 221–22), which produces a pulse for each X-ray photon. Diffraction is controlled by the

Bragg equation (sec. 13.2.2), but in this case the interplanar spacing (d) remains fixed and the diffraction angle θ is a measure of the wavelength (λ). Nondispersive XRF (also called energy-dispersive in Europe) has the advantage of involving a simpler instrument (eliminating the diffracting crystal and using a semiconductor counter to detect X rays and determine their wavelength), and radioactive sources rather than an X-ray tube may be used to generate the radiation. The technique can determine multiple elements at the same time, thus in theory being rather fast; however, it needs longer counting times and may be less accurate and less sensitive than energy (wavelength)-dispersive methods, especially with elements of low atomic number (below 26). Ballié and Stern (1984) used energy-dispersive XRF and report the ability to study objects with sizes up to 50 square inches without damage.

13.3.2.3 ATOMIC ABSORPTION SPECTROSCOPY

Atomic absorption spectroscopy (Slavin 1968; McLaughlin 1977), or AAS, is a relatively new technique developed in the 1950s. Elements are identified by their absorption rather than their emission of energy (fig. 13.10). A light source includes a hollow cathode containing a small amount of the element being investigated. When an electrical current is passed, the lamp emits visible or near-ultraviolent monochromatic light of a defined wavelength characteristic of that element, which is shone through a flame. The sample material is dissolved in a solution, aspirated in a fine spray, and atomized in the flame; the atoms of the element to be determined in the spray absorb a portion of the light. After passing through the sample, the light beam is focused on a monochromator fitted with a photomultiplier detector system. The amount of light absorbed (measured by the photomultiplier) determines the concentration of the element in the sample. Only one element can be identified at a time, and a separate lamp (emitting light at the wavelength characteristic of the element to be analyzed) must be used for each one. This procedure is

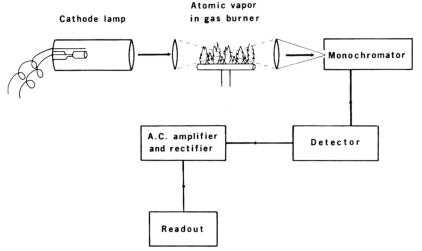

Figure 13.10 Schematic diagram of components of a flame atomic absorption spectrometer system. After McLaughlin 1977, fig. 1.

known as flame AAS; a flameless procedure is also available, which uses approximately 20 mg of solid sample placed in carbon-rod atomizer cups.

Both techniques are slightly damaging; the more common flame technique requires that samples of 10 mg to 1 g be ground into a powder and dissolved in an acid solution (see Bomgardner 1981). The very high dilution of the sample (up to 500 times) poses potential problems with contamination as well as making it difficult to detect very rare elements, but nonetheless the technique is useful on minor and trace elements (to ca. 10 ppm) with a high precision of ± 2%. AAS can be used to identify approximately fifty elements; it cannot be used to identify nonmetals or rare earths.

Atomic absorption spectrometry is inexpensive, uses simple equipment, and can be used and interpreted with minimal training. For qualitative analysis—determining the presence/absence of a particular element—the results are immediate. The technique has generally high sensitivity (which varies with each element) and precision; with carefully prepared standards it can achieve high accuracy. For determining only a few elements in a sample it is very useful. In general it is most useful for analyzing elements in amounts between the rather large quantities suitable for XRF and the very low ultratrace concentrations of neutron activation analysis.

The disadvantages of the technique are several, the chief being that it is very inefficient for multiple element determinations. (Multielement cathode tubes exist, however, and may be improved.) In addition, diluting the sample in acid is an unpleasant and time-consuming procedure and poses the risk of contamination. Although there are problems in identifying very rare elements because of the high dilutions, microconcentration techniques can largely overcome these, but they may require large samples. An additional difficulty is the possibility that another element in the solution will interfere with the absorption of the element of interest in the flame, thus making quantitative determinations inaccurate. In general, however, the problem of interference is generally lower than in emission methods (McLaughlin 1977, 375–79).

Atomic absorption was used comparatively little in early ceramic characterization studies, but its applications are increasing (Bower, Bromund, and Smith 1975; Hatcher et al. 1980; Tubb, Parker, and Nickless 1980; Torres, Arie, and Sandoval 1984; see also Winefordner 1971 and Gritton and Magalousis 1978 for discussion of methods).

13.3.2.4 NEUTRON ACTIVATION ANALYSIS

Neutron activation analysis (Kruger 1971; Goles 1977), usually abbreviated NA, NAA, or INAA (for instrumental NAA), is a technique that was first used in the 1930s and first applied to archaeological artifacts in the late 1950s (Sayre and Dodson 1957; Sayre, Murrenhoff, and Weick 1958; Emeleus 1960; Perlman and Asaro 1969). For many reasons it has emerged as the most significant technique in trace element artifact studies. The method requires a source of thermal (low-energy, or slow) neutrons, usually a particle accelerator or a nuclear reactor with research functions, typically the latter. This restricts the locations where NAA can be carried out, and in fact most artifact studies are performed at only a small number of major research laboratories scattered over the world.

In activation analysis, a small sample of the artifact (for ceramics it is usually a ground powder) is placed in a glass or plastic vial and introduced (together with standards for calibration) into the reactor core, where the nuclei of the atoms are excited by bombardment with neutrons at a controlled rate for a brief period (see Goles 1977, 356–57). This bombardment changes the elements into unstable radioactive isotopes, which then decay by emitting several kinds of radiation, eventually forming stable isotopes. The rate of decay varies from element to element and is characterized by the time required for half of the amount initially present to decay (the half-life). Elements can be partially separated by varying the time between the neutron bombardment and the measurement of emitted radiation. Immediately following the bombardment, the elements with short half-lives dominate the radiation; later their activity has died away and the elements with longer half-lives can conveniently be studied.

As the radioactive isotopes decay, they emit several kinds of radiation, of which gamma rays are the most important for NAA. The gamma rays have sharply defined energies (wavelengths) characteristic of each element, and this energy is measured by either scintillation detectors (which have high efficiency) or Ge(Li) semiconductor detectors (providing better resolution) in a gamma spectrometer apparatus. Signals from the detector go to a system of amplifiers and a multichannel (2,000–4,000 channels) pulse-height analyzer, which stores and displays data as a spectrum of number of counts versus energy. Usually the sample is analyzed several times after decay periods of increasing lengths, to identify elements with different half-lives. By determining the energy levels of the emitted gamma rays, the individual elements in the sample can be identified; by calculating their intensities (the number of gamma photons), their concentrations can be estimated.

Neutron activation analysis is extremely sensitive, able to detect about seventy-five of the ninety-two naturally occurring elements (Bishop, Rands, and Holley 1982, 292) in minor, trace, and ultratrace amounts. The method involves little sample preparation time, the tiny (50–100 mg) samples of clay or sherd being powdered and irradiated in glass or plastic containers. Although the technique requires removing samples and hence damages the artifact, the small sample size keeps the damage minimal, and even exhibit vessels have been analyzed by sampling the underside (see sec. 10.3.2.3). With extremely small objects such as coins or beads, the entire specimen can be irradiated, though it becomes radioactive: this then becomes effectively (if temporarily) a destructive technique.

The advantages of neutron activation analysis are many. Sample size is very small (although representativeness may be a problem), and preparation time is low. The method has been completely automated, so many samples and many elements can be determined simultaneously (although the long decay times necessary for those with long half-lives does extend the analysis procedure into many months). NAA is extremely sensitive, sometimes to concentrations as low as parts per billion, and because neutrons and gamma rays penetrate deeply into a variety of materials it can analyze the entire specimen. For trace amounts the technique usually suffers from few matrix effects. The accuracy of quantitative determinations can usually be given within ± 5%, or sometimes ± 1%.

The disadvantage of the method is chiefly its exorbitant cost, which can run to four hundred dollars per sample for complete analysis of twenty to thirty elements. Not only does the cost limit access to the technique, but the necessity of a reactor facility also restricts its availability. Finally, samples are rendered radioactive (though for only relatively short periods if the initial irradiation is brief), and this must be taken into consideration in their selection for analysis.

13.3.2.5 X-RAY MILLIPROBE

One technique that has a great deal of potential but is used comparatively little is the milliprobe (Banks and Hall 1963). This method is essentially point-focused X-ray fluorescence spectrometry and can be considered a cross between that technique and the microprobe, discussed below.

As in X-ray fluorescence analysis, a beam of primary exciting X rays is directed onto a specimen, but in the milliprobe the X rays are collimated into a narrow beam, usually less than 1 mm in diameter. The secondary X rays produced in the specimen are thus emitted from a very small area of the sample, so that the technique effectively permits analysis of small areas such as individual inclusions. As in conventional X-ray fluorescence spectrometry, the primary X rays are of low energy, so that the beam analyzes only the surface of the material rather than the entire bulk specimen.

This method has one distinctive advantage—that specimens are placed outside the spectrometer apparatus rather than inside it, so that artifacts of any size and shape can be analyzed. Furthermore, there is no elaborate sample preparation. Size and shape are not important in quantitative calculations as they are in XRF analysis. Elements above atomic number 14 (silicon) can be analyzed. This technique has seen little use in archaeology, however, despite its promise.

13.3.2.6 PROTON-INDUCED X-RAY EMISSION

Proton-induced X-ray emission analysis, or PIXE (Kullerud et al. 1979; Clayton, Cohen, and Duerden 1981), is a relatively new technique of chemical analysis in which protons rather than X-ray photons are used to excite the specimen. Flat cross sections of sherds can be used, or ground powder can be formed into pellets for analysis, and the proton beam can be focused down to a diameter at least as small as 1 mm (Rye and Duerden 1982, 60).

The technique is sensitive to a large number of elements, which can be analyzed simultaneously; in addition, very small samples are needed, and the specimens can be processed automatically. Accuracies of approximately ± 5% have been reported in analyses of major and trace constituents of Papuan pottery, using elements of atomic number 13 (aluminum) and above (Rye and Duerden 1982, 61).

A significant disadvantage of the technique is the relatively high cost of the equipment, restricting its availability.

13.3.2.7 MÖSSBAUER SPECTROSCOPY

Mössbauer spectroscopy, or nuclear gamma resonance spectroscopy (Wertheim 1964; Cohen 1976; Gibb 1976), is a rather esoteric absorption analysis technique based on the Mössbauer effect, discovered in 1958. This refers to the "recoil-free" production of gamma rays of particular energies from a radioactive source. Some radioactive isotopes undergo transitions whereby in an excited state they emit gamma rays and end up in a ground state, having lost only energy (not mass or charge). In this loss energy is usually imparted to the emitting nucleus as the gamma rays are emitted: this is called recoil energy. However, in a ceramic the atom is part of a crystalline lattice or glassy network. The phonons (vibrational energy states of the solid) are quantized, and if the gamma ray energy is small in comparison with the quanta, no recoil energy is lost; the gamma ray possesses the full energy of the nuclear transition both in emission and in absorption. This is known as recoil-free emission or absorption, and the radiation emitted or absorbed has a very sharply defined energy. Only a few isotopes meet the conditions.

As in atomic absorption, the source and absorber of gamma rays in Mössbauer spectroscopy is an isotope of the element to be identified; and the technique measures the amount of the element present in the sample by how much it absorbs gamma rays. The valence or chemical state of the element may differ between the sample and the source, and these differences in energy will affect the degree of absorption. Mössbauer spectroscopy introduces a very small amount of motion to the source, dispersing the energy of the emitted gamma rays, and this permits measurement of absorption as a function of velocity or energy. What is shown in the resultant Mössbauer spectrum is a graph of the amount of gamma rays transmitted (i.e., those not absorbed) versus their energy or velocity in this movement.

Although a number of isotopes exhibit the Mössbauer effect, including Fe, Ni, Al, and Zn (Kempe and Templeman 1983, 36), the technique has very limited applications, and in ceramics it is primarily used to study iron-bearing materials. Thus iron is the element of particular interest in pottery studies (see Tite 1972, 291–95; Kostikas, Simopoulos, and Gangas 1976; Maniatis, Simopoulos, and Kostikas 1982; Hess and Perlman 1974; Gancedo et al. 1985), and particularly the ferric/ferrous (Fe^{3+}/Fe^{2+}) ratio may be investigated using the ^{57}Fe isotope.

For analysis of iron, Mössbauer spectroscopy utilizes as a source of energy an isotope that can emit a gamma particle without recoil, such as ^{57}Fe. The source contains the radioactive isotope ^{57}Co, which decays to an excited state of the stable iron isotope ^{57}Fe, which in turn is transformed to its unexcited ground state by recoil-free emission of gamma rays. The absorbing material, that is, the sample under investigation, must also contain iron, in which there is about 2% of ^{57}Fe, in orber to absorb the gamma rays.

Mössbauer spectrometry utilizes a source of gamma rays, usually a thin foil of radioactive isotope, an absorber (i.e., the sample), and a scintillation-detection system. Among the many important properties of the Mössbauer spectrum are (Olsen 1975, 595–608) the size of the absorption peak (which is a function of the number of nuclei in the sample); the line width (it is desirable to have a narrow line, which is a function of half-life, as well as experimental factors); the isomer shift, or shift in the location of the peak in the spectrum (a function of the electron charge density at the nucleus and therefore of its chemical environment); the quadrupole splitting (a division of the main peak into, in the case of iron, two components as a result of an electric field gradient at the nucleus, and therefore a function of the crystal symmetry); and the magnetic field splitting, which occurs with ferrimagnetic iron compounds.

Mössbauer spectroscopy cannot be used qualitatively to identify the constituents of a substance: it must start with a gamma-emitting isotope of the element to be investigated. It is also limited in quantitative use, indicating only the relative concentrations of various iron minerals. The method is best used to determine the valence states of iron in a sample. This information is useful in characterizing raw and fired clays or pigments, in studying the firing temperatures of iron-rich ceramics (such as terra-cottas, with 5–10% iron in their composition; see sec. 14.3), in investigating the authenticity of art objects, or even in provenience studies (see Keisch 1974; Cousins and Dharmawardena 1969). The method can accommodate whole artifacts without sample damage and thus is nondestructive (Keisch 1974).

Mössbauer spectroscopy is nonquantitative and relatively time-consuming (requiring 2–4 hours). Thus far it has been restricted to studying the nature of one element, iron, in artifactual specimens. Given the abundance of iron as a constituent of pottery, however, the suggested but thus far largely unexplored applications in provenience and archaeothermometric studies may be highly significant in the future.

13.3.2.8 X-Ray Photoelectron Spectroscopy

X-ray photoelectron spectroscopy (or XPS; sometimes also called electron spectroscopy for chemical analysis, or ESCA; Lambert and McLaughlin 1976; Berrin and Sundahl 1971, 603–6) uses an intense beam of unmonochromated X rays to excite the sample. The sample emits photoelectrons from the inner shells of the atom, and the characteristic binding energy (BE) required to free these electrons from their orbitals is the basis for identifying elements in the sample. A given element may have several BE levels, and the intensity of the peak on the energy spectrum from XPS analysis is a function of its concentration in the sample after correction for matrix effects.

XPS analysis can be used not only for the heavier elements but also for all elements below atomic number 10 except hydrogen and helium, and thus an important advantage is that it can detect carbon (see Gillies and Urch 1983). In addition, the technique analyzes all elements simultaneously. It can be used for major and minor constituents, but is not useful for concentrations below approximately 0.5% (Lambert and McLaughlin 1976, 178). XPS is used for surface examination only, measuring a maximum depth of approximately 50 Å; for examining artifact surfaces the technique is nondestructive, but for bulk composition a small (ca. 1 mg) powdered sample is required.

Disadvantages of XPS are its relatively high cost and the fact that it can be used only for semiquantitative determinations. In addition, it is not suitable for trace or ultratrace analyses.

13.4 Structural and Microstructural Characterization

13.4.1 Electron Microscopy

The mineral and chemical characterization of pottery can also be enhanced by electron microscopes (McConnell 1977), first used in the 1930s, although some of their more interesting variants developed considerably later. These instruments not only yield qualitative and quantitative chemical and mineral data, but also permit visual examination of microstructural features and are particularly well suited to fine-grained materials such as ceramics and clay products. As a result, they are often successfully used in relatively simple characterization studies without much training or expertise in the more technical aspects of the equipment.

An electron microscope consists of three primary systems: an electron-optical system, a vacuum system, and a detection and display system (Bates 1971, 420–23). Monochromatic (traveling on a single wavelength) electrons are generated from a hot-filament electron gun and accelerated through a high voltage within a vacuum. A complex system of electromagnetic condenser and objective lenses demagnifies the beam of electrons, focusing it onto the specimen as a narrow beam. The specimen, also contained in the vacuum, is placed on a stage that can be rotated and tilted and often can be heated for observing structural changes at high temperatures. Additional lenses magnify the electron beam leaving the specimen and send it to a detection and display system, which usually shows the results on a fluorescent screen or records them photographically.

13.4.1.1 TRANSMISSION AND SCANNING ELECTRON MICROSCOPES

In the transmission electron microscope, or TEM (Tufts 1971), electrons traveling at high energies (between 20 and 1 MeV) are directed onto the specimen, which may be a very thin section of the actual specimen itself or, commonly, a replica of the specimen surface made of a strip of plastic or carbon (see Tite 1972, 244). The electrons hitting the specimen are scattered several ways, sending signals that—after magnification up to 300,000 times—reach a fluorescent screen or a photographic plate or film. If the actual sample substance is used, some of the electrons are transmitted and some are scattered "coherently," which means they are diffracted: directed to the detector along specific paths of propagation by the periodic spacing of the lattice planes in the specimen. The specimen may be observed directly through "bright field" or "dark field" illumination, created by inserting apertures into the back focal plane of one of the lenses so that only certain diffracted spectra are allowed to form the image.

Samples can also be studied by selected area electron diffraction, in which the electron beam is focused onto a tiny area about 1 μm in diameter, which can be smaller by a factor of ten in the most modern instruments. This technique is in principle identical to X-ray diffraction and provides a basis for identifying the mineral constituents. In materials with as many constituents as ceramics, however, particularly low-fired ceramics, electron diffraction may be too complex a technique, and the TEM is more often used to study surface microstructural characteristics by the replica/shadowing technique. This method was used, for example, in investigating the slips and paints on Greek and Samian wares (Hofmann 1962).

The scanning electron microscope, or SEM (Thornton 1968; Bates 1971) has, in addition to the lens-vacuum detection system described above, two sets of scanning coils that permit the sharply focused electron beam to move across a specimen and analyze a series of areas. To accomplish this the surface has to be made conductive, usually by coating it with a thin film of gold or carbon. Compared with the transmission electron microscope, the electron beam of the SEM is accelerated at a lower voltage; it has a greater depth of field, lower magnification (up to 50,000 times), and, most important, does not require thin sections, because it operates by reflection. The scanning electron microscope has been of great use in illuminating the size and shape of particulate matter in ceramic materials, including slips (Tite et al. 1982) and the clay platelets themselves (see Bates 1964; Brown 1964), as well as in identifying structural changes in the fabric that accompany sintering, which are useful in assessing firing temperatures (Tite and Maniatis 1975a; Tite et al. 1982; see sec. 14.3).

13.4.1.2 ELECTRON MICROPROBE

Several "microprobe" instruments are known, some operating via ions, lasers, and protons (Andersen 1973; Kane 1973), but perhaps the best known is the electron microprobe (Reed 1975; Long 1977; Lewis 1971), developed in the late 1940s and early 1950s (Birks 1971, 5–19). Also called the electron probe or the electron probe microanalyzer (EPMA), this instrument may be considered a combination of the scanning electron microscope and X-ray fluorescence apparatus. That is, the technique utilizes the SEM apparatus, in which a specimen is bombarded with a focused beam of high-energy electrons that can scan its surface. Rather than investigating the image caused by secondary or backscattered electrons, however, the microprobe technique is like XRF because the analysis uses the fluorescent X rays emitted by the sample (fig. 13.11). When the electron beam is focused on a small area of the specimen, secondary X rays are emitted at wavelengths characteristic of the particular element that is excited. These X rays are analyzed in terms of their characteristic energies or wavelengths by an energy-dispersive detector. The intensity of the X rays depends on the concentration of the element in the sample, so quantitative determinations can be made using appropriate corrections and data reduction systems. Many electron microprobes are combined scanning microscope/microprobe devices.

The technique is destructive; a small sample must be removed from the artifact, polished, and coated with a metal film to make it electrically conductive. Electron microprobe analysis can be used to detect elements with atomic numbers greater than 12 (magnesium), although with special conditions elements down to 5 (boron) can be analyzed. These can be accurately detected in major, minor, and trace quantities (commonly to 100 ppm, sometimes lower).

The primary advantage of the technique is its extraordinary versatility; it can be used for both point analyses and composite or bulk analyses and to analyze particular tiny points of a specimen, such as inclusions, or glazes or pigments (Steinberg and Kamilli 1984). As in X-ray fluorescence, the beam penetrates only 2–10 μm below the surface of the specimen. The technique also can analyze "transects" comparing elemental concentrations across a boundary, as from paint to interface to body (DeAtley 1986), and can create an "elemental map" of the distribution of a particular element across the entire sample visible on the fluorescent screen (Kamilli and Steinberg 1985,

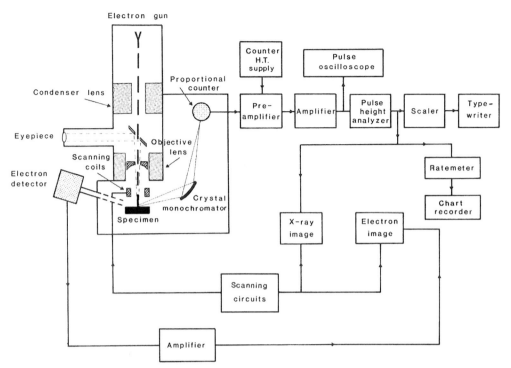

Figure 13.11   Schematic diagram of components of an electron probe microanalyzer. After Long 1977, fig. 5.

325–27). These capabilities are particularly useful for analyzing the chemical composition of a clay matrix while excluding the elements in clastic inclusions. With respect to microstructural (noncompositional) characterization, the microprobe can also investigate texture, phase relationships, changes on firing, and defects (Ruddlesden 1967; Ruddlesden and Airey 1967).

Disadvantages of the method (see Ruddlesen 1967 for a review) include some aspects of sample preparation: a sample several millimeters in diameter must be extracted from the artifact; poorly consolidated materials must be impregnated, and powders must be embedded in a solid. In addition, the sample must be flat and polished. Additional problems are those associated with X-ray fluorescence analysis: only the surface is analyzed, and quantitative determinations may be confused by the size and shape of the specimen, which must be flat.

13.4.2   X-Ray Radiography

X-ray radiography and xeroradiography are essentially photographic techniques in which an object is placed within the beam of X rays produced by a high-voltage X-ray tube; the X rays passing through the object are allowed to make contact with a photographic film. In conventional X-ray radiography, the developed film is a "shadowgraph" displaying variations in contrast, that is, light and dark areas, as a function of differential absorption of the X rays. These differences are caused by both the structure of the object (its thickness) and its composition (constituents of high atomic number absorb more X rays, thus appearing as dark areas on the film). Several early studies considered the application of X-ray radiography to archaeological pottery (Titterington 1933, 1951), noting that quartz inclusions, for example, were not visible on the film.

Xeroradiography creates an electrostatic image on a selenium-coated plate (Alexander and Johnston 1982). The principal advantage of this technique over conventional film radiography is that it yields greater contrast and detail and hence sharper images, particularly of edges or profiles.

In pottery studies, both techniques are useful for studying the orientation, size, quantity, and distribution of particulate matter (Braun 1982); for determining the technique of manufacture (see Rye 1977, 1981, 68–70; Foster 1985); for revealing details of construction (Alexander and Johnston 1982); and for identifying forgeries or areas of reconstruction (Meyers 1978).

13.5   References

Ahrens and Taylor 1961
Alexander and Johnston 1982
Andersen 1973
Bailey and Stevens 1960
Ballié and Stern 1984
Bamps 1883
Banks and Hall 1963
Bates 1971
Bates 1964
Berrin and Sundahl 1971
Bertin 1978
Birks 1971
Bishop, Rands, and Holley 1982
Blatt 1982
Bomgardner 1981
Bower, Bromund, and Smith 1975
Bradley 1964
Braun 1982
Brewer 1964
Brown 1964
Catling, Blin-Stoyle, and Richards 1961
Chayes 1956
Clayton, Cohen, and Duerden 1981
Cohen 1976
Courtois 1976
Cousins and Dharmawardena 1969
Cullity 1967
DeAtley 1986
Dickson 1966
Emeleus 1960
Enriquez, Danon, and Beltrao 1979
Farnsworth and Ritchie 1938
Flamini and de Lorenzo Flamini 1985
Folk 1966

Foster 1985
Francaviglia, Minardi, and Palmieri 1975
Franklin and Vitali 1985
Frechette 1971
Freestone, Meeks, and Middleton 1985
Gancedo et al. 1985
Gibb 1976
Gillies and Urch 1983
Goffer 1980
Goles 1977
Gould 1971
Grim 1968
Grim and Bradley 1948
Gritton and Magalousis 1978
Hall 1963
Hancock 1985
Hatcher et al. 1980
Hawley 1929
Hench and Gould 1971
Hess and Perlman 1974
Hodder 1974a
Hodges 1963
Hofmann 1962
Kamilli and Steinberg 1985
Kane 1973
Keisch 1974
Kempe and Harvey 1983
Kempe and Templeman 1983
Kerr 1977
Kingery 1974
Kleeman 1967
Kostikas, Simopoulos, and Gangas 1976

Kruger 1971
Kullerud et al. 1979
Lambert and McLaughlin 1976
Lewis 1971
Long 1977
McConnell 1977
Mackenzie 1964
McLaughlin 1977
Magetti 1982
Maniatis, Simopoulos, and Kostikas 1982
Mason and Berry 1968
Meinholz 1983
Meschel 1978
Meyers 1978
Middleton, Freestone, and Leese 1985
Muir 1977
Muller, L. 1977
Neumann 1977
Norrish and Chappell 1977
Olsen 1975
Orphanides 1985
Peacock, 1967, 1970, 1971, 1977
Perlman and Asaro 1969
Phillips 1971
Rankin 1971
Reed 1975
Reeves and Brooks 1978
Rice 1974

Rich and Kunze 1964
Ritchie 1937
Ruddlesden 1967
Ruddlesden and Airey 1967
Rye 1976, 1977, 1981
Rye and Duerden 1982
Sayre and Dodson 1957
Sayre, Murrenhoff, and Weick 1958
Shackley 1975
Shepard 1976
Slavin 1968
Spiel et al. 1945
Steinberg and Kamilli 1984
Taylor 1960
Thornton 1968
Tite 1972
Tite et al. 1982
Tite and Maniatis 1975a
Titterington 1933, 1951
Torres, Arie, and Sandoval 1984
Tubb, Parker, and Nickles 1980
Tufts 1971
Wandibba 1982
Ware 1971
Wertheim 1964
Williams 1977, 1979, 1983
Winefordner 1971
Woods 1986
Zussman 1977
Zussman, ed., 1977

14 Special Topics in Ceramic Characterization Studies

Ceramic materials typically are characterized for descriptive or determinative purposes, and the object may be qualitative or quantitative—to identify the constituents in the material, to determine their amounts, or both. Characterization also commonly measures the properties of the finished product, either for more precise description, for example, of color or hardness, or to assess use-related properties such as strength, porosity, and thermal stress resistance.

In studying archaeological pottery, the techniques and findings of ceramic characterization often have an additional goal: understanding the manufacture of the pottery. In archaeological terms this includes several distinct objectives, only a few of which are discussed here. One is to identify inclusions in the paste and discover whether they were added intentionally as temper. A second objective is to determine provenience—where the ceramic was made. Archaeothermometric studies are undertaken to find the temperature of firing, and dating and authentication studies may be carried out to determine the antiquity of a piece.

14.1 What Is "Temper"?

"Temper" is perhaps the most used, abused, and imprecise term employed in archaeological and technological descriptions of pottery. Differences in tempering materials have stood as a primary basis for distinguishing all manner of classificatory units of pottery, from varieties to types to groups to wares. The terms is used rather casually in pottery studies: everyone seems to know generally what it is, but there is little agreement on a precise definition, a problem noted as early as the 1930s (March 1934; see also Arnold 1974).

Archaeologists use "temper" both as a noun and as a verb. As a noun it refers to the coarse components in a paste, usually assumed to have been added by potters to modify the properties of the clay; it is similar to words modern studio or commercial ceramists use for particulate matter added to a

Table 14.1 Characteristics of Some Common Kinds of Temper

Characteristics	Shell		Carbo-nate	Sherd	Mica	Organic	Crushed Rock	Volcanic Ash	Quartz Sand	Biosilica
	Calcined	Uncal-cined								
Advantages										
Platy—blocks crack propagation	x	x			x					
Angular—adds strength				x			x	x		x
Crushes easily	x									x
Has low or comparable thermal expansion	x				x					
Increases porosity						x				
Disadvantages										
Platy—prone to laminar fractures	x	x			x					
Hard to crush or process		x	x	x			x			
Rehydrates after firing	x	x	x							
May weaken body by shape or porosity						x			x	
Shape[a]	P	P	I,S,R	I,A	P	I,P	A	A	R,S,I	A
Natural abundance in clays[b]	N	M	Y	N	M	N	M	N	Y	M

[a]P = platy; S = smooth; I = irregular; A = angular; R = rounded.
[b]Y = commonly found in quantities sufficient to act as temper; M = may occur in variable to moderate quantities in clays, may or may not be sufficient for tempering; N = does not commonly occur in clays.

clay, which may be called grog or filler (Brody 1979, 7–8). As a verb, temper refers to the action of adding that material. Both usages are closely tied to the dictionary definition of the word: as a verb, "to bring to the proper texture, consistency, hardness, etc., by mixing with something or treating in some way"; as a noun, "something used to temper a mixture."

Whether it is called temper, grog, or something else, the subject of discussion here is a substance in a clay that modifies its properties when wet or dry as well as during and after firing. A seemingly endless variety of materials may be added to clay for these purposes (see table 14.1; also chap. 5; Shepard 1976, 26–27; Rye 1981, 31–36). Some tempers are organic materials of either plant or animal origin or composition. Plant materials include grass or plant fibers, chaff or straw, cattail fuzz, and plant silica, to name a few types. Material of animal origin includes shell, sponge spicules, and dung, which is actually largely plant material (see London 1981). Mineral tempers are the most common and variable, including various types of crushed rock (limestone, sandstone, andesite, trachyte, basalt, schist, etc.), sand (usually quartz), and volcanic ash. Finally, material of human origin is also used, such as ground potsherds or brick (referred to as grog); in addition, modern potters may use fiberglass or expanded plaster aggregate (Brody 1979, 7–8).

The properties these materials modify include workability, drying characteristics, firing behavior, and final fired characteristics. For example, additions to the paste may increase or decrease plasticity or stickiness, reduce shrinkage in drying, lower the vitrification point in firing, or increase the strength of the fired piece (see chaps. 3 and 4 for the influence of particulate matter on clay properties).

14.1.1   Problems in Terminology

For archaeologists, problems in the proper use of the term temper have arisen for several reasons. One problem focuses on the identification and description of temper, which is usually based on the size and visibility of particles. Archaeologically, in examining a fired sherd or vessel, only relatively coarse inclusions are clearly identifiable as materials that modify the properties of a clay paste. Yet a variety of other substances may have been added, including salt, dung, and other clays. For example, some Pakistani potters use two parts of a relatively coarse clay "tempered" with one part of a finer plastic clay (Rye and Evans 1976, 20). Such mixing of clays is likely in areas where large deposits of relatively coarse residual clays are common (Bishop, Rands, and Holley 1982, 317; also Buko 1984, 360–61). Even the water added to make the dry clay plastic (Rye 1976, 121–23) can in the strictest sense be considered a tempering agent. Many of these additions to clays leave little to no readily visible trace in the fired sherd, and hence they are effectively excluded from discussions of temper constituents; yet they modify the original clay's workability, drying, firing, and use-related properties.

A second difficulty is behavioral and concerns how the particles came to be present in the clay. The definition of temper implies that potters added these substances intentionally to modify the properties of the clay for manufacture and use. In commercial pottery, and in traditionally made products today, the addition of materials as temper is empirically verifiable. But much of what is called temper in the archaeological literature may constitute inclusions naturally present in the original clay material, not added independently at all. The clay may have been selected purposefully to take advantage of this natural temper.

Third, setting aside for a moment the question whether the substance was naturally present in the clay, the notion of temper has a quantitative implication—that it is present in sufficient amounts to modify the clay properties. It is important to acknowledge that small amounts of material may have been incorporated accidentally while processing the clay (grinding, soaking, wedging) for manufacture. Although even these small amounts may sometimes be characteristic of a particular paste (Shepard 1936, 438), they are not temper in the sense of either being intentional additions or existing in sufficient quantity to modify the clay properties. Similar incorporation of lumps of dried clay during mixing has occasionally been noted in descriptions of "clay-tempered" pastes (see Weaver 1963; Shepard 1964; Porter 1964; Whitbread 1986).

The final problem is determining what constitutes untempered pottery. Pottery may have considerable quantities of sizable inclusions that are naturally present rather than added by the potter: behaviorally, this is "untempered" clay, but technically and functionally the inclusions modify its properties. On the other hand, very fine paste pottery materials are often spoken of as untempered because they have few visible coarse inclusions. Yet these may contain abundant natural (but fine) particles, as do the spiculite clays of the Southeastern U.S. (Borremans and Shaak 1986). Or they may be mixtures of two clays, one or neither having coarse particles; in this case the mixing itself is an act of tempering.

Defining temper is more than a semantic quibble, because the deliberate combining of raw materials into a pottery paste has significant stylistic, technological, and functional implications for the pottery-making process and for the uses of the products (see Shepard 1964). For example, the ceramic classificatory units that archaeologists base on temper distinctions (see sec. 9.1.1) are presumed to have chronological, ethnic, spatial, social, and functional significance and represent the traditional foundation for regional historical sequences and outlines of cultural interactions. More important, the choice of tempering materials is assumed to represent a consistent or normative pattern, and thus the regular covariation of particular tempering agents with particular vessel forms or styles is seen as culture specific.

For these purposes it is in some senses immaterial how the temper came to be in the clay, whether the potter selected clay with particular kinds of inclusions or added them to the clay. The observable fact of covariation exists regardless of the behavior involved. On the other hand, for certain purposes the behavior is critical. For example, the associations of paste/temper/form/style may permit some provenience determinations (see sec. 14.2), both distinguishing local from intrusive tradewares, and locating specific source materials. It also is important in relating groups of unknown sherds to known kiln materials or raw resources and to the history of manufacturing technology. Finally, the kinds, sizes, and shapes of tempering materials are important in determining pottery functions and performance characteristics (see chaps. 7 and 12), a growing interest.

14.1.2 Distinguishing Natural from Added Substances

In general, the critical distinction in discussing temper is whether the materials are naturally present or were added by the potter (to modify the clay properties), and this distinction is particularly difficult. Four characteristics are usually considered in determining the origin of the particles: the identity of the material and the particle shape, size range, and amount. (Clearly these criteria do not reveal whether two or more clays were mixed as a tempering practice, however.)

Identifying the inclusions in pottery is usually a matter of recognizing that many materials can occur naturally in clays, either as residues of the parent material in primary clays or as particulate matter incorporated during transportation and rebedding of sedimentary clays. The primary categories of inclusions that can be assumed to be added to clays rather than occurring naturally are rock fragments, grog (crushed fired clay), volcanic ash, and most kinds of vegetable matter, which are distinguished chiefly by their "casts" and by the large amount of pore space they leave in the fabric after being burned out during firing. Although this seems to clarify the temper issue by putting many materials clearly into the "added" category, such is not the case. Quartz and calcite (often as sand or "grit"), mica, sponge spicules, and even shell often occur naturally and abundantly in clay deposits.

Although a wide variety of materials can occur either as added temper or as natural inclusions in clays, their status can sometimes be differentiated by careful observation of their size, shape, and quantity (see Braun 1982 for a discussion of X-ray radiographic images in quantitative temper analysis). In the case of shell, for example, although small amounts of whole or broken shells of terrestrial or freshwater snails, mollusks, or foraminifera may be present in sedimentary clays or beach sands, in most cases where shell is added as temper it is present in relatively large quantities (ca. 20%–30%).

Furthermore, because many mollusk shells are difficult to crush, they are often calcined or heated, which makes it much easier: shell [aragonite] changes to calcite when it is heated to about 500°C, with a concomitant expansion, and the structural changes make crushing easier. In addition, calcite has a lower coefficient of thermal expansion (sec. 12.4.1) than aragonite, making it more suitable as a temper for cooking vessels. If shell is calcined at higher temperatures (at or above 750°C), however, and then added to clay and fired, the subsequent rehydration of the decomposition product (CaO) with atmospheric water and then CO_2 after cooling will lead to lime popping. On the other hand, prefiring to 750°C will prevent evolution of CO_2 on firing, with its effects of increasing porosity and bloating.

Mica is not uncommon in pottery, but because it is a common inclusion in clays it is not likely to have been added as temper unless the particle sizes and quantities are large. Mica may remain in primary clays after weathering from a parent deposit, and at times a considerable amount may be present. When mica is abundant in pottery, it is likely that the pottery was made from a micaceous clay or tempered with crushed micaceous rock (e.g., a micaceous schist) rather than being tempered with mica alone (Shepard 1976, 162).

Calcite (as distinct from limestone) may be added to clays as temper in crystalline or cryptocrystalline form, but it may also be a natural inclusion. Such clays are usually marly sedimentary clays that were deposited, for example, in lacustrine or riverine environments in a limestone (or other carbonate) geological region. The distinction between marly clays and calcite as temper is based on both quantity and shape: particles in calcareous sedimentary clays will be rounded from the action of transport and deposit and are usually rather fine grained because the mineral readily fractures along cleavage planes.

The greatest problem in distinguishing added temper from natural inclusions is the presence of quartz sand. Typically the shape of the grains is the basis for such distinctions. Pronounced angularity of the grains is interpreted as meaning a rock was crushed and hence that the quartz was added, whereas rounded grains are taken as evidence of alteration during transport as part of a sedimentary clay deposit. This distinction does not always hold up, however, because angular particles may be present in primary clays or in sedimentary clays deposited relatively close to a parent material.

Questions concerning quartz in pottery are particularly intractable in areas of sandy soils, such as Florida, where clay deposits are likely to have a considerable admixture of quartz sand and sand is also likely to be one of the most available tempering agents. In such situations the most useful analytical recourse may be granulometry—consideration of the particle sizes in the ceramic. A clear division in the frequency distribution of coarse (and angular) fragments versus small (and rounded) particle sizes may suggest that the coarse, angular particles were added to a fine sandy clay. On the other hand, if all particles are in the very fine sand-to-silt size range, it is more likely that they were naturally present in the clay deposit.

All these observations are guidelines, however, and in many circumstances it will be impossible to distinguish between natural and added inclusions in a sherd.

14.1.3   Alternative Terms

Given the burden of inferences deriving from a vague term such as temper, it is not surprising that several writers have treated the problem and recommended other terms. March (1934, 16) proposed the term aplastic, and Shepard (1976, 25) advocated restricting the term temper to definitely added inclusions; she prefers to use "*nonplastic* . . . in a general sense and for material of indeterminate source." Besides aplastic and nonplastic, other suggested terms are inclusion, additive, aggregate, modifier, filler, grog, and opening material. None of these alternatives is completely satisfactory, however.

Aplastic and nonplastic avoid the issue of whether the substance was deliberately added or was naturally present, although the expressed contrast with "plastic" constituents has a subtle connotation of intended function. In addition, these terms do not accommodate the possibility that the added materials were themselves plastic or enhanced plasticity. For example, clay minerals such as attapulgite and very fine organic substances such as dung or blood (which increase plasticity and perhaps also adhesiveness through the presence of gel-forming hydrated organic polymers; London 1981, 193; Stimmell and Stromberg 1986, 248) may have been added to a clay; this is not uncommon ethnographically. Once in the paste, however, added clays may or may not have functioned as plasticizers (compare Arnold 1971, 35–36, with Rye and Evans 1976, 20).

The term inclusions (see Rye 1981, 31–32) explicitly avoids dealing with how the material in question got into the clay, but the term is sometimes taken to imply that it is present as grains or particulate matter of some size. In addition, organics or salt added to the clay might be visible only as "negative" inclusions—as casts or voids—after firing.

Additive, aggregate, modifier, filler (Bennett 1974, 81–82), binder, grog (Norton 1970, 96), and opening material are all terms that are perhaps more common among studio or commercial ceramists than among archaeologists, and understandably all of these refer to deliberate additions rather than to materials occurring naturally in the clay. Binder refers to organic materials added for workability and green strength (Norton 1970, 99; see sec. 3.3.3). The term grog has a very special usage among archaeologists and ceramists alike;

meaning crushed prefired and "prereacted" clay materials such as potsherds or brick, it therefore refers to one *kind* of temper, and not to the generic or functional material itself. In Southeast Asia, potters prepare grog temper "from scratch" by mixing clay with rice chaff, firing it, and then crushing the material into small bits to use in making vessels (Solheim 1965, 259). Elsewhere, the availability of ancient sherds to be ground up for temper is an important factor for Shipibo-Conibo potters in deciding where to settle (DeBoer and Lathrap 1979, 111).

The term "opening material" has been suggested to emphasize the function of inclusions, that is, their role in increasing porosity so as to facilitate even drying, firing, and thermal shock resistance (Woods 1986, 170). Among French and Spanish speakers, the term *degraissant* or *desgrasante* (literally, "degreaser"; see Balfet, Fauvet-Berthelot, and Monzon 1983, 51) also calls attention to one of the functions of temper, reducing the clay's stickiness, but this is not its sole or primary function.

Arnold (1974, 45) has suggested redefining or abandoning the term temper, preferring more correct if somewhat cumbersome descriptions such as clay "modified by the potter using . . ." versus "naturally occurring nonplastics." A more recent attempt at defining temper is based primarily on using size criteria to distinguish inclusions from the paste or matrix (Magetti 1982, 122). In this scheme temper consists of all solid phases of the ceramic with a diameter greater than 0.015 mm and may be differentiated into artificial temper (if "added artificially") or natural temper if naturally present in the clay. It might be noted, however, that this particle size is within the silt range in most classifications (see fig. 2.2), and one could question to what extent potters' additions would be so finely sorted. A diameter of 0.05 mm might be a more appropriate boundary.

These recent turns in the thinking on temper are headed in the right direction. Although studies of archaeological pottery focus on the cultural aspects (the behavior of manufacture and use), it is important to recognize the distinction between characterizing a material and drawing behavioral inferences from that characterization.

Microscopic and chemical analyses provide qualitative and quantitative data on what constituents are present and in what amounts and sizes. This information, supplemented by additional data from geology or ceramic science, permits inferences about cultural significance, such as whether certain component phases of the pottery are inclusions added to the paste, whether they have plastic properties, and what effects they would have had on workability, drying, firing, and use. After such determinations, finally, it is possible to assess the likelihood that these materials were deliberately added by the potter to temper the clay.

In its traditional meaning, temper is a behavioral inference drawn from an analytical observation, not the observation itself, and this suggests that the term should be used very carefully if at all to refer to particulate matter in the paste of archaeological pottery. Most nonchemical characterization analyses directed toward what is commonly called temper focus on identifying inclusions. Inclusions may be mineral or organic, large or small, plastic or nonplastic. They may be present in the natural clay selected by the potter or additions to it; if added, the term inclusions is neutral on whether the incorporation was intentional. For these reasons inclusions is a more appropriate term than temper in studies of the pastes of archaeological pottery, covering virtually all circumstances except the mixing of two (or more) clay substances to form the paste.

14.2 Provenience Studies

An important objective in ancient pottery studies, and a critical first step in studying pottery production, is to determine where the objects were produced. For much of the historical period this poses little difficulty, since a variety of documents and known kiln sites attest the location of former pottery manufacturing areas. For much of prehistory, however, such information is maddeningly elusive: questions on the location of production sites, the types of wares fabricated there, and the organizational arrangements of production, while related, pose unique difficulties for analysis and interpretation (table 14.2). Yet identifying the location of pottery production is critical for many reasons; for example, without this information it is difficult to pursue studies of distribution and exchange successfully.

As discussed in section 6.2.1, one traditional way to determine the geographical source of ancient pottery has been to note the spatial occurrence of pottery styles: applying the so-called criterion of abundance, gravity model, or culture-area concept places the locus of manufacture in the zone where the ware most frequently occurs. Another approach has been based on the spatial disposition of artifacts related to ceramic production, such as kilns, molds, wasters, unfired vessels, and smoothing and shaping tools. The presence of quantities of these items, singly or together, in an area is a reasonably unambiguous indicator of a production locus.

In the past several decades a widely popular physicochemical approach has been used to locate the origins of particular kinds of pottery by characterizing the composition of the ceramic and comparing it with the composition of pottery of known origin or with raw resources. These provenience (or provenance) studies or sourcing studies attempt to find the geographical source or provenience of the pottery through its chemical or mineral characterization (see Rapp 1985). Provenience studies are commonly used on many artifacts besides pottery, including those made of obsidian (Dixon 1976; Stross et al. 1976), turquoise (Weigand, Harbottle, and Sayre 1977), jade (Hammond et al. 1977), steatite or soapstone (Kohl, Harbottle, and Sayre 1979; Allen, Luckenbach, and Holland 1975), and chert (Luedtke 1979; see also Cummins 1983, 185–90).

14.2.1 Assumptions and Procedures

The underlying assumption of provenience studies is referred to as the "provenience postulate" (Weigand, Harbottle, and Sayre 1977, 24; Rands and Bishop 1980, 19) and is usually formulated in terms of chemical composition. Briefly stated, the provenience postulate holds that differences between distinct sources of raw materials can be recognized analytically and that com-

Table 14.2   Errors in Identifying Intrusive Pottery

Intrusive Element Source	Characteristics of Materials	Characteristics of Technique and Style	Basis for Differentiation
I. Raw materials nonlocal	A. All nonlocal	1. Local techniques and styles	Local style on nonlocal materials
		2. Imitation of foreign style and technique	Identification depends on ability to discern imperfect imitation
		3. Mixed local and nonlocal techniques/styles	Elements of local technique or style identify the pottery as locally made
	B. Nonlocal resources used with local materials	All of the above possibilities	Elements of local resources identify the products as local, together with elements of technique or style
II. Nonlocal potters working in the area	A. Resources imported	1. Made in their native (nonlocal) tradition	Indistinguishable from an intrusive item from a nonlocal center of manufacture
		2. Technique and style modified by local tradition	Elements of local technique and style identify the pottery as locally made
		3. Local techniques and styles adopted	Same as above
	B. Using some local and nonlocal resources	Any of the above possibilities	Identified by local materials, further confirmed by local elements of technique or style
	C. Only local resources	1. Made in their native (nonlocal) tradition	Identified by local resources
		2. Native tradition modified by local practices	Identified by local resources, further confirmed by local elements of technique or style
		3. In local tradition	Indistinguishable from local products
III. Nonlocal style adopted by local potters	A. Nonlocal resources imported	Duplication of I.A.2	
	B. Combining local and nonlocal resources	Duplication of I.B	
	C. Only local materials used		Characteristics of local materials identify pottery as locally made

Source: After Shepard 1976, table 11.

positional variations will be greater *between* sources than *within* sources (see Bishop, Rands, and Holley 1982, 301). In other words, if clay source X is used to make pottery type A, and a different source Y is used for type B, then if A and B pottery types are analyzed chemically, it should be apparent that they were made from different clays. This postulate does not specify any necessary relation between a raw clay and a fired product made of that clay, however, and thus identifying clay sources X or Y in the manufacture of pottery types A and B is a separate task.

In general terms, provenience analysis begins with compositional characterization (see chap. 10) of the artifacts of unknown origin. Ideally this should be carried out by both chemical (sec. 13.3) and mineralogical (sec. 13.2) techniques, but in practice the studies frequently analyze only the minor, trace, and ultratrace chemical elements.

Chemical analysis is most successfully applied to fine-textured, apparently untempered pottery, although even fine paste pottery can sometimes benefit from petrographic examination (compare Bishop and Rands 1982, 331–14, with Prag et al. 1974, 157–66). Chemical methods are less suited to characterization of very coarse, sandy pastes because of their extreme inhomogeneity.

With coarse-textured and tempered pottery it is advisable to make careful use of both chemical and mineral techniques. Sometimes petrographic analysis alone is sufficient to determine regions of resource procurement and hence manufacture (see Peacock 1970; Shepard 1942a, 1965), because mineral inclusions may be distinctive enough that a particular geological locale can be specified. Petrographic analysis is most informative for differentiating local from "intrusive" pastes in the following circumstances (Shepard 1976, 165): extensive exchange of stylistically similar pottery over broad regions; "importation" of pottery in such large quantities that local manufacture seems more logical; poor preservation of sherds, preventing examination of surface finish or decoration; and recognition of unusual inclusions in initial sorting that suggest nonlocal manufacture.

Although chemical and petrographic methods have usually been used for ceramic sourcing studies, other approaches have also been employed. One study has used the shape of the artificially induced (by gamma-ray irradiation) thermoluminescence glow curves (see sec. 14.4.2.3) to determine origins of New World majolicas (Vaz and Cruxent 1975), and a study of Finnish pottery has utilized diatoms to pinpoint origins (Matiskainen and Alhonen 1984). In addition, although provenience studies usually focus on the body of the ceramic, the surface composition and characteristics (slips, glazes, or paints) as analyzed by microprobe (sec. 13.4.1.2 may also be distinctive, as with terra sigillata ware (Ballié and Stern 1984).

Provenience analyses are not complete with the chemical analysis of the pottery. The data from these physicochemical analyses are next subjected to a variety of multivariate statistical transformations such as discriminant function or cluster analysis (see Bieber et al. 1976; Bishop, Harbottle, and Sayre 1982) to form groupings of similar materials (fig. 14.1), sometimes called "paste compositional reference units," or PCRUs (Bishop, Harbottle, and Sayre 1982, 290). These groups may be the basis for some simple kinds of provenience interpretations that do not push the limits of inference very far beyond the compositional characterization itself. For example, the goal may be merely to describe the composition of the typical pottery at a site and to compare the groupings of pottery created by the compositional data (fig. 14.2). These groups are then used in discriminating indigenous or local from foreign or trade wares or in distinguishing imitations by means of nonlocal constituents.

Provenience analyses more usually compare the composition of the unknown specimens with that of materials of more precisely known provenience, using the same analytical methods and physicochemical properties.

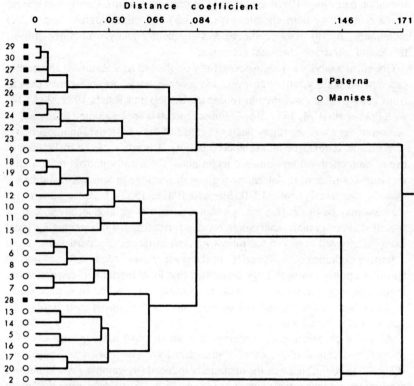

Figure 14.1 Dendrogram depicting results of hierarchical agglomerative cluster analysis of minor and trace element concentrations in samples of pottery from two sites, Paterna and Manises, Spain. The two compositional groups are clearly separated. After Jornet, Blackman, and Olin 1985, fig. 9.

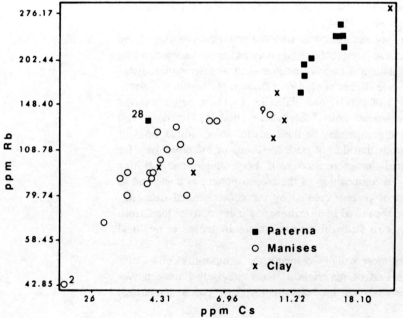

Figure 14.2 Scatter diagram showing separation of Paterna and Manises pottery samples (plus clay samples) on the basis of concentrations of Rb versus Cs. After Jornet, Blackman, and Olin 1985, fig. 10.

These known materials may be of two kinds. One set of data may be obtained by analyzing samples of clays and tempers taken from the geological "resource procurement zones" in the region where the pottery of interest occurs (Hancock 1984; Bishop and Rands 1982; Buko 1984; Adan-Bayewitz and Perlman 1985). This endeavor is fraught with difficulties because of problems with exhaustion of or variations in clay beds or because the original clay composition is altered by the potter in making a pot (see below).

A second procedure, common in Europe, is to use as the knowns a set of pottery recovered either from a specific site or from particular workshops. These "reference groups" consist of materials from identified production locations, such as finished products (sometimes signed) or kiln wasters, and unknown or questionable specimens are compared against these (rather than against the raw geological resources) to obtain a provenience attribution or determine authenticity. This approach has been used in the study of terra sigillata (Widemann et al. 1975; postmedieval Continental European pottery (Poole and Finch 1972), and Romano-British ware (Tubb, Parker, and Nickless 1980).

Finally, the two bodies of characterization data—on unknown sherds and on known resources or ceramics—are compared statistically to determine the likelihood that the unknown compositional groups and the reference groups drawn from the resource zones or workshop materials represent a single (or an identifiable number of) geological/geochemical population(s).

It should be evident that with respect to provenience as a cultural problem, each approach has a slightly different emphasis. Comparisons with resources are directed not toward identifying the location of the human activity of creating the artifacts, but rather toward identifying the geographical source region of the raw materials—clay, temper, and pigments—and how they are used. This is an approach aligned with ceramic ecology (sec. 10.2.3) and with resource specialization (sec. 6.2.3). In comparing data against workshop materials or sherds of known manufacturing origin, provenience analyses endeavor to group unknown ceramics with knowns (a procedure closer to site specialization) but do not always reveal patterns of resource use within and between production units. Furthermore, the composition of pottery at a site is not necessarily constant through time if there is a very long occupation (cf. Attas, Fossey, and Yaffe 1982), since different clays may be used and even the same clay source can vary from one part of the bed to another. In any case, in both approaches provenience is identified primarily as a geochemical (or petrological) problem, not a cultural one.

It is not surprising, therefore, that most of the advances and developments in provenience studies have occurred in two areas—instrumentation and statistics. Advances in the instrumentation have brought greater sensitivity and precision in element analysis, while refinements of the statistical transformations of the enormous amounts of quantitative data have yielded automated mathematical techniques for grouping sherds by composition in statistically meaningful ways. These developments are complex and not easily summarized (the interested reader is referred to original papers on the topic [e.g., Ward 1974; Bieber et al. 1976; Wilson 1978, 226–33; Bishop, Harbottle, and Sayre 1982], and the mathematically inclined might start with Doran and Hodson 1975). The techniques essentially attempt to subdivide the overall assemblage into discrete groups in such a way as to minimize variation within the groups and maximize it among groups. The demands for precision this analysis places on experimental techniques may be summarized in an equation that models all the components of variation in a compositional analysis, expressed as the mathematical quantity of variance (Bishop, Harbottle, and Sayre 1982, 273; Bieber et al. 1976, 68–70): $S_T^2 = S_N^2 + S_S^2 + S_A^2$.

In this equation, S_T^2 is the total variance in determinations of the quantities of a particular element in a sample, representing the sum of the natural, sampling, and analytic variances. S_N^2 is the "natural variance," representing the naturally occurring variation in concentration of a particular element in a material. S_S^2 is the "sampling variance," arising from errors in estimating the quantity of an element owing to problems in sampling the sherd; S_A^2 is the "analytic variance," arising from errors in the quantitative measurements of the analysis procedure, including detection, calibration, interferences, and data processing. S_S^2 and S_A^2 represent the controllable part of the variance; S_N^2 is that part inherent in the particular materials being studied. The sampling error can be made very small by careful work. A requirement that the analytic and sampling errors introduce a contribution of 10% or less into the overall standard deviation of the results suggests a practical criterion for the analytic precision: $S_A^2 \leq \frac{1}{4}S_N^2$. In some cases of very homogeneous materials, the desirable level of analytic precision for provenience studies is on the order of 1%–2% (Wilson 1978, 222), but in many cases precision of only 7%–10% is acceptable (Harbottle 1982, 70). Instrumentational and statistical refinements in analytic methods have reduced the errors of S_A^2 to these desirably low levels, while larger sample sizes (see sec. 10.3.2), repeated analyses, and careful calibration with standards can reduce both S_A^2 and S_S^2.

14.2.2   Confounding Issues in Provenience Studies

Data on chemical composition have been used for decades (sec. 10.2.1) to differentiate classes of pottery as well as to compare the finished artifact with raw resources. Much of the inspiration for this work comes from obsidian studies, where comparisons between artifact and source are relatively simple. Obsidian is volcanic glass, and the worldwide occurrence of flows or outcrops of this material is limited to volcanic geological zones. As a glass it is compositionally rather homogeneous both within an artifact and within a flow, the one caveat being that flows sometimes occur repeatedly in the same spot, and though compositionally distinct they may have been quarried indiscriminately (see Bowman, Asaro, and Perlman 1973; Taylor 1977; Perlman 1984). More significantly, the chemical composition of obsidian is not altered by the addition or subtraction of substances during artifact manufacture. In addition, once the obsidian sources in a region have been adequately characterized, they can often be differentiated by a relatively few elements or element ratios. The provenience postulate, in other words, is straightforward in its operation.

In pottery manufacture, however, many factors complicate the relationship between the composition of the clay source and that of the finished pottery (see Wilson 1978 and Bishop, Rands, and Holley 1982 for reviews). Indeed, vessels made from the same clay may differ compositionally. For this reason efforts to link pottery (even fine-textured, untempered pottery) to specific clay resources by chemical composition alone have experienced considerable difficulties, and most provenience studies have instead compared unknown pottery with pottery from known locations.

One problem is that clays are ubiquitous, particulate sediments rather than geographically isolated, solid outcrops. They are highly variable from deposit to deposit in their chemical and mineralogical constituents, partly because many different clay minerals exist, but also because weathering, transport, and redeposit of the material lead to complex mixing. By their very nature, clay materials lack the relative depositional and compositional integrity characteristic of obsidians.

In addition, manufacturing a vessel involves various steps, including selecting clay, cleaning it, perhaps blending different clays, adding various substances as temper, and firing it; all of these procedures have the potential for increasing S_N^2 and S_S^2 in the variance equation (sec. 14.2.1). These procedures also distort the relationship between a raw clay and the vessels made from it and call into question the assumption that variations between sources are greater than those within sources even after temper has been added. Additional sources of variation may be caused by element alterations during use or in the postuse depositional environment. Despite the instrumental and statistical sophistication evident at the data-processing stage of most provenience studies, it is not difficult to see that when these problems are related to "real-life" pottery-making behavior they can interfere with efforts to understand pottery production (see Rice 1978b; Arnold et al. 1978; Bishop, Rands, and Holley 1982).

The confounding factors in provenience analysis can be considered from two directions: from the viewpoint of physicochemical analysis and from the viewpoint of the behavior involved in manufacturing a pot. Because most of the attention to these factors has been analytic, more data are to be found on geochemical precision than on the relation between making a pot and variations in constituents. To a certain extent the confounding problems are less severe with petrographic than chemical characterization, because these procedures take into account some aspects of manufacturing behavior by considering texture, particle size and orientation, and so forth, as well as suggesting the mineral basis for the chemical constituents of the products.

14.2.2.1 SELECTING ELEMENTS FOR ANALYSIS

One of the most critical issues in chemical analysis is selecting the elements by which individual ceramic groups are to be differentiated and compared with known and characterized materials (clays or kiln products). In general, a very large number of elements—as many as thirty-five to forty—are identified because it is not known beforehand which elements are unique to which geological source. Not knowing which constituents will discriminate between groups, one should have a large selection of element concentrations to choose from in order to establish clear differences between groups in statistically multivariate space. The actual discriminations between groups can often be based on a smaller number of elements, sometimes as few as four (Tubb, Parker, and Nickless 1980). The elements selected for characterizing the samples should be good discriminators, have good analytic precision, and be reliable in terms of contamination in the postdepositional environment.

Elements that are good discriminators differ consistently *between* pottery made of different resources while having little variation *within* a single type. Certain element ratios—for example, the ratio of scandium to iron (Brooks et al. 1974; Harbottle 1975)—are useful in differentiating materials because they meet this criterion. In general, however, it is preferable to use absolute concentrations rather than ratios of elements in chemical characterization (Bishop, Rands, and Holley 1982, 300; Wilson 1978, 228). In addition, the elements should ideally be present in the ceramic in large enough quantities to be measured reliably.

Although the two major chemical constituents of clays, alumina and silica, are not always useful in differentiating deposits because of overlapping concentration ranges (as well as the extremely short half-life of alumina as measured in neutron activation analysis), other major and minor constituents such as iron, potassium, magnesium, and sodium frequently are useful. Elements that have been found to be particularly good discriminators include scandium, iron, sodium, potassium, cesium, thorium, and hafnium, while tantalum, cobalt, manganese, cerium, chromium, lanthanum, europium, barium, and arsenic have also been cited (Winther-Nielsen et al. 1981, 86, 87). In selecting elements it is generally wise to eliminate (or correct statistically for) those that have correlated occurrences, on the basis that one should seek independent variables (Perlman and Asaro 1969, 31; see also Wilson 1978). Among the possible correlations are nickel and chromium (Harbottle 1970); potassium, rubidium, cesium, and barium, which tend to substitute for each other in K-feldspars; calcium and strontium, which occur together in limestone; and finally the rare earth elements, which often occur in correlated quantities.

Analytic precision in detection and measurement of the chemical elements within a ceramic is largely a function of the interaction of the element and instruments used in the analysis (see chap. 13), because individual instruments vary in their ability to detect different elements. Using neutron activation analysis (NAA), Harbottle (1982, 70) grouped elements into three categories according to their precision (standard deviation). The "best-behaved" elements, having standard deviations of only 1%, were iron, thorium, chromium, sodium, and potassium; almost as good, with standard deviations of 2%–4%, were cobalt, barium, samarium, and manganese. The determination of titanium and calcium concentrations by NAA using [47]Sc has been found to be unreliable (Hancock 1985). X-ray fluorescence is more suitable than NAA for detecting some elements, such as calcium, magnesium, and titanium (see Bishop, Rands, and Holley 1982, 290); in the case of PIXE analysis, sodium, manganese, copper, and zinc were found to be *un*satisfactorily analyzed (Rye and Duerden 1982, 60, 61).

The elements selected should also occur reliably in nature. This may be a question of the heterogeneity of geochemical distribution or of differential occurrence within a particular clay deposit. Three elements that have been found to occur unreliably under certain conditions are manganese (Bishop, Rands, and Holley 1982, 292), lutecium (Harbottle 1982, 70), and zirconium (Rye and Duerden 1982, 61). Few studies have sampled large clay beds to determine the variation in element occurrences, in part because of the problems of determining the vertical and horizontal extent of the deposit so as to establish the boundaries for sampling. One such study (Buko 1984, 353, 355) included thirteen samples taken from several vertically and horizontally varied locations within a large loess clay deposit outside Sandomierz, Poland. Of six elemental oxides, the greatest differences occurred with CaO, while little difference was found in the distribution of Al_2O_3 and K_2O.

Alteration or contamination of the pottery sample relates both to the environment of burial (pH, humidity, temperature) and to the sampling procedure and has implications for choice of elements analyzed.

In the burial environment, a variety of processes may alter the chemical composition of the pottery. Soil pH may cause leaching, which removes the alkali metals and also particularly calcium, sodium, zinc, cobalt, and barium (Bieber et al. 1976; Freeth 1967; Sayre, Chan, and Sabloff 1971). Also, cation exchange reactions within the burial environment (Hedges and McLellan 1976) can affect calcium and sodium as well as potassium and magnesium. This may be more serious with low-fired or underfired sherds (Tubb, Parker, and Nickless 1980, 165), because without vitrification the fabric is characterized by an open structure with high internal surface area and reactive phases (Freestone, Meeks, and Middleton 1985, 175). Recent studies have explored in greater detail the alteration of a ceramic during burial, and the data are equivocal. Some studies have suggested that rather than being removed by leaching, in certain circumstances calcium may be secondarily deposited by mineralization or recrystallization (Prag et al. 1974, 158; Courtois 1976), as may manganese (Freeth 1967) and phosphate (Freestone, Meeks, and Middleton 1985). Of particular concern is whether such alteration or (re)deposit may occur only on the surfaces of sherds (Franklin and Vitali 1985) or in cores as well (Freestone, Meeks, and Middleton 1985).

In sampling, removing samples with steel or tungsten carbide drills or burrs has been known to contaminate the sample with tungsten, cobalt, or tantalum. Samples should be taken from the cores rather than the surfaces of sherds, because in general the surfaces are more subject to contamination (Franklin and Vitali 1985), and though careful examination of the physical condition of sherds is an important first step to a physicochemical characterization study, it does not guarantee freedom from internal alterations.

14.2.2.2 COMPARING SHERDS AND CLAYS

Several studies have treated the potential sources of variation between clays and fired ceramics (for some examples, see Freeth 1967; Olin and Sayre 1971, 200; Brooks et al. 1974; Bishop 1975, 1980; Rice 1976a, 330–39, 1978b; Bishop, Rands, and Holley 1982, 294–95; Arnold et al. 1978; Butzer 1974; Buko 1984; Hancock 1984; Adan-Bayewitz and Perlman 1985). They have almost always, however, used different sample materials and rather small numbers of specimens, and thus there has been little or no systematic exploration of these problems with suitably sized sample sets.

Of all the possible sources of variation, the most significant is chemical inhomogeneities correlated with the kind and size of particles. Translated into potters' behavior in handling their clays, this involves either removing certain relatively large size-grades of particulate matter or adding such material. Either can cause serious difficulties for provenience analyses that involve comparing sherds with raw clay resources. Before undertaking a provenience analysis of pottery, it is important to determine whether such clay modifying was part of the producers' repertoire. These determinations will usually require textural investigation (by means of petrography) of the potsherds to determine the kinds, sizes, shapes, and quantities of inclusions; studying the local geology and soils; and sampling local clay resources to examine their naturally occurring inclusions.

The intentional cleaning, sieving, winnowing, or levigation of a natural clay removes coarse particulate matter or clastics, and only the fine fractions (usually clay, silt, and possibly fine sand-sized particles) are used to make the pottery. The consequences of this practice for altering the relationship between clays and sherds depend on the nature of the minerals removed. If what is removed is largely quartz sand, there may be little change in chemical composition (except for silicon), but if feldspars, heavy minerals, and dark-colored mafic (ferromagnesian) minerals are removed the trace-chemical composition could change considerably. One experimental analysis of unrefined and refined clays suggested drastic changes in the element concentrations in the refining process, but no data are provided on the actual chemistry or mineralogy of the samples (Attas, Yaffe, and Fossey 1977, 41). An additional problem is that highly mobile ions such as sodium and potassium may also be selectively removed during refining (Bishop, Rands, and Holley 1982, 296). One solution to these characterization problems is to analyze coarse and fine fractions of sherds separately (Fillières, Harbottle, and Sayre 1984) before comparison with possible clay sources. At the same time, alterations in chemical composition call attention to the need for mineral analysis as well as chemical analysis in provenience studies.

A second consideration in relating chemical composition to particle size concerns the addition of coarse particulate matter to the clay to eliminate stickiness, open up the pore structure, reduce shrinkage, hasten drying, and alter firing and postfiring use-related properties (see chaps. 3 and 4). These tempering ingredients (sec. 14.1) are of several kinds—including sand, rock, shell, organic matter, and even other clays as well as water—and each can have a different effect on the overall chemical composition of the product. Few of these effects have been investigated systematically or in detail, however.

One possible problem in chemical analysis concerns tempering one clay with another clay material. Although this procedure is widely known ethnographically (e.g., DeBoer and Lathrap 1979; Arnold 1971; Rye and Evans 1976, 20), it has received little attention in the literature on compositional analysis of archaeological pottery. In one study where mixing of clays was known to occur, the element composition of the final product reflected the proportions of elements in the two clays that were combined (Brooks et al. 1974, 54). In another archaeological study, incompatibilities between the chemical composition and the petrographic characteristics of the ancient ceramic products led to the conclusion that clays of different types had been mixed by the potters (Buko 1984).

The water added to make a clay plastic may contribute certain ions to the final product. Water contains soluble salts of various elements, including sodium, potassium, magnesium, calcium, and iron, and although the water and the anions tend to volatilize on firing, these cations may remain in the clay. To a certain extent this is probably not a problem, since the chemical composition of local water sources might be expected to be largely comparable to that of soil moisture or groundwater within the region. In areas where seawater rather than fresh water might have been added to clays (see Rye and Duerden 1982, 61–63), however, variations in chlorine and bromine have been noted between sample clays and the fired clay products, so these elements are not reliable for sourcing.

Sand is a common category of inclusions in clay and pottery. Although it has long been claimed that quartz sand will simply "dilute" the element content of the product (Sayre, Chan, and Sabloff 1971, 174; Olin and Sayre 1971, 200; Bishop, Rands, and Holley 1982, 295), especially when present in amounts less than 25% (Brooks et al. 1974, 55), there is no such thing as pure quartz sand. Most sands contain varying amounts of heavy or accessory minerals, some of which are high enough in trace elements to be mined industrially. For example, the sands of northeastern Florida near Jacksonville were mined between 1916 and 1929, and in some places up to the present day, for their heavy minerals, especially ilmenite, rutile, zircon, and monazite (Calver 1957, 15–25); monazite sands are high in thorium and other rare elements, and zircon is high in zirconium and hafnium (e.g., see Hancock 1984, 214).

Volcanic sands, too, contain quantities of heavy minerals with distinctive chemical compositions (see Rice 1978b, 527–34), as do many types of igneous and metamorphic rocks (sandstone, basalt, trachyte, etc.) that may be crushed and added to the clay as temper. Other added ingredients include calcite, limestone, and crushed sherd, and in all these examples the minor and trace elements in these materials will supplement those of the clay. Thus these materials have a potential for distorting any hypothetical one-to-one relation between clay and ceramic product, but their actual effect has not been measured systematically.

A third potential cause of variations in the relation between the element composition of a clay and a ceramic vessel is the firing process. There is some evidence that the effects of firing temperature and atmosphere on composition are negligible (Brooks et al. 1974, 54; Rice 1978b, 534–35; Attas, Yaffe, and Fossey 1977, 41; Tubb, Parker, and Nickless, 162–65), the variations being within the natural range of occurrence of the element in the clay. On the other hand, during firing a variety of volatile substances may be lost; these include primarily water and organics (carbon) at the low temperatures or early stages of firing, together with the decomposition of calcite at 700–800°C. At higher temperatures a variety of elements may volatilize and be lost, such as chlorine, bromine, sulfur, strontium, lead, and mercury (see Rye and Duerden 1982, 64; Poole and Finch 1972). To a certain extent the degree and effect of such losses will be a function of the original firing temperature, with more losses at higher temperatures (over about 850°C). At lower temperatures the sherds will have lost fewer elements, but they will also retain some cation exchange capability that may predispose them to adsorb elements from the burial environment (see Hedges and McLellan 1976).

To compensate for some of the many sources of variation between clays and archaeologically recovered pottery, different types of sample pretreatment may be recommended before chemical analysis (see Wilson 1978, 224–25). Some investigators have soaked sherds in distilled water to leach out elements acquired from the burial environment or to bring samples to similar condition with respect to water-soluble constituents (Sayre, Chan, and Sabloff 1971, 168). Another procedure is to prefire samples at temperatures of 700 to 1000°C, a practice sometimes recommended to eliminate the "diluting" effect of organic matter, water, and volatiles (such as SO_2 or the CO_2 from carbonates) in low-fired sherds. In all cases removing areas of surface contamination is very important.

The inhomogeneity of low-fired ceramics, usually a consequence of coarse materials added to the clays as well as the lack of vitrification, gives rise to problems of sampling in provenience studies (sec. 10.3.2.3). A general rule of thumb is that the more heterogeneous the population (e.g., the composition of a given category of pottery), the larger the sample required for representativeness. This stricture applies both to selecting a sample from a collection of sherds and to taking a sample of the paste of an individual sherd. In sampling collections, one suggestion has been to use between ten and thirty sherds in order to establish the compositional pattern of a particular ceramic group, depending on the apparent homogeneity of that group (Catling 1961, 36).

In sampling sherds for neutron activation analysis, generally several tiny samples of a few hundred milligrams are removed from the core of the sherd; these are mixed, then combined for analysis. But in the case of relatively coarsely crystalline material, such as much traditional pottery, the sample volume should be much greater because of the inhomogeneity caused by differences in chemical composition of the different mineral constituents, which also vary in particle size and abundance in the sherd. In the chemical analysis of rocks, for example, sample sizes are determined by average grain size. It has been estimated that samples on the order of several hundred grams to several kilograms (Reeves and Brooks 1978, 5), ground and subsampled, may be necessary for representative analysis. Needless to say, such criteria are not met in pottery trace-element studies.

14.2.3   Provenience and Production

Thus far, provenience studies are largely exercises in physicochemical characterization and have done little to shed light on production arrangements in the past. If provenience is identified in terms of geochemical groupings, the question that remains is how to pass beyond resource or site specialization (see sec. 6.2.3) and address producer specialization. Ideally, some correspondence should be sought between the geochemical groupings and human behavior so that, for example, the groupings might represent patterns of choosing and using resources within individual producer units.

Production is generally reconstructed at present in terms of a geological/geochemical data set that, by principles of least cost, represents a zone that is hypothetically or actually relatively near identified clay or temper sources. It has been noted that "according to least cost principles, the bulky materials used in fabricating pottery—the clay and temper—are less likely to have been obtained from a distant location in preindustrial societies than the clays or pigments used for finishing and decorating" (Rye 1981, 12; also Bishop, Rands, and Holley 1982, 315–16). The empirical basis for this assumption comes from a survey of procurement distances in the ethnographic literature on pottery making (sec. 5.2; Arnold 1980, 1985, 32–60). It was found that potters tend to obtain their resources from a "preferred territory of exploitation" extending a relatively short distance from their working locations: 85% of 110 potting communities used clay and temper resources obtained within a radius of only 7 km although distances may extend as much as 50 km from the manufacturing location.

These data have been incorporated into a scheme of five clay procurement strategies (Bishop, Rands, and Holley 1982, 316–18) in order to relate variability in pottery reference groups to the way potters exploit that environment. (1) In a nondiscriminating strategy, many clays are used, with no clear preference for any one. (2) In discriminating procurement, a single valued resource is used; the pottery manufacturing location is likely to be near the deposit, but which factor determines the choice of the other is a chicken-and-egg question. (3) A specializing strategy is a particular instance of discriminating procurement: several clays are employed, but each is selected for specific use-related properties in making different kinds of pottery. (4) A compounding strategy involves mixing clays to obtain desirable properties; this may be common in areas of residual or primary clays rather than sedimentary clays. (5) Finally, importing strategies involve procuring clay—either directly or through a second party—from very distant sources. This last situation is a nightmare to contemplate in light of traditional provenience objectives and assumptions.

There are numerous inadequacies in this scheme, both as a summary of the ethnographic record and as an aid in interpreting geochemical provenience data. The hypothesis of a single procurement strategy per community, while a convenient assumption for provenience studies, does not take into consideration many other kinds of decisions potters make individually or as a group. Furthermore, although the scheme of procurement strategies may appear to inject the variable of human behavior and selectivity into geochemical provenience studies, it has not been tested with either ethnographic or archaeological data. Its chief contribution thus far is adding the element of relative distance in efforts to model the relations between producer and resources.

In most provenience studies, the socioeconomic questions concerning production—the decision-making, organizational, and social-structural components that are ultimately of archaeological interest—seem to be viewed as epiphenomenal. In this regard it is important to include data on variability in cultural attributes of pottery, such as form, decoration, and thickness, as well as composition, in the study of pottery provenience. Computerized clustering programs are available for analyzing mixed-level (combined quantitative chemical and qualitative cultural) data, and these are very useful in refining provenience interpretations (Rice and Saffer 1982; Philip and Ottaway 1983)). Although identifying specific clay resources used in making specific kinds of pottery may well be an unattainable objective, the decision-making, organiza-

Table 14.3   Comparison of Archaeothermometric Techniques

Technique or Property	Advantages	Disadvantages	Temperature Range
Color (refiring specimens)	Simple Requires no prior knowledge of clay mineral constituents Minimal equipment—kiln and color charts	Sensitive to variations in time and atmosphere Organic material may confuse interpretations Requires damage to or destruction of sample Simple estimate; low accuracy	500°C+
Porosity	May be relatively simple, depending on method used Requires no prior knowledge of clay mineral composition Gives a composite indication of temperature as a function of vitrification	Requires damage to or destruction of sample Results are a function of granulometry Results affected by leaching, mineralization, or recrystallization	900°C+
Mössbauer spectroscopy	Relatively nondestructive Based on iron, a relatively common constituent Gives relatively fine temperature discriminations	Time-consuming Requires comparison with clays Less useful or not applicable with nonferruginous (< 5% Fe) clays	750–1100°C
Electron spin resonance	Useful for low temperatures (< 600°C)	Requires comparison with clays Requires expensive equipment	< 600°C
Petrography Quartz inversion		Must have quartz inclusions Unreliable—may not have visible manifestations in pottery Destructive—requires thin sectioning	~ 573°C
Anisotropy of matrix	Observations can be made in connection with general petrographic study	Requires thin sectioning and petrographic microscope	< 850°C
Calcite decomposition	Can be observed without a petrographic microscope	Calcite must be present Range of decomposition is wide	700–900°C

tional, or social-structural components of the economic process of production and distribution are well worth additional scrutiny.

14.3   Archaeothermometry: Estimating Firing Temperature

One aspect of pottery manufacture that has received considerable attention is archaeothermometry, the determination of the temperature at which the pottery was fired, sometimes also called the initial firing temperature (or ift). The subject has been the focus of an international symposium in Berlin, Ceramic Firing Temperatures and Their Determination through Experimental Archaeology (Hoffman and Goldmann 1979, cited in Matson 1982, 21). A wide variety of analytic methods have been brought to bear on this problem (table 14.3), including observations of physical and chemical properties, but most procedures address the mineralogical characteristics of the pottery. Some of the common approaches to pottery-firing temperature are surveyed below; more detailed discussion of the characterization techniques themselves is provided in chapters 11, 12, and 13.

Table 14.3 *(cont.)*

Technique or Property	Advantages	Disadvantages	Temperature Range
Scanning electron microscope	Provides information on both degree of vitrification and firing temperature Does not require comparable information on clays	Expensive equipment Destruction of sample (for refiring)	800°C+
X-ray diffraction	Provides both low- and high-temperature firing estimates Especially useful on illites, 500–950°C Especially useful on calcareous clays	Must know clay mineral constituent(s) Not good on kaolinites, 600–1000°C No information on vitrification Complex equipment	Best below 500° or above 900°C
Thermal reactions			
Differential thermal analysis (DTA)	Useful for low to midrange firing temperatures	Must know clay mineral constituent(s) Estimates complicated when other mineral constituents (temper) react thermally Not for high-temperature estimates	250–900°C
Thermal gravimetric analysis (TGA)		Must know clay mineral constituent(s) Useful only at a narrow temperature range No information on vitrification Elaborate equipment No low- or high-temperature estimates	500–700°C
Thermal expansion analysis	Accurate to ± 30°C Good for high temperatures Detects vitrification in addition to temperature	Problems with "bloating" Requires correction for deviation of rate of heating Very complex process of refiring Problems if calcite is present	800°C+

Note: See text for explanation.

14.3.1 Physical Properties

Perhaps the simplest procedures for estimating the original conditions of firing of prehistoric pottery relate to the physical properties of color and porosity. These properties are usually measured by refiring sherd fragments in a laboratory under controlled conditions (rate of temperature increase, atmosphere, soaking period, etc.). The principle is that after a clay has been heated to several hundred degrees Celsius or above and then cooled, the physical and chemical transformations its constituents experience will be halted or frozen at the point of maximum heating. These processes will not be resumed upon reheating—thus continuing to alter the properties of the sherd—until this temperature is exceeded. If a sherd can be sacrificed for destructive analysis, it can be broken into several fragments and each one refired in an appropriate atmosphere in an electric kiln at a different temperature. The widest possible range of temperatures is desirable for refiring, for example, using 50° or 100° increments from 400 to 1000°C or above (see Hammond 1971, 15–16). (Refiring experiments are also useful for estimating the original firing temperatures of glazed wares: small fragments of the glaze are heated, e.g., in a heating microscope, and the temperature is noted when they soften and melt into a bead.)

To use color for estimating original firing temperature, the color of the original sherd is measured (see chap. 11) and then compared with the refired sequence. If, for example, there is little to no change in color of fragments refired at 700°C or less, but marked changes occur in those refired to 800°C and above, then it is likely that the sherds were originally fired at between 700 and 800°C. Depending on the change in value (grayness) of the color after refiring, it may or may not be possible to say something about the general atmosphere (oxidizing or nonoxidizing) of original firing.

In heavily carbonaceous clays, color changes may not take place until after the organic matter has burned out, which may require a relatively long duration and/or high temperature of firing (sec. 4.2.1). In such cases it will be very difficult to interpret the refiring data accurately as distinguishing between the original temperature of firing, the atmosphere of firing, and its duration. The utility of refiring tests can be enhanced if local clays have been collected and fired in a temperature sequence, for the resultant data then form a background or standard for comparison of color development of refired sherds as a function of firing temperature (as well as time and atmosphere).

Refiring tests are probably not particularly useful at temperatures below 500°C (and perhaps not below 700°C), because at or below these temperatures the color changes are likely to be largely a function of organic content. Refiring color changes were successfully employed by Matson (1971) as part of a larger study of the original firing temperatures of Seleucia pottery and figurines, and they revealed that different firing techniques were used for each category. In his study, Matson found that another property useful for estimating the firing temperature of sherds—especially by comparison with local clays—was the percentage of weight lost on refiring; changes in hardness were concluded to be of limited value (cf. Fabre and Perinet 1973).

Porosity is another physical property that has some utility for estimating firing temperature, again by comparing the original value with that obtained on refired sherd fragments. As a clay begins to sinter and vitrify during firing at elevated temperatures, its pores begin to shrink (secs. 4.3.1 and 12.2); apparent porosity thus decreases with increasing temperature of firing. The original apparent porosity of the sherds is measured, then fragments are refired under controlled conditions at a sequence of temperature intervals likely to span the original firing temperature. After cooling, apparent porosity is remeasured on the fragments. The lowest temperature that marks a change in porosity, that is, the point at which the percentage of moisture absorbed begins to decrease, exceeds that at which the sherd was probably fired. A series of seventeenth-century "red biscuit ware" sherds from England were refired above 850°C and the changes in porosity were measured; it was estimated that the original firing temperatures had been in the range of 1000–1175°C (Plant 1970). In another study, porosimetry was one of several techniques used for estimating the initial firing temperature of fifty-seven European sherds

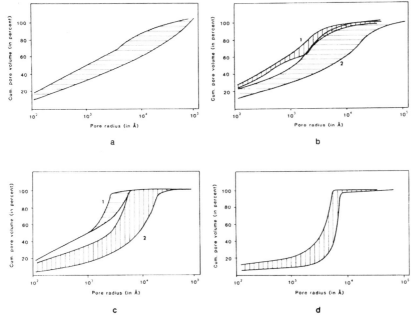

Figure 14.3   Pore-size distribution of pottery fired at different initial firing temperatures (ift): *a,* coarse Dacian sherds with ift of 500–600°C; *b,* coarse pottery with ift approximately 700°C (b1, Romanian and Assyrian, b2, Dacian); *c,* fine pottery with ift of about 900°C (c1, Celtic pottery, c2, Hellenistic, Roman, and Dacian pottery); *d,* fine Roman and Dacian pottery with ift above 900°C. After Morariu, Bogdan, and Ardelean 1977, figs. 1–4.

(Morariu, Bogdan, and Ardelean 1977). Distributions of pore sizes (the pore structure) could be correlated with firing time/temperature characteristics, revealing that better (higher) firing results in smaller average pore size and a more homogeneous pore structure with a narrower size distribution (fig. 14.3).

Porosity measurements will not provide useful estimates of firing temperature on extremely low-fired sherds (below 500–600°C), because changes in porosity may be affected by postdepositional leaching and rehydration of clay minerals, and also by granulometry (Courtois 1976; Magetti 1982, 126, 129; Plant 1970). The method is most appropriate for relatively high-fired wares, those fired at 900°C or more; under some conditions it may be useful as low as 800°C.

Another physical (and mineral) property that can give a clue to relative firing temperature is the state of carbonate minerals in the pottery. If a ware is tempered with calcite or uncalcined shell and is fired to approximately 750°C or above, the $CaCO_3$ will dissociate, which can cause spalling of the surfaces (known as lime popping), as the particles of CaO remaining later rehydrate from normal atmospheric humidity. With firing temperatures of 900°C or higher, however, the CaO reacts with other constituents and does not cause spalling. If the surfaces of calcite-tempered vessels show conical spalls with white specks at their centers (see Vitelli 1984, figs. 1 and 2), it can be inferred that the firing temperature was between 750 and 900°C (see Magetti 1982, 128).

14.3.2   Chemical Analysis

One method of chemical analysis used in estimating firing temperatures of ancient pottery is Mössbauer spectroscopy (see sec. 13.3.2.7), which is especially useful for analyzing changes in the Fe_2O_3/FeO ratio with firing. Two features of the Mössbauer spectrum are important in archaeothermometric studies: the separation of the two lines of the doublet peaks of the Fe^{2+} and Fe^{3+} ions ("quadrupole splitting") and the line positions of magnetic iron oxides and hydroxides (magnetic ratio). To estimate the firing temperature of prehistoric sherds, the Mössbauer spectra obtained for sherds must be compared with spectra measured on local clays likely to have been used in manufacture of the pottery. Mössbauer spectroscopy is relatively new in archaeological applications, and there is some suggestion that it may provide relatively fine temperature discriminations, especially at or above 900°C (Maniatis, Simopoulos, and Kostikas 1982; see also Bouchez et al. 1974).

Electron spin resonance (ESR) has been in use for many years in solid state physics but has only recently begun to be applied to archaeometric problems, in particular to determining pottery firing temperatures (Warashina, Higashimura, and Maeda 1981) and to dating (Ikeya 1978). ESR detects atomic-level magnetic moments, which include paramagnetic ions such as the transition metal or rare earth ions, and also other electronic states with unpaired electronic spins, such as electrons trapped at anion vacancies and similar defects in the crystal lattice, or oxygen ions with a missing electron. In the presence of a magnetic field, microwave-frequency electromagnetic radiation is absorbed by these atomic magnetic moments. In practice the specimen is subjected to microwaves of a given frequency and the magnetic field is varied, resulting in an absorption spectrum that has magnetic field instead of frequency as the variable. The various ions and defects absorb at characteristic values of the magnetic field. The absorptions are usually not single peaks but complex patterns that depend on the crystalline surroundings, again adding to the power to characterize the ion or defect and to locate it within the crystal structure. Differences in valence state produce easily recognizable differences.

Firing-temperature studies observe changes in valence or crystal structure through changes in the ESR spectra as the clay is fired and the various reactions occur. To estimate the firing temperature of a particular sherd or set of sherds, two techniques are available. In the first, samples of the clay the pottery was made from must be available. Archaeothermometric estimates are made by comparing the ESR after a series of firings of the clay with the ESR of the pottery. The initial firing temperature of the pottery is the temperature of firing of the clay that gives the best match. In the other technique, the pottery is refired at successively higher temperatures and the temperatures at which major changes in peak intensities occur suggests the original firing temperature of the ceramic.

14.3.3   Mineralogy

By far the most common approaches to determining ancient firing temperatures are based on the mineralogy of the sherd. Some of these use microscopic techniques, another uses X-ray diffraction, and several are founded on thermal changes in the mineral components of the clays.

With respect to optical petrographic methods (sec. 13.2.1), one possibility for low-fired pottery is the alpha-beta quartz inversion, which occurs at about 573°C. This inversion is accompanied by a slight expansion of the mineral, which might be expected to cause cracking of either the mineral or the surrounding matrix. Shepard (1936, 424–25), however, notes that in all the sherds she has examined she has never seen any petrographic changes in the pots or in the quartz itself that would correlate with this transformation. This is partly because the change in the quartz is reversible, but more significant is that at temperatures in the range of 575–600°C the fabric is still highly porous and is undergoing a series of expansion and shrinkage changes as the clay minerals dehydrate.

Another point of observation is the anisotropy or isotropy of the clay matrix; an anisotropic matrix is nonvitrified and retains its optical properties (chiefly birefringence), suggesting firing temperatures below the vitrification point (below ca. 850°C; Brisbane 1981, 234, citing Peacock 1971). Experiments suggested that kaolin becomes isotropic (vitrified) at higher temperatures than montmorillonite (Shepard 1936, 428; see also sec. 4.2.2), but since pottery is usually a mixture of clay minerals this is not likely to be an accurate clue to firing temperature.

Changes in the properties of the micas—chlorite, muscovite (Shepard 1936, 427), and "black" mica (biotite; Sabine 1958, cited in Williams 1983, 305)—have also been used as a basis for estimating firing temperature. Similarly, the transformation from green to brown hornblende at approximately 750°C can suggest whether the original firing was above or below this temperature (McGovern 1986, 35).

More success has been achieved with scanning electron microscope (SEM) techniques (sec. 13.4.1.1). The SEM has been used to examine the internal morphology, especially the extent of vitrification and pore structure, and compare these features on sherds and refired specimens. This procedure was tested on a set of sherds, all Near Eastern pottery types manufactured from calcareous clays. The SEM investigation showed that the collection could be divided into four groups differentiated by firing temperature ranges estimated by the degree of vitrification (Tite and Maniatis 1975a). It is not necessary to know beforehand the chemical or mineralogical composition of the sherds being tested, nor is it necessary to have local clays for comparison. Because fragments of the sherds are refired for analysis, this method can be supplemented by other observations such as color and especially porosity, which also is affected by vitrification. There is some question about the effectiveness of this method at certain temperature ranges; for example, below 800°C there is little precision to the estimates, because vitrification has not begun, and in calcareous clays there is little variability in extent of vitrification between 850 and 1050°C (Tite et al. 1982, 112).

Determination of ancient firing temperatures by X-ray diffraction (sec. 13.2.2) is based on changes that take place in clays upon heating. As discussed in chapter 4, when clay minerals are heated, progressive dehydroxylation changes their crystalline structure and the spacing of the atomic planes.

The temperatures at which these changes occur differ among the clay minerals. If the specific clay mineral composition of a particular piece of pottery is known, the temperature of firing can be determined by identifying the thermally induced crystalline transformations that have taken place in the mineral as an indication of firing temperatures met or exceeded. X-ray diffraction can be used for both low- or high-temperature firing, but it is not very satisfactory at intermediate temperatures of 500–900°C. At low firing temperatures—below 500°C when the clay still retains part of its lattice structure—the method is relatively straightforward; it tells the clay mineral(s) present and the thermally induced changes that have taken place, so one can infer firing temperature. Firing temperatures above 900°C can be estimated either by identifying the high-temperature minerals such as mullite or cristobalite that recrystallize from the clay and other minerals present or by other mineral phases that form at known high temperatures owing to large amounts of elements such as manganese or especially calcium in the system (Bimson 1969; Perinet 1960; Magetti 1982).

Between approximately 500 and 800/900°C the crystal lattice of clay minerals is generally lost, and the resultant amorphous material will not usually diffract X rays, so the technique is of dubious utility for archaeothermometric purposes. This is not universally true, however, as Magetti (1982) has shown. Although kaolinite is generally useless for estimating firing temperature between 600 and 1000°C, illite clays are informative between 500 and 950°C, and in calcareous clays the formation of calcium silicates in the range of 850–900°C provides another clue to ancient firing temperatures.

14.3.4   Thermal Analysis

Several methods of determining firing temperatures of ancient pottery measure the thermal behavior, principally physical changes, occurring when clay minerals are heated under laboratory conditions. Differential thermal analysis, thermogravimetric analysis, and thermal expansion analysis are all closely related (sec. 13.2.3).

Differential thermal analysis, or DTA, measures changes in the temperature of a pottery sample while it is being heated to approximately 1000°C. These changes are measured against the temperature of a standard, an inert or nonthermally reactive substance such as aluminum oxide (Al_2O_3) that is heated at the same time, and the differences are recorded as a series of peaks. Positive peaks indicate higher temperatures in the pottery than in the standard and register exothermic (heat-producing) reactions; examples are the combustion of organic matter and the formation of high-temperature minerals. Negative peaks mark lower temperatures in the pottery than in the standard and denote endothermic (heat-absorbing) reactions such as loss of mechanically and chemically combined water. The changes that occurred in the clay mineral during the original firing will leave no record of peaks on experimental reheating, and thus significant temperature differentials between sample and standard begin when the original firing temperature is exceeded.

There are several problems in using DTA to estimate firing temperature.

Sherds fired above approximately 900–1000°C (or to vitrification) have had their clay structure altered to such a degree that DTA is not useful. Also, to identify the peaks and reactions one must know the clay mineral constituents, because the same reactions occur at different temperatures in different minerals. In relatively low-fired vessels in which these changes occur, the process can be used to identify the minerals and thus estimate the firing temperature.

Related to this issue is the common belief that clays fired between 500 and 800°C lose their crystalline structure almost completely, so that mineral and mineral-based archaeothermometric determinations cannot be made. Recent work by Magetti (1982), however, has shown that these limitations may vary with individual clay minerals, and Kingery (1974) has shown that sherds fired in this temperature range may rehydrate, making such measurements possible (see also Grim and Bradley 1948). Thus the range of DTA for estimating firing temperatures may be broader than previously supposed. Additional extensions (or complications) of the technique may exist where other minerals in the clay, for example, added as temper, also undergo thermal reactions; although knowing the temperatures at which these reactions occur may be useful in estimating firing temperature, there may be confusion in separating them from clay minerals (see Isphording 1974, 482).

Thermogravimetric analysis (TGA) is in some ways comparable to DTA, for it measures changes in a clay during controlled reheating, but in this case the changes recorded are not in temperature but in weight. The important change accompanies the dehydroxylation of the clay, the loss of chemically combined water, and this occurs typically in the range of 500–700°C. A change in the sample weight, indicating water loss in that temperature range, means the sherds were not originally fired to a temperature high enough to dehydrate them completely, and the original firing temperature was below 500–700°C. Confounding the interpretation of these temperature ranges, of course, is the fact that the clay may rehydrate during burial (see Flamini and de Lorenzo Flamini 1985). Like DTA, TGA requires that the clay mineral constituent(s) be known (see Schweizer 1971).

Measuring thermal expansion is yet another way to estimate original firing temperatures (see Tite 1969). The variable recorded in this procedure is the expansion and shrinkage that occur when a clay or sherd sample is heated under controlled conditions. This heating erases any changes that might have taken place in the sherd during deposition. The sherd exhibits the normal linear thermal expansion as the temperature rises and then begins to expand more rapidly at about 573°C because of the alpha-beta quartz inversion (assuming the presence of quartz). At some higher temperature, the expansion ceases and shrinkage begins. The temperature where shrinkage begins (T_a, the shrinkage temperature) signifies the beginning of sintering, and at this point the laboratory refiring has exceeded the temperature of the original firing. The sherd is then heated a second time to a temperature 50°C above the temperature at which shrinkage was noted and held for one hour, then the temperature at which shrinkage begins is remeasured. One can estimate the original firing temperature from the first shrinkage temperature by calculating the difference between them from the difference between the second firing and shrinkage temperatures.

If shrinkage begins at a temperature immediately higher than the 573°C quartz inversion, the vessel probably was not originally fired at a temperature high enough to start vitrification, and thus thermal expansion can only reveal that the firing temperature was less than 700°C. Thermal expansion analysis is therefore useful only for relatively high-temperature firings (>800°C), in which the beginning of shrinkage signals the resumption of the sintering process as the original firing temperature is exceeded. Experiments with thermal expansion analysis on European, Greek, Near Eastern, and Chinese pottery (Tite 1969, 141; see also Roberts 1963; Heimann 1982) have yielded estimates of firing temperatures as high as 1200°C for Ubaid pottery and 1000–1200°C for Samian ware, with accuracies of ± 20–30°C.

14.3.5 Summary

A great deal of analytical expertise has been devoted to developing ways to assess the original firing temperature of a sherd. Yet each method has particular drawbacks, and indeed a number of problems are inherent in the entire enterprise.

One difficulty is that many of these methods depend upon prior knowledge of the clay mineral constituents of the sherd. Many sherds are composed of several clays (together with a variety of mineral inclusions), and the multiplicity of peaks involved in X-ray diffraction and thermal methods can make the results difficult to interpret. In addition, many of these mineral-based methods are not useful for firing temperatures above 500–700°C.

A related problem is that the instrumental methods often focus primarily on temperatures in the range of low firing, below 600°C, while others are best suited to estimating temperatures above 900°C. It is difficult to find techniques that are reliable in the 600–900°C range.

Regardless of temperature range, the accuracy of the methods usually has an uncertainty anywhere between ± 30 and ± 100°C (Tite et al. 1982, 113). This means that if an original firing temperature is estimated to be 800°C, one can really say only that it was probably fired between 700 and 900°C.

Several of the methods, such as SEM and porosity determinations, are particularly useful because they register not only the firing temperature, but also the extent of vitrification. As such, they consider the important roles that microstructure and mineral or chemical additions play in developing the physical properties scrutinized in assessing firing temperature.

By observing vitrification as well as firing temperature, these methods measure not only a technical property of the ceramic but also cultural and functional characteristics. If vitrification is consistently attained, this reflects advanced development of firing control among the potters as well as the society's demand for hard, nonporous vessels. The difficulty is that the temperature at which clays begin to sinter is highly variable, given their refractoriness, impurities, and the atmosphere of firing; vitrification may occur over a temperature range of 200°C (Tite and Maniatis 1975a).

The characteristics of a fired ware, especially its vitrification, are a function not only of the firing temperature but of the duration of firing (both rate of heating and soaking time) and the atmosphere (see chap. 4). Tite and Mani- atis (1975a, 122) have pointed out that if a vessel was fired in a reducing rather than an oxidizing atmosphere, the actual firing temperature could be as much as 50°C lower than the experimental estimate; if it was fired with a shorter heating and soaking time, the temperature of firing may be 50°C higher than the estimate.

In addition, Roberts (1963) notes that if ancient firings were at all like con- temporary nonindustrial firings, the vessels were probably heated to a peak temperature and then, rather than being held at that temperature for any length of time, allowed to cool almost immediately. Much of the sintering may therefore have taken place at temperatures that were high but below the maxi- mum. Regardless of whether temperatures were sufficient to initiate sintering, the temperatures attained in nonindustrial firings—bonfires and kilns alike— are apt to fluctuate considerably. Even within kilns, temperature differentials of as much as 100°C may exist from top to bottom or from the center to sides (see, e.g., Mayes 1961, 1962).

A last point is that many postdepositional processes—leaching, mineral re- crystallization, rehydration—may affect the properties measured to estimate the firing temperatures of clay vessels. Thus what are measured are the cur- rent properties of the sherd; but one may ask whether these are equivalent to the ancient properties and hence a valid basis for estimating firing temperature.

The final character of a fired clay product will depend on its composition (the clay minerals and the kind, amount, and size of impurities), the time of firing (rate of heating, soaking time, total firing time), and the atmosphere of firing. All of these may be highly variable in nonindustrial pottery manufac- ture. With all this in mind, it is appropriate to question the significance of firing-temperature estimates for single sherds (Tite 1969, 141) and to ask, as Tite et al. (1982, 113) have done, why there is such a need to determine the precise temperature of firing. It is not intrinsically significant or necessary to know how high any individual sherd was fired. Rather, the consistent attain- ment of a particular firing range or level within a particular category of ce- ramic provides a useful clue to potters' general control over the firing process and the desired qualities of the products.

One must remember, however, that to focus on a single aspect of firing tech- nology, such as temperature, can be misleading, because the final product de- pends on the interaction of many variables, not all of which were necessar- ily rigorously controlled. The concept of "equivalent firing temperature" (Roberts 1963, 21; Tite 1969) has been suggested as more appropriate than attempting to determine precise temperatures of prehistoric firings. Similarly, the notion of "work heat" (Nelson 1984, 270) calls attention to the need to consider both temperature and time in understanding the character of a finished ceramic object.

14.4 Dating and Authentication

One of archaeologists' traditional objectives in excavating ancient sites is to date them, and pottery has long been an important tool in chronology build- ing. Its abundance at archaeological sites throughout the world, its many functions, easy transportability, and endless shapes and decorations all combine to make pottery a very sensitive instrument for delineating stylistic changes through time and for tracing cultural relation. Thus pottery is often used for dating other things—construction episodes, burials, occupation layers, and so forth—by its associations. In many cases, however, it is necessary to determine the date of manufacture of a vessel itself, either as an aid in dating sites and burials by association or to prove the vessel's antiquity and authenticity in situations where modern forgery is suspected.

Two categories of dating methods are used in archaeology: relative and chronometric (Michels 1973; Michael and Ralph 1971; Fleming 1976). Relative dating suggests whether an object is younger or older than something else or contemporaneous; the date is not in calendar years. Chronometric (or absolute) dating does provide an age in years for the object; this is often accompanied by a plus-or-minus statistical and—if properly done—systematic error factor (standard deviation) of the estimated date. The date is then properly read as a range of time within which it is likely that the object was made and used. Radiocarbon dating is a common chronometric technique in archaeology.

Late

Early

14.4.1 Relative Dating

Relative dating has two major subdivisions, cross-dating and sequence dating, and both have long had important applications for prehistoric pottery.

In artifact cross-dating, a particular pottery or stone or metal object well known at one site or region is recovered at another, showing that the two sites or areas are approximately contemporaneous. A useful concept in cross-dating is the horizon style, a recognizable art style that has a very wide geographical distribution and a relatively brief temporal duration (see Willey and Phillips 1958, 32). Horizon styles may be represented by portable artifacts (such as pottery) that might have been trade objects, or they may appear in styles of buildings, burials, or manufacturing technologies that indicate movement of people (artisans) or ideas or both over a wide area.

An important example of sequence dating is seriation, which in its simplest sense means ordering items in a series. One basis for the ordering is similarities in decorative or formal attributes of the pottery, and this kind of seriation is called "similiary seriation" (Rowe 1961). Stylistic similiary seriation of pottery is particularly associated with Sir Flinders Petrie (1899) in his study of nine hundred predynastic Egyptian burial lots (fig. 14.4) and was subsequently applied to American materials by Kroeber (1916) in the Southwestern United States.

Seriation becomes a dating method when the sequence is interpreted as the temporal dimension. In this usage it is not the stylistic similarities that are of interest, but rather how frequently particular categories of pottery occur at the

Figure 14.4 One of the earliest examples of stylistic similiary seriation, Sir Flinders Petrie's chronological ordering of Predynastic Egyptian tombs was based on associated pottery. After Sharer and Ashmore 1979, fig. 10.3.

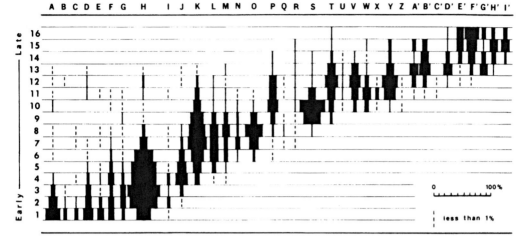

Figure 14.5 A typical example of a frequency seriation of thirty-five pottery types (A–I) in sixteen levels (1–16) in a midden, the levels arranged chronologically by stratigraphic order. The increase and decrease in popularity of each type through time results in a lens-shaped or "battleship-shaped" pattern. After Sharer and Ashmore 1979, fig. 10.2.

different locations being seriated. In a graph of time versus frequency, ordering these data yields a series of lens-shaped or "battleship-shaped" curves for each category (fig. 14.5), in which the width is proportional to the changing occurrence of the category through time as it grows and then declines in popularity (e.g., Ford 1962). As seriation has become increasingly quantitative, the frequencies of artifactual categories may be transformed into abundance, similarity, or dissimilarity matrices by calculating coefficients of similarity or dissimilarity of the data (see Orton 1980, 81–88). It is then possible to use a variety of multivariate statistical procedures (see Michels 1973, 66–82) such as multidimensional scaling to determine if there is any linear or scalar component to the data (see Matson and True 1974; Drennan 1976).

In all types of seriation, it is important to remember that because it is only a relative dating method, seriation does not provide an absolute date for any point in the continuum. Indeed, to be effective at all a seriation must have one end anchored to provide either a known starting point or ending point (a terminus post or ante quem) of the ordering. Furthermore, time is only one interpretation of the underlying linearity, and other continua—such as geographic distance—may order seriated data.

In historical times, workshop or factory records or other data may provide detailed information on when particular kinds of pottery were available, and this has been incorporated into a formula for dating sites bearing this pottery. The mean ceramic date formula (South 1977, 215–74) was developed to date historical-period sites in the Americas and requires knowing such information for European pottery types found at these sites. The formula uses the following equation:

$$Y = \frac{\sum_{i=1}^{n} X_i \cdot f_i}{\sum_{i=1}^{n} f_i},$$

where Y = mean ceramic date, X_i = median date for a given type (known through records), f_i = frequency of each type, and n = number of types in the sample. This formula, in other words, dates an occupation by the weighted mean of the dates of the European pottery. Besides the requirement of knowing the range of dates for each type, the formula is most successfully applied to samples of large size. Although originally developed for use with well-dated European types, it has also been used to date protohistoric and historical-period aboriginal sites (Grange 1984).

A similar principle underlies pipestem dating (Binford 1962b), which uses the fact that the stem holes of the kaolin tobacco pipes found at early historical sites in North America get progressively smaller between 1620 and 1800. The mean diameter of pipestems found at a particular site is calculated and substituted in a regression formula of diameter versus years, yielding the mean date of the sample.

14.4.2 Chronometric Dating

Chronometric techniques yield dates in absolute time, in either calendar years or calibrated years. These dating methods are applicable to a wide variety of archaeological materials, including organic materials (radiocarbon dating), obsidian (hydration dating), wooden beams (dendrochronology), and magnetic iron oxides (archaeomagnetic dating), to name a few. Of the many chronometric dating methods available to archaeologists, three are of varying usefulness with ceramic materials: radiocarbon, archaeomagnetism, and thermoluminescence dating (see also Waddell and Fountain 1984 for a discussion of the Ca-diffusion method).

14.4.2.1 RADIOCARBON DATING

Radiocarbon dating is one of several chronometric techniques based on the radioactive decay of certain isotopes (atoms of a given element having the same number of protons in their nuclei but different numbers of neutrons and very slightly different chemical properties). This dating method utilizes the ratio of radioactive ^{14}C and the stable isotope of carbon, ^{12}C, in the world's carbon exchange reservoir. ^{14}C is formed by cosmic rays in the upper levels of the earth's atmosphere. Oxidized to carbon dioxide, it circulates rapidly throughout the lower atmosphere, including the air and oceans, and is incorporated in all terrestrial life through photosynthesis.

The archaeological dating method (Fleming 1976, 56–85; Ralph 1971; Ralph, Michael, and Han 1973) is based primarily on this latter process: living organisms, particularly plants, constantly take in carbon dioxide that has a known proportion of radioactive ^{14}C to stable ^{12}C. When the organism dies, this exchange process ceases; the ^{14}C trapped within the organism meanwhile continues to decay to ^{14}N (with the emission of a beta particle) at a known rate, and thus the ratio of ^{14}C to ^{12}C gradually declines. The rate of decay is such that half of the total amount present is lost every 5,730 years (later recalculated to 5,568); this figure represents the element's half-life, which is equivalent to the decay of approximately 1% of the material every 83 years.

The amount of ^{14}C remaining in the ancient specimen to be dated is determined by counting the rate of emission of beta particles as ^{14}C decays to ^{14}N. This figure, taken together with the half-life of radioactive carbon, gives the age of the specimen since it ceased taking in carbon dioxide.

Although radiocarbon dating is most commonly used on wood, bone, shell, or plant materials (Ralph 1971, 3–7), it has also been applied experimentally to pottery containing 1% or more organic matter, such as dung or *caraipé* temper (Ralph 1971, 8; Taylor and Berger 1968). Initial samples showed a very wide range of accuracies, however, some samples being very close to estimated archaeological ages while others ranged between much too old and too young. This called attention to the fact that carbon in a ceramic can arise not only from cultural causes related to the age of the vessel (tempering or use) but also from noncultural causes such as incorporation of organics in the original clay deposit or postdepositional alteration of the sherds, including post-1944 "bomb" carbon (DeAtley 1980). In addition, because of the generally low organic content of pottery, as much as several kilograms of sherds need to be crushed to obtain sufficient samples for dating. Recently, however, ^{14}C content has been measured by accelerator or high-energy mass spectrometry (AMS/HEMS) using instruments consisting of a tandem van de Graf accelerator coupled with a mass spectrometer (Taylor et al. 1984, 352). This technique has a much better signal-to-noise ratio than beta counting and hence can deal with much smaller amounts of carbon and much older samples. This sensitivity makes radiocarbon dating of ceramics a practical reality.

14.4.2.2 ARCHAEOMAGNETIC DATING

Archaeomagnetic dating is based on thermoremanent magnetism (TRM) of the ferrimagnetic minerals widely present in clays or clayey soils. In unfired clays, the direction of magnetization of individual grains of hematite and magnetite is random, but when the clay is heated to a dull red heat, the magnetization direction changes as a result of thermal agitation. Some of the grains will be magnetized parallel to the earth's magnetic field. On cooling that magnetic orientation remains in place (thermoremanent magnetism). The resultant magnetic field may also be useful in locating buried and hence invisible subterranean kilns or other burned features through proton magnetometry (see Aitken 1961, 20–28).

For dating, either the direction or the intensity of the thermoremanent magnetism may be measured to determine the date of the heating event and hence the antiquity of the object.

The direction of magnetism is defined in terms of declination (the angle between magnetic north and geographic north) and inclination (the angle between the magnetic field direction and the horizontal plane). Thus, to date objects by the magnetic direction method, the objects must be in situ and undisturbed since the heating. Furthermore, this method requires that the unknown be compared against an independently established (dated) "secular variation" curve that traces the long-term changes in declination and inclination within a particular region, because both properties are extremely localized (dependent on latitude and longitude).

Archaeomagnetic dating by magnetic direction can be used to date kilns or other burned areas associated with ancient firing (e.g., Aitken and Weaver 1962), but it is not satisfactory with portable materials. The method requires samples of burned material about 10 by 10 cm, and they should be removed from their location by someone well trained to make precise measurements of the orientation of the in situ samples before removal.

Magnetic intensity can also be used for dating. Intensity varies with latitude (being greater at the poles than at the equator) and, like magnetic direction dating, must have an independent secular variation curve. Because it does not require information on the orientation of the sample, intensity dating has the advantage of not needing in situ specimens, so it can be applied to individual pottery vessels, figurines, bricks, or sherds (see Aitken 1958; Aitken and Weaver 1962, 4–5). It is a destructive method, however, requiring a few cubic centimeters of material that is heated to successively higher temperatures; thus it is not suitable for dating display specimens.

Regardless of which technique is used, the success of archaeomagnetic dating depends on many factors, not the least being detectable changes in the secular variation curve within a particular archaeological period. For example, dating kilns of the Roman period in Europe (A.D. 50–350) by this method has shown little promise because there is little or no change in magnetic declination and inclination (Tite 1972, 147).

One difficulty with the intensity method arises from the dependence of TRM on the oxidation state of the iron: when sherds are successively reheated their oxidation state may change. For example, gray or black sherds, which may contain reduced iron, will gradually be oxidized at the low temperatures of reheating for magnetic dating. If the iron is already oxidized, the problem may be less severe. A related difficulty is caused by reduction in the size of magnetic particles when minerals in low-fired clays are rehydrated in the burial environment (see Enriquez, Danon, and Beltrao 1979; Barbetti et al. 1977). Finally, it has been found that most pottery exhibits an "intrinsic anisotropy" in acquiring magnetization that is related to preferred orientation of particles and the method of forming the ware, and these anisotropy effects require some correction (Aitken et al. 1981).

The intensity method is best applied to pottery that has been oxidation-fired at temperatures well above 600°C. The accuracy of the method has been claimed to be within ± 5%–15% (Tite 1972, 146).

14.4.2.3 THERMOLUMINESCENCE DATING

Thermoluminescence (or TL) dating measures the light emitted during experimental heating of a ceramic material to about 500°C. Like magnetic intensity dating, the method can be used on individual ceramic objects rather than their contexts.

Crystalline geological substances are exposed to low levels of ionizing radiation that comes from cosmic rays and, more specifically, from the decay of small amounts of radioactive materials present within them. Part of the energy from this radioactive decay is accumulated and stored as trapped electrons and electron "holes" in imperfections or at impurity ions in the crystal lattice of materials. A "hole" is an electron state that is normally occupied but has the electron missing; obviously, trapped electrons are created simultaneously.

Figure 14.6 Thermoluminescence (TL) glow curves for various pottery samples: *a,* natural glow curve from a fine-grain pottery sample; *b,* glow curve from natural TL (of *a*) plus TL induced by laboratory irradiation; *c,* glow curve from irradiated portion of coarse-grained crystalline minerals extracted from pottery; *d,* glow curve of quartz grains taken from *c* (note intense peak at 110°C and overlapping peaks at 325 and 375°C); *e,* background incandescence. After Fleming 1976, figs. 5.5(*i*) and 5.6.

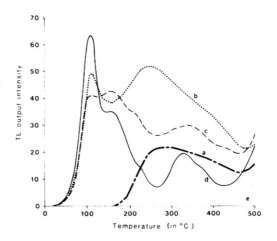

Pottery is usually made from a mixture of clay and inclusions, and all have been accumulating radiation energy since their geological formation. When this mixture is fired to temperatures of approximately 500°C or higher, the heat frees the trapped electrons and holes. They escape, some of them recombining and emitting light or thermoluminescence during the heating process. Firing the pottery in principle (see below) returns the clay and inclusions to a zero level of stored electrons and holes and restarts the accumulation of new trapped electrons and holes in the crystalline imperfections and impurity ions.

Ancient pottery can then be heated experimentally in a laboratory up to a temperature of approximately 500°C (at which point normal incandescence appears as a dull red glow visible to the naked eye). The amount of light emitted in this reheating (plotted in a "glow curve" of intensity versus temperature; fig. 14.6) will be proportional to the age of the piece since its last heating (presumably its original firing), when the geological TL was lost and the baseline was reset (see Fleming 1976, 110–32; Tite 1972, 114–29; Aitken 1985).

Several kinds of radiation impinge on pottery and are important in TL measurements; these include alpha, beta, and gamma rays and small amounts of cosmic radiation. These categories establish the radiation dose received by the pottery since its original firing: they govern the amount of free electrons and holes that will be trapped in imperfections and impurities and hence the TL that will be emitted on experimental reheating.

Alpha, beta, and gamma rays are emitted by radioactive isotopes (primarily ^{238}U, ^{232}Th, and ^{40}K) both within the mineral constituents of the ceramic itself and also within the surrounding burial matrix. They differ, however, in how far they can travel from their emitting sources: gamma rays have a very large range, measurable in centimeters; beta particles may travel up to 2 mm; and alpha particles travel only short distances, from 20 to 50 μm. (The recoil of atomic nuclei after emission of alpha particles is the basis for another dating method, alpha-recoil dating, as measured on muscovite mica inclusions in pottery; see Garrison, McGimsey, and Zinke 1978.) The alpha and beta particles therefore come effectively only from within the ceramic. Gamma and cosmic rays are external sources of radiation coming into the pottery from outside, and of these, gamma rays are by far the more significant. Gamma rays penetrating the pottery originate in impurities in the soil in which the pot was buried, and they may be accumulated from as far as 30 cm around the artifact.

Two techniques are employed primarily in TL dating: the fine-grain technique and the inclusion technique (see Aitken 1985, 17–28). Each emphasizes a different aspect of the composition of the pottery according to grain size, because different size components receive different kinds of radiation. Both techniques require that a sample of the ceramic material be removed, crushed, and carefully separated into size or density fractions, or both, and sometimes the sample is given further treatments (see Bell and Zimmerman 1978 for a discussion of quartz etching, for example). The dating procedure is thus a damaging one, and sample preparation is rather complex for both techniques. It is important to have at least two samples from a single artifact for the multiple steps of the procedure.

The fine-grain technique (Zimmerman 1971) uses very fine particle fractions of 1–5 μm. Particles this tiny are subjected to all the radiation dose components, including alpha, beta, and gamma radiation. The inclusion technique (Fleming 1970) uses larger grains (ca. 90–105 μm and up), chiefly quartz although feldspar is also used (Aitken 1985, 180–83). The major difference between this technique and that using fine particles is that the larger particle size effectively eliminates the contribution of alpha radiation to the experimentally determined dose and subsequent calculations. Other variants of TL sample selection and dating procedures include a subtraction technique (Fleming and Stoneham 1973a; Aitken 1985, 29, 184–85), a radioactive inclusion technique using zircon (Zimmerman, Yuhas, and Meyers 1974; Sutton and Zimmerman 1976; Aitken 1985, 172–78), and a calibration-free technique (Wang and Zhou 1983).

The age of a ceramic as determined by TL is expressed as:

$$\text{Age} = \frac{\text{``Natural'' TL}}{S \times R},$$

where S = sensitivity and R = dose rate. The "natural" TL is the stored TL accumulated since the last heating to about 500°C or above (the pottery firing event). In dating a ceramic by TL, the first step is to heat one sample of an artifact to about 500°C in the laboratory to determine its natural TL or paleodose. The graph of light emitted (as detected by a photomultiplier) versus increasing temperature is called the TL glow curve. This sample is then reheated to determine what proportion of that light was caused by normal incandescence, at temperatures usually beginning about 450°C.

Sensitivity, S, to alpha, beta, gamma, and cosmic radiation is determined by measuring the "induced" TL after additional samples of the artifact have been given a series of irradiations in the laboratory; these irradiated samples are then heated, and their glow curves (combining natural TL plus induced TL) are measured. Such a series is necessary to establish that the sensitivity is independent of dose. Determining the dose rate R requires measuring concentrations of radioactive constituents for each sherd; it also necessitates assessing the contribution of the surrounding burial soil environment, particularly the gamma radiation, usually accomplished by burying a dosimetry monitor in place of the artifact for one year.

It should be noted that each artifact has to be independently calibrated for its own TL sensitivity and dose rate. There is no regional or worldwide standard for dosage for these kinds of radiation.

TL dating of pottery has had, in its most successful applications, an accuracy of about ± 5%–15% (see Aitken and Alldred 1972; Aitken 1976, 1985; Tite and Waine 1962; Fleming and Stoneham 1973b, 244). There have been, however, numerous problems in dosimetry and complicating factors in the relation between TL emission and age (see Fleming 1976, 118–27; Tite 1972, 123–35) that have prevented the technique from achieving its potentially wide use. Among the most useful applications of the TL dating method to clay artifacts has been authenticating important art objects.

An additional obstacle is that TL may be sensitive to original firing temperatures, particularly with reference to the behavior of the quartz inclusions (Han 1975). Thus pottery fired at low temperatures may not have lost all its original geological TL and returned to a zero level; these samples may then yield anomalously early dates. It is not inconceivable that the structural transformations occurring as quartz is heated (see chap. 4) and the ability of low-fired clays to rehydrate and regain their original lattice structures could also play a part here. Finally, there may be complications if the ceramic piece was moved from the fire while it was still hot. These considerations for TL dating also pertain to determinations of original firing temperature (see Handy and Gaines 1975).

14.4.3 Authentication

In many situations an object is dated not for the purpose of dating a broader stylistic phenomenon or an associated cultural occupation, but to determine whether the object itself is a genuine antiquity or a modern forgery. This is a particular concern for museums and art historians, both for verifying the technological, stylistic, iconographic, and historical significance of the object and from a financial viewpoint—to avoid paying substantial sums to acquire, display, and insure art objects that turn out to be falsifications. All manner of evidence is thus brought to bear on the problem of authentication, including scientific dating and characterization techniques.

Falsifying antiquities is not new, and ceramic materials seem particularly susceptible. In the sixteenth-century New World, it is reported that enterprising individuals in the Aztec capital of Tenochtitlan made souvenirs for the Spanish conquerors, and large quantities of fake antique vessels and figurines were made during the nineteenth century (see Batres 1909; Ekholm 1964; Pasztory 1982, 90–92; Boone 1982).

Fakes are sometimes manufactured inexpensively and often rather shoddily and may be sold openly as reproductions. In other cases painstaking effort may be devoted to faithful replication of the original, including experimenting with raw materials for paste and pigments, careful attention to stylistic and iconographic detail, and simulated aging. The sale of well-made forged antiquities is highly lucrative and may develop from a small practical joke (see Bruhns and Hammond 1983) or from a legitimate interest in reproducing an ancient technological process (see Donnan 1982, 50, 142; Sawyer 1982, 33). Although technological and iconographic errors often help experienced authenticators recognize a forgery, in many cases the work is so skillful that it is nearly impossible to determine by stylistic factors alone whether the piece is genuine (see Shaplin 1978, 49–50; Fleming 1973). The problem of stylistic verisimilitude is especially acute if forgers have access to the molds used in forming genuine objects, as is apparently the case with some T'ang unglazed figurines (Fleming 1974).

In such situations one must turn to other means of ascertaining antiquity or authenticity (or both). These two problems are related but distinct: an object may be genuinely old (as opposed to a modern forgery), but authenticity also implies attribution to a particular culture or artisan, which is a separate matter. In many cases authenticity determinations are special cases of characterization studies.

TL dating has been widely used for determining the age of an object, which is one basis for evaluating its authenticity (see Rogers 1973 for a general discussion; also Aitken, Moorey, and Ucko 1971; Shaplin 1978; Fleming 1974; Zimmerman, Yuhas, and Meyers 1974). In many authentication problems, TL dating is precise enough, for instance, to distinguish a genuinely ancient piece from a relatively recent forgery. For pottery vessels a problem with TL is that the gamma dose rate (or other environmental data) cannot be determined from the surrounding burial medium because the site of recovery of many museum-quality vessels is unknown. The radioactive inclusion technique largely obviates this difficulty, however. Another problem arises if the piece has been refired (e.g., to eliminate fireclouding or enhance its colors) or X-rayed as part of examination of the object, because these processes alter or destroy the natural TL accumulated since the original firing.

Finally, because accuracy rates are sometimes very low (a high spread of values in repeated testing), it may be possible to establish the antiquity of a piece but not to date it precisely enough to establish its authenticity. For example, the core of the bronze horse in the Metropolitan Museum of Art was dated using zircon, quartz, and fine grains. Though it was determined that the piece was indeed old, the wide range of TL dates obtained did not settle whether it is a classic Greek sculpture of the fifth century B.C. (Zimmerman, Yuhas, and Meyers 1974). It is of interest that not only ceramic figurines and vessels but other materials associated with fired clays, such as bronzes with clay casting cores, can be dated by TL (Fleming and Fagg 1977).

Besides TL, a variety of characterization procedures (see chap. 13) have been used to determine the antiquity and authenticity of ceramic objects. X-ray radiography, for example, can reveal whether a ceramic object is complete or has been damaged and then restored with plaster or other substances and repainted (Meyers 1978, 83). Mössbauer spectroscopy has been used to detect forgeries among sixteenth-to-nineteenth-century terra-cotta figurines (Keisch 1974, 201). The glazes on Chinese pottery have been investigated in several ways. X-ray fluorescence, for example, has been used to identify different ratios of manganese and cobalt in blue glazes on a series of Chinese porcelains (Yap and Tang 1984). And microstructural examination of the glazes allows relative dating by the size and structure of the tiny bubbles (Paine and Young 1953).

14.5 References

Adan-Bayewitz and Perlman 1985
Aitken 1958, 1961, 1976, 1985
Aitken et al. 1981
Aitken and Alldred 1972
Aitken, Moorey, and Ucko 1971
Aitken and Weaver 1962
Allen, Luckenbach, and Holland 1975
Arnold 1971, 1974, 1980, 1985
Arnold et al. 1978
Attas, Fossey, and Yaffe 1982
Attas, Yaffe, and Fossey 1977
Balfet, Fauvet-Berthelot, and Monzon 1983
Ballié and Stern 1984
Barbetti et al. 1977
Batres 1909
Bell and Zimmerman 1978
Bennett 1974
Bieber et al. 1976
Bimson 1969
Binford 1962b
Bishop 1975, 1980
Bishop, Harbottle, and Sayre 1982
Bishop and Rands 1982
Bishop, Rands, and Holley 1982
Boone 1982
Borremans and Shaak 1986
Bouchez et al. 1974
Bowman, Asaro, and Perlman 1973
Braun 1982
Brisbane 1981
Brody 1979
Brooks et al. 1974
Bruhns and Hammond 1983
Buko 1984
Butzer 1974
Calver 1957
Catling 1961
Courtois 1976
Cummins 1983
DeAtley 1980
DeBoer and Lathrap 1979
Dixon 1976
Donnan 1982

Doran and Hodson 1975
Drennan 1976
Ekholm 1964
Enriquez, Danon, and Beltrao 1979
Fabre and Perinet 1973
Fillières, Harbottle, and Sayre 1984
Flamini and de Lorenzo Flamini 1985
Fleming 1970, 1973, 1974, 1976
Fleming and Fagg 1977
Fleming and Stoneham 1973a,b
Ford 1962
Franklin and Vitali 1985
Freestone, Meeks, and Middleton 1985
Freeth 1967
Garrison, McGimsey, and Zinke 1978
Grange 1984
Grim and Bradley 1948
Hammond et al. 1977
Hammond 1971
Han 1975
Hancock 1984, 1985
Handy and Gaines 1975
Harbottle 1970, 1975, 1982
Hedges and McLellan 1976
Heimann 1982
Hoffman and Goldmann 1979
Ikeya 1978
Isphording 1974
Jornet, Blackman, and Olin 1985
Keisch 1974
Kingery 1974
Kohl, Harbottle, and Sayre 1979
Kroeber 1916
London 1981
Luedtke 1979
McGovern 1986
Magetti 1982
Maniatis, Simopoulos, and Kostikas 1982
March 1934
Matiskainen and Alhonen 1984
Matson 1971, 1982

Matson and True 1974
Mayes 1961, 1962
Meyers 1978
Michael and Ralph 1971
Michels 1973
Morariu, Bogdan, and Ardelean
    1977
Nelson 1984
Norton 1970
Olin and Sayre 1971
Orton 1980
Paine and Young 1953
Pasztory 1982
Peacock 1970, 1971
Périnet 1960
Perlman 1984
Perlman and Asaro 1969
Petrie 1899
Philip and Ottaway 1983
Plant 1970
Poole and Finch 1972
Porter 1964
Prag et al. 1974
Ralph 1971
Ralph, Michael, and Han 1973
Rands and Bishop 1980
Rapp 1985
Reeves and Brooks 1978
Rice 1976a, 1978b
Rice and Saffer 1982
Roberts 1963
Rogers 1973
Rowe 1961
Rye 1976, 1981
Rye and Duerden 1982
Rye and Evans 1976
Sabine 1958
Sawyer 1982
Sayre, Chan, and Sabloff 1971

Schweizer 1971
Shaplin 1978
Sharer and Ashmore 1979
Shepard 1936, 1942a, 1964, 1965,
    1976
Solheim 1965
South 1977
Stimmell and Stromberg 1986
Stross et al. 1976
Sutton and Zimmerman 1976
Taylor 1977
Taylor and Berger 1968
Taylor et al. 1984
Tite 1969, 1972
Tite et al. 1982
Tite and Maniatis 1975a
Tite and Waine 1962
Tubb, Parker, and Nickless 1980
Vaz and Cruxent 1975
Vitelli 1984
Waddell and Fountain 1984
Wang and Zhou 1983
Warashina, Higashimura, and
    Maeda 1981
Ward 1974
Weaver 1963
Weigand, Harbottle, and Sayre 1977
Whitbread 1986
Widemann et al. 1975
Willey and Phillips 1958
Williams 1983
Wilson 1978
Winther-Nielsen et al. 1981
Woods 1986
Yap and Tang 1984
Zimmerman 1971
Zimmerman, Yuhas, and Meyers
    1974

Epilogue

Turn, turn, my wheel! What is begun
At daybreak must at dark be done,
To-morrow will be another day;
To-morrow the hot furnace flame
Will search the heart and try the frame
And stamp with honor or with shame
These vessels made of clay.

H. W. Longfellow, *Keramos*

Continuity and Change in the Modern World

15

The number of communities of potters who make traditional ceramic forms, using traditional materials and traditional techniques, is fast dwindling. Few if any of these peoples or their craft products have remained untouched during the past six centuries of colonial, missionary, and other institutional expansionism around the globe. Third and Fourth World societies have been rapidly incorporated into twentieth-century international economic and political structures, transforming the potter's craft, or in some cases, bringing its extinction. This chapter examines change and continuity among potters and pottery and their implications for studies of prehistoric pottery.

15.1 Change in Pottery Systems

Although expansionist state societies and institutions have impinged on rural commodity production and distribution for the past four millennia, prehistoric acculturation was not of the same magnitude as the events of more recent history. Since the late fifteenth century, the Age of Exploration, the world has seen the founding of exploitative commercial colonies over the entire globe, transfers of production technology on an unprecedented scale, and most recently, imposition of a worldwide monetary economy.

It is not unreasonable to ask why the changes of the modern world have transformed traditional pottery making. Part of the answer lies in the nature of systems in general and cultural systems in particular: because all the components of any system are related and interactive, changing one changes the others. Thus, with the integration of First, Second, Third, and Fourth World societies into an international economy, the stage is set for far-reaching ramifications into even small-scale rural, nonindustrial economic enterprises such as traditional pottery making (see Barnett 1953 and Foster 1962 for dis-

449

cussions of societal and individual aspects of cultural changes and material innovation). Traditional pottery production is an infinitesimal cog in the international economic wheel, yet even in this insignificant area the repercussions of broader changes are felt.

These social and economic changes are complex and interrelated, occurring at different times and in different ways; there are differences not only from area to area but also from craft to craft within a single region (see papers in Graburn 1976). International economic integration has involved four significant transformations influencing pottery making as well as many other crafts. These include imposition of a cash economy, better communication and transportation facilities, the ready availability of substitutes for traditional utilitarian craft products, and an increase in national and international tourism. Improved methods of industrial manufacture, new products, and more efficient transportation have made cheap, mass-produced articles of plastic, metal, or china more widely available even in rural areas. These articles cannot be easily acquired by traditional methods of exchange or barter, since they are part of the money economy imposed through other means, but handmade craft items such as pottery have provided economically marginal peoples with sources of cash. Furthermore, the growing influx of tourists wanting souvenirs of their travels among "primitive" peoples in exotic locales has meant a steady stream of buyers for these goods.

Although these processes have stimulated interest in pottery making in many places, other independent factors have often operated to the detriment of the craft (see chap. 6). Fuel shortages, for example as a result of deforestation, have played a significant role in the decline or abandonment of pottery making or have required elaborate arrangements to obtain nontraditional fuels, often from some distance. In addition, the lure of urban life—education, jobs, and advancement—has drawn many from the younger generations out of pottery making into alternative economic endeavors, especially in rural regions. In Guinhilaran, Philippines, pottery making has declined in all generations in one family:

> The women, when interviewed, gave the following reasons for quitting pottery making: (1) age, (2) illness, (3) need to do other things such as housework, and (4) the lack of a man to get clay for them. As for the working children it would seem that the availability of better economic opportunities was the deciding factor. This reason is frequently given to explain why male potters will leave off potting for almost any other job. Informants say that women have to be potters since they can't get away from the home. This is, of course, another way of stating that wage work, when available, is open mostly to men. (Scheans 1977, 22–23)

15.1.1   Changes in the Products: The "Arts of Acculturation"

A great deal of the pottery produced today by traditional potters consists of relatively unchanged utilitarian or domestic vessels for local consumption. Much of it, however, shows some transformation to accommodate the modern market, and a large body of this material is regarded as "art" rather than as more prosaic "craft" products. Most of this art falls into a category known as the "arts of acculturation" (Graburn 1976), which subsumes many media, including painting, carving, weaving, jewelry, and other items besides pottery. A variety of additional labels are used for these modern items: some, such as folk, popular, transitional, ethnic, provincial, commercial, urban, or souvenir art, are more or less neutral in their connotations; other terms, such as tourist art and airport art, are distinctly pejorative. Regardless, all emphasize contrasts between the producing and consuming sectors of the society with respect to these products; they call attention to both the stimuli for their development and the transformations that have taken place in the finished objects.

One of the best theoretical statements of how and why changes occur in traditional artisan activities arose from a study of the extinction of aboriginal New World art motifs after the Spanish conquest (Kubler 1961). A critical factor underlying the relative amounts of change is the symbolic content of the art, and this is particularly important for a craft such as pottery, which has varying—but often high—degrees of integration between symbolic and utilitarian forms.

> The triumph of one culture over another is usually marked by the virtual cessation of the art of the vanquished, and its replacement by the art of the conqueror. When the offending objects and monuments finally cease to correspond to any living behavior, they become symbolically inert. They then are "safe" to play with in recombinations emptied of previous vital meanings, as in tourist souvenirs, antiquarian reconstructions, or archaizing revivals.
> . . . The linguistic separation of the populace into Spanish- and Indian-speaking groups strengthened the emerging division of colonial society as exploiting and exploited groups. Under these conditions, all symbolic expressions, including those of native origin, eventually became reinforcements of the power of the colonial state. As such, they are extensions of European art rather than native survivals. (Kubler 1961, 15)

The arts of acculturation have been grouped into a number of classes (Graburn 1976, 5–8), depending on their sources of inspiration (the minority versus the dominant society) and their intended consumers (within or outside the producing society); to some extent, the degree of financial profit versus aesthetic motivation for their creation is also integrated into these categories. Although it is often difficult to demarcate categories, three are perhaps most important with respect to pottery: functional, commercial, and souvenir art or wares.

Functional art or ware is largely directed toward the producing society and consists of pieces that have remained generally faithful to traditional materials, shapes, decorations, and uses in that society. It may be found in areas where relative geographical or cultural isolation has precluded continual economic contacts with tourists or art buyers, or it may be produced along with items that are more clearly oriented to an exterior market. In contrast, both commercial and souvenir art or ceramic wares are directed toward external groups who purchase them. The products represent varying balances of traditional standards against accommodation to a variety of needs of those consumers (or the artisan's perceptions of those needs). Of the two, souvenir or tourist ware is less valued, because standards of production are often lowered so the output will sell profitably (inexpensively and in quantity).

As recognized implicitly, if not always explicitly, to be successful souvenirs should be cheap and portable as well as understandable, dustable, and sometimes useful (Graburn 1976, 15). In accordance with these guidelines, the products of acculturation frequently are markedly different from traditional items, reflecting several trends (e.g., see Graburn 1976, 15–23): miniaturization, elaboration, simplification, secularization, and archaism or falsification. In ceramics these trends affect the products' shapes, sizes, and decorations as well as the kinds and quantities produced.

Miniaturization means making items for commercial sale smaller than normal, a particular advantage that both allows the artisan to transport more of the items to the selling area and lets the tourist buyer (or art dealer) fit more of them into a suitcase. Sometimes the objects are simply scaled-down versions of traditional forms, and sometimes they are actual miniatures (fig. 15.1): tiny jars and bowls that would fit in a dollhouse. In functional categories of wares, smaller utilitarian forms may correlate with acculturation situations, in which social stress is compounded by population dislocations and reductions through war or disease. Alternatively, if nuclear households join into extended family units, vessels may increase in size, as happened in the Southwestern United States, where the capacity of historical period Hopi bowls was as much as 100% larger than that of prehistoric counterparts (Turner and Lofgren 1966, 125).

Elaboration (perhaps better called innovation or syncretization) is the tendency to create entirely new nontraditional objects or to combine new elements with elements of the traditional ware. Sometimes this involves subtle combinations of characteristics. For example, the broad category of aboriginal "Colono-Indian" or "colono ware" pottery (Ferguson 1980), produced in the southeastern United States during the seventeenth and eighteenth centuries, shows a mixing of European shapes with traditional Indian traits as well as African characteristics (especially decoration), probably associated with intermarriage between Europeans and Indians and with African slaves' having been brought into the region. In the Dominican Republic, local Indian potters (perhaps under Spanish direction) produced wheel-thrown and hand-modeled wares exhibiting Arawak designs on European forms (Ortega and Fondeur 1978). Similar syncretism between European and indigenous ceramics has been noted in contact period wares in the Andes (Tschopik 1950, 205), where glazes and European motifs sometimes appear on traditional Inca aryballoid jars, and in sixteenth-century Mexico City (Lister and Lister 1982, 34–40).

In other cases, particularly in response to modern demands, the innovations are more direct, as in forms that replicate Western objects such as ashtrays, candle holders, or planters; they may also include figurines of animals or people. In Chinautla, Guatemala, for example, which had been famous throughout the highlands for large whiteware *tinajas*, the new so-called urban ware (Reina and Hill 1978, 262) now includes crèches, candle holders, doves, chickens, angels, madonnas, ashtrays, and a wide variety of nontraditional bowls, jars, and other containers (fig. 15.2).

Figure 15.1 (*right*) A young potter in Margaurites, Crete, throwing miniature jars "off the hump" on a kick wheel. Photograph by Lynnette Hesser.

Figure 15.2 (*below*) A pottery stall in the main market in Guatemala City, the middle two shelves displaying "urban ware," such as vases, candle holders (including *angelitos*), flowerpots, and a variety of dishes. Note the white slip and appliquéd flower decoration of this pottery, made in the community of Chinautla, to the north of the city. The lower shelf holds utilitarian glazed wares made in the western Guatemala highlands.

Sometimes the innovation is not in ceramic forms but in decoration and may represent a syncretism of materials (the use of acrylic or poster paints), nontraditional motifs (appliquéd grape clusters on some of the Chinautla urban pottery), or techniques (modeled, appliquéd, or painted embellishments added to formerly plain or simply decorated objects). Balfet comments (see Rice 1984b, 293) on the inverse correlation between decoration and technical quality in North Africa: in one kind of pottery known for its excellent technical quality, decoration gradually disappeared, whereas in commercial ceramics based on tourist demand "the decoration spreads across the whole surface, but at the same time the technical quality of the pottery deteriorates."

Inspirations for pottery innovations may come from many sources. The potter's own imagination and experience, including comic books, concrete statues (Scheans 1977, 29), company calendars (Scheans 1977, 112–13), or ancient vessels from museums or nearby archaeological sites often lead to new forms and decorations. Individual buyers frequently give potters drawings or models to copy. More elaborate technical innovations may be stimulated by direct patronage, one of the most famous examples being the development of the first European porcelain in the early eighteenth century under the patronage of Augustus, elector of Saxony (Wykes-Joyce 1958, 136–42).

The trends toward both miniaturization and innovation in modern pottery making—which increase the object's appeal to collectors—have unfortunate consequences for those who wish to study museum collections of ceramics. Many collections tend to emphasize small, unusual, or highly decorated objects (DeBoer 1985, 355–56), which are not necessarily representative of either the range of products manufactured by potters in a given community or the range of objects in household use.

Simplification in pottery refers primarily to changes in finishing and decoration. It is most commonly seen in the reduced attention devoted to particularly time-consuming steps such as burnishing, polishing, slipping, or decorating. Simplification has been widely noted as accompanying social upheavals and dislocations, such as European conquest or contact in central Mexico (Charlton 1968, 98, 1976, 521), Venezuela (Cruxent and Rouse 1959, 58–59), and North Dakota (Deetz 1965).

In modern times, simplification is not necessarily characteristic of products directed toward an art market, since art patrons may pay top prices for well-executed examples of a craft because of their aesthetic value. It does, however, tend to characterize tourist art. Shipibo potters in eastern Peru, for example, known for the very intricate fine-line painted decoration on their wares (fig. 15.3), have increasingly simplified the decoration on tourist pottery, reducing the number of brushstrokes, sometimes omitting the fine-line work entirely and at other times emphasizing broad areas of color to heighten the visual impact of a piece at a distance (Lathrap 1976, 203–4). Simplification within tourist wares has the advantage, for the producers, of speeding up production for an undiscerning market; for their own functional use artisans may maintain higher standards (e.g., Lathrap 1976, 207).

Secularization is the tendency to remove or diminish the symbolic content of objects or their decoration, often as part of a rationale for allowing them to enter a broader exterior market. As a traditional society is transformed and

Figure 15.3 Exterior design of a contemporary Conibo (Peru) *kënpo ani* (a large communal drinking bowl), painted in black and red on white. Diameter 29 cm. After Lathrap 1976, fig. 62.

norms and beliefs break down during acculturation (see Kubler 1961), many sacred objects used in rituals lose their special significance and may be shown or sold to outsiders. Proscriptions still linger on many objects, however, such as Laguna and Acoma Pueblo ceremonial bowls with their distinctive stepped rim, which cannot be sold beyond the in-group (see Gill 1976, 107). Secularization can be linked to formal and decorative simplification or elaboration of traditional shapes and decoration by the symbolic content or messages contained in the elements. To the extent that the symbolic content is in direct conflict with those of the dominant society (e.g., "pagan" religion versus Christianity in certain areas), its survival within the acculturative art will vary. It may be suppressed and disappear if it conflicts sharply (e.g., veneration of "idols" of wood or pottery), or it may undergo a transformation to a more neutral form or be a focal point of regional or ethnic expression (see below).

In archaism and falsification ancient elements—shapes, themes, motifs—are incorporated into later products, although the two processes generally arise from somewhat different motives. Archaism has sometimes been stimulated by anthropologists or archaeologists (Brody 1976, 74) who encourage local potters to adopt ancient styles in order to illuminate their heritage and provide a new source for creative variations. Archaism may also be stimulated by patrons of modern artisans or by dealers in their products, who sometimes have antiquarian intersts. And of course archaism may simply be an expression of the interests of individuals, rather than being suggested by an outsider, resulting from an appreciation of past techniques or technologies and how they were employed. The meaning of the ancient styles has largely been lost, and because they are "symbolically inert" their production is little threat to the dominant society.

While archaism may be born of the purest aesthetic motives, it often enjoys considerable success in the marketplace, and this economic success may give rise to more intensive use of ancient styles: instead of incorporating elements of earlier shapes, techniques, or motifs into contemporary styles, potters may attempt exact duplication of ancient vessels and styles. Such endeavors to create reproductions for sale to museums or tourists may be government sponsored, aiming to encourage the development of local crafts and foster appreciation of their heritage while at the same time providing a suitable alternative to the illegal sale of genuine antiquities. Mexico, for example, has a history of creating reproductions of pottery vessels and figurines, which are stamped with a government stamp and sold at modest prices.

Falsification is the reverse of the coin, in which skilled potters turn out replicas of artifacts that are virtually indistinguishable from genuine antiquities stylistically (see Bruhns and Hammond 1983). The business of making antiques is an old one, as indicated by Père d'Entrecolles's description of the creation of imitation porcelains at Jingdezhen, and making them look old is an important part of the process:

> There is nothing peculiar in the manufacture of these kinds of porcelain beyond that they are covered with a glaze made of yellow stone, mingled with the ordinary glaze, the latter predominating in the mixture, which gives the porcelain a sea green colour. When it is fired it is placed in a very rich broth made of chicken and other meats; in this it is baked a second time, and after that it is put in the foulest drain that can be found and left for a month or more. On issuing from this drain it passes for three or four hundred years old, or at any rate for a representative of the preceding Ming dynasty, when porcelain of this colour and thickness was appreciated at Court.
> (Quoted in Hobson 1976, 83–84)

Forgeries are typically sold as genuine ancient objects, often fetching handsome prices. It is not infrequent that they cannot be identified as forgeries by stylistic criteria, but only by modern dating methods (see sec. 14.4.3).

15.1.2   Changes in the Society

Changes in the quantities, kinds, and attributes of pottery do not occur at random. They are responses to changes within the society that impinge on individual potters as well as on the consumers or users of the ceramic products (see Foster 1965b; Nicklin 1971; Rice 1984b). These social and economic changes may come from within the society or may arise from the relation between the traditional society and the broader national or international community.

As mentioned above, the kinds and quantities of pottery manufactured by traditional potters may change in response to the transition to a cash economy. Potters are typically of lower socioeconomic status, so most often a lack of cash stimulates innovation (see sec. 15.2). Sometimes the availability of cash may spur changes, however. In Dangtalan, Philippines, the sudden cash influx brought by the opening of a gold mine nearby meant that villagers could buy prized plastic water containers instead of ceramic water jars, and the number of such jars in the village declined from eighty-eight in 1976 to fifty-two.in 1980 (Longacre 1985, 345). Similar preference for nontraditional containers is characteristic of Bé, Cameroon (David and Hennig 1972, 25), where both potters and pottery are held in low esteem. In Yucatán, as a result of the decline in demand for traditional pottery in general, the customary pattern of product specialization, in which individual potters make only one or a small number of forms, is breaking down (Thompson 1958, 115).

The effects of acculturation are not confined to changes in production: traditional distribution patterns may be considerably altered as well. For example, the traditional *kula* cycle by which pottery manufactured in the Amphlett Islands was traded to the Trobriand Islands has been disrupted by European politicoeconomic meddling and by the replacement of seagoing canoes with motorized launches (Lauer 1971, 199).

Cash and transportation are certainly powerful motivations, but they are not the only ones. Other forces have a considerable part in fomenting changes in production, and these include value orientations, individualism, and a sense of ethnic identity.

One of the most powerful forces underlying ceramic change in acculturative situations is the difference between the values of the traditional and the dominant societies. A particularly good example is Chinautla, Guatemala, where traditional views of pottery manufacture and other behavior are exemplified by the importance of *costumbre,* or custom. Chinautla is described as a closed corporate community that places great value on traditional practices and conformity to communitywide standards of behavior (Reina 1966; Reina and Hill 1978, 231–51). Proximity to Guatemala City, the capital of the country, with its Ladino consumers and foreign tourists, however, has inexorably drawn the potters of Chinautla into the international economic web. With this opening of the closed community structure, potters have gradually broken away from the restrictions imposed by their *costumbre,* broadening their repertoire of shapes and techniques beyond the traditional *tinajas* that once identified a potter as a good Chinautleca. This has not been an easy transition, because the necessary emphasis on innovation to meet the demands of an urban market has constituted a rejection of *costumbre* and of the corporate identity. For this reason, innovators themselves have been socially rejected (see, e.g., Reina 1963; also Díaz 1966, 213. Another example comes from Sardinia, where a potter who changed the grate in his kiln to a nontraditional type that reduced wastage was ostracized by his colleagues; Annis 1985, 244).

As ceramic products move into a broader economic framework new statuses develop, attracting skilled, ambitious, and innovative individuals by the promise of a more prestigious role in society. Sometimes this may simply constitute an increase in the esteem with which contemporaries regard a particular potter's work; other times a particular artisan or village may draw public acclaim for creating a particular style. The beautiful blackware of San Ildefonso Pueblo in New Mexico, for example, was widely copied after its creation by Maria and Julian Martinez.

Changed status is also illustrated by potters in Los Pueblos, Mexico, where success is measured materially rather than through artistic recognition—by ownership of a truck. Trucks make potters far more independent, and they save labor in all stages of producing and marketing pots, from acquiring and processing the clay to obtaining fuel and transporting the products to market (Papousek 1981, 120).

Related to the changes in value systems and status is a transformation in the role of the individual producer, with a greater emphasis on innovation and effort. Craft production, and the economic success that results, is coming to be seen as an individual matter rather than a manifestation of community solidarity. This trend may be shown in several ways: artisans more often sign their wares, and they may jealously guard their own formulas for forming, decorating, and firing pottery. On an international level, the competition and intrigue surrounding the beginnings of porcelain manufacture in Europe in the eighteenth century probably constitute the most extreme example (Wykes-Joyce 1958, 136–222), but similar attitudes can be seen on a smaller scale in potting villages today. For example, in both Chinautla, Guatemala, and Tzintzuntzan, Mexico, producing tourist wares for a wide market has led to a competitive spirit that emphasizes individual "ownership" of ideas and secrets for new products. Procedures for firing the new pottery styles particularly inspire possessiveness: in Chinautla, for example, these steps

> have been perfected by some of the best potters and are kept secret by the family. So, each potter involved in the production of urban ware finds out on her own how to succeed. "Intelligence is needed," remarked a potter, "before these innovations take place." In the solitude of each household and in the conservative ways of the community, each family guards their findings jealously. Producing urban ware is, after all, an individual pursuit, not yet a community tradition. (Reina and Hill 1978, 264–65; see also Foster 1965b, 57–58)

Ethnographic and ethnoarchaeological accounts of pottery making often report the considerable influence, often community- or regionwide, of individuals in accepting the challenges of a new market with different standards and redirecting their artistic output toward that market. Potters such as Maria of San Ildefonso (Marriott 1948) and Nampeyo of Hano in the Southwestern United States, Margarita of Chinautla, Guatemala (Reina and Hill 1978, 258), and Natividad Pena of Tzintzuntzan, Mexico (Foster 1948a, 95–99), for example, were significant in transforming their craft. These individuals—as well as such potters as Wasëmëa in Peru (Lathrap 1976, 203) and Àbátàn in Africa (Thompson 1969), who upheld more traditional standards, or the powerful monopolist Don Asunción in Los Pueblos (Papousek 1981, 102–5), who influenced the production and marketing relationships of potters and middlemen—illuminate the role of strong personalities in economic development in ways that will never be achievable for the archaeological record of prehistoric ceramic change.

Although some ceramic changes in modern products have been stimulated by the creative artistry of particular potters, others have been brought about by institutional organizations attempting to develop a viable ceramic industry. For example, in Mexico in the late 1960s several attempts were made to stimulate indigenous *artesanias*, or arts and crafts, in order to preserve the Mexican cultural heritage and encourage economic progress. These programs tried to organize potters into cooperatives or employ them in factories, offered technical and financial assistance, and sought markets for the products. In Los Pueblos the efforts had little success, however, primarily because of shortages of funds for paying the workers and very limited markets for the products (Papousek 1981, 87–100). In Atolo, Philippines, the National Cottage Industry Board introduced a pivoted turntable to modernize the pottery industry there, and though potters initially bought the turntables they quickly discarded them. They said thàt "there was no time advantage to be gained and that they didn't want to pay seven pesos for such an item when *tagang* [a supporting and turning device], made from broken vessels, cost nothing" (Scheans 1977, 112). Government intervention seems to have achieved more with the artisan center in La Chamba, Columbia, established by the Ministry of Economic Development in that country, which undertook international marketing of the wares (Litto 1976, 148–49). And Michael Cardew's highly successful twenty-year program in Nigeria was initiated at the government's behest to start potteries in the country and produce serviceable glazed wares (Cardew 1969, 1985, 33).

A final point about changes in pottery manufacture in the modern world is how far pottery is regionalized and may become part of an ethnic identity. Regionalization refers to local or regional specializations in particular crafts or products within a craft, such as incised or polychrome decoration, blackwares versus redwares, jars versus bowls, and so forth. Local and regional manufactures are closely identified with corporate community identities, in part because of the messages carried by the decorative and formal stylistic content of pottery and other crafts (see chap. 8; also Wobst 1977), which distinguish members of the in-group from outsiders. This also reflects behavioral patterns of long standing, including use of resources, techniques of manufacture, and patterns of using the objects, such as different ways of carrying water jars (e.g., see Reina and Hill 1978, 238–42).

In modern times these messages are of increasing importance as society becomes more and more pluralistic and as movement out of traditional communities into urban areas and beyond threatens their existence. With outward-directed messages, such as tourist ware, regional or ethnic authenticity may be important to salability: for undiscriminating casual tourist buyers, symbols of the exotic or the ethnic are likely to be either limited or highly generalized. Similarly, commercial art wares may do well either through adherence to traditional styles or by creative innovation at the behest of patrons and dealers.

In the case of internally directed identifiers, archaism or revivalism—calling up styles and forms of earlier periods—are important in symbolizing ethnic cohesiveness and pride. Traditional markers of minority ethnic groups frequently cross boundaries, however, being borrowed by the dominant group to promote tourism by displaying recognizable symbols of exotic precolonial or non-Western cultures.

15.2 Continuity in Pottery Systems

It has frequently been alleged that potters as a group are extremely conservative and resistant to change. This judgment has been made from two perspectives: study of contemporary potters and their attitudes toward introduced modernization schemes, and study of how changes in archaeological pottery correspond to changes in the broader social system. Numerous archaeologists, for example, have investigated the correlation between ceramic change in the archaeological record and known political, economic, or religious disjunctions in the historical record and have concluded that ceramics are surprisingly unresponsive to changing social circumstances (Tschopik 1950, 217; Adams 1979; van der Merwe and Scully 1971, 184).

The complexity of the changes in ceramic production discussed above belies this facile judgment of stubborn conservatism by potters, and consequently in their products. Pottery changes qualitatively and quantitatively as well as through substitution and integration: that is, formal, decorative, or technological categories of pottery may be added, lost, substituted, or recombined. In fact it is these changes that have allowed archaeologists to outline many of the cultural transitions in the history of occupation and in the development and spread of civilization throughout the world.

One point that is immediately apparent is that change occurs differently in different categories of pottery. For example, art pottery for commercial or tourist or other external markets can be extremely flexible and responsive to the whims and fluctuations of outside purchasers. Both its production and its sale tend to be regarded as individual matters rather than reflections of corporate identity, and potters adapt to outside forces as individuals rather than as part of a general group response. Whereas art pottery is innovative, however, more traditional functional or utilitarian categories of pottery, used within the producing society for cooking or storage, are likely to change more slowly. In this latter context, where traditional internal group practices and relations are confronted and challenged, barriers to change and innovations can be strong. These barriers may be cultural, social, or psychological (see Foster 1962).

Traditional utilitarian pottery may resist change because the uses and contents of the pots change little, but also because in colonial or acculturation situations utilitarian vessels have little or no overt symbolic loading that a dominant group would suppress as threatening. For this reason, New World native culture after the Conquest has been said to survive primarily in language or technical/economic patterns (Kubler 1961, 30), including utilitarian pottery manufacture and use. An example comes from Puebla, Mexico, where traditional Indian pottery and foods were adopted by Spaniards, who also introduced new technical features (such as the wheel and glazing). By the middle of the nineteenth century the former pattern of separate Indian and Spanish manufacture of utilitarian wares had ended, and during a time of social and economic change a black-and-red glazed cooking ware emerged as a marker of "traditional group consciousness and of a new national identity" (Kaplan and Levine 1981, 871; cf. Charlton 1976, 523 for a similar example in the Teotihuacán valley).

It is also apparent that different kinds and degrees of change (or lack of change) are associated with different ways of organizing production and probably also with the status of the producers (see Balfet 1965). The same responsiveness to change may be given different connotations depending on production mode, however. Household producers of utilitarian or domestic wares for intragroup use are often described as tradition-bound and conservative. In workshop production units, on the other hand, similar adherence to a set of specific procedures and products, whether in mass manufacture of utilitarian vessels or tourist curios, is described with some approbation in terms of efficiency and standardization.

15.2.1 Continuity in the Society

Because of the close relationship between any utilitarian or craft product and its social milieu, it follows that some attention should be given to the social context that encourages or discourages change.

Many factors within a social system help maintain tradition in pottery manufacture and retard change (see Rice 1984b). Traditional values and *costumbre*, for example, are backed by social sanctions against anyone who violates community standards and norms, and this is a powerful mechanism for conservatism (see Reina and Hill 1978). Similarly, production in the family household or the barrio intensifies these forces and sanctions (see Díaz 1966). Social scientists might base their explanations on sanctions and such, but to the potters themselves the persistence of tradition is much simpler, and "Why?" is met with amused incredulity: as potters in Bé, Cameroon, explained, "pots were made in the Bé style because that is how pots are made at Bé" (David and Hennig 1972, 27; see Fontana et al. 1962, 49, for a similar reaction in the American Southwest). Individual innovations and secrets are antithetical to this production ethos.

The alleged resistance to innovation among potters is sometimes attributed to a conservative "basic personality structure." For example, a program of directed culture change was initiated in Tzintzuntzan, Michoacán, Mexico, where approximately two-thirds of the families are potters. Because the potting families were slower to accept innovations that were farmers or fishermen, Foster concluded (1962, 143–44) that "the conservatism of Tzintzuntzan reflects a basic conservatism in the psychological make-up of potters in other parts of the world. As a rule-of-thumb guide to community development work, I would suggest that new community development programs avoid pottery-making villages as initial targets." It is doubtful, however, that such a conservative worldview can be postulated on an international level, or that the concept of "limited good" (Foster 1965a; see also Papousek 1981, 45–51) is a direct cause for retaining traditional ceramic styles. More closely related are their relatively low socioeconomic status and lack of cash reserves to invest in capital equipment (see chap. 6). Even comparatively cheap tools may be rejected as an unnecessary expense, as Scheans (1977, 112) noted about potters' reluctance to buy pivoted turntables when they could use broken vessels as supports for shaping.

The use life (sec. 9.3) and frequency of production of vessel categories can also be related to conservatism and rates of change. DeBoer (1984, 557), for example, observed that among the Shipibo-Conibo small vessels in constant use, such as beer mugs, are replaced frequently, whereas large jars are replaced less frequently and so old ones differ considerably from modern examples. He suggested an inverse relation between rate of change and frequency of production.

Although Western products of plastic and metal are more durable than pottery and hence usually are eagerly sought as replacements for pottery jars and bowls (see Longacre 1985, 345; David and Hennig 1972, 24), this is not invariably so. In the late 1940s in rural Costa Rica metal cooking pots were scarce and costly, and the preference for pottery vessels was strengthened by "the belief commonly evidenced by the country housewife that aluminum utensils 'evaporate' or disappear over a hot fire" (Stone 1950, 278).

Many of the reasons for continuity in traditional ceramics are technological. For example, the clay, temper, and pigment resources in an area are effectively fixed. Potters' practices constitute proven adaptations to the mechanical and thermal properties of those resources, developed by long experimentation. Altering standard procedures in processing clay and in forming and firing the vessels may constitute unnecessary and potentially disastrous tinkering with a safe and effective procedure. Innovations such as wheels or kilns are risks—short-term risks of failure with an individual vessel or batch of vessels, and long-term risks in using scarce cash for such a sizable capital investment. Where the risk is great, potters are less likely to innovate.

A particularly powerful force for maintaining tradition in pottery manufacture is customary motor patterns—habitual postures, actions, and ways of doing things. Motor patterns are resistant to change because they are related not only to the positions in which implements are used, but to the shapes and sizes of the implements themselves. With respect to pottery, the conservative force of motor patterns is most significant in forming vessels and in using them.

Customary methods of forming pottery vessels, whether coiling, molding, or throwing, require a highly coordinated set of movements learned by experience over a long period, and they also require eyes and fingers trained to recognize appropriate texture, thickness, and smoothness of the clay at various stages. New techniques, most commonly introduced in efforts at modernization, are frequently resisted because the unfamiliar new movements seem awkward and inefficient. For example, several efforts to introduce the potter's wheel in various pottery-making locales, despite assurances of increased output, have had little success (Foster 1962, 87–88, 1965b, 51). Arnold (1979, 735) suggested that the integration of new motor habits into a potting industry takes place slowly, needing about two generations. In some situations, however, manufacturing techniques may be much more flexible; for example, pressure to conform to village standards (*costumbre*) may force a woman from another village to abandon her own ways and adopt those of her new husband's village, as in the case of painted decoration on Shipibo cloth (Roe 1980). Charlton (1976, 523) notes that in the Teotihuacán Valley, Mexico, the technique of glazing earthenwares was widely accepted after its introduction in the seventeenth century, but potters preferred to use traditional mold-making techniques rather than the wheel, a preference that continues today.

Ways of using and carrying traditional pottery vessels are also subject to conservatism. Communities in the Guatemalan highlands have different modes of carrying *tinajas*, or water jars (fig. 15.4): balanced on the head,

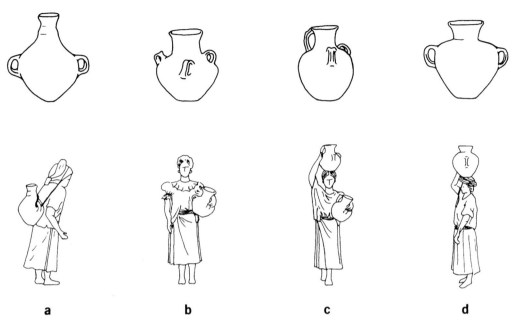

a   **b**   **c**   **d**

Figure 15.4   Different styles of *tinajas* (water carrying jars) in highland Guatemala and different ways of carrying them: *a,* northwest highlands; *b,* eastern highlands; *c,* southeast coast; *d,* north-central highlands. After Reina and Hill 1978, map 10.

resting on the hip, or supported on the back by a tumpline (Reina and Hill 1978, 242). These motor patterns are paralleled by differences in size and shape of the jars, particularly in center of gravity, volume, and weight. They are reflected in consumer preferences, and communities identify with their own traditional jar shapes and reject those of other areas.

Dietary patterns also influence continuity in traditional utilitarian vessels for cooking and storage. Like motor habits, diet is extremely stable and resistant to change, and in contact situations it may be easier to adopt local foods (and utensils) than to import these items from long distances. In modern societies the people who continue to use pottery vessels for cooking and water storage are often poor and rural and therefore more likely to maintain traditional foodways. Low socioeconomic status, combined with *costumbre* and traditional food preparation and preferences, will favor retention of traditional vessel shapes. People the world over believe that food staples such as rice or beans taste better when cooked in traditional earthenware ollas and that water is fresher when cooled in pottery jars rather than aluminum or enamel containers (see Foster 1965b, 55; Deal 1983, 143; Fontana et al. 1962, 30; Solheim 1965, 257). A variant of this sentiment comes from the nineteenth-century southeastern United States, where earthenwares were used for specialty cooking among the upper classes: it was said that "okra soup was always inferior if cooked in any but an old Indian pot" (Ferguson 1980, 21).

Many of these factors come together in the role of pottery manufacture and use in ritual and ceremonial life. Religion is a powerful force for conservatism, and this effect will be felt where pottery vessels have important religious functions: traditional pottery ritual vessels are unlikely to be replaced by modern industrial products. In Bombay, for example, potters are a traditional occupational caste whose products are essential in various Hindu festivals and ceremonies. The religiously defined demand for pottery within the society has contributed to their "traditional and conservative outlook" (Lynch 1979, 7).

15.2.2   Continuity in the Products

Forces of *costumbre*, adherence to familiar motor habits, traditional diets, and use of customary clay resources—all establish a cultural context of continuity that fosters a corresponding continuity of styles in the utilitarian vessels produced. As discussed above (sec. 15.1), nonutilitarian, nontraditional art wares or tourist items produced for outside consumers respond sensitively to the demands of the marketplace. Utilitarian or domestic vessels, on the other hand, are quite different: produced for internal use, they adhere to traditional standards and change relatively little.

To study continuity and change in pottery, it is useful to describe the objects in terms of four major attributes or subsystems of variation: characteristics of decoration, technology, performance or use, and form. Variation and change occur differently in each system (Adams 1979; Rice 1984b, 261–63).

Of these four pottery subsystems, decoration is probably least stable and most susceptible to change. Decorative styles usually are meant to be highly visible, and they have a high symbolic content in terms of both the internal significance of the motifs and their arrangements and the messages they send to outsiders. Because of this high symbolic load, it is likely that traditional decorative elaboration in a variety of goods would be actively suppressed by a dominant society or colonial power and that new elements would be borrowed or created by the subordinate group.

As noted above, under cultural stress decoration frequently becomes simplified, with treatments being abandoned or greatly reduced in complexity. This simplification accompanies the loss of symbolic meaning of the decorative elements. There is some evidence that stylistic arrangements or design structures have more continuity and communitywide persistence than do more easily modified decorative motifs (see sec. 8.3.2). Their survival depends on how far traditional ritual beliefs, practices, and paraphernalia have survived contacts or modernization efforts.

Technological and performance variables of pottery, on the other hand, tend to resist change. These variables relate to the composition of the ceramic, how it is formed and fired, and how well it performs its designated uses, such as cooking. Because potters generally tend to continue using the same clay source, which is usually nearby (see sec. 5.2.1), and because of the primacy of clays and tempers in pottery making as well as the long-standing adaptations in subsequent shaping, drying, and firing operations, ceramic resources are one of the most stable elements of a pottery-producing system.

Technological and performance characteristics resist change despite sometimes dramatic cultural upheavals in part because, unlike decorative variables, they are almost entirely devoid of symbolic content. Technological attributes of utilitarian pottery have no inherent or overt meaning except as they constitute the customary raw materials (pigments, etc.) for such stylistic messages. There is therefore no strong impetus for destroying them or curtailing the behavior that perpetuates them.

The resource selection and preparation involved in pottery making are the basis for vessel's performance characteristics. These include physical, mechanical, and thermal properties such as porosity, strength, and resistance to thermal stress (see chaps. 7 and 13). Technological variables and performance characteristics are thus closely related to another conservative force in pottery use: dietary patterns, including customary tastes and ways of preparing traditional foods.

Like technological variables, the shapes of traditional domestic pottery are conservative and resist change. Primary vessel shape characteristics reflect methods of forming (the molding technique, of course, accommodates no changes unless the molds themselves are altered or no longer used), uses (e.g., cooking in, versus over, a fire), and customary actions (such as the way a water jar is carried). These behaviors, themselves relatively slow to change, are reflected in the primary shapes and in the use-related qualities (see chap. 7), such as ease of carrying or resistance to tipping, conferred by proportions and dimensions. The shape and size of vessels may be heavily dependent on the properties of the clay used for them, as it was in Sardinia: when one customary clay source was exhausted, potters had to move closer to another source of clay that was of inferior quality, and large vessels either could no longer be made or had to be reduced in size (Annis 1985, 253). Secondary form characteristics and sizes of vessels may vary—indeed, several sizes of the same shape may be made for preparing different quantities of food for different occasions—but the basic shapes show considerable stability.

It is thus important to highlight the forces for conservatism in the manufacture of two major categories of traditional utilitarian pottery vessels: the water jar (Reina and Hill 1978, 238–43; Nicklin 1971, 20–21) and the cooking pot (Rye 1981, 27). The conservatism of these forms derives from several factors: (1) the familiar flavor imparted to water stored or food cooked in them (as a consequence of the clay composition and porosity); (2) the motor patterns used in carrying them or in preparing traditional foods; (3) in water-carrying jars, the messages of group identification sent by the shape and any decoration; and (4) in cooking pots, the adaptation of the round shape to thermal stress resistance. Add to these specific factors the low socioeconomic status of people who continue to use clay household utensils, their traditional dietary preferences, and their lack of exposure to variation or means of modifying their foodways (whether because of age, sex, or cost), and a powerful set of circumstances exists to maintain continuity and stability in utilitarian pottery manufacture.

Although utilitarian forms seem most likely to be conservative, underlying continuities can also be detected through syncretism in nonutilitarian forms. An interesting example of continuity covarying with change is the translation of ancient carved stone animal figures into the popular ceramic bulls manufactured today in Peru.

The *toros de Pucará* are produced in the village of Pupuja, near Pucará, in the Department of Puno in the southern Andes. They range from several inches to a foot or more in length and may be completely covered with a green glaze or left unglazed. If unglazed, they are covered with a white slip, and red paint or areas of green glaze or both are used to decorate the face and body.

These small ceramic figurines seem to have developed out of stone figures of alpacas or llamas, called *conopas*, carved by the Incas. Originally shown reclining, with a flat base and no legs, these figures had a small hole in the back to hold offerings. During the late eighteenth century there was a change in these objects; reclining stylized alpacas continued to be made, but in glazed ceramic (Stastny 1979, 60). In the early nineteenth century reclining or flat-based ceramic bulls rather than native camelids were created (Stastny 1979, 104–5), and sometime later standing bulls with short legs, covered with glaze, began to be made. As these bulls evolve through time the legs progressively lengthen from the traditional legless Inca stone model (Stastny 1979, 60).

Cattle were introduced into the New World by the Spaniards in the sixteenth century, and the bull gradually replaced the llama as a beast of burden. In addition, the bull became an important symbol of fertility in southern Peru, replacing felines (pumas) in modern Quechua myth (Stastny 1979, 105–7). Various rituals associated with feasting and fertility involve bulls. In one the loose folds of skin on the bull's neck are pierced to draw sacrificial blood, *chicha* (local liquor) is rubbed on its nostrils, and chilies are tied under its tail. As a result of these irritants the animal licks its nostrils and raises its tail, and these are precisely the characteristics of the modern pottery *toros*.

The small pottery bulls are appealing to tourists, but they also can be found widely in both rural and urban (e.g., Cusco) areas of Peru. Pairs of them decorate the roof ridges of houses as symbols of luck and fertility, and they are often placed on each side of a cross (fig. 15.5).

15.3   Implications for Archaeology

Archaeologists pursue many courses in seeking to understand ancient pottery manufacture and use. Physicochemical analyses of pottery (see chaps. 13 and 14) are highly informative, but they tell only part of the story. Much can be learned from ethnographic and ethnoarchaeological studies of modern potters, and the ways they form, decorate, fire, market, and use wares in their societies (chaps. 5–9). The documentation of pottery manufacture and use in the ethnographic present of the past century or so has been invaluable. These descriptions record a craft that is disappearing in modern times, and the wealth of data is enormously useful for drawing analogies with the manufacture, distribution, and use of pottery in times past.

Because archaeologists have traditionally used variations in styles and forms of pottery to develop site and regional chronologies, there is a special preoccupation with ceramic change through time. In this area analogies between past and present may need to be treated with caution. The ubiquity, duration, and intensity of contacts between Western societies and indigenous peoples raise some concerns about the legitimacy of certain aspects of both

Figure 15.5 Small painted pottery bulls from   roof ornament in modern Cusco, Peru. See
Pucará flank a cross with hanging pots as a   text for details.

specific and general analogies between prehistoric and modern pottery producers and their products. No pottery-producing society has remained untouched
by twentieth-century economics. In prehistoric times, before the advent of
cheap metal or plastic containers, when utensils for rich and poor alike were
ceramic, could it be said, as now, that "the hallmark of the successful potter is
to have stopped potting" (David and Hennig 1972, 252; see also Papousek
1984, 526)?

Although it is usually simple to differentiate the products touched by such
contacts—prehistoric New World populations did not make models of cathe-
drals or bulls or angels—this is not always so clear. The changes in decorative
strategies among Shipibo-Conibo potters have been relatively long-standing
and have included creating unusual forms to attract collectors. These exotics
have found their way into many European collections (Vossen 1969; cited in
Lathrap 1976, 207; also DeBoer 1985, 355–56). Such atypical collections are
not suitable for study of traditional ceramic manufactures, as Lathrap
remarks, though they certainly provide an important means of documenting
the transition of the craft. No doubt similar cautions apply to other large museum collections of wares produced after a substantial modern art market
was created.

Some of the changes outlined as characteristic of recent modernization may
be largely confined to the conditions of the twentieth century: the ease of
international travel and communication, for example, stimulating miniaturization for tourist curios and falsification for the art market. Yet other processes
may apply cross-culturally and cross-temporally. For example, the extremely
slow change in domestic cooking and storage wares seems widespread. It is
no doubt by some intuitive recognition of this that archaeologists have gener-

ally ignored plain utilitarian pottery in favor of decorated wares in building chronologies.

While miniaturization may be most closely associated with twentieth-century mass production of airport art, other types of change in pottery forms, decoration, technology, and uses may be more universally applicable. One likely possibility is that different processes of change (simplification, syncretism, elaboration, secularization) may accompany different contact or acculturation situations (military, economic, religious, etc.), but this has not been explored in any detail. A particular problem in pottery, which is a continuing source of argument among archaeologists, is distinguishing local from nonlocally produced objects (see sec. 14.2): in many situations a given foreign style may be imported into area A, or it may be copied locally by area A potters, or a group of foreign potters may reside in area A and produce their native style. Imitation, innovation, elaboration, and syncretism all play roles in these circumstances, but they are difficult to isolate archaeologically.

There is always a lag between the occurrence of an event and the time when its impact is fully felt in various alterations to the accustomed pattern. This lag must be added to the typically coarse-grained chronologies prehistoric archaeologists are forced to work with, in which it is rare to find identified intervals of less than a century. It is thus virtually impossible to correlate ceramic changes one-to-one with significant political, economic, or religious events in a culture (see Adams 1979). More subtle factors also militate against easy recognition of such a correlation: high values placed on tradition or *costumbre*, low status of potters, and lack of access to innovations, to name a few.

Modernization in the twentieth century has "opened" heretofore "closed" traditional communities and integrated them into national and international economic networks. We do not know to what extent similar processes might have operated in ancient times—for example, accompanying urbanization or the development and spread of state societies. Although the processes might have been the same in the past, the transformation doubtless took longer than the one or two generations over which these events take place today. Thus while modern analogies can shed light on how acculturation affects the ceramic craft, it is questionable that any incidence of state expansion in earlier times is equivalent in scale to post–fifteenth-century European colonization.

All these considerations combine to make it frustratingly difficult to understand the changes in pottery over the past millennia. One must have some awareness of historical and contextual differences between past and present to evaluate how far modern potters are appropriate analogies for prehistoric artisans. Nonetheless, modern potters and their products provide a singularly valuable connection with an art, a craft, and an industry whose roots go back at least ten thousand years. It is by incorporating ethnographic insights into technological and archaeological studies that this tradition can be most fruitfully illuminated.

15.4 References

Adams 1979
Annis 1985
Arnold 1979
Balfet 1965
Barnett 1953
Brody 1976
Bruhns and Hammond 1983
Cardew 1969, 1985
Charlton 1968, 1976
Cruxent and Rouse 1959
David and Hennig 1972
Deal 1983
DeBoer 1984, 1985
Deetz 1965
Díaz 1966
Ferguson 1980
Fontana et al. 1962
Foster 1948a, 1962, 1965a,b
Gill 1976
Graburn 1976
Hobson 1976
Kaplan and Levine 1981
Kubler 1961
Lathrap 1976
Lauer 1971

Lister and Lister 1982
Litto 1976
Longacre 1985
Lynch 1979
Marriott 1948
Nicklin 1971
Ortega and Fondeur 1978
Papousek 1981, 1984
Reina 1963, 1966
Reina and Hill 1978
Roe 1980
Rice 1984b
Rye 1981
Scheans 1977
Solheim 1965
Stastny 1979
Stone 1950
Thompson 1969
Thompson 1958
Tschopik 1950
Turner and Lofgren 1966
van der Merwe and Scully 1971
Vossen 1969
Wobst 1977
Wykes-Joyce 1958

Glossary

This glossary was prepared with reference to the following works:

American Geological Institute
　　1962　*Dictionary of geological terms.* Garden City, N.Y.: Doubleday.
Fournier, R.
　　1981　*Illustrated dictionary of pottery form.* New York: Van Nostrand Reinhold.
Hamer, F.
　　1975　*The potter's dictionary of materials and techniques.* London: Pitman.
Perkins, W. W., ed.
　　1984　*Ceramic glossary 1984.* Columbus, Ohio: American Ceramic Society.
Savage, G., and H. Newman
　　1976　*An illustrated dictionary of ceramics.* New York: Van Nostrand Reinhold.

absorption　the process by which a liquid is drawn into and fills the pores of a permeable, porous body.

accuracy　the correctness of a quantitative determination as a function of experimental procedures, standards, calibration, and possible systematic errors.

additive　an organic or mineral material mixed with a clay by the potter to modify its properties in forming, drying, and firing; sometimes used interchangeably with *temper* or related terms; see also *aplastic, grog, inclusion, nonplastic, temper.*

adsorption　the capacity of a material to accept and retain another substance (such as moisture) on its surface.

aggregate　an inert component such *grog* or potter's *flint* in ceramic bodies, especially *triaxial bodies,* analogous to the archaeological term *temper;* also called filler.

aging　storing prepared ceramic material (usually a wet, plastic clay body) to improve its working properties by thorough wetting of particles, slow compression, bacterial action (called souring), and other poorly understood processes.

alkaline glaze　a relatively low-fired glaze with a high concentration of alkali metal elements (especially Na, K, or Li) in its composition, often having wood ash as a significant constituent.

471

anisotropic   having physical properties that vary in different directions, particularly important in modifying the drying and firing behavior of ceramics and in crystal optics (petrographic study) of ceramic materials.

aplastic   particulate matter in a clay body that does not contribute to plasticity or that reduces the plasticity of the clay; one of several terms used for *temper,* but lacking implications of either natural occurrence or deliberate addition by the potter; see also *additive, grog, inclusion, nonplastic, temper.*

apparent porosity   the relation of the open pore space to the bulk volume of a clay body, expressed in percent.

archaeomagnetism (archaeomagnetic dating)   a method of absolute dating of undisturbed archaeological features by measuring their magnetic alignments (inclination and declination) and comparing them with known schedules of past magnetic alignments within a region.

archaeometry   the segment of archaeological science that applies the methods of chemistry and physics to the analysis of archaeological artifacts, features, and sites.

archaeothermometry   measurement of any of several properties of ancient pottery (including color, *porosity,* shrinkage, degree of *vitrification,* etc.) in order to determine the temperature range of its original firing.

Arretine   a widely copied and traded Roman earthenware made at Arretium (Arezzo), Italy, characterized by a distinctive lustrous red slip and molded, impressed decoration; see also *Samian, terra sigillata.*

assemblage   an archaeologist's grouping of artifacts (such as pottery) from a site by form and function, assumed to represent the material culture of a single occupation or cultural episode.

atmosphere (kiln)   the gases in the air in the environment of heating and cooling clay articles, particularly with reference to the availability of oxygen; see also *oxidation, reduction.*

attapulgite   one of several hydrous-magnesian clays with a lathlike or fibrous particle shape, characterized by a chainlike rather than a sheetlike atomic structure; related to *palygorskite.*

attribute   a feature or characteristic of style, form, or technology of an artifact that forms the basis for analysis, as in classification; also called a variable.

attribute state   the value or score of a particular artifact with respect to a particular attribute or any of several alternative values; sometimes used interchangeably with *attribute.*

ball clay   a fine-textured, highly plastic sedimentary clay, usually composed of the mineral *kaolinite,* typically containing considerable organic matter and firing white or cream.

band   a design *element* or fundamental part that is continued or repeated along a straight line that, on pottery, most commonly encircles the vessel but may also be vertical or diagonal.

base   (1) the underside of a vessel, or that part of a vessel in contact with the surface it rests on during normal use; sometimes called the *foot;* (2) chemistry: an alkali substance, a metal oxide with *pH* above 7.

base exchange capacity   *ion* exchange or replacement; the capacity of *colloidal* inorganic materials, such as clays, to *adsorb* ions on their surfaces from the surrounding medium and to replace or exchange them with other ions in the medium.

bat (batt)   a slab, disk, or board of plaster, fired clay, asbestos, or other slightly porous material used to dry a wet clay body by absorbing moisture from it, as a support in shaping an object from the clay, or as a detachable wheel head.

binder   a substance, usually organic, added to a clay or glaze to increase its *green* strength.

birefringence   the property of some crystals (*anisotropic* crystals) to split a beam of light into two beams that pass through the crystal at different speeds, producing characteristic optical effects seen under crossed nicols in a *polarizing microscope;* the difference between the largest and smallest *refractive indexes.*

biscuit (bisque)   unglazed fired pottery, awaiting glazing: the first or preliminary firing of a ware that is subsequently glazed and refired in the *glost* firing.

body   (1) clay or a mixture of clay and *inclusions* (*temper*) that is suitable for forming vessels or that has been fired into a vessel; often used interchangeably with *fabric, ware,* or *paste* and being closest to paste; (2) that portion of a vessel between the *orifice* and the *base,* also sometimes called the belly.

Bragg equation   a statement specifying the angle at which X rays are reflected from a crystal, as a function of the crystal-lattice spacing and the wavelength of the X rays: $n\lambda = 2d \sin \theta$, where λ is wavelength, d is the lattice spacing, and θ is the reflection angle.

burnish   a method of producing a luster on an unfired clay surface by rubbing it while *leather-hard* with a hard, smooth object to compact and align the surface particles.

casting   a process for forming a ceramic object by pouring a clay slip into a hollow, porous (usually plaster) mold and leaving it there long enough for a layer of clay to settle and thicken on the mold wall. The remaining slip is poured off, and the object is removed from the mold when it has dried. Also called slip casting or solid casting.

categorization   an aspect of the classificatory process that consists of creating groupings within a previously unclassified set of objects (as opposed to assigning objects to existing classes).

celadon   a blue-green or gray-green, reduction fired, iron-containing feldspathic glaze; a stoneware ceramic having a glaze with a soft blue-green or gray-green color and satiny texture, similar to jade, produced by relatively low temperatures and reduction firing. High-quality celadons are particularly associated with the Song dynasty of China (A.D. 1127–79).

ceramics (or ceramic)   (1) materials manufactured of silicates and formed by application of heat; (2) the research and applied fields developed around ceramic products; (3) the art or technique of producing articles by applying heat to inorganic and nonmetallic materials, usually clays; (4) in art and archaeology, high-fired, usually *vitrified* cooking and serving utensils and art objects (as distinct from *pottery*).

characteristic points   points on the contours of a vessel silhouette or vertical section marking angles (corner points) or curvature (inflection points), used in one system of classifying vessel shapes.

characterization   the qualitative and quantitative description of the composition and structure of a material so as to evaluate its properties and uses.

china clay   another name for kaolin clay, usually used specifically for a white-firing primary clay.

chroma   saturation, purity, or strength of color; in the *Munsell* system, chroma is the horizontal dimension, denoting the presence or absence of gray.

chronometric   a category of dating methods that yield ages in years; also called absolute dating. Contrasts with relative dating methods, which yield "younger than" or "older than" dates.

classification   ordering objects into groups based on their degree of similarity with one another; classifications of pottery may be *folk classifications* or *devised classifications,* the latter being more common in archaeology; compare *typology.*

clay   (1) one of several hydrous alumina-silicate minerals that are formed by decomposition of rock, chiefly granite, and have the property of *plasticity;* (2) an extremely fine particle size grade, less than 0.002 mm in diameter; (3) soil composed of 35%–40% particles in the fine particle size grade (less than 0.002 mm in diameter); (4) a fine-grained earthy material that becomes plastic and malleable when wet and hardens with the application of heat.

cleavage   the tendency of some minerals to split along planes determined by their crystalline structure.

coefficient of thermal expansion   a mathematical quantity (known as α) giving the ratios of linear or volume expansion of a material occurring with a change in temperature, expressed in inches of change ($\times 10^{-6}$) per inch of length per °C.

coil fracture   a smooth-edged circumferential breakage characteristic of coiled vessels in which the coils were poorly bonded, resulting in planes of weakness.

coiling   the method of hand building an object of clay by successive additions of ropes or coils of clay (variants include *ring building*, spiral coiling, and segmental coiling).

collar   a raised and extended *orifice* that begins at or just above the point of maximum diameter of the vessel and does not significantly reduce the opening relative to the body diameter.

colloid   a stable suspension of small particles (usually 1 μm or less in diameter) of some substance in a fluid.

colorant   a chemical element that contributes color to a mixture; unglazed, low-fired pottery is colored chiefly by carbon, iron, and manganese, whereas a broader range of colors occurs in glazes; see also *pigment, stain*.

complex shape   a vessel shape that in silhouette is marked by two or more *characteristic points* of inflection, or changes in curvature, or by both corner and inflection points.

composite shape   a vessel shape that in silhouette is marked by *characteristic points* of angles or corners, and lacks inflection points.

compound   a substance comprising atoms of two or more elements, having relatively fixed composition and properties.

compression   the *stress* of a crushing force applied to a material.

conductivity, thermal   the ability of a material to conduct heat, symbolized by k; the rate of heat flow through a material, expressed as BTU per square foot per °F, or as watts per meter per °K.

cones (pyrometric cones)   small, elongated pyramids made of controlled mixtures of ceramic materials in a numbered sequence that soften and bend when heated under specific conditions. When cones are placed in a kiln during firing, their bending provides an index of heat treatment and proper firing.

configuration   the arrangement of decorative *motifs* on a vessel so as to fill a spatial division and form the design.

core (coring)   a black or gray zone in the interior cross section of a vessel wall, usually associated with incomplete removal of carbonaceous matter from the clay during relatively low-temperature firing; not to be confused with black coring at high temperatures, which results from trapped gases and may lead to bloating.

countercharge   color reversal; a term used in *symmetry* analysis of painted designs, in which colors alternate through repetition of fundamental parts.

crawling   a defect in which the *glaze* separates from the body during drying or firing (e.g., around a prefiring crack), leaving unglazed areas.

crazing   a defect characterized by a fine network of cracks in the *glaze*, occurring when the glaze is in tension because it shrinks more than the body.

critical point   the point in the drying of a clay article at which *shrinkage water* has been removed, shrinkage has largely ceased, and the piece is rigid and *leather-hard;* also referred to as the critical moisture content.

crystal   a material with atoms distributed in an orderly array (a lattice structure), having characteristic optical and physical properties.

crystal lattice water   chemically combined water (as hydroxyls) held as an integral part of the layer structure of clay minerals, as distinct from *interlayer water*, normally lost only with heating the clay to temperatures between 450 and 600°C.

decay model (fall-off model)   a graphic representation of economic exchange in which the frequency of occurrence of a commodity at a number of sites is plotted against the distance of those sites from the source of the commodity.

deflocculate   to disperse a fine clay suspension so that particles repel each other and the substance becomes more fluid, for example, by adding a substance (a defloc-culant) such as sodium carbonate that changes the electric charge of the particles. A deflocculated solution, such as a casting slip, tends not to settle and has a low *viscosity*.

dehydroxylation   removal of OH^{1-} ions (chemically combined water) from the crystalline structure of minerals, as in the dehydroxylation of clays by application of heat.

dendrogram   a treelike diagram resulting from a type of multivariate statistical analysis called cluster analysis, which depicts the mathematical relations of greater or lesser similarity between a set of entities based on their *attributes*.

density   the weight of an object per unit volume, expressed as grams per cubic centimeter or pounds per cubic foot. **Apparent density** is computed from the apparent volume, that is, the true volume plus the volume of closed pores; **bulk density** refers to the overall volume including open and closed pores; **true density** is computed from true volume and excludes all pores.

design structure   the layout or arrangement of a design; the way the surface area to be decorated is conceptualized, for example, whether subdivided and bounded, and the arrangement of *elements* and *motifs* within that layout.

devised classification   a formal scheme of categories of entities developed by and used within a particular scientific discipline to order a set of data; compare *folk classification*.

diffraction   the scattering of radiant energy (e.g., X rays) by the edges, points, or planes of a substance, the spacings of which are comparable to the wavelength of the radiation, so that particles can be identified by such scattering.

diversity   a concept in ecology that describes the structure of a population of entities by number, size, and/or proportion of constituent categories. Akin to the quantity of variance, diversity may be measured by a number of mathematical diversity indexes.

docking   soaking a freshly fired article in cold water for a short period to prevent or reduce spalling of the ware if it contains calcareous inclusions.

dunting   cracking that occurs in a fired ware as a result of thermal stresses. More specifically, cracking that occurs if a ware is cooled too rapidly or that appears on refiring *bisque* ware through 400–600°C, with the expansion of quartz.

earthenware   a glazed or unglazed nonvitreous ceramic material, usually lowfired, porous, and permeable, and red or brown in color.

element   (1) a substance that cannot be decomposed into other substances; (2) chemistry: a substance all of whose atoms have the same atomic number; (3) style: the smallest component of a design that is manipulated as a single unit.

endothermic reaction   a chemical reaction that absorbs heat or requires heat in order to occur, such as the *dehydroxylation* of a clay.

engobe   a slip coating applied to a ceramic body before glazing to impart a desired color or smooth texture to the surface; sometimes used synonymously with *slip*.

equivalent firing temperature   an estimate of the level of firing of a ceramic (usually ancient) that takes into consideration the time and atmosphere conditions of firing as well as temperature.

ethnoarchaeology   the study of the material culture of living peoples by archaeologists in order to understand processes of manufacture, distribution, use, and discard and, by analogy, similar processes in the past.

exothermic reaction   a chemical reaction that liberates heat, such as the burning of fuel (oxidation of carbon).

extensibility   the ability of a material to be deformed without cracking or forming planes of weakness.

fabric   the composition of a fired ceramic, including clay, inclusions, and pores and excluding surface treatment; often used synonymously with *body, paste,* or *ware.*

faience   (1) earthenware with an opaque tin-lead glaze; a French term for earthenware manufactured at the Renaissance center of Faenza, Italy; (2) a blue-green, nonpottery, glazed silicate material manufactured in Dynastic Egypt.

fall-off model   see *decay model.*

fettle   to trim rough edges, casting or mold marks, and other imperfections from dry or *leather-hard* ware before firing.

film water   water that surrounds and separates platelets in a clay/water mass and makes the mass plastic; see also *shrinkage water.*

firebox   the combustion chamber of a *kiln* (usually one fired by wood), typically beneath the ware chamber.

firecloud   a darkened area on a vessel's surface resulting from uneven firing and the deposit of carbon in the pores during firing, characteristic of firings in which fuel and vessels are in immediate proximity.

fit   the dimensional adjustment of a glaze (less frequently, of a slip) to a clay body, specifically with reference to their respective *thermal expansions* and contractions and resultant stresses, which may cause flaws in the coating.

flint   a micro- or cryptocrystalline form of silica (SiO_2) containing some water and very fine pores, added to clay as an inert filler or *aggregate.*

flocculation   the agglomeration or coming together of particles in a suspension, such as a slip, forming "flocs" and causing the suspension to thicken or settle.

flux   a substance in a clay body, slip, or glaze that lowers the melting point of the mixture and promotes *vitrification.*

folk classification   the grouping and naming of entities according to elicited native categories, as distinguished from *devised classifications.*

foot   the *base* of a ceramic vessel, usually a ringlike projection formed by tooling or by adding a coil.

frit   a mixture of two or more materials, fused by heating to a melt, which after rapid cooling is ground into a powder and used as an ingredient in glazes. Ingredients in a frit are usually individually soluble in water or weak acid and may be toxic (e.g., lead) without fritting.

glass   a silicate mixture that has been heated to a melt and then cooled to a solid without crystallizing.

glaze   a glassy coating melted onto the surface of a ceramic article, applied as a liquid suspension to a ware that has usually been fired once (*biscuit*) and is subsequently refired (*glost*).

glaze fit   see *fit.*

glost (glost fire)   glaze firing; the firing process in which a glazed ware is fired, usually having already been fired once (the *bisque* firing) before application of the glaze.

green   formed but unfired ceramic articles or their properties; used as greenware, green strength, etc.

grog   prefired clay (or potsherds), crushed or ground to small particle size and added to a clay as a type of *temper* to modify its properties; also called filler.

half-life   the period of time in which half the number of atoms in a radioactive element decay or disintegrate by emission of charged particles from their nuclei, thus changing into a new element.

hardness   the resistance of a material to mechanical deformation, especially indentation, scratching, abrasion, or crushing; also the elasticity of a material. Many hardness tests exist for ceramic materials; for archaeological pottery the most commonly used is *Mohs' scale*.

heavy mineral   an accessory detrital mineral present in generally small particle sizes and quantities in most rocks, which has high specific gravity (greater than 2.89).

hue   the first quality of a color corresponding to its perception as visible light as red, blue, green, etc.; in *Munsell* nomenclature, hue refers to different pages or sheets corresponding to radii of the color cylinder model.

hygroscopic   the ability or tendency of a material (e.g., CaO) to take up moisture readily from the surrounding air or other moist materials.

illite   a group of clay minerals having a three-layer, nonexpanding structure similar to that of well-crystallized micas.

inclusion   particulate matter, usually mineral in nature, present in a clay or fabric, either naturally or added by the potter; often used synonymously with *temper*.

interaction hypothesis   the proposition that the similarity (or frequency) of decorative elements shared between social groups is proportional to the direction and intensity of interaction between those groups.

interference colors   the colors visible in minerals viewed through crossed nicols in a *polarizing microscope* when the mineral causes the weakening or destruction of certain wavelengths of a beam of light.

interlayer water   water that exists between the unit layers of the three-layer clay minerals; the last water to be lost in drying.

inversion   a transformation or change of phase, typically in a solid, from one polymorphic form to another with different atomic structure and bonding; see also *quartz inversion*.

ion   an atom or group of atoms with an electric charge, either positive (cation) or negative (anion).

isotopes   nuclides or elements having an identical number of protons in their nuclei but differing in their number of neutrons. The isotopes of an element have different atomic weights (mass), very similar chemical properties, and identical atomic structures.

isotropic   having the same properties in all directions, usually with reference to optical properties but also pertaining to physical properties such as shrinkage.

jigger   to form an article of ceramic flatware by means of a rotating mold and profile tool; the machine by which such a process is accomplished. Usually the mold has the contour of the interior and the profile tool has the contour of the exterior surface, but sometimes the term is used interchangeably with *jolly* without specifying the article formed or which surface is shaped by which apparatus.

jolly (jolley)   to form ceramic hollowware by a machine similar to a *jigger*, but the rotating mold forms the outside while a profile forms the interior.

kaolinite   a common clay mineral having a two-layer structure of silica and alumina and the ideal chemical composition $Al_2O_3 \cdot 2SiO_2 \cdot 2H_2O$; the principal mineral of the kaolin clay (also called *china clay*) group.

kiln   an enclosed or partially enclosed construction for firing ceramic materials. Kilns may be labeled on the basis of the characteristics of construction or by their firing characteristics. Some important types of kilns include: **bottle** (an updraft kiln with a narrow chimney, shaped like a bottle); **clamp** (open-topped updraft kiln, of semipermanent construction, usually with intermixed fuel and ware); **climbing**

(kiln set along a slope to aid the draft); **continuous** (in which ware is fed continuously into the kiln on a track, moving through it during firing); **downdraft** (an enclosed periodic kiln in which the heat is passed to the top of the kiln, then the draft carries it down through the ware); **intermittent** (a kiln that is loaded, fired, cooled, and then unloaded before firing a new batch); **muffle** (a kiln constructed so that the ware is not directly subjected to the radiant heat from the flame or heating elements); **periodic** (intermittent); **pit** (a clamp that is excavated partially into the ground); **scove** (an updraft kiln usually having no permanent parts); **tunnel** (a type of continuous kiln); **updraft** (a kiln in which the heat or flame passes upward through the ware and then is vented outside).

lattice water   see *crystal lattice water.*

leather-hard   clay that is dried to the *critical point* so that individual clay particles touch and the body is rigid, but retaining sufficient moisture to be carved or joined (e.g., by *luting* with slip).

levigation   separating fine from coarser material, such as clays, by mixing with a liquid (water) and washing down a series of traps, allowing the coarser material to settle.

lime popping (lime blowing)   a surface defect on ware containing inclusions of calcium carbonate ($CaCO_3$, as limestone, shell, or calcite). When fired to temperatures between about 650 and 900°C, the calcium carbonate decomposes and after cooling the lime (CaO) rehydrates with an accompanying expansion. This expansion exerts sufficient stress to spall the surface and sometimes may cause the entire article to disintegrate.

lip   the edge or margin of the *orifice* of a vessel; sometimes refers more specifically to a modification of a rim of a vessel for pouring.

lute   to join together two *leather-hard* pieces of a vessel by using slip as a glue.

maiolica (majolica)   earthenware covered with an opaque tin-lead glaze, best known from fifteenth- to nineteenth-century Europe. The name comes from the island of Majorca, from which Italy obtained these wares in trade, but the term is commonly used as a technological class without reference to origins of the ware. Delft ware and *faience* are two types of tin-lead glazed earthenwares that fall under the rubric maiolica.

marl   a calcareous clay; a mixture of clay and particles of calcite, dolomite, and/ or shell.

maturity   the range of temperature and time (the maturing range) at which a clay body fires to desired qualities of hardness, porosity, and serviceability; the temperature and time at which a glaze develops qualities of bonding (to the body), stability, strength, and texture.

metakaolin   dehydroxylated kaolin, formed after firing *kaolinite* above approximately 500°C. Metakaolin is nonplastic and has lost most of its crystalline structure, but it can rehydrate and revert to kaolinite.

microstructure   the arrangement of *phases* of a material; in a ceramic, the internal arrangement of crystalline and amorphous materials, pores, and boundaries between them.

mineral   a homogeneous, inorganic, naturally occurring solid with a characteristic chemical composition and a regularly ordered atomic structure.

mode   a classificatory term referring to *attributes* (of a set of artifacts) that are judged to be behaviorally and culturally significant as reflections of operating standards for the manufacture and use of the artifacts.

modulus of elasticity (E, or Young's modulus)   a measure of the rigidity of a material or its ability to withstand *stress* without deformation. Ceramics typically have high elastic moduli.

Mohs' scale   an ordinal *hardness* scale developed in the nineteenth century for minerals, consisting of a series of increasingly hard minerals from 1 (talc) to 10 (diamond). The minerals in the scale are drawn across the test piece to determine which mineral is sufficiently hard to mark the ceramic, thus measuring *scratch hardness.*

montmorillonite   a common clay mineral of the *smectite* group, having a small particle size and an expanding lattice.

motif   a fixed combination of design *elements* that forms a larger component of the decoration.

mouth   the *orifice* or opening of a hollowware vessel.

Munsell charts   a series of charts published by the Munsell Color Company for the standardized identification and description of colors; color is divided into three components, *hue, value,* and *chroma,* and individual *shades, tints,* and *tones* are represented by rows of small color chips.

neck   the part of a vessel between the *shoulder* and the *rim,* typically characterized by a marked constriction of the maximum body diameter; where there is little constriction, the region is often called a *collar.*

nonplastic   material in a clay, whether naturally present or added by the potter, mineral or organic, which by virtue of generally large particle size lacks the property of plasticity and often reduces the plasticity and stickiness of the clay; see also *additive, aggregate, aplastic, inclusion, temper.*

orifice   the *mouth* or opening of a vessel, usually hollowware.

oxidation   the combining of an atom or ion with oxygen, usually resulting in the loss of electrons; a firing atmosphere characterized by an abundance of free oxygen, which combines with elements (such as iron) in the body and yields clear colors of the ceramic body; see also *reduction.*

oxide   a compound of oxygen plus another element.

paint   the action of applying a *pigment* (not the pigmenting material itself).

palygorskite   a group of hydrous-magnesian clay minerals characterized by a distinctive rodlike or needlelike shape related to chaining rather than sheetlike arrangement of atoms. Palygorskite is related to *attapulgite* but magnesium is replaced by aluminum.

parting agent   a material, such as sand, ash, or dry clay, sprinkled over a mold or working surface to prevent wet clay from sticking; sometimes refers to wax spread over metal.

paste   a clay or mixture of clay and added materials, often used synonymously with *fabric, body,* or *ware.* Technically paste differs from *fabric* because it does not include *pores* and differs from *ware* because it excludes surface treatment.

pattern   any design with regularly repeated parts; roughly synonymous with *symmetry* as a type of analysis of pottery design.

permeability   the capacity of a material to transmit a fluid, measured as the amount of liquid passing through a given thickness in a given time.

petrography   the microscopic study and description of rocks or other mineral material (such as ceramics) by optical properties.

petrology   the study of the natural history of rocks, including their origins, alterations, and decay, and description of their present condition.

pH   the relative alkalinity or acidity of a solution, measured as the negative logarithm of hydrogen ion activity (or concentration).

phase   a homogeneous, physically distinct portion of a nonhomogeneous system.

phyllosilicate   a layered *silicate* mineral; the major category of clay minerals, composed of those with a regular ordering of layers of silica and alumina structural components.

pigment   a coloring material, usually a mixture of *colorants*, clay, water, and a *binder;* may be organic or inorganic.

plagioclase   one of several soda-lime feldspar minerals, a common rock-forming mineral group.

plasticity   the property of a material that enables it to be shaped when wet and to hold this shape when the shaping force is removed.

plasticity, water of   the water required for a clay material to develop optimal *plasticity.*

plastic limits   the range in the amount of water that may be added to a dry clay in order to develop a satisfactorily plastic mass; see also *working range.*

pleochroism   the property of a material of differentially absorbing light that vibrates in different directions as it passes through a crystal; the change in color of a mineral viewed under uncrossed nicols in a *polarizing microscope.*

point count   a method of determining the quantity of grains or inclusions in a material by counting individual grains of different phases along a line (or within a transect) as the specimen is viewed in a microscope.

polarizing microscope (petrographic microscope)   a microscope that incorporates filters to modify the vibration direction of light as it passes through a thinly ground section of a mineral and permits characterization of that mineral by its optical properties.

polish   a glossy luster on the surface of an unglazed ceramic article, produced by rubbing it while *leather-hard* with a yielding tool; lacks the individual parallel facets characteristic of *burnishing.*

porcelain   a fine, vitrified, high-fired ceramic body, usually translucent and white, that may be used for pottery or for a variety of industrial and scientific products.

pore water   mechanically combined water remaining in the pores and capillaries of a clay article after shrinkage is completed and particles come into contact with each other.

porosity   the volume of pores contained within a solid, such as a ceramic object, measured as *true* or *apparent porosity.* In most pottery studies open or apparent porosity is measured.

pottery   low-fired, nonvitrified objects including cooking, serving, and storage vessels (as distinct from high-fired *ceramics*); one of several industries within the ceramic field, including manufacture of tableware, utensils, and tiles.

precision   the dispersion of a set of measured values; the reproducibility of a technique.

preferred orientation   a systematic orientation of platy or acicular crystals in which the crystals are aligned parallel to their long axis.

primary clay (residual clay)   a clay deposit located on its geological site of formation by weathering from a parent rock (as opposed to a *secondary* or transported clay).

profile   a type of illustration of ceramic objects based on the vertical cross section, showing wall thickness and details of lip, rim, and base configuration.

props   shelf supports for kilns, made of *refractory* material.

provenience (provenance)   the geographical or geological origin or source of an artifact; an analysis carried out with the aim of discovering such origins, usually by chemical and/or mineralogical *characterization* of the composition of the artifacts in question and comparison with raw materials in a particular area of interest.

pyrometric cones   see *cones.*

quartz inversion   a change in the atomic structure and bonding of quartz during heating. One inversion (from α to β) occurs at 573°C, the second (to tridymite) at 867°C, and the third (to cristobalite) at 1250°C.

rare earth   one of a series of relatively scarce metallic elements having atomic numbers from 57 (lanthanum) to 71 (lutecium), also known as the lanthanide elements.

reduction (reducing atmosphere)   a chemical reaction characterized by addition of electrons (as contrasted with oxidation); an atmosphere of firing in which oxygen is removed from substances or materials, for example, because of reducing agents such as hydrogen, carbon, or carbon monoxide.

refractive index   the ratio of the velocity of light in air to its velocity in a given medium, such as a mineral, which bends or refracts the light and thereby changes its direction and velocity.

refractory   ceramic materials, usually high in alumina and silica, that can withstand high temperatures and are slow to melt.

residual clay   a clay weathered in place, remaining in association with its parent rock; a *primary clay* as distinguished from a *secondary clay.*

rilling   the spiral ridges or striations around the interior or exterior surface of a vessel thrown on a wheel, formed by finger pressure in "lifting" the clay; also called throwing marks.

rim   the area between the *lip* or margin and the side wall or *neck* of a vessel; sometimes used interchangeably with lip, especially if there is no change of orientation between the lip and neck or wall.

ring building   a type of *coiling* in which individual coils or annular rings are placed as separate "courses" to build up a vessel.

saggar (sagger, seggar)   a container made of *refractory* clay used to protect clay articles and glazes from flames and gases during firing.

Samian   a red-slipped Roman ware made in molds with relief decoration between 100 B.C. and A.D. 300. Named after the island of Samos, the ware was also widely copied in Gaul; see also *Arretine, terra sigillata.*

sampling   the process of selecting a small number of units from a larger whole, called the population.

sand   a particle size grade ranging from 2 mm to 0.05 mm in diameter; often incorrectly used to refer to the composition of a detrital sediment, one composed of quartz.

scratch hardness   a measure of relative hardness of pottery, obtained by comparison with minerals of known hardness (*Mohs' scale*). A mineral harder than the pottery will scratch it, but it will be unmarked by a mineral that is less hard.

secondary clay   a clay deposit that has been moved away from the original parent from which it weathered and is redeposited (as contrasted with a *primary* or *residual clay*).

sensitivity   the limits of detection of an analytical technique, such as a chemical analysis, phrased as either the smallest quantity of material detectable or the lowest atomic number of elements that can be analyzed.

sepiolite   a clay mineral with a spongy, fibrous, or lathlike structure related to *palygorskite;* meerschaum.

seriation   one of several techniques archaeologists use to determine the similarity of artifacts or sets of artifacts and then to place them in a series, their order being interpreted as relative age.

shade   a variation of a color produced by adding black.

shear   a type of *stress* or force in which parts of a body slip or slide relative to each other.

sherd (potsherd, shard)   a term archaeologists use to refer to a broken fragment of pottery.

shivering   a defect caused by compressive stress, resulting in incomplete coverage or peeling of the *glaze.*

shoulder   the upper part of the body of a restricted vessel; that portion between the maximum diameter and the *orifice* or *neck*.

shrinkage water   the portion of mechanically combined water that separates the clay particles in a clay/water mass and, when lost during drying, contributes to shrinkage of the body; see also *film water*.

silicate   a compound in which SiO_4 tetrahedrons are major constituents. Clays, for example, are alumina-silicates in which the tetrahedrons are joined primarily as sheets.

silt   a particle size grade in which particles are between 0.05 and 0.002 mm in diameter; a sediment consisting of 80% or more silt-sized particles and less than 12% clay-sized particles.

sinter   a process of adhesion and densification (but not complete fusion or vitrification) of a particulate material upon heating close to but below the melting point.

skeuomorph   an object made of one kind of material, such as pottery, that imitates in shape and decorative detail objects made of other materials, such as metal, wood, leather, or gourd.

slip   a fluid suspension of fine clay and water, used to coat a body before firing or poured into a mold to cast a piece; a nonvitreous coating on a pottery vessel; see also *engobe*.

smectite   a group of clay minerals having a three-layer structure consisting of two silica layers with an alumina layer between, characterized by expandability and relatively high base exchange. Common smectite clay minerals include *montmorillonite*, bentonite, and saponite.

soaking period   the time during which the highest temperature of firing is sustained.

social interaction theory   see *interaction hypothesis*.

specialization   the practice of a particular economic activity by a relatively small number (as compared with total output or market) of skilled individuals who engage in it for their primary livelihood.

spectrometry   methods of chemical characterization based on analysis of the electromagnetic spectrum of radiant energy emitted by the sample (emission spectrometry) or absorbed by it (absorption spectrometry) under specified conditions.

spur   kiln furniture consisting of triangular supports placed to prevent glazed ware from sticking to shelves of the kiln in firing; sometimes called *stilts* or trivets.

stain   a prepared, *fritted* compound of coloring *oxides*, alumina, and a flux used as a glaze *colorant* or for overglaze and underglaze decoration.

standardization   the lack of variation or reduced variation in attributes of composition, form, and style within a particular category of artifact, such as pottery.

stilt   kiln furniture consisting of small clay tripods used for holding glazed ware in a kiln; sometimes called *spurs* or cockspurs.

stoneware   a vitreous or semivitreous ceramic ware, usually gray, brown, or white, and frequently glazed.

strain   elastic deformation owing to *stress;* change in dimension per unit dimension.

stress   an applied force, measured per unit area. Significant stresses in ceramics include *tensile, compression, transverse,* and impact stresses.

style   (1) a manner or mode of expression or the character of that expression; (2) a visual representation, specific to a particular time and place, that transmits information about the identity of the makers and the context of use. Style usually refers to decorative or surface embellishment, but it may also refer to a constellation of technological traits.

symmetry   a property of design based on the spatial position of the geometric figure(s) constituting the fundamental part of the design, and on the movement of the figure(s) across a line or around a point axis (e.g., translation, reflection, rotation, and slide reflection).

taxonomic classification   a formal classification scheme, often hierarchical (e.g., the *type-variety system*), that specifies inclusion relations and results in the creation of *types*.

temper   to mix or modify to a proper consistency; a material—mineral or organic, but usually nonplastic—added to a clay to improve its working, drying, or firing properties; see also *additive, aggregate, aplastic, inclusion, nonplastic.*

tensile strength   the ability of a material such as a ceramic to withstand a tensile load, or forces pulling in opposite directions.

terra-cotta   an earthenware body, unglazed, usually red, relatively coarse and porous, and low fired; sculptural or architectural articles made from such an earthenware body.

terra sigillata   a red-slipped earthenware associated with Roman Europe. Although the name means "stamped" (from *sigillum*), the term is sometimes used to refer to a red earthenware slip or "slip glaze" having the same properties as its ancient counterpart; see also *Arretine, Samian.*

texture   (1) the proportion, size, shape, and orientation characteristics of *phases* in a clay body; (2) the general character of a fired *fabric* as viewed in cross section, described in terms of particle size (fine vs. coarse), characteristics of fracture (friable, blocky), and density (dense vs. porous); (3) sometimes, the surface quality of a vessel.

thermal conductivity (*k*)   the ability of a material to conduct heat, measured as the rate of heat flow through unit area per unit temperature gradient.

thermal expansion   the change in size (length or volume) of a material with increasing temperature of firing; see also *coefficient of thermal expansion.*

thermal fatigue   the delayed failure of a ceramic as a consequence of thermal stress, caused by the cumulative effect of repeated cycles of heating and cooling.

thermal gradient   a temperature differential between the surfaces and interior of the walls of a vessel that may exist during firing, cooling, or use with heat.

thermal shock resistance   the ability of a ceramic object to withstand sudden changes in temperature or repeated cycles of heating and cooling (*thermal stress*) without damage.

thermal stress   internal stresses in a ceramic body arising from repeated subjection to temperature changes and the resulting thermal expansion and contraction of the components in the body.

thermoluminescence (TL)   the light released when an object is heated, apart from normal incandescence; a technique of determining the age of an object, such as a fired clay, by measuring the amount of light energy released on experimental heating to about 500°C, that amount being proportional to the time elapsed since the object was last heated.

thermoremanent magnetism   the magnetism of a ferrimagnetic material (such as an iron-bearing clay) after it has been heated, which retains an alignment corresponding to the earth's magnetic field at the time of heating and is used in archaeomagnetic dating of the material.

thin section   a piece of rock or ceramic, ground to extreme thinness (0.03 mm) and mounted between glass slides, usually for study in a *polarizing microscope.*

throat   the base of a *neck* or *collar* on a vessel, or the point of maximum diameter restriction of a neck or collar.

throw   to form a ceramic object on a potter's *wheel*, making use of the centrifugal force produced by rapid rotation of the wheel.

tint   a variation of a color produced by adding white to it, characterized by low saturation.

tone   a mixture of light (white) and shade (black) with a color.

tournette   a small pivoted turntable used as a revolving support for hand building vessels, but lacking the weight for sustained rotation and the centrifugal force for *throwing* on the true potter's *wheel*.

trace elements   an element present in very small amounts in the earth's crust (in amounts less than 0.1%). Elements present in amounts less than 1 ppm are sometimes called ultratrace.

transition element   an element in the middle of the long periods (rows) of the periodic table, many of which (especially Ti, V, Cr, Mn, Fe, Co, Ni, and Cu) are important coloring agents in glazes.

transverse stress   flexural stress; a stress or force causing bending.

triaxial body   a modern prepared clay body consisting of a clay, an *aggregate* or filler (e.g., *flint* or *grog*), and a *flux*.

true porosity   total porosity; the total proportion of the bulk volume of a material occupied by pores, both open and closed. True porosity cannot be easily measured in a ceramic, and usually *apparent porosity* is measured.

type   a nonrandom cluster of attributes; an internally cohesive class of items formally defined by a consistent association of *attributes* (or *attribute states*) and set off from other classes by discontinuities in attribute states.

type-variety system   a standardized system of pottery classification that defines a hierarchy of increasingly inclusive classes, from varieties (minimal units) through *types* and groups, to *wares*.

typology   a theoretically oriented classification directed toward solving a problem; see also *classification*.

underglaze   a type of colored decoration applied to raw or *biscuit* ware before the glaze coating is applied.

value   the intensity, brilliance, or lightness/darkness of a color. In the *Munsell* system, value is the vertical dimension, varying from dark to light.

viscosity   the resistance of a fluid to shear or flow; the thickness or stiffness of a fluid (such as a slip or glaze) causing it to resist being stirred or not to flow (run) once applied to a body.

visible spectrum   that portion of the range of energies (vibrations or wavelengths) of the electromagnetic spectrum that is perceived by the human eye as visible light, generally defined as consisting of wavelengths of 400 to 700 μm.

vitrification   the action or process of becoming glass; the high-temperature process whereby the particles within a mass fuse, closing the surface pores and forming a homogeneous, impervious mass without deformation.

void   an open space in a pottery fabric; pore.

volatilize   vaporize; to convert to a vapor or to the state of a gas, as with the heat of firing.

ware   a ceramic material in the raw or fired state (e.g., greenware, *earthenware, stoneware*, etc); a class of pottery whose members share similar technology, fabric, and surface treatment.

waster   vessels or sherds from vessels damaged in manufacturing, particularly in firing, as by overfiring, underfiring, warping, or bloating.

water of plasticity   see *plasticity, water of*.

water smoking   preheating; the initial phase of the firing cycle in which all mechanically held water in the clay piece is volatilized and removed by slow heating to about 120°C.

wedge   variously described as to knead or mix a plastic clay body with the hands or feet or to cut and rejoin the mass before kneading, in order to eliminate air pockets, randomize the orientation of particles, compress the mass, and provide a uniform distribution of moisture.

wheel (potter's wheel)   a pivoted device capable of sustained rotation (usually by means of a flywheel) upon which a potter builds a vessel making use of centrifugal force produced at high rotation speeds to aid in lifting and shaping the piece to its final form. May be driven mechanically (by kicking or by turning with a stick) or electrically.

work heat ratio   the effect of a particular amount of heat in a particular amount of time on the firing of a ceramic, registered by pyrometric cones but not by temperature alone.

working range   the variable amounts of water that may be added to a dry clay to make it satisfactorily plastic; see also *plastic limits*.

Young's modulus (E)   a measure of the rigidity of a material; see also *modulus of elasticity*.

yield point   the force or stress at which deformation or flow begins to take place in a clay/water system.

References

Abascal, R.

1975 Los hornos prehispanicos en la región de Tlaxcala. *Mesa Redonda* 13: 189–98 (Mexico, Sociedad Mexicana de Antropología).

Adams, W. Y.

1979 On the argument from ceramics to history: A challenge based on evidence from medieval Nubia. *Current Anthropology* 20(4):727–44.

Adan-Bayewitz, D., and I. Perlman

1985 Local pottery provenience studies: A role for clay analysis. *Archaeometry* 27(2):203–17.

Ahrens, L. H., and S. R. Taylor

1961 *Spectrochemical analysis.* 2d ed. London: Pergamon.

Aitken, M. J.

1958 Magnetic dating—I. *Archaeometry* 1:16–20.

1961 *Physics and archaeology.* New York: Interscience.

1976 Thermoluminescent age evaluation and assessment of error limits: Revised system. *Archaeometry* 18(2):233–38.

1985 *Thermoluminescence dating.* London: Academic Press.

Aitken, M. J., P. A. Alcock, G. D. Bussell, and C. J. Shaw

1981 Archaeomagnetic determination of the past geomagnetic intensity using ancient ceramics: Allowance for anisotropy. *Archaeometry* 23(1):53–64.

Aitken, M. J., and J. C. Alldred

1972 The assessment of error limits in thermoluminescent dating. *Archaeometry* 14(2):257–67.

Aitken, M. J., P. R. S. Moorey, and P. J. Ucko

1971 The authenticity of vessels and figurines in the Hacilar style. *Archaeometry* 13(2):89–141.

Aitken, M. J., and G. H. Weaver

1962 Magnetic dating: Some archaeomagnetic measurements in Britain. *Archaeometry* 5:4–18.

Aldenderfer, M. S., and R. K. Blashfield

1984 *Cluster analysis.* Beverly Hills, Calif.: Sage.

487

Alexander, R. E., and R. H. Johnston
1982   Xeroradiography of ancient objects: A new imaging modality. In *Archaeological ceramics*, ed. J. S. Olin and A. D. Franklin, 145–54. Washington, D.C.: Smithsonian Institution.

Allen, R. O., A. H. Luckenbach, and G. C. Holland
1975   The application of instrumental neutron activation analysis to a study of prehistoric steatite artifacts and source materials. *Archaeometry* 17(1):69–83.

Allen, W. L., and J. B. Richardson III
1971   The reconstruction of kinship from archaeological data: The concepts, the methods, and the feasibility. *American Antiquity* 36(1):41–53.

Amberg, C. R., and J. Hartsook
1946   Effect of design factors on thermal-shock resistance of cooking ware. *Bulletin of the American Ceramic Society* 25:448–52.

Amiran, R.
1965   The beginnings of pottery-making in the Near East. In *Ceramics and man*, ed. F. R. Matson, 240–47. Chicago: Aldine.

Amiran, R., and D. Shenhav
1984   Experiments with an ancient potter's wheel. In *Pots and potters: Current approaches in ceramic archaeology*, ed. P. M. Rice, 107–12. UCLA Institute of Archaeology Monograph 24. Los Angeles: University of California.

Andersen, C. A., ed.
1973   *Microprobe analysis*. New York: John Wiley.

Anderson, A.
1984   *Interpreting pottery*. New York: Pica Press.

Anderson-Stojanovic, V. R.
1982   Computer-assisted analysis of pottery at Stobi, Yugoslavia. *Journal of Field Archaeology* 9:336–48.

Annis, M. B.
1985   Resistance and change: Pottery manufacture in Sardinia. *World Archaeology* 17(2):240–55.

Anseau, M. R., M. Deletter, and F. Cambier
1981   The separation of sintering mechanisms for clay-based ceramics. *Transactions of the British Ceramic Society* 80:142–46.

Arayaphong, D., M. G. McLaren, and G. W. Phelps
1984   Role of sub-sieve mica in ceramic clays. *Bulletin of the American Ceramic Society* 63:1181–85.

Arnold, C. J.
1981   Early Anglo-Saxon pottery: Production and distribution. In *Production and distribution: A ceramic viewpoint*, ed. H. Howard and E. Morris, 243–55. International Series 120. Oxford: British Archaeological Reports.

Arnold, D. E.
1971   Ethnomineralogy of Ticul, Yucatán, potters: Etics and emics. *American Antiquity* 36(1):20–40.
1972   Native pottery making in Quinua, Peru. *Anthropos* 67:858–72.
1974   Some principles of paste analysis and interpretation: A preliminary formulation. *Journal of the Steward Anthropological Society* 6(1):33–47.
1975a   Ceramic ecology of the Ayacucho basin, Peru: Implications for prehistory. *Current Anthropology* 16(2):183–206.
1975b   Ecological variables and ceramic production: Toward a general model. In *Primitive art and technology*, ed. J. S. Raymond et al., 92–108. Alberta: University of Calgary.
1978   Ethnography of pottery-making in the Valley of Guatemala. In *The ceramics*

of Kaminaljuyú, Guatemala, ed. R. K. Wetherington, 327–400. University Park: Pennsylvania State University Press.

1979 Comment on Adams. *Current Anthropology* 20(4):735.

1980 Localized exchange: An ethnoarchaeological perspective. In *Models and methods in regional exchange,* ed. R. E. Fry, 147–50. SAA Papers 1. Washington, D.C.: Society for American Archaeology.

1983 Design structure and community organization in Quinua, Peru. In *Structure and cognition in art,* ed. D. K. Washburn, 56–73. Cambridge: Cambridge University Press.

1984 Social interaction and ceramic design: Community-wide correlates in Quinua, Peru. In *Pots and potters: Current approaches in ceramic archeology,* ed. P. M. Rice, 133–61. UCLA Institute of Archaeology Monograph 24. Los Angeles: University of California Press.

1985 *Ceramic theory and cultural process.* Cambridge: Cambridge University Press.

Arnold, D. E., P. M. Rice, W. A. Jester, W. N. Deutsch, B. K. Lee, and R. I. Kirsch

1978 Neutron activation analysis of contemporary pottery and pottery materials from the Valley of Guatemala. In *The ceramics of Kaminaljuyú, Guatemala,* ed. R. K. Wetherington, 543–86. University Park: Pennsylvania State University Press.

Arrott, C. R.

1953 La cerámica moderna, hecha a mano en Santa Apolonia. *Antropología e Historia de Guatemala* 5:3–10.

Asboe, Rev. W.

1946 Pottery in Ladakh, western Tibet. *Man* 46:9–10.

Ashley, H. E.

1909 The colloidal matter of clay and its measurement. *U.S. Geological Survey Bulletin* 388:1–62.

Attas, M., J. M. Fossey, and L. Yaffe

1982 Variations of ceramic composition with time: A test case using Lakonian pottery. *Archaeometry* 24(2):181–90.

1984 Corrections for drill-bit contamination in sampling ancient pottery for neutron activation analysis. *Archaeometry* 26(1):104–7.

Attas, M., L. Yaffe, and J. M. Fossey

1977 Neutron activation analysis of Early Bronze Age pottery from Lake Vouliagméni, Perakhóra, Central Greece. *Archaeometry* 19(1):33–43.

Bailey, E. H., and R. E. Stevens

1960 Selective staining of K-feldspar and plagioclase on rock slab and thin sections. *American Mineralogist* 45:1020–25.

Baines, J.

1985 Color terminology and color classification: Ancient Egyptian color terminology and polychromy. *American Anthropologist* 87(2):282–97.

Balfet, H.

1965 Ethnographical observations in North Africa and archaeological interpretation: The pottery of the Mahgreb. In *Ceramics and man,* ed. F. R. Matson, 161–77. Chicago: Aldine.

Balfet, H., M.-F. Fauvet-Berthelot, and S. Monzon

1983 *Pour la normalisation de la description des poteries.* Paris: CNRS.

Ballié, P. J., and W. B. Stern

1984 Non-destructive surface analysis of Roman terra sigillata: A possible tool in provenance studies? *Archaeometry* 26(1):62–68.

Bamps, A.
    1883   La céramique américaine au point de vue des éléments constitutifs de sa pâte et de sa fabrication. *Congrès International des Américanistes* 5:274–81.
Bankes, G.
    1980   *Moche pottery from Peru.* London: British Museum.
    1985   The manufacture and circulation of paddle and anvil pottery on the north coast of Peru. *World Archaeology* 17(2):269–77.
Banks, M., and E. T. Hall
    1963   X-ray fluorescent analysis in archaeology: The "milliprobe." *Archaeometry* 6:31–36.
Barbetti, M. F., M. W. McElhinny, D. J. Edwards, and P. W. Schmidt
    1977   Weathering processes in baked sediments and their effects on archaeomagnetic field intensity measurements. *Physics of the Earth and Planetary Interiors* 13:346–54.
Barbour, W. T.
    1976   A new way of identifying producers of Teotihuacán figurines. Manuscript, Department of Anthropology, State University of New York, Buffalo.
Barna, G.
    1967   Plasticity of clay minerals. *Bulletin of the American Ceramic Society* 46: 1091–93.
Barnett, H. G.
    1953   *Innovation: The basis of cultural change.* New York: McGraw-Hill.
Baroody, E. M., E. M. Simons, and W. H. Duckworth
    1955   Effect of shape on thermal fracture. *Journal of the American Ceramic Society* 38(1):38–43.
Bates, S. R.
    1971   Scanning electron microscopy. In *Characterization of ceramics*, ed. L. L. Hench and R. W. Gould, 419–34. New York: Marcel Dekker.
Bates, T. F.
    1964   The application of electron microscopy in soil clay mineralogy. In *Soil clay mineralogy: A symposium*, ed. C. I. Rich and G. W. Kunze, 125–47. Chapel Hill: University of North Carolina Press.
Batres, L.
    1909   *Antiguedades mejicanas falsificadas.* Mexico: Soria.
Baumhoff, M. A., and R. F. Heizer
    1959   Some unexploited possibilities in ceramic analysis. *Southwestern Journal of Anthropology* 15:308–15.
Beals, R. L
    1975   *The peasant marketing system of Oaxaca, Mexico.* Berkeley: University of California.
Beaudry, M. C., J. Long, H. M. Miller, F. D. Neiman, and G. W. Stone
    1983   A vessel typology for early Chesapeake ceramics: The Potomac Typological System. *Historical Archaeology* 17:18–39.
Beazley, J. D.
    1945   *Potter and painter in ancient Athens.* Oxford: Oxford University Press.
Beck, C. W.
    1984   Smithsonian Archaeometric Research Collections and Records (SARCAR). *Journal of Field Archaeology* 11:341–43.
Beck, C. W., ed.
    1974   *Archaeological chemistry.* Advances in Chemistry 138. Washington, D.C.: American Chemical Society.

Beck, C. W., C. A. Fellows, and E. MacKennan
1974 Nuclear magnetic resonance spectrometry in archaeology. In *Archaeological chemistry*, ed. C. W. Beck, 226–35. Advances in Chemistry 138. Washington, D.C.: American Chemical Society.

Bell, W. T., and D. W. Zimmerman
1978 The effect of HF acid etching on the morphology of quartz inclusions for thermoluminescence dating. *Archaeometry* 20(1):63–65.

Benfer, R. A.
1975 Sampling and classification. In *Sampling in archaeology*, ed. J. W. Mueller, 227–47. Tucson: University of Arizona Press.

Bennett, M. A.
1974 *Basic ceramic analysis*. Contributions in Anthropology no. 6. Portales: Eastern New Mexico University Press.

Benson, E.
1974 Gestures and offerings. In *Proceedings, Primera Mesa Redonda de Palenque*, vol. 1, ed. M. G. Robertson. Pebble Beach, Calif.: Robert Louis Stevenson School.

Berlin, B., and P. Kay
1969 *Basic color terms: Their universality and evolution*. Berkeley: University of California Press.

Berrin, L., and R. C. Sundahl
1971 Characterization of ceramic surfaces. In *Characterization of ceramics*, ed. L. L. Hench and R. W. Gould, 583–624. New York; Marcel Dekker.

Bertin, E. P.
1978 *Introduction to X-ray spectrometric analysis*. New York: Plenum.

Bieber, A. M., Jr., D. W. Brooks, G. Harbottle, and E. V. Sayre
1976 Application of multivariate techniques to analytical data on Aegean ceramics. *Archaeometry* 18(1):59–74.

Bimson, M.
1956 The technique of Greek black and terra sigillata red. *Antiquaries Journal* 36:200.
1969 The examination of ceramics by X-ray powder diffraction. *Studies in Conservation* 14:85–89.

Binford, L. R.
1962a Archaeology as anthropology. *American Antiquity* 28(2):217–26.
1962b A new method for calculating dates from kaolin pipe stem samples. *Southeastern Archaeological Conference Bulletin* 9(1):19–21.
1964 A consideration of archaeological research design. *American Antiquity* 29(4):425–41.
1965 Archaeological systematics and the study of culture process. *American Antiquity* 31(2):203–10.

Birks, L. S.
1971 *Electron probe microanalysis*. 2d ed. New York: Wiley-Interscience.

Birmingham, J.
1975 Traditional potters of the Kathmandu valley: An ethnoarcheological study. *Man*, n.s., 10:370–86.

Bischoff, H., and J. Viteri Gamboa
1972 Pre-Valdivia occupations on the southwest coast of Ecuador. *American Antiquity* 37(4):548–51.

Bishop, R. L.
1975 Western lowland Maya ceramic trade: An application of nuclear chemi-

cal and geological data analysis. Ph.D. diss., Southern Illinois University, Carbondale.

1980   Aspects of ceramic compositional modeling. In *Models and methods in regional exchange*, ed. R. E. Fry, 47–66. SAA Papers 1. Washington, D.C.: Society for American Archaeology.

Bishop, R. L., G. Harbottle, and E. V. Sayre

1982   Chemical and mathematical procedures employed in the Maya Fine Paste ceramics project. In *Analyses of Fine Paste ceramics: Excavations at Seibal, Department of El Petén, Guatemala*, ed. J. A. Sabloff, 272–82. Memoirs of the Peabody Museum, vol. 15, no. 2, Cambridge, Mass.: Peabody Museum.

Bishop, R. L., and R. L. Rands

1982   Maya Fine Paste ceramics: A compositional perspective. In *Analysis of Fine Paste ceramics: Excavations at Seibal, Department of El Petén, Guatemala*, ed. J. A. Sabloff, 283–314. Memoirs of the Peabody Museum, vol. 15, no. 2. Cambridge, Mass.: Peabody Museum.

Bishop, R. L., R. L. Rands, and G. R. Holley

1982   Ceramic compositional analysis in archaeological perspective. In *Advances in archaeological method and theory*, ed. M. B. Schiffer, 5:275–330. New York: Academic Press.

Blandino, B.

1984   *Coiled pottery, traditional and contemporary ways.* Radnor, Pa.: Chilton.

Blashfield, R. K., and J. G. Draguns

1976   Toward a taxonomy of psychopathology: The purpose of psychiatric classification. *British Journal of Psychiatry* 129:574–83.

Blatt, H.

1982   *Sedimentary petrology.* San Francisco: W. H. Freeman.

Bloor, E. C.

1957   Plasticity: A critical survey. *Transactions of the British Ceramic Society* 56:423–81.

Bomgardner, D. L.

1981   Atomic absorption spectroscopy applications for ceramic analysis. In *Scientific studies in ancient ceramics*, ed. M. J. Hughes, 93–101. BAR Occasional Paper 19. London: British Museum.

Boone, E. H., ed.

1982   *Falsifications and misreconstructions of pre-Columbian art.* Washington, D.C.: Dumbarton Oaks.

Borremans, N. T., and G. D. Shaak

1986   A preliminary report on investigations of sponge spicules in Florida "chalky" paste pottery. In *Papers in ceramic analysis*, ed. P. M. Rice. *Ceramic Notes* 3:125–31.

Bostanci, E. Y.

1959   Researches on the Mediterranean coast of Anatolia: A new Paleolithic site at Beldibi near Antalya. *Anatolia* 4:129–77.

Bouchez, R., J. M. D. Cooey, R. Coussement, et al.

1974   Mössbauer study of firing conditions used in the manufacture of the grey and red ware of Tureng Tepe. *Journal de Physique* 35:861–65.

Bowen, T., and E. Moser

1968   Seri pottery. *Kiva* 33:89–132.

Bower, N. W., R. H. Bromund, and R. H. Smith

1975   Atomic absorption for the archaeologist: An application from Pella of the Decapolis. *Journal of Field Archaeology* 2:389–98.

Bowie, S. H. U., and P. R. Simpson
1977 Microscopy: Reflected light. In *Physical methods in determinative mineralogy.* 2d ed., ed. J. Zussman, 109–265. London: Academic Press.

Bowman, H. R., F. Asaro, and I. Perlman
1973 Composition variations in obsidian sources and the archaeological implications. *Archaeometry* 15(1): 123–27.

Bowyer, D.
1972 Chromatography analyses for lipids in clay. Appendix D in *Myrtos, an early Bronze Age settlement in Crete,* by P. Warren, 330–31. London: Thames and Hudson.

Bradley, W. F.
1964 X-ray diffraction analysis of soil clays and structures of clay minerals. In *Soil clay mineralogy: A symposium,* ed. C. I. Rich and G. W. Kunze, 113–24. Chapel Hill: University of North Carolina Press.

Bradley, W. F., and R. E. Grim
1961 Mica clay minerals. In *The X-ray identification and crystal structures of clay minerals,* ed. G. W. Brindley, 208–41. Monographs. London: Mineralogical Society of Great Britain.

Brainerd, G. W.
1942 Symmetry in primitive conventional design. *American Antiquity* 8(2): 164–66.
1958 *The archaeological ceramics of Yucatán.* Anthropological Records, vol. 19. Berkeley: University of California Press.

Braithwaite, M.
1982 Decoration as ritual symbol: A theoretical proposal and an ethnographic study in southern Sudan. In *Symbolic and structural archaeology,* ed. I. Hodder, 80–88. Cambridge: Cambridge University Press.

Braun, D. P.
1980 Experimental interpretation of ceramic vessel use on the basis of rim and neck formal attributes. In *The Navajo Project, archaeological investigations,* ed. D. Fiero, R. Munson, et al. Research Paper 11. Flagstaff: Museum of Northern Arizona.
1982 Radiographic analysis of temper in ceramic vessels: Goals and initial methods. *Journal of Field Archaeology* 9: 183–92.
1983 Pots as tools. In *Archaeological hammers and theories,* ed. J. A. Moore and A. S. Keene, 107–34. New York: Academic Press.
1985 Ceramic decorative diversity and Illinois Woodland regional integration. In *Decoding prehistoric ceramics,* ed. B. A. Nelson, 128–53. Carbondale: Southern Illinois University Press.

Bray, A.
1982 Mimbres Black-on-white, melamine or Wedgwood? A ceramic use-wear analysis. *Kiva* 47(3): 133–49.

Brew, J. O.
1946 The uses and abuses of taxonomy. In *Archaeology of Alkali Ridge, southeastern Utah,* 44–66. Papers of the Peabody Museum, vol. 21. Cambridge, Mass.: Peabody Museum.

Brewer, R.
1964 Structure and mineral analysis of soils. In *Soil clay mineralogy: A symposium,* ed. C. I. Rich and G. W. Kunze, 77–112. Chapel Hill: University of North Carolina Press.

Brill, R. H., ed.
1971 *Science and archaeology.* Cambridge: MIT Press.

Brindley, G. W.

1961   The chlorite minerals. In *The X-ray identification and crystal structures of clay minerals*, ed. G. W. Brindley, 242–96. Monographs. London: Mineralogical Society of Great Britain.

Brindley, G. W., ed.

1951   *X-ray identification and structures of clay minerals*. Monographs. London: Mineralogical Society of Great Britain.

1961   *The X-ray identification and crystal structures of clay minerals*. Monographs. London: Mineralogical Society of Great Britain.

Brindley, G. W., and K. Robinson

1946   The structure of kaolinite. *Mineralogical Magazine* 27:242–53.

Brindley, G. W., et al.

1951   The nomenclature of the clay minerals. *American Mineralogist* 36:370–71.

Brisbane, M. A.

1981   Incipient markets for early Anglo-Saxon ceramics: Variations in levels and modes of production. In *Production and distribution: A ceramic viewpoint*, ed. H. Howard and E. Morris, 229–42. International Series 120. Oxford: British Archaeological Reports.

Brody, H.

1979   *The book of low-fire ceramics*. New York: Holt, Rinehart and Winston.

Brody, J. J.

1976   The creative consumer: Survival, revival and invention in Southwest Indian arts. In *Ethnic and tourist arts: Cultural expressions from the Fourth World*, ed. N. H. H. Graburn, 70–84. Berkeley: University of California Press.

Bromund, R. H., N. W. Bower, and R. H. Smith

1976   Inclusions in ancient ceramics: An approach to the problem of sampling for chemical analysis. *Archaeometry* 18(2):218–21.

Brongniart, A.

1844   *Traité des arts céramiques*. Paris: Dessain et Tolra.

Bronitsky, G.

1982   Clay workability: A pilot study. *Archaeological Society of Virginia Quarterly Bulletin* 37:65–72.

1986   The use of materials-science techniques in the study of pottery construction and use. In *Advances in archaeological method and theory*, ed. M. B. Schiffer, 9:209–76. Orlando, Fla.: Academic Press.

Bronitsky, G., and R. Hamer

1986   Experiments in ceramic technology: The effects of various tempering materials on impact and thermal-shock resistance. *American Antiquity* 51(1):89–101.

Brooks, D., A. M. Bieber, Jr., G. Harbottle, and E. V. Sayre

1974   Biblical studies through activation analysis of ancient pottery. In *Archaeological chemistry*, ed. C. W. Beck, 48–80. Advances in Chemistry 138. Washington, D.C.: American Chemical Society.

Brothwell, D., and E. Higgs, eds.

1963   *Science in archaeology*. New York: Basic Books.

Brown, G., and I. Stephen

1959   Expanding-lattice minerals. *Mineralogical Magazine* 32:251–53.

Brown, J. L.

1964   Laboratory techniques in the electron microscopy of clay minerals. In *Soil clay mineralogy: A symposium*, ed. C. I. Rich and G. W. Kunze, 148–69. Chapel Hill: University of North Carolina Press.

Brownell, W. E.

1949   Fundamental factors influencing efflorescence of clay products. *Journal of the American Ceramic Society* 32(12):375–89.

Broyles, B.
1968   Reconstructed designs from Swift Creek Complicated Stamped sherds. *Southeastern Archaeological Conference Bulletin* 8:49–55.

Bruhns, K. O., and N. Hammond
1983   A visit to Valdivia. *Journal of Field Archaeology* 10:485–87.

Brush, C. F.
1965   Pox pottery: Earliest identified Mexican ceramic. *Science* 149:194–95.

Buerger, M. J., and J. S. Lukesh
1937   Wallpaper and atoms. *Technology Review* 39:338–42.

Buessem, W. R.
1955   Thermal shock testing. *Journal of the American Ceramic Society* 38(1):15–17.

Buko, A.
1984   Problems and research prospects in the determination of the provenance of pottery. *World Archaeology* 15(3):348–65.

Bullen, R. P., and J. B. Stoltman, eds.
1972   Fiber-tempered pottery in southeastern United States and northern Colombia: Its origins, context, and significance. *Florida Anthropologist* 25(2), part 2.

Bunzel, R.
1972   *The Pueblo potter: A study of creative imagination in primitive art.* New York: Dover. (originally published 1929.)

Burke, J. E.
1985   A history of the development of a science of sintering. In *Ancient technology to modern science*, ed. W. D. Kingery, 315–33. Ceramics and Civilization, vol. 1. Columbus, Ohio: American Ceramic Society.

Burnham, F., and M. A. Tuttle
1945   Influence of variable amounts of New York talc, flint and calcined clay on serviceability of glazed cooking-ware bodies. *Journal of the American Ceramic Society* 28(3):72–75.

Burton, W.
1906   *Porcelain: Its nature, art, and manufacture.* London: B. T. Batsford.

Bushell, S. W.
1910   *Description of Chinese pottery and porcelain.* Oxford: Clarendon Press.

Butterworth, B.
1956   Lime blowing: Some notes on the literature. *Transactions of the British Ceramic Society* 55:532–44.

Butzer, K.
1974   Modern Egyptian pottery clays and Predynastic buff ware. *Journal of Near Eastern Studies* 33:377–82.

Caley, E. R.
1949   Klaproth as a pioneer in the chemical investigation of antiquities. *Journal of Chemical Education* 26:242–47.
1951   Early history and literature of archaeological chemistry. *Journal of Chemical Education* 28:64–66.

Calver, J. L.
1957   *Mining and mineral resources.* Bulletin no. 39. Tallahassee: Florida Geological Survey.

Cardew, M.
1969   *Pioneer pottery.* New York: St. Martin's Press.
1985   The fatal impact. *Ceramics Monthly* 33(6):33–38.

Carriveau, G. W.
1980   Contamination of hard-fired ceramics during sampling with diamond burrs. *Archaeometry* 22(2):209–10.

Carter, G. F., ed.
  1978   *Archaeological chemistry.* Vol. 2. Advances in Chemistry 171. Washington, D.C.: American Chemical Society.
Caso, A., and I. Bernal
  1952   *Urnas de Oaxaca.* Memorias 2. Mexico City: Instituto Nacional de Antropología e Historia.
Castillo Tejero, N., and J. Litvak
  1968   *Un sistema de estudio para formas de vasijas.* Technología 2. Mexico City: Departamento de Prehistória, Instituto Nacional de Antropología e Historia.
Catling, H. W.
  1961   Spectrographic analysis of Mycenaean and Minoan pottery: Introductory note. *Archaeometry* 3:31–33.
Catling, H. W., A. E. Blin-Stoyle, and E. E. Richards
  1961   Spectrographic analysis of Mycenaean and Minoan pottery. *Archaeometry* 4:31–38.
Catling, H. W., E. E. Richards, and A. E. Blin-Stoyle
  1961   Correlations between composition and provenance of Mycenaean and Minoan pottery. *Annals of the British School at Athens* 58:94–115.
Chagnon, N.
  1968   *Yanomamö: The fierce people.* New York: Holt, Rinehart and Winston.
Chandler, H.
  1981   Thermal stress in ceramics. *Transactions of the British Ceramic Society* 80:191–95.
Chang, K.-C.
  1977   *The archaeology of ancient China.* 3d ed. rev. New Haven: Yale University Press.
  1983   *Art, myth, and ritual: The path to political authority in ancient China.* Cambridge: Harvard University Press.
Charlton, T.
  1968   Post-Conquest Aztec ceramics: Implications for archaeological interpretation. *Florida Anthropologist* 21:96–101.
  1969   Texcoco fabric-marked pottery, tlateles, and salt-making. *American Antiquity* 34(1):73–76.
  1976   Contemporary central Mexican ceramics: A view from the past. *Man* 11(4):517–25.
Chase, P. G.
  1985   Whole vessels and sherds: An experimental investigation of their quantitative relationship. *Journal of Field Archaeology* 12:213–18.
Chayanov, A. V.
  1966   *The theory of peasant economy.* Homewood, Ill.: Irwin.
Chayes, F.
  1956   *Petrographic modal analysis.* New York: John Wiley.
Chernela, J.
  1969   In praise of the scratch: The importance of aboriginal abrasion on museum ceramic ware. *Curator* 12:174–79.
Cheung, K.-Y.
  1983   Recent archaeological evidence relating to the origin of Chinese characters. In *The origins of Chinese civilization,* ed. K. N. Keightley, 323–91. Berkeley: University of California Press.
Christenson, A. L., and D. W. Read
  1977   Numerical taxonomy, R-mode factor analysis, and archaeological classification. *American Antiquity* 42(2):163–79.

Chu, G. P. K.
1968 Microstructure of complex ceramics. In *Ceramic microstructures: Their analysis, significance, and production,* ed. R. M. Fulrath and J. A. Pask, 828–62. New York: John Wiley.

Clancy, J. J.
1961 Chemical analysis of residue from Indian Hill ceramic pot. *Massachusetts Archaeological Society Bulletin* 22:44–46.

Clarke, D.
1968 *Analytical archaeology.* London: Methuen.

Clayton, E., D. D. Cohen, and P. Duerden
1981 Thick target PIXE analysis and yield curve calculations. *Nuclear Instruments and Methods* 180:541–48.

Coble, R.
1958 Effect of microstructure on the mechanical properties of ceramic materials. In *Ceramic fabrication processes,* ed. W. D. Kingery, 213–28. Cambridge: MIT Press.

Coble, R. L., and W. D. Kingery
1955 Effect of porosity on thermal stress fracture. *Journal of the American Ceramic Society* 38(1):33–37.

Cochran, W. G.
1963 *Sampling techniques.* London: Chapman and Hall.

Coe, M. D.
1973 *The Maya scribe and his world.* New York: Grolier Club.
1978 *The lords of the underworld.* Princeton: Princeton University Press.

Cohen, R. L., ed.
1976 *Applications of Mössbauer spectroscopy.* Vol 1. London: Academic Press.

Colton, H. S.
1951 Hopi pottery firing temperatures. *Plateau* 24:73–76.
1953 *Potsherds: An introduction to the study of prehistoric southwestern ceramics and their use in historic reconstruction.* Flagstaff: Museum of Northern Arizona.

Condamin, J., F. Formenti, M. O. Metais, M. Michel, and P. Blond
1976 The application of gas chromatography to the tracing of oil in ancient amphorae. *Archaeometry* 18(2):195–202.

Conkey, M. W.
1978 Style and information in cultural evolution: Toward a predictive model for the Paleolithic. In *Social archaeology: Beyond subsistence and dating,* ed. C. L. Redman, M. J. Berman, E. V. Curtin, et al., 61–85. New York: Academic Press.

Cook, S.
1984 Peasant economy, rural industry, and capitalist development in the Oaxaca valley, Mexico. *Journal of Peasant Studies* 12(1):3–40.

Cooke, R. G.
1985 Ancient painted pottery from Panama. *Archaeology* 38(4):33–39.

Cordell, A. S.
1984 *Ceramic technology at a Weeden Island period archaeological site in north Florida.* Ceramic Notes no. 2. Gainesville: Florida State Museum.

Courtois, L.
1976 *Examen au microscope pétrographique des céramiques archéologiques.* Notes et Monographies Techniques no. 8. Paris: Centre de Recherches Archéologiques.

Cousins, D. R., and K. G. Dharmawardena
1969 Use of Mössbauer spectroscopy in the study of ancient pottery. *Nature* 223:732–33.

Cowgill, G. L.

1964   The selection of samples from large sherd collections. *American Antiquity* 29(4):467–73.

1982   Clusters of objects and associations between variables: Two approaches to archaeological classification. In *Essays on archaeological typology*, ed. R. Whallon and J. A. Brown, 30–55. Evanston, Ill.: Center for American Archaeology Press.

Crandall, W. B., and J. Ging

1955   Thermal shock analysis of spherical shapes. *Journal of the American Ceramic Society* 38(1):44–54.

Cronin, C.

1962   An analysis of pottery design elements indicating possible relationships between three decorated types. In *Chapters in the prehistory of eastern Arizona*, ed. P. Martin, 105–14. Fieldiana: Anthropology, vol. 53. Chicago: Field Museum of Natural History.

Crossland, L. B., and M. Posnansky

1978   Pottery, people, and trade at Begho, Ghana. In *The spatial organisation of culture*, ed. I. Hodder, 77–89. Pittsburgh: University of Pittsburgh Press.

Cruxent, J. M., and I. Rouse

1959   *An archaeological chronology of Venezuela*. Social Science Monographs no. 6. Washington, D.C.: Pan American Union.

Cullity, B.D.

1967   *Elements of X-ray diffraction*. Reading, Mass.: Addison-Wesley.

Cummins, W. A.

1983   Petrology of stone axes and tools. In *The petrology of archaeological artefacts*, ed. D. R. C. Kempe and A. P. Harvey, 171–226. Oxford: Clarendon Press.

Curtis, F.

1962   The utility pottery industry of Bailén, southern Spain. *American Anthropologist* 64(3):486–503.

Dal, P. H., and W. J. Berden

1965   Bound water on clay. *Science of Ceramics* 2:59.

d'Albis, A.

1985   Steps in the manufacture of the soft-paste porcelain of Vincennes, according to the books of Hellot. In *Ancient technology to modern science*, ed. W. D. Kingery, 257–71. Ceramics and Civilization, vol. 1. Columbus, Ohio: American Ceramic Society.

David, N.

1972   On the life span of pottery, type frequencies, and archaeological inference. *American Antiquity* 37(1):141–42.

1981   The design of archaeological processing systems with special reference to that employed at Lake Vouliagméni, Greece. *Journal of Field Archaeology* 9:237–41.

David, N., and H. Hennig

1972   The ethnography of pottery: A Fulani case seen in archaeological perspective. Module 21. Reading, Mass.: Addison-Wesley.

Davidge, R. W., and G. Tappin

1967   Thermal shock and fracture in ceramics. *Transactions of the British Ceramic Society* 66:405–22.

Deal, M.

1983   Pottery ethnoarchaeology among the Tzeltal Maya. Ph.D. diss., Simon Fraser University.

DeAtley, S. P.

1980 Radiocarbon dating of ceramic materials: Progress and prospects. *Radiocarbon* 22(3):987–93.

1986 Mix and match: Traditions of glaze paint preparation at Four Mile Ruin, Arizona. In *Technology and style*, ed. W. D. Kingery, 297–329. Ceramics and Civilization, vol. 2. Columbus, Ohio: American Ceramic Society.

DeBoer, W. R.

1974 Ceramic longevity and archaeological interpretation: An example from the upper Ucayali, Peru. *American Antiquity* 39(2):335–43.

1980 Vessel shape from rim sherds: An experiment on the effect of the individual illustrator. *Journal of Field Archaeology* 7:131–35.

1984 The last pottery show: System and sense in ceramic studies. In *The many dimensions of pottery: Ceramics in archaeology and anthropology*, ed. S. E. van der Leeuw and A. C. Pritchard, 527–71. CINGULA 7. Amsterdam: Institute for Pre- and Proto-history, University of Amsterdam.

1985 Pots and pans do not speak, nor do they lie: The case for occasional reductionism. In *Decoding prehistoric ceramics*, ed. B. A. Nelson, 347–57. Carbondale: Southern Illinois University Press.

DeBoer, W. R., and D. Lathrap

1979 The making and breaking of Shipibo-Conibo ceramics. In *Ethnoarchaeology: Implications of ethnography for archaeology*, ed. C. Kramer, 102–38. New York: Columbia University Press.

DeBoer, W. R., and J. A. Moore

1982 The measurement and meaning of stylistic diversity. *Ñawpa Pacha* 20: 147–62.

DeBruin, M., P. J. M. Korthoven, A. J. VanderSteen, J. P. W. Houtman, and R. P. W. Duin

1976 The use of trace element concentrations in the identification of objects. *Archaeometry* 18(1):75–84.

Deetz, J. F.

1965 *The dynamics of stylistic change in Arikara ceramics.* Illinois Studies in Anthropology no. 4. Urbana: University of Illinois Press.

1967 *Invitation to archaeology.* Garden City, N.Y.: Natural History Press.

Deevey, E. S., Jr.

1970 In defense of mud. *Bulletin of the Ecological Society of America* 51(1):5–8.

Demont, M., and P. Centlivres

1967 Poteries et potiers d'Afghanistan. *Bulletin Annuel du Musée et Institut d'Ethnographie de la Ville de Genève* 10:23–67.

Díaz, M. N.

1966 *Tonalá: Conservatism, responsibility, and authority in a Mexican town.* Berkeley: University of California Press.

Dickinson, B. M., and K. F. Hartley

1971 The evidence of potters' stamps on Samian ware and on mortaria for the trading connections of Roman York. In *Soldier and civilian in Roman Yorkshire*, ed. R. M. Butler, 127–42. Leicester: Leicester University Press.

Dickson, J. A. D.

1966 Carbonate identification and genesis as revealed by staining. *Journal of Sedimentary Petrology* 36:491–505.

Dinsdale, A., J. Camm, and W. T. Wilkinson

1967 The mechanical strength of ceramic tableware. *Transactions of the British Ceramic Society* 66:367–404.

Dittert, A. E., Jr., and F. Plog
  1980   *Generations in clay: Pueblo pottery of the American Southwest.* Flagstaff, Ariz.: Northland Press.
Dixon, J. E.
  1976   Obsidian characterization studies in the Mediterranean and Near East. In *Advances in obsidian glass studies,* ed. R. E. Taylor, 288–333. Park Ridge, N.J.: Noyes.
Donnan, C. B.
  1965   Moche ceramic technology. *Ñawpa Pacha* 3:115–38.
  1971   Ancient Peruvian potters' marks and their interpretation through ethnographic analogy. *American Antiquity* 36(4):460–65.
  1978   Antiguas marcas alfareras y su interpretación a través la analogía etnográfica. In *Tecnología andina,* ed. R. Ravines, 439–46. Lima: Instituto de Estudios Peruanos.
  1982   The identification of a Moche fake through iconographic analysis. In *Falsifications and misreconstructions of pre-Columbian art,* ed. E. H. Boone, 37–50, 142. Washington, D.C.: Dumbarton Oaks.
Donnan, C. B., and C. W. Clewlow, eds.
  1974   *Ethnoarchaeology.* UCLA Institute of Archaeology, Archaeological Survey, Monograph 4. Los Angeles: University of California Press.
Doran, J. E., and F. R. Hodson
  1975   *Mathematics and computers in archaeology.* Cambridge: Harvard University Press.
Douglas, M.
  1955   *Purity and danger.* New York: Frederick A. Praeger.
Dow, M. M.
  1985   Agricultural intensification and craft specialization: A nonrecursive model. *Ethnology* 24(2):137–52.
Drennan, R. D.
  1976   A refinement of chronological seriation using nonmetric multidimensional scaling. *American Antiquity* 41(3):290–302.
Drier, R. W.
  1939   A new method of sherd classification. *American Antiquity* 5(1):31–35.
Duma, G.
  1972   Phosphate content of ancient pots as indication of use. *Current Anthropology* 13(1):127–31.
Dumont, L.
  1952   A remarkable feature of south Indian pot-making. *Man* 52:81–83.
Dunnell, R.
  1971   *Systematics in prehistory.* New York: Free Press.
  1978   Style and function: A fundamental dichotomy. *American Antiquity* 43(2):192–202.
Earle, T. K.
  1977   A reappraisal of redistribution: Complex Hawaiian chiefdoms. In *Exchange systems in prehistory,* ed. T. K. Earle and J. E. Ericson, 213–29. New York: Academic Press.
  1981   Comment on Rice. *Current Anthropology* 22(3):230–31.
Egloff, B. J.
  1973   A method for counting ceramic rim sherds. *American Antiquity* 38(3):351–53.
Ekholm, G. F.
  1964   The problem of fakes in pre-Columbian art. *Curator* 7:19–32.

Ellen, R. F.
1979   Introductory essay. In *Classifications in their social contexts*, ed. R. F. Ellen and D. Reason, 1–32. New York: Academic Press.

Ellen, R. F., and I. C. Glover
1974   Pottery manufacture and trade in the Central Moluccas, Indonesia: The modern situation and historical implications. *Man*, n.s., 9:353–79.

Emeleus, V. M.
1960   Neutron activation analysis of Samian ware sherds. *Archaeometry* 3:16–19.

Emeleus, V. M., and G. Simpson
1960   Neutron activation analysis of ancient Roman potsherds. *Nature* 185:196.

Englebrecht, W.
1978   Ceramic patterning between New York Iroquois sites. In *The spatial organisation of culture*, ed. I. Hodder, 141–52. Pittsburgh: University of Pittsburgh Press.

Enriquez, C. R., J. Danon, and M. da C. M. C. Beltrao
1979   Differential thermal analysis of some Amazonian archaeological pottery. *Archaeometry* 21(2):183–86.

Ericson, J. E., D. Read, and C. Burke
1972   Research design: The relationships between the primary functions and the physical properties of ceramic vessels and their implications for ceramic distributions on an archaeological site. *Anthropology UCLA* 3:84–95.

Erickson, J. E., and E. G. Stickel
1973   A proposed classification system for ceramics. *World Archaeology* 4(3):357–67.

Evans, R. K.
1978   Early craft specialization: An example from the Balkan Chalcolithic. In *Social archaeology: Beyond subsistence and dating*, ed. C. L. Redman, M. J. Berman, E. V. Curtin, et al., 113–29. New York: Academic Press.

Fabre, M., and G. Périnet
1973   Mesure de la dureté de pâtes céramiques calcaires. *Bulletin de la Société Française de Céramique* 99:39–49.

Farnsworth, M.
1964   Greek pottery: A mineralogical study. *American Journal of Archaeology* 68:221–28.

Farnsworth, M., and P. D. Ritchie
1938   Spectrographic studies in ancient glass: Egyptian glass, mainly of the Eighteenth Dynasty, with special reference to its cobalt content. *Technical Studies in the Field of Fine Arts* 6:154–73.

Feinman, G., S. Upham, and K. Lightfoot
1981   The production step measure: An ordinal index of labor input in ceramic manufacture. *American Antiquity* 46(4):871–84.

Felts, W. M.
1942   A petrographic examination of potsherds from ancient Troy. *American Journal of Archaeology* 46:237–44.

Ferguson, L.
1980   Looking for the "Afro" in Colono-Indian pottery. In *Archaeological perspectives on ethnicity in America*, ed. R. L. Schuyler, 14–28. Farmingdale, N.Y.: Baywood.

Fewkes, V. J.
1940   Methods of pottery manufacture. *American Antiquity* 6(2):172–73.
1941   The function of the paddle and anvil in pottery making. *American Antiquity* 7(2):162–64.

Fillières, D., G. Harbottle, and E. V. Sayre
  1984   Neutron-activation study of figurines, pottery, and workshop materials from the Athenian Agora, Greece. *Journal of Field Archaeology* 10:55–69.
Fina, A.
  1985   Porcelain plasticity update. *Ceramics Monthly* 33(6):104–5.
Fischer, J. L.
  1961   Art styles as cultural cognitive maps. *American Anthropologist* 63(1):79–93.
Flamini, A., and P. de Lorenzo Flamini
  1985   Discrimination between Etruscan pottery and recent imitations by means of thermal analyses. *Archaeometry* 27(2):218–24.
Flannery, K. V., ed.
  1976   *The early Mesoamerican village*. New York: Academic Press.
Fleming, S. J.
  1970   Thermoluminescent dating: Refinement of the quartz inclusion method. *Archaeometry* 12(2):133–45.
  1973   Thermoluminescence and glaze studies of a group of T'ang dynasty ceramics. *Archaeometry* 15(1):31–52.
  1974   Thermoluminescent authenticity studies of unglazed T'ang dynasty ceramic tomb goods. *Archaeometry* 16(1):91–95.
  1976   *Dating in archaeology*. New York: St. Martin's.
Fleming, S. J., and B. E. B. Fagg
  1977   Thermoluminescent dating of the Udo bronze head. *Archaeometry* 19(1): 86–88.
Fleming, S. J., and D. Stoneham
  1973a The subtraction technique of thermoluminescent dating. *Archaeometry* 15(2):229–38.
  1973b Thermoluminescent authenticity study and dating of Renaissance terracottas. *Archaeometry* 15(2):239–48.
Folk, R. L.
  1966   A review of grain-size parameters. *Sedimentology* 6:73–93.
Fontana, B. L., W. J. Robinson, C. W. Cormack, and E. E. Leavitt, Jr.
  1962   *Papago Indian pottery*. American Ethnological Society, Monograph 37. Seattle: University of Washington Press.
Ford, J. A.
  1938   Report of the conference on southeastern pottery typology. Mimeographed, Museum of Anthropology, Ann Arbor.
  1953   Measurements of some prehistoric design developments in the southeastern states. *Anthropological Papers of the American Museum of Natural History*, vol. 44, pt. 3.
  1962   *A quantitative method of deriving cultural chronology*. Technical Manual no. 1. Washington, D.C.: Pan American Union.
Fossey, J. M., D. Sedgwick, and M. Attas
  1982   The Lake Vouliagméni (Perakhóra) recording system for pottery revisited: An answer to Nicholas David. *Journal of Field Archaeology* 9:241–47.
Foster, G. M.
  1948a *Empire's children: The people of Tzintzuntzan*. Institute of Social Anthropology Publication no. 6. Washington, D.C.: Smithsonian Institution.
  1948b Some implications of modern Mexican mold-made pottery. *Southwestern Journal of Anthropology* 4:356–70.
  1956   Resin coated pottery in the Philippines. *American Anthropologist* 58(4): 732–33.

1959 The Coyotepec molde and some associated problems of the potter's wheel. *Southwestern Journal of Anthropology* 15:63–63.

1960 Life-expectancy of utilitarian pottery in Tzintzuntzan, Michoacán, Mexico. *American Antiquity* 25(4):606–9.

1962 *Traditional cultures and the impact of technological change.* New York: Harper and Row.

1965a Peasant society and the image of limited good. *American Anthropologist* 67(2):293–315.

1965b The sociology of pottery: Questions and hypotheses arising from contemporary Mexican work. In *Ceramics and man*, ed. F. R. Matson, 43–61. Chicago: Aldine.

1967 *Tzintzuntzan: Mexican peasants in a changing world.* Boston: Little, Brown.

Foster, G. V.

1985 Identification of inclusions in ceramic artifacts by xeroradiography. *Journal of Field Archaeology* 12:373–76.

Foster, M. D.

1953 Geochemical studies of clay minerals. 2. Relation between ionic substitution and swelling in montmorillonites. *American Mineralogist* 38:994–1006.

Fourest, H. P.

1980 *Delftware: Faience production at Delft.* New York: Rizzoli Books.

Fournier, R.

1981 *Illustrated dictionary of pottery form.* New York: Van Nostrand Reinhold.

Francaviglia, V., M. E. Minardo, and A. Palmieri

1975 Comparative study of various samples of Etruscan bucchero by X-ray diffraction, X-ray spectrometry, and thermoanalysis. *Archaeometry* 17(2):223–31.

Franchet, L.

1911 *Céramique primitive: Introduction a l'étude de la technologie.* Paris: Paul Guenther.

Franken, H. J.

1971 Analysis of methods of potmaking in archaeology. *Harvard Theological Review* 64:227–55.

Franklin, U. M., and V. Vitali

1985 The environmental stability of ancient ceramics. *Archaeometry* 27(1):3–15.

Frechette, V. D.

1971 Petrographic analysis. In *Characterization of ceramics*, ed. L. L. Hench and R. W. Gould, 257–71. New York: Marcel Dekker.

Freeman, L. G.

1962 Statistical analysis of painted pottery pottery types from upper little Colorado drainage. In *Chapter in the prehistory of eastern Arizona, I*, ed. P. Martin et al., 87–104. Fieldiana: Anthropology, vol. 53. Chicago: Field Museum of Natural History.

Freeman, L. G., and J. A. Brown

1964 Statistical analysis of Carter Ranch pottery. In *The prehistory of eastern Arizona, II*, ed. P. Martin et al., 126–54. Fieldiana: Anthropology, vol. 55. Chicago: Field Museum of Natural History

Freestone, I. C., N. D. Meeks, and A. P. Middleton

1985 Retention of phosphate in buried ceramics: An electron microbeam approach. *Archaeometry* 27(2):161–77.

Freeth, S. J.

1967 A chemical study of some Bronze Age pottery and sherds. *Archaeometry* 10:104–19.

Friedrich, M. H.
1970   Design structure and social interaction: Archaeological implications of an ethnographic analysis. *American Antiquity* 35(3):332–43.

Frierman, J. D.
1980   Ceramic archaeometry, objectivity in ceramic studies, and ceramic education. *Faenza* 66:199–203.

Froese, P.
1985   Pottery classification and sherd assignment. In *Decoding prehistoric ceramics*, ed. B. A. Nelson, 229–42. Carbondale: Southern Illinois University Press.

Gancedo, J. R., M. Gracia, A. Hernandez-Laguna, C. Ruiz Garcia, and J. Palomares
1985   Moessbauer spectroscopic, chemical and mineralogical characterization of Iberian pottery. *Archaeometry* 27(1):75–82.

Gardin, J.-C.
1980   *Archaeological constructs: An aspect of theoretical archaeology.* Cambridge: Cambridge University Press.

Garrison, E. G., C. R. McGimsey III, and O. H. Zinke
1978   Alpha-recoil tracks in archaeological ceramic dating. *Archaeometry* 20(1): 39–46.

Gaudette, H. E., J. J. Eades, and R. E. Grim
1966   The nature of illite. In *Proceedings of the Thirteenth National Clay Conference*, 33–48. New York: Pergamon Press.

Gibb, T. C.
1976   *Principles of Mössbauer spectroscopy.* London: Chapman and Hall.

Gifford, J. C.
1960   The type-variety method of ceramic classification as an indicator of cultural phenomena. *American Antiquity* 25(3):341–47.
1976   *Prehistoric pottery analysis and the ceramics of Barton Ramie in the Belize Valley.* Memoirs of the Peabody Museum, vol. 18. Cambridge, Mass.: Peabody Museum.

Gifford, C., and W. Smith
1978   *Gray corrugated pottery from Awatovi and other Jeddito sites in northeastern Arizona.* Papers of the Peabody Museum, vol. 69. Cambridge, Mass.: Peabody Museum.

Gill, M. C.
1981   The potter's mark: Contemporary and archaeological pottery of the Kenyan Southeastern Highlands. Ph.D. diss., Boston University.

Gill, R. R.
1976   Ceramic arts and acculturation at Laguna. In *Ethnic and tourist arts: Cultural expressions from the Fourth World*, ed. N. H. H. Graburn, 102–13. Berkeley: University of California Press.

Gillies, K. J. S., and D. S. Urch
1983   Spectroscopic studies of iron and carbon in black surfaced ware. *Archaeometry* 25(1):29–44.

Glick, D. P.
1936   The microbiology of aging clays. *Journal of the American Ceramic Society* 19:169–75.

Goffer, Z.
1980   *Archaeological chemistry: A sourcebook on the applications of chemistry to archaeology.* New York: John Wiley.

Goggin, J. M.
1970   The Spanish olive jar, an introductory study. In *Papers in Caribbean anthropology*. Publications in Anthropology no. 62. New Haven: Yale University Press.

Goles, G. G.

1977   Instrumental methods of neutron activation analysis. In *Physical methods of determinative mineralogy,* ed. J. Zussman, 343–69. London: Academic Press.

Gordon, E.

1977   *Collecting Chinese export porcelain.* New York: Universe Books.

Goudineau, C.

1968   *La céramique arétine lissé.* Paris.

Gould, R. A.

1978   *Explorations in ethnoarchaeology.* Albuquerque: University of New Mexico Press.

Gould, R. A., and P. J. Watson

1982   A dialogue on the meaning and use of analogy in ethnoarchaeological reasoning. *Journal of Anthropological Archaeology* 1(4):355–81.

Gould, R. W.

1971   X-ray diffraction. In *Characterization of ceramics,* ed. L. L. Hench and R. W. Gould, 135–76. New York: Marcel Dekker.

Graburn, N. H. H.

1976   Introduction: Arts of the Fourth World. In *Ethnic and tourist arts: Cultural expressions from the Fourth World,* ed. N. H. H. Graburn, 1–32. Berkeley: University of California Press.

Graham, W. A.

1922   Pottery in Siam. *Journal of the Siam Society* 16:1–27.

Grange, R. T., Jr.

1984   Dating Pawnee sites by the ceramic formula method. *World Archaeology* 15(3):274–93.

Graves, M. W.

1981   Ethnoarchaeology of Kalinga ceramic design. Ph.D. diss., University of Arizona.

1985   Ceramic design variation within a Kalinga village: Temporal and spatial processes. In *Decoding prehistoric ceramics,* ed. B. A. Nelson, 9–34. Carbondale: Southern Illinois University Press.

Greer, J. W.

1977   Geometric methods for computing vessel diameters. *Southwestern Lore* 43:25–28.

Greger, H. H., and M. Berg

1956   Instrument for measuring workability of clay-water systems. *Journal of the American Ceramic Society* 39(3):98–103.

Griffin, J. B.

1965   Ceramic complexity and cultural development: The eastern United States as a case study. In *Ceramics and man,* ed. F. R. Matson, 104–13. Chicago: Aldine.

Griffiths, D. M.

1978   Use marks on historic ceramics: A preliminary study. *Historical Archaeology* 12:78–81.

Grim, R. E.

1939   Relation of the composition to the properties of clays. *Journal of the American Ceramic Society* 22:141–51.

1950   Modern concepts of clay materials. *Journal of Geology* 50:225–75.

1962   *Applied clay mineralogy.* New York: McGraw-Hill.

1965   The clay mineral concept. *American Ceramic Society Bulletin* 44:687–92.

1968   *Clay mineralogy.* 2d ed. New York: McGraw-Hill.

Grim, R. E., and W. F. Bradley

1948   Rehydration and dehydration of the clay minerals. *American Mineralogist* 33:50–59.

Grim, R. E., and F. L. Cuthbert
1945   Some clay-water properties of certain clay minerals. *Journal of the American Ceramic Society* 28(3):90–95.

Grim, R. E., and G. Kulbicki
1961   Montmorillonite: High temperature reaction and classification. *American Mineralogist* 46:1329–69.

Grim, R. E., and R. A. Rowland
1942   Differential thermal analysis of clay minerals and other hydrous materials. *American Mineralogist* 27:746–61.

Grimshaw, R. W.
1971   *The chemistry and physics of clays and other ceramic materials*. 4th ed. New York: John Wiley.

Gritton, V., and N. M. Magalousis
1978   Atomic absorption spectroscopy of archaeological ceramic materials. In *Archaeological chemistry*, vol. 2, ed. G. F. Carter, 258–70. Advances in Chemistry 171. Washington, D.C.: American Chemical Society.

Grout, F. F.
1906   Methods of determining plasticity. *West Virginia Geological Survey* 3:40.

Grove, D. C., and D. E. Buge
1978   Prehistoric demography, behavior, and ancient pottery. *Journal of Irreproducible Results* 24(4):21–23.

Groves, M.
1960   Motu pottery. *Journal of the Polynesian Society* 69(1):3–22.

Gruner, J. W.
1932   The crystal structure of kaolinite. *Zeitschrift für Kristallographie* 83:75–88.

Guthe, C. E.
1925   *Pueblo pottery making*. New Haven: Yale University Press.

Hagstrum, M. B.
1985   Measuring prehistoric ceramic craft specialization: A test case in the American Southwest. *Journal of Field Archaeology* 12:65–75.

Hall, E. T.
1963   Physical methods of chemical analysis. In *The scientist and archaeology*, ed. E. Pyddoke, 168–92. London: Phoenix House.

Hally, D. J.
1983a   The interpretive potential of pottery from domestic contexts. *Midcontinental Journal of Archaeology* 8(2):163–96.

1983b   Use alteration of pottery vessel surfaces: An important source of evidence in the identification of vessel function. *North American Archaeologist* 4(1):3–26.

1986   The identification of vessel function: A case study from northwest Georgia. *American Antiquity* 51(2):267–95.

Hamer, F.
1975   *The potter's dictionary of materials and techniques*. London: Pitman.

Hammond, N.
1982   *Ancient Maya civilization*. New Brunswick, N.J.: Rutgers University Press.

Hammond, N., A. Aspinall, S. Feather, J. Hazelden, T. Gazard, and S. Agrell
1977   Maya jade: Source location and analysis. In *Exchange systems in prehistory*, ed. T. K. Earle and J. E. Ericson, 35–67. New York: Academic Press.

Hammond, P. C.
1971   Ceramic technology of South-west Asia, Syro-Palestine: Iron IIb, Hebron. *Science and Archaeology* 5:11–21 (Stafford, England).

Han, M. C.
1975   Effects of alpha and X-ray doses and annealing temperatures upon pottery dating by thermoluminescence. *MASCA Newsletter* 11(1):1–3.

Hancock, R. G. V.

1984   On the source of clay used for Cologne Roman pottery. *Archaeometry*
26(2):210–17.

1985   Neutron activation analysis of ceramics: Problems with titanium and calcium. *Archaeometry* 27(1):94–101.

Handy, J. L., and A. M. Gaines

1975   The thermal behaviour of clays and possible methods of determining firing
temperatures of pottery. *MASCA Newsletter* 11(1):4–5.

Harbottle, G.

1970   Neutron activation analysis of potsherds from Knossos and Mycenae. *Archaeometry* 12(1):23–34.

1975   Activation analysis study of ceramics from the Capacha (Colima) and Opeño
(Michoacán) phases of West Mexico. *American Antiquity* 40(4):453–58.

1982   Provenience studies using neutron activation analysis: The role of standardization. In *Archaeological ceramics*, ed. J. S. Olin and A. D. Franklin, 67–77.
Washington, D.C.: Smithsonian Institution.

Hardin, M. A.

1977   Individual style in San José pottery painting: The role of deliberate choice.
In *The individual in prehistory*, ed. J. N. Hill and J. Gunn, 109–36. New York:
Academic Press.

1983   The structure of Tarascan pottery painting. In *Structure and cognition in art*,
ed. D. K. Washburn, 8–24. Cambridge: Cambridge University Press.

1984   Models of decoration. In *The many dimensions of pottery: Ceramics in archaeology and anthropology*, ed. S. E. van der Leeuw and A. C. Pritchard,
573–614. CINGULA 7. Amsterdam: Institute for Pre- and Proto-History, University of Amsterdam.

Hart, K.

1982   On commoditization. In *From craft to industry: The ethnography of proto-
industrial cloth production*, ed. E. N. Goody, 38–49. Cambridge: Cambridge
University Press.

Hartley, B. R.

1966   Gaulish potters' stamps. *Antiquities Journal* 46:102–3.

Hasselman, D. P. H.

1963   Elastic energy at fracture and surface energy as design criteria for thermal
shock. *Journal of the American Ceramic Society* 46(11):535–40.

1969   Unified theory of thermal shock fracture initiation and crack propagation in
brittle ceramics. *Journal of the American Ceramic Society* 52(11):600–604.

Hasselman, D. P. H., and R. M. Fulrath

1968   Mechanical properties of continuous matrix, dispersed phase ceramic systems. In *Ceramic microstructures*, ed. R. M. Fulrath and J. A. Pask, 343–78.
New York: John Wiley.

Hatch, J. W., S. L. Whittington, and B. Dyke

1982   A simulation approach to the measurement of change in ceramic frequency
seriation. *North American Archaeologist* 3(4):333–50.

Hatcher, H., R. E. M. Hedges, A. M. Pollard, and P. M. Kenrick

1980   Analysis of Hellenistic and Roman fine pottery from Benghazi. *Archaeometry* 22(2):133–51.

Hawley, F. M.

1929   Prehistoric pottery pigments in the Southwest. *American Anthropologist*
31(4):731–54.

1930   Chemical examination of prehistoric smudged wares. *American Anthropologist* 32(3):500–502.

Hay, R. L.
    1960   Rate of clay formation and mineral alteration in a 4000-year old volcanic ash soil on St. Vincent, B.W.I. *American Journal of Science* 258:354–68.

Hayden, B., and A. Cannon
    1984   Interaction inferences in archaeology and learning frameworks of the Maya. *Journal of Anthropological Archaeology* 3(4):325–67.

Hearn, M. K.
    1979   An ancient Chinese army rises from underground sentinel duty. *Smithsonian* 10(8):39–51.

Hedges, R. E. M., and M. McLellan
    1976   On the cation exchange capacity of fired clays and its effect on the chemical and radiometric analysis of pottery. *Archaeometry* 18(2):203–6.

Hedges, R. E. M., and P. R. S. Moorey
    1975   Pre-Islamic ceramic glazes at Kish and Nineveh in Iraq. *Archaeometry* 17(1):25–43.

Heimann, R. B.
    1977   A simple method for estimation of the macroporosity of ceramic sherds by a replica technique. *Archaeometry* 19(1):55–56.
    1982   Firing technologies and their possible assessment by modern analytical methods. In *Archaeological ceramics*, ed. J. S. Olin and A. D. Franklin, 89–96. Washington, D.C.: Smithsonian Institution.

Helms, M.
    1979   *Ancient Panama: Chiefs in search of power*. Austin: University of Texas Press.

Hench, L. L.
    1971   Introduction to the characterization of ceramics. In *Characterization of ceramics*, ed. L. L. Hench and R. W. Gould, 1–5. New York: Marcel Dekker.

Hench, L. L., and E. C. Etheridge
    1982   *Biomaterials: An interfacial approach*. Biophysics and Bioengineering Series, vol. 4. New York: Academic Press.

Hench, L. L., and R. W. Gould, eds.
    1971   *Characterization of ceramics*. New York: Marcel Dekker.

Hendricks, S. B.
    1942   Lattice structure of clay minerals and some properties of clays. *Journal of Geology* 50:276–90.

Henrickson, E. F., and M. M. A. McDonald
    1983   Ceramic form and function: An ethnographic search and an archaeological application. *American Anthropologist* 85(3):630–43.

Herron, M. K.
    1986   A formal and functional analysis of St. Johns series pottery from two sites in St. Augustine, Florida. In *Papers in ceramic analysis*, ed. P. M. Rice. *Ceramic Notes* 3:31–45.

Hess, J., and I. Perlman
    1974   Mössbauer spectra of iron in ceramics and their relation to pottery colors. *Archaeometry* 16(2):137–52.

Hill, J. N.
    1970   *Broken K Pueblo: Prehistoric social organization in the American Southwest*. Anthropological Papers no. 18. Tucson: University of Arizona Press.
    1977   Individual variability in ceramics and the study of prehistoric social organization. In *The individual in prehistory*, ed. J. N. Hill and J. Gunn, 55–108. New York: Academic Press.

1985   Style: A conceptual evolutionary framework. In *Decoding prehistoric ceramics*, ed. B. A. Nelson, 362–85. Carbondale: Southern Illinois University Press.

Hill, J. N., and R. K. Evans
1972   A model for classification and typology. In *Models in archaeology*, ed. D. L. Clarke, 231–73. London: Methuen.

Hill, J. N., and J. Gunn, eds.
1977   *The individual in prehistory.* New York: Academic Press.

Ho, Y.-M., and D. L. Huddle
1976   Traditional and small-scale culture goods in international trade and employment. *Journal of Development Studies* 12:232–51.

Hobson, R. L.
1976   *Chinese pottery and porcelain: An account of the potter's art in China from primitive times to the present day.* New York: Dover.

Hodder, B. W.
1962   The Yoruba rural market. In *Markets in Africa*, ed. P. Bohannon and G. Dalton, 103–17. Evanston, Ill.: Northwestern University Press.

Hodder, I.
1974a   The distribution of two types of Romano-British coarse pottery in the west Sussex region. *Sussex Archaeological Collections* 112:86–96.
1974b   Regression analysis of some trade and marketing patterns. *World Archaeology* 6(2):172–89.
1974c   Some marketing models for Romano-British coarse pottery. *Britannia* 5:340–59.
1977   The distribution of material culture items in the Baringo District, western Kenya. *Man* 12:239–69.
1978   Social organisation and human interaction: The development of some tentative hypotheses in terms of material culture. In *The spatial organisation of culture*, ed. I. Hodder, 199–269. Pittsburgh: University of Pittsburgh Press.
1979a   Pottery distributions: service and tribal areas. In *Pottery and the archaeologist*, ed. M. Millett, 7–23. Occasional Publication no. 4. London: Institute of Archaeology.
1979b   Social and economic stress and material culture patterning. *American Antiquity* 44(3):446–54.
1980   Trade and exchange: Definitions, identification and function. In *Models and methods in regional exchange*, ed. R. E. Fry, 151–56. SAA Papers 1. Washington, D.C.: Society for American Archaeology.
1981   Pottery production and use: A theoretical discussion. In *Production and distribution: A ceramic viewpoint*, ed. H. Howard and E. Thomas, 215–20. International Series 120. Oxford: British Archaeological Reports.
1982   *Symbols in action: Ethnoarchaeological studies of material culture.* Cambridge: Cambridge University Press.

Hodder, I., and C. Orton
1976   *Spatial analysis in archaeology.* Cambridge: Cambridge University Press.

Hodges, H.
1963   The examination of ceramic materials in thin section. In *The scientist and archaeology*, ed. E. Pyddoke, 101–10. London: Phoenix House.
1974   The medieval potter: Artisan or artist? In *Medieval pottery from excavations*, ed. V. I. Evian, H. Hodges, and J. G. Hurst, 33–40. New York: St. Martin's Press.
1976   *Artifacts: An introduction to early materials and technology.* London: John Baker.

Hodson, F. R.

1969   Searching for structure within multivariate archaeological data. *World Archaeology* 1(1):90–105.

1982   Some aspects of archaeological classification. In *Essays on archaeological typology*, ed. R. Whallon and J. A. Brown, 21–29. Evanston, Ill.: Center for American Archaeology Press.

Hoffman, B.

1983   Die Rolle handwerklicher Verfahren bei der Formgebung in Serien hergestellter reliefverzierter Terra Sigillata. Ph.D. diss., Ludwig-Maximilian University, Munich.

Hoffman, B., and K. Goldmann

1979   Brenntechniken von Keramik und ihre Wiedergewinnung durch experimentelle Archäologie (Proceedings of a 1977 symposium on ceramic firing techniques and their determination through experimental archaeology). *Acta Praehistorica et Archaeologica* 9/10 (Berlin, Verlag Volker Spiess).

Hofman, V.

1962   The chemical basis of ancient Greek vase painting. *Angewandte Chemie* 1:341–50.

Holdridge, D. A.

1952   The effect of moisture content on the strength of unfired ceramic bodies. *Transactions of the British Ceramic Society* 51:401.

1956   Ball clays and their properties. *Transactions of the British Ceramic Society* 55:369–440.

Hole, F.

1984   Analysis of structure and design in prehistoric ceramics. *World Archaeology* 15(3):326–47.

Holm, B.

1982   *Northwest Coast Indian art.* Seattle: University of Washington Press.

Horton, D., and J. Berman

1941   Appendix I: Preliminary report on the technological analysis of Meillac and Carrier sherds. In *Culture of the Ft. Liberté region, Haiti*, by I. Rouse, 169–72. Yale University Publications in Anthropology no. 24. New Haven: Yale University Press.

Howard, H.

1981   In the wake of distribution: Towards an integrated approach to ceramic studies in prehistoric Britain. In *Production and distribution: A ceramic viewpoint*, ed. H. Howard and E. Morris, 1–30. International Series 120. Oxford: British Archaeological Reports.

Howard, H., and E. Morris, eds.

1981   *Production and distribution: A ceramic viewpoint.* International Series 120. Oxford: British Archaeological Reports.

Howry, J. C.

1976   Fires on the mountain: Ceramic traditions and marketing in the highlands of Chiapas, Mexico. Ph.D. diss., Harvard University.

Hughes, M. J., ed.

1981   *Scientific studies in ancient ceramics.* BAR Occasional Paper 19. London: British Museum.

Hulthén, B.

1974   On choice of element for determination of quantity of pottery. *Norwegian Archaeological Review* 7:1–5.

Hurd, G. S.

1976   Anthropological interpretations of ceramic technologies: A comparison of two Yucatec towns. Ph.D. diss., Department of Anthropology, University of California, Irvine, California.

Ichikawa, Y., T. Nagatomo, and N. Hagahara
1978   Thermoluminescent dating of Jōmon pattern pottery from Taishaka valley. *Archaeometry* 20(2): 171–76.

Ikawa-Smith, F.
1980   Current issues in Japanese archaeology. *American Scientist* 68(2): 134–45.

Ikeya, M.
1978   Electron spin resonance as a method of dating. *Archaeometry* 20(2): 147–58.

Irwin, G.
1974   Carved paddle decoration of pottery and its capacity for inference in archaeology: An example from the Solomon Islands. *Journal of the Polynesian Society* 83(3): 368–71.
1977   The emergence of Mailu as a central place in the prehistory of coastal Papua. Ph.D. diss., Australian National University.

Isphording, W. C.
1974   Combined thermal and X-ray diffraction technique for identification of ceramic ware temper and paste materials. *American Antiquity* 39(3): 477–83.

Jeancon, J. A.
1923   *Excavations in the Chama Valley, New Mexico.* Bureau of American Ethnology Bulletin 81. Washington, D.C.: Smithsonian Institution.

Jernigan, E. W.
1986   A non-hierarchical approach to ceramic decoration analysis: A Southwestern example. *American Antiquity* 51(1): 3–20.

Joesink-Mandeville, L.
1973   The importance of gourd prototypes in the analysis of Mesoamerican ceramics. *Katunob* 8(3): 47–53.

Johns, C.
1963   Gaulish potters' stamps. *Antiquities Journal* 43: 288–89.
1977a   *Arretine and Samian pottery.* London: British Museum.
1977b   A group of Samian wasters from Les-Martres-de-Veyre. In *Roman pottery studies in Britain and beyond*, ed. J. Dore and K. Greene, 235–46. BAR Series 30. Oxford: British Archaeological Reports.

Johnson, A. L.
1949   Surface area and its effect on exchange capacity of montmorillonite. *Journal of the American Ceramic Society* 32(6): 210–14.

Johnson, A. L., and W. G. Lawrence
1942   Fundamental study of clay. 4. Surface area and its effect on exchange capacity of kaolinite. *Journal of the American Ceramic Society* 25(12): 344–46.

Johnson, A. L., and F. H. Norton
1941   Fundamental study of clay. 2. Mechanism of deflocculation in the clay-water system. *Journal of the American Ceramic Society* 24(6): 189–203.

Johnson, G. A.
1973   *Local exchange and early state development in southwestern Iran.* Anthropological Papers no. 51. Ann Arbor: Museum of Anthropology, University of Michigan.

Johnson, R.
1976   Some observations on flint v. silica sand in pottery bodies. *Transactions of the British Ceramic Society* 75: 1–5.

Johnson, S. M., J. A. Pask, and J. S. Moya
1982   Influence of impurities in high temperature reactions of kaolinite. *Journal of the American Ceramic Society* 65(1): 31–35.

Johnston, R. H.

1977   The development of the potter's wheel: An analytical and synthesizing study. In *Material culture: Styles, organization, and dynamics of technology*, ed. H. Lechtman and R. S. Merrill, 169–210. New York: West.

1984   An abandoned pottery at Guellala on the Island of Djerba, Tunisia: A hermeneutic approach to ethnoarchaeology. In *Pots and potters: Current approaches in ceramic archaeology*, ed. P. M. Rice, 81–94. UCLA Institute of Archaeology Monograph 24. Los Angeles: University of California Press.

Jornet, A., J. Blackman, and J. Olin

1985   Thirteenth to eighteenth century ceramics from the Paterna-Manises area (Spain). In *Ancient technology to modern science*, ed. W. D. Kingery, 235–55. Ceramics and Civilization, vol. 1. Columbus, Ohio: American Ceramic Society.

Joukowsky, M.

1978   Computer use in pottery studies at Aphrodisias. *Journal of Field Archaeology* 5:431–42.

1980   *A complete manual of field archaeology*. Englewood Cliffs, N.J.: Prentice-Hall.

1982   Ceramic processing: An appraisal of the Lake Vouliagméni recording system and the issues addressed by Nicholas David. *Journal of Field Archaeology* 9:248–51.

Kaiser, T. M.

1984   Vinca ceramics: Economic and technological aspects of late Neolithic pottery production in southeast Europe. Ph.D. diss., University of California, Berkeley.

Kamilli, D. C., and A. Steinberg

1985   New approaches to mineral analysis of ancient ceramics. In *Archaeological geology*, ed. G. Rapp, Jr., and J. A. Gifford, 313–30. New Haven: Yale University Press.

Kane, W. T.

1973   Applications of the electron microprobe in ceramics and glass technology. In *Microprobe analysis*, ed. C. A. Andersen, 241–70. New York: John Wiley.

Kaplan, F. S.

1985   The measuring, mapping, and meaning of pots. *American Anthropologist* 87(2):357–64.

Kaplan, F. S., and D. M. Levine

1981   Cognitive mapping of a folk taxonomy of Mexican pottery: A multivariate approach. *American Anthropologist* 83(3):868–84.

Kardos, J., L. Kriston, O. Morozova, T. Trager, K. Zimmer, and E. Jerem

1985   Scientific investigations of the Sopron-Krautacker Iron Age pottery workshop. *Archaeometry* 27(1):83–93.

Keeling, P. S.

1965   The nature of clay. *Journal of the British Ceramic Society* 2:236–42.

Keighley, J.

1973   Some problems in the quantitative interpretation of ceramic data. In *The explanation of culture change: Models in prehistory*, ed. C. Renfrew, 131–36. Pittsburgh: University of Pittsburgh Press.

Keisch, B.

1974   Mössbauer effect spectroscopy without sampling: Application to art and archaeology. In *Archaeological chemistry*, ed. C. W. Beck, 186–206. Advances in Chemistry 138. Washington, D.C.: American Chemical Society.

Keller, W. D.

1964   Processes of origin and alteration of clay minerals. In *Soil clay mineralogy:*

A symposium, ed. C. I. Rich and G. W. Kunze, 3–76. Chapel Hill: University of North Carolina Press.

Kempe, D. R. C., and A. P. Harvey, eds.

1983 *The petrology of archaeological artefacts*. Oxford: Clarendon Press.

Kempe, D. R. C., and J. A. Templeman

1983 Techniques. In *The petrology of archaeological artefacts*, ed. D. R. C. Kempe and A. P. Harvey, 26–52. Oxford: Clarendon Press.

Kempton, W.

1981 *The folk classification of ceramics: A study of cognitive prototypes*. New York: Academic Press.

Kennard, F., and W. Williamson

1971 Transverse strength of ball clay. *Bulletin of the American Ceramic Society* 50:745–48.

Kerr, P. F.

1977 *Optical mineralogy*. New York: McGraw-Hill.

Kidder, A. V.

1927 Southwestern archaeological conference. *Science* 66:486–91.

1931 *The pottery of Pecos*. Vol. 1. Papers of the Southwestern Expedition, Phillips Academy. New Haven: Yale University Press.

Kidder, J. E.

1968 *Prehistoric Japanese arts: Jōmon pottery*. Tokyo: Kodansha International.

Kingery, W. D.

1955 Factors affecting thermal stress resistance of ceramic materials. *Journal of the American Ceramic Society* 38(1):3–15.

1960 *Introduction to ceramics*. New York: John Wiley.

1974 A note on the differential thermal analysis of archaeological ceramics. *Archaeometry* 16(1):109–11.

Kingery, W. D., ed.

1985 *Ancient technology to modern science*. Ceramics and Civilization, vol. 1. Columbus, Ohio: American Ceramic Society.

Kingery, W. D., H. K. Bowen, and D. R. Uhlmann

1976 *Introduction to ceramics*. 2d ed. New York: John Wiley.

Kingery, W. D., and J. Francl

1954 Fundamental study of clay. 13. Drying behavior and plastic properties. *Journal of the American Ceramic Society* 37(12):596–602.

Kingery, W. D., and D. Smith

1985 The development of European soft-paste (frit) porcelain. In *Ancient technology to modern science*, ed. W. D. Kingery, 273–92. Ceramics and Civilization, vol. 1. Columbus, Ohio: American Ceramic Society.

Kingery, W. D., and P. Vandiver

1986 *Ceramic masterpieces: Art, structure and technology*. New York: Free Press.

Kirchner, H.

1979 *Strengthening of ceramics*. New York: Marcel Dekker.

Kirkby, A., and M. Kirkby

1976 Geomorphic processes and the surface survey of archaeological sites in semi-arid areas. In *Geoarchaeology*, ed. D. Davidson and M. Shackley, 229–53. London: Duckworth.

Kirkpatrick, M.

1978 The application of the type-variety method of ceramic analysis to a collection of contemporary pottery from Metepec, Mexico. M.A. thesis, Temple University.

Kleeman, A. W.
   1967   Sampling error in the chemical analysis of rocks. *Journal of the Geological Society of Australia* 14:43–47.
Klemptner, L. J., and P. F. Johnson
   1986   Technology and the primitive potter: Mississippian pottery development seen through the eyes of a ceramic engineer. In *Technology and style*, ed. W. D. Kingery, 251–71. Ceramics and Civilization, vol. 2. Columbus, Ohio: American Ceramic Society.
Kluckhohn, C.
   1960   The use of typology in anthropological theory. In *Men and cultures*, ed. A. F. C. Wallace, 134–40. Philadelphia: University of Pennsylvania Press.
Kohl, P. L., G. Harbottle, and E. V. Sayre
   1979   Physical and chemical analyses of soft stone vessels from Southwest Asia. *Archaeometry* 21(2):131–59.
Kohler, T. A.
   1978   Ceramic breakage rate simulation: Population size and the southeastern chiefdom. *Newsletter of Computer Archaeology* 14:1–15 (Tempe, Arizona State University).
Kostikas, A., A. Simopoulos, and N. H. Gangas
   1976   Analysis of archaeological artifacts. In *Applications of Mössbauer spectroscopy*, ed. R. L. Cohen. London: Academic Press.
Kramer, C., ed.
   1979   *Ethnoarchaeology: Implications of ethnography for archaeology.* New York: Columbia University Press.
Krieger, A. D.
   1944   The typological concept. *American Antiquity* 9(3):271–88.
Kroeber, A. L.
   1916   Zuñi potsherds. *Anthropological Papers of the American Museum of Natural History* 18(1):7–37.
Kruger, P.
   1971   *Principles of activation analysis.* New York: John Wiley.
Kubler, G.
   1961   On the colonial extinction of the motifs of pre-Columbian art. In *Essays in pre-Columbian art and archaeology*, ed. S. K. Lothrop, 14–34. Cambridge: Harvard University Press.
Kullerud, G., R. M. Steffen, P. C. Simms, and F. A. Rickey
   1979   Proton induced X-ray emission (PIXE)—a new tool in geochemistry. *Chemical Geology* 25:245–56.
Lackey, L.
   1981   *The pottery of Acatlán: A changing Mexican tradition.* Norman: University of Oklahoma Press.
Lacovara, P.
   1985   The ethnoarchaeology of pottery production in an Upper Egyptian village. In *Ancient technology to modern science*, ed. W. D. Kingery, 51–60. Ceramics and Civilization, vol. 1. Columbus, Ohio: American Ceramic Society.
Laird, R. T., and W. Worcester
   1956   The inhibiting of lime blowing. *Transactions of the British Ceramic Society* 55:545–63.
Lambert, J. B., ed.
   1984   *Archaeological chemistry.* Vol. 3. Advances in Chemistry 205. Washington, D.C.: American Chemical Society.

Lambert, J. B., and C. D. McLaughlin

1976 X-ray photoelectron spectroscopy: A new analytical method for the examination of archaeological artifacts. *Archaeometry* 18(2):169–80.

Landon, M.

1959 Dimensional determination from potsherds. *Bulletin of the Massachusetts Archaeological Society* 20:46.

Lathrap, D. W.

1973 Gifts of the cayman: Some thoughts on the subsistence base of Chavin. In *Variation in anthropology*, ed. D. W. Lathrap and J. Douglas, 91–105. Urbana: Illinois Archaeological Survey.

1976 Shipibo tourist art. In *Ethnic and tourist arts: Cultural expressions from the Fourth World*, ed. N. H. H. Graburn, 197–207. Berkeley: University of California Press.

1983 Recent Shipibo-Conibo ceramics and their implications for archaeological interpretation. In *Structure and cognition in art*, ed. D. K. Washburn, 25–39. Cambridge: Cambridge University Press.

Lauer, P. K.

1970 Amphlett Islands pottery trade and the kula. *Mankind* 7:165–76.

1971 Changing patterns of pottery trade to the Trobriand Islands. *World Archaeology* 3(2):197–209.

Laufer, B.

1917 The beginnings of porcelain in China. Field Museum of Natural History Publication 192. *Anthropological Series* 15(2):75–179.

Lawrence, W. G., and R. R. West

1982 *Ceramic science for the potter.* 2d ed. Radnor, Pa.: Chilton.

Layard, A. H.

1853 *Discoveries in the ruins of Nineveh and Babylon.* New York: G. Putnam.

Leach, B.

1976 *A potter's book.* London: Faber and Faber.

LeBlanc, S. A., and P. J. Watson

1973 A comparative statistical analysis of painted pottery from seven Halafian sites. *Paleorient* 1:117–33.

Lechtman, H.

1977 Style in technology—some early thoughts. In *Material culture: Styles, organization, and dynamics of technology*, ed. H. Lechtman and R. Merrill, 3–20. New York: West.

LeFree, B.

1975 *Santa Clara pottery today.* Albuquerque: University of New Mexico Press.

Leroi-Gourhan, A.

1968 The evolution of Paleolithic art. *Scientific American* 218(2):58–70.

Levey, M., ed.

1967 Archaeological chemistry: A symposium. Philadelphia: University of Pennsylvania Press.

Levin, E., C. Robbins, and H. McMurdie

1964 *Phase diagrams for ceramists.* Columbus, Ohio: American Ceramic Society.

Lewis, R.

1971 Electron microprobe. In *Characterization of ceramics*, ed. L. L. Hench and E. C. Etheridge, 505–27. New York: Marcel Dekker.

Li Guozhen and Zhang Xiqiu

1986 The development of Chinese white porcelain. In *Technology and style*, ed. W. D. Kingery, 217–36. Ceramics and Civilization, vol. 2. Columbus, Ohio: American Ceramic Society.

Li Hu Hou

　　1985　Characteristic elements of Longquan greenware. *Archaeometry* 27(1): 53–60.

Li Jiazhi

　　1985　The evolution of Chinese pottery and porcelain technology. In *Ancient technology to modern science*, ed. W. D. Kingery, 135–62. Ceramics and Civilization, vol. 1. Columbus, Ohio: American Ceramic Society.

Lieberman, S. J.

　　1980　Of clay pebbles, hollow clay balls, and writing: A Sumerian view. *American Journal of Archaeology* 84(3):339–58.

Linares de Sapir, O.

　　1969　Diola pottery of the Fogny and the Kasa. *Expedition* 11:2–11.

Linné, S.

　　1957　Technical secrets of American Indians. *Journal of the Royal Anthropological Institute* 87:149–64.

　　1965　The ethnologist and the American Indian potter. In *Ceramics and man*, ed. F. R. Matson, 20–42. Chicago: Aldine.

Linton, R.

　　1944　North American cooking pots. *American Antiquity* 9(4):369–80.

Lischka, J. J.

　　1978　A functional analysis of Middle Classic ceramics at Kaminaljuyú. In *The ceramics of Kaminaljuyú, Guatemala*, ed. R. Wetherington, 223–78. University Park: Pennsylvania State University Press.

Lister, F. C., and R. H. Lister

　　1982　*Sixteenth century Maiolica pottery in the Valley of Mexico*. Anthropological Papers no. 39. Tucson: University of Arizona.

Littman, E.

　　1980　Maya Blue—a new perspective. *American Antiquity* 45(1):87–100.

Litto, G.

　　1976　*South American folk pottery*. New York: Watson-Guptill.

Lobert, H. W.

　　1984　Types of potter's wheels and the spread of the spindle-wheel in Germany. In *The many dimensions of pottery: Ceramics in archaeology and anthropology*, ed. S. E. van der Leeuw and A. C. Pritchard, 203–30. CINGULA 7. Amsterdam: Institute for Pre- and Proto-history, University of Amsterdam.

London, G.

　　1981　Dung-tempered clay. *Journal of Field Archaeology* 8:189–95.

Long, J. V. P.

　　1977　Electron probe microanalysis. In *Physical methods in determinative mineralogy*. 2d ed., ed. J. Zussman, 273–341. London: Academic Press.

Longacre, W. A.

　　1964　Sociological implications of the ceramic analysis. In *Chapters in the prehistory of eastern Arizona, II*, ed. P. Martin et al., 155–70. Fieldiana: Anthropology, vol. 55. Chicago: Field Museum of Natural History.

　　1970　*Archaeology as anthropology: A case study*. Anthropological Papers no. 17. Tucson: University of Arizona Press.

　　1981　Kalinga pottery, an ethnoarchaeological study. In *Pattern of the past*, ed. I. Hodder, G. Isaac, and N. Hammond, 49–66. Cambridge: Cambridge University Press.

　　1985　Pottery use-life among the Kalinga, northern Luzon, the Philippines. In *Decoding prehistoric ceramics*, ed. B. A. Nelson, 334–46. Carbondale: Southern Illinois University Press.

Lothrop, S. K.

1927 *The potters of Guatajiagua, Salvador.* Indian Notes, vol. 4, no. 1. New York: Museum of the American Indian, Heye Foundation.

Loughlin, N.

1977 Dales ware: A contribution to the study of Roman coarse pottery. In *Pottery and early commerce: Characterization and trade in Roman and later ceramics,* ed. D. P. S. Peacock, 85–146. London: Academic Press.

Lowenstein, J. G.

1986 Westerwald salt-glazed stoneware. In *Technology and style,* ed. W. D. Kingery, 383–95. Ceramics and Civilization, vol. 2. Columbus, Ohio: American Ceramic Society.

Luedtke, B.

1979 The identification of sources of chert artifacts. *American Antiquity* 44(4): 744–57.

Lustig-Arecco, V.

1975 *Technology: Strategies for survival.* New York: Holt, Rinehart, and Winston.

Lynch, O. M.

1979 Potters, plotters, prodders in a Bombay slum: Marx and meaning or meaning versus Marx. *Urban Anthropology* 8:1–27.

McConnell, J. D. C.

1977 Electron microscopy and electron diffraction. In *Physical methods in determinative mineralogy,* ed. J. Zussman, 475–527. London: Academic Press.

McDowell, I. C., and W. Vose

1952 Observations upon the dry strength of clays and clay bodies. *Transactions of the British Ceramic Society* 51:511.

McGovern, P. E.

1986 Ancient ceramic technology and stylistic change: Contrasting studies from Southwest and Southeast Asia. In *Technology and Style,* ed. W. D. Kingery, 33–52. Ceramics and Civilization, vol. 2. Columbus, Ohio: American Ceramic Society.

McGregor, J. C.

1941 *Southwestern archaeology.* New York: Wiley.

Mackenzie, R. C.

1964 The thermal investigation of soil clays. In *Soil clay mineralogy: A symposium,* ed. C. I. Rich and G. W. Kunze, 200–245. Chapel Hill: University of North Carolina Press.

McLaughlin, R. J. W.

1977 Atomic absorption spectroscopy. In *Physical methods in determinative mineralogy,* 2d ed., ed. J. Zussman, 371–89. London: Academic Press.

McNabb, A., and M. E. Duncan

1967 Firing-deformation of ceramic bodies. *Bulletin of the American Ceramic Society* 46:514–20.

McPherron, A.

1967 *The Juntunen site and late Woodland prehistory of the upper Great Lakes area.* Anthropological Papers no. 30. Ann Arbor: Museum of Anthropology, University of Michigan.

Maerz, A., and M. R. Paul

1950 *Dictionary of color.* 2d ed. New York: McGraw-Hill.

Magetti, M.

1982 Phase analysis and its significance for technology and origin. In *Archaeological ceramics,* ed. J. S. Olin and A. D. Franklin, 121–33. Washington, D.C.: Smithsonian Institution.

Majidzadeh, Y.
  1975–77 The development of the pottery kiln in Iran from prehistoric to historical periods. *Paleorient* 3:207–19.
Malinowski, B.
  1922 · *Argonauts of the western Pacific.* London: Routledge.
Man, E. H.
  1894 Nicobar pottery. *Journal of the Anthropological Institute* 23:21–27.
Maniatis, Y., A. Simopoulos, and A. Kostikas
  1982 The investigation of ancient ceramic technologies by Mössbauer spectroscopy. In *Archaeological ceramics,* ed. J. S. Olin and A. D. Franklin, 97–108. Washington, D.C.: Smithsonian Institution.
Maniatis, Y., A. Simopoulos, A. Kostikas, and V. Perdikatsis
  1983 Effect of reducing atmosphere on minerals and iron oxides developed in fired clays: The role of Ca. *Journal of the American Ceramic Society* 66(11):773–81.
March, B.
  1934 *Standards of pottery description.* Occasional Contributions no. 3. Ann Arbor: Museum of Anthropology, University of Michigan. (Reprinted 1967.)
Marquis, J.
  1952 A general paper on glaze defects. *Journal of the Canadian Ceramic Society* 21:45–50.
Marriott, A.
  1948 *Maria: The potter of San Ildefonso.* Norman: University of Oklahoma Press.
Marshall, C.
  1955 A new concept of clay plasticity. *Bulletin of the American Ceramic Society* 34:54–56.
Mason, B.
  1966 *Principles of geochemistry.* 3d ed. New York: John Wiley.
Mason, B., and L. G. Berry
  1968 *Elements of mineralogy.* San Francisco: W. H. Freeman.
Matiskainen, H., and P. Alhonen
  1984 Diatoms as indicators of provenance in Finnish sub-Neolithic pottery. *Journal of Archaeological Science* 11:147–57.
Matson, F. R.
  1937 Pottery. Appendix in *The Younge site: An archaeological record from Michigan,* by E. F. Greenman, 99–124. Occasional Contributions no. 6. Ann Arbor: Museum of Anthropology, University of Michigan.
  1939 A technological study of the unglazed pottery and figurines from Seleucia on the Tigris. Ph.D. diss., University of Michigan, Ann Arbor.
  1952 The contribution of technical ceramic studies to American archaeology. In *Prehistoric pottery of the eastern United States,* no. 2, pp. 1–7. Ann Arbor: University of Michigan.
  1963 Some aspects of ceramic technology. In *Science in archaeology,* ed. D. Brothwell and E. Higgs, 592–602. New York: Basic Books.
  1965 Ceramic ecology: An approach to the study of the early cultures of the Near East. In *Ceramics and man,* ed. F. R. Matson, 202–17. Chicago: Aldine.
  1971 A study of temperatures used in firing ancient Mesopotamian pottery. In *Science and archaeology,* ed. R. Brill, 65–80. Cambridge: MIT Press.
  1972 Ceramic studies. In *The Minnesota Messenian expedition: Reconstructing a Bronze Age regional environment,* ed. W. A. McDonald and G. R. Rapp, Jr., 200–224. Minneapolis: University of Minnesota Press.
  1973 The potters of Chalkis. In *Classics and the classical tradition,* ed. E. N.

Borza and R. W. Carruba, 117–42. University Park: Pennsylvania State University Press.

1974   The archaeological present: Near Eastern potters at work. *American Journal of Archaeology* 78:345–47.

1975a   Technological studies of Egyptian pottery—modern and ancient. In *Recent advances in science and technology of materials,* ed. A. Bishay, 3:129–39. New York: Plenum.

1975b   Archaeological ceramic study possibilities with a thermal gradient furnace. In *Archaeological chemistry,* ed. C. W. Beck, 34–47. Advances in Chemistry 138. Washington, D.C.: American Chemical Society.

1982   Archaeological ceramics and the physical sciences: Problem definition and results. In *Archaeological ceramics,* ed. J. S. Olin and A. D. Franklin, 19–28. Washington, D.C.: Smithsonian Institution.

Matson, F. R., ed.

1965   *Ceramics and man.* Chicago: Aldine.

Matson, R. G., and D. L. True

1974   Site relationships at Quebrada Tarapacá, Chile: A comparison of clustering and scaling techniques. *American Antiquity* 39(1):51–74.

Matthiae, P.

1977   Tell Mardikh: The archives and palace. *Archaeology* 30(4):244–53.

May, P., and M. Tuckson

1982   *The traditional pottery of Papua New Guinea.* Sydney: Bay Books.

Mayes, P.

1961   The firing of a pottery kiln of a Romano-British type at Boston, Lincolnshire. *Archaeometry* 4:4–18.

1962   The firing of a second pottery kiln of Romano-British type at Boston, Lincolnshire. *Archaeometry* 5:80–92.

Medley, M.

1976   *The Chinese potter: A practical history of Chinese ceramics.* Oxford: Phaidon.

Meggers, B. J., and C. Evans.

1966   A transpacific contact in 3000 B.C. *Scientific American* 214(1):28–35.

Mehran, F., K. A. Muller, and W. J. Fitzpatrick

1981   Characterization of particle orientations in ceramics by electron paramagnetic resonance. Communications of the American Ceramic Society. *Journal of the American Ceramic Society* 64(10):C129–30.

Meinholz, N. M.

1983   The preparation of thin sections for the FAI-270 project. Appendix 2 in *Thin section analysis of ceramics from the Robinson's Lake site,* by J. W. Porter. FAI-270 Archaeological Mitigation Project, Petrographic Report no. 1. Urbana-Champaign: University of Illinois.

Mellaart, J.

1964   A Neolithic city in Turkey. *Scientific American* 210(4):94–104.

1965   Anatolian pottery as a basis for cultural synthesis. In *Ceramics and man,* ed. F. R. Matson, 218–239. Chicago: Aldine.

Mera, H. P.

1937   *The rain bird: A study in Pueblo design.* Memoirs of the Laboratory of Anthropology no. 2. Santa Fe. (Reprinted New York: Dover, 1970.)

Mercer, H. C.

1897   The kabal, or potter's wheel of Yucatán. University of Pennsylvania, Free Museum of Science and Art, *Bulletin* 2:63–70.

Meschel, S. V.
 1978   Chemistry and archaeology: A creative bond. In *Archaeological chemistry*, vol. 2, ed. G. F. Carter, 1–24. Advances in Chemistry 171. Washington, D.C.: American Chemical Society.

Messing, S. D.
 1957   Further comments on resin-coated pottery: Ethiopia. *American Anthropologist* 59(1):134.

Meyers, P.
 1978   Applications of X-ray radiography in the study of archaeological objects. In *Archaeological chemistry*, vol. 2, ed. G. F. Carter, 79–96. Advances in Chemistry 171. Washington, D.C.: American Chemical Society.

Michael, H. N., and E. D. Ralph, eds.
 1971   *Dating techniques for the archaeologist*. Cambridge: MIT Press.

Michels, J. W.
 1973   *Dating methods in archaeology*. New York: Seminar Press.

Middleton, A. P., I. C. Freestone, and M. N. Leese
 1985   Textural analysis of ceramic thin sections: Evaluations of grain sampling procedures. *Archaeometry* 27(1):64–74.

Mikami, T.
 1979   *The art of Japanese ceramics*. New York: Weatherhill.

Miller, D.
 1981   The relationship between ceramic production and distribution in a central Indian village. In *Production and distribution: A ceramic viewpoint*, ed. H. Howard and E. Morris, 221–28. International Series 120. Oxford: British Archaeological Reports.
 1985   *Artefacts as categories: A study of ceramic variability in central India*. Cambridge: Cambridge University Press.

Millett, M.
 1979a   An approach to the functional interpretation of pottery. In *Pottery and the archaeologist*, ed. M. Millett, 35–48. Occasional Publication no. 4. London: Institute of Archaeology.
 1979b   How much pottery? In *Pottery and the archaeologist*, ed. M. Millett, 77–80. Occasional Publication no. 4. London: Institute of Archaeology.

Millon, R.
 1970   Teotihuacán: Completion of map of giant ancient city in the Valley of Mexico. *Science* 170:1077–82.

Millot, G.
 1942   Rélations entre la constitution et la genèse des roches sédimentaires argileuses. In *Géologie appliquée et prospection minière*, vol. 2. Nancy, France.
 1979   Clay. *Scientific American* 240(4):76–83.

Mills, J. S., and R. White
 1977   Natural resins of art and archaeology: Their sources, chemistry, and identification. *Studies in Conservation* 22:12–31.

Moore, F.
 1961   The mechanism of moisture movement in clays with particular reference to drying: A concise view. *Transactions of the British Ceramic Society* 60:517–39.

Morariu, V. V., M. Bogdan, and I. Ardelean
 1977   Ancient pottery: Its pore structure. *Archaeometry* 19(2):187–92.

Morgan, L. H.
 1877   *Ancient society*. New York: World.

Morris, C.
 1974   Reconstructing patterns of non-agricultural production in the Inca economy:

Archaeology and documents in institutional analysis. In Reconstructing complex societies, ed. C. Moore, 49–60. *Bulletin of the American School of Oriental Research*, no. 20 (suppl.).

Morris, E. H.
  1917   The place of coiled ware in Southwestern pottery. *American Anthropologist* 19(1):24–29.

Mueller, J. W., ed.
  1975a   Archaeological research as cluster sampling. In *Sampling in archaeology*, ed. J. W. Mueller, 33–41. Tucson: University of Arizona Press.
  1975b   *Sampling in archaeology*. Tucson: University of Arizona Press.

Muir, I. D.
  1977   Microscopy: Transmitted light. In *Physical methods in determinative mineralogy*, ed. J. Zussman, 35–108. London: Academic Press.

Muller, J.
  1977   Individual variation in art styles. In *The individual in prehistory*, ed. J. N. Hill and J. Gunn, 23–38. New York: Academic Press.
  1984   Mississippian specialization and salt. *American Antiquity* 49(3):489–507.

Muller, L. D.
  1977   Mineral separation. In *Physical methods in determinative mineralogy*, 2d ed., ed. J. Zussman, 1–34. London: Academic Press.

Munn, N.
  1966   Visual categories: An approach to the study of representational systems. *American Anthropologist* 68(4):936–950.

Munsell Color Company
  1975   Munsell soil color charts. Baltimore, Md.: Munsell Color Company.

Museum of Qin Shi Huang
  1981   *Qin Shi Huang pottery figures of warriors and horses*. Corpus of Data no. 1. Shaanxi, China: Museum of Qin Shi Huang.

Musty, J. W. G., and L. C. Thomas
  1962   The spectrographic examination of English and Continental medieval glazed pottery. *Archaeometry* 5:38–52.

Naroll, R.
  1962   Floor area and settlement population. *American Antiquity* 27(4):587–98.

Nash, M.
  1966   *Primitive and peasant economic systems*. Scranton, Pa.: Chandler.

National Academy of Sciences
  1980   *Firewood crops: Shrub and tree species for energy production*. Washington, D.C.: National Academy of Sciences.

Nelson, B. A.
  1981   Ethnoarchaeology and paleodemography: A test of Turner and Lofgren's hypothesis. *Journal of Anthropological Research* 37(2):107–29.
  1985   Reconstructing ceramic vessels and their systemic contexts. In *Decoding prehistoric ceramics*, ed. B. A. Nelson, 310–29. Carbondale: Southern Illinois University Press.

Nelson, G. C.
  1984   *Ceramics: A potter's handbook*. 5th ed. New York: CBS College Publishing.

Neumann, B. S.
  1977   Thermal techniques. In *Physical methods in determinative mineralogy*, 2d ed., ed. J. Zussman, 605–62. London: Academic Press.

Nicholson, P. T., and H. L. Patterson
  1985a   Ethnoarchaeology in Egypt: The Ballâs pottery project. *Archaeology* 38(3):52–59.

1985b   Pottery making in Upper Egypt: An ethnoarchaeological study. *World Archaeology* 17(2):222–39.

Nickerson, D.

1948   Color and its description. *Bulletin of the American Ceramic Society* 27(2): 47–55.

Nicklin, K.

1971   Stability and innovation in pottery manufacture. *World Archaeology* 3(1): 13–48.

1979   The location of pottery manufacture. *Man* 14:436–58.

1981a   Ceramic pyrometry: Two Ibibio examples. In *Production and distribution: A ceramic viewpoint*, ed. H. Howard and E. Morris, 347–59. International Series 120. Oxford: British Archaeological Reports.

1981b   Pottery production and distribution in southeast Nigeria. In *Production and distribution: A ceramic viewpoint*, ed. H. Howard and E. Morris, 169–86. International Series 120. Oxford: British Archaeological Reports.

Noble, J. V.

1966   *The techniques of painted Attic pottery.* New York: Watson-Guptill.

1972   An unusual Attic baby feeder. *American Journal of Archaeology* 76(4): 437–38.

Nordenskiöld, E.

1983   *The cliff dwellers of the Mesa Verde.* Stockholm.

Norrish, K., and B. W. Chappell

1977   X-ray fluorescence spectrometry. In *Physical methods in determinative mineralogy*, 2d ed., ed. J. Zussman, 201–72. London: Academic Press.

Norton, F. H.

1938   Instrument for measuring workability of clays. *Journal of the American Ceramic Society* 21:33–36.

1948   Fundamental study of clay. 8. A new theory for the plasticity of clay-water masses. *Journal of the American Ceramic Society* 31(8):236–40.

1952   *Elements of ceramics.* Cambridge: Addison-Wesley.

1970   *Fine ceramics, technology and applications.* New York: McGraw-Hill.

Norton, F. H., and F. B. Hodgdon

1931   The influence of time on the maturing of temperature of whiteware bodies. *Journal of the American Ceramic Society* 14:177.

Norton, F. H., and A. L. Johnson

1944   Fundamental study of clay. 5. Nature of the water film in a plastic clay. *Journal of the American Ceramic Society* 27(3):77–80.

Ochsenschlager, E.

1974   Mud objects from al-Hiba. *Archaeology* 27(3):162–74.

Ogan, E.

1970   Nasioi pottery making. *Journal of the Polynesian Society* 79:86–90.

Oldfather, W. A.

1920   A note on the etymology of the word "ceramic." *Journal of the American Ceramic Society* 3:537–42.

Olin, J. S., ed.

1982   *Future directions in archaeometry: A round table.* Washington, D.C.: Smithsonian Institution.

Olin, J. S., and A. D. Franklin, eds.

1981   *Archaeological ceramics.* Washington, D.C.: Smithsonian Institution.

Olin, J. S., and E. V. Sayre

1971   Compositional categories of some English and American pottery of the American colonial period. In *Science and archaeology*, ed. R. H. Brill, 196–209. Cambridge: MIT Press.

Oliver, D.
1955   *A Solomon Island society.* Cambridge: Harvard University Press.
Olsen, E. D.
1975   *Modern optical methods of analysis.* New York; McGraw-Hill.
Orphanides, A. G.
1985   Radioanalytical techniques in archaeology: Pottery and raw clay analysis. Nicosia, Cyprus: AGO Publications.
Ortega, E., and C. Fondeur
1978   *Estudio de la cerámica del período indo-hispano de la Antigua Concepción de la Vega.* Serie Científica 1. Santo Domingo, D.R.: Fundación Ortega Alvarez.
Orton, C.
1980   *Mathematics in archaeology.* Cambridge: Cambridge University Press.
1982   Computer simulation experiments to assess the performance of measures of quantity of pottery. *World Archaeology* 14(1):1–19.
Osgood, C.
1951   Culture: Its empirical and non-empirical character. *Southwest Journal of Anthropology* 7:202–14.
Oswalt, W. H.
1973   *Habitat and technology.* New York: Holt, Rinehart and Winston.
Otto, J.
1975   Status differences and the archaeological record: A comparison of planter, overseer, and slave sites from Cannons Point plantation (1794–1861), St. Simons Island, Georgia. Ph.D. diss., University of Florida.
Paine, R. T., and W. J. Young
1953   A preliminary report on the sub-surface structure of glazes of Kuan and Kuan-type wares. *Far Eastern Ceramic Bulletin* 5(3):2–20.
Palmatary, H. C.
1950   *The pottery of Marajo Island, Brazil.* Transactions of the American Philosophical Society, n.s., vol. 39, part 3. Philadelphia: American Philosophical Society.
Papousek, D. A.
1981   *The peasant potters of Los Pueblos.* Assen: Van Gorcum.
1984   Pots and people in Low Pueblos: The social and economic organization of pottery. In *The many dimensions of pottery: Ceramics in archaeology and anthropology,* ed. S. E. van der Leeuw and A. C. Pritchard, 475–526. CINGULA 7. Amsterdam: Institute for Pre- and Proto-history, University of Amsterdam.
Pask, J. A.
1953   Measurement of dry strength of clay bodies. *Journal of the American Ceramic Society* 36(9):313–18.
Pastron, A. G.
1974   Preliminary ethnoarchaeological investigations among the Tarahumara. In *Ethnoarchaeology,* ed. C. B. Donnan and C. W. Clewlow, Jr., 93–114. UCLA Institute of Archaeology Monograph 4. Los Angeles: University of California Press.
Pasztory, E.
1982   Three Aztec masks of the god Xipe. In *Falsifications and misreconstructions of pre-Columbian art,* ed. E. H. Boone, 77–105. Washington, D.C.: Dumbarton Oaks.
Patrick, M., A. J. de Koning, and A. B. Smith
1985   Gas liquid chromatographic analysis of fatty acids in food residues from ceramics found in the southwestern Cape, South Africa. *Archaeometry* 27(2):231–36.

Payne, W. O.

1982   Kilns and ceramic technology of ancient Mesoamerica. In *Archaeological ceramics*, ed. J. S. Olin and A. D. Frankiln, 189–92. Washington, D.C.: Smithsonian Institution.

Peacock, D. P. S.

1967   The heavy mineral analysis of pottery: A preliminary report. *Archaeometry* 10:97–100.

1970   The scientific analysis of ancient ceramics: A review. *World Archaeology* 1(3):375–89.

1971   Petrography of certain coarse pottery. In Excavations at Fishbourne, 1961–1969, ed. B. Cunliffe. *Research Report of the Society of Antiquaries* 27:255–59.

1977   Ceramics in Roman and medieval archaeology. In *Pottery and early commerce: Characterization and trade in Roman and later ceramics*, ed. D. P. S. Peacock, 21–33. London: Academic Press.

1981   Archaeology, ethnology and ceramic production. In *Production and distribution: A ceramic viewpoint*, ed. H. Howard and E. Morris, 187–94. International Series 120. Oxford: British Archaeological Reports.

1982   *Pottery in the Roman world: An ethnoarchaeological approach.* London: Longmans.

Peacock, D. P. S., ed.

1977   *Pottery and early commerce: Characterization and trade in Roman and later ceramics.* London: Academic Press.

Périnet, G.

1960   Contribution de la diffraction des rayons X à l'évaluation de la température de cuisson d'une céramique. In *Transactions of the Seventh International Ceramic Congress*, 371–76. London.

Perkins, W. W., ed.

1984   *Ceramic glossary 1984.* Columbus, Ohio: American Ceramic Society.

Perlman, I.

1984   Modern neutron activation analysis and ancient history. In *Archaeological chemistry*, vol. 3, ed. J. B. Lambert, 117–32. Advances in Chemistry 205. Washington, D.C.: American Chemical Society.

Perlman, I., and F. Asaro

1969   Pottery analysis by neutron activation. *Archaeometry* 11:21–53.

Petrie, W. M. F.

1899   Sequences in prehistoric remains. *Journal of the Royal Anthropological Institute of Great Britain and Ireland* 29:295–301.

Phelps, G. W., and S. G. Maguire, Jr.

1956   Water as a ceramic raw material. *Bulletin of the American Ceramic Society* 35:422–26.

Philip, G., and B. S. Ottaway

1983   Mixed data cluster analysis: An illustration using Cypriot hooked-tang weapons. *Archaeometry* 25(2):119–33.

Phillips, P.

1958   Application of the Wheat-Gifford-Wasley taxonomy to Eastern ceramics. *American Antiquity* 24(2):117–25.

Phillips, W. R.

1971   *Mineral optics: Principles and techniques.* San Francisco: W. H. Freeman.

Phillipson, D.

1974   Iron Age history and archaeology in Zambia. *Journal of African History* 15(1):1–25.

Picolpasso, C. C.
1934   *The three books of the potter's art.* Trans. B. Rackham and A. Van de Put. London: Victoria and Albert Museum.

Pielou, E. C.
1974   *Ecological diversity.* Halifax: Dalhousie University Press.

Plant, R. J.
1970   A study of the moisture absorbed by biscuit pottery as a means of determining the approximate firing temperature. *Science and Archaeology* 4:19–20 (Stafford, England).

Plog, F.
1977   Modeling economic exchange. In *Exchange systems in prehistory,* ed. T. K. Earle and J. E. Ericson, 127–40. New York: Academic Press.

Plog, S.
1976   Measurement of prehistoric interaction between communities. In *The early Mesoamerican village,* ed. K. V. Flannery, 255–72. New York: Academic Press.
1978   Social interaction and stylistic similarity: A reanalysis. In *Advances in archaeological method and theory,* 1:143–82. New York: Academic Press.
1980   *Stylistic variation in prehistoric ceramics: Design analysis in the American Southwest.* New York: Cambridge University Press.
1982   Issues in the analysis of stylistic variation: Reply to Washburn and Ahlstrom. *Kiva* 48(1–2):123–31.
1985   Estimating vessel orifice diameters: Measurement methods and measurement error. In *Decoding prehistoric ceramics,* ed. B. A. Nelson, 243–53. Carbondale: Southern Illinois University Press.

Polanyi, K.
1957   The economy as instituted process. In *Trade and market in the early empires,* ed. K. Polanyi, C. Arensberg, and H. Pearson, 243–69. Glencoe, Ill.: Free Press.

Poole, A. B., and L. R. Finch
1972   The utilization of trace chemical composition to correlate British postmedieval pottery with European kiln site materials. *Archaeometry* 14(1):79–91.

Porada, E.
1984   Pottery in scenes of the period of Agade? In *Pots and potters: Current approaches in ceramic archaeology,* ed. P. M. Rice, 21–25. UCLA Institute of Archaeology Monograph 24. Los Angeles: University of California Press.

Porter, J. W.
1964   Comment on Weaver's "Technological analysis of lower Mississippi ceramic materials." *American Antiquity* 29(4):520–21.

Potts, D.
1981   The potter's marks of Tepe Yahya. *Paleorient* 7:107–19.

Prag, A. J. N. W., F. Schweizer, J. L. L. Williams, and P. A. Schubiger
1974   Hellenistic glazed wares from Athens and southern Italy: Analytical techniques and implications. *Archaeometry* 16(2):154–87.

Proulx, D. A.
1968   *Local differences and time differences in Nasca pottery.* Publications in Anthropology, vol. 5. Berkeley and Los Angeles: University of California Press.

Pyddoke, E.
1963   *The scientist and archaeology.* London: Phoenix House.

Pyne, N.
1976   The fire-serpent and were-jaguar in Formative Oaxaca: A contingency table analysis. In *The early Mesoamerican village,* ed. K. V. Flannery, 272–82. New York: Academic Press.

Quirarte. J.
  1979   The representation of underworld processions in Maya vase painting: An iconographic study. In *Maya archaeology and ethnohistory*, ed. N. Hammond and G. R. Willey, 116–48. Austin: University of Texas Press.

Ralph, E. K.
  1971   Carbon-14 dating. In *Dating techniques for the archaeologist*, ed. H. N. Michael and E. K. Ralph, 1–48. Cambridge: MIT Press.

Ralph, E. K., H. N. Michael, and M. C. Han
  1973   Radiocarbon dates and reality. *MASCA Newsletter* 9:1–20.

Rands, R. L., and R. L. Bishop
  1980   Resource procurement zones and patterns of ceramic exchange in the Palenque region, Mexico. In *Models and methods in regional exchange*, ed. R. E. Fry, 19–46. SAA Papers 1. Washington, D.C.: Society for American Archaeology.

Rankin, P.
  1971   General analytical chemistry. In *Characterization of ceramics*, ed. L. L. Hench and R. W. Gould, 9–38. New York: Marcel Dekker.

Rapp, G., Jr.
  1977   Archaeological geology. *Geotimes* 22:16.
  1985   The provenance of artifactual raw materials. In *Archaeological geology*, ed. G. Rapp, Jr., and J. A. Gifford, 353–75. New Haven: Yale University Press.

Rapp, G., Jr., and J. A. Gifford
  1985   *Archaeological geology*. New Haven: Yale University Press.

Rathbun, W. J.
  1979   Impressed and incised decoration on early Japanese pottery. In *Decorative techniques and styles in Asian ceramics*, ed. M. Medley, 34–46. Colloquies on Art and Archaeology in Asia no. 8. London: University of London.

Rathje, W., D. A. Gregory, and F. M. Wiseman
  1978   Trade models and archaeological problems: Classic Maya examples. In *Mesoamerican communication routes and cultural contacts*, ed. T. A. Lee, Jr., and C. Navarette, 147–75. Provo, Utah: New World Archaeological Foundation.

Redman, C. L.
  1974   *Archaeological sampling strategies*. Module in Anthropology no. 55. Reading, Mass.: Addison-Wesley.
  1977   The "analytical individual" and prehistoric style variability. In *The individual in prehistory*, ed. J. N. Hill and J. Gunn, 23–38. New York: Academic Press.
  1978a Multivariate artifact analysis: A basis for multidimensional interpretations. In *Social archaeology: Beyond subsistence and dating*, ed. C. L. Redman, M. J. Berman, E. V. Curtin, et al., 159–92. New York: Academic Press.
  1978b *The rise of civilization*. San Francisco: W. H. Freeman.

Redman, C. L., and J. E. Myers
  1981   Interpretation, classification, and ceramic production: A medieval North African case study. In *Production and distribution: A ceramic viewpoint*, ed. H. Howard and E. Morris, 285–307. International Series 120. Oxford: British Archaeological Reports.

Reed, S. J. B.
  1975   *Electron microprobe analysis*. Cambridge: Cambridge University Press.

Reeves, R. D., and R. R. Brooks
  1978   *Trace element analysis of geological materials*. New York: John Wiley.

Reichel-Dolmatoff, G.
  1961   Puerto Hormiga: Un complejo prehistórico marginal de Colombia. *Revista Colombiana de Antropología* 10:347–54.

Reid, K. C.

1984   Fire and ice: New evidence for the production and preservation of Late Archaic fiber-tempered pottery in the middle-latitude lowlands. *American Antiquity* 49(1):55–76.

Reina, R. E.

1963   The potter and the farmer: The fate of two innovators. *Expedition* 5(4): 18–31.

1966   *The law of the saints: A Pokomam pueblo and its community culture.* New York: Bobbs-Merrill.

Reina, R. E., and R. M. Hill II

1978   *The traditional pottery of Guatemala.* Austin: University of Texas Press.

Renfrew, C.

1977a   Alternative models for exchange and spatial distribution. In *Exchange systems in prehistory*, ed. T. K. Earle and J. Ericson, 71–90. New York: Academic Press.

1977b   Production and exchange in early state societies: The evidence of pottery. In *Pottery and early commerce: Characterization and trade in Roman and later ceramics*, ed. D. P. S. Peacock, 1–20. London: Academic Press.

Renfrew, C., J. E. Dixon, and J. R. Cann

1968   Further analysis of Near Eastern obsidians. *Proceedings of the Prehistoric Society* 34:319–31.

Rhodes, D.

1968   *Kilns: Design, construction, and operation.* Philadelphia: Chilton Books.

1973   *Clay and glazes for the potter.* 2d ed. Philadelphia: Chilton Books.

Rice, P. M.

1974   Comment on Weymouth's "X-ray diffraction analysis of prehistoric pottery." *American Antiquity* 39(4):619–20.

1976a   Ceramic continuity and change in the Valley of Guatemala: A study of whiteware pottery production. Ph.D. diss., Pennsylvania State University.

1976b   Rethinking the ware concept. *American Antiquity* 41(4):538–43.

1978a   Ceramic continuity and change in the Valley of Guatemala. In *The ceramics of Kaminaljuyú, Guatemala*, ed. R. K. Wetherington, 401–510. University Park: Pennsylvania State University Press.

1978b   Clear anwers to vague questions: Some assumptions of provenience studies of pottery. In *The ceramics of Kaminaljuyú, Guatemala*, ed. R. K. Wetherington, 511–42. University Park: Pennsylvania State University Press.

1981   Evolution of specialized pottery production: A trial model. *Current Anthropology* 22(3):219–40.

1982   Pottery production, classification, and the role of physicochemical analyses. In *Archaeological ceramics*, ed. J. S. Olin and A. D. Franklin, 47–56. Washington, D.C.: Smithsonian Institution.

1984a   Ceramic diversity: Implications for production and use. Paper presented at the forty-ninth annual meeting of the Society for American Archaeology, Portland, Oregon.

1984b   Some reflections on change in pottery producing systems. In *The many dimensions of pottery: Ceramics in archaeology and anthropology*, ed. S. E. van der Leeuw and A. C. Pritchard, 231–93. CINGULA 7. Amsterdam: Institute for Pre- and Proto-history, University of Amsterdam.

1985   Maya pottery techniques and technology. In *Ancient technology to modern science*, ed. W. D. Kingery, 113–32. Ceramics and Civilization, vol. 1. Columbus, Ohio: American Ceramic Society.

Rice, P. M., ed.

1984   *Pots and potters: Current approaches in ceramic archaeology.* UCLA Institute of Archaeology Monograph 24. Los Angeles: University of California Press.

Rice, P. M., and A. S. Cordell

1986   Weeden Island pottery: Style, technology, and production. In *Technology and style*, ed. W. D. Kingery, 273–95. Ceramics and Civilization, vol. 2. Columbus, Ohio: American Ceramic Society.

Rice, P. M., and M. E. Saffer

1982   Cluster analysis of mixed-level data: Pottery provenience as an example. *Journal of Archaeological Science* 9(4): 395–409.

Rich, C. I., and G. W. Kunze, eds.

1964   *Soil clay mineralogy: A symposium.* Chapel Hill: University of North Carolina Press.

Richards, E. E.

1959   Preliminary spectrographic investigation of some Romano-British mortaria. *Archaeometry* 2: 21–31.

Richards, T. W.

1895   The composition of Athenian pottery. *American Chemical Journal* 17: 152–54.

Richter, G.

1976   *Attic red-figure vases.* New Haven: Yale University Press.

Ridgway, R.

1912   *Color standards and color nomenclature.* Baltimore: Hoen.

Ries, H.

1927   *Clays: Their occurrence, properties and uses.* 3d ed. New York: John Wiley.

Riley, J. A.

1981   The late Bronze Age Aegean and the Roman Mediterranean: A case for comparison. In *Production and distribution: A ceramic viewpoint,* ed. H. Howard and E. Morris, 133–43. International Series 120. Oxford: British Archaeological Reports.

Rinne, F.

1924   An X-ray investigation of some finely divided minerals, artificial products, and dense rocks. *Zeitschrift für Kristallographie* 60: 55–69.

Ritchie, P. D.

1937   Spectrographic studies on ancient glass: Chinese glass, from pre-Han to T'ang times. *Technical Studies in the Field of Fine Arts* 5: 209–20.

Roberts, J. P.

1963   Determination of the firing temperature of ancient ceramics by measurement of thermal expansion. *Archaeometry* 6: 21–25.

Robicsek, F., and D. M. Hales

1981   *The Maya Book of the Dead: The ceramic codex.* Charlottesville: University of Virginia Art Museum.

Robinson, G.

1968a   Design of clay bodies for controlled microstructure. *Bulletin of the American Ceramic Society* 47: 477–80.

1968b   Design of clay bodies for controlled microstructure. 2. Clay aggregate bodies. *Bulletin of the American Ceramic Society* 47: 548–53.

Roe, P. G.

1980   Art and residence among the Shipibo Indians of Peru: A study in microacculturation. *American Anthropologist* 82(1): 42–71.

Rogers, F. E.
  1973 Chemistry and art: Thermoluminescence and forgery. *Journal of Chemical Education* 50:388.
Ross, C. S.
  1928 The mineralogy of clays. *First International Congress of Soil Scientists* 4:555–56.
Ross, C. S., and S. B. Hendricks
  1945 Minerals of the montmorillonite group. *U.S. Geological Survey, Professional Paper* 205B:23–79.
Ross, C. S., and P. F. Kerr
  1931a The clay minerals and their identity. *Journal of Sedimentary Petrology* 1:55–65.
  1931b The kaolin minerals. *U.S. Geological Survey, Professional Paper* 165E: 151–75.
Roth, R. S., T. Negas, and L. P. Cook
  1983 *Phase diagrams for ceramists.* Vol. 5. Columbus, Ohio: American Ceramic Society.
Rottländer, R. C. A.
  1967 Is provincial Roman pottery standardized? *Archaeometry* 9:76–91.
  1968 Standardization of Roman provincial pottery. 2. Function of the decorative collar on Form Drag. 38. *Archaeometry* 10:35–46.
Rottländer, R. C. A., and H. Schlichtherle
  1983 Analyse frühgeschichtlicher Gefäbinhalte. *Naturwissenschaften* 70:30–38.
Rouse, I.
  1960 The classification of artifacts in archaeology. *American Antiquity* 25(3): 313–23.
Rowe, J. H.
  1961 Stratigraphy and seriation. *American Antiquity* 26(3):324–30.
Ruddlesden, S. N.
  1967 Applications of the electron probe microanalyser to ceramics. 1. Potentialities of the instrument. *Transactions of the British Ceramic Society* 66:587–98.
Ruddlesden, S. N., and A. C. Airey
  1967 Applications of the electron probe microanalyser to ceramics. 2. Analysis of defects in ware. *Transactions of the British Ceramic Society* 66:599–606.
Ryan, W.
  1965 Factors influencing the dry strength of clays and bodies. *Transactions of the British Ceramic Society* 64:275–85.
Rye, O. S.
  1976 Keeping your temper under control. *Archaeology and Physical Anthropology in Oceania* 11(2):106–37.
  1977 Pottery manufacturing techniques: X-ray studies. *Archaeometry* 19(2): 205–11.
  1981 *Pottery technology: Principles and reconstruction.* Washington, D.C.: Taraxacum.
Rye, O. S., and P. Duerden
  1982 Papuan pottery sourcing by PIXE: Preliminary studies. *Archaeometry* 24(1):59–64.
Rye, O. S., and C. Evans
  1976 *Traditional pottery techniques of Pakistan: Field and laboratory studies.* Smithsonian Contributions to Anthropology no. 21. Washington, D.C.: Smithsonian Institution.

Sabine, P. A.
  1958   Black mica in the pottery fabric. In Excavation of a medieval settlement at
         Beere, North Tawton, Devon, by E. M. Jepe and R. I. Threlfall. *Medieval Ar-
         chaeology* 2:140.
Sabloff, J. A.
  1975   *Excavations at Seibal: Ceramics.* Memoirs of the Peabody Museum, vol.
         13, no. 2. Cambridge, Mass.: Peabody Museum.
Sabloff, J. A., and R. E. Smith
  1969   The importance of both analytic and taxonomic classification in the type-
         variety system. *American Antiquity* 34(3):278–85.
  1972   Ceramic wares in the Maya area: A clarification of an aspect of the type-
         variety system and presentation of a formal model for comparative use. *Estudios
         de Cultura Maya* 8:97–115 (Mexico).
Sackett, J. R.
  1977   Style, function, and artifact variability in Paleolithic assemblages. In *The
         explanation of culture change*, ed. C. Renfrew, 317–25. Pittsburgh: University of
         Pittsburgh Press.
Sahlins, M.
  1972   *Stone Age economics.* New York: Aldine-Atherton.
  1976   Colors and cultures. *Semiotica* 16:1–22.
Salmang, H.
  1961   *Ceramics, physical and chemical fundamentals.* Trans. Marcus Frances.
         London: Butterworths.
Sanders, H. P.
  1973   Pore size distribution determinations in Neolithic, Iron Age, Roman and
         other pottery. *Archaeometry* 15(2):159–61.
Santley, R. S.
  1982   Final field report, Matacapán project: 1982 season. Manuscript. Department
         of Anthropology, University of New Mexico.
Saunders, R.
  1986   Pottery manufacture and design symbolism of Late Swift Creek Phase ce-
         ramics at Kings Bay, Georgia. In *Papers in ceramic analysis*, ed. P. M. Rice. *Ce-
         ramic Notes* 3:145–98.
Savage, G., and H. Newman
  1976   *An illustrated dictionary of ceramics.* New York: Van Nostrand Reinhold.
Sawyer, A. R.
  1982   The falsification of ancient Peruvian slip-decorated ceramics. In *Falsifica-
         tions and misreconstructions of Pre-Columbian art*, ed. E. H. Boone, 19–36.
         Washington, D.C.: Dumbarton Oaks.
Sayre, E. V., L.-H. Chan, and J. A. Sabloff
  1971   High-resolution gamma ray spectroscopic analyses of Fine Orange pottery.
         In *Science and archaeology*, ed. R. H. Brill, 165–81. Cambridge: MIT Press.
Sayre, E. V., and R. E. Dodson
  1957   Neutron activation study of Mediterranean potsherds. *American Journal of
         Archaeology* 61:35–41.
Sayre, E. V., A. Murrenhoff, and C. F. Weick
  1958   *Non-destructive analysis of ancient pot sherds through neutron activation.*
         Report BNL-508. Upton, N.Y.: Brookhaven National Laboratory.
Schapiro, M.
  1953   Style. In *Anthropology today*, ed. A. L. Kroeber et al., 287–312. Chicago:
         University of Chicago Press.

Scheans, D. J.
1977   *Filipino market potteries.* Monograph no. 3. Manila: National Museum.
Schiffer, M. B.
1976   *Behavioral archaeology.* New York: Academic Press.
Schmandt-Besserat, D.
1974   The use of clay before pottery in the Zagros. *Expedition* 16(2):11–17.
1977a   The beginnings of the use of clay in Turkey. *Anatolian Studies* 27:133–50.
1977b   The earliest uses of clay in Syria. *Expedition* 19(3):28–42.
1978   The earliest precursor of writing. *Scientific American* 238(6):50–59.
Schramm, E., and F. P. Hall
1936   The fluxing effects of feldspar in whiteware bodies. *Journal of the American Ceramic Society* 19:159–68.
Schumann, T.
1942   Oberflächenverzierung in der antiken Töpferkunst, Terra Sigillata und Griechische Schwartzrotmalerei. *Berichte de Deutsche Keramischen Gesellschaft* 23:408–26.
Schumpeter, J. A.
1961   *The theory of economic development: An inquiry into profits, capital, credit, interest, and the business cycle.* Trans. R. Opie. New York: Oxford.
Schwartz, B.
1952   Fundamental study of clay. 12. A note of the effect of the surface tension of water on the plasticity of clay. *Journal of the American Ceramic Society* 35(2):41–43.
Schweizer, F.
1971   Investigation of firing temperature. Appendix to The authenticity of vessels and figurines in the Hacilar style. *Archaeometry* 13(2):131–37.
Scripture, E. W., Jr., and E. Schramm
1926   The deflocculation of clay slip and related properties. *Journal of the American Ceramic Society* 9:174–84.
Sears, W. H., and J. B. Griffin
1951   Fiber-tempered pottery of the Southeast. In *Prehistoric pottery of the eastern United States,* ed. J. B. Griffin. Ann Arbor: University of Michigan Press.
Sedgwick, D., J. M. Fossey, and M. Attas
1980   The pottery recording system used at Lake Vouliagméni, Perakhóra, central Greece. *Journal of Field Archaeology* 7:136–46.
Shackley, M. L.
1975   *Archaeological sediments: A survey of analytical methods.* New York: John Wiley.
1982   Gas chromatographic identification of a resinous deposit from a sixth century storage jar and its possible identification. *Journal of Archaeological Science* 9:305–6.
Shangraw, C. F.
1977   Early Chinese ceramics and kilns. *Archaeology* 30(6):382–93.
1978   *Origins of Chinese ceramics.* New York: China Institute in America.
Shapiro, G.
1983   Site variability in the Oconee province: A late Mississippian society of the Georgia Piedmont. Ph.D. diss., University of Florida.
1984   Ceramic vessels, site permanence, and group size: A Mississippian example. *American Antiquity* 49(4):696–712.
Shaplin, P. D.
1978   Thermoluminescence and style in the authentication of ceramic sculpture from Oaxaca, Mexico. *Archaeometry* 20(1):47–54.

Sharer, R. J., and W. Ashmore
    1979   *Fundamentals of archaeology.* Menlo Park, Calif.: Benjamin/Cummings.
Shennan, S. J., and J. D. Wilcock
    1975   Shape and style variation in central German bell beakers. *Science and Archaeology* 15:17–31.
Shepard, A. O.
    1936   Technology of Pecos pottery. In *The pottery of Pecos*, vol. 2, ed. A. V. Kidder and A. O. Shepard. Papers of the Phillips Academy Southwestern Expedition 7:389–587. Andover.
    1939   Technology of La Plata pottery. Appendix in *Archaeological studies in the La Plata District*, by E. H. Morris. Publication 519. Washington, D.C.: Carnegie Institution of Washington.
    1942a   *Rio Grande glaze paint ware: A study illustrating the place of ceramic technological analysis in archaeological research.* Publication 526, Contributions to Anthropology 39. Washington, D.C.: Carnegie Institution of Washington.
    1942b   Technological notes on the pottery of San Jose. Appendix to *Excavations at San Jose, British Honduras*, by J. E. S. Thompson. Publication 506. Washington, D.C.: Carnegie Institution of Washington.
    1946   Technological notes. In *Excavations at Kaminaljuyú*, ed. A. V. Kidder, J. D. Jennings, and E. M. Shook, 261–77. Publication 561. Washington, D.C.: Carnegie Institution of Washington.
    1948a   *Plumbate: A Mesoamerican trade ware.* Publication 573. Washington, D.C.: Carnegie Institution of Washington.
    1948b   *The symmetry of abstract design, with specific reference to ceramic decoration.* Publication 574. Washington, D.C.: Carnegie Institution of Washington.
    1962   Ceramic development of the lowland and highland Maya. Thirty-fifth Congreso Internacional de Americanistas, *Actas* 1:249–62 (Mexico City).
    1964   Temper identification: "Technological sherd-splitting" or an unanswered challenge. *American Antiquity* 29(4):518–20.
    1965   Rio Grande glaze-paint pottery: A test of petrographic analysis. In *Ceramics and man*, ed. F. R. Matson, 62–87. Chicago: Aldine.
    1976   *Ceramics for the archaeologist.* Washington, D.C.: Carnegie Institution of Washington.
Shepard, A. O., and D. Horton
    1939   Conference on archaeological technology in ceramics. *American Antiquity* 4(4):358–59.
Shepard, A. O., and H. E. D. Pollock
    1977   Maya Blue: An updated record. In *Notes from a ceramic laboratory*, 65–100. Washington, D.C.: Carnegie Institution. (originally published 1971.)
Shotton, F. W., and G. L. Hendry
    1979   The developing field of petrology in archaeology. *Journal of Archaeological Science* 6:75–84.
Shubnikov, A. V., and V. A. Koptsik
    1974   *Symmetry in science and art.* New York: Plenum.
Silver, H. R.
    1979   Ethnoart. *Annual Review of Anthropology* 8:267–307.
Simpkins, D. L., and D. J. Allard
    1986   Isolation and identification of Spanish moss fiber from a sample of Stallings and Orange series ceramics. *American Antiquity* 51(1): 102–17.
Slavin, W.
    1968   *Atomic absorption spectroscopy.* New York: John Wiley.

Smith, C.

1974   Economics of marketing systems: Models from economic geography. *Annual Review of Anthropology* 3:167–201.

Smith, M. F., Jr.

1983   The study of ceramic function from artifact size and shape. Ph.D. diss., University of Oregon.

1985   Toward an economic interpretation of ceramics: Relating vessel size and shape to use. In *Decoding prehistoric ceramics,* ed. B. A. Nelson, 254–309. Carbondale: Southern Illinois University Press.

Smith, R. E.

1955   *Ceramic sequence at Uaxactún, Guatemala.* Vol. 1. MARI publication no. 20. New Orleans: Tulane University.

Smith, R. E., G. R. Willey, and J. C. Gifford

1960   The type-variety concept as a basis for the analysis of Maya pottery. *American Antiquity* 25(3):330–40.

Smith, W.

1962   Schools, pots, and potters. *American Anthropologist* 64(6):1165–78.

Sokal, R. R., and P. H. A. Sneath

1963   *Principles of numerical taxonomy.* San Francisco: W. H. Freeman.

Solheim, W. G., II

1952   Oceanian pottery manufacture. *Journal of East Asiatic Studies* 1:1–39.

1954   Ibanag pottery manufacture in Isabela, Philippines. *Journal of East Asiatic Studies* 3:305–7.

1960   The use of sherd weights and counts in the handling of archaeological data. *Current Anthropology* 1(4):325–29.

1965   The functions of pottery in Southeast Asia: From the present to the past. In *Ceramics and man,* ed. F. R. Matson, 254–73. Chicago: Aldine.

1984   Pottery and the prehistory of northeast Thailand. In *Pots and potters: Current approaches to ceramic archaeology,* ed. P. M. Rice, 95–105. UCLA Institute of Archaeology Monograph 24. Los Angeles: University of California Press.

South, S.

1977   *Method and theory in historical archaeology.* New York: Academic Press.

Southward, J. A., and D. C. Kamilli

1983   Preliminary study of selected ceramics from the Cerén house. Appendix 7-B in *Archaeology and volcanism in Central America,* ed. P. D. Sheets, 147–51. Austin: University of Texas Press.

Spaulding, A. C.

1953a   Review of "Measurements of some prehistoric design developments in the southeastern states" by J. A. Ford. *American Anthropologist* 55(4):588–91.

1953b   Statistical techniques for the discovery of artifact types. *American Antiquity* 18(4):305–13.

1982   Structure in archaeological data: Nominal variables. In *Essays on archaeological typology,* ed. R. Whallon and J. A. Brown, 1–20. Evanston, Ill.: Center for American Archaeology Press.

Speck, F. G.

1931   Birch-bark in the ancestry of pottery forms. *Anthropos* 26:407–11.

Spiel, S., L. H. Berkelheimer, J. A. Pask, and B. Davies

1945   *Differential thermal analysis—its application to clays and other aluminous minerals.* Technical Paper 664. Washington, D.C.: U.S. Bureau of Mines.

Spinks, C. N.

1965   *The ceramic wares of Siam.* Bangkok: Siam Society.

Spriggs, M., and D. Miller
1979   Ambon-Lease: On study of its contemporary pottery making and its archaeological relevance. In *Pottery and the archaeologist*, ed. M. Millett, 25–34. Occasional Publication no. 4. London: Institute of Archaeology.

Staehelin, W.
1965   *The book of porcelain: The manufacture, transport, and sale of export porcelain in China during the eighteenth century, illustrated by a contemporary series of Chinese watercolors.* London: Lund Humphries.

Stanislawski, M.
1978   If pots were mortal. In *Explorations in ethnoarchaeology*, ed. R. A. Gould, 201–28. Albuquerque: University of New Mexico Press.

Stanislawski, M., and B. Stanislawski
1978   Hopi and Hopi-Tewa ceramic tradition networks. In *The spatial organisation of culture*, ed. I. Hodder, 61–76. Pittsburgh: University of Pittsburgh Press.

Stark, B. L.
1985   Archaeological identification of pottery-production locations: Ethnoarchaeological and archaeological data in Mesoamerica. In *Decoding prehistoric ceramics*, ed. B. A. Nelson, 158–94. Carbondale: Southern Illinois University Press.

Starkey, P.
1977   *Saltglaze.* London: Pitman.

Stastny, F.
1979   *Las artes populares del Peru.* Madrid: Ediciones Edubanco.

Steinberg, A., and D. C. Kamilli
1984   Paint and paste studies of selected Halaf sherds from Mesopotamia. In *Pots and potters: Current approaches in ceramic archaeology*, ed. P. M. Rice, 187–208. UCLA Institute of Archaeology Monograph 24. Los Angeles: University of California Press.

Stern, T.
1951   *Pamunkey pottery making.* Southern Indian Studies 3. Chapel Hill: University of North Carolina Press.

Steward, J. H.
1954   Types of types. *American Anthropologist* 56(1):54–57.

Stimmell, C., and R. L. Stromberg
1986   A reassessment of Thule Eskimo ceramic technology. In *Technology and style*, ed. W. D. Kingery, 237–50. Ceramics and Civilization, vol. 2. Columbus, Ohio: American Ceramic Society.

Stokes, R. J.
1968   Mechanical behavior of polycrystalline ceramics. In *Ceramic microstructures*, ed. R. M. Fulrath and J. A. Pask, 379–405. New York: John Wiley.

Stone, D.
1950   Notes on present-day pottery making and its economy in the ancient Chorotegan area. *Research Records* 1:269–80 (Middle American Research Institute, Tulane University).

Stross, F., and F. Asaro
1984   Time's wheel runs back or stops: Potter and clay endure. In *Pots and potters: Current approaches in ceramic archaeology*, ed. P. M. Rice, 179–86. UCLA Institute of Archaeology Monograph 24. Los Angeles: University of California Press.

Stross, F., T. R. Hester, R. F. Heizer, and R. N. Jack
1976   Chemical and archaeological studies in Mesoamerican obsidians. In *Advances in obsidian glass studies*, ed. R. E. Taylor, 240–58. Park Ridge, N.J.: Noyes.

Sturtevant, W. C.
 1964 Studies in ethnoscience. In Transcultural studies in cognition, ed. A. K. Romney and R. D'Andrade, 99–131. *American Anthropologist* 66, no. 3, part 2.
Sutton, S. R., and D. W. Zimmerman
 1976 Thermoluminescent dating using zircon grains from archaeological ceramics. *Archaeometry* 18(2): 125–34.
Talbott, P. T.
 1984 Prospecting for clay. *Bulletin of the American Ceramic Society* 63: 1047–50.
Tankersley, K., and J. Meinhart
 1982 Physical and structural properties of ceramic materials utilized by a Fort Ancient group. *Midcontinental Journal of Archaeology* 7: 225–43.
Tatje, T. A., and R. Naroll
 1973 Two measures of societal complexity: An empirical cross-cultural comparison. In *A handbook of method in cultural anthropology*, ed. R. Naroll and R. Cohen, 766–833. New York: Columbia University.
Taylor, J. C. M.
 1960 Impregnation of rocks for sectioning. *Geological Magazine* 97: 261.
Taylor, R. E., ed.
 1977 *Advances in obsidian glass studies.* Park Ridge, N.J.: Noyes.
Taylor, R. E., and R. Berger
 1968 Radiocarbon dating of the organic portion of ceramic and wattle-and-daub house construction materials of low carbon content. *American Antiquity* 33(3): 363–66.
Taylor, R. E., D. J. Donahue, T. H. Zabel, P. E. Damon, and A. J. T. Jull
 1984 Radiocarbon dating by particle accelerator: An archaeological perspective. In *Archaeological chemistry*, vol. 3, ed. J. B. Lambert, 333–56. Advances in Chemistry 205. Washington, D.C.: American Chemical Society.
Taylor, W. W., Jr.
 1948 *A study of archaeology.* Memoir no. 69. Washington, D.C.: American Anthropological Association.
Theuvenin, H., R. P. Bullen, and M. Sanoja
 1970 Ceramic terminology: Equivalent French-English-Spanish terms. In *Proceedings of the Third International Congress for the Study of Pre-Columbian Cultures of the Lesser Antilles, 1969*, 4–7. Grenada: Grenada National Museum.
Thompson, H. A.
 1984 The Athenian vase-painters and their neighbors. In *Pots and potters: Current approaches in ceramic archaeology*, ed. P. M. Rice, 7–19. UCLA Institute of Archaeology Monograph 24. Los Angeles: University of California Press.
Thompson, R.
 1969 Àbátàn: a master potter of the Ègbádò Yorùbá. In *Tradition and creativity in tribal art*, ed. D. P. Biebuyck, 120–82. Berkeley: University of California Press.
Thompson, R. H.
 1958 Modern Yucatecan Maya pottery making. Memoirs of the SAA, no. 15. *American Antiquity* 23, no. 4, part 2.
Thornton, P. R.
 1968 *Scanning electron microscopy.* London: Chapman and Hall.
Tichane, R.
 1983 *Ching-tê-chên: View of a porcelain city.* Painted Post: New York State Institute for Glaze Research.
Tite, M. S.
 1969 Determination of the firing temperature of ancient ceramics by measurement of thermal expansion: A reassessment. *Archaeometry* 11: 132–43.

1972   *Methods of physical examination in archaeology.* London: Seminar Press.

Tite, M. S., M. Bimson, and I. C. Freestone

1982   An examination of the high gloss surface finishes on Greek Attic and Roman Samian wares. *Archaeometry* 24(2):117–26.

Tite, M. S., I. C. Freestone, N. D. Meeks, and M. Bimson

1982   The use of scanning electron microscopy in the technological examination of ancient ceramics. In *Archaeological ceramics,* ed. J. S. Olin and A. D. Franklin, 109–20. Washington, D.C.: Smithsonian Institution.

Tite, M. S., and Y. Maniatis

1975a   Examination of ancient pottery using the scanning electron microscope. *Nature* 257:122–23.

1975b   Scanning electron microscopy of fired calcareous clays. *Transactions of the British Ceramic Society* 74:19–22.

Tite, M. S., and J. Waine

1962   Thermoluminescent dating: A re-appraisal. *Archaeometry* 5:53–79.

Titterington, P. F.

1933   Has the X-ray a place in the archaeological laboratory? *American Anthropologist* 35(2):145–86.

1951   Applications of X-ray to archaeology. In *Essays on archaeological methods,* ed. J. B. Griffin, 94–96. Anthropological Papers no. 8. Ann Arbor: Museum of Anthropology, University of Michigan.

Toll, H. W.

1981   Ceramic comparisons concerning redistribution in Chaco Canyon, New Mexico. In *Production and distribution: A ceramic viewpoint,* ed. H. Howard and E. Morris, 83–122. International Series 120. Oxford: British Archaeological Reports.

Torres, L. M., A. W. Arie, and B. Sandoval

1984   Provenance determination of Fine Orange Maya ceramic figurines by flame atomic absorption spectrometry: A preliminary study of objects from Jaina (Campeche) and Jonuta (Tabasco), Mexico. In *Archaeological chemistry,* vol. 3, ed. J. B. Lambert, 193–213. Advances in Chemistry 205. Washington, D.C.: American Chemical Society.

Trachsler, W.

1965   The influence of metalworking on prehistoric pottery: Some observations on Iron Age pottery of the Alpine region. In *Ceramics and man,* ed. F. R. Matson, 140–51. Chicago: Aldine.

Tschopik, H.

1950   An Andean ceramic tradition in historical perspective. *American Antiquity* 15(3):196–218.

Tubb, A., A. J. Parker, and G. Nickless

1980   The analysis of Romano-British pottery by atomic absorption spectrophotometry. *Archaeometry* 22(2):153–71.

Tufts, C. F.

1971   Transmission electron microscopy and electron diffraction. In *Characterization of ceramics,* ed. L. L. Hench and R. W. Gould, 177–218. New York: Marcel Dekker.

Tuggle, H. D.

1970   Prehistoric community relations in east-central Arizona. Ph.D. diss., University of Arizona.

Turner, C. G., II, and L. Lofgren

1966   Household size of prehistoric western Pueblo Indians. *Southwestern Journal of Anthropology* 22:117–32.

van der Leeuw, S. E.

1977 Towards a study of the economics of pottery making. *Ex Horreo* 4:68–76.

1984 Pottery manufacture: Some complications for the study of trade. In *Pots and potters: Current approaches in ceramic archaeology,* ed. P. M. Rice, 55–69. UCLA Institute of Archaeology Monograph 24. Los Angeles: University of California Press.

van der Leeuw, S. E., and A. C. Pritchard, eds.

1984 *The many dimensions of pottery: Ceramics in archaeology and anthropology.* CINGULA 7. Amsterdam: Institute for Pre- and Proto-history, University of Amsterdam.

van der Merwe, N. J., and R. T. K. Scully

1971 The Phalaborwa story: Archaeological and ethnographic investigation of a South African Iron Age group. *World Archaeology* 3(2):178–96.

Van de Velde, P., and H. R. Van de Velde

1939 The black pottery of Coyotepec, Oaxaca, Mexico. *Southwest Museum Papers,* no. 13.

Vandiver, P. B.

1982 Technological change in Egyptian faience. In *Archaeological ceramics,* ed. J. S. Olin and A. D. Franklin, 167–79. Washington, D.C.: Smithsonian Institution.

Vandiver, P. B., and W. D. Kingery

1984 Composition and structure of Chinese Song dynasty celadon glazes from Longquan. *Ceramic Bulletin* 63(4):612–16.

Vandiver, P. B., and C. G. Koehler

1986 Structure, processing, properties, and style of Corinthian transport amphoras. In *Technology and style,* ed. W. D. Kingery, 173–215. Ceramics and Civilization, vol. 2. Columbus, Ohio: American Ceramic Society.

Van Esterik, P.

1979 Symmetry and symbolism in Ban Chiang painted pottery. *Journal of Anthropological Research* 35:495–508.

Van Olphen, H.

1963 *An introduction to clay colloid chemistry.* New York: Interscience.

1966 Maya Blue: A clay-organic pigment. *Science* 154:645–46.

Van Vlack, L.

1964 *Physical ceramics for engineers.* Reading, Mass.: Addison-Wesley.

Vaz, J. E., and J. M. Cruxent

1975 Determination of the provenience of majolica pottery found in the Caribbean area using its gamma ray induced thermoluminescence. *American Antiquity* 40(1):71–81.

Vescelius, G. S.

1960 Archaeological sampling: A problem of statistical inference. In *Essays in the science of culture in honor of Leslie White,* ed. G. Dole and R. Carneiro, 457–70. New York: Thomas Y. Crowell.

Vince, A. G.

1977 The medieval and post-medieval ceramic industries of the Malvern region: The study of a ware and its distribution. In *Pottery and early commerce: Characterization and trade in Roman and later ceramics,* ed. D. P. S. Peacock, 257–305. London: Academic Press.

1981 The medieval pottery industry in southern England: Tenth to thirteenth centuries. In *Production and distribution: A ceramic viewpoint,* ed. H. Howard and E. Morris, 309–22. International Series 120. Oxford: British Archaeological Reports.

Vitelli, K. D.
    1984   Greek Neolithic pottery by experiment. In *Pots and potters: Current approaches in ceramic archaeology*, ed. P. M. Rice, 113–31. UCLA Institute of Archaeology Monograph 24. Los Angeles: University of California Press.

Von Bothmer, D.
    1985   *The Amasis painter and his world: Vase painting in sixth century B.C. Athens*. New York: Thames and Hudson.

Vossen, R.
    1969   Archäologische Interpretation und Ethnographischer Befund. Ph.D. diss., University of Hamburg.

Voyatzoglou, M.
    1974   The jar makers of Thrapsano in Crete. *Expedition* 16:18–24.

Waddell, C., and J. C. Fountain
    1984   Calcium diffusion: A new dating method for archaeological materials. *Geology* 12:24–26.

Wagner, P.
    1960   *The human use of the earth*. Glencoe, Ill.: Free Press.

Wahl, M. F.
    1965   High-temperature phases of three-layer clay minerals and their interactions with common ceramic materials. *Bulletin of the American Ceramic Society* 44:676.

Walker, G. F.
    1961   Vermiculite minerals. In *X-ray identification and crystal structures of clay minerals*, ed. G. W. Brindley, 297–324. London: Mineralogical Society of Great Britain.

Wallis, F. S., and E. D. Evens
    1934   Report on the heavy minerals contained in the coarse Pant-y-Saer pottery. In The excavation of a hut group at Pant-y-Saer in the parish of Wanfair-Mathafarn-Eithaf, Anglesey. *Archaeologia Cambrensis* 89:29–32.

Wandibba, S.
    1982   Experiments in textural analysis. *Archaeometry* 24(1):71–75.

Wang, W., and Z. Zhou
    1983   Thermoluminescence dating of Chinese pottery. *Archaeometry* 25(2): 99–106.

Warashina, T., T. Higashimura, and Y. Maeda
    1981   Determination of the firing temperature of ancient pottery by means of ESR spectrometry. In *Scientific studies in ancient ceramics*, ed. M. J. Hughes, 117–28. BAR Occasional Paper no. 19. London: British Museum.

Ward, G. K.
    1974   A systematic approach to the definition of sources of raw material. *Archaeometry* 16(1):41–53.

Ware, R. K.
    1971   Thermal analysis. In *Characterization of ceramics*, ed. L. L. Hench and R. W. Gould, 273–305. New York: Marcel Dekker.

Warren, P.
    1972   *Myrtos: An early Bronze Age settlement in Crete*. London: Thames and Hudson.

Warshaw, S. I., and R. J. Seider
    1968   Triaxial porcelains—strength and microstructural relations. In *Ceramic microstructures*, ed. R. M. Fulrath and J. A. Pask, 559–71. New York: John Wiley.

Washburn, D. K.
    1977   *A symmetry analysis of upper Gila area ceramic design*. Papers of the Peabody Museum no. 68. Cambridge, Mass.: Peabody Museum.

1978 A symmetry classification of Pueblo ceramic design. In *Discovering past behavior: Experiments in the archaeology of the American Southwest,* ed. P. Grebinger, 102–21. New York: Gordon and Breach.

1983 Symmetry analysis of ceramic design: Two tests of the method on Neolithic material from Greece and the Aegean. In *Structure and cognition in art,* ed. D. K. Washburn, 138–64. Cambridge: Cambridge University Press.

Washburn, D. K., and R. V. N. Ahlstrom

1982 Review of Plog, "Stylistic analysis in prehistoric ceramics." *Kiva* 48(1–2): 117–23.

Washburn, D. K., and R. G. Matson

1985 Use of multidimensional scaling to display sensitivity to spatial and chronological change: Examples from Anasazi prehistory. In *Decoding prehistoric ceramics,* ed. B. A. Nelson, 75–101. Carbondale: Southern Illinois University Press.

Washburn, E. W.

1921 Porosity. 1. Purpose of the investigation. 2. Porosity and the mechanism of absorption. *Journal of the American Ceramic Society* 4:916–22.

Washburn, E. W., H. Ries, and A. L. Day

1920 Reports of the committee on definition of the term "ceramics." *Journal of the American Ceramic Society* 3:526–36.

Watson, P. J.

1977 Design analyses of painted pottery. *American Antiquity* 42(3):381–93.

Weaver, E. C.

1963 Technological analysis of prehistoric Mississippi ceramic materials: A preliminary report. *American Antiquity* 29(1):49–56.

Weigand, P. C.

1969 Modern Huichol ceramics. In *Mesoamerican studies.* Research Records. Carbondale: Southern Illinois University.

Weigand, P. C., G. Harbottle, and E. V. Sayre

1977 Turquoise sources and source analysis: Mesoamerica and the Southwestern U.S.A. In *Exchange systems in prehistory,* ed. T. K. Earle and J. E. Ericson, 15–34. New York: Academic Press.

Weiss, G.

1971 *The book of porcelain.* Trans. J. Seligman. New York: Praeger.

Weissner, P.

1984 Reconsidering the behavioral basis for style: A case study among the Kalahari San. *Journal of Anthropological Archaeology* 3:190–234.

Wentworth, C. K.

1922 A scale of grade and class terms for clastic sediments. *Journal of Geology* 30:377–92.

1933 Fundamental limits to the sizes of clastic grains. *Science* 77:633–34.

Werner, O.

1972 Ethnoscience 1972. *Annual Review of Anthropology* 1:271–308.

Wertheim, G. K.

1964 *Mössbauer effect: Principles and applications.* New York: Academic Press.

West, H. W. H., and R. W. Ford

1967 An empirical drying test. *Transactions of the British Ceramic Society* 66: 511–21.

Weyl, W. A.

1941 Phosphates in ceramics. 2. Role of phosphorus in bone china. *Journal of the American Ceramic Society* 24(8):245–47.

Whallon, R.

1968 Investigations of late prehistoric social organization in New York State. In

New perspectives in archaeology, ed. S. Binford and L. Binford, 223–44. Chicago: Aldine.

1972   A new approach to pottery typology. *American Antiquity* 37(1):13–33.

1982   Variables and dimensions: The critical step in quantitive typology. In *Essays on archaeological typology*, ed. R. Whallon and J. A. Brown, 127–61. Evanston, Ill.: Center for American Archaeology Press.

Whallon, R., and J. A. Brown

1982   Preface. In *Essays on archaeological typology*, ed. R. Whallon and J. A. Brown, xv–xix. Evanston, Ill.: Center for American Archaeology Press.

Wheat, J. B., J. C. Gifford, and W. W. Wasley

1958   Ceramic variety, type cluster, and ceramic system in Southwestern pottery analysis. *American Antiquity* 24(1):34–47.

Whitaker, I., and E. Whitaker

1978   *A potter's Mexico.* Albuquerque: University of New Mexico Press.

Whitbread, I. K.

1986   The characterisation of argillaceous inclusions in ceramic thin sections. *Archaeometry* 28(1):79–88.

Whitehouse, D.

1980   Protomajolica. *Faenza* 66:77–83.

Whittemore, J. W.

1935   Mechanical method for the measurement of the plasticity of clays and mixtures of clays. *Journal of the American Ceramic Society* 18:352–59.

Whittemore, O., and G. Halsey

1983   Pore structure characterized by mercury porosimetry. In *Materials science research*, ed. D. Rossington, R. Condrate, and R. Snyder, 147–58. Advances in Materials Characterization, vol. 15. New York: Plenum.

Whittlesey, S. M.

1974   Identification of imported ceramics through functional analysis of attributes. *Kiva* 40:101–12.

Widemann, F., M. Picon, F. Asaro, H. V. Michel, and I. Perlman

1975   A Lyons branch of the pottery-making firm of Ateius of Arezzo. *Archaeometry* 17(1):45–59.

Will, E. L.

1977   The ancient commercial amphora. *Archaeology* 30(4):264–70.

Willey, G. R.

1966   *An introduction to American archaeology.* Vol. 1. *North and Middle America.* Englewood Cliffs, N.J.: Prentice-Hall.

Willey, G. R., T. P. Culbert, and R. E. W. Adams

1967   Maya lowland ceramics: A report from the 1965 Guatemala City conference. *American Antiquity* 32(3):289–315.

Willey, G. R., and P. Phillips

1958   *Method and theory in American archaeology.* Chicago: University of Chicago Press.

Willey, G. R., and J. A. Sabloff

1980   *A history of American archaeology*, 2d ed. San Francisco: W. H. Freeman.

Williams, B., W. Williams, and J. McMillan

1985   Notes on some clays used for pottery in ancient Nubia. In *Ancient technology to modern science*, ed. W. D. Kingery, 43–50. Ceramics and Civilization, vol. 1. Columbus, Ohio: American Ceramic Society.

Williams, D. F.

1977   The Romano-British black burnished industry: An essay on characterization by heavy mineral analysis. In *Pottery and early commerce*, ed. D. P. S. Peacock, 163–220. London: Academic Press.

1979   The heavy mineral separation of ancient ceramics by centrifugation: A preliminary report. *Archaeometry* 21(2):177–82.

1983   Petrology of ceramics. In *The petrology of archaeological artefacts*, ed. D. R. C. Kempe and A. P. Harvey, 301–29. Oxford: Clarendon.

Williamson, W. O.

1947   Some observations on the behavior of water in ceramic materials. *Transactions of the British Ceramic Society* 46:77.

Wilson, A. L.

1978   Elemental analysis of pottery in the study of its provenance: A review. *Journal of Archaeological Science* 5:219–36.

Wilson, J. G.

1973   The addition of talc and asbestos to pot clay by past and present inhabitants of Karamoja district in Uganda and adjoining districts of Kenya. *Man* 8(3): 300–302.

Winefordner, J. D.

1971   Atomic absorption flame spectrometry. In *Characterization of ceramics*, ed. L. L. Hench and R. W. Gould, 89–132. New York: Marcel Dekker.

Winterhalder, B., R. Larsen, and R. B. Thomas

1974   Dung as an essential resource in a highland Peruvian community. *Human Ecology* 2:89–104.

Winther-Nielsen, M., K. Conradsen, K. Heydorn, and V. Mejdahl

1981   Investigation of the number of elements required for provenance studies of ceramic materials. In *Scientific studies in ancient ceramics*, ed. M. J. Hughes, 85–92. BAR Occasional Paper 19. London: British Museum.

Wobst, H. M.

1977   Stylistic behavior and information exchange. In *For the director: Research essays in honor of James B. Griffin*, ed. C. E. Cleland, 317–42. Anthropological Papers no. 61. Ann Arbor: Museum of Anthropology, University of Michigan.

Wolfe, A.

1969   Social structural basis of art. *Current Anthropology* 10(1):3–44.

Wolkodoff, V. E., L. E. Ferreira, and R. E. Weaver

1968   Ceramic surfaces and relationship to internal microstructures. In *Ceramic microstructures*, ed. R. M. Fulrath and J. A. Pask, 297–309. New York: John Wiley.

Woods, A. J.

1986   Form, fabric, and function: Some observations on the cooking pot in antiquity. In *Technology and style*, ed. W. D. Kingery, 157–72. Ceramics and Civilization, vol. 2. Columbus, Ohio: American Ceramic Society.

Wormington, H. M., and A. Neal

1951   *The story of Pueblo pottery*. Museum Pictorial no. 2. Denver: Museum of Natural History.

Worrall, W. E.

1956   The organic matter in clays. *Transactions of the British Ceramic Society* 55:689–705.

Wright, H. T., and G. A. Johnson

1975   Population, exchange, and early state formation in southwestern Iran. *American Anthropologist* 77(2):267–89.

Wykes-Joyce, M.

1958   *Seven thousand years of pottery and porcelain*. New York: Philosophical Library.

Yap, C. T., and S. M. Tang
   1984   X-ray fluorescence analysis of modern and recent Chinese porcelains. *Archaeometry* 26(1):78–81.
Young, W. J., and F. E. Whitmore
   1957   Analysis of oriental ceramic wares by non-destructive X-ray methods. *Far Eastern Ceramic Bulletin* 9:1–27.
Zaslow, B.
   1977   A guide to analyzing prehistoric ceramic decorations by symmetry and pattern mathematics. In *Pattern mathematics and archaeology*, ed. G. A. Clarke. Tempe: Arizona State University Press.
   1981   *Pattern dissemination in the prehistoric Southwest and Mesoamerica*. Anthropological Research Papers no. 25. Tempe: Arizona State University Press.
Zaslow, B., and A. E. Dittert
   1976   The symmetry and pattern mathematics displayed in Hohokam ceramic painting. *Journal of the Arizona Academy of Sciences* 11:9.
Zhang Fukang
   1985   The origin and development of traditional Chinese glazes and decorative ceramic colors. In *Ancient technology to modern science*, ed. W. D. Kingery, 163–80. Ceramics and Civilization, vol. 1. Columbus, Ohio: American Ceramic Society.
Zhou Zhen-xi
   1985   The origin and early use of throwing wheel in manufacturing of pottery in ancient China. Paper presented at the second international conference on ancient Chinese pottery and porcelain, Beijing.
Zimmerman, D. W.
   1971   Thermoluminescent dating using fine grains from pottery. *Archaeometry* 13(1):29–52.
Zimmerman, D. W., and J. Huxtable
   1971   Thermoluminescence dating of Upper Paleolithic fired clay from Dolní Věstonice. *Archaeometry* 13(1):53–57.
Zimmerman, D. W., M. P. Yuhas, and P. Meyers
   1974   Thermoluminescence authenticity measurements on core material from the bronze horse of the New York Metropolitan Museum of Art. *Archaeometry* 16(1):19–30.
Zussman, J.
   1977   X-ray diffraction. In *Physical methods in determinative mineralogy*, 2d ed., ed. J. Zussman, 392–473. London: Academic Press.
Zussman, J., ed.
   1977   *Physical methods in determinative mineralogy*. 2d ed. London: Academic Press.

Index

Absorption, 351
Acatlán (Mexico) potters, 119, 162, 176
Access to vessel contents, 225–26
Accuracy (of analytical methods), 390, 434, 440, 443, 444. *For comparison of individual methods, see each method and* 374–75 (table 13.1)
Adiok, 133
Afghan potters, 174
Aggregate, 75, 118, 366, 411. *See also* Inclusions; Temper
Aging clay, 63, 119
Albite, 35, 96
Alkali feldspars. *See* Potash feldspars
Allophane, 43
Alumina
  in clay composition, 40, 390
    ball clays, 51
    kaolinite, 45
    lath structure clays, 50
    refractory clays, 51
    smectites, 48
  in clay origins, 34
  octahedrons, 41, 42 (fig. 2.5)
  in provenience studies, 420
Amphlett Island potters, 193, 457
Amphorae, 231, 234, 240
Andean potters, 188, 316
Anion, 41, 423, 430. *See also* Ionic substitutions
Anistropy
  in archaeothermometry, 426 (table 14.3), 431
  of crystals, 378

in magnetism, 440
in physical properties (*see* Preferred [particle] orientation)
Anorthite, 35, 96, 97
Aplastic, as term, 411
Appliqué, 148
Archaeological record formation. *See* Site formation processes
Archaeomagnetic dating, 439–40
Archaeometry, 310
Archaeothermometry, 386, 400, 402, 406, 426–27 (table 14.3), 428–35. *See also names of individual techniques*
  problems in, 434–35
Archaism, 455–56, 459
Arikara pottery, 253 (fig. 8.7)
Arretine ware, 18. *See also* Maker's marks; Samian ware
  levigation tanks, 118
  production mode, 186, 202
  slip, 49
Arts of acculturation, 450–56
  commercial, 451
  functional, 451
  souvenir, 451–52 (*see also* Tourist market, production for)
Assemblage, 293–301. *See also* Breakage/replacement rates; Metal and plastic containers; Use-life
  archaeological approaches to, 300–301
  composition, 295
  size, 294–95
Asymmetrical design, 261
Atmosphere of firing, 81

543